American Plays and
Musicals on Screen

American Plays and Musicals on Screen

650 Stage Productions and Their Film and Television Adaptations

THOMAS S. HISCHAK

McFarland & Company, Inc., Publishers
Jefferson, North Carolina, and London

LIBRARY OF CONGRESS CATALOGUING-IN-PUBLICATION DATA

Hischak, Thomas S.
American plays and musicals on screen : 650 stage productions
and their film and television adaptations / Thomas S. Hischak.
p.   cm.
Includes bibliographical references and index.

ISBN 0-7864-2003-0 (illustrated case binding : 50# alkaline paper) ∞

1. American drama—Film and video adaptations.
2. Musicals—United States—Film and video adaptations.
3. Motion pictureplays—History and criticism.
4. Theater—United States.
5. Film adaptations.
I. Title.
PS338.M67H57   2005   791.43'6—dc22   2004022967

British Library cataloguing data are available

Cover image: Barbara Bel Geddes and Ben Gazzara in the 1955 Broadway
production of *Cat on a Hot Tin Roof* (Photofest);
background © 2005 Corbis Images

Manufactured in the United States of America

McFarland & Company, Inc., Publishers
Box 611, Jefferson, North Carolina 28640
www.mcfarlandpub.com

For Sandi and Bruce

Contents

Preface

The movies have been borrowing from Broadway since the first film studios on Long Island were cranking away at one-reel moving pictures and coercing stage stars and directors to cross the East River and provide their services. When the movies got longer, filmmakers needed more substantial plots to sustain the action, so they started borrowing stories as well as personnel from Broadway. For a short time it was possible to work in both media: shoot movies during the day and perform on stage at night. The Marx Brothers, for instance, were making the film of *The Cocoanuts* in 1929 while playing evenings and matinees in *Animal Crackers* on Broadway. Had the movie capital remained in the New York City area, America's film industry today would be similar to Great Britain's, where top artists can do theatre and make films (and television) without leaving the London metropolis.

But it was not to be. In the United States, with Hollywood and the movies on one coast and Broadway on the other, the crossover between the two involved geography as well as career transitions. Everyone agrees that plays and films are different, but no one has ever found an unshakeable explanation of exactly why something works in one medium but not the other. Yes, theatre is verbal and movies are visual. But many great plays depend on visuals, while some movie classics are beloved primarily for their talk. It is a commonplace that stage actors need to have a voice while movie stars need to have a look. Yet many performers make the transition easily from one medium to the other. Another generality: Broadway directors create pictures on a stage, while Hollywood directors choose what to focus on. But there are as many ways to direct a movie as there are theories on acting and directing. If a foolproof formula existed that could distinguish what elements of a play would be sure to work on the screen, there would be fewer mistakes and fewer embarrassing results. But there is no formula, and the history of plays-to-films is filled with inexplicable duds and triumphs.

This book allows the reader to look at what worked and what didn't. Six hundred and fifty American plays and musicals, from the pre–Civil War years to the end of the twentieth century, are cited, with their screen and television versions following them. The data about the plays and movies are objective, but the commentary after each title is necessarily somewhat subjective. Did the transition from stage to screen work? That is often a matter of opinion. Opinions may be formed on a reasonable basis, however, and this book attempts to make that basis clear by describing what changes occurred, determining the strengths and weaknesses of each version, and relating how the end product was received. I have attempted to insure that the evaluations offered are a consensus of opinions rather than my own personal preference.

For each play, the information provided refers to the original New York production: date, theatre, author, major cast members and the characters they played, director, producer, and length of the run in number of performances. For musical plays, the authors of the score, some of the song titles, and the choreographer are added. Films are listed with these credits: date, studio, authors of the screenplay, cast and characters, director, and producer. Movie musicals include the same additional information as theatre musicals. When the title of the movie differs from the stage title, that fact is indicated. The commentary also mentions screen productions not listed, such as silent shorts or a television broadcast on kinescope.

Selecting which plays and films to include has been a difficult task. I have tried to be as comprehensive as possible, but I cannot claim that *every* play turned into a movie or television production is here. Such a book would never be possible or accurate. There are probably hundreds of films made from both popular and obscure plays that are lost or missing or just fallen into obscurity. Many films have been made from plays that were never produced or published; still others may be based on scripts that had a short, unrecorded production somewhere and then were picked up by a film company. I have found several movies that said in their credits, "based on a play by...," yet no record of the play seems to exist. (A famous example: *Casablanca* was based on a play, *Everybody Comes to Rick's*, that seems never to have been produced.) But I can say with confidence that every notable playwright, genre, and time period is covered, along with hundreds of less familiar titles. The 650 plays discussed give a comprehensive *vision* of American theatre, if not an exhaustive *list*.

Some other clarifications: Only American plays and musicals are listed, but foreign films based on those works are sometimes included or at least mentioned. Productions on television are included only if they were made in a studio or on location and are not a videotaping of the actual stage production. For example, the excellent video versions of Stephen Sondheim's *Sweeney Todd, the Demon Barber of Fleet Street* or *Sunday in the Park with George* are not included, but the 1958 television production of *Wonderful Town*, with Rosalind Russell recreating her stage performance of five years earlier, is considered a new production and is included.

Finally, a note about the number of performances given for theatre productions. In the early years of the twentieth century, a run of 100 performances was considered a milestone and the play was regarded as a major hit. By the Depression years, 100 performances did not guarantee box office success, and a hit was closer to 150 performances for plays and 300 for musicals. By the end of the century a musical that could not run 800 times or a play with fewer than 300 performances was often listed as a box office failure. So it is worth noting that when a 1906 play runs 250 performances it is a giant hit; a 1996 play with the same number of performances probably lost a lot of money.

I would like to acknowledge the research assistance I received from Mark Robinson, Sandi Zecchini, and Bruce Deal; the help of the librarians at local public and college libraries; and the consistent and unquestioning support of my family.

The Plays and Films

Abe Lincoln in Illinois

October 15, 1938 (Plymouth Theatre), a drama by Robert Sherwood. *Cast*: Raymond Massey (Abe Lincoln), Muriel Kirkland (Mary Todd), Albert Phillips (Stephen Douglas), Adele Longmire, Frank Andrews, John Payne, Kevin McCarthy, George Christie, Calvin Thomas, Howard Da Silva, Wendell K. Philips. *Director*: Elmer Rice. *Producer:* Playwrights' Company. 472 performances. Pulitzer Prize.

(RKO 1940). *Screenplay*: Grover Jones, Robert Sherwood. *Cast*: Raymond Massey (Abe Lincoln), Ruth Gordon (Mary Todd), Gene Lockhart (Stephen Douglas), Mary Howard, Alan Baxter, Minor Watson, Howard Da Silva, Harvey Stephens. *Director*: John Cromwell. *Producer*: Max Gordon.

(TV 1964). *Teleplay:* Robert Haurtung. *Cast:* Jason Robards (Abe Lincoln), Kate Reid (Mary Todd), Jack Bittner (Stephen Douglas), Burt Brinckerhoff, Staats Cotsworth, Nan McFarland, Hiram Sherman, Mildred Trares. *Director:* George Schaefer.

Robert Sherwood's play is an intelligent, cliché-free biographical drama of Lincoln's life from his days as a young man in Kentucky until he leaves for Washington to be inaugurated president. While politics are frequently foremost in the story (including the famous debates with Stephen Douglas), domestic episodes are just as effective, such as the death of his gentle fiancée Ann Rutledge and his marriage to the volatile Mary Todd. Raymond Massey found the role of his career as Lincoln, playing it on Broadway, on an extensive tour, and in the 1940 film version. (Sardonic wit George S. Kaufman once quipped that Massey wouldn't be "satisfied until he's assassinated.") The film is tastefully done with some laudable acting (particularly Ruth Gordon as the difficult Mary) but lacks excitement. Most moviegoers preferred the previous year's more theatrical (and more fictional) bio-pic *Young Mr. Lincoln* with Henry Fonda as the lawyer Lincoln. Abbreviated television versions of *Abe Lincoln in Illinois* were made in 1945 and 1957 and a well-acted telecast in 1964 boasted a superb performance by Jason Robards as the president-to-be. Because of its large cast and many scenic locations, the play is not frequently revived, though there were commendable New York productions in 1963 with Hal Holbrook and 1993 with Sam Waterston in the title role.

Abie's Irish Rose

May 23, 1922 (Fulton Theatre), a comedy by Anne Nichols. *Cast*: Robert B. Williams (Abie Levy), Marie Carroll (Rosemary Murphy), Alfred Wiseman (Solomon Levy), John Cope (Patrick Murphy), Harry Bradley (Fr. Whalen), Mathilde Cottrelly, Bernard Gorcey, Howard Lang. *Director*: Laurence Marston. *Producer:* Anne Nichols. 2,327 performances.

(Paramount 1928). *Screenplay*: Herman J. Mankiewicz, etc. *Cast*: Charles "Buddy" Rogers (Abie Levy), Nancy Carroll (Rosemary Murphy), Jean Hersholt (Solomon Levy), J. Farrell MacDonald (Patrick Murphy), Nick Cogley (Fr. Whalen), Bernard Gorcey, Ida Kramer, Camillus Pretal, Rosa Rosanova. *Director-producer*: Victor Fleming.

3

(United Artists 1946). *Screenplay*: Anne Nichols. *Cast*: Joanne Dru (Rosemary Murphy), Richard Norris (Abie Levy), Michael Chekhov (Solomon Levy), J. M. Kerrigan (Patrick Murphy), Emory Parnell (Fr. Whalen), Eric Blore, George E. Stone, Vera Gordon, Art Baker. *Director:* A. Edward Sutherland. *Producers*: A. Edward Sutherland, Bing Crosby.

Jewish Abie Levy secretly marries the Irish Catholic Rosemary Murphy in a Methodist ceremony, knowing their religious fathers would never consent to the union. When the two families find out, a series of comic complications (as well as subsequent Jewish and Catholic marriage ceremonies) follow. Matters are not resolved until Rosemary gives birth to "twinses" that are named Patrick and Rebecca and everyone is satisfied. The comedy did not open to the scathing reviews that were later heaped on the play, yet neither critics nor audiences were very enthusiastic. But mobster Arnold Rothstein liked the domestic comedy and bankrolled it until it eventually became the longest-running play on Broadway. Neither of the two film versions, a silent one in 1928 featuring heartthrobs Buddy Rogers and Nancy Carroll and a rather dull 1946 remake with lackluster leads Joanne Dru and Richard Norris, was able to repeat the stage play's success. Yet in 1972 the television sitcom series *Bridget Loves Bernie*, using the same premise, was very popular; it is believed that pressure from groups that objected to the religious stereotypes encouraged the network to cancel the show after one season even though it had high ratings.

About Face see *Brother Rat*

About Last Night see *Sexual Perversity in Chicago*

Accent on Youth

December 25, 1934 (Plymouth Theatre), a comedy by Samson Raphaelson. *Cast*: Nicholas Hannen (Steven Gaye), Constance Cummings (Linda Brown), Theodore Newton (Dickie Reynolds),

Eleanor Hicks, Ernest Lawford, Irene Purcell. *Director*: Benn W. Levy. *Producer:* Crosby Gaige. 229 performances.

(Paramount 1935). *Screenplay*: Claude Binyon, Herbert Fields. *Cast*: Sylvia Sidney (Linda Brown), Herbert Marshall (Steven Gaye), Philip Reed (Dick Reynolds), Holmes Herbert, Catherine Doucet, Astrid Allwyn, Ernest Cossart, Lon Chaney, Jr. *Director*: Wesley Ruggles. *Producer*: Douglas MacLean.

Mr. Music (Paramount 1950). *Screenplay:* Arthur Sheekman. *Score:* Johnny Burke, James Van Heusen. *Cast:* Bing Crosby (Paul Merrick), Nancy Olsen (Katherine Holbrook), Charles Coburn, Ruth Hussey, Tom Ewell, Ida Moore, Robert Stack, Peggy Lee, Groucho Marx, Marge and Gower Champion, Dorothy Kirsten. *Songs:* Life Is So Peculiar; Accidents Will Happen; Mr. Music; And You'll Be Home; High on the List. *Director*: Richard Haydn. *Producer:* Robert L. Welch.

But Not for Me (Paramount 1959). *Screenplay:* John Michael Hayes. *Cast:* Clark Gable (Russell Ward), Carroll Baker (Ellie Brown), Lilli Palmer, Lee J. Cobb, Barry Coe, Thomas Gomez, Charles Lane. *Director:* Walter Lang. *Producers:* William Perlberg, George Seaton.

When a middle-aged playwright writes a romance about a man in love with a much younger woman, life copies art and he falls for his younger secretary. The lightweight comedy opened to a mixed press but found an audience on Broadway and for many years in summer stock. The 1935 film was faithful to the play's modest ambitions and a likable cast made for some delightful moments. It was successful enough at the box office that the property was musicalized for the screen in 1950 as *Mr. Music* with Bing Crosby as a middle-aged songwriter in love with his younger secretary Nancy Olsen who keeps trying to get him off the golf course and back to the piano. The charm of the original may have been lost but some warm and cozy songs and a few bright guest star appearances made for a mild musical entertainment. Both music and much of the comedy were dropped when the plot was recycled once again in 1959 as *But Not for Me*, a romance about aging producer Clark Gable and his secretary Carroll Baker. The mature Gable still has a twinkle in his eye but there is little else to recommend in the tired tale.

The Actress see *Years Ago*

Adam and Eva

September 13, 1919 (Longacre Theatre), a comedy by Guy Bolton, George Middleton. *Cast*: Berton Churchill (James King), Otto Kruger (Adam Smith), Ruth Shepley (Eva), Reginald Mason, Ferdinand Gottschalk, Richard Sterling, Courtenay Foote. *Producers:* F. Ray Comstock, Morris Gest. 312 performances.

(MGM/Cosmopolitan 1923). *Screenplay*: Luther Reed, etc. *Cast*: Tom Lewis (James King), Marion Davies (Eva King), T. Roy Barnes (Adam), William Norris, Percy Ames, Leon Gordon, Luella Gear. *Director*: Robert G. Vignola.

A millionaire, fed up with his family's careless overspending, takes off for one of his rubber plantations and leaves the business in the hands of the bright Adam Smith who manages to curtail the family's indulgences (he steals their jewels and even lies to them that the business went bust) and even wins the heart of the heiress daughter. This sunny domestic comedy was one of the biggest hits of the season and remained a favorite in little theatres and summer stock for decades. The 1923 silent film starred Marion Davies as the daughter so the plot was altered to feature her comic talents, which were considerable. Yet as successful as the film and Davies were, her benefactor William Randolph Hearst preferred to see her in serious roles so she would infrequently get to shine in comedies such as this.

The Adding Machine

March 19, 1923 (Garrick Theatre), a drama by Elmer Rice. *Cast*: Dudley Digges (Mr. Zero), Helen Westley (Mrs. Zero), Margaret Wycherly (Daisy), E. G. Robinson (Shrdlu), Irving Dillon (Boss), Elise Bartlett, William M. Griffith. *Producer:* Theatre Guild. 72 performances.

(Universal 1969). *Screenplay*: Jerome Epstein. *Cast*: Milo O'Shea (Mr. Zero), Phyllis Diller (Mrs. Diller), Billie Whitelaw (Daisy), Julian Glover (Shrdlu), Sydney Chaplin, Raymond Huntley, Phil Brown, Paddie O'Neil. *Director-producer*: Jerome Epstein.

One of the American theatre's finest examples of expressionism, the fable tells of the plight of long-time clerk Mr. Zero who is fired from his job, murders his employer, is tried and executed, than finds himself briefly in heaven before he must return to life and repeat the whole process over and over again through time. While the Broadway production was far from a financial blockbuster, it was one of the most discussed plays of the decade (particularly its bold expressionistic sets and lighting) and has always been of interest to educational and experimental theatre groups. Hollywood was never interested in filming such a dour, leftist tale so the play was not put on screen until 1969. The ambitious movie aims high but its naturalistic presentation of the material is an obvious mistaken and the fascinating performances end up being more a curiosity than involving.

Advise and Consent

November 17, 1960 (Cort Theatre), a drama by Loring Mandel. *Cast*: Ed Begley (Orrin Knox), Chester Morris (Bob Munson), Kevin McCarthy (Van Ackerman), Richard Kiley (Brig Anderson), Sally Kemp, Barnard Hughes, Conrad Bain, Tom Shirley, Judson Laire, Joan Whetmore, Staats Cotsworth. *Director*: Franklin Schaffner. *Producers:* Robert Fryer, Lawrence Carr. 212 performances.

(Columbia 1962). *Screenplay*: Wendell Mayes. *Cast*: Henry Fonda (Robert A. Leffingwell), Charles Laughton (Sen. Seabright Cooley), Walter Pidgeon (Sen. Robert D. Munson), Don Murray (Sen. Brig Anderson), Franchot Tone (President), Lew Ayres (Harley M. Hudson), Peter Lawford (Sen. Lafe Smith), Gene Tierney (Dolly Harrison), Burgess Meredith, Paul Ford, Eddie Hodges, Inga Swenson, George Grizzard. *Director-producer*: Otto Preminger.

Allen Drury's best-selling novel about backroom politics in Washington made for a theatrical tour de force, especially given the strong cast and first-class production. The President tries to push his man into the political arena as Secretary of State and before matters are concluded, there is blackmail, last minute double crossing, and suicide. The powerful exposé even included an episode about a senator's homosexual past, a shocking aspect of the novel that was boldly retained for the stage and the 1962 film. An all-star cast was assembled for the movie and performances ranged from Charles Laughton's juicy Southern senator (it was his last screen appearance) to the understated portrayal of the President by Franchot Tone. While some critics thought the documentary-like approach to the piece did not work with the sizzling melodrama, most agreed that the long talky movie was very absorbing and it remains so, even in light of *All the President's Men* and other later political films.

After the Fall

January 23, 1964 (ANTA Washington Square Theatre), a play by Arthur Miller. *Cast*: Jason Robards (Quentin), Barbara Loden (Maggie), Salome Jens (Holga), Mariclare Costello, Virginia Kaye, Paul Mann, David Wayne, Hal Holbrook, Ralph Meeker. *Director*: Elia Kazan. *Producer*: Repertory Theatre of Lincoln Center. 208 performances.

(TV 1974). *Teleplay*: Arthur Miller. *Cast*: Christopher Plummer (Quentin), Faye Dunaway (Maggie), Bibi Andersson (Holga), Mariclare Costello, Murray Hamilton, Addison Powell, Nancy Marchand, Lee Richardson. *Director-producer*: Gilbert Cates.

Arthur Miller's most autobiographical play concerns the prosperous lawyer Quentin who is haunted by his memories of the past, including the witch hunts of the 1950s and his failed marriage to the beautiful but insecure actress Maggie who committed suicide. First produced two years after Miller's ex-wife Marilyn Monroe took her own life, the play was both praised and criticized for its obvious attempt to explain the complex and tragic Miller-Monroe relationship. Yet the drama is more introspective than sensational and Quentin is far from an apologetic spokesman. Robards was outstanding in the role and the Elia Kazan production also boasted other fine qualities. The television version in 1974 was able to better handle Miller's many short cinematic-like scenes and for some critics it was an improvement over the play. Christopher Plummer is very accomplished as Quentin but Faye Dun-

away's Maggie is only a surface rendering of what Barbara Loden brought to the character on stage.

Agnes of God

March 30, 1982 (Music Box Theatre), a drama by John Pielmeier. *Cast*: Elizabeth Ashley (Dr. Martha Livingstone), Geraldine Page (Mother Miriam Ruth), Amanda Plummer (Agnes). *Director*: Michael Lindsay-Hogg. *Producers:* Kenneth Waissman, etc. 599 performances.

(Columbia 1985). *Screenplay*: John Pielmeier. *Cast*: Jane Fonda (Dr. Martha Livingstone), Anne Bancroft (Mother Miriam Ruth), Meg Tilly (Agnes), Anne Pitoniak, Winston Rekert. *Director*: Norman Jewison. *Producers*: Patrick Parker, Norman Jewison.

Although this was a rather preposterous little drama that raised more questions than it had the ability to answer, the three-character play was a showcase for three actresses willing to chew the scenery with aplomb and they did. Newcomer Amanda Plummer was quite eerie and mesmerizing as the young nun who gives birth to a baby and is accused of murdering it. But Geraldine Page as the mother superior and Elizabeth Ashley as the psychiatrist looking into the affair got their juicy moments as well. Presented on a bare stage, the economical show fascinated audiences for almost two years. The 1985 movie was opened up and beautifully filmed and the performances this time were less flamboyant but just as effective. In many ways the movie is more satisfying than the play, though the logic of much of the story still baffles.

Ah, Wilderness!

October 2, 1933 (Guild Theatre), a comedy by Eugene O'Neill. *Cast*: George M. Cohan (Nat Miller), Elisha Cook, Jr. (Richard Miller), Marjorie Marquis (Essie Miller), Ruth Gilbert (Muriel McComber), Gene Lockhart (Sid Davis), Eda Heinemann, Richard Sterling, John Wynne. *Director*: Philip Moeller. *Producer:* Theatre Guild. 289 performances.

(MGM 1935). *Screenplay*: Frances Goodrich, Albert Hackett. *Cast*: Lionel Barrymore (Nat

Miller), Eric Linden (Richard Miller), Spring Byington (Essie Miller), Wallace Beery (Sid), Cecilia Parker (Muriel McComber), Mickey Rooney, Charley Grapewin. *Director*: Clarence Brown. *Producers*: Clarence Brown, Hunt Stromberg.

Summer Holiday (MGM 1944). *Screenplay*: Frances Goodrich, Albert Hackett. *Score*: Harry Warren, Ralph Blane. *Cast*: Mickey Rooney (Richard Miller), Gloria De Haven (Muriel Mc-Comber), Walter Huston (Nat Miller), Marilyn Maxwell, Selena Royale, Frank Morgan, Agnes Moorehead, Jackie Jenkins, Anne Francis. *Songs*: It's Our Home Town; Afraid to Fall in Love; The Stanley Steamer; I Think You're the Sweetest Kid I've Ever Known; Spring Isn't Everything. *Director*: Rouben Mamoulian. *Producer*: Arthur Freed.

Eugene O'Neill's only comedy is a warm, nostalgic piece of Americana about a well-adjusted family and its minor trials and troubles during the Fourth of July holiday. Although lighter and more optimistic in tone than his other works, O'Neill's characterizations are just as vivid and actors have always relished playing these endearing small-town folk. The focus of the original Broadway production was on George M. Cohan as the father, his only major non-musical role in a play he didn't write himself. The piece is continually revived and has not dated in its sincerity and charm. Sunny nostalgia was a specialty of Hollywood and the 1935 film glows with affection and tenderness as some of the screen's favorite character actors shine throughout. The movie was successful enough that MGM put together a similar small-town family with the Andy Hardy films, a series of sixteen movies made between 1937 and 1958. Mickey Rooney, who played one of the kids in *Ah, Wilderness!*, was usually cast as Andy and he played the central adolescent in the 1944 musical film version of the O'Neill play called *Summer Holiday*. It is an uneven film with some wonderful performances (particularly Walter Huston as the father) alongside some strained ones. The Harry Warren-Ralph Blane score produced no hits but is very skillful and some numbers, such as "The Stanley Steamer," are rather contagious. A 1955 television version of *Ah, Wilderness!* featured Leon Ames as the father and in 1976 a fine production staged by Arvin

Brown was broadcast on television as well. The 1959 Broadway musical *Take Me Along* was also based on O'Neill's play but had a new score by Bob Merrill.

Alias Jimmy Valentine

January 21, 1910 (Wallack's Theatre), a play by Paul Armstrong. *Cast*: H. B. Warner (Lee Randall/Jimmy Valentine), Laurette Taylor (Rose Lane), Frank Monroe (Detective Doyle), Alma Sedley (Kitty), Charles E. Graham, James E. Wilson. *Director*: Edward E. Rose. *Producer*: Lieber & Co. 155 performances.

(World Film Corporate 1915). *Screenplay*: Maurice Tourneur. *Cast*: Robert Warwick (Jimmy Valentine), Ruth Shepley (Rose Fay), Robert Cummings (Detective Doyle), Frederick Truesdell, Johnny Hines, D. J. Flanagan. *Director*: Maurice Tourneur. *Producer*: William A. Brady.

(Metro Pictures 1920). *Cast*: Bert Lytell (Jimmy Valentine), Vola Vale (Rose Lane), Wilton Taylor (Detective Doyle), Eugene Pallette, Marc Robbins, Robert Dunbar. *Directors*: Edward Mortimer, Arthur Ripley. *Producer*: Maxwell Karger.

(MGM 1928). *Screenplay*: Sarah Y. Mason, A. P. Younger. *Cast*: William Harris (Jimmy Valentine), Lionel Barrymore (Detective Doyle), Leila Hyams (Rose), Karl Dane, Tully Marshall, Howard Hickman. *Director*: Jack Conway.

O. Henry's short story "A Retrieved Reformation," about a former safe cracker who gives up his alias as a bank employee when he rescues a child locked in a bank vault, was fashioned into one of the most popular plays of the 1910s. The engrossing melodrama was particularly popular on the road where it toured for much of the decade and the play was revived again on Broadway in 1921. Three films were made from the piece: silent versions in 1915 and 1920 and in 1928 MGM made its first partial talkie with its version starring stage actor Lionel Barrymore as the detective who discovers the safe cracker's true identity. The story is still an intriguing one and it is surprising that later sound films weren't made of it.

All My Sons

January 29, 1947 (Coronet Theatre), a drama by Arthur Miller. *Cast*: Ed Begley (Joe Keller),

Arthur Kennedy (Chris Keller), Beth Merrill (Kate Keller), Lois Wheeler (Anne Deever), Karl Malden (George Deever), John McGovern, Hope Cameron, Dudley Sadler, Peggy Meredith, Eugene Steiner. *Director*: Elia Kazan. *Producer:* Harold Clurman. 328 performances.

(Universal 1948). *Screenplay*: Chester Erskine. *Cast*: Edward G. Robinson (Joe Keller), Burt Lancaster (Chris Keller), Mady Christians (Kate Keller), Louisa Horton (Anne Deever), Howard Duff (George Deever), Frank Conroy, Lloyd Gough, Arlene Francis, Harry Morgan, Elizabeth Fraser. *Director*: Irving Reis. *Producer*: Chester Erskine.

(TV 1986). *Teleplay*: Arthur Miller. *Cast*: James Whitmore (Joe Keller), Aidan Quinn (Chris Keller), Michael Learned (Kate Keller), Joan Allen (Anne Deever), Zeljko Ivanek (George Deever), Joanna Miles, Alan Scarfe, Layne Coleman. *Director*: Jack O'Brien. *Producers*: John Blanchard, Michael Brandman.

Arthur Miller's first stage success is a domestic drama about a father who willingly sold defective airplane engine parts to the government during World War Two in order to save his business and secure a future for his sons. But his deception ends up destroying the family and he takes his own life. This taut, tightly constructed play in the Ibsen mold remains one of Miller's best pieces of realism even as it foreshadows his more expressionistic later works like *Death of a Salesman* (qv).

Splendid stage revivals have been consistent but the 1948 film shows how the play can be reduced to stilted melodrama when handled poorly. Edward G. Robinson is masterful as the father and Burt Lancaster has his moments as his embittered son, but much of the theatrics come across as artificial. There was a British television version in 1955 with Albert Dekker and Patrick McGoohan as father and son and in 1986 James Whitmore and Aidan Quinn were featured in a first-rate television production carefully directed by Jack O'Brien.

All Over

May 1, 1971 (Martin Beck Theatre), a play by Edward Albee. *Cast*: Jessica Tandy (Wife), Colleen Dewhurst (Mistress), Madeleine Sher-

wood (Daughter), James Ray (Son), George Voskovec (Best Friend), Betty Field (Nurse), Neil Fitzgerald. *Director*: John Gielgud. *Producers:* Richard Barr, etc. 42 performances.

(TV 1976). *Teleplay*: Edward Albee. *Cast*: Anne Shropshire (Wife), Myra Carter (Mistress), Anne Lynn (Daughter), Pirie MacDonald (Son), William Prince (Best Friend), Margaret Thomson (Nurse), David Peterson, David J. Skal. *Directors*: John Desmond, John Edwards, Peter Weidner. *Producers*: Phylis Geller, Jac Venza.

One of Edward Albee's most straightforward works, this intimate drama concerned the friends and relatives that gather when a famous man lies dying in his mansion. His wife, mistress, best friend, and children reminisce, argue, and lament until a doctor comes out to inform them that it is "all over." The plotless piece had some striking characterizations but most critics found the play lifeless and dull and it closed in a month. Yet there were no complaints about the powerhouse cast and infrequent revivals have also proven the play to be a strong vehicle for actors. The 1976 television production was a studio recreation of a revival done at the Hartford Stage in Connecticut. While it boasts no major stars, the acting is nonetheless engrossing and the video is interesting in its own quiet way.

All the Way Home

November 30, 1960 (Belasco Theatre), a drama by Tad Mosel. *Cast*: Arthur Hill (Jay Follet), Colleen Dewhurst (Mary Follet), Lillian Gish (Catherine Lynch), John Megna (Rufus), Aline MacMahon (Aunt Hannah Lynch), Lylah Tiffany, Dorrit Kelton, Art Smith, Tom Wheatley, Georgia Simmons. *Director*: Arthur Penn. *Producers:* Fred Coe, Arthur Cantor. 334 performances. Pulitzer Prize.

(Paramount 1963). *Screenplay*: Philip H. Reisman, Jr. *Cast*: Robert Preston (Jay Follet), Jean Simmons (Mary Follet), Helen Carew (Mary's Mother), Pat Hingle (Ralph Follet), Aline MacMahon (Hannah), John Cullum, Michael Keanrey. *Director*: Alex Segal. *Producer*: David Susskind.

(TV 1971). *Teleplay*: Tad Mosel. *Cast:* Joanne Woodward (Mary Follet), Richard Kiley (Jay Follet), Pat Hingle (Ralph Follet), Eileen Heckart

(Hannah), Shane Nickerson, James Woods, Barnard Hughes, Betty Garde. *Director:* Fred Coe. *Producer:* David Susskind.

(TV 1981). *Teleplay:* Tad Mosel. *Cast:* Sally Field (Mary Follet), William Hurt (Jay Follet), Ned Beatty (Ralph Follet), Polly Holliday (Hannah), Ellen Corby, Jeremy Licht, Betty Garrett, Michael Horton. *Director:* Delbert Mann. *Producer:* Charles Raymond.

James Agee's novel *A Death in the Family* has more characterization than plot and the stage version was deemed by some critics more static than theatrical. Yet the portrayal of a family dealing with the sudden death of the father in a car accident was quite stirring on stage, particularly because of the superior cast. Much the same can be said about the film and two television versions of the work. Robert Preston gives a surprisingly subdued performance as the father in the 1963 movie and Jean Simmons is just as effective as his young wife. An outstanding cast was assembled for the 1971 television production though it lacked the atmosphere of the film. The 1981 television remake struck some critics as more melodramatic than tragic though some of the performances were commendable.

American Buffalo

February 16, 1977 (Ethel Barrymore Theatre), a drama by David Mamet. *Cast:* Robert Duvall (Teach), Kenneth McMillan (Don Dubrow), John Savage (Bobby). *Director:* Ulu Grosbard. *Producers:* Edgar Lansbury, Joseph Beruh. 135 performances.

(Goldwyn 1996). *Screenplay:* David Mamet. *Cast:* Dustin Hoffman (Teach), Dennis Franz (Don Dubrow), Sean Nelson (Bobby). *Director:* Michael Correate. *Producer:* Gregory Mosher.

David Mamet's first Broadway play is a salty character piece about three small-time crooks planning and then abandoning the theft of a rare, valuable coin. Mamet's slangy, colorful language gives the play its rhythm and drive and the piece has remained a favorite showcase for actors. The original production was mostly praised but only found an audience for a modest run. Subsequent revivals, particularly two on Broad-

way with Al Pacino, found much more success. The 1996 movie was basically a filmed play with the action pretty much confined to the junk shop where the heist is being planned. It may have made for static filmmaking but, as on stage, it is the acting that counts and Dustin Hoffman, Dennis Franz, and Seal Nelson provide all the theatrics needed.

The American Clock

November 20, 1980 (Biltmore Theatre), a play by Arthur Miller. *Cast:* William Atherton (Lee Baum), Joan Copeland (Rose Baum), John Randolph (Moe Baum), Rosanna Carter, Salem Ludwig, David Chandler, Marilyn Caskey, Francine Beers, Robert Harper. *Director:* Vivian Matalon. *Producers:* Jack Garfein, etc. 12 performances.

(TV 1993). *Teleplay:* Frank Galati. *Cast:* Loren Dean (Younger Lee Baumler), John Randolph (Older Lee Baumler), Mary McDonnell (Rose Baumler), David Straithairn (Young Arthur Huntington), Darren McGavin (Older Arthur Huntington), Felton Perry, John Rubinstein, Eddie Bracken, Jim Dale. *Director:* Bob Clark. *Producer:* Leanne Moore.

Playwright Arthur Miller called this panoramic look at the Great Depression "a mural for the theatre" and it was very cinematic with its many short scenes and dozens of characters. One family was central in the drama but most of the play was more like a documentary with a very wide scope. Some critics found the work intriguing, others dismissed it as scattered and the production folded after twelve performances. The play had been more successful earlier at the Spoloto Festival in South Carolina and many felt it was the New York production that was at fault. Playwright Frank Galati reworked the material and it fared better as a television play in 1993 with its focus on the central family and the flashback sequences more clearly presented.

An American Daughter

April 13, 1997 (Cort Theatre), a play by Wendy Wasserstein. *Cast:* Kate Nelligan (Lyssa Dent Hughes), Peter Riegert (Walter Abrahamson),

Lynne Thigpen (Judith B. Kaufman), Hal Holbrook (Sen. Alan Hughes), Penny Fuller (Chubby Hughes), Cotter Smith, Elizabeth Marvel, Bruce Norris, Andrew Dolan, Peter Benson. *Director*: Daniel Sullivan. *Producer:* Lincoln Center Theatre. 88 performances.

(TV 2000). *Teleplay*: Wendy Wasserstein. *Cast*: Christine Lahti (Lyssa Dent Hughes), Tom Skerritt (Walter), Lynne Thigpen (Judith B. Kaufman), Stanley Anderson (Sen. Alan Hughes), Cynthia Harris (Chubby Hughes), Jay Thomas, Mark Feuerstein, Blake Lindsley. *Director*: Sheldon Larry. *Producers*: Abby Adams, etc.

One of the few plays specifically about women and politics, Wendy Wasserstein's comedy-drama was uneven and sometimes didactic but her usual talent for vibrant characterization and fertile ideas was in evidence. When a celebrated health care expert is nominated by the president of the nation for the post of Surgeon General, the press descends on her and her family and twist her past and her pubic statements into a scandal. One of the highlights of the well-acted production was Lynn Thigpen's performance as an outspoken African American Jewish doctor trying to conceive a child. Thigpen got to reprise the role in the 2000 television production which was very faithful to the play. It was a little less talky than the stage original but most of Wasserstein's potent ideas and sprightly dialogue remained.

Anastasia

December 29, 1954 (Lyceum Theatre), a play by Guy Bolton, Marcelle Maurette. *Cast*: Viveca Lindfors (Anna), Joseph Anthony (Prince Bournine), Eugenie Leontovich (Dowager Empress), Dorothy Patten, David J. Stewart, Hurd Hatfield, William Callan, Boris Tumarin. *Director*: Alan Schneider. *Producer:* Elaine Perry. 272 performances.

(Fox 1956). *Screenplay*: Arthur Laurents, Guy Bolton. *Cast*: Ingrid Bergman (Anastasia), Yul Brynner (Prince Bournine), Helen Hayes (Dowager Empress), Akim Tamiroff, Martita Hunt, Felix Aylmer, Sacha Pitoeff. *Director*: Anatole Litvak. *Producer*: Buddy Adler.

The French play about the lost Romanoff daughter was adapted by Guy Bolton into a Broadway melodrama and, regardless of what critics thought of the part-history, part-fictional tale, all agreed that the scene between the young Anya and her grandmother, the Dowager Empress, was riveting theatre. It was also the highlight of the 1956 film in which Ingrid Bergman and Helen Hayes played together beautifully. A 1967 television version featured Julie Harris as Anya and Lynn Fontanne as the Dowager and their chemistry was also remarkable. Sadly, it was Fontanne's last public performance. In 1965 *Anastasia* was turned into the unsuccessful Broadway musical drama *Anya* using music by Rachmaninoff for the score.

Angels in America

Part One: Millennium Approaches. May 4, 1993; *Part Two: Perestroika*. November 23, 1993 (Walter Kerr Theatre), a play in two parts by Tony Kushner. *Cast*: Ron Leibman (Roy Cohn), Stephen Spinella (Prior Walter), Joe Mantello (Louis Ironson), David Marshall Grant (Joe Pitt), Marcia Gay Harden (Harper Pitt), Jeffrey Wright (Belize, etc.), Kathleen Chalfant (Hannah Pitt, etc.), Ellen McLaughlin (Angel, etc.). *Director*: George C. Wolfe. *Producers:* Gordon Davidson, etc. Part One: 367 performances; Part Two: 216 performances. Pulitzer Prize, Tony Award.

(TV 2003). *Teleplay*: Tony Kushner. *Cast*: Al Pacino (Roy Cohn), Justin Kirk (Prior Walter), Ben Shenkman (Louis Ironson), Patrick Wilson (Joe Pitt), Mary-Louise Parker (Harper Pitt), Meryl Streep (Hannah Pitt, etc.), Jeffrey Wright (Belize, etc.), Emma Thompson (Angel, etc.), James Cromwell, Brian Markinson, Robin Weigert. *Director*: Mike Nichols. *Producer*: Celia Costas.

Surely the most ambitious American drama of the decade, this two-part epic was subtitled a "Gay Fantasia on National Themes" by playwright Tony Kushner and he was as good as his word, dealing with gay America, politics, sex, marriage, religion, family, and fantasy. The play's many plots overlapped and eventually tied together as such diverse characters as Mormons, leftists, politicians, ghosts, angels, and conservatives found themselves intertwined in each other's lives. The play was first seen in London and Los Angeles before finding critical (if not financial) success on Broadway. Some cast members played both male and female characters and the versatility of the actors was among the play's many merits. Plans to condense the long drama into one movie were abandoned and HBO opted to film the entire work for television. The result was one of the finest of all television dramas. Kushner opened up and expanded sections of the epic and director Mike Nichols filmed the realistic drama with a surreal flavor that used all the best cinema techniques. Only Jeffrey Wright, who played the gay nurse Belieze and other roles, was retained for the television version but all the movie stars used in the new cast had considerable stage credits. Al Pacino's gross, funny Roy Cohn may have been the finest performance of his career and Meryl Streep's multiple characterizations were also a marvel. But all of the television cast were superb and the result was a superior American play captured magnificently on the small screen.

Animal Crackers

October 23, 1928 (44th Street Theatre), a musical comedy by George S. Kaufman, Morrie Ryskind. *Score:* Bert Kalmar, Harry Ruby. *Cast:* Groucho Marx (Capt. Spalding), Chico Marx (Emanuel Ravelli), Harpo Marx (Professor), Zeppo Marx (Jamison), Margaret Dumont (Mrs. Rittenhouse), Bobby Perkins, Milton Watson, Bernice Ackerman, Alice Wood. *Songs:* Hooray for Captain Spaulding; Who's Been Listening to My Heart?; Long Island Low-Down; When Things Are Bright and Rosy; Musketeers. *Director:* Oscar Eagle. *Choreographer:* Russell E. Markert. *Producer:* Sam H. Harris. 191 performances.

(Paramount 1930). *Screenplay:* George S. Kaufman, Morrie Ryskind. *Score:* Bert Kalmar, Harry Ruby, Shelton Brooks, etc. *Cast:* Groucho Marx (Capt. Spalding), Chico Marx (Emanuel Ravelli), Harpo Marx (Professor), Zeppo Marx (Jamison), Margaret Dumont (Mrs. Rittenhouse), Lillian Roth, Hal Thompson, Louis Sorin. *Songs:* Hooray for Captain Spaulding; Why Am I So Romantic?; Collegiate; Some of These Days. *Director:* Victor Heerman.

The story may have revolved around a stolen painting at a Long Island mansion, but the real entertainment came from the presence of the Marx Brothers in their third (and last) Broadway musical. Groucho played the African explorer Captain Spalding and Chico and Harpo were a pair a harmless henchmen who get caught up in the theft. Comic anarchy took over for much of the evening and the team became famous for never doing the same show twice. It was filmed in the Astoria Studios in Queens where conditions were far from sophisticated. But despite the artificial sets, awkward dance numbers, and the stagy quality, the movie remains thoroughly delightful whenever the Brothers are center stage.

The Animal Kingdom

January 12, 1932 (Broadhurst Theatre), a comedy by Philip Barry. *Cast:* Leslie Howard (Tom Collier), Lora Baxter (Cecilia Henry), Frances Fuller (Daisy Sage), Ilka Chase (Grace Macomber), G. Albert Smith, Frederick Forrester, William Gargan. *Director:* Gilbert Miller. *Producers:* Gilbert Miller, Leslie Howard. 183 performances.

(RKO 1932). *Screenplay:* Horace Jackson. *Cast:* Leslie Howard (Tom Collier), Myrna Loy (Cecilia Henry), Ann Harding (Daisy Sage), Ilka Chase (Grace), William Gargan, Neil Hamilton, Henry Stephenson. *Directors:* Edward H. Griffith, George Cukor. *Producer:* David O. Selznick.

One More Tomorrow (Warner 1946). *Screenplay:* Charles Hoffman, etc. *Cast:* Ann Sheridan (Christie Sage), Dennis Morgan (Tom Collier), Alexis Smith (Cecilia), Jack Carson, Jane Wyman, Reginald Gardiner, John Loder, Marjorie Gateson. *Director:* Peter Godfrey. *Producer:* Henry Blanke.

This stylish comedy of manners was playwright Philip Barry at his most introspective. A successful publisher decides to discard his artist mistress and marry a proper girl, only to find his new wife so manipulative that she forces him back into the arms of his previous lover. Leslie Howard shone as the publisher as he nicely balanced the wit and pathos of the piece. He repeated his performance in the 1932 film and was given fine support by Myra Loy and Ann Harding as the two women in his life. The unusually intelligent comedy was remade in 1946 under the title *One More Tomorrow* and it was unusually hollow. Dennis Morgan was a rich playboy who buys up Ann Sheridan's magazine in order to romance her and no one much cared what happened to them after that. Lacking Barry's style and sensibility (as well as dialogue), the film turned the comedy into a dull curiosity.

Anna Christie

November 2, 1921 (Vanderbilt Theatre), a drama by Eugene O'Neill. *Cast*: Pauline Lord (Anna), Frank Shannon (Mat Burke), George Marion (Chris Christopherson), Eugenie Blair (Marthy Owen), James C. Mack, Ole Anderson. *Producer*: Arthur Hopkins. 177 performances. Pulitzer Prize.

(First National 1923). *Screenplay*: Bradley King. *Cast*: Blanche Sweet (Anna), William Russell (Matt Burke), George F. Marion (Chris Christopherson), Eugenie Besserer (Marthy), Chester Conklin, Ralph Yearsley, George Siegmann. *Directors*: John Griffith Wray, Thomas H. Ince. *Producer*: Thomas H. Ince.

(MGM 1930). *Screenplay*: Frances Marion. *Cast*: Greta Garbo (Anna), Charles Bickford (Matt Burke), George F. Marion (Chris Christopherson), Marie Dressler (Marthy), James C. Mack, Lee Phelps, Jack Baxley. *Director-producer*: Clarence Brown.

Eugene O'Neill's early drama is perhaps more romantic and optimistic than most of his other works but it is no less powerful. The former prostitute Anna returns to her father in New York City and falls in love with the rough but tenderhearted sailor Mat. When he finds out about her past Mat rejects her, but Anna make no apologies and wins him back by her direct and fearless ways. The beloved actress Pauline Lord captured the enigmatic quality of Anna and her characterization introduced a tougher kind of heroine to the American stage. The drama was first filmed in 1923 with silent screen star Blanche Sweet as Anna but the more famous version was the 1930 movie that marked Greta Garbo's first talkie. The promotion ads announced "Garbo Talks!" and moviegoers anxiously awaited for the exotic screen star to utter her first words on screen. When she spoke in her low, weary voice

Garbo immediately became a star all over again. The film is actually rather primitive and static and only the fine acting gives it any distinction. Garbo reprised her Anna in a German film in 1931 and in 1936 a very early television production was made with Flora Robson in the title role. A British television version in 1957 featured Diane Cilento as Anna and a young, unknown Sean Connery as the sailor Mat. That same year the play was turned into the Broadway musical hit *New Girl in Town* with Gwen Verdon as a dancing Anna. Its score was by Bob Merrill who had also written the songs for the other O'Neill musical *Take Me Along*, based on *Ah, Wilderness!* (qv).

Anna Lucasta

August 30, 1944 (Mansfield Theatre), a drama by Philip Yordan. *Cast*: Hilda Simms (Anna Lucasta), Earle Hyman (Rudolph), Frederick O'Neal (Frank), Alice Childress, Rosetta LeNoire, Canada Lee. *Director*: Harry Wagstaff Gribble. *Producer*: John J. Wildberg. 957 performances.

(Columbia 1949). *Screenplay*: Arthur Laurents. *Cast*: Paulette Goddard (Anna Lucasta), William Bishop (Rudolf Strobel), Broderick Crawford (Frank), Oscar Homolka, John Ireland, Will Geer, Gale Page, Mary Wickes. *Director*: Irving Rapper. *Producer*: Philip Yordan.

(Longridge Enterprises 1958). *Screenplay*: Philip Yordan. *Cast*: Eartha Kitt (Anna), Sammy Davis, Jr. (Danny Johnson), Frederick O'Neal (Frank), Rex Ingram (Joe Lucasta), Georgia Burke, Rosetta LeNoire. *Director*: Arnold Laven. *Producer*: Sidney Harmon.

This drama, about a former prostitute who returns home to start a new life and falls in love with a man who is unaware of her past, had more than a passing resemblance to Eugene O'Neill's *Anna Christie* (qv) yet the play had its own merits. The Polish family Anna returns to is filled with interesting characters and the relationship between Anna and her beau is more detailed. No producer would pick up the drama except the American Negro Theatre Company so playwright Philip Yordan rewrote the piece and made Anna an African American who walked the streets of Brooklyn before returning to her family in Pennsylvania. The production featured a cast of promising black actors and was a surprise hit, one of the longest-running plays of the 1940s. Ironically, the first movie version in 1949 restored the Polish-American characters and Paulette Goddard was commendable as Anna, but the slow-paced drama rarely rose above domestic melodrama. An impressive all-black cast was used in the 1958 remake and the result was somewhat more satisfying. Eartha Kitt may have been fairly one-dimensional as Anna but Rex Ingram as her father and others in the cast gave powerful performances.

Anne of the Thousand Days

December 8, 1948 (Shubert Theatre), a drama by Maxwell Anderson. *Cast*: Rex Harrison (Henry VIII), Joyce Redman (Anne Boleyn), Robert Duke (Percy), Percy Waram (Cardinal Wolsey), Wendell K. Philips (Cromwell), John Merivale, Allan Stevenson, John Williams. *Director*: H. C. Potter. *Producer*: Playwrights' Company. 288 performances.

(Universal 1969). *Screenplay*: Bridget Boland, etc. *Cast*: Richard Burton (Henry VIII), Genevieve Bujold (Anne Boleyn), Anthony Quayle (Cardinal Wolsey), John Colicos (Cromwell), Irene Papas, Michael Hordern, Katherine Blake. *Director*: Charles Jarrott. *Producer*: Hal B. Wallis.

What made this costume drama about Anne Boleyn and her 1000-day courtship and marriage to Henry VIII more than routine was playwright Maxwell Anderson's use of blank verse in the dialogue. While some critics found it stuffy, others thought the writing lively and interesting and the familiar characters vividly portrayed. Most agreed that Rex Harrison, in his first major Broadway role, was outstanding. Because the play was only a modest success and the 1933 film *The Private Life of Henry VIII* with Charles Laughton as Henry was so well remembered, Hollywood passed on filming Anderson's play until 1969. It was given splendid production values but rarely was the historical movie very exciting. Richard Burton is a surprisingly low-key Henry but Genevieve Bujold shines radiantly as Anne. Excellent

performances by the polished supporting cast certainly helped. The film was very popular with the public yet the original play is hardly ever revived.

Annie

April 21, 1977 (Alvin Theatre), a musical comedy by Thomas Meehan. *Score:* Charles Strouse, Martin Charnin. *Cast:* Andrea McArdle (Annie), Dorothy Loudon (Miss Hannigan), Reid Shelton (Oliver Warbucks), Sandy Faison (Grace Farrell), Robert Fitch (Rooster), Barbara Erwin (Lily), Raymond Thorne, Laurie Beechman. *Songs:* Tomorrow; You're Never Fully Dressed Without a Smile; It's a Hard-Knock Life; Maybe; Little Girls; Easy Street. *Director:* Martin Charnin. *Choreographer:* Peter Gennaro. *Producers:* Mike Nichols, etc. 2,377 performances. Tony Award.

(Columbia 1982). *Screenplay:* Carol Sobieski. *Score:* Charles Strouse, Martin Charnin. *Cast:* Aileen Quinn (Annie), Albert Finney (Oliver Warbucks), Carol Burnett (Miss Hannigan), Tim Curry (Rooster), Bernadette Peters (Lily), Ann Reinking (Grace Farrell), Edward Herrmann, Geoffrey Holder. *Songs:* Tomorrow; You're Never Fully Dressed Without a Smile; It's a Hard-Knock Life; Maybe; Little Girls; Easy Street; Let's Go to the Movies. *Director:* John Huston. *Choreographer:* Arlene Phillips. *Producer:* Ray Stark.

(TV 1999). *Teleplay*: Irene Mecchi. *Score*: Charles Strouse, Martin Charnin. *Cast*: Alice Morton (Annie), Victor Garber (Daddy Warbucks), Kathy Bates (Miss Hannigan), Alan Cummings (Rooster), Kristin Chenoweth (Lily), Audra McDonald (Grace), Ernie Sabella, Dennis Howard. *Songs*: Tomorrow; You're Never Fully Dressed Without a Smile; It's a Hard-Knock Life; Maybe; Little Girls; Easy Street. *Director-choreographer*: Rob Marshall. *Producer*: John Whitman.

A highly professional, well-crafted musical comedy that never takes itself too seriously, *Annie* not only enjoyed a long run on Broadway and on tour but remains one of the most produced musicals by school, community, and summer theatres. Thomas Meehan's well-plotted libretto took one-dimensional cartoon characters and turned them into vibrant musical comedy creations. From the villainous Miss Hannigan to the sweet but spunky orphan herself, the characters easily move from jokes to songs to pathos.

Meehan's original plot dealt with some crooks trying to cash in on Annie's new-found prestige as the favorite of billionaire Daddy Warbucks. It was a slight but enjoyable story that easily lent itself to vivacious musical numbers, some of them capturing the slaphappy optimism of the Depression years. Columbia paid a record $9.5 million for the screen rights and another $52 million on the production and the dismal result just about bankrupted the studio. Poor choices in script, director, and star have accurately been cited as the reason for the film's failure to please either audiences or critics. Yet there are a few delicious performances to be found in the movie, particularly Carol Burnett as Hannigan and Bernadette Peters and Tim Cury as her cronies. But so much about the film version is so wrong-headed that there is some truth to the belief that *Annie*, more than any other film, signaled the death of the movie musical. Disney made an abridged television version in 1999 with Alice Morton as Annie, Victor Garber as Warbucks, and Kathy Bates as Hannigan and it often managed to capture the spirit of the original stage show. The script was abridged and changed (with mixed results) but for the most part it was the sprightly musical that the movie should have been. The stage sequels *Annie II* and *Annie Warbucks* both failed.

Annie Get Your Gun

May 16 1946 (Imperial Theatre), a musical comedy by Herbert Fields, Dorothy Fields. *Score:* Irving Berlin. *Cast:* Ethel Merman (Annie Oakley), Ray Middleton (Frank Butler), Marty May, William O'Neal, Kenny Bowers, Lea Penman, Harry Belaver, Lubov Roudenko. *Songs:* They Say It's Wonderful; You Can't Get a Man With a Gun; There's No Business Like Show Business; I Got Lost in His Arms; Doin' What Comes Natur'lly; I Got the Sun in the Morning; My Defenses Are Down; Anything You Can Do; Moonshine Lullaby; The Girl That I Marry. *Director:* Joshua Logan. *Choreographer:* Helen Tamiris. *Producers:* Rodgers and Hammerstein. 1,147 performances.

(MGM 1950). *Screenplay:* Sidney Sheldon. *Score:* Irving Berlin. *Cast:* Betty Hutton (Annie Oakley), Howard Keel (Frank Butler), Louis Calhern, J. Carroll Naish, Edward Arnold, Benay Venuta,

Keenan Wynn, Chief Yowlachie. *Songs:* They Say It's Wonderful; You Can't Get a Man With a Gun; There's No Business Like Show Business; Doin' What Comes Natur'lly; I Got the Sun in the Morning; My Defenses Are Down; The Girl That I Marry; Anything You Can Do. *Director:* George Sidney. *Choreographer:* Robert Alton. *Producer:* Arthur Freed.

Both Irving Berlin's and Ethel Merman's longest-running Broadway hit, this musical biography of sharpshooter Annie Oakley was tailor made for its star but it has found favor over the years with other performers as well. Jerome Kern was slated to score the project but after his untimely death producers Rodgers and Hammerstein persuaded Berlin to do the songs. It turned out to be his greatest score and was filled with future standards. It was also his first score in the new integrated style introduced by *Oklahoma!* (qv) and the veteran songwriter proved he could write memorable tunes for the new Broadway as well as the old. Merman's Annie was tough, funny, and endearing, and her supporting cast was first rate. Judy Garland was contracted to play the sharpshooter in the film and even completed some scenes before illness and instability forced the studio to begin again with Betty Hutton as Annie. At her best in broad, supporting roles, Hutton played up the comedy in the part and her singing delivery sometimes slipped into her trademark air raid siren voice. It is a wild, manic performance but not a very satisfying one. Ten of the stage score's songs were kept for the film and the movie was given huge, expensive production values. Yet much of the spectacle is underwhelming and the film is poorly paced. On the plus side, Howard Keel, in his screen debut, played Annie's rival and love interest and he was both solid and believable. The film itself was very popular (the top grossing picture of the year) but does not hold up very well. There was an abridged television version of the musical in 1957 with Mary Martin and John Raitt as the quarreling couple and in 1967 a stage revival with Merman reprising her Annie was recreated in a television studio. Both versions are stagy and sometimes awkward but they are important records of two of Broadway's greatest stars playing one of the musical theatre's most flavorful parts.

Anniversary Waltz

April 7, 1954 (Broadhurst Theatre), a comedy by Jerome Chodorov, Joseph Fields. *Cast*: Macdonald Carey (Bud Walters), Kitty Carlisle (Alice Walters), Phyllis Povah, Howard Smith, Warren Beringer, Mary Lee Dearring, Pauline Myers. *Director*: Moss Hart. *Producers:* Joseph M. Hyman, Bernard Hart. 615 performances.

Happy Anniversary (United Artists 1959). *Screenplay*: Joseph Fields, Jerome Chodorov. *Cast*: David Niven (Chris Walters), Mitzi Gaynor (Alice Walters), Phyllis Povah, Carl Reiner, Loring Smith, Monique Van Vooren, Elizabeth Wilson, Patty Duke. *Director*: David Miller. *Producer*: Ralph Fields.

A slapdash comedy of questionable taste, this surprise hit was about a married couple who mistakenly reveal to their children that they had premarital sex. In the contrived plot, the offspring broadcast the news on television and all hell breaks out. One of the first plays to recognize the new medium of television, it made its opinion of the tube clear when the husband smashes the family television set ... more than once. The 1959 movie was called *Happy Anniversary* and it was no improvement over the play. A likable cast strains itself with feeble results though it is interesting to see the young Patty Duke take on comedy after her recent success in the dramatic *The Miracle Worker* (qv).

Another Language

April 25, 1932 (Booth Theatre), a play by Rose Franken. *Cast*: Margaret Wycherly (Mrs. Hallam), Glenn Anders (Victor Hallam), Dorothy Stickney (Stella Hallam), John Beal (Jerry Hallam), Margaret Hamilton (Helen Hallam), Herbert Duffy, Irene Cattell, Maude Allan, Wyrley Birch, Hal K. Dawson, William Pike. *Director-producer*: Arthur J. Beckhard. 348 performances.

(MGM 1933). *Screenplay*: Herman J. Mankiewicz, Donald Ogden Stewart, Gertrude Purcell. *Cast*: Helen Hayes (Stella Hallam), Robert Montgomery (Victor Hallam), Louise Closser Hale (Mother Hallam), John Beal (Jerry Hallam), Margaret Hamilton (Helen Hallam), Henry Travers, Willard Robertson, Irene Cattell, Minor Watson. *Director*: Edward H. Griffith. *Producer*: Walter Wanger.

Playwright Rose Franken's usual insight into women and their ability to control men was at the center of this drama about a domineering mother whose grip on her grown children is not broken until her outspoken daughter-in-law puts her foot down. The slight but engrossing play was well received by both press and theatregoers and it ran nearly a year during the darkest days of the Depression. A strong cast (including a few members of the Broadway company) was the highlight of the 1933 film which gave Helen Hayes one of her too-few opportunities to shine on screen. As dated as the domestic drama has become, there is still something fascinating about its view of determined women.

Another Part of the Forest

November 20, 1946 (Fulton Theatre), a play by Lillian Hellman. *Cast*: Patricia Neal (Regina Hubbard), Leo Genn (Ben Hubbard), Percy Waram (Marcus Hubbard), Mildred Dunnock (Lavinia Hubbard), Scott McKay (Oscar Hubbard), Margaret Philips, Paul Ford, Jean Hagen. *Director*: Lillian Hellman. *Producer:* Kermit Bloomgarden. 182 performances.

(Universal 1948). *Screenplay*: Vladimir Pozner. *Cast*: Fredric March (Marcus Hubbard), Ann Blyth (Regina Hubbard) Dan Duryea (Oscar Hubbard), Edmond O'Brien (Ben Hubbard), Florence Eldridge (Lavinia Hubbard), John Dull, Dona Frake, Betsy Blair, Fritz Leiber. *Director*: Michael Gordon. *Producer*: Jerry Bresler.

Lillian Hellman's prequel to her popular drama *The Little Foxes* (qv) attempts to explain how the grasping Hubbard family got that way. Blockade running and extortion with the enemy during the Civil War brought the family their fortune but they are not content. Soon they are blackmailing each other for more and only the hard, cold Regina is content to wait until the next play to get what she wants. Although it was well received by the critics, audiences were not as interested in the Hubbards the second time around. The talky play was made into a talky movie in 1948 yet the sterling cast is never less than provocative.

Any Wednesday

February 18, 1964 (Music Box Theatre), a comedy by Muriel Resnik. *Cast*: Don Porter (John Cleves), Sandy Dennis (Ellen Gordon), Rosemary Murphy (Dorothy Cleves), Gene Hackman (Cass Henderson). *Director*: Henry Kaplan. *Producers:* George W. George, etc. 982 performances.

(Warner 1966). *Screenplay*: Julius P. Epstein. *Cast*: Jane Fonda (Ellen Gordon), Jason Robards (John Cleves), Dean Jones (Cass Henderson), Rosemary Murphy (Dorothy Cleves), Ann Prentiss, Jack Fletcher. *Director*: Robert Ellis Miller. *Producer*: Julius P. Epstein.

This "sleeper" comedy hit was slight in plot and ideas but had a slick amiability that was right for the time. A spoiled, pampered husband writes off his mistress as a tax exemption and he gets his comeuppance from both wife and lover. The critics mostly scowled but audiences kept the harmless comedy running for nearly three years. The 1966 film version is sluggishly paced but Jason Robards and Jane Fonda are personable enough to make much of it entertaining. A highlight in both the stage and screen productions is Rosemary Murphy as the droll wife who doesn't seem much concerned about her husband's infidelity.

Anything Goes

November 21, 1934 (Alvin Theatre), a musical comedy by Guy Bolton, P. G. Wodehouse, Howard Lindsay, Russel Crouse. *Score:* Cole Porter. *Cast:* William Gaxton (Billy Crocker), Ethel Merman (Reno Sweeney), Victor Moore (Rev. Dr. Moon), Bettina Hall (Hope Harcourt), Vera Dunn, Leslie Barrie, Helen Raymond. *Songs:* I Get a Kick Out of You; Anything Goes; All Through the Night; You're the Top; Blow, Gabriel, Blow; Be Like the Bluebird; The Gypsy in Me. *Director:* Howard Lindsay. *Choreographer:* Robert Alton. *Producer:* Vinton Freedley. 420 performances.

(Paramount 1936). *Screenplay:* Guy Bolton, Howard Lindsay, Russel Crouse. *Score:* Cole Porter, etc. *Cast:* Bing Crosby (Billy Crocker), Ethel Merman (Reno Sweeney), Ida Lupino (Hope Harcourt), Charles Ruggles (Rev. Dr. Moon), Arthur Treacher, Grace Bradley, Richard Carle, Margaret Dumont, Keye Luke. *Songs:* I Get a Kick Out of You; Anything Goes; Moonburn; My Heart and I; You're the Top; Blow, Gabriel, Blow; Sailor Beware. *Director:* Lewis Milestone. *Producer*: Benjamin Glazer.

(Paramount 1956). *Screenplay:* Sidney Sheldon. *Score:* Cole Porter, Jimmy Van Heusen, Sammy Cahn. *Cast:* Bing Crosby (Bill Benson), Donald O'Connor (Ted Adams), Mitzi Gaynor (Patsy Blair), Jeanmaire (Gaby Duval), Phil Harris, Kurt Kasznar, Richard Erdman, Walter Sande. *Songs:* I Get a Kick Out of You; All Through the Night; You're the Top; Blow, Gabriel, Blow; It's De-Lovely; You Gotta Give the People Hoke; A Second-Hand Turban and a Crystal Ball. *Director:* Robert Lewis. *Choreographers:* Nick Castle, Ernie Flatt, Roland Petit. *Producer:* Robert Emmett Dolan

Perhaps the most revived musical from the 1930s, this Broadway blockbuster almost didn't happen. P. G. Wodehouse and Guy Bolton wrote a silly libretto about an ocean liner that experiences a bomb threat then is washed up on a desert island. Cole Porter completed the score and the show was cast when the authors left for a project in London. But when the liner *S. S. Morro Castle* caught fire off the coast of New Jersey and 125 people died, the producers knew they had to scrap their plot or cancel the production. Director Howard Lindsay and press agent Russel Crouse quickly cobbled together a new libretto using the same sets, costumes, songs and cast, the result being a surprisingly coherent musical comedy about romance and harmless gangsters on the high seas. Ethel Merman played an evangelist-turned-nightclub-singer, William Gaxton was a stowaway trying to win his sweetheart on board, and Victor Moore was the befuddled gangster who never seems to make the FBI's Top Ten most wanted list. The show ran over a year during the Depression and was filmed twice, neither time very satisfactorily. The 1936 version was faithful to the original, keeping a good portion of the score as well as Merman who got to singer "I Get a Kick Out of You" and "You're the Top" (with laundered lyrics). Bing Crosby and Ida Lupino as the lovers and Charles Ruggles as the gangster gave competent but not exceptional performances. A 1956 remake tossed out the plot and half of the score and came up with a contrived vehicle for Crosby and Donald O'Connor as two producers looking for a new leading lady for their next show. They discover Jeanmaire and Mitzi Gaynor but nothing much happens aside from pleasant production numbers. Neither movie version seems to have hurt the popularity of *Anything Goes*; it's revived on stage all the time.

Arsenic and Old Lace

January 10, 1941 (Fulton Theatre), a comedy by Joseph Kesselring. *Cast*: Josephine Hull (Abby Brewster), Jean Adair (Martha Brewster), Allyn Joslyn (Mortimer Brewster), Boris Karloff (Jonathan Brewster), John Alexander (Teddy), Edgar Stehli, Helen Brooks. *Director*: Bretaigne Windust. *Producers:* Howard Lindsay, Russel Crouse. 1,444 performances.

(Warner 1944). *Screenplay*: Julius J. Epstein, Phillip G. Epstein. *Cast*: Cary Grant (Mortimer Brewster), Josephine Hull (Abby Brewster), Jean Adair (Martha Brewster), Raymond Massey (Jonathan Brewster), John Alexander (Teddy), Priscilla Lane, Jack Carson, Peter Lorre, Edward Everett Horton, James Gleason. *Director-producer*: Frank Capra.

(TV 1969). *Cast:* Helen Hayes (Abby Brewster), Lillian Gish Martha Brewster), Bob Crane (Mortimer Brewster), Fred Gwynne (Jonathan Brewster), David Wayne (Teddy), Sue Lyon, Richard Deacon, Jack Gilford, Billy De Wolfe. *Director:* Robert Scheerer.

One of the longest-running plays in the American theatre, this farce continues to please not because its characters or dialogue are of any interest but because of its wacky premise: two sweet old ladies murder off a series of old gentlemen who seem unhappy with life. Legend has it that Joseph Kesselring wrote the piece as a serious thriller and that producers Howard Lindsay and Russel Crouse rewrote it as broad comedy. For decades the dark comedy has remained a favorite with all kinds of producing groups, from Broadway to high schools. Frank

Capra's 1944 screen version opened the story up somewhat and kept the piece moving in a broad, rapid manner. Cary Grant, as the nephew Mortimer who discovers what his two elderly aunts are up to, gives a fever-pitch performance filled with so many double takes that he seems like a cartoon; possibly his best and worst comic portrayal. Josephine Hull and Jean Adair played the aunts on stage and on screen and they are the glue that holds the story together. The film also boasts a variety of delightful character actors in playful supporting roles. A very abridged version of the play was shown on television in 1955 and in 1969 the comedy was reset in the 1960s and clumsily altered. (Newspaper drama critic Mortimer became a television critic.) It is indeed unfortunate that this version was so misguided for it had a first-rate cast, including Helen Hayes and Lillian Gish as the aunts.

As Is

March 10, 1985 (Circle Theatre), a play by William M. Hoffman. *Cast*: Jonathan Hogan (Rich), Jonathan Hadary (Saul), Steven Gregan (Chet), Lou Liberatore, Lily Knight, Claris Erickson, Mary Myers, Ken Kliban. *Director*: Marshall W. Mason. *Producer:* Circle Repertory Company. 49 performances.

(TV 1986). *Teleplay*: William M. Hoffman. *Cast*: Robert Carradine (Rich), Jonathan Hadary (Saul), Doug Annear (Chet), Colleen Dewhurst, Joanna Miles, Alan Scarfe. *Director*: Michael Lindsay-Hogg. *Producer*: Iris Merlis.

One of the first and best plays about the AIDS epidemic, this powerful drama did not preach or place blame but instead concentrated on the way the disease altered the relationship between lovers, family members, and friends. The Off Broadway production had a limited run but the play transferred to Broadway for a few months and was frequently presented by schools and other groups across the country. The 1986 television production is mostly studio bound and edited so that it resembles a documentary but the characters still come across with compassion and the piece remains very effective.

At War with the Army

March 8, 1949 (Booth Theatre), a farce by James B. Allardice. *Cast*: Gary Merrill (Sgt. Robert Johnson), Maxine Stuart (Millie), William Mendrek (Captain Caldwell), Sara Seegar (Mrs. Caldwell), George Mosel, Ernest Sarracino, Jerry Jarrett, Mike Kellin, Ty Perry, Mitchell Agruss, Kenneth Forbes. *Director*: Ezra Stone. *Producers*: Henry May, Jerome E. Rosenfeld. 151 performances.

(Paramount 1951). *Screenplay*: Fred K. Finklehoffe. *Cast*: Dean Martin (Sgt. Vic Puccinelli), Jerry Lewis (Pfc. Alvin Korwin), Mike Kellin (Sgt. McVey), Polly Bergen (Helen Palmer), Jimmie Dundee (Eddie), Dick Stabile, Tommy Farrell, Frank Hyers. *Director*: Hal Walker. *Producer*: Fred K. Finklehoffe.

This military farce was filled with the usual barracks high jinks and colorful Army types and it found some favor with post-war theatregoers. In 1944 a sergeant at a training camp in Kentucky is anxious to go overseas and join in the fighting but Army red tape and a local girl friend stand in his way. The comedy was rewritten by the studio as a vehicle for Dean Martin and Jerry Lewis; it was the team's first starring roles on screen. Many of the comic bits from the play survived (including a running gag with a Coke machine with a mind of its own) and the two comic are entertaining without being overwhelming. Yet the public heartily embraced Martin and Lewis and their long screen partnership began.

Auntie Mame

October 31, 1956 (Broadhurst Theatre), a comedy by Jerome Lawrence, Robert E. Lee. *Cast*: Rosalind Russell (Mame Dennis), Polly Rowles (Vera Charles), Peggy Cass (Agnes Gooch), Robert Smith, Jan Handzlik, Robert Higgins, Yuki Shimoda. *Director*: Morton Da Costa. *Producers*: Robert Fryer, Lawrence Carr. 639 performances.

(Warner 1958). *Screenplay*: Betty Comden, Adolph Green. *Cast*: Rosalind Russell (Mame Dennis), Coral Browne (Vera Charles), Peggy Cass (Agnes Gooch), Forrest Tucker, Fred Clark, Jan Handzlik, Roger Smith, Patrick Knowles, Lee Patrick, Joanna Barnes. *Director*: Morton Da Costa. *Producers*: Robert Fryer, Lawrence Carr.

Author Patrick Dennis first introduced the wacky, life-affirming Auntie Mame in a novel and she would return as a play, a film, a musical, and a film musical. Jerome Lawrence and Robert E. Lee took the episodic book, about how Mame raised her nephew in unconventional ways, and created a loose, episodic stage comedy out of the material that moved like a series of blackout sketches. Rosalind Russell scored a triumph as the irrepressible aunt and her animated performance was reprised in the 1958 movie. Although the film was too slowly paced and some scenes dragged on, Russell kept the production afloat and the picture was very popular at the box office. A decade later the property was turned into the Broadway musical *Mame* (qv).

Avanti!

January 31, 1968 (Booth Theatre), a comedy by Samuel Taylor. *Cast*: Robert Reed (Alexander Ben Claiborne), Keith Baxter (Baldassare Pantaleone), Jennifer Hilary (Alison Ames), Betsy Von Furstenburg (Helen Claiborne), Rik Pierce. *Director*: Nigel Patrick. *Producers*: Morris Jacobs, Jerome Whyte. 21 performances.

(United Artists 1972). *Screenplay*: I. A. L. Diamond, Billy Wilder. *Cast*: Jack Lemmon (Wendell Armbruster) Juliet Mills (Pamela Piggot), Clive Revill (Carlo Carlucci), Edward Andrews, Gianfranco Barra, Pippo Franco. *Producer-director*: Billy Wilder.

This gimmicky comedy was about infidelity across the generations. When an American businessman goes to Rome to bring back the body of his father, he learns that the old boy had been going there yearly to have an affair with an English woman. She has died in the same car accident as the father and her daughter arrives to claim the body. Soon the daughter and the American are lovers and plan to continue the parents' annual trysts. The comedy was not well received by the press or the public, though Keith Baxter was praised for his funny Italian "Baldo" who knows how to arrange everything. Although the play failed on Broadway, Hollywood bought the property as a vehicle for Jack Lemmon. But the chemistry between Lemmon and Juliet Mills as the English daughter is tepid and the contrived aspects of the plot seem even more obvious on screen. But again the liveliest moments in the film come from the Italian fixer, played with relish by Clive Revill.

Awake and Sing!

February 19, 1935 (Belasco Theatre), a play by Clifford Odets. *Cast*: Stella Adler (Bessie), John Garfield (Ralph), Morris Carnovsky (Jacob), Luther Adler (Moe Axelrod), Phoebe Brand (Hennie), Art Smith, Sanford Meisner, J. E. Bromberg, Roman Bohnen. *Director*: Harold Clurman. *Producer:* Group Theatre. 184 performances.

(TV 1972). *Teleplay*: Clifford Odets. *Cast*: Ruth Storey (Bessie), Robert Lipton (Ralph), Leo Fuchs (Jacob), Walter Matthau (Moe Axelrod), Felicia Farr (Hennie), Ron Rifkin, Martin Ritt, Milton Selzer, John Myhers. *Directors*: Robert Hopkins, Norman Lloyd. *Producer*: Norman Lloyd.

A landmark play in more ways than one, Clifford Odets's domestic drama was the first major American work that looked at a Jewish family without sentiment, jokes, or clichés. The mother Bessie Berger dominates her lower-income household, destroying the dreams of her son and the happiness of her daughter in her efforts to survive the Depression. The original production was a triumph for the ambitious Group Theatre and one of the earliest examples of the American acting Method. Because of its anti-establishment and leftist views, Hollywood avoided any efforts to film the play. In 1972 a television production featured a mostly unknown cast (though Walter Matthau shone as the bitter and crippled war vet Moe) but captured the flavor of 1930s socialist theatre. Revivals of the drama are sporadic and the difficult piece has been known to sometimes wallow in agit prop, other times to still astound with its vibrant characters and ideas.

The Awful Truth

September 18, 1922 (Henry Miller Theatre), a comedy by Arthur Richman. *Cast*: Ina Claire (Lucy Warriner), Bruce McRae (Norman Satterly), Paul Harvey (Daniel Leeson), Raymond Walburn (Rufus Kempster), Louise Mackintosh, Cora Witherspoon. *Producer*: Charles Frohman. 144 performances.

(Pathé Exchange 1929). *Screenplay*: Horace Jackson, Arthur Richman. *Cast*: Ina Claire (Lucy Warriner), Henry Daniell (Norman Warriner), Theodore Van Eltz (Edgar Trent), Paul Harvey (Dan Leeson), Blanche Frederici, Judith Vosselli, John Roach. *Director*: Marshall Neilan. *Producer*: Maurice Revnes.

(Columbia 1937). *Screenplay*: Vina Delmar, Sidney Buchman. *Cast*: Irene Dunne (Lucy Warriner), Cary Grant (Jerry Warriner), Ralph Bellamy (Dan Leeson), Alexander D'Arcy (Armand Duvalle), Cecil Cunningham, Molly Lamont, Esther Dale. *Director-producer*: Leo McCarey.

Let's Do It Again (Columbia 1953). *Screenplay*: Mary Loos, Richard Sale. *Cast*: Jane Wyman (Constance Stuart), Ray Milland (Gary Stuart), Aldo Ray (Frank McGraw), Leon Ames, John Helmore, Valerie Bettis, Karen Booth. *Director*: Alexander Hall. *Producer*: Oscar Saul.

This early example of the divorced-couple-falling-back-in-love comedy, repeated many times later on stage and screen, was filmed four times, each version making changes liberally and with mixed results. The play was a vehicle for Ina Claire who played the divorcée Lucy who wishes to marry a stuffy conservative so she persuades her ex-husband to convince her fiancé of her unstained character. It was a contrived plot but it served to bring the former couple together with plenty of knowing laughs along the way. Since most of the fun was in the dialogue, the 1925 silent movie with Agnes Ayers and Warner Baxter was only a pale copy of the original. Claire got to repeat her scatterbrained performance as Lucy in a 1929 talkie with Henry Daniell as her ex and it is a primitive but enjoyable record of what the play must have sounded like. The most popular movie version, a 1937 comedy with Irene Dunne and Cary Grant, practically rewrote the whole play, concentrating on the courtroom divorce trial and adding some delightful dialogue and plot twists. But it still came down to the quarreling couple getting back together again. The story was further diluted and musicalized in 1953 as *Let's Do It Again* with Jane Wyman and Ray Milland as married songwriters who agree to split but are rematched after a couple of musical numbers.

Babes in Arms

April 14, 1937 (Shubert Theatre), a musical comedy by Richard Rodgers, Lorenz Hart. *Score:* Richard Rodgers, Lorenz Hart. *Cast:* Mitzi Green (Billie Smith), Wynn Murray (Baby Rose), Ray Heatherton (Val LaMar), Alfred Drake, Nicholas Brothers, Duke McHale, Ray McDonald, Grace McDonald, Dan Dailey. *Songs:* My Funny Valentine; The Lady Is a Tramp; Where or When; All at Once; Way Out West; Johnny One Note; Babes in Arms; I Wish I Were in Love Again. *Director:* Robert Sinclair. *Choreographer:* George Balanchine. *Producer:* Dwight Deere Wiman. 289 performances.

(MGM 1939). *Screenplay:* Jack McGowan, Kay Van Riper. *Score:* Richard Rodgers, Lorenz Hart, Nacio Herb Brown, Arthur Freed, etc. *Cast:* Mickey Rooney (Mickey Moran), Judy Garland (Patsy Barton), June Preisser (Rosalie Essex), Charles Winninger (Joe Moran), Guy Kibbee (Judge Black), Betty Jaynes, Grace Hayes, Douglas McPhail, Margaret Hamilton, Henry Hull, John Sheffield, Rand Brooks. *Songs:* Babes in Arms; Where or When; God's Country; You Are My Lucky Star; Good Morning; I Cried for You; I'm Just Wild About Harry. *Director-choreographer:* Busby Berkeley. *Producer:* Arthur Freed.

After Irving Berlin's *Annie Get Your Gun* (1946), no other Broadway musical introduced as any standards as this Rodgers and Hart show. Such terrific songs as "I Wish I Were in Love Again," "The Lady Is a Tramp," and "My Funny Valentine" were gems in a loosely-plotted tale about the teenage children of down-and-out vaudevillians who put on a show to raise money. The cast was young and energetic and the production numbers did justice to the score. Surprisingly, the studio cut all the famous songs and only used "Where or When" and the title number in the film version, a "let's-put-on-a-show" vehicle for Mickey Rooney and Judy Garland. The movie score is filled out with some old favorites and it remains a

very enjoyable musical even if it does not come close to the Broadway show. The film was popular enough to launch a whole series of Rooney-Garland musicals, most of them slight variations on this first entry.

Babes in Toyland

October 13, 1903 (Majestic Theatre), a "musical extravaganza" by Glen MacDonough. *Score:* Victor Herbert, Glen MacDonough. *Cast:* William Norris (Alan), Mabel Barrison (Jane), George W. Denham (Uncle Barnaby), Dore Davidson (Master Toymaker), Bessie Wynn, Hattie Delaro, Nella Webb. *Songs:* Toyland; I Can't Do the Sum; Go To Sleep, Slumber Deep; March of the Toys. *Director-choreographer:* Julian Mitchell. *Producers:* Fred R. Hamlin, Julian Mitchell. 192 performances.

(MGM 1934). *Screenplay:* Nick Grinde, Frank Butler. *Score:* Victor Herbert, Glen MacDonough, etc. *Cast:* Stan Laurel (Stannie Dum), Oliver Hardy (Ollie Dee), Charlotte Henry (Little Bo-Peep), Felix Knight (Tom-Tom), Johnny Downs (Little Boy Blue), Jean Darling (Curly Locks), Florence Roberts. *Songs:* Toyland; I Can't Do the Sum; Go To Sleep, Slumber Deep; March of the Toys; Who's Afraid of the Big Bad Wolf? *Directors:* Charles Rogers, Gus Meins. *Producer:* Hal Roach.

(Buena Vista 1961). *Screenplay:* Joe Rinaldi, Ward Kimball, Lowell S. Hawley. *Score:* Victor Herbert, Glen MacDonough, etc. *Cast:* Ray Bolger (Barnaby), Tommy Sands (Tom Piper), Annette Funicello (Mary Contrary), Ed Wynn (Toymaker), Mary McCarty (Mother Goose), Henry Calvin, Gene Sheldon, Tommy Kirk. *Songs:* I Can't Do the Sum; Castle in Spain; Toyland; The Forest of No Return; March of the Toys; The Workshop Song. *Director:* Jack Donohue. *Choreographer:* Tommy Mahoney. *Producer:* Walt Disney.

(TV 1986). *Teleplay:* Paul Zindel. *Score:* Victor Herbert, Glen MacDonough, Leslie Bricusse. *Cast:* Drew Barrymore (Lisa Piper), Keanu Reeves (Jack), Pat Morita (Toymaker), Richard Mulligan (Barnaby), Eileen Brennan, Jill Schoelen, Googie Gress. *Director:* Clive Donner. *Choreographer:* Eleanor Fazan. *Producers:* Tony Ford, etc.

Because it was always a favorite with children and families, this musical fantasy was the most revived of Victor Herbert's operettas. Two children, escaping by boat from their wicked Uncle Barnaby, are shipwrecked in Toyland where they are helped by various Mother Goose characters. The show was sometimes closer to a revue, with its sensational if disjointed musical numbers, than a book musical but it never failed to please for half a century. The first movie version in 1934 featured Laurel and Hardy as inept toymakers and the plot was greatly altered but not improved. Yet during its fast-paced seventy-nine minutes all the musical highlights of the original were there. In 1954 an abridged version of the musical was broadcast on television with a cast that included Wally Cox, Jack E. Leonard, and Dave Garroway. Walt Disney's 1962 movie, his first live-action musical feature, turned the youngsters into squeaky clean teenagers Annette Funicello and Tommy Sands who, as naively as they behaved, could not capture the innocence of the characters. Ed Wynn as the Toymaker is delightful and there are some enjoyable production numbers, but much of the film is a colorful bore. Even less satisfying is a 1986 television version with Drew Barrymore and Keanu Reeves as the kids, Pat Morita as the Toymaker, and Richard Mulligan as Barnaby. It is a charmless production that doesn't seem to understand operetta or children. On the other hand, there is much to recommend in a 1997 animated movie version with familiar voices on the soundtrack, most memorably Christopher Plummer as Barnaby. Only a few of the Herbert songs are used but the animation and storytelling are top flight.

Baby Doll see 27 Wagons Full of Cotton

Baby Mine

August 23, 1910 (Daly's Theatre), a comedy by Margaret Mayo. Cast: Marguerite Clark (Zoie Hardy), Ernest Glendinning (Albert Hardy), Walter Jones (Jimmy Jinks), Ivy Troutman (Aggie), John E. Mackin, E. D. Cromwell, Harry H. Hart. Producer: William A. Brady. 287 performances.

(Goldwyn 1917). Screenplay: Doty Hobart. Cast:

Madge Kennedy (Zoie), Frank Morgan (Alfred), John Cumberland (Jimmie), Kathryn Adams (Aggie), Jack Ridgeway, Sonia Marcelle, Nellie Fillmore. Directors: Hugo Ballin, John S. Robertson.

(MGM 1927). Screenplay: Sylvia Thalberg, etc. Cast: Karl Dane (Oswald Hardy), George K. Arthur (Jimmy Hemingway), Charlotte Greenwood (Emma), Louise Lorraine. Director-producer: Robert Z. Leonard.

When marital trouble brews over a simple misunderstanding, the imaginative Zoie decides to win her husband back with a baby. Her husband's best friend helps her locate some babies and soon three infants are in their charge as three mothers come looking for them. This slaphappy farce was a hit on Broadway and Madge Kennedy was featured in the silent film in 1917. But more interesting to watch is a young Frank Morgan as the hassled husband. A 1927 remake was a vehicle for the comedy team of Karl Dane and George K. Arthur whose clowning with the infants and a midget overrode much of the original plot.

Baby, the Rain Must Fall see The Traveling Lady

The Bachelor Father

February 28, 1928 (Belasco Theatre), a comedy by Edward Childs Carpenter. Cast: C. Aubrey Smith (Sir Basil Winterton), June Walker (Tony Flagg), Rex O'Malley (Geoffrey Trent), Adriana Dori (Maria Credaro), Howard Bouton, Geoffrey Kerr, David Glassford. Director-producer: David Belasco. 263 performances.

(Cosmopolitan/MGM 1931). Screenplay: Laurence E. Johnson. Cast: Marion Davies (Antoinette Flag), C. Aubrey Smith (Sir Basil Winterton), Ray Milland (Geoffrey Trent), Ralph Forbes (John Ashley), Guinn Williams, Doris Lloyd, Edgar Norton. Director: Robert Z. Leonard. Producers: Marion Davies, Robert Z. Leonard.

The titled aristocrat Basil Winterton has never been married but he has fathered several illegitimate children over the years. He sends his attorney to locate the now-grown offspring and when they assemble at his mansion they are a colorful and diverse lot. But soon all start to get along famously and the bachelor dad helps each one in his or her career pursuits. What might have been an off-color joke turned into a pleasant comedy hit on Broadway and a popular film. Crusty forever-old C. Aubrey Smith played the father both on stage and on screen in 1931 and his droll performance was in merry contrast to the livewire children he produced. Marion Davies is particularly sparkling as the slang-talking Tony. The 1957–1962 television series *Bachelor Father* only shared the title with the play and film. John Forsythe played an unmarried attorney who becomes guardian to an orphaned niece. (No illegitimate children existed on television at that time.)

The Bad Seed

December 8, 1954 (46th Street Theatre), a drama by Maxwell Anderson. *Cast*: Nancy Kelly (Christine Penmark), Patty McCormack (Rhoda Penmark), Eileen Heckart (Mrs. Daigle), John O'Hare, Evelyn Varden, Lloyd Gough, Joan Croydon, Joseph Holland. *Director*: Reginald Denham. *Producer:* Playwrights' Company. 332 performances.

(Warner 1956). *Screenplay*: John Lee Mahin. *Cast:* Nancy Kelly (Christine Penmark), Patty McCormack (Rhoda Penmark), Eileen Heckart (Mrs. Daigle), Henry Jones, Evelyn Varden, William Hopper, Paul Fix, Jesse White. *Director-producer*: Mervyn LeRoy.

(TV 1986). *Teleplay:* George Eckstein. *Cast:* Blair Brown (Christine Penmark), Christa Denton (Rhoda Penmark), Carol Lucatell (Mrs. Daigler), David Carradine, Lynn Redgrave, Richard Kiley, Carrie Wells, David Ogden Stiers. *Director:* Paul Wendkos. *Producer:* George Eckstein.

William March's novel, about a sweet nine-year-old girl who murders people, was adapted by Maxwell Anderson into a chiller that entertained Broadway audiences for nearly a year. The ending of the piece was particularly ironic: the mother realizes what her daughter is doing so she gives the girl an overdose and then shoots herself. But the gunshot awakes the neighbors and the girl is saved, smiling and ready to continue to murder those that annoy her. Much of the stage cast was retained for the 1956 film, including riveting performances by Nancy Kelly and Patty McCormack as mother and daughter. But Hollywood's idea of poetic justice would not allow the young murderess to get away scot free so the movie has an epilogue in which the youngster is struck dead by lightning when she goes out in a thunderstorm. It is an unintentionally funny ending to a very serious thriller and has been the butt of many jokes over the years. The 1986 television version was well acted and closer to the original play even though it was opened up a bit and characters were added. But it did retain Anderson's ironic ending. Interestingly, a decade later a grown-up McCormick played a mother who murders others to further the welfare of her daughter in *Mommy* (1995).

The Ballad of the Sad Cafe

October 30, 1963 (Martin Beck Theatre), a play by Edward Albee. *Cast*: Colleen Dewhurst (Amelia Evans), Lou Antonio (Marvin), Michael Dunn (Cousin Lymon), Roscoe Lee Browne (Narrator), William Prince, Enid Markey, William Duell, Bette Henritze. *Director*: Alan Schneider. *Producers:* Lewis Allen, Ben Edwards. 123 performances.

(Merchant-Ivory 1991). *Screenplay*: Michael Hirst. *Cast*: Vanessa Redgrave (Miss Amelia), Keith Carradine (Marvin), Cork Hubbert (Cousin Lymon), Rod Steiger, Austin Pendleton, Beth Dixon, Mert Hatfield, Anne Pitoniak. *Director*: Simon Callow. *Producer*: Ismail Merchant.

Carson McCullers's odd but tender story, about a demanding Southern misfit and her love-hate relationships with her ex-con husband and her dwarfish cousin, was dramatized with skill by Edward Albee and the delicate character study was well received by the critics if not the public. Over the years the play was revived by various theatre groups but was not filmed until 1993. The result struck some as overwrought and overacted, others as a powerful drama. Regardless, the screen cast was never less than fascinating even if one didn't quite buy the characters.

The Band Wagon

June 3, 1931 (New Amsterdam Theatre), a musical revue with sketches by George S. Kaufman, Howard Dietz. *Score:* Arthur Schwartz, Howard Dietz. *Cast:* Adele and Fred Astaire, Frank Morgan, Helen Broderick, Tilly Losch, Philip Loeb, John Barker. *Songs:* Dancing in the Dark; I Love Louisa; New Sun in the Sky; Hoops; High and Low; Sweet Music. *Director:* Hassard Short. *Choreographer:* Albertina Rasch. *Producer:* Max Gordon. 260 performances.

(MGM 1953). *Screenplay:* Betty Comden, Adolph Green. *Score:* Howard Dietz, Arthur Schwartz. *Cast:* Fred Astaire (Tony Hunter), Cyd Charisse (Gabrielle Gerard), Oscar Levant (Lester Marton), Nanette Fabray (Lily Marton), Jack Buchanan (Jeffrey Cordova), James Mitchell, Thurston Hall. *Songs:* That's Entertainment; By Myself; Dancing in the Dark; I Love Louisa; New Sun in the Sky; Triplets; I'll Guess I'll Have to Change My Plan; High and Low; Something to Remember You By; A Shine on Your Shoes. *Director:* Vincente Minnelli. *Choreographer:* Michael Kidd. *Producer:* Arthur Freed.

Generally considered the best Broadway revue of the 1930s, this show was a musical and comic treat with masterful visuals. Dietz and Schwartz wrote the memorable songs that were sung and danced by a dream cast. The production itself was sometimes the star as its twin turntables kept the snappy show moving. Revues were infrequently filmed and when they were the sketches were usually dropped and a plot was added to tie the musical numbers together. The screen version of *The Band Wagon* only kept the title, the songs (augmented by others by Dietz and Schwartz), and Fred Astaire from Broadway. The witty screenplay by Comden and Green was a wry satire on show business, making fun of a Broadway producer who wishes to forego entertainment and create art. Jack Buchanan was delightfully stuffy as the producer, Nanette Fabray and Oscar Levant played a pair of authors not unlike Comden and Green, and Astaire and Cyd Charisse provided the romance and the dancing. The film overflows with unforgettable production numbers, from the comic "Triplets" to the sublime "Dancing in the Dark" to the the droll "Girl Hunt" ballet. The movie's only new song,

Dietz and Schwartz's "That's Entertainment," characterized the whole show, as it later came to represent the Hollywood musical in general.

Barbara Frietchie

October 23, 1899 (Criterion Theatre), a drama by Clyde Fitch. *Cast:* Julia Marlowe (Barbara Frietchie) J. H. Gilmour (Capt. Trumbull), Arnold Daly (Jack Negly), Lionel Adams (Arthur Frietchie), W. J. Le Moyne (Col. Negly), George Woodard (Mr. Frietchie), Algernon Tassin, Dodson Mitchell. *Director:* William Seymour. *Producer:* Charles Frohman. 83 performances.

(Popular Plays and Players 1915). *Screenplay:* Clarence J. Harris. *Cast:* Mary Miles Minter (Barbara Frietchie), Guy Coombs (Capt. Trumball), Fraunie Fraunholz (Jack Negly), Wallace Scott (Arthur Frietchie), Frederick Heck (Col. Negly), Mrs. Thomas Whiffen, Lewis Sealy, Anna Q. Nilsson, Myra Brooks. *Director:* Herbert Blaché. *Producers:* Herbert Blaché, etc.

(Regal 1924). *Screenplay:* Lambert Hillyer. *Cast:* Florence Vidor (Barbara Frietchie), Edmund Lowe (William Trumball), Emmett King, Joseph Bennett, Charles Delaney, Louis Fitzroy. *Director:* Lambert Hillyer. *Producer:* Thomas H. Ince.

Loosely based on a real person who was immortalized in a poem by John Greenleaf Whittier, the Civil War drama provide plenty of romance, suspense, and action for Broadway audiences. Feisty Barbara supports the Union even though most of the town of Frederick, Maryland, displays the Confederate flag. She dares to fall in love with a Yankee Captain, helps hide her wounded brother from the enemy, shoots a pistol out of the hands of a Southerner who tries to harm her sweetheart, and even waves the Stars and Stripes when Confederate General Stonewall Jackson comes to town. For all her spunkiness, Barbara is shot by her spurned Confederate lover who is then executed by his own father under Jackson's orders. The romantic melodrama strayed far from the facts (the real Barbara was ninety-six years old and bedridden when Jackson came to Frederick) but was a rousing entertainment that pleased audiences in New York and on the road. Two silent film versions were made and, emphasizing the action as well as the love scenes, both were popular. The play was later turned into the successful Broadway operetta *My Maryland* with a score by Sigmund Romberg and Dorothy Donnelly.

Barefoot in the Park

October 23, 1963 (Biltmore Theatre), a comedy by Neil Simon. *Cast:* Elizabeth Ashley (Corrie Bratter), Robert Redford (Paul Bratter), Mildred Natwick (Mrs. Banks), Kurt Kasznar (Victor Velasco), Herb Edelman, Joseph Keating. *Director:* Mike Nichols. *Producer:* Saint Subber. 1,530 performances.

(Paramount 1967). *Screenplay:* Neil Simon. *Cast:* Jane Fonda (Corrie Bratter), Robert Redford (Paul Bratter), Mildred Natwick (Mrs. Banks), Charles Boyer (Victor Velasco), Herb Edelman, Mabel Albertson, Fritz Feld, Doris Roberts. *Director:* Gene Saks. *Producer:* Hal B. Wallis.

(TV 1981). *Teleplay:* Neil Simon. *Cast:* Richard Thomas (Paul Bratter), Bess Armstrong (Corrie Bratter), Barbara Barrie (Mrs. Banks), Hans Conried (Victor Velasco), James Cromwell.

Neil Simon's first long-run Broadway hit, this engaging look at a pair of newlyweds discovering their first incompatibilities was slight on plot but filled with knowing jokes and likable characters. Newcomer Redford got to reprise his young, staid lawyer Paul on screen and never returned to the stage again. Ashley was dropped for Hollywood's favorite kookie ingenue at the time, Jane Fonda. Yet, just as she had on stage, Natwick stole the show as the quietly frustrated mother of the bride. The oddball neighbor from upstairs was given a crusty East European flavor by character actor Kasznar on Broadway and Boyer did his suave Continental thing on screen, though many found it a bit flat. But most agreed that Simon did a creditable job opening up his play for the screen, only his second screenplay effort. The film was popular and remains one of his best stage-to-screen projects. A 1981 television production featured Bess Armstrong and Richard Thomas as the Bratters, with able support by Barbara Barrie and Hans Conried as the mother and Velasco; many

thought Thomas and Conried outshone the previous performers of the roles. A 1970 television series based on the comedy, boldly featuring an African American cast, only lasted thirteen episodes.

The Bat

August 23, 1920 (Morosco Theatre), a mystery drama by Mary Roberts Rinehart, Avery Hopwood. *Cast:* Effie Ellsler (Cornelia Van Gorder), May Vokes (Lizzie), Anne Morrison, Edward Ellis, Richard Barrows. *Director:* Collin Kemper. *Producers:* Wagenhals and Kemper. 867 performances.

(United Artists 1926). *Screenplay:* George Marion, etc. *Cast:* Emily Fitzroy (Cornelia Van Gorder), Louise Fazenda (Lizzie), Jack Pickford, Eddie Beranger, Charles Herzinger, Robert McKim. *Director-producer:* Roland West.

The Bat Whispers (United Artists 1930). *Screenplay:* Roland West. *Cast:* Grayce Hampton (Cornelia Van Gorder), Chester Morris (Detective Anderson), Maude Eburne (Lizzie), Richard Tucker, DeWitt Jennings, Spencer Charters. *Director:* Roland Young. *Producer:* Joseph M. Schenck.

The Bat (Liberty 1959). *Screenplay:* Crane Wilbur. *Cast:* Agnes Moorehead (Cornelia Van Gorder), Vincent Price (Dr. Malcolm Wells), Lenita Lane (Lizzie), Gavin Gordon, John Sutton, Darla Hood. *Director:* Crane Wilbur. *Producer:* C. J. Tevlin.

One of the classic "haunted house" stage thrillers, this popular attraction was based on Mary Roberts Rinehart's story "The Circular Staircase" and was a hit in New York, in revival, on the road, and with amateur groups for decades. The aged spinster Cornelia Van Gorder rents a summer home that belonged to a now-dead banker who may have hidden stolen funds in the house. When various characters show up looking for the money, mysterious things start to occur and soon not even the detective Cornelia has hired can be trusted. A comic highlight of the production was the constantly terrified maid Lizzie and the actress playing her often stole the show. A silent film version in 1915 greatly abridged the story but a 1926 movie was faithful to the play and had its fair share of chills. In 1930 it was remade as *The Bat Whispers* but there was little to recommend except some interesting visuals, including a 70mm widescreen process called Magnifilm. The 1959 remake was again called *The Bat* but the old hysterics were rather outdated by then, as was some of the acting. The next year an abridged version of the thriller was shown on television with a cast headed by Helen Hayes, Jason Robards, and Margaret Hamilton. It also showed its age but the performances were admirable.

The Bat Whispers see *The Bat*

Beau Brummell

May 19, 1890 (Madison Square Theatre), a play by Clyde Fitch. *Cast*: Richard Mansfield (Beau Brummell), Agnes Miller (Mariana Vincent), D. H. Harkins (Prince of Wales), W. J. Ferguson, F. W. Lander. *Producer*: A. M. Palmer, Richard Mansfield. 150 performances.

(Warner 1924). *Screenplay*: Dorothy Farnum. *Cast*: John Barrymore (Beau Brummell), Mary Astor (Lady Marjorie), Willard Lewis (Prince of Wales), Carmel Myers, Irene Rich, Alec B. Francis, William Humphrey. *Director*: Harry Beaumont.

(MGM 1954). *Screenplay*: Karl Tunberg. *Cast*: Stewart Granger (Beau Brummell), Elizabeth Taylor (Lady Patricia), Peter Ustinov (Prince of Wales), Robert Morley (King George III), James Donald, James Hayter, Rosemary Harris, Paul Rogers, Noel Willman. *Director*: Curtis Bernhardt. *Producer*: Sam Zimbalist.

Booth Tarkington's novel, about the well-dressed dandy of Regency England who is the cream of society until he offends the Prince of Wales, was turned into a stage vehicle for the popular actor Richard Mansfield and he kept it in his repertoire for decades. The costume piece has always thrilled audiences with its lavishness, humor, romance, and intrigue. The final scene, in which an elderly, impoverished, forgotten Brummell holds an imaginary dinner party with phantoms from his past, is also a theatrical tour de force. A silent film in 1915

with James Young abridged the story beyond recognition. John Barrymore had his first important screen role in the 1924 silent remake and it immediately made him a film star. The most opulent, though less satisfying, screen version was the 1954 film with Stewart Granger as the London playboy. Despite a first-class cast and marvelous production values, the old tale shows its age and much of the movie comes across as artificial.

Bell, Book and Candle

November 14, 1950 (Ethel Barrymore Theatre), a comedy by John Van Druten. *Cast*: Lilli Palmer (Gillian Holroyd), Rex Harrison (Shep Henderson), Scott McKay (Nicky Holroyd), Jean Adair (Miss Holroyd), Larry Gates. *Director*: John Van Druten. *Producer*: Irene Mayer Selznick. 233 performances.

(Columbia 1958). *Screenplay*: Daniel Taradash. *Cast*: James Stewart (Shepherd Henderson), Kim Novak (Gillian Holroyd), Jack Lemmon (Nicky Holroyd), Ernie Kovacs, Hermione Gingold, Elsa Lanchester, Janice Rule. *Director*: Richard Quine. *Producer*: Julian Blaustein.

A stylish comedy about modern-day witchcraft, this unusual play managed to balance romance and fantasy while giving its stars a juicy vehicle. Gillian uses her magical powers to ensnare the man she loves, the publisher Shep. But when her brother and aunt, who are also witches, spill the beans about her powers to Shep, Gillian has to swear off witchcraft to keep the man she loves. Rex Harrison and Lilli Palmer were so proficient as Shep and Gillian that the Broadway production faltered after they returned to England. But the comedy was a success on the road and was given revivals across the country. A film was not made until 1958 and most of the charm was gone. Much blame was put on the very unbewitching performance by Kim Novak as Gillian but most of the cast was at odds with the material: James Stewart seemed lost as Shep and Jack Lemmon was too overpowering in the supporting role of the brother. Yet some of the play survives the lackluster screen treatment and there are moments (usually provided by Hermione Gingold and Ernie Kovacs) that amuse.

A Bell for Adano

December 6, 1944 (Cort Theatre), a drama by Paul Osborn. *Cast*: Fredric March (Maj. Victor Joppolo), Everett Sloane (Sgt. Borth), Bruce MacFarlane (Capt. Purvis), Margo (Tina), Tito Vuolo (Giuseppe Ribaudo), Gilbert Mack, Alexander Granach, Rolfe Sedan, Leon Rothier. *Director*: H. C. Potter. *Producer*: Leland Hayward. 296 performances.

(Fox 1945). *Screenplay*: Norman Reilly Raine, Lamar Trotti. *Cast*: John Hodiak (Maj. Victor Joppolo), Gene Tierney (Tima Tomasino), William Bendix (Sgt. Borth), Harry Morgan (Capt. Purvis), Glenn Langan, Richard Conte, Stanley Praeger. *Director*: Henry King. *Producers*: Louis D. Lighton, Lamar Trotti.

When the Allies free the Sicilian town of Adano from the Nazis, the Italian-American Major Joppolo is put in charge of running the town. He is quickly accepted and beloved by the locals even though the American officers above Joppolo are not popular. When the major disobeys his superiors he is transferred, but not before Joppolo has replaced the town bell that had been melted down by the Nazis. Paul Osborn adapted John Hersey's novel into a tight, moving drama and Frederic March was roundly cheered for his performance as Joppolo. A film was quickly made while the subject was still topical and the result was a pleasant but routine movie. Handsome but uninteresting John Hodiak played Joppolo and a romance with Italian local Gene Tierney was emphasized. But the supporting characters give the picture some life and the sentiments of the time are nicely captured.

The Belle of New York

September 28, 1897 (Casino Theatre), a musical comedy by Hugh Morton (aka C.M.S. McLellan). *Score*: Gustave Kerker, Hugh Morton. *Cast*: Edna May (Violet Gray), Harry Davenport (Harry Bronson), Dan Daly (Ichabod Bronson), David Warfield (Karl von Pumpernick), George Fortescue, Phyllis Rankin. *Songs*: At Ze Naughty Folies Bergere; Teach Me How to Kiss, Dear; They All Follow Me; The Anti-Cigarette League; She Is the Belle of New York; The Purity Brigade. *Director-Producer*: George W. Lederer. *Choreographer*: Signor Francioli. 64 performances.

(MGM 1952). *Screenplay*: Robert O'Brien, Irving Ellinson. *Score*: Harry Warren, Johnny Mercer. *Cast*: Fred Astaire (Charlie Hill), Vera-Ellen (Angela Bonfils), Marjorie Main (Mrs. Phineas Hill), Keenan Wynn (Max Ferris), Alice Pearce, Clinton Sundberg. *Songs*: Baby Doll; Seeing's Believing; Thank You, Mr. Currier, Thank You, Mr. Ives; When I'm Out With the Belle of New York; I Wanna Be a Dancin' Man; Let a Little Love Come In. *Director*: Charles Walters. *Choreographer*: Robert Alton. *Producer*: Arthur Freed.

Here is a rare instance of an American musical failing to find success on Broadway but becoming a hit in Europe. The plot concerned a spendthrift New York playboy who is cast out by his rich father but is taken up by a Salvation Army gal who reforms him. The writing was light and playful, as was the score. But Broadway audiences didn't buy it and the show closed in two months. Yet when it was presented in London, the musical ran over two years and it was later a hit across the continent. A silent film version was made in 1919 with Marion Davies and Etienne Giradot but it took Hollywood another thirty-three years to get around to remaking it with sound. The entire stage score was scrapped and the plot slightly altered with Fred Astaire as the playboy and Vera-Ellen as his reformer. The new score by Harry Warren and Johnny Mercer introduced the hit "Baby Doll" and there were clever production numbers for the other songs, such as Astaire dancing in the clouds in "Seeing Is Believing" and the use of old prints in "Thank You, Mr. Currier, Thank You, Mr. Ives." The story may creak a bit along the way but there is enough bright spots to make the movie watchable.

Bells Are Ringing

November 29,1956 (Shubert Theatre), a musical comedy by Betty Comden, Adolph Green, *Score*: Jule Styne, Betty Comden, Adolph Green. *Cast*: Judy Holliday (Ella Peterson), Sydney Chaplin (Jeff Moss), Jean Stapleton (Sue), Eddie Lawrence (Sandor), Dort Clark, George S, Irving, Peter Gennaro. *Songs*: Just in Time; The Party's Over; Long Before I Knew You; It's a Perfect Relationship; I'm Going Back; I Met a Girl; Hello, Hello There. *Director*: Jerome Robbins. *Choreographers*: Jerome Robbins, Bob Fosse. *Producer*: Theatre Guild. 924 performances.

(MGM 1960). *Screenplay:* Betty Comden, Adolph Green, *Score:* Jule Styne, Betty Comden, Adolph Green. *Cast:* Judy Holliday (Ella Peterson), Dean Martin (Jeff Moss), Jean Stapleton (Sue), Eddie Foy, Jr. (Sandor), Dort Clark, Frank Gorshin, Fred Clark. *Songs:* Just in Time; The Party's Over; It's a Perfect Relationship; I'm Going Back; I Met a Girl; Better Than a Dream. *Director:* Vincente Minnelli. *Choreographer:* Charles O'Curran. *Producer:* Arthur Freed.

Judy Holliday had her greatest musical triumph with this likable piece about a telephone answering service operator who falls for one of her clients before she even meets him. The show was a star vehicle for Holliday (written for her by her old performing partners Comden and Green) and she was onstage for most of the evening, helped by a handful of hit songs. The movie version gave her a chance to recreate her performance and it is a glowing, endearing record of her stage success. Jean Stapleton, as the owner of the service, also got to repeat her stage role and she is memorable. Dean Martin, on the other hand, makes a lightweight leading man and his laid-back performance is best enjoyed by devout Martin fans. Director Vincente Minnelli opened up the stage piece for the screen and incorporated many New York locations into the filming. The Broadway production featured some memorable dance routines staged by Bob Fosse and Jerome Robbins; but there is very little dancing in the film and what is there is not very impressive.

Bent

December 2, 1979 (New Apollo Theatre), a play by Martin Sherman. *Cast:* Richard Gere (Max), David Dukes (Horst), David Marshall Grant (Rudy), James Remar, Michael Gross, George Hall. *Director:* Robert Allan Ackerman. *Producers:* Jack Schlissel, Steven Steinlauf. 240 performances.

(Goldwyn 1997). *Screenplay:* Martin Sherman. *Cast:* Clive Owen (Max), Lothaire Bluteau (Horst), Brian Webber (Rudy), Ian McKellan, Nikolai Coster Waldau, Mick Jagger, Jude Law, Rupert Graves. *Director:* Sean Mathias. *Producers:* Dixie Linder, Michael Solinger.

An uncompromising and unsentimental look at how homosexuals were treated by the Nazis, this powerful drama was first produced in London but its author Martin Sherman was American. When Hitler decides to purge Germany of homosexuality, storm troopers murder Max's lover then send Max to a concentration camp where gay prisoners are treated even worst than the Jews. Yet despite the hellish conditions, Max finds camaraderie and love with a fellow prisoner before they are both destroyed. While the grim drama may have had difficulty finding an audience on Broadway, the presence of movie star Richard Gere as Max helped turn the play into a modest hit. (Once Gere left, the production only lasted a month.) The 1997 British film cast unknowns in the leads and familiar faces in the supporting roles but the acting is consistently strong. Yet the movie itself is rather stagy and unimaginative, rarely finding the power of the stage work.

Berkeley Square

November 4, 1929 (Lyceum Theatre), a drama by John L. Balderston. *Cast:* Leslie Howard (Peter Standish), Margalo Gillmore (Helen Pettigrew), Valerie Taylor (Kate Pettigrew), Alice John, Ann Freshman, Louise Prussing, Henry Warwick, Lucy Beaumont. *Directors-Producers:* Gilbert Miller, Leslie Howard. 229 performances.

(Fox 1933). *Screenplay:* Sonya Levien, John Balderston. *Cast:* Leslie Howard (Peter Standish), Heather Angel (Helen Pettigrew), Valerie Taylor (Kate Pettigrew), Irene Brown, Beryl Mercer, Colin Keith-Johnston, Alan Mowbray. *Director:* Frank Lloyd. *Producer:* Jesse L. Lasky.

I'll Never Forget You (Fox 1951). *Screenplay:* Ranald MacDougall. *Cast:* Tyrone Power (Peter Standish), Ann Blyth (Helen Pettigrew), Michael Rennie, Dennis Price, Beatrice Campbell. *Director:* Roy Ward Baker. *Producer:* Sol C. Siegel.

This romantic fantasy, about a man who goes back in time and falls in love with a long-gone woman, would later be copied in other plays and films, but none had the intelligence and sense of awe as this original. John Balderston got the idea for the play from an unfinished work by Henry James called *A Sense of the Past.* American Peter Standish is in London to get married but when he becomes fascinated with he Berkeley Square townhouse he is staying at, he is transplanted to 1784 where he fails to fit into society but becomes enamored by Helen Pettigrew. After he is forced to return to the 20th century, Standish finds out that Helen died soon after he left. He breaks off his engagement and stays in the townhouse where he feels connected to his lost love. Leslie Howard found both the romanticism and tragedy in the role and his performance helped the play to become a hit. He reprised his Peter Standish in the 1933 film and it is a marvelous performance in every way. The rest of the film is also quite accomplished, avoiding mawkish melodrama and costume triviality. The story was remade as *I'll Never Forget You* in 1951 and suffers in comparison. The acting is disappointing and the romance is more sentimental. The movie does have interesting visuals, though, beginning in black and white and moving into color when Peter enters the 18th century, the opposite approach usually taken with flashbacks.

Best Foot Forward

October 1, 1941 (Ethel Barrymore), a musical comedy by John Cecil Holm. *Score:* Hugh Martin, Ralph Blane. *Cast:* Rosemary Lane (Gale Joy), Gil Stratton (Bud Hooper), Marty May (Jack Haggerty), Nancy May Walker (Blind Date), Maureen Cannon, June Allyson, Kenny Bowers, Jack Jordan, Tommy Dix. *Songs:* Buckle Down, Winsocki; Just a Little Joint With a Jukebox; The Three B's; What Do You Think I Am?; Ev'ry Time. *Director-producer:* George Abbott. *Choreographer:* Gene Kelly. 326 performances.

(MGM 1953). *Screenplay:* Irving Brecher, Fred Finklehoffe. *Score:* Hugh Martin, Ralph Blane. *Cast:* Lucille Ball (Lucille Ball), Tommy Dix (Bud Hooper), William Gaxton (Jack O'Riley), Nancy Walker (Blind Date), Virginia Weidler (Helen Schlessinger), June Allyson, Kenny Bowers, Gloria DeHaven, Jack Jordan. *Songs:* Buckle Down, Winsocki; The Three B's; Alive and Kicking; Wish I May, Wish I Might; Ev'ry Time; Three Men on a Date; You're Lucky. *Director:* Edward Buzzell. *Choreographer:* Charles Walters. *Producer:* Arthur Freed.

Here is a musical with an academic setting that is not about the big football game.

Instead it deals with the problems that arise when a student invites a movie star to his school prom and, needing the publicity, she accepts. The Broadway production boasted a tuneful score and a cast of young and up-and-coming talents. Several of them were retained for the film version which kept most of the libretto and score as well. Of particular interest was Nancy Walker as the wisecracking Blind Date. Because the war was on, the setting for the film was changed to a military school; aside from that it is a fairly faithful adaptation of a Broadway hit on the screen.

The Best Little Whorehouse in Texas

April 17, 1978 (Entermedia Theatre), a musical comedy by Larry L. King, Peter Masterson. *Score:* Carol Hall. *Cast:* Carlin Glynn (Mona Stangley), Henderson Forsythe (Ed Earl Dodd), Delores Hall (Jewel), Jay Garner (Governor, etc.), Pamela Blair, Susan Mansur. *Songs:* Twenty Fans; A Li'l Ole Bitty Pissant Country Place; Hard Candy Christmas; Girl, You're a Woman; Side Step; Bus From Amarillo; Good Old Girl; Twenty-Four Hours of Lovin'; The Aggie Song. *Directors:* Peter Masterson, Tommy Tune. *Choreographer:* Tommy Tune. *Producers:* Stevie Philips, Universal Pictures. 1,703 performances.

(Universal/RKO 1982). *Screenplay:* Larry L. King, Peter Masterson, Colin Higgins. *Score:* Carol Hall, etc. *Cast:* Burt Reynolds (Ed Earl Dodd), Dolly Parton (Mona Stangley), Dom DeLuise (Melvin P. Thorpe), Charles Durning (Governor), Jim Nabors, Lois Nettleton, Theresa Merritt, Robert Mandan, Barry Corbin, Noah Berry. *Songs:* Twenty Fans; I Will Always Love You; A Li'l Ole Bitty Pissant Country Place; Hard Candy Christmas; Side Step; The Aggie Song; Sneakin' Around. *Director:* Colin Higgins. *Choreographer:* Tony Stevens. *Producers:* Colin Higgins, etc.

An unlikely hit, this country-western musical ran on the strength of Tommy Tune's inventive choreography and a tuneful score by Carol Hall. The broad satire on Texas politics and how an old established cat house was closed by the righteous right had a simple charm, despite its provocative title. Hollywood stuck with the title but tended to clean up the play's honesty, casting the middle-aged principal characters with glamourous movie stars and giving the piece a happy ending. Few of the Broadway talents were involved in the film and it certainly shows. But then there is Charles Durning stealing the show as a side-stepping governor who loves being so slippery; it's a star turn that almost saves the movie. A musical sequel, called *The Best Little Whorehouse Goes Public*, was a quick flop on Broadway in 1994.

The Best Man

March 31, 1960 (Morosco Theatre), a drama by Gore Vidal. *Cast*: Melvyn Douglas (William Russell), Lee Tracy (Arthur Hockstadter), Frank Lovejoy (Joseph Cantwell), Leora Dana, Kathleen Maguire, Karl Weber, Ruth McDevitt, Joseph Sullivan. *Director*: Joseph Anthony. *Producer:* Playwrights' Company. 520 performances.

(United Artists 1964). *Screenplay*: Gore Vidal. *Cast*: Henry Fonda (William Russell), Cliff Robertson (Joe Cantwell), Lee Tracy (Arthur Hockstadter), Margaret Leighton, Edie Adams, Kevin McCarthy, Shelley Berman, Ann Sothern, Gene Raymond, Mahalia Jackson. *Director*: Franklin Schaffner. *Producers*: Stuart Millar, Lawrence Turman.

Potent dialogue and vivid characterizations made this political drama one of the best of its genre. An idealistic liberal and a shrewd senator are major contenders for the presidential nomination but the support of the outspoken ex-president upsets the balance of power. Gore Vidal's central characters were thought by many at the time to represent Adlai Stevenson, Joseph McCarthy, and Harry Truman, but the play has remained stimulating theatre decades after those parallels have faded. The drama is an actors' showcase and both the Broadway production and the 1964 film boasted splendid acting. (Lee Tracy's President was a highlight of both the play and the film.) The movie concentrates on talk rather than action but it is nonetheless engrossing entertainment.

Between Two Worlds see Outward Bound

Beyond the Horizon

February 2, 1920 (Morosco Theatre), a play by Eugene O'Neill. *Cast*: Richard Bennett (Robert Mayo), Edward Arnold (Andrew Mayo), Helen MacKellar (Ruth Atkins), Mary Jeffrey, Louise Closser Hale, Elfin Finn. *Director*: Homer Saint-Gaudens. *Producer:* John D. Williams. 111 performances. Pulitzer Prize.

(TV 1975). *Teleplay*: Eugene O'Neill. *Cast*: Richard Backus (Robert Mayo), James Broderick (Andrew Mayo), Maria Tucci (Ruth Atkins), Geraldine Fitzgerald, John Houseman, John Randolph. *Directors*: Richard Hauser, Michael Kahn. *Producer*: Lindsay Law.

Eugene O'Neill's first full length play, this drama about disillusionment may be said to usher in the modern era for the American theatre. Two brothers love the same girl; one goes off to sea while the other stays behind and marries her. But happiness eludes all three as their dissatisfaction is handed down to the next generation, eventually destroying them all. The powerful characterizations and tragic temperament of the play were strikingly new in its day and, while revivals must contend with some stiff dialogue here and there, it remains a remarkable American drama. The 1975 television version was shot in a studio with a stylized, even artificial look. But the acting throughout is exemplary and the power of the original is evident.

Beyond Therapy

January 1, 1981 (Marymount Manhattan Theatre), a comedy by Christopher Durang. *Cast*: Stephen Collins (Bruce), Sigourney Weaver (Prudence), Kate McGregor-Stewart, Nick Stannard, Jim Borelli, Jack Gilpin, Conan McCarty. *Director*: Jerry Zaks. *Producer:* Phoenix Theatre. 30 performances.

(New World 1987). *Screenplay*: Robert Altman, Christopher Durang. *Cast*: Jeff Goldblum (Bruce), Julie Haggerty (Prudence), Glenda Jackson, Tom Conti, Christopher Guest, Genevieve Page, Cris Campion. *Director*: Robert Altman. *Producer*: Steven Huft.

A disjointed but very funny comedy about people's dependency on their psychiatrists, Christopher Durang's comedy struggled

Off Broadway and later on Broadway to find an audience but with little success. Yet as the years passed the satiric piece was frequently produced by groups across the country. At the suggestion of her shrink, Prudence moves in with the gay Bruce, which does not please his lover Bob at all. But eventually all three learn to think for themselves and to move beyond therapy. As in most Durang plays, the sprightly dialogue and outrageous characters were more inspired than the plotting. But both the talk and the people fell flat in the misguided 1987 movie version. An impressive cast fumbles badly and director Robert Altman seems to have no idea how to handle the material. Most fascinating is how the humor disappears on the screen. Because of this critical and box office bomb, Durang's other works have very rarely been filmed.

The Big Knife

February 24, 1949 (National Theatre), a drama by Clifford Odets. *Cast*: John Garfield (Charlie Castle), Nancy Kelly (Marion Castle), Paul McGrath (Smiley Coy), Reinhold Schunzel (Nat Dazinger), William Terry (Buddy Bliss), J. Edward Bromberg (Marcus Hoff), Joan McCracken (Dixie Evans), Theodore Newton, Mary Patton. *Director*: Lee Strasberg. *Producer:* Dwight Deere Wiman. 108 performances.

(Aldrich & Assoc. 1955). *Screenplay*: James Poe. *Cast*: Jack Palance (Charles Castle), Ida Lupino (Marion Castle), Wendell Corey (Smiley Coy), Everett Sloane (Nat Danzinger), Paul Laughton (Buddy Bliss), Rod Steiger (Hoff), Shelley Winters (Dixie Evans), Jean Hagen, Ilka Chase, Wesley Addy. *Director-producer*: Robert Aldrich.

One of the most ruthless condemnations of Hollywood ever written, Clifford Odets's melodrama paints studio manipulators as no better than mobsters. Film actor Charlie Castle wants out of his studio contract but his boss reminds him that they covered up a scandal when he had his fling with a loose woman and the two accidentally killed a little girl while on a drunken spree in the car. The woman with him in the car was given a movie contract to shut her up but now she wants to squeal so the studio plans to kill her. It is all too much for Charlie so he kills himself. Critics dismissed the play as turgid melodrama but audiences were intrigued. The 1955 movie boasts some fine performances, though none could be called subtle, and there is something still fascinating about the overheated piece. Television versions were made in 1959 with Patrick McGoohan as Charlie and in 1988 with Peter Gallagher as the hero. The later is probably the best handling of the script, the acting usually more intense than flamboyant.

Biloxi Blues

March 28, 1985 (Neil Simon Theatre), a comedy by Neil Simon. *Cast*: Matthew Broderick (Eugene Jerome), Barry Miller (Arnold Epstein), Bill Sadler (Sgt. Merwin J. Toomey), Matt Mulhern, Alan Ruck, Penelope Ann Miller, Randall Edwards. *Director*: Gene Saks. *Producers:* Emanuel Azenberg, etc. 524 performances. Tony Award.

(Universal 1988). *Screenplay*: Neil Simon. *Cast*: Matthew Broderick (Eugene Jerome), Christopher Walken (Sgt. Toomey), Corey Parker (Arnold Epstein), Matt Mulhern, Casey Siemaszko, Penelope Ann Miller, Park Overall, Michael Dolan. *Director*: Mike Nichols. *Producer*: Ray Stark.

Having been applauded for his portrayal of the teenage hero Eugene in *Brighton Beach Memoirs* (qv), Matthew Broderick returned to the character and played him as a young Army recruit in this second play of Neil Simon's trilogy about his past. Eugene is stationed in boot camp in Biloxi, Mississippi, where he meets up with anti–Semitism, homosexuality, prostitution, and even young love. Yet the script is playful and lighthearted as Eugene observes everything with a wry sense of humor and tucks it all away for his later writing career. The Broadway production was top-notch in every category and, in addition to Broderick and others, there was a standout performance by Barry Miller as the smart, caustic Jew Epstein. Simon wrote the screenplay for the 1988 movie and stuck closely to the original except for diminishing the role of Epstein and giving his big scene to Broderick, who reprised his Eugene for the screen. Some of the acting in the film disappoints but for the most part it is a funny and truthful memoir.

The Bird of Paradise

January 8, 1912 (Daly's Theatre), a play by Richard Walton Tully. *Cast*: Laurette Taylor (Luana), Lewis S. Stone (Paul Wilson), Guy Bates Post (Dean), Theodore Roberts, Pamela Gaythorne, Robert Harrison. *Director-producer*: Oliver Morosco. 112 performances.

(RKO 1932). *Screenplay*: Leonard Praskins, etc. *Cast*: Dolores del Rio (Luana), Joel McCrea (Johnny), John Halliday (Mac), Richard Skeets Gallagher (Chester), Bert Roach, Lon Chaney, Jr., Napoleon Pukui. *Director*: King Vidor. *Producer*: David Selznick.

(Fox 1951). *Screenplay*: Delmer Daves. *Cast*: Debra Paget (Kalua), Louis Jourdan (Andre Laurence), Jeff Chandler (Tenga), Everett Sloane, Prince Lei Lani, Otto Waldis. *Director-producer*: Delmer Daves.

This exotic Hawaiian romance made Laurette Taylor into a major stage star. She played the island princess Luana who falls in love with a scientist studying the island. They wed and remain on the island but the loss of his career and the cultural differences drive him into depression. When the volcano Kilaua erupts, Luana takes it as a sign that the gods are angry so she throws herself into the boiling crater to appease the gods and set her husband free. The original production boasted magnificent scenery and special effects, including bubbling lava flowing down from the volcano. The Broadway run was modest but the drama was even more successful on the road where it toured for years The first movie version in 1932 featured Dolores del Rio as Luana and her screen appeal helps disguise some of the film's melodramatic awkwardness. (Her nude bathing scene in this pre-code picture certainly added to her appeal.) The 1951 remake lacks star performances but the scenery is lovely (both movies were filmed on location in Hawaii) and the production values throughout commendable. But Debra Paget and Louis Jourdan create few sparks together and the handling of the island natives and their ceremonies is ludicrous.

The Birth of a Nation see The Clansman

Black Girl

June 16, 1971 (Theatre de Lys), a play by J. E. Franklin. *Cast*: Kishasha (Billie Jean), Arthur French (Earl), Minnie Gentry (Mu'Dear), Lorraine Ryder, Gloria Edwards, Louise Stubbs, Loretta Greene. *Director*: Shauneille Perry. *Producers:* New Federal Theatre, etc. 234 performances.

(Cinerama 1972). *Screenplay*: J. E. Franklin. *Cast*: Peggy Pettit (Billie Jean), Brock Peters (Earl), Claudia McNeil (Mu'Dear), Leslie Uggams (Netta), Louise Stubbs, Gloria Edwards, Ruby Dee, Loretta Greene. *Director*: Ossie Davis. *Producer*: Lee Savin.

A superior, but little known, drama about African Americans, it is, in some ways, a rural version of *A Raisin in the Sun* (qv) but the play has plenty of distinction of its own. In a small Texas town Billie Jean drops out of high school and works as a dancer in a bar, dreaming of becoming a ballet artist someday. Her dysfunctional family cannot help her but her worldy-wise grandmother does and Billie Jean sets off to pursue her dream. The original Off Broadway production was beautifully acted, just as the 1972 movie featured some of the finest African American actors in the business. Claudia McNeil, who was so memorable as the mother in *A Raisin in the Sun*, played the grandmother on screen and it is another sterling performance.

Blue Denin

February 27, 1958 (Playhouse Theatre), a play by James Leo Herlihy, William Noble. *Cast*: Carol Lynley (Janet Willard), Burt Brinkerhoff (Arthur Bartley), Chester Morris (Maj. Bartley), June Walker (Jessie Bartley), Pat Stanley (Lillian Bartley), Warren Berlinger (Ernie Lacey). *Director*: Joshua Logan. *Producers:* Barbara Wolferman, James Hammerstein. 166 performances.

(Fox 1959). *Screenplay*: Philip Dunne, Edith R. Sommer. *Cast*: Carol Lynley (Janet Willard), Brandon De Wilde (Arthur Bartley), Macdonald Carey (Maj. Bartley), Marsha Hunt (Jessie Bartley), Nina Shipman (Lillian Bartley), Warren Berlinger (Ernie), Buck Class, Vaughn Taylor. *Director*: Philip Dunne. *Producer*: Charles Brackett.

Considered a truthful depiction of teenagers in its day, this domestic drama may have been a bit contrived in spots but was an honest attempt to capture the lingo and attitudes of the younger generation. Teenager Arthur finds out his girl friend Janet is pregnant and with his pal Ernie forges his father's name on a check to pay for an abortion. Of course the truth eventually comes out and parents and son are forced to try and understand each other. The play was thought to be in questionable taste by the studios so the tale was laundered somewhat for the 1959 screen version (the movie ends with wedding bells for the teen couple) but it was still one of the few Hollywood efforts to look at that generation. Carol Lynley and Brandon De Wilde are agreeably sincere as the central couple though some of the older folks come across as more stereotypic than necessary.

Blue Jeans

October 6, 1890 (14th Street Theatre), a melodrama by Joseph Arthur. *Cast*: Jennie Yeamans (June), Robert Hilliard (Perry Bascom), George Fawcett (Ben Boone), Judith Berolde (Sue Eudaly). 176 performances.

(Metro 1917). *Screenplay*: June Mathis, Charles A. Taylor. *Cast*: Viola Dana (June), Robert Walker (Perry Bascom), Clifford Bruce (Ben Boone), Sally Crute (Sue Eudaly), Henry Hallman (Col. Risener), Russell Simpson, Margaret McWade. *Director*: John H. Collins.

This long-forgotten melodrama was not only wildly popular in its day but introduced to the American stage one of the most famous of all suspense scenes and inspired a best-selling song. Politics and marriage are intertwined in the rural drama in which an unscrupulous congressman commits bigamy and, in order to silence the man who can betray him, the crooked politician knocks out his rival in an empty sawmill and ties him to the belt that moves him toward a large, spinning saw. But the heroine breaks down the door and rescues him at the last moment. The plight of one of the female characters, who leaves home for the big city and disgraces her family, was turned into the 1891 popular sentimental ballad "The Picture That Is Turned to the Wall" which sold

thousands of copies of sheet music. *Blues Jeans* had a long run in New York and remained popular on tour for decades. When it became a silent film in 1917, the sawmill scene was again the climax of the picture. Other movies copied the scene, though none were directly based on the stage play.

Bodies, Rest and Motion

December 21, 1986 (Mitzi E. Newhouse Theatre), a play by Roger Hedden. *Cast*: Laurie Metcalf (Beth), W. H. Macy (Nick), Andrew McCarthy (Sid), Christina Moore (Carol), Lois Smith, Larry Bryggman, Carol Schneider. *Director*: Billy Hopkins. *Producer:* Lincoln Center Theatre. 22 performances.

(Fine Line 1993). *Screenplay*: Roger Hedden. *Cast*: Bridget Fonda (Beth), Phoebe Cates (Carol), Tim Roth (Nick), Eric Stoltz (Sid), Alicia Witt, Sandra Ellis Lafferty, Peter Fonda. *Director*: Michael Steinberg. *Producers*: Alan Mindel, etc.

Four aimless people in a run-down Connecticut town search for love and meaning in their dreary lives; the only thing giving them satisfaction is watching television. The quirky, low-key comedy-drama was more an acting exercise than a fully-formed play but the cast was interesting to watch. The 1993 movie set the actionless action in a remote Arizona town but the aimlessness was the same. Again, the performances are more worthy of attention than the vehicle.

Boom see *The Milk Train Doesn't Stop Here Anymore*

Born Yesterday

February 4, 1946 (Lyceum Theatre), a comedy by Garson Kanin. *Cast*: Judy Holliday (Billie Dawn), Paul Douglas (Harry Brock), Gary Merrill (Paul Verrall), Larry Oliver, Mona Bruns, Otto Hulett. *Director*: Garson Kanin. *Producer:* Max Gordon. 1,642 performances.

(Columbia 1950). *Screenplay*: Albert Mannheimer. *Cast*: Judy Holliday (Billie Dawn), Broderick Crawford (Harry Brock), William Holden (Paul Verrall), Howard St. John, Frank Otto. *Director*: George Cukor. *Producer*: S. Sylvan Simon.

(Touchstone-Hollywood 1993). *Screenplay*: Douglas McGrath. *Cast*: Melanie Griffith (Emma "Billy" Dawn), John Goodman (Harry Brock), Don Johnson (Paul Verrall), Edward Herrmann, Max Perlich, Michael Ensign, Sally Quinn. *Director*: Luis Mandoki. *Producer*: D. Constantine Conte.

This classic American comedy introduced one of the great comic characters, the not-so-dumb blonde Billie Dawn who becomes someone to reckon with once she starts using her head. She is the mistress of wealthy junk dealer Harry Brock who hires Paul to educate the floozie. Billie not only learns about books but about life and soon she is calling the shots. The play made a star out of Judy Holliday, an unknown who took over the role when Jean Arthur quit before opening. The comedy ran nearly four years, toured extensively, and is frequently revived by all kinds of theatre groups. Holliday got to reprise her funny, knowing Billie in the 1950 film (and won a Oscar for it) and she was ably supported by Broderick Crawford as Harry and William Holden as Paul. An abridged television version in 1956 featured Mary Martin as Billie. The 1993 remake was updated and dumbed down, never rising above a sit-com level and losing energy as it dragged along. Melanie Griffith is no Holliday (but who is?) but she has a nice rapport with (then-husband) Don Johnson as Paul while John Goodman huffs and puffs predictably as Harry.

The Boss

January 30, 1911 (Astor Theatre), a drama by Edward Sheldon. *Cast*: Holbrook Blinn (Michael R. Regan), Emily Stevens (Emily), Henry Weaver (Griswold), Howard Estabrook (Donald), Frank Sheridan, Kenneth Hill, Henry Sargent, Ruth Benson. *Directors*: Holbrook Blinn, William A. Brady. *Producer*: William A. Brady. 88 performances.

(Brady Picture Plays 1915). *Screenplay*: Edward Sheldon. *Cast*: Holbrook Blinn (Michael R. Regan), Alice Brady (Emily), Charles S. Abbe (Griswold), William Marion, Bert Starkey. *Director*: Emile Chautard. *Producer*: William A. Brady.

Disturbing and thrilling in its day, this "problem play" by the innovative playwright Edward Sheldon still packs a punch on the rare occasions when it is revived. The corrupt businessman Michael R. Regan will destroy the Griswold family unless the attractive daughter Emily marries him to give him social position. Against her father's wishes she does but she warns Regan that it will not be a marriage of love. Eventually Griswald family members and others gang up and expose Regan's criminal practices. He plans to flee to Canada but Emily urges him to stay and take his medicine. He then realizes she has grown to love him. Many of the issues of the play were lost in the abbreviated 1915 film version, though character actor favorite Holbrook Blinn got to reprise his Regan on screen.

Bought and Paid For

September 26, 1911 (Playhouse Theatre), a play by George Broadhurst. *Cast*: Julia Dean (Virginia Blaine), Charles Richman (Robert Stafford), Frank Craven (James Gilley), Marie Nordstrom (Fanny Blaine), John Sharon, Allen Atwell. *Director*: Edward Elsner. *Producer:* William A. Brady. 431 performances.

(Brady Picture Plays 1916). *Screenplay*: Frances Marion. *Cast*: Alice Brady (Vivian Blaine), Josephine Drake (Fanny Blaine), Frank Conlon (Jimmy Gilly), Montagu Love (Robert Stafford). *Director*: Harley Knoles. *Producer*: William A. Brady.

(Famous Players 1922). *Screenplay*: Clara Beranger. *Cast*: Agnes Ayers (Virginia Blaine), Jack Holt (Robert Stafford), Walter Hiers (James Gilley), Leigh Wyant (Fanny Blaine), Ethel Wales, George Kuwa, Bernie Frank. *Director*: William C. de Mille. *Producer*: Adolph Zukor.

A domestic drama that often rises above melodramatics, this look at a troubled marriage was unusually frank for its time. When humble telephone operator Virginia agrees to marry millionaire Robert Stafford she is not aware of his drinking problem. Soon after their wedding he gets drunk and demands sexual favors, saying she is "bought and paid for." Virginia locks herself in the bedroom and the next day, when he is sober and repentant, the two agree to use their brains and their love for each other to work out their problems. Two silents films were made from the play, a 1916 movie with Alice Brady as Vivian (read Virginia) and one in 1922 starring Agnes Ayers as the young wife. There is a bit of sensationalism in both films but they remain true to the play's issues.

Boy Meets Girl

November 27, 1935 (Cort Theatre), a comedy by Bella and Samuel Spewack. *Cast*: Allyn Joslyn (Robert Law), Jerome Cowan (J. Carlyle Benson), Charles McClelland (Larry Toms), James MacColl (Rodney), Joyce Arling, Peggy Hart, Royal Beal, Everett H. Sloane. *Director-producer*: George Abbott. 669 performances.

(Warner 1938). *Screenplay*: Sam and Bella Spewack. *Cast*: James Cagney (Robert Law), Pat O'Brien (J. Carlyle Benson), Marie Wilson (Susan Seabrook), Dick Foran (Larry Toms), Ralph Bellamy (C. Elliott Friday), Bruce Lester (Rodney Bevan), Frank McHugh, Paul Clark, Ronald Reagan, Penny Singleton. *Director*: Lloyd Bacon. *Producer*: George Abbott.

One of the earliest and best stage farces about Hollywood, the comedy centered on two madcap screenwriters who must write a vehicle for a fading cowboy movie star. Since an unmarried waitress at the studio is pregnant, the two writers get power of attorney and co-star the infant opposite the cowboy. The baby becomes an even bigger star than the cowboy so he plans on marrying the waitress and adopting the child until the kids gives him the measles. The waitress ends up marrying a film extra (who is a British aristocrat in disguise) and the two writers are left to dream up a new "boy meets girl" story. The Spewacks based their central characters on the lively, unconventional writers Ben Hecht and Charles MacArthur who were in Hollywood at the time, yet all the people in the comedy were delicious, satiric types. George Abbott directed the large, noisy farce which was a hit with the critics and the public, running two years. Much of the playful mayhem can be found in the 1938 movie with James Cagney and Pat O'Brien as the zany writers. It is a loud and fast-paced romp but most of it holds up as screwball fun.

The Boys from Syracuse

November 23, 1938 (Alvin Theatre), a musical comedy by George Abbott. *Score:* Richard Rodgers, Lorenz, Hart. *Cast:* Eddie Albert (Antipholus of Syracuse), Jimmy Savo (Dromio of Syracuse), Wynn Murray (Luce), Teddy Hart (Dromio of Ephesus), Ronald Graham (Antipholus of Ephesus), Muriel Angelus (Adriana), Marcy Wescott (Luciana), Betty Bruce, Burl Ives. *Songs:* Dear Old Syracuse; Falling in Love With Love; This Can't Be Love; Sing for Your Supper; Oh, Diogenes!; He and She; What Can You Do With a Man?; The Shortest Day of the Year. *Director-producer:* George Abbott. *Choreographer:* George Balanchine. 235 performances.

(Universal 1940). *Screenplay:* Leonard Spigelgass, Charles Grayson. *Score:* Richard Rodgers, Lorenz, Hart. *Cast:* Allan Jones (Antipholus of Syracuse/Ephesus), Joe Penner (Dromio of Syracuse/Ephesus), Martha Raye (Luce), Irene Hervey (Adriana), Rosemary Lane (Phyllis)), Charles Butterworth, Alan Mowbray, Eric Blore. *Songs:* Falling in Love With Love; This Can't Be Love; Sing for Your Supper; He and She; Who Are You? *Director:* Edward Sutherland. *Choreographer:* Dave Gould. *Producer:* Jules Levey.

Perhaps the most revived of all Rodgers and Hart musicals, this playful, anachronistic version of Shakespeare's *The Comedy of Errors* boasted a hilarious mistaken identity plot and one of the team's finest scores. While twin brothers are mistaken for each other in the ancient town of Ephesus, their twin servants are likewise confused as wives become jealous and a new romance grows between one brother and his supposed sister-in-law. With its trunkful of song hits, the show remains a favorite with audiences. Yet the movie version, which cut or abridged the famous score until the piece didn't even feel like a musical, quickly disappeared from memory. Martha Raye makes a funny shrew of a wife and the final chariot race has some fun moments, but otherwise there is little to recommend in the film. It is believed that the poor screen version hurt the stage work and *The Boys from Syracuse* was little revived until a popular Off Broadway production in 1963 put it back into the repertory.

The Boys in the Band

April 15, 1968 (Theatre Four), a play by Mart Crowley. *Cast*: Kenneth Nelson (Michael), Frederick Combs (Donald), Cliff Gorman (Emory), Leonard Frey (Harold), Laurence Luckinbill (Hank), Keith Prentice, Peter White, Reuben Greene, Robert la Tourneaux. *Director*: Robert Moore. *Producers:* Richard Barr, Charles Woodward, Jr. 1,000 performances.

(Fox 1970). *Screenplay*: Mart Crowley. *Cast*: Kenneth Nelson (Michael), Frederick Combs (Donald), Cliff Gorman (Emory), Leonard Frey (Harold), Laurence Luckinbill (Hank), Keith Prentice, Peter White, Reuben Greene, Robert la Tourneaux. *Director*: William Friedkin. *Producer*: Mart Crowley.

A group of homosexuals throw a birthday party for their mutual friend Harold but a straight man shows up and eventually the fun turns sour and the games of truth raise disturbing realities. The first mainstream American play about contemporary gays may have dated somewhat but in its day it was provocative and fascinating. While this group of self-pitying men may not have been indicative of most gays, the play was an unapologetic look at an alternate lifestyle. The entire Off Broadway cast recreated their roles in the 1970 movie which made no efforts to open up the action outside of the New York apartment setting. Yet the result is riveting cinema and effectively claustrophobic rather than stagy. Standouts in the excellent cast are Cliff Gorman's outrageous Emory and Leonard Frey's quietly seething Harold.

The Boys Next Door

November 23, 1987 (Lambs Theatre), a play by Tom Griffin. *Cast*: Dennis Boutsikaris (Jack), Joe Grifasi (Arnold Wiggins), Josh Mostel (Norman Bulansky), Christine Estabrook (Sheila), William Jay (Lucien P. Smith), Joe Urla (Barry Klemper), Ed Setrakian, John Wylie, Laurinda Barrett. *Director*: Josephine R. Abady. *Producers:* Jay H. Fuchs, A. Joseph Tandet. 168 performances.

(TV 1996). *Teleplay*: William Blinn. *Cast*: Tony Goldwyn (Jack), Nathan Lane (Norman Bulansky), Michael Jeter (Arnold Wiggins), Robert Sean Leonard (Barry Klemper), Mare Winningham (Sheila), Courtney B. Vance (Lucien P. Singer), Elizabeth Wilson, Lynne Thigpen, Richard Jenkins. *Director*: John Erman. *Producer*: Hallmark Home Entertainment.

A comedy-drama that portrays various levels of mental disorders, this Off Broadway work approached its subject with humor and honesty rather than sentiment or romanticism. The social worker Jack monitors four outpatients living together in an apartment and while his job brings him a lot of stress and frustration, he also finds the foursome funny and inspiring at times. The play tends to be episodic but all of the scenes, both hilarious and tragic, are equally effective. The 1996 television production was given an all-star cast and the performances were splendid, particularly Nathan Lane's doughnut-obsessive Norman and Michael Jeter's eccentric paranoid Arnold. The adaptation was faithful to the original and the comic-tragic tone of the play was maintained.

Brewster's Millions

December 31, 1906 (New Amsterdam Theatre), a play by Winchell Smith, Byron Ongley. *Cast*: Edward Abeles (Montgomery Brewster), Mary Ryan (Peggy Gray), George Probart, Sumner Gard,, Willard Howe, Emily Lytton, George Spelvin. *Directors*: Frederick Thompson, Winchell Smith. *Producers:* Thompson and Dundy.163 performances.

(Lasky Feature Play Co. 1914). *Screenplay*: Winchell Smith, Byron Ongley. *Cast*: Edward Abeles (Monty Brewster), Joseph Singleton, Sydney Deane, Miss Bartholomew, Mabel Van Buren. *Directors*: Oscar Apfel, Cecil B. DeMille. *Producer*: Jesse L. Lasky.

(Famous Players 1921). *Screenplay*: Walter Woods. *Cast*: Fatty Arbuckle (Monty Brewster), Betty Rose Clarke, Fred Huntley, Marian Skinner, James Corrigan. *Director*: Joseph Henabery. *Producer*: Jesse L. Lasky.

(British and Dominion 1935). *Screenplay*: Arthur Wimperis, etc. *Cast*: Jack Buchanan (Jack Brewster), Lili Damita, Nancy O'Neil, Sydney Fairbrother, Amy Veness, Fred Emney. *Director*: Thornton Freeland. *Producer*: Herbert Wilcox.

(Small Prod. 1945). *Screenplay*: Sig Herzig, Charles Rogers. *Cast*: Dennis O'Keefe (Monty Brewster), Eddie Anderson, Helen Walker, Gail

Patrick, Mischa Auer, June Havoc *Director*: Allan Dwan. *Producer*: Edward Small.

(Universal 1985). *Screenplay*: Herschel Weingrod, Timothy Harris. *Cast*: Richard Pryor (Montgomery Brewster), John Candy, Lonette McKee, Stephen Collins, Jerry Orbach, Pat Hingle, Tovah Feldshuh. *Director*: Walter Hill. *Producers*: Lawrence Gordon, Joel Silver.

This contrived but audience-pleasing farce was not only a stage hit but spurned at least seven movies. Mortimer Brewster inherits one million dollars but he must spend it all at once, not giving it to charity and keeping the inheritance a secret. To add to the far-fetched plot, Brewster gets a handful of friends to help him spend the money and all kinds of problems come up over letting the secret out. The silly comedy was popular in New York and on the road for several seasons, followed by silent screen versions in 1914, 1921 (with Fatty Arbuckle as Brewster) and 1926 (a slight variation on the plot starring Bebe Daniels called *Miss Brewster's Millions*). The first talkie in 1935 was British and featured Jack Buchanan as Brewster; it was popular enough to be remade in Hollywood in 1945 with Dennis O'Keefe. In Great Britain the 1961 movie *Three on a Spree* used the same premise. The 1985 screen version again called *Brewster's Millions* used the old tale as a vehicle for Richard Pryor who played a baseball player who must spend one million dollars a day for thirty days. He got help from some talented co-stars but the comedy was as ridiculous as its predecessors. Interesting footnote: in the original stage production, co-author Winchell Smith used the fictitious name George Spelvin in the playbill program to disguise the real name of an actor. Smith continued the ploy in other productions, the name caught on, and it is still widely used in theatre today.

Brigadoon

March 13, 1947 (Ziegfeld Theatre), a musical play by Alan Jay Lerner. *Score*: Frederick Loewe, Alan Jay Lerner. *Cast*: David Brooks (Tommy Albright), Marion Bell (Fiona MacLaren), Pamela Britten (Meg Brockie), Lee Sullivan (Charlie Dalrymple), James Mitchell (Harry Beaton),

George Keane (Jeff Douglas), William Hansen. *Songs*: The Heather on the Hill; Almost Like Being in Love; I'll Go Home With Bonnie Jean; Come to Me, Bend to Me; There But for You Go I; Brigadoon; Waiting for My Dearie; My Mother's Wedding Day. *Director*: Robert Lewis. *Choreographer*: Agnes de Mille. *Producer*: Cheryl Crawford. 581 performances.

(MGM 1954). *Screenplay*: Alan Jay Lerner. *Score*: Frederick Loewe, Alan Jay Lerner. *Cast*: Gene Kelly (Tommy Albright), Cyd Charisse (Fiona MacLaren), Van Johnson (Jeff Douglas), Elaine Stewart (Jane Ashton), Virginia Bosler (Meg Brockie), Barry Jones, Hugh Laing, Albert Sharpe. *Songs*: The Heather on the Hill; Almost Like Being in Love; I'll Go Home With Bonnie Jean; Brigadoon; Waiting for My Dearie. *Director*: Vincente Minnelli. *Choreographer*: Gene Kelly. *Producer*: Arthur Freed.

Lerner and Loewe's first hit, this fantasy was overflowing with romance in both its plot and songs. The setting of a Scottish village that has escaped the modern world was ideal for the sudden love that grows between the American tourist Tommy and the local lass Fiona. There was magic in the plot but just as much in the lyrical score filled with both Broadway and Scottish-flavored songs. But magic on screen is problematic and few movie musicals have managed it. (*The Wizard of Oz* is the great exception.) Filmed in a studio rather than on location, the film version looks artificial without ever looking magical. The dancing is more 1950s Hollywood than timeless Highlands and none of the performances are very enjoyable save Van Johnson's wry, cynical Jeff. This is an awkward movie musical in just about every aspect; the only redeeming element is the romantic, lush (but radically cut) stage score. In 1966 a television version with Robert Goulet, Sally Ann Howes, Edward Villela, and Peter Falk cut much of the score and the libretto yet what remained was truer to the Broadway hit than anything in the movie. The production is obviously filmed in a studio yet it theatrically captures the Highlands feel of the piece.

Brighton Beach Memoirs

March 17, 1983 (Alvin Theatre), a comedy by Neil Simon. *Cast*: Matthew Broderick (Eugene Jerome),

Elizabeth Franz (Kate), Joyce Van Patten (Blanche), Zeljko Ivanek (Stanley), Peter Michael Goetz (Jack), Jodi Thelen. *Director*: Gene Saks. *Producers*: Emanuel Azenberg, etc.1,299 performances.

(Universal 1986). *Screenplay*: Neil Simon. *Cast*: Jonathan Silverman (Eugene Jerome), Blythe Danner (Kate), Judith Ivey (Blanche), Brian Drillinger (Stanley), Bob Dishy (Jack), Lisa Waltz, Stacey Glick. *Director*: Gene Saks. *Producer*: Ray Stark.

The first in a trilogy of autobiographical plays by Neil Simon, this warm-hearted memoir had a tough interior as a Jewish family fights the Depression and each other in an overcrowded house in Brooklyn. Young Eugene Jerome hopes to be a writer and keeps a diary filled with Simon-like wisecracks. But there is true frustration and even bitterness here as the family slowly falls apart. Matthew Broderick became a star playing the young Eugene but the whole cast was very proficient, under the sure direction of Gene Saks. Yet when he directed the 1986 film, much of the magic disappeared. Jonathan Silverman makes a funny if hollow Jerome, Blythe Danner and Judith Ivey do not convince as Jewish sisters, yet Bob Dishy is surprisingly understated as the weary father. While Simon's screenplay is true to his stage work, there is nothing very special about the film. The story of Eugene was continued in *Biloxi Blues* (qv) and *Broadway Bound* (qv).

Broadway

September 16, 1926 (Broadhurst Theatre), a melodrama by Philip Dunning, George Abbott. *Cast:* Robert Gleckler (Steve Crandall), Sylvia Field (Billie Moore), Lee Tracy (Roy Lane), Paul Porcasi, John Wray, Clara Woodbury, Mildred Wall, William Foran. *Directors*: Philip Dunning, George Abbott. *Producer:* Jed Harris. 603 performances.

(Universal 1929). *Screenplay:* Edward T. Lower, Jr., Charles Furthman. *Score:* Con Conrad, Sidney Mitchell, Archie Gottler. *Cast:* Glenn Tryon (Roy Lane), Merna Kennedy (Billie Moore), Thomas E. Jackson (Dan McCorn), Paul Porcasi, Robert Ellis, Evelyn Brent. *Songs:* Broadway; Hittin' the Ceiling; The Chicken or the Egg; A Little Love

Song; Hot Footin' It. *Director:* Paul Fejos. *Choreographer:* Maurice L. Kusell. *Producer:* Carl Laemmle, Jr.

(Universal 1942). *Screenplay:* Felix Jackson, Don Bright. *Score:* Joe Young, Sam Lewis, Harry Akst, etc. *Cast:* George Raft (George), Janet Blair (Billie), Pat O'Brien (Dan McCorn), Broderick Crawford, Marjorie Rambeau, S. Z. Sakall, Edward Brophy. *Songs:* Dinah; I'm Just Wild About Harry; Sweet Georgia Brown; The Darktown Strutters Ball; Alabamy Bound; Some of These Days. *Director:* William A. Seiter. *Producer:* Bruce Manning.

One of the long runs of the 1920s, this melodrama was set in the Paradise Night Club where a gangster and a hoofer are both after the same chorus girl and matters are complicated by a murder of a fellow mobster and the revenge his moll takes on the culprit. It was a solid story but the play's wide appeal came from the colorful character types that peopled the script and the slangy Broadway lingo that peppered the dialogue. The play was not a musical, though the club's orchestra was heard offstage during much of the action. The first movie version added a score of new songs and, as performed at the club, they turned the melodrama into a musical. Yet much of the tough, gritty quality of the stage work survived and the film managed to succeed in both genres. When *Broadway* was remade in 1942, old standards were used for the club's production numbers and the 1920s tale was told in flashback by George Raft remembering his youth. Solid acting by some expert character actors kept the melodrama potent even as the period songs fit nicely into the action.

A condensed version of the melodrama was broadcast in television in 1955 with Martha Hyer as the central chorine.

Broadway Bound

December 4, 1986 (Broadhurst Theatre), a comedy by Neil Simon. *Cast:* Jonathan Silverman (Eugene Jerome), Linda Lavin (Kate), John Randolph (Ben), Jason Alexander (Stanley), Phyllis Newman (Blanche). *Director*: Gene Saks. *Producer:* Emanuel Azenberg. 756 performances.

(TV 1992). *Teleplay*: Neil Simon. *Cast*: Anne Bancroft (Kate), Corey Parker (Eugene Jerome),

Jonathan Silverman (Stanley), Hume Cronyn (Ben), Michele Lee (Blanche), Jerry Orbach (Jack). *Director*: Paul Bogart. *Producer*: Terry Nelson.

Neil Simon's autobiographical trilogy concludes with this comedy-drama about the young man Eugene Jerome trying to begin his writing career on radio. He and his brother Stanley write comedy sketches as their family is falling apart: dad wants to leave mom, Socialist grandpa refuses to live with his daughter in Florida, and Eugene's love life is in turmoil. Yet the piece was basically optimistic and there was a lovely scene in which Eugene's mother recalled the day long ago when she danced with George Raft and then mother and son recreate the moment. More a character study than the previous works in the trilogy, the Broadway production boasted a superior cast, most memorably Linda Lavin as the unsentimental mother and John Randolph as the tragicomic grandfather. Jonathan Silverman, who had played Eugene in the movie of *Brighton Beach Memoirs*, was the older Eugene but he played older brother Stanley in the 1992 television version. Anne Bancroft was predictable as the mother and Hume Cronyn was quite moving as grandpa. But the television production is often flat and forced, a far cry from the wistful magic that Broadway had witnessed.

Broadway Rhythm see Very Warm for May

Broken Glass

April 25, 1994 (Booth Theatre), a play by Arthur Miller. *Cast*: Ron Rifkin (Phillip Gellberg), Amy Irving (Sylvia Gellberg), David Dukes (Dr. Harry Hyman), Frances Conroy (Margaret Hyman), George N. Martin (Stanton Case), Lauren Klein (Harriet). *Director*: John Tillinger. *Producers*: Robert Whitehead, etc. 73 performances.

(TV 1996). *Teleplay*: David Holman, David Thacker. *Cast*: Mandy Patinkin (Dr. Harry Hyman), Elizabeth McGovern (Margaret Hyman), Henry Goodman (Phillip Gellburg), Margot Leicester (Sylvia Gellburg), Julia Swift,

Ed Bishop, Nitzan Sharron, Mark Lambert. *Director*: David Thacker. *Producer*: Fiona Finlay.

One of Arthur Miller's many near-misses late in his career, this drama was often extraordinarily potent and, with all its faults, was still the work of a master playwright. In 1938 Brooklyn, Sylvia, the wife of a Jewish banking clerk, suddenly become paralyzed from the waist down yet the doctors can find nothing physically the matter with her. But under psychoanalysis it is revealed that Sylvia's husband is filled with self hatred at being a Jew and that her paralysis occurred when she heard about the "night of broken glass" in Germany in which the Nazis torched many synagogues. The Broadway production had many merits, including Amy Irving's poignant Sylvia, but the play was received with lukewarm enthusiasm by the press and the public. The 1996 television version offered a clearer, more direct approach to the tale and again there was some commendable acting yet still it failed to fully satisfy.

Brother Rat

December 16, 1936 (Biltmore Theatre), a comedy by John Monks, Jr., Fred Finklehoffe. *Cast*: Eddie Albert (Bing Edwards), José Ferrer (Dan), Frank Albertson (Billy), Kathleen Fitz (Kate Rice), Ezra Stone, Robert Griffith, Robert Foulk, Curtis Burnley Railing, Richard Clark. *Director-producer*: George Abbott. 575 performances.

(Warner 1938). *Screenplay*: Richard Macaulay, Jerry Wald. *Cast*: Eddie Albert (Bing Edwards), Wayne Morris (Billy Randolph), Ronald Reagan (Dan Crawford), Priscilla Lane (Joyce Winfree), Johnnie Davis, Jane Bryan, Jane Wyman, Henry O'Neill. *Director*: William Keighley. *Producers*: George Abbott, Robert Lord.

About Face (Warner 1952). *Screenplay*: Peter Milne. *Score*: Charles Tobias, Peter De Rose. *Cast*: Eddie Bracken (Boff Roberts), Gordon MacRae (Tony Williams), Dick Wesson (Dave Crouse), Virginia Gibson (Betty Long), Phyllis Kirk, Joel Grey, Larry Keating. *Songs*: If Someone Had Told Me; I'm Nobody; Piano, Bass and Drums; Spring Has Sprung. *Director*: Roy Del Ruth. *Producer*: William Jacobs.

One in a long line of comedies set on a campus, this lighthearted romp takes place at a military school where the top athlete

Bing Edwards has a secret: he is married. Anxious for money, he competes for an athletics prize but when Bing learns that his wife is pregnant he panics and loses the big baseball game and the award. But he does win a cash prize for being the first father in the class. Much of the play's humor came from Bing's two pals, played by José Ferrer and Frank Albertson who, along with Eddie Albert as the hero, launched their careers with this show. Albert made his screen debut playing Bing in the 1938 film and the comedy was so successful he played Bing again in the post-graduation sequel *Brother Rat and a Baby* (1940). Hollywood musicalized the original story as *About Face* in 1952 but the tired story and forgettable score gave the promising cast nothing worthwhile to do.

Buffalo Bill and the Indians see *Indians*

Bus Stop

March 2, 1955 (Music Box Theatre), a drama by William Inge. *Cast*: Kim Stanley (Cherie), Albert Salmi (Bo Decker), Elaine Stritch (Grace), Crahan Denton (Virgil Blessing), Phyllis Love (Elma Duckworth), Anthony Ross (Dr. Gerald Lyman), Lou Polan (Will Masters), Patrick McVey (Carl). *Director*: Harold Clurman. *Producer:* Robert Whitehead. 478 performances.

(Fox 1956). *Screenplay*: George Axelrod. *Cast*: Marilyn Monroe (Cherie), Don Murray (Bo Decker), Betty Field (Grace), Arthur O'Connell (Virgil Blessing), Robert Bray (Carl), Hope Lange (Elma Duckworth), Eileen Heckart (Vera), Hans Conreid, Casey Adams. *Director*: Joshua Logan. *Producer*: Buddy Adler.

Travelers on a bus in the midwest are forced to wait out a blizzard in a lonely restaurant and bus stop and, in a somewhat Chekhovian manner, the characters reveal themselves while waiting to move on with their lives. The central character is no-talent nightclub singer Cherie who is being wooed by the naive cowboy Bo but she wants nothing to do with him. Only after their forced wait do they begin to discover what the other is really like and they start to truly

fall in love. Kim Stanley's Cherie was highly praised and the comedy-drama enjoyed a long run on Broadway. The 1956 film opened up the story considerably, showing events leading up to the encounters at the bus stop. Marilyn Monroe, in what is arguably her finest performance, brought more humor to the role of Cherie yet there was something touchingly pathetic about her as well. She gets strong support from Don Murray, Arthur O'Connell, and others and Joshua Logan's firm direction keeps the story moving efficiently. A television series in 1961-1962 was loosely based on the play; different characters appeared each week as patrons of a bus stop diner with Marilyn Maxwell as the proprietor Grace. A 1982 television version of the original play featured Margo Kidder as Cherie and Tim Matheson as Bo.

But Not for Me see *Accent on Youth*

Butterflies Are Free

October 21, 1969 (Booth Theatre), a comedy by Leonard Gershe. *Cast*: Keir Dullea (Don Baker), Blythe Danner (Jill Tanner), Eileen Heckart (Mrs. Baker), Paul Michael Glaser. *Director*: Milton Katselas. *Producers:* Arthur Whitelaw, etc. 1,128 performances.

(Columbia 1972). *Screenplay*: Leonard Gershe. *Cast*: Goldie Hawn (Jill Tanner), Edward Albert (Don Baker), Eileen Heckart (Mrs. Baker), Paul Michael Glaser, Michael Warren. *Director*: Milton Katselas. *Producer*: M. J. Frankovich.

This slick, manipulative little comedy was a surprise success on Broadway where an estimable cast made it very appealing to audiences looking for a feel-good story with an easy message. Although he is blind, Don Baker gets his own Manhattan apartment and tries to break away from his domineering mother. He even finds himself having a fling with the kookie next-door neighbor Jill who is fun-loving but noncommittal. When Jill considers leaving him, Don plans to retreat back to his home and his mother. But Jill merrily returns so all ends well. Newcomer

Blythe Danner was applauded as Jill and veteran Eileen Heckart was also impressive as Mrs. Baker. Heckart got to reprise her role in the 1972 movie (and won an Oscar for it) but Jill was played by the new Hollywood favorite Goldie Hawn who specialized in likable scatterbrains. Playwright Leonard Gershe, who was an experienced screenwriter (this was his only play), opened the slight piece up for the screen and it was equally enjoyable if equally emptyheaded.

Bye Bye Birdie

April 14, 1960 (Martin Beck Theatre), a musical comedy by Michael Stewart. *Score:* Charles Strouse, Lee Adams. *Cast:* Dick Van Dyke (Albert Peterson), Chita Rivera (Rose Grant), Susan Watson (Kim MacAfee), Paul Lynde (Mr. MacAfee), Kay Medford (Mae Peterson), Dick Gautier (Conrad Birdie), Michael J, Pollard, Marijane Maricle. *Songs:* Put on a Happy Face; Kids; Got a Lot of Livin' to Do; One Boy; Baby, Talk to Me; One Last Kiss; How Lovely to Be a Woman; Rosie; The Telephone Hour. *Director-choreographer:* Gower Champion. *Producer:* Edward Padula. 607 performances. Tony Award.

(Columbia 1963). *Screenplay:* Irving Brecher. *Score:* Charles Strouse, Lee Adams. *Cast:* Ann-Margret (Kim MacAfee), Dick Van Dyke (Albert Peterson), Janet Leigh (Rose Grant), Paul Lynde (Mr. MacAfee), Maureen Stapleton (Mae Peterson), Jesse Pearson (Conrad Birdie), Bobby Rydell, Ed Sullivan. *Songs:* Put on a Happy Face; Kids; Got a Lot of Livin' to Do; One Boy; Bye Bye Birdie; One Last Kiss; How Lovely to Be a Woman; Rosie; The Telephone Hour. *Director:* George Sidney. *Choreographer:* Onna White. *Producer:* Fred Kohlmar.

(TV 1995). *Teleplay*: Michael Stewart. *Score:* Charles Strouse, Lee Adams. *Cast*: Jason Alexander (Albert Peterson), Vanessa Williams (Rose Alvarez), Tyne Daly (Mrs. Peterson), Chynna Phillips (Kim McAfee), George Wendt (Mr. McAfee), Sally Mayes (Mrs. McAfee), Marc Kudisch (Conrad Birdie), Vicki Lewis, Jason Gaffney. *Songs:* Put on a Happy Face; Kids; Got a Lot of Livin' to Do; One Boy; A Giant Step; One Last Kiss; How Lovely to Be a Woman; Rosie; The Telephone Hour; A Mother Doesn't Matter Anymore; Let's Settle Down. *Director*: Gene Saks. *Choreographer*: Ann Reinking. *Producers*: Tim Bell, etc.

What started as a silly high school musical meant for amateur groups ended up on Broadway as a surprise hit and launched the careers of songwriters Charles Strouse and Lee Adamas and director-choreographer Gower Champion. The lighthearted plot about an Elvis Presley-like singing star being drafted into the army was based on fact but the musical never took itself very seriously and still is a favorite with schools and amateur theatres. Dick Van Dyke as the singer's agent and Paul Lynde as a harried father got to repeat their roles in the 1963 screen version but they were secondary to Ann-Margret who, in the supporting role of teenager Kim, was showcased in the movie. The film made her a Hollywood star but it just about destroyed the Broadway musical in the process, cutting half of the songs and turning parts of the plot into cheap farce. It is a sometimes funny, tuneful movie but only a shadow of the Broadway show. A 1995 television version with Jason Alexander and Vanessa Williams as agent and girl friend was more faithful to the stage original but surprisingly dull and lifeless. The cast and creative team were filled with talent but for some reason the slaphappy show that every high school in America had presented with success didn't work on the small screen.

Cabaret

November 20, 1966 (Broadhurst Theatre), a musical play by Joe Masteroff. *Score:* John Kander, Fred Ebb. *Cast:* Jill Haworth (Sally Bowles), Joel Grey (Master of Ceremonies), Bert Convy (Clifford Bradshaw), Jack Gilford (Her Schultz), Lotte Lenya (Fraulein Schneider), Peg Murray, Edward Winter. *Songs:* Cabaret; Wilkommen; Two Ladies; Don't Tell Mama; If You Could See Her Through My Eyes; Tomorrow Belongs to Me; Married; Meeskite; It Couldn't Please Me More; Perfectly Marvelous; The Money Song. *Director-producer:* Harold Prince. *Choreographer:* Ron Field. 1,165 performances. Tony Award.

(Allied Artists/ABC 1972). *Screenplay:* Jay Presson Allen. *Score:* John Kander, Fred Ebb. *Cast:* Liza Minnelli (Sally Bowles), Michael York (Brian Roberts), Joel Grey (Master of Ceremonies), Marisa Berenson, Helmut Griem, Fritz Wepper. *Songs:* Cabaret; Wilkommen; Two Ladies; Mein Herr; If You Could See Her Through My Eyes; Tomorrow Belongs to Me;

Money, Money; Maybe This Time. *Director-choreographer:* Bob Fosse. *Producer:* Cy Feuer.

One of the outstanding musical plays of the 1960s, this gritty, uncompromising look at the rise of the Nazis in Germany and how it affects a handful of characters was both traditional and innovative. The two plots, one involving English cabaret singer Sally Bowles and American writer Cliff and the other an autumnal romance between a Jewish fruit merchant and his landlady, were presented in a straightforward manner but were punctuated by scenes from the local Kit Kat Klub where the musical numbers commented on the play's action. Holding the show together was the slim and slimy Master of Ceremonies played with chilling familiarity by Joel Grey. Harold Prince staged the musical in a Brechtian manner and Kander and Ebb wrote two scores: a set of character songs for the plot and pastiche numbers for the cabaret. Despite its dark and disturbing tone, *Cabaret* was a hit and remains potent in revival. Grey was the only artist from the Broadway production to be retained for the screen version. The screenplay kept only parts of the libretto and returned to the source material—Christopher Isherwood's *Berlin Stories* which had been dramatized earlier as *I Am a Camera* (qv)—for a new subplot about a Jewish heiress and her fortune-seeking suitor. All of the character songs were cut, limiting the musical numbers to the cabaret, and Sally became an American as Cliff (changed to Brian) was made British in order to accommodate the casting of Liza Minnelli and Michael York. Yet for all the changes, the movie is faithful to the original in temperament and quality and stands as a classic in its own right. Much of the power came from Bob Fosse's incisive direction and choreography but the cast is excellent, the new Kander and Ebb songs are first rate, and the film is a visual triumph of cinematography and editing.

Cabin in the Sky

October 25, 1940 (Martin Beck Theatre), a musical fantasy by Lynn Root. *Score:* Vernon Duke, John Latouche. *Cast:* Ethel Waters (Petunia Jackson), Todd Duncan (Lawd's General), Dooley Wilson (Little Joe Jackson), Katherine Dunham (Georgia Brown), Rex Ingram (Lucifer Jr.), J. Rosamond Johnson. *Songs:* Cabin in the Sky; Taking a Chance on Love; Honey in the Honeycomb; Love Turned the Light Out; Do What You Wanna Do. *Directors:* George Balanchine, Albert Lewis. *Choreographer:* George Balanchine. *Producer:* Albert Lewis. 156 performances.

(MGM 1943). *Screenplay:* Joseph Schrank. *Score:* Vernon Duke, John Latouche, Harold Arlen, E. Y. Harburg. *Cast:* Ethel Waters (Petunia Jackson), Eddie Anderson (Little Joe Jackson), Lena Horne (Georgia Brown), Rex Ingram (Lucifer Jr.), Kenneth Spencer (Lawd's General), John Bubbles, Louis Armstrong, Ford Buck. *Songs:* Cabin in the Sky; Taking a Chance on Love; Honey in the Honeycomb; Happiness is a Thing Called Joe; Life's Full of Consequence. *Director:* Vincente Minnelli. *Choreographer:* Busby Berkeley. *Producer:* Arthur Freed.

This musical "Negro folk tale" is arguably the best example of its genre, combining warmth and humor as it relates the fable of the idler Little Joe who is saved from death and given a second chance by the "Lawd" to reform his ways. Ethel Waters was superb as his steadfast wife Petunia and the Duke-Latouche score was filled with musical gems. The film version was director Vincente Minnelli's first screen effort yet it has a masterfully stylized look and a firm handling of the material. The screenplay altered the playscript slightly, putting the whole tale in the context of a dream so that audiences would accept the fantasy elements. Waters got to reprise her life-affirming Petunia and Joe, played by Dooley Wilson on stage, was given a playful interpretation by Eddie "Rochester" Anderson on screen. In a featured supporting role, Lena Horne as Lucifer's seductive helper is in top form. Only three of the Broadway songs were kept but the new ones included the indelible "Happiness Is a Thing Called Joe." A rare and wonderful piece of musical theatre was accurately and lovingly recaptured on film.

Cactus Flower

December 8, 1965 (Royale Theatre), a comedy by Abe Burrows. *Cast:* Lauren Bacall (Stephanie),

Barry Sullivan (Julian), Brenda Vaccaro (Toni), Burt Brinckerhoff, Arny Freeman, Robert Moore. *Director*: Abe Burrows. *Producer:* David Merrick. 1,234 performances.

(Columbia 1969). *Screenplay*: I. A. L. Diamond. *Cast*: Walter Matthau (Julian), Ingrid Bergman (Stephanie), Goldie Hawn (Toni), Rick Lenz, Jack Weston, Vito Scotti, Irene Hervey. *Director*: Gene Saks. *Producer*: M. J. Frankovich.

Abe Burrows adapted a French "boulevard comedy" by Pierre Barillet and Jean Pierre Gredy into an all–American comedy that became a long-run hit. A philandering dentist has lied to his mistress that he is married in order to avoid commitment, but when he wants to finally tie the knot he must convince his staid nurse to play the role of his wife so he can divorce her. The nurse blossoms during the charade and the dentist ends up with her. Lauren Bacall as the nurse was the prime attraction but the comedy was also popular with her many replacements. The 1969 film featured Ingrid Bergman in the role but the movie was stolen by newcomer Goldie Hawn who won an Oscar as the perky mistress. I. A. L. Diamond's screenplay may have been less adventuresome than his better work but he opened up the play nicely and the comedy is entertaining without being very memorable.

The Caine Mutiny see *The Caine Mutiny Court-Martial*

The Caine Mutiny Court-Martial

January 20, 1954 (Plymouth Theatre), a play by Herman Wouk. *Cast*: Henry Fonda (Lt. Barney Greenwald), John Hodiak (Lt. Stephen Maryk), Lloyd Nolan (Lt. Cmdr. Queeg), Ainslie Pryor (Lt. Cmdr. John Challee), Russell Hicks (Capt. Blakely), Robert Gist (Lt. Thomas Keefer), Paul Birch, Eddie Firestone, Carles Nolte. *Director*: Charles Laughton. *Producer:* Paul Gregory. 415 performances.

The Caine Mutiny (Columbia 1954). *Screenplay*: Stanley Roberts. *Cast*: Humphrey Bogart (Lt.

Comdr. Queeg), José Ferrer (Lt. Barney Greenwald), Van Johnson (Lt. Steve Maryk), Fred MacMurray (Lt. Tom Keefer), E. G. Marshall (Lt. Cmdr. Challee), Robert Francis, May Wynn, Tom Tully, Lee Marvin, Claude Atkins. *Director*: Edward Dmytryk. *Producer*: Stanley Kramer.

The Caine Mutiny Court-Martial (TV 1988). *Screenplay*: Herman Wouk. *Cast*: Eric Bogosian (Lt. Barney Greenwald), Jeff Daniels (Lt. Steve Maryk), Brad Davis (Lt. Cmdr. Queeg), Peter Gallagher (Lt. Cmdr. John Challee), Michael Murphy (Capt. Blakely), Kevin O'Connor (Lt. Thomas Keefer), Daniel Jenkins, Danny Darst, Ken Michaels. *Director*: Robert Altman. *Producers*: Robert Altman, John Flaxman.

Herman Wouk's novel *The Caine Mutiny*, about a mutiny aboard a Navy vessel during World War Two and the trial that followed, was ideal fodder for a movie but the court-martial scenes in the book were so detailed and theatrical that Wouk fashioned them into a play. A lieutenant is on trial for taking over the U.S.S. *Caine* from the captain during a typhoon, citing naval regulations regarding an incompetent captain. Lt. Greenwald takes the case and proves the captain to be neurotic and even self-dillusional, though in the end Greenwald blames some of the other officers for the unhappy events. Despite its lack of action, the talky courtroom drama was gripping theatre and, aided by an outstanding cast (Henry Fonda as Greenwald and Lloyd Nolan as the captain, in particular), the play ran over a year. That same year a film version of the complete novel was made and, though the trial section was much abbreviated, it was still the climax of the story. Humphrey Bogart gave one of his best performances as the paranoid captain and the whole movie focused on him. A television version of *The Caine Mutiny Court-Martial* in 1955 was greatly abridged but it did give Nolan a chance to reprise his performance on screen; he was given commendable support by Barry Sullivan and Frank Lovejoy. A 1988 television production of the play was also admirable. It featured Eric Bogosian as Greenwald and Brad Davis in a very different interpretation of the captain.

California Suite

June 10, 1976 (Eugene O'Neill Theatre), a comedy by Neil Simon. *Cast*: Tammy Grimes (Hannah/ Diana/Gert), George Grizzard (William/ Sidney/Stu), Jack Weston (Marvin/Mort), Barbara Barrie (Millie/Beth). *Director*: Gene Saks. *Producer*: Emanuel Azenberg, Robert Fryer. 445 performances.

(Rastar 1978). *Screenplay*: Neil Simon. *Cast*: Jane Fonda (Hannah), Alan Alda (Bill) Maggie Smith (Diana), Michael Caine (Sidney), Walter Matthau (Marvin), Elaine May (Millie), Herb Edelman, Richard Pryor, Bill Cosby. *Director*: Herbert Ross. *Producer*: Ray Stark.

The four comic playlets all set in the Beverly Hills Hotel may not have been as entertaining as the three one-act comedies Neil Simon had set earlier in the Plaza Hotel for *Plaza Suite* (qv), but an amusing cast and smart direction made the evening a success. The most memorable of the foursome was a funny-sad playlet about an English actress in Los Angeles for the Academy Awards ceremony and her bisexual husband. She doesn't win the award but the couple reach an understanding of sorts. Maggie Smith and Michael Caine were brilliant as the same couple in the 1978 film. (Ironically, Smith *did* win an Oscar for her performance.) Much of the rest of the movie is either routine or annoying, African American comics Bill Cosby and Richard Pryor coming out of it the worst for wear.

Call Me Madam

October 12, 1950 (Imperial Theatre), a musical comedy by Howard Lindsay, Russel Crouse. *Score*: Irving Berlin. *Cast*: Ethel Merman (Sally Adams), Paul Lukas (Cosmo Constantine), Russell Nype (Kenneth Gibson), Galina Talva, Pat Harrington, Nathaniel Frey, Alan Hewitt, Tommy Rall. *Songs*: You're Just in Love; The Hostess With the Mostes' on the Ball; They Like Ike; Marrying for Love; It's a Lovely Day Today; The Best Thing for You; Can You Use Any Money Today? 644 performances. *Director*: George Abbott. *Choreographer*: Jerome Robbins. *Producer*: Leland Hayward.

(Fox 1953). *Screenplay*: Arthur Sheekman. *Score*: Irving Berlin. *Cast*: Ethel Merman (Sally Adams), George Sanders (Cosmo Constantine), Donald O'Connor (Kenneth Gibson), Vera-Ellen, Billy DeWolfe, Walter Slezak. *Songs*: You're Just in Love; The Hostess With the Mostes' on the Ball; What Chance Have I With Love?; Marrying for Love; It's a Lovely Day Today; The Best Thing for You; Can You Use Any Money Today? *Director*: Walter Lang. *Choreographer*: Robert Alton. *Producer*: Sol C. Siegel.

Arguably Ethel Merman's best screen performance, her sassy and warm society hostess Sally Adams gave the Broadway belter a rare opportunity to recreate one of her stage roles on film. Appointed as ambassador to the tiny country of Lichtenburg, the outgoing Sally charms the foreign nation, falls in love with a gentlemanly minister, and even helps her assistant woo a princess. It was more a pliable story than an inspired one but Irving Berlin's tuneful score and Merman's panache made it seem like pure gold. The screen version was faithful to both libretto and score but most importantly it allowed Merman to show moviegoers why she was one of Broadway's biggest stars.

Call Me Mister

April 18, 1946 (National Theatre), a musical revue with sketches by Arnold Auerbach, Arnold B. Horwitt. *Score*: Harold Rome. *Cast*: Betty Garrett, Jules Munshin, Bill Callahan, Lawrence Winters, Paula Bane, Maria Karnilova, George S. Irving. *Songs*: The Face on the Dime; Call Me Mister; South America, Take It Away; Goin' Home Train; The Red Ball Express. *Director*: Robert H. Gordon. *Choreographer*: John Wray. *Producers*: Melvin Douglas, Herman Levin. 734 performances.

(Fox 1951). *Screenplay*: Albert E. Lewin, Burt Styler. *Score*: Harold Rome, Sammy Fain, Mack Gordon, etc. *Cast*: Betty Grable (Kay Hudson), Dan Dailey (Shep Dooley), Danny Thomas (Stanley), Dale Robertson, Benay Venuta, Richard Boone, Jeffrey Hunter. *Songs*: Call Me Mister; Goin' Home Train; Japanese Girl Like American Boy; Lament to the Pots and Pans; Love Is Back in Business; I'm Gonna Love That Guy. *Director*: Lloyd Bacon. *Choreographer*: Busby Berkeley. *Producer*: Fred Kohlmar.

With a cast made up mostly of ex–GIs and USO workers, this musical revue about soldiers returning to civilian life after the war was both ribald and sobering. Some numbers lampooned the homecoming situation while others memorialized the memory of FDR or lamented the plight of African Americans denied employment in the post-war boom. It was a significant Broadway entry and audiences supported it for over two years. The 1952 movie version only kept three of the stage songs and added a tiresome plot about a quarreling couple putting on a camp show during the Korean War. It was a routine backstager with a capable but unexceptional cast but, while the stage revue was very vocal in its ideas, the film had nothing to say.

Camelot

December 3, 1960 (Majestic Theatre), a musical play by Alan Jay Lerner. *Score:* Frederick Loewe, Alan Jay Lerner. *Cast:* Richard Burton (King Arthur), Julie Andrews (Guenevere), Robert Goulet (Lancelot), Roddy McDowell, Robert Coote, Me'l Dowd. *Songs:* If Ever I Would Leave You; Camelot; How to Handle a Woman; Before I Gaze at You Again; The Lusty Month of May; I Loved You Once in Silence; I Wonder What the King Is Doing Tonight?; The Simple Joys of Maidenhood; What Do the Simple Folks Do? *Director:* Moss Hart. *Choreographer:* Hanya Holm. *Producers:* Alan Jay Lerner, Frederick Loewe, Moss Hart. 873 performances.

(Warner 1967). *Screenplay:* Alan Jay Lerner. *Score:* Frederick Loewe, Alan Jay Lerner. *Cast:* Richard Harris (King Arthur), Vanessa Redgrave (Quenevere), Franco Nero (Lancelot), David Hemmings, Lionel Jeffries, Laurence Naismith. *Songs:* If Ever I Would Leave You; Camelot; How to Handle a Woman; The Lusty Month of May; I Loved You Once in Silence; I Wonder What the King Is Doing Tonight?; The Simple Joys of Maidenhood; What Do the Simple Folks Do?; Then You May Take Me to the Fair. *Director:* Joshua Logan. *Producer:* Jack L. Warner.

Riding on the success of *My Fair Lady*, much of the same creative team was reunited for this ambitious musicalization of T. H. White's mammoth book *The Once and Future King* about Arthur and the knights of the Round Table. Alan Jay Lerner's libretto could only cover parts of the novel so as lengthy as the musical was it seemed rather choppy and incomplete in sections. But some scenes were beautifully realized and the

Lerner-Loewe score was outstanding. So was the cast, with Richard Burton making an impressive Arthur, Julie Andrews showing eloquent maturity as Guenevere, and newcomer Robert Goulet in full voice as Lancelot. *Camelot* opened to mixed notices but audiences favored it and the problematic show still thrills in revival. Lerner did some judicious rewriting for the screen version, cutting most of the fantasy and setting the whole story as a flashback so that the tragic incidents near the end were foreshadowed. Although the performances did not equal the stage cast, Vanessa Redgrave made a surprisingly witty and lyrical Guenevere. Much of *Camelot* disappoints on the screen but, like the play, it is filled with intriguing ideas and noteworthy elements.

Can-Can

May 7, 1953 (Shubert Theatre), a musical comedy by Abe Burrows. *Score:* Cole Porter. *Cast:* Lilo (La Mome Pistache), Gwen Verdon (Claudine), Peter Cookson (Aristede Forestier), Hans Conreid (Boris), Erik Rhodes (Hilaire), C. K. Alexander, Phil Leeds. *Songs:* I Love Paris; It's All Right With Me; Come Along With Me; C'est Magnifique; Never Give Anything Away; Can-Can. *Director:* Abe Burrows. *Choreographer:* Michael Kidd. *Producers:* Cy Feuer, Ernest Martin. 892 performances.

(Fox 1960). *Screenplay:* Dorothy Kingsley, Charles Lederer. *Score:* Cole Porter. *Cast:* Frank Sinatra (Francois Durnais), Shirley MacLaine (Simone Pistache), Maurice Chevalier (Paul Barriere), Louis Jourdan (Philipe Forestier), Juliet Prowse (Claudine). *Songs:* I Love Paris; It's All Right With Me; Come Along With Me; C'est Magnifique; Let's Do It; Just One of Those Things; You Do Something to Me; Can-Can. *Director:* Walter Lang. *Choreographer:* Hermes Pan. *Producer:* Jack Cummings.

One of the many Cole Porter musicals set in Paris, this one concerned the scandalous can-can dance which was censored by the authorities in the 1890s. Madame Pistache runs a dance hall that performs the outlawed dance, Forestier is the young judge sent to investigate, and the two fall in love and together fight the status quo. More interesting was a subplot featuring Gwen Verdon as a dancer being wooed by two jealous suitors. In her first major Broadway role, Verdon stopped the show with her two production numbers and became a star. The Porter score is filled with lovely gems but the screen version sabotaged it, using the haunting "I Love Paris" only under the credits, cutting or abridging other numbers, and adding outside Porter tunes that did not fit. Abe Burrows's lively stage libretto was altered to the point of illogic and even the superstars cast could not save the movie. Verdon was passed over for Juliet Prowse who, history repeating itself, provided the only memorable moments in the film.

Captain Jinks and the Horse Marines

February 4, 1901 (Garrick Theatre), a comedy by Clyde Fitch. *Cast*: Ethel Barrymore (Mme. Trentoni), H. Reeves-Smith (Capt. Robert Carrolton Jinks), Mrs. Thomas Whiffen (Mrs. Jinks), Lucile Watson (Mrs. Stonington), Charles Bryant, Fanny Burt, Eugene Jepson. *Director*: Clyde Fitch. *Producer:* Charles Frohman. 168 performances.

(Essanay Film Co. 1916). *Screenplay*: Clyde Fitch. *Cast*: Anna Murdock (Mme. Trentoni), Richard Travers (Capt. Robert Carrolton Jinks), Laura Frankenfield (Mrs. Jinks), John Junior, Edmund Cobb, Camille D'Arcy, Ernest Maupain. *Director*: Fred E. Wright.

This stylish comedy is most remembered as the play that made Ethel Barrymore a Broadway star. She played Mme. Trentoni, a young and beautiful prima donna who is the toast of New York. Captain Jinks makes a wager with his friends that he can win her heart and he does, but when she finds out about the bet the courtship cools until the captain convinces her that what started as a dare turned into true love. Very popular in its day, the lightweight romance is an apt example of the kind of shows that dominated Broadway before Eugene O'Neill and others changed its direction. Barrymore did not make many films until later in her career so the 1916 movie featured Anna Murdock as Trentoni and she caused few sparks. It has lavish and romantic production values but was not a runaway hit like the play.

Carmen Jones

December 2, 1943 (Broadway Theatre), a musical play by Oscar Hammerstein. *Score:* Georges Bizet, Oscar Hammerstein. *Cast:* Muriel Smith (Carmen), Luther Saxon (Joe), June Hawkins, Carlotta Franzell, Glenn Bryant, Cosy Cole. *Songs:* Dat's Love; Beat Out Dat Rhythm on a Drum; Stan' Up and Fight; Dere's a Café on de Corner; My Joe. *Directors:* Hassard Short, Charles Friedman. *Choreographer:* Eugene Loring. *Producer:* Billy Rose. 502 performances.

(Fox (1954). *Screenplay:* Harry Kleiner. *Score:* Georges Bizet, Oscar Hammerstein. *Cast:* Dorothy Dandridge (Carmen), Harry Belafonte (Joe), Olga James, Pearl Bailey, Diahann Carroll, Joe Adams, Brock Peters. *Songs:* Dat's Love; Beat Out Dat Rhythm on a Drum; Stan' Up and Fight; Dere's a Café on de Corner; My Joe. *Director-producer:* Otto Preminger. *Choreographer:* Herbert Ross.

Oscar Hammerstein's retelling of the opera *Carmen* with African American characters was done with taste and talent and the new-old opera was a hit on Broadway. During World War Two, Carmen works in a parachute factory in the South and bewitches the colonel Joe who arrests her then runs off with her. Their tempestuous affair is filled with jealousy and bitterness and ends tragically. On stage it all worked as the larger-than-life characters matched the pulsating Bizet music given rhythmic new lyrics by Hammerstein. But the film version employs realism in its setting and acting and, despite fine efforts all around, it is uncomfortably melodramatic. Dorothy Dandridge is a sultry temptress but Harry Belafonte's Joe seems too naive and, when he turns to rage, unconvincing. Recent productions in Europe have shown that *Carmen Jones* still works on the stage; the film reminds us how easily the material can fail.

Carousel

April 19, 1945 (Majestic Theatre), a musical play by Oscar Hammerstein. *Score:* Richard Rodgers, Oscar Hammerstein. *Cast:* John Raitt (Billy Bigelow), Jan Clayton (Julie Jordan), Jean Darling (Carrie Pipperidge), Eric Mattson (Enoch Snow), Christine Johnson (Nettie), Mervyn Vye (Jigger Craigin), Bambi Linn, Jean Casto. *Songs:*

If I Loved You; June Is Bustin' Out All Over; You'll Never Walk Alone; Soliloquy; What's the Use of Wond'rin?; A Real Nice Clambake; When the Children Are Asleep; Blow High, Blow Low. *Director:* Rouben Mamoulian. *Choreographer:* Agnes de Mille. *Producer:* Theatre Guild. 890 performances.

(Fox 1954). *Screenplay:* Henry Ephron, Phoebe Ephron. *Score:* Richard Rodgers, Oscar Hammerstein. *Cast:* Gordon MacRae (Billy Bigelow), Shirley Jones (Julie Jordan), Cameron Mitchell (Jigger Craigin), Barbara Ruick (Carrie Pepperidge), Claramae Turner (Nettie), Robert Rounseville (Enoch Snow), Gene Lockhart, Susan Luckey, Audrey Christie. *Songs:* If I Loved You; June Is Bustin' Out All Over; You'll Never Walk Alone; Soliloquy; What's the Use of Wond'rin?; When the Children Are Asleep; A Real Nice Clambake. *Director:* Henry King. *Choreographers:* Rod Alexander, Agnes de Mille. *Producer:* Henry Ephron.

Arguably Rodgers and Hammerstein's finest musical, this dark operetta has never been as popular as the team's other major hits because it is often too subtle, too operatic, and too disturbing. Based on the Hungarian play *Liliom*, the story is an unromantic view of a failed marriage. The wooing of carousel barker Billy Bigelow and mill worker Julie has lush music but it is continually foreboding; his death in a robbery is far from surprising and even the optimistic ending that encourages his daughter to face life's cruelties is far from escapist. The original production ran two and a half years (less than a third of the run of *Oklahoma!*) and *Carousel* has seen several revivals over the years. But it remains a problematic show and probably the least likely to make a satisfying film. The 1956 version was successful in its first release but today is considered the least accomplished Rodgers and Hammerstein film. Frank Sinatra was slated to play Billy but at the last minute it went to Gordon MacRae who is totally out of his element unless he is singing. The rest of the cast is admirable but little else in the movie is. The rewritten script (told as a flashback from heaven) is awkward and sometimes downright silly. But most of the stage score is here to enjoy and some of the dancing is noteworthy. All in all, a great disappointment of a film. A television version in 1967

with Robert Goulet and Mary Grover as Billy and Julie abbreviated the musical so much that it seemed more like a series of highlights from *Carousel*. Yet some of the musical numbers were still very effective and it reminded audiences how moving the material still was.

The Cat and the Canary

February 7, 1922 (National Theatre), a thriller by John Willard. *Cast*: Florence Eldridge (Annabelle West), Edmund Elton (Hendricks), Henry Hull (Paul Jones), Blanche Friderici, John Willard, Beth Franklin, Harry D. Southard, Percy Moore, Ryder Keane. *Producer:* Kilbourn Gordon. 349 performances.

(Universal 1927). *Screenplay*: Alfred A. Cohn, etc. *Cast*: Laura La Plante (Annabelle West), Creighton Hale (Paul Jones), Forrest Stanley, Tully Marshall, Gertrude Astor, Flora Finch, Arthur Carewe. *Director*: Paul Leni.

The Cat Creeps (Universal 1930). *Screenplay:* Gladys Lehrman, William Hurlbut. *Cast:* Helen Twelvetrees (Annabelle West), Raymond Hackett (Paul), Neil Hamilton (Charles Wilder), Jean Hersholt (Dr. Patterson), Montagu Love, Blanche Friderici, Elizabeth Patterson. *Directors:* Rupert Julian, John Willard. *Producer:* Carl Laemmle, Jr.

The Cat and the Canary (Paramount 1939). *Screenplay*: Walter de Leon, Lynn Starling. *Cast*: Bob Hope (Wally Campbell), Paulette Goddard (Joyce Norman), Gale Sondergaard (Miss Lu), Douglass Montgomery (Charlie Wilder), John Beal, George Zucco. *Director*: Elliott Nugent. *Producer*: Arthur Hornblow, Jr.

The Cat and the Canary (Gala/Grenadier 1979). *Screenplay*: Radley Metzger. *Cast*: Honor Blackman (Susan Sillsby), Michael Callan (Paul Jones), Edward Fox (Hendricks), Wendy Hiller (Allison Crosby), Beatrix Lehmann, Olivia Hussey, Daniel Massey, Carol Lynley. *Director*: Radley Metzger. *Producer*: Richard Gordon.

One of the first (and best) of the "let's-scare-the-heroine-to-death" thrillers, the play was set in an appropriately creepy mansion during a thunderstorm. Young Annabelle will inherit a fortune only if she stays sound of mind so of course evil relatives and assorted crooks make every attempt to drive her insane. After running a year on Broadway, the melodrama was popular on the road and then with little theatres for decades. The first film version was a very atmospheric 1927 silent movie featuring Laura LaPlante as the terrified heroine. The look of the film was distinctive and other filmmakers would later copy it for haunted house movies. A 1938 talkie, titled *The Cat Creeps*, was a close copy of the play and silent movie and it was effective without being as accomplished as the earlier efforts. There was sufficient humor in the play and the films to relieve tension but comedy was in the forefront during the 1939 remake, called *The Cat and the Canary,* which gave Bob Hope his first starring screen role. As he assists heroine Paulette Goddard keep her sanity, Hope cracked the kind of one-liners that he would become famous for. The whole movie is well written and directed and features a delectable supporting cast. A first-class cast was also assembled for the 1979 British remake but most of the comedy and the chills were missing. Mildly entertaining, the movie is best enjoyed if one is unfamiliar with its better predecessors.

The Cat and the Fiddle

October 15, 1931 (Globe Theatre), a "musical love story" by Otto Harbach. *Score:* Jerome Kern, Otto Harbach. *Cast:* Georges Metaxa (Victor Florescu), Bettina Hall (Shirley Sheridan), Odette Myrtil, Eddie Foy, Jr., José Ruben, Doris Carson, George Meader, Lawrence Grossmith. *Songs:* Try to Forget; The Night Was Made for Love; She Didn't Say Yes; I Watch the Love Parade; Poor Pierrot; One Moment Alone. *Director:* José Ruben. *Choreographer:* Albertina Rasch. *Producer:* Max Gordon. 395 performances.

(MGM 1934). *Screenplay:* Bella and Samuel Spewack. *Score:* Jerome Kern, Otto Harbach. *Cast:* Jeanette MacDonald (Shirley Sheridan), Ramon Novarro (Victor Florescu), Frank Morgan, Charles Butterworth, Jean Hersholt, Vivienne Segal, Joseph Cawthorn, Frank Conroy, Sterling Holloway. *Songs:* Try to Forget; The Night Was Made for Love; She Didn't Say Yes; I Watch the Love Parade; Don't Ask Us Not to Sing; One Moment Alone. *Director:* William K. Howard. *Choreographer:* Albertina Rasch. *Producer:* Bernard Hyman.

Best described as a modern operetta, this romance between an American jazz composer and a Rumanian operetta composer both in Brussels flowed musically like the old genre but had a more cohesive story. Just as the two types of music need to blend, so too the two characters compromised to find happiness. Jerome Kern and Otto Harbach wrote the intoxicating songs and the show was a success even during the darkest days of the Depression. Surprisingly, Hollywood kept the entire score for the film version; not so surprisingly, the studio altered the plot and came up with a clichéd tale that climaxed with the operetta star walking out on opening night and songwriter Jeanette MacDonald stepping in á la *42nd Street.* But when it sings the movie is very pleasing.

The Cat Creeps see The Cat and the Canary

Cat on a Hot Tin Roof

March 24, 1955 (Morosco Theatre), a drama by Tennessee Williams. *Cast:* Ben Gazzara (Brick), Barbara Bel Geddes (Margaret), Burl Ives (Big Daddy), Mildred Dunnock (Big Mama), Madeleine Sherwood, Pat Hingle. *Director:* Elia Kazan. *Producer:* Playwrights' Company. 694 performances. Pulitzer Prize.

(MGM 1958). *Screenplay:* Richard Brooks, James Poe. *Cast:* Elizabeth Taylor (Maggie), Paul Newman (Brick), Burl Ives (Big Daddy), Judith Anderson (Big Mama), Madeleine Sherwood, Jack Carson. *Director:* Richard Brooks. *Producer:* Lawrence Weingarten.

(TV 1976). *Teleplay:* Tennessee Williams *Cast:* Natalie Wood (Maggie), Robert Wagner (Brick), Laurence Olivier (Big Daddy), Maureen Stapleton (Big Mama), Jack Hedley, Mary Peach. *Director:* Robert Moore. *Producers:* Derek Granger, Laurence Olivier.

(TV 1985). *Teleplay:* Tennessee Williams. *Cast:* Jessica Lange (Maggie), Tommy Lee Jones (Brick), Rip Torn (Big Daddy), Kim Stanley (Big Mama), Penny Fuller, David Dukes. *Director:* Jack Hofsiss.

Tennessee Williams's classic potboiler about a scheming and lying family of wealth on the Mississippi delta has some of his most colorful characters: the determined, sexually frustrated Maggie, her seething alcoholic husband Brick, the gross and self-dillusional Big Daddy, and others. It has always been a showcase for vivacious acting and many celebrated stars performed it over the years. The original production was considered shocking with its racy talk and many references to homosexuality. Barbara Bel Geddes and Ben Gazzara, as Maggie and Brick, were dynamic foils for each other but Burl Ives as the forceful Big Daddy often stole the show. Ives got to reprise the role in the 1958 film that had to tone down the more vulgar aspects of the play and even suggested a happy ending for Maggie and Brick. Elizabeth Taylor and Paul Newman as the incompatible couple may have laid it on a bit thick at times but the chemistry between the two is pure movie magic. The rest of the cast is excellent and the story remains cinematic even as it rarely leaves a few rooms in the mansion. Broadway revivals of the play have been plentiful and there were also two noteworthy television productions as well. Natalie Wood and Robert Wagner as Maggie and Brick were admirable in the 1976 version but Laurence Olivier's Big Daddy struck some as too forced and artificial. The 1985 television production had more consistently fine acting, with Jessica Lange and Tommy Lee Jones as the central couple and Rip Torn giving a distinctive interpretation as Big Daddy. But the pace is a bit too languid and the production never builds up much steam.

The Cemetery Club

May 15, 1990 (Brooks Atkinson Theatre), a play by Ivan Menchell. *Cast*: Eileen Heckart (Lucille), Doris Belack (Doris), Elizabeth Franz (Ida), Lee Wallace (Sam), Judith Granite (Mildred). *Director*: Pamela Berlin. *Producer:* Howard Hurst, etc. 56 performances.

(Touchstone 1993). *Screenplay*: Ivan Menchell. *Cast*: Ellen Burstyn (Esther), Olympia Dukakis (Doris), Diane Ladd (Lucille), Danny Aiello (Ben), Lainie Kazan, Jeff Howell, Christina Ricci, Bernie Casey. *Director*: Bill Duke. *Producer*: David Brown, etc.

Three middle-aged Jewish widows, who make monthly visits together to the cemetery, start to wonder if they are missing something out of life so two of them make efforts to find male companionship. Zippy one-liners alternate with sentiment as a romance blossoms but a contrived ending (one of the widows suddenly dies) sobers up the surviving women. The cast was exceptional but even expert performances could not hide the thinness of the play. Pretty much dismissed by the press and the public, the comedy-drama was later more popular with community theatre groups. The 1993 film also boasted a strong (if rather gentile) cast and the story was opened up a bit to fill out the tale, but the result was as forgettable as the stage play.

Chapter Two

December 4, 1977 (Imperial Theatre), a comedy by Neil Simon. *Cast*: Judd Hirsch (George Schneider), Anita Gillette (Jennie Malone), Cliff Gorman (Leo Schneider), Ann Wedgeworth (Faye Medwick). *Director*: Herbert Ross. *Producer:* Emanuel Azenberg. 857 performances.

(Columbia 1979). *Screenplay*: Neil Simon. *Cast*: James Caan (George Schneider), Marsha Mason (Jennie Malone), Joseph Bologna (Leo Schneider), Valerie Harper (Faye Medwick), Alan Fudge, Judy Farrell. *Director*: Robert Moore. *Producer*: Ray Stark.

One of Neil Simon's first and most successful attempts to move in a more serious direction, this middle-aged romance between a writer-widower and a divorced actress was both funny and touching. The two meet by accident on the phone and the jokes fly back and forth with characteristic Simon ingenuity. But once the two of them wed, the fear of true happiness without his deceased wife threatens the marriage until the two come to an understanding. The autobiographical play was based on Simon's relationship with actress Marsha Mason after the death of his wife so the honesty in the writing was often quite poignant. Judd Hirsch, in his first starring Broadway role, was sparkling and unromantic as the writer and Anita Gillette made a warm and personable partner for him. The comedy-drama ran on Broadway for nearly three years, followed by many regional productions. The 1979 movie was a misguided bore, poorly paced, clumsily opened up, and oddly cast. In an uncomfortable bit of casting, Marsha Mason played herself and was believable if nothing else. But dashing James Caan as the confused writer is tedious even when punching the one-liners. One of Simon's best works was botched beyond recognition.

Chicago

December 30, 1926 (Music Box Theatre), a satirical comedy by Maurine Watkins. *Cast*: Francine Larrimore (Roxie Hart), Edward Ellis (Billy Flynn), Isabelle Winlocke (Mrs. Morton), Juliette Crosby (Velma), Charles Halton (Amos), Eda Heinemann, Charles A. Bickford, Robert Barrat. *Director*: George Abbott. *Producer:* Sam H. Harris. 172 performances.

Roxie Hart (Fox 1942). *Screenplay*: Nunnally Johnson. *Cast*: Ginger Rogers (Roxie Hart), Adolphe Menjou (Billy Flynn), George Chandler (Amos Hart), Phil Silvers (Babe), Iris Adrian (Gertie Baxter), Spring Byington (Mary Sunshine), Nigel Bruce, Lynn Overman, Helene Reynolds. *Director*: William Wellman. *Producer*: Nunnally Johnson.

Chicago. June 3, 1975 (46th Street Theatre), a musical comedy by Fred Ebb, Bob Fosse. *Score:* John Kander, Fred Ebb. *Cast:* Gwen Verdon (Roxie Hart), Chita Rivera (Velma Kelly), Jerry Orbach (Billy Flynn), Mary McCarty (Mama Morton), Barney Martin (Amos). *Songs:* All That Jazz; Nowadays; Razzle Dazzle; Class; All I Care About; The Cell Block Tango; Roxie; My Own Best Friend; Mr. Cellophane. *Director-choreographer:* Bob Fosse. *Producers:* Robert Fryer, James Cresson. 898 performances.

Chicago. (Miramax 2002). *Screenplay:* Bill Condon. *Score:* John Kander, Fred Ebb. *Cast:* Renée Zellweger (Roxie Hart), Catherine Zeta-Jones (Velma Kell), Richard Gere (Billy Flynn), John C. Reilly (Amos), Queen Latifah (Mama Morton), Christine Baranski, Taye Diggs, Colm Feore. *Songs:* All That Jazz; Nowadays; Class; All I Care About; Roxie; My Own Best Friend; Mr. Cellophane; I Move On. *Director-choreographer:* Rob Marshall. *Producers*: Craig Zadan, etc. Academy Award.

The enduring tale of murderess Roxie Hart and how celebrity and "razzle dazzle" can overcome justice and truth began as a satirical play by Maurene Watkins that commented on the current fascination with purple journalism. The piece was exaggerated and smart-alecky and appealed to theatregoers in the Roaring Twenties. A 1927 silent film version featured Phyllis Haver as Roxie and remained fairly faithful to the source material. The 1941 movie, retitled *Roxie Hart*, featured Ginger Rogers as the title murderess and some of the wit and sass of the original remained, particularly in Rogers's performance and in the machinations of Adolphe Menjou as her slippery lawyer. Director-choreographer Bob Fosse collaborated with songwriters Kander and Ebb on the 1975 Broadway show that they labeled a "musical vaudeville." The tale was told as a series of variety turns, the action stopping as each song and dance was announced. The score was a brilliant pastiche of 1920s songs and often served to comment on the tale rather than continue the story. With Broadway favorites Gwen Verdon as Roxie, Chita Rivera in the enlarged role of fellow murderess Velma Kelly, and Jerry Orbach as the shyster lawyer, the stage was filled with talent. But after its initial run, *Chicago* faded from memory and it wasn't until a popular 1997 revival on Broadway and the road that a film version came to be. Screenwriter Bill Condon and director-choreographer Rob Marshall solved the problem of the disjointed vaudeville show by making each of the numbers occur in the mind of the heroine. By cutting from her imagination to the brutal reality of the situation, the movie was able to go places the musical play never could. A superior cast (all of whom did their own singing and dancing) and expert production values made this late movie musical an outstanding addition to the old genre.

Children of a Lesser God

March 30, 1980 (Longacre Theatre), a drama by Mark Medoff. *Cast*: John Rubenstein (James Leeds), Phyllis Frelich (Sarah Norman), Lewis Merken, William Frankfather, Scotty Bloch. *Director*: Gordon Davidson. *Producers*: Emanuel Azenberg, etc. 887 performances. Tony Award.

(Paramount 1986). *Screenplay*: Hesper Anderson. *Cast*: William Hurt (James Leeds), Marlee Matlin (Sarah Norman), Piper Laurie, Philip Bosco, Allison Gompf, John F. Cleary, Philip Holmes, Bob Hiltermann. *Director*: Randa Haines. *Producers*: Patrick Palmer, Burt Sugarman.

This is one of the very few plays to concern itself with deaf characters and it did so in an unsentimental and truthful manner. A teacher at a school for the death courts and marries a hearing impaired woman but the relationship is stormy because he must learn to separate pity from love. Because some members of the cast were deaf actors, any artificiality was replaced by some very eloquent scenes. The play was a critical and popular success and the 1986 movie was also a hit, though most agreed that it packed less punch since the film was often sluggish and sometimes preachy. Marlee Matlin, a deaf actress making her screen debut, won an Oscar for her fervent, uncompromising performance and it is the most accomplished aspect of the movie.

The Children's Hour

November 20, 1934 (Maxine Elliott's Theatre), a drama by Lillian Hellman. *Cast*: Anne Revere (Martha Dobie), Katharine Emery (Karen Wright), Katherine Emmett (Mrs. Amelia Tilford), Florence McGee (Mary Tilford), Robert Keith (Dr. Joseph Cardin), Aline McDermott, Barbara Beals. *Director-producer*: Herman Shumlin. 691 performances.

These Three (United Artists 1936). *Screenplay*: Lillian Hellman. *Cast*: Miriam Hopkins (Martha Dobie), Merle Oberon (Karen Wright), Joel McCrea (Dr. Joseph Cardin), Alma Kruger (Mrs. Amelia Tilford), Bonita Granville (Mary Tilford), Catherine Doucet, Marcia Mae Jones, Margaret Hamilton. *Director*: William Wyler. *Producer*: Samuel Goldwyn.

The Children's Hour (United Artists/Mirisch 1961). *Screenplay*: Lillian Hellman. *Cast*: Audrey Hepburn (Karen Wright), Shirley MacLaine (Martha Dobie), James Garner (Dr. Joseph Cardin), Fay Bainter (Mrs. Amelia Tilford), Karen Balkin (Mary Tilford), Miriam Hopkins, Veronica Cartwright, Hope Summers. *Director*: William Wyler. *Producer*: William and Robert Wyler.

Hellman's first play, a disturbing tale of a schoolgirl taking revenge on two of her teachers by suggesting a lesbian relationship, was the sensation of the theatre season. The first film version in 1936 dared not even hint at homosexuality so Hellman rewrote the script, the rumor now being about a heterosexual affair one teacher has with the other's fiancé. It made for a mild melodrama but the fine acting and skillful direction allowed it to seem bold and exciting. Hellman and director William Wyler got to redo the piece in 1961, returning to the original playscript and the lesbian scandal, but the result was less satisfying. The issues were still potent but the playwriting showed its age. Interestingly, Miriam Hopkins, who had portrayed one of the accused teachers in 1936, played a meddling aunt in the remake.

Child's Play

February 17, 1970 (Royale Theatre), a drama by Robert Marasco. *Cast*: Ken Howard (Paul Reese), Fritz Weaver (Jerome Malley), Pat Hingle (Joseph Dobbs), David Rounds, Peter MacLean, Michael McGuire, Mark Hall, Patrick Shea. *Director*: Joseph Hardy. *Producer:* David Merrick. 342 performances.

(Paramount 1972). *Screenplay*: Leon Prochnik. *Cast*: James Mason (Jerome Malley), Robert Preston (Joseph Dobbs), Beau Bridges (Paul Reis), David Rounds, Ron Weyand, Charles White, Kate Harrington. *Director*: Sidney Lumet. *Producer*: David Merrick.

A thriller without a murder or murderer, this masterful melodrama was a hit on Broadway but it has pretty much been forgotten since, even the notable film version largely neglected. In a Catholic boys boarding school, evil has broken out in the form of unprovoked attacks by students on other students. The rival factions within the faculty parallel the incidents with the students and eventually it is determined that the evil is growing out of adult hatred, not student pranks. A fascinating, if rather puzzling, melodrama, the original production featured a spooky setting and a superb cast. The 1972 movie seemed even more confusing than the play but again the acting was splendid. For some reason the studio gave the picture a very limited release then it quickly disappeared.

The Chorus Lady

September 1, 1906 (Savoy Theatre), a comedy by James Forbes. *Cast*: Rose Stahl (Patricia O'Brien), Wilfred Lucas (Dan Mallory), Francis Byrne (Dick Crawford), Eva Dennison (Nora O'Brien), Alice Leigh (Mrs. O'Brien), Giles Shine, Margaret Wheeler, Thomas Maguire. *Director*: James Forbes. *Producer*: Henry B. Harris. 315 performances.

(Lasky Feature Play Co. 1915). *Screenplay*: Marion Fairfax. *Cast*: Cleo Ridgely (Patricia O'Brien), Wallace Reid (Danny Mallory), Marjorie Daw (Nora O'Brien), Richard Grey (Dick Crawford), Mrs. Lewis McCord. *Director*: Frank Reicher. *Producer*: Jesse L. Lasky.

(Regal 1924). *Screenplay*: Bradley King. *Cast*: Margaret Livingston (Patricia O'Brien), Alan Roscoe (Dan Mallory), Virginia Lee Corbin (Nora O'Brien), Philo McCullough (Dick Crawford), Mervyn LeRoy, Lillian Elliott, Lloyd Ingraham, Eve Southern. *Director*: Ralph Ince.

This very popular melodrama started as a short story by James Forbes about a chorus girl in New York who gets involved in some criminal mischief and romantic triangles before giving up the theatre and settling down on the farm. Vaudevillian Rose Stahl had the tale turned into a variety sketch for her and it went over so well she had Forbes write a full-length play version. It was a resounding success on Broadway and later on the road and two silent film versions were made. Cleo Ridgely played the title chorine in the 1915 movie and Margaret Livingston essayed the role in 1924. Moviegoers' fascination with backstage stories made both films popular. But the story was considered old hat by the time sound came in and audiences became more interested in the more knowing kind of chorines found in *The Broadway Melody* (1929) and *The Gold Diggers* movies.

A Chorus Line

April 15, 1975 (Public Theatre), a musical by James Kirkwood, Nicholas Dante. *Score:* Marvin Hamlisch, Edward Kleban. *Cast:* Donna McK-echnie (Cassie), Priscilla Lopez (Diana), Kelly Bishop (Sheila), Robert LuPone (Zach), Sammy Williams, Pamela Blair, Wayne Cilento. *Songs:* What I Did for Love; I Can Do That; At the Ballet; I Hope I Get It; The Music and the Mirror; Nothing; Dance: Ten—Looks: Three; One. *Director-choreographer:* Michael Bennett. *Producer:* Joseph Papp. 6,137 performances. Pulitzer Prize, Tony Award.

(Embassy/Polygram 1985). *Screenplay:* Arnold Schulman. *Score:* Marvin Hamlisch, Edward Kleban. *Cast:* Michael Douglas (Zach), Alyson Reed (Cassie), Terrence Mann, Cameron English, Vicki Frederick, Audrey Landers, Gregg Burge, Nicole Fosse, Janet Jones, Matt West, Justin Reed, Pam Klinger, Michelle Johnston. *Songs:* What I Did for Love; I Can Do That; Let Me Dance for You; At the Ballet; Dance: Ten—Looks: Three; Surprise, Surprise; One. *Director:* Richard Attenborough. *Choreographer:* Jeffrey Hornaday. *Producers:* Cy Feuer, Ernest Martin.

Few Broadway musicals were as beloved as this tribute to the dancers in the chorus line and no musical had such a unique birth. Created from taped discussions with dancers then fashioned into a show during rehearsals, the concept musical defied all the usual requirements such as plot, character development, and spectacle. But Michael Bennett's crazy ideas worked on stage and audiences everywhere identified with those gypsies trying to sell themselves and be accepted for more than a job. If this was all problematic for the stage, it was just about impossible for the screen and no film version of *A Chorus Line* was likely to please its legions of fans. But the movie version that eventually was made was flatter and more lackluster than even the skeptics imagined. Few of the auditionees were engaging, little of the dancing was of interest, and nowhere was to be found the joy and admiration that had overflowed from the Broadway stage. The film was released, generally panned, and disappeared; meanwhile *A Chorus Line* continued to run on Broadway and in touring companies across the country for several more years.

The Clansman

January 8, 1906 (Liberty Theatre), a play by Thomas Dixon, Jr. *Cast*: Holbrook Blinn, George

Bee Jackson, Joseph Woodburn, Albert Lovern, Henry Riley, Grayce Scott, Samuel Hyams. *Director*: Frank Hatch. *Producer:* George H. Brennan. 51 performances.

The Birth of a Nation (Griffith 1915). *Screenplay*: D. W. Griffith, etc. *Cast*: Henry B. Walthall (Col. Ben Cameron), Lillian Gish (Elsie Stoneman), Mae Marsh (Flora Cameron), Miriam Cooper (Margaret Cameron), Mary Alden, Ralph Lewis, George Siegman, Donald Crisp, Raoul Walsh, Eugene Pallette. *Director-producer*: D. W. Griffith.

In a Southern town during Reconstruction, an African American rabble rouser joins with some carpetbaggers to get the recently-freed Negroes to terrorize the community. But the Ku Klux Klan organizes and puts down the rebellion, in turn terrorizing the blacks. During the play's modest run, an African American group objected to the stilted melodrama, calling it "evil propaganda." But even that notoriety was not enough to interest playgoers and the play pretty much disappeared from memory. In 1915 D. W. Griffith turned to the Thomas Dixon, Jr. novel the play was based on as the inspiration for his feature length film *The Birth of a Nation*, the cinema's first and most influential movie epic. The screenplay covers the story of two families during the Civil War and only the last reels are close to the stage play. African Americans protested then, and have continued to object, to the racist treatment of Negroes in the film, several of them played by white actors in blackface. As in the play, the Ku Klux Klan is seen as the savior of the white race and that also has bothered many over the decades. Yet there is no denying the power of the film and the many innovations it made in moviemaking. As for the original play, it remains forgotten. Footnote of interest: when the film was first released it was titled *The Clansman*; it's more grandiose title came a little later.

Clarence

September 20, 1919 (Hudson Theatre), a comedy by Booth Tarkington. *Cast*: Alfred Lunt (Clarence), Helen Hayes (Cora), Mary Boland (Mrs. Wheeler), John Flood (Mr. Wheeler), Glenn Hunter, Elsie Mackay. *Director*: Frederick Stanhope. *Producer:* George C. Tyler. 300 performances.

(Famous Players 1922). *Screenplay*: Clara Beranger. *Cast*: Wallace Reid (Clarence), Mary McAvoy (Cora), Agnes Ayres (Violet Pinney), Kathlyn Williams (Mrs. Wheeler), Edward Martindel (Mr. Wheeler), Robert Agnew, Adolphe Menjou, Bertram Jones. *Director*: William C. de Mille. *Producer*: Jesse L. Lasky.

(Paramount 1937). *Screenplay*: Grant Garett, Seena Owen. *Cast*: Roscoe Karnes (Clarence), Eleanore Whitney (Cora), Spring Byington (Mrs. Wheeler), Eugene Pallette (Mr. Wheeler), Johnny Downs, Inez Courtney, Charlotte Wynters, Richard Powell. *Director*: George Archainband.

While this breezy comedy by Booth Tarkington is mostly remembered today as the play that made Alfred Lunt a stage star and started Helen Hayes playing a series of flappers on Broadway, the play was very popular in its own right and has proven in revival to be one of the best American comedies of the period. The shy veteran Clarence is taken in by the chaotic, eccentric Wheeler family and before the final curtain he has brought order to their lives and won the heart of the governess. Hayes played a teenage whirlwind and the scenes between her and Lunt were pure gold. A silent film version in 1922 featured Wallace Reid as Clarence and it had its charm but most of the play's fun was in the dialogue. The 1937 talkie remake, with Roscoe Karnes as the title character, retained much of Tarkington's playful stage talk and the movie captured some of the fun of the Broadway original.

Claudia

February 12, 1941 (Booth Theatre), a comedy by Rose Franken. *Cast*: Dorothy McGuire (Claudia Naughton), Donald Cook (David Naughton), Frances Starr (Mrs. Brown), Frank Tweddell, John Williams, Adrienne Gessner. *Director*: Rose Franken. *Producer:* John Golden. 722 performances.

(Fox 1943). *Screenplay*: Morrie Ryskind. *Cast*: Dorothy McGuire (Claudia Naughton), Robert Young (David Naughton), Ina Claire (Mrs. Brown), Reginald Gardiner, Olga Baclanova,

Jean Howard. *Director*: Edmund Goulding. *Producer*: William Perlberg.

Claudia Naughton is a married woman but acts like a dithering teenager, unsure of her sexual self and doing rash things like selling their restored colonial home to an opera singer without even telling her ever-patient husband. But when Claudia learns that her mother is dying, maturity sets in and she becomes a true wife and mother. Rose Franken's works were often dismissed as "women's plays" but this comedy has some dangerous truths underneath the surface. Dorothy McGuire was animated and adept as Claudia and she got to reprise her performance in the 1943 movie, her screen debut. The story is expertly opened up for the film and the cast is uniformly commendable. It too was labeled a "women's picture" but was very popular and has held up as one of the best of that genre. A movie sequel called *Claudia and David* (1946) again starred McGuire and Robert Young as the couple, this time dealing with a baby, and it too is very entertaining even it it stoops to contrived melodrama on occasion.

Clear All Wires

September 14, 1932 (Times Square Theatre), a comedy by Bella and Samuel Spewack. *Cast*: Thomas Mitchell (Buckley Joyce Thomas), Dorothy Mathews (Dolly Winslow), Dorothy Tree (Kate Nelson), Eugene Sigaloff (Prince Tomofsky), Pauline Achmatova (Eugenie Smirnova), Harry Tyler, Charles Romano. *Director-producer:* Herman Shumlin. 93 performances.

(MGM 1933). *Screenplay*: Delmer Daves, Bella and Samuel Spewack. *Cast*: Lee Tracy (Buckley Joyce Thomas), Una Merkel (Dolly Winslow), Benita Hume (Kate Nelson), Eugene Sigaloff (Prince Alexander), James Gleason, Alan Edwards, Ari Kutai. *Director*: George W. Hill. *Producer*: Herman Shumlin.

A fast-paced satire about journalism, international politics, and Soviet Russia, this slam-bang farce was filled with various comic characters and smart-aleck laughs. Newsman Buckley Joyce Thomas has a reputation for making news so that he has something to report on. Sent to Moscow by his paper, he writes fictitious stories about camping with the soldiers in Manchuria and even tries to assassinate a leftover Romanoff. When he is wounded in the attempt, Buckley becomes a hero until he is found out, so off he goes to fresh journalistic pastures. Although the frantic comedy was well received by the press, its run during the darkest days of the Depression was relatively short. Thomas Mitchell was particularly applauded for his sly, manipulating Buckley, as was Lee Tracy as Buckley in the 1933 movie. It also is fast-paced and well acted but parts get more tiring than exhilarating. The film expands on the locales so sometimes the comedy seems like a Cook's tour around the world. The play served as the basis for the popular Cole Porter musical *Leave It to Me!* on Broadway in 1938.

Cobra

April 22, 1924 (Hudson Theatre), a drama by Martin Brown. *Cast*: Judith Anderson (Elsie Van Zile), Louis Calhern (Jack Race), Ralph Morgan (Tont Dorning), William B. Mack, Clara Moores. *Producer:* L. Lawrence Weber. 224 performances.

(Ritz-Carlton Pictures 1925). *Screenplay*: Anthony Coldeway. *Cast*: Rudolph Valentino (Count Rodrigo Torriani), Nita Naldi (Elsie Van Zile), Casson Ferguson (Jack Dorning), Hector Sarno, Claire de Lorez, Gertrude Olmstead. *Director*: Joseph Henabery.

This sultry melodrama made a stage star of Judith Anderson and introduced one of Broadway's most famous *femme fatales* in the character of the predatory Elsie Van Zile. She comes from a small town to New York to look up her old friend Jack. (Elsie hears he has money). But when she meets his richer friend Tony, Elsie throws over Jack and seduces Tony and marries him. After a few years she is bored with Tony and has an illicit rendezvous at a hotel. She dies there when a fire breaks out and Tony, going through all of her love letters from various men, realizes the truth about this cobra-like woman. The critics balked but audiences enjoyed the play, the naughty character, and Anderson's seething performance. When the

1925 silent film was made, it bore little resemblance to the play. Made as a vehicle for Rudolph Valentino, the focus was now on an Italian playboy who enjoys a series of women until he comes up against the vampy Elsie played by Nita Naldi. Valentino gives one of his best performances but, ironically, his fans were not impressed and the picture failed at the box office. Yet it has lavish, very elegant production values and is still very enjoyable.

The Cocoanuts

December 8, 1925 (Lyric Theatre), a musical comedy by George S. Kaufman, Morrie Ryskind. *Score:* Irving Berlin. *Cast:* Groucho Marx (Henry W. Schlemmer), Chico Marx (Willie the Wop), Harpo Marx (Silent Sam), Zeppo Marx (Jamison), Margaret Dumont (Mrs. Potter), John Barker, Frances Williams, Mabel Withee, Brox Sisters. *Songs:* Florida by the Sea; A Little Bungalow; Lucky Boy; The Monkey Doodle-Doo. *Director:* Oscar Eagle. *Choreographer:* Sammy Lee. *Producer:* Sam H. Harris. 276 performances.

(Paramount 1929). *Screenplay:* Morrie Ryskind. *Score:* Irving Berlin. *Cast:* Groucho Marx (Henry W. Schlemmer), Chico Marx (Willie the Wop), Harpo Marx (Silent Sam), Zeppo Marx (Jamison), Margaret Dumont (Mrs. Potter), Oscar Shaw, Mary Eaton, Kay Francis, Cyril Ring, Basil Ruysdael, Sylvan Lee. *Songs:* My Dreams Come True; Florida by the Sea; The Tale of a Shirt; The Monkey Doodle-Doo. *Directors:* Joseph Santley, Robert Florey. *Choreographer:* Sammy Lee. *Producer:* Walter Wanger.

Although the story was set in land speculation-crazy Florida and the plot concerned two lovers kept apart by a crook who has the boy falsely accused of stealing Margaret Dumont's jewels, all that really mattered were the Marx Brothers who interrupted the proceedings for a series of hilarious sight and sound gags. Irving Berlin's score was not noteworthy (the best song in the show, "Always," was cut before opening because librettist George S. Kaufman didn't like it) and the production numbers were rather tired looking. But the show ran on the strength of the renowned vaudeville clowns. Filmed under early, primitive conditions in a studio is Astoria during the

day while the Brothers were performing *Animal Crackers* on Broadway at night, the film version of *The Cocoanuts* introduced the team to movie audiences and they were an instant hit. The clanking early sound cameras were so noisy that they had to be enclosed in glass booths so the cinematography is very static. And the stage-like sets, awkward staging, and dance numbers are similarly wooden. But the movie is still highly entertaining when it captures the Marx Brothers doing one of their zany routines.

Collected Stories

May 20, 1997 (Manhattan Theatre Club), a play by Donald Margulies. *Cast*: Maria Tucci (Ruth Steiner), Debra Messing (Lisa Morrison). *Director*: Lisa Peterson. *Producer:* Manhattan Theatre Club. 80 performances.

(TV 2002). *Teleplay*: Donald Margulies. *Cast*: Linda Lavin (Ruth Steiner), Samantha Mathis (Lisa Morrison). *Director*: Gilbert Cates. *Producer*: Dennis E. Doty.

The young writer Lisa has a series of private tutorials with the famous short story writer Ruth Steiner and as the years go by they become friend and rivals. This penetrating two-actor piece was a showcase for two ambitious actresses and for potent ideas about literature. The original Off Broadway production was well received and after its limited engagement was revived with Uta Hagen and Lorca Simmons as teacher and pupil. The faithful television production in 2002 made no efforts to open up the material and relied on the riveting performances by Linda Lavin and Samantha Mathis. Alternately funny and sobering, both play and film are exceptionally masterful.

The Colored Museum

November 2, 1986 (Public Theatre), a revue by George C. Wolfe. *Cast*: Danitra Vance, Loretta Devine, Tommy Hollis, Reggie Montgomery, Vickilyn Reynolds. *Director*: L. Kenneth Richardson. *Producer:* New York Shakespeare Festival. 198 performances.

(TV 1991). *Teleplay*: George C. Wolfe. *Cast*: Danitra Vance, Linda Hopkins, Kevin Jackson, Reggie

Montgomery, Victor Love, Loretta Devine, Tommy Hollis, Vickilyn Reynolds. *Directors*: Andrew Carl Wilk, George C. Wolfe.

Director-playwright George C. Wolfe first came to the attention of New York playgoers with this dark comic revue consisting of eleven "exhibits" about African American culture. The sketches were sometimes highly satiric, such as a spoof of *A Raisin in the Sun* (qv), sometimes very moving, as with a piece about a Vietnam casualty lamenting the America his black brethren must return to. The Off Broadway show was the talk of the town and a decade later Wolfe was running the Public Theatre. The 1991 television production includes most of the vignettes but the performances seem too overpowering for the camera and both the comic and tragic moments are too overwrought to be truly effective. Most of the original cast made the studio version so it was more a matter of degree than talent.

Come Back, Little Sheba

February 15, 1950 (Booth Theatre), a drama by William Inge. *Cast*: Shirley Booth (Lola), Sidney Blackmer (Doc), Joan Lorring (Marie), Lonny Chapman (Turk). *Director*: Daniel Mann. *Producer:* Theatre Guild. 190 performances.

(Paramount 1952). *Screenplay*: Ketti Frings. *Cast*: Shirley Booth (Lola), Burt Lancaster (Doc), Terry Moore (Marie), Richard Jaeckel (Turk), Philip Ober, Edwin Max. *Director*: Daniel Mann. *Producer*: Hal B. Wallis.

(TV 1977). *Teleplay*: William Inge. *Cast*: Joanne Woodward (Lola), Laurence Olivier (Doc), Carrie Fisher (Marie), Nicholas Campbell (Turk), Patience Collier, William Hootkins, Bob Sherman. *Director*: Silvio Narizzano. *Producers*: Derek Granger, Laurence Olivier.

The slovenly housewife Lola is a bit of a child-wife, married to a recovering alcoholic, chatting endlessly with neighbors, and still waiting for her puppy Sheba to return, though the dog ran off years ago. When her husband Doc gets too interested in their pretty young boarder Marie, jealousy drives him back to drink. But by the end the couple is left alone and returns to their quiet desperation. While some critics carped

about the play, all agreed that Shirley Booth was giving the performance of her career. Sidney Blackmer's Doc was also a poignant picture of reserved frustration, arguably his finest performance as well. William Inge's play has proven stageworthy in many revivals across the country. The 1952 movie allowed Booth to put her marvelous portrayal on film and she won an Oscar for it. Burt Lancaster's Doc is less impressive (he is far too young for the role) and the movie is rather stagy at times, but there is still much to appreciate. A 1977 television production featured Joanne Woodward as Lola and it is a funny-pathetic portrayal that is very different from Booth's. Laurence Olivier's Doc is fascinating to watch, even if one suspects there is more technique here than heartfelt emotion.

Come Back to the Five and Dime, Jimmy Dean, Jimmy Dean

February 18, 1982 (Martin Beck Theatre), a play by Ed Graczyk. *Cast*: Sandy Dennis (Mona), Cher (Sissy), Karen Black (Joanne), Kathy Bates (Stella May), Mark Patton, Gena Ramsel, Marta Heflin, Ann Risley, Dianne Turley Travis, Ruth Miller. *Director*: Robert Altman. *Producers*: Dan Fisher, etc. 52 performances.

(Viacom 1982). *Screenplay*: Ed Graczyk. *Cast*: Sandy Dennis (Mona), Cher (Sissy), Karen Black (Joanne), Kathy Bates (Stella May), Mark Patton, Gena Ramsel, Marta Heflin, Ann Risley, Sudie Bond, Ruth Miller. *Director*: Robert Altman. *Producer*: Scott Bushnell.

This oddball comedy-drama struck most critics are more ridiculous than believable but there was no question it was a top-flight showcase for lively performances. In a drugstore in McCarthy, Texas, in 1975, a reunion of the local James Dean fan club brings out the best and the worst of the women who adored the movie star who had filmed *Giant* nearby twenty years earlier. Surprising revelations, cockeyed claims to fame, and dashed hopes are unearthed by the end of the play. After a little-seen Off Off Broadway production in 1980, the play was given an all-star revival on Broadway two years later. Although it was far from a hit, most of the cast and creative staff were involved in the 1982 movie which had an odd fascination of its own. Robert Altman's creative direction turned the filmed-play into a visually interesting piece of moviemaking, even if the source material was still questionable.

Come Blow Your Horn

February 22, 1961 (Brooks Atkinson Theatre), a comedy by Neil Simon. *Cast*: Hal March (Alan Baker), Warren Berlinger (Buddy Baker), Lou Jacobi (Mr. Baker), Pert Kelton (Mrs. Baker), Arlene Golonka, Sarah Marshall. *Director*: Stanley Praeger. *Producers*: William Hammerstein, Michael Ellis. 677 performances.

(Paramount 1963). *Screenplay*: Norman Lear. *Cast*: Frank Sinatra (Alan Baker), Tony Bill (Buddy Baker), Lee J. Cobb (Mr. Baker), Molly Picon (Mrs. Baker), Barbara Rush, Jill St. John, Dan Blocker, Phyllis McGuire. *Director*: Bud Yorkin. *Producers*: Norman Lear, Bud Yorkin.

Neil Simon's first Broadway play is a routine comedy about the generation gap but its amusing characters and risible dialogue foreshadow his later comic accomplishments. Two brothers, who work for their father in the plastic fruit business, rebel against old-fashioned ways; but after a few comic squabbles with the folks, everyone is resigned to each other. While the press was only moderately supportive, audiences immediately responded to Simon's brand of humor and the play ran nearly two years. The 1963 movie was rewritten to focus on Frank Sinatra as the elder son but the funniest performances were those by Molly Picon and Lee J. Cobb as the parents. It is a lighthearted and enjoyable film, though its ideas about bachelor swingers have dated poorly.

Come Out of the Kitchen

October 23, 1916 (Cohan Theatre), a comedy by A. E. Thomas. *Cast*: Ruth Chatterton (Olivia Daingerfield), Bruce McRae (Burton Crane), Robert Ames (Charles Daingerfield), Charles Trowbridge (Paul), Barbara Milton (Elizabeth),

Marguerite St. John, Alice Lindahl, William H. Sams, Walter Connolly. *Producer-director:* Henry Miller. 224 performances.

(Famous Players 1919). *Screenplay*: Clara Beranger. *Cast*: Marguerite Clark (Claudia Daingerfield), Eugene O'Brien (Bruce Crane), Bradley Barker (Paul), Frances Kaye (Elizabeth), Albert Hackett (Charles Daingerfield), George Stevens, May Kitson. *Director*: John S. Robertson. *Producer*: Jesse L. Lasky.

When an aristocratic Southern family finds themselves broke, they lease their plantation to a rich Yankee and, against their better wishes, become his house servants. But the beautiful and practical daughter Olivia keeps up the family's spirits and ends up marrying the Yankee, thereby keeping the homestead in the family. A delightful comedy based on a story by Alice Duer Miller, this was one of producer Henry Miller and star Ruth Chatterton's biggest hits. A 1919 silent screen version featured Marguerite Clark as Olivia (now called Claudia) but no talkie was later made of the tale. The premise of the wealthy posing as servants would return in other plays and films, most memorably the British movies *Come Out of the Pantry* (1935) and *Spring in Park Lane* (1948).

Command Decision

October 1, 1947 (Fulton Theatre), a drama by William Wister Haines. *Cast*: Paul Kelly (Gen. K. C. Dennis), Jay Fassett (Maj. Gen. Roland Kane), Paul McGrath (Brig. Gen. Clifton Garnett), Edmond Ryan (Elmer Brockhurst), Stephen Elliott (Col. Edward Martin), James Whitmore (Sgt. Evans), John Randolph, Lewis Martin, William Layton. *Director*: John O'Shaughnessy. *Producer:* Kermit Bloomgarden. 409 performances.

(MGM 1948). *Screenplay*: George Froeschel, William Laidlaw. *Cast*: Clark Gable (Brig. Gen. K. C. Dennis), Walter Pidgeon (Maj. Gen. Roland Kane), Van Johnson (Sgt. Immanuel Evans), Brian Donlevy (Brig. Gen. Clifton Garnett), Charles Bickford (Elmer Brockhurst), John Hodiak (Col. Edward Martin), Edward Arnold, Marshall Thompson, Richard Quine, Cameron Mitchell. *Director*: Sam Wood. *Producer*: Sidney Franklin.

William Wister Haines wrote this World War Two tale in 1945 as a play but when producers feared it was too soon after its events to appeal to theatregoers he turned it into a novel. The story was finally seen on stage in 1947 and proved to be very popular. Without ever leaving the office headquarters of the driven, suicidal General Dennis, this drama about bombing missions setting out from England was gripping theatre. Dennis sends his men on hopeless raids as he himself takes on dangerous missions without listening to his fellow officers. The faithful 1948 film boasted some outstanding acting and was opened up effectively for the screen. But the movie was soon overshadowed by *Twelve O'Clock High* (1949), another film about a demanding commander of bombing missions, and is little remembered today.

Compulsion

October 24, 1957 (Ambassador Theatre), a drama by Meyer Levin. *Cast*: Dean Stockwell (Judd Steiner), Roddy McDowell (Artie Straus), Michael Constantine (Jonathan Wilk), Howard Da Silva (Horn), Stefan Gierasch, Gerald Gordon, Barbara Loden, Roger De Koven, Ben Astar, Chris Gampel, Elliott Sullivan. *Director*: Alex Segal. *Producer*: Michael Myerberg. 140 performances.

(Fox 1959). *Screenplay*: Richard Murphy, Meyer Levin. *Cast*: Dean Stockwell (Judd Stein), Bradford Dillman (Artie Straus), Orson Welles (Jonathan Wilk), E. G. Marshall (DA Harold Horn), Diana Varsi, Martin Milner, Richard Anderson, Robert Simon, Ed Binns, Wilton Graf. *Director*: Robert Fleischer. *Producer*: Richard D. Zanuck.

Meyer Levin wrote a book about the infamous 1924 Leob-Leopold murder case, in which two upper-class law students murdered a cousin for the fun of it, and it was a bestseller so he later fashioned the complex tale into a play with many characters and scene changes. The young criminals were renamed Artie Straus and Judd Stein on the stage and, as played by Roddy McDowell and Dean Stockwell, they were an odd but intriguing pair. The real killers were defended by renowned lawyer Clarence Darrow, changed to Jonathan Wilk in the drama

and played by Michael Constantine. Positive reviews helped the play run over four months but the expensive production lost money. The 1950 screen version retained Stockwell from the Broadway production and he was supported by Bradford Dillman as Artie and Orson Wells as Wilk. It is an expert film adaptation with gripping performances throughout. In fact, many felt it made a stronger movie than a play. The true story had already inspired Alfred Hitchcock's experimental film *Rope* (1948) and would later turn up again in the movie thriller *Swoon* (1992).

The Connection

July 15, 1959 (Living Theatre), a play by Jack Gelber. *Cast*: Warren Finnerty (Leach), Carl Lee (Cowboy), Barbara Winchester (Sister Salvation), John McCurry (Sam), Jerome Raphael (Solly), Ira Lewis, Leonard Hicks. *Director*: Judith Malina. *Producer*: Living Theatre Company. 722 performances.

(Allen/Clarke 1961). *Screenplay*: Jack Gelber. *Cast*: Warren Finnerty (Leach), Carl Lee (Cowboy), Barbara Winchester (Sister Salvation), Jerome Raphael (Solly), William Redfield (Jim Dunn), James Anderson, Garry Goodrow, Henry Proach, Roscoe Lee Browne. *Director*: Shirley Clarke. *Producers*: Lewis Allen, Shirley Clarke.

Few Off Broadway plays had as much impact on its era as this slice-of-life look at a group of drug addicts killing time in a "pad" while they wait for the dealer Cowboy to bring their narcotics. The talk was unstructured and potent and, with its jazz background score, it created a powerful glimpse into an unseen world. Without opening up the action, the screen version took on a documentary feel as filmmaker Jim Dunn pays for the drugs and is allowed to film the addicts as they wait. The odd and potent play made for an equally unique movie.

The Copperhead

February 18, 1918 (Shubert Theatre), a drama by Augustus Thomas. *Cast*: Lionel Barrymore (Milt Shanks), Doris Rankin (Mrs. Shanks/Madeline), Harry Hadfield (Rev. Andrews), Eugenie Woodward (Grandma Perley), Raymond Hackett (Joey), Gladys Burgette, Evelyn Archer, Thomas Carrigan. *Producer:* John D. Williams. 120 performances.

(Maigne 1920). *Screenplay*: Charles Maigne. *Cast*: Lionel Barrymore (Milt Shanks), William P. Carlton (Lt. Tom Hardy), Doris Rankin (Mrs. Shanks/Madeline), Leslie Stowe (Rev. Andrews), Carolyn Lee (Grandma Perley), Arthur Rankin (Joey), Francis Joyner, N. Schroell. *Director-producer*: Charles Maigne.

Playwright Augustus Thomas turned Frederick Landis's novel *The Glory of His Country* into a affecting vehicle for Lionel Barrymore who gave perhaps his greatest stage performance as the seeming-pacifist Milt Shanks. Because he remains silent on the issues of the day, Shanks is suspected by his neighbors in rural Illinois of being a Confederate sympathizer or even a rebel spy. It is not until years later that he reveals to his granddaughter that he was a spy for the North and he even has a grateful letter from Abe Lincoln to prove it. Opening on Broadway during World War One, the drama was seen by some as a plea for pacifism, by others a patriotic work. But they all agreed that Barrymore was outstanding and so he got to recreate the role of Shanks in a 1920 silent film version. He had been making movies on and off since 1911 and the success of *The Copperhead* encouraged him to do more; by 1925 he left the stage permanently for Hollywood.

Coquette

November 8, 1927 (Maxine Elliot's Theatre), a drama by George Abbott, Ann Preston Bridgers. *Cast*: Helen Hayes (Norma Besant), Eliot Cabot (Michael Jeffrey), Charles Waldron (Dr. Besant), Una Merkle (Betty Lee Reynolds), Andrew Lawlor, Jr., Gaylord Pendleton, Phyllis Tyler, G. Albert Smith. *Director*: George Abbott. *Producer:* Jed Harris. 366 performances.

(Pickford Corp. 1929). *Screenplay*: John Grey, etc. *Cast*: Mary Pickford (Norma Besant), Johnny Mack Brown (Michael Jeffrey), John St. Polis (Dr. Besant), Matt Moore, William Janney, George Irving, Louise Beavers, Henry Kolker. *Director*: Sam Taylor. *Producers*: Sam Taylor, Mary Pickford.

A domestic drama that secured Helen Hayes's position as one of the foremost Broadway stars of her era, the play concerned a zesty flapper name Norma who sleeps with the man she wants to marry. When her father refuses to accept him as a son-in-law, Norma blurts out the truth about their sexual relations. The father allows the marriage but later in anger shoots the young man. Rather than be subject to the physical exam that will prove the loss of her virginity, Norma kills herself. As purple as the drama seems today, it was a considerable hit in its day because of Hayes's luminous performance. In fact, the Broadway production would have run longer except Hayes revealed that she and her husband were expecting a baby so the "act of God" forced the show to close. The 1929 screen version of the play was an early talkie in which Mary Pickford made her sound film debut. "America's Sweetheart" cut off her curls, bobbed her hair, and played the liberated Norma with abandon. She won an Oscar for the performance but audiences were disappointed and missed the sweet innocent Pickford. After a few more films she would retire from the screen permanently.

Counsellor-at-Law

November 6, 1931 (Plymouth Theatre), a drama by Elmer Rice. *Cast*: Paul Muni (George Simon), Anna Kostant (Regina), Louise Prussing, Marvin Kline, Conway Washburne, Gladys Feldman. *Director*: Elmer Rice. *Producer:* Elmer Rice. 397 performances.

(Universal 1933). *Screenplay*: Elmer Rice. *Cast*: John Barrymore (George Simon), Bebe Daniels (Regina), Doris Kenyon, Isabel Jewell, Melvyn Douglas, Onslow Stevens, Thelma Todd, Mayo Methot. *Director*: William Wyler. *Producer*: Carl Laemmle, Jr.

Peopled with lawyers, clerks, defendants, and witnesses, this lively play was a microcosm of the legal world just as Elmer Rice's *Street Scene* (qv) was of a New York neighborhood. George Simon is an East Side Jew who has risen to the top of his profession and has married into society. But bigoted people of wealth conspire to bring him down and only with the help of his loving secretary does he survive. At the center of all the hubbub was Paul Muni giving an electrifying performance as George. The 1933 film featured John Barrymore as the lawyer (Muni had actually turned down the role because he was afraid of being typecast as Jews in the movies) and it was one of his finest screen portrayals. William Wyler directed with precision and the large cast of characters overflowed with energy. Although both play and movie were hits, the drama is little revived because of its demanding production values.

The Country Girl

November 10, 1950 (Lyceum Theatre), a drama by Clifford Odets. *Cast*: Uta Hagen (Georgie), Steven Hill (Bernie Dodd), Paul Kelly (Frank Elgin), Joseph Sullivan, Peter Kass, Louis Veda Quince, Joseph Sullivan. *Director*: Clifford Odets. *Producer:* Dwight Deere Wiman. 235 performances.

(Paramount 1954). *Screenplay*: George Seaton. *Score:* Ira Gershwin, Harold Arlen. *Cast*: Bing Crosby (Frank Elgin), Grace Kelly (Georgie Elgin), William Holden (Bernie Dodd), Anthony Ross, Gene Reynolds. *Songs*: The Search Is Through; The Land Around Us; It's Mine, It's Yours. *Director*: George Seaton. *Producer*: William Perlberg.

Frank Elgin has ruined his acting career through drink but his wife Georgie and the understanding director Bernie Dodd get him back on stage and Frank's a hit. Georgie and Bernie begin to fall into a romance but she sticks with her husband, knowing her leaving him will send him back to the bottle. This intimate drama is Clifford Odets's his least political work and it has often been revived because of the strong, demanding roles it provides for actors. Hollywood had its eye on the box office when it reworked the play into a 1954 vehicle for Bing Crosby who played Frank, now a singer on the outs. A handful of songs were written for Crosby to sing in clubs but the picture doesn't have the look or feel of a musical. Several critics deemed the film dreary but it was very popular, helped by the presence of the three top stars. Grace Kelly, as the unglamorous Georgie, gave arguably her best screen performance (and won an Oscar) and William Holden was solid and appealing as Bernie. A first-rate 1973 television production, which used the original stage script, starred Jason Robards as Frank, Shirley Knight as Georgie, and George Grizzard as Bernie. Less effective but still worthwhile was a 1982 television remake with Dick Van Dyke as Frank, Faye Dunaway as Georgie, and Ken Howard as Bernie.

The County Chairman

November 24, 1903 (Wallack's Theatre), a comedy by George Ade. *Cast*: Maclyn Arbuckle (Jim Hackler), Charles Fisher (Judge Rigby), Earle Brown (Tillford Wheeler), Miriam Nesbitt (Lucy Rigby), Edward Chapman (Jefferson Briscoe), Anna Buckley, George Ricketts, Fred Santley, Harry Holman, John J. Meehan, Rose Beaudet. *Director*: George Marion. *Producer:* Henry W. Savage. 222 performances.

(Famous Players 1914). *Screenplay*: Allan Dwan. *Cast*: Maclyn Arbuckle (Jim Hackler), William Lloyd (Elias Rigby), Harold Lockwood (Tillford Wheeler), Daisy Robinson (Lucy Rigby), Willis P. Sweatnam, Helen Aubrey. *Director*: Allan Dwan. *Producer*: Jesse L. Lasky.

(Fox 1934). *Screenplay*: Sam Hellman, Gladys Lehman. *Cast:* Will Rogers (Jim Hackler), Evelyn Venable (Lucy Rigby), Kent Taylor (Ben Harvey), Louise Dresser (Mrs. Rigby), Mickey Rooney (Freckles), Stepin Fetchit, Berton Churchill. *Director:* John Blystone. *Producer*: Edward Butcher.

This comedy about small-town politics was very popular on Broadway and on the road but the only memorable aspect of the play to survive is the raucous, funny civic chairman Jim Hackler, a character who would be copied and reused in many later plays and movies. The rotund stage favorite Macklyn Arbuckle (not to be confused with the equally large comic "Fatty" Arbuckle who starred in many comic film shorts) triumphed as Hackler on Broadway and he appeared in the 1914 silent movie as well. Of course, much of Hackler's humor was verbal so the film only gives a hint of what Arbuckle's stage performance was like. Will

Rogers played Hackler in the 1934 talkie and he is his characteristically wry self but not the broad, outrageous politician that propelled the play.

The Cowboy Quarterback
see *Elmer the Great*

The Cradle Snatchers

September 7, 1925 (Music Box Theatre), a comedy by Russell Medcraft, Norma Mitchell. *Cast*: Margaret Dale (Kitty Ladd), Mary Boland (Susan Martin), Edna May Oliver (Ethel Drake), Humphrey Bogart (Jose Vallejo), Mary Loane, Raymond Guion, Stanley Jessup, Raymond Hackett, Cecil Owen. *Director*: Sam Forrest. *Producer*: Sam H. Harris. 485 performances.

(Fox 1927). *Screenplay*: Sarah Y. Mason. *Cast*: Louise Fazenda (Kitty), Diane Ellis (Susan), Nick Stuart, Arthur Lake, Franklin Pangborn, J. Farrell MacDonald, Dorothy Philips. *Director*: Howard Hawks. *Producer*: William Fox.

When a wife discovers that her husband and his two cronies' weekend sporting trips involve more infidelity than sport, she arranges for the three wives to have their own fling. They invite a trio of college boys to a party and the champagne flows until the three husbands enter. The boys leave to seek younger companions and the married couples are left to reconcile with each other. The fast-paced, broad comedy was a hit with the press and the public and the sparking cast was roundly applauded, in particular a young Humphrey Bogart as one of the college lads. The silent screen version in 1927 is of interest because it was directed by Howard Hawks and already his talent for fast and furious comedy is evident. In 1941 the play was later turned into the Cole Porter Broadway musical *Let's Face It!* (qv).

Craig's Wife

October 12, 1925 (Morosco Theatre), a drama by George Kelly. *Cast*: Chrystal Herne (Harriet Craig), Charles Trowbridge (Walter Craig), Anne Sutherland (Miss Austen), Josephine Hull (Mrs. Frazier), Arling Alcine, Arthur Shaw. *Di-*rector: George Kelly. *Producer:* Rosalie Stewart. 360 performances. Pulitzer Prize.

(Pathé Exchange 1928). *Screenplay*: George Kelly. *Cast*: Irene Rich (Mrs. Craig), Warner Baxter (Walter Craig), Jane Keckley (Miss Austen), Mabel Van Buren (Mrs. Frazier), Virginia Bradford, Carroll Nye, Lilyan Tashman, George Irving. *Director*: William C. de Mille.

(Columbia 1936). *Screenplay*: Mary McCally, George Kelly. *Cast*: Rosalind Russell (Harriet Craig), John Boles (Walter Craig), Billie Burke (Mrs. Frazier), Jane Darwell, Dorothy Wilson, Thomas Mitchell, Alma Kruger. *Director*: Dorothy Arzner. *Producer*: Edward Chodorov.

Harriet Craig (Columbia 1950). *Screenplay*: Anne Froelick, James Gunn. *Cast:* Joan Crawford (Harriet Craig), Wendell Corey (Walter Craig), Allyn Joslyn (Billy Birkmire), Lucile Watson (Celia Fenwick), Fiona O'Shiel (Mrs. Fazier), William Bishop, K. T. Stevens, Raymond Greenleaf. *Director:* Vincent Sherman. *Producer:* William Dozier.

The center of this domestic drama was a domineering, irritating woman who was both unique and very familiar to playgoers. Harriet Craig runs her household with an iron hand, telling her passive husband what he can and cannot do and always putting her precious house and its furnishings above everything and everyone else. But Mr. Craig and his aunt know Harriet has gone too far when she will not let them help a neighbor attempting suicide because she doesn't want a scandal. By the final curtain Craig's wife is alone and friendless. Broadway favorite Chrystal Herne was chilling as Harriet and the disturbing drama ran a year. Irene Rich played her in the 1928 silent movie but more memorable was the 1936 talkie in which Rosalind Russell scored her first screen hit as the pushy Harriet. She is surrounded by a first-class cast and the adaptation from stage to screen is quite accomplished. The piece was remade as a vehicle for Joan Crawford and, titled *Harriet Craig*, it was also true to the play, even if the film was less impressive than the earlier talkie.

Crimes of the Heart

November 4, 1981 (John Golden Theatre), a play by Beth Henley. *Cast*: Mary Beth Hurt (Meg),

Lizbeth MacKay (Lenny), Mia Dillon (Babe), Peter MacNichol, Raymond Baker, Sharon Ullrick. *Director*: Melvin Bernhardt. *Producers:* Warner Theatre Productions, etc. 535 performances. Pulitzer Prize.

(De Laurentis-Fields-Sugarman 1986). *Screenplay*: Beth Henley. *Cast*: Diane Keaton (Lenny), Jessica Lange (Meg), Sissy Spacek (Babe), David Carpenter, Sam Shepard, Tess Harper, Hurd Hatfield. *Director*: Bruce Beresford. *Producer*: Freddie Fields.

A Southern Gothic comedy filled with risible eccentric characters, this surprise hit was one of the most produced works across the country for a time. The three McGrath sisters in a small Mississippi town have always been talked about but when Babe shoots her husband because she "didn't like his looks," the locals really have something to gossip about. Before the day is over the threesome have fought, reminisced, cried, and laughed enough that they know they will survive this latest McGrath crisis. The humor was sometimes outrageous, always honest, and occasionally wistful. The largely unknown cast from Off Broadway were featured on Broadway with great success but Hollywood went with established screen stars for the 1986 film. Sissy Spacek was ideally suited for the naive, incongruous Babe and Jessica Lange was believable as the self-dillusional Meg, but attractive Diane Keaton never convinced as the spinsterish, overlooked Lennie. Playwright Beth Henley's screenplay stuck close to the stage script but the movie was only mildly interesting where the play had been a joyous roller coaster ride.

Critic's Choice

December 14, 1960 (Ethel Barrymore Theatre), a comedy by Ira Levin. *Cast*: Henry Fonda (Parker Ballantine), Georgeann Johnson (Angela Ballantine), Eddie Hodges (John Ballantine), Mildred Natwick (Charlotte Orr), Virginia Gilmore (Ivy London), Murray Hamilton, Billie Allen. *Director-producer:* Otto Preminger. 189 performances.

(Warner 1963). *Screenplay*: Jack Sher. *Cast*: Bob Hope (Parker Ballantine), Lucille Ball (Angela Ballantine), Ricky Kelman (John Ballantine), Jessie Royce Landis (Charlotte Orr), Marilyn Maxwell (Ivy London), Rip Torn, John Dehner,

Jim Backus. *Director*: Don Weiss. *Producer*: Frank P. Rosenberg.

When a celebrated theatre critic finds out his wife is writing a play, he scoffs until it is optioned for Broadway and he finds himself reviewing it. His damning notice nearly breaks up the marriage but eventually the husband and wife reconcile even if critic and playwright fail to agree. There were many inside theatre jokes in the lightweight script and the comedy tended toward the brainy rather than the belly laugh. The show managed to entertain audiences for six months on the strength of its adroit cast, particularly Henry Fonda as the husband-critic. The 1963 movie was opened up and dumbed down so it hardly seemed to be about the theatre anymore. Bob Hope was miscast as the critic, cracking jokes that the character would pan rather than punch. Lucille Ball had her moments as the playwright-wife but the most enjoyable performances came from the supporting cast.

The Crucible

January 22, 1953 (Martin Beck Theatre), a drama by Arthur Miller. *Cast*: Arthur Kennedy (John Proctor), Beatrice Straight (Elizabeth Proctor), Madeleine Sherwood (Abigail Williams), Fred Stewart (Rev. Samuel Parris), E. G. Marshall (Rev. Hale), Walter Hampden (Danforth), Jenny Egan (Mary Warren), Jean Adair (Rebecca Nurse), Philip Coolidge, Janet Alexander, Raymond Bramley, Jacqueline Andre, Joseph Sweeney. *Director*: Jed Harris. *Producer:* Kermit Bloomgarden. 197 performances. Tony Award

(TV 1967). *Teleplay*: Arthur Miller. *Cast*: George C. Scott (John Proctor), Colleen Dewhurst (Elizabeth Proctor), Tuesday Weld (Abigail Williams), Melvyn Douglas (Danforth), Fritz Weaver, Will Geer, Cathleen Nesbitt, Catherine Burns. *Director*: Alex Segal.

(Fox 1996). *Screenplay*: Arthur Miller. *Cast*: Daniel Day Lewis (John Proctor), Winona Ryder (Abigail Williams), Joan Allen (Elizabeth Proctor), Bruce Davison (Rev. Parris), Paul Scofield (Danforth), Karron Graves (Mary Warren), Rob Campbell (Rev. Hale), Charlayne Woodard, Elizabeth Lawrence, Frances Conroy. *Director*: Nicholas Hytner. *Producers*: Robert A. Miller, David Picker.

Arthur Miller's historical drama about the Salem witch trials of 1692 opened during the McCarthy witch hunts in government and media and there was no mistaking the parallels that the playwright was making. Several critics dismissed the drama as political preaching, though most commended the superb cast and excellent production values. Time has proven the play much more than a liberal reaction to a national paranoia about Communism. In fact, young audiences (the play is often taught and performed in schools) who know nothing of the 1950s events have no trouble appreciating the drama on its own terms. One of Miller's most produced works, *The Crucible* approaches tragedy as few American plays do. Afraid of its inflammatory reputation, no Hollywood version was made for forty-three years, though there was a French film adaptation in 1956 with Yves Montand and Simone Signoret recreating the roles they had played on the Paris stage. A splendid television production in 1967 was very compelling in all regards, particularly for performances by George C. Scott and Colleen Dewhurst in the leading roles. There was a British television version in 1980 featuring Michael N. Harbour then finally an American film in 1996 that stayed pretty close to the original script. Miller's screenplay opened the tale up somewhat but the most powerful moments were those directly from the stage. British actors Daniel Day-Lewis and Paul Scofield shone alongside American performers Joan Allen, Winona Ryder, and others and the picture had an authentic New England look that added to the potency of the story.

The Crucifer of Blood

September 28, 1978 (Helen Hayes Theatre), a melodrama by Paul Giovanni. *Cast*: Paxton Whitehead (Sherlock Holmes), Glenn Close (Irene St. Claire), Timothy Landfield (Dr. Watson), Nicolas Surovy (Capt. Neville St. Claire), Christopher Curry, Andrew Davis, Edward Zang, Tuck Milligan, Dwight Schultz. *Director*: Paul Giovanni. *Producers:* Lester Osterman, etc. 228 performances.

(TV 1991). *Teleplay*: Paul Giovanni, Fraser C. He-ston. *Cast*: Charlton Heston (Sherlock Holmes), Richard Jonson (Dr. Watson), Susannah Harker (Irene St. Claire), Edward Fox (Alistair Ross), John Castle (Neville St. Claire), Simon Callow (Inspector Lestrade), Clive Wood, James Coyle, Kaleem Janjua. *Director-producer*: Fraser C. Heston.

This very British Sherlock Holmes thriller was written, produced, and performed by Americans but it felt like the real thing, from its foggy London streets to its Limehouse opium den. The daughter of a British officer comes to Holmes to find her missing father and the search leads to a thirty-year-old death pact made in India, a curse that has followed its victims halfway around the world, and a gripping climax with two boats in chase down the Thames. The spectacular Broadway version featured a fine cast alongside its impressive scenic effects but the expensive production failed to pay off after its six-month run. Hollywood passed on the property and not until a dozen years later did it appear on television with Charlton Heston as a robust (and not very British) Holmes. The melodrama transferred to the small screen with little trouble yet, curiously, the production values were disappointing, especially to those who recalled the Broadway original.

The Cuckoos see The Ramblers

Curse of the Starving Class

February 14, 1978 (Public Theatre), a play by Sam Shepard. *Cast*: Olympia Dukakis (Ella), James Gammon (Weston), Ebbe Roe Smith (Wesley), Pamela Reed (Ella), Michael J. Pollard, Kenneth Walsh, Eddie Jones, John Aquino, Raymond Barry. *Director*: Robert Woodruff. *Producer:* New York Shakespeare Festival. 62 performances.

(TV 1994). *Teleplay*: Bruce Beresford. *Cast*: James Woods (Weston), Kathy Bates (Ella), Henry Thomas (Wesley), Kristin Fiorella (Emma), Randy Quaid, Louis Gossett, Jr. *Director*: J. Michael McClary. *Producer*: William S. Gilmore.

One of Sam Shepard's darkest but also funniest plays, this view of an aimless rural family who is starving for meaning and not food is both quirky and satiric. Moving from absurdism to a heightened kind of realism, Shepard began a new facet of his career with this play. The shabby father, the dreamy but burnt out mother, and the two anxious but confused children were all a part of Shepard's vision of a decaying America that either intrigued or disgusted audiences. The original Off Broadway production had a limited run but the script would see many revivals across the nation, including a long-running New York production in 1985. The comedy-drama was adapted for television in 1994 and featured Kathy Bates who had shone in the 1985 revival. She is the only one who seems to understand the comedy in the piece for it is mostly a slow and drawn out production that comes across as pointless as it is depressing.

Daddy Long-Legs

September 28, 1914 (Gaiety Theatre), a comedy by Jean Webster. *Cast*: Ruth Chatterton (Judy Abbott), Charles Waldron (Jervis Pendleton), Harry Dodd (Cyrus Wycoff), Cora Witherspoon (Sally McBride), Charles Trowbridge (James McBride), Edward Howard, Conway Wingfield. *Director-producer*: Henry Miller. 264 performances.

Daddy Long Legs (Mary Pickford Co. 1919). *Screenplay*: Agnes Christine Johnston. *Cast*: Mary Pickford (Judy Abbott), Mahlon Hamilton (Jervis Pendleton), Audrey Chapman (Sally McBride), Marshall Neilan (Jimmie McBride), Percy Haswell, Mila Davenport, Fay Lempost, Lillian Langdon. *Director*: Marshall Neilan. *Producer*: Mary Pickford.

Daddy Longlegs (Fox 1931). *Screenplay*: Sonya Levien. *Cast*: Janet Gaynor (Judy Abbott), Warner Baxter (Jervis Pendleton), Una Merkel, John Arledge, Claude Gillingwater, Louise Closser Hale. *Director*: Alfred Santell.

Daddy Longlegs (Fox 1955). *Screenplay*: Phoebe & Henry Ephron. *Score*: Johnny Mercer. *Cast*: Leslie Caron (Julie Andre), Fred Astaire (Jervis Pendleton), Fred Clark, Thelma Ritter, Terry Moore, Charlotte Austin, Larry Keating. *Songs*: Something's Gotta Give; Dream; Sluefoot. *Director*: Jean Negulesco. *Producer*: Samuel G. Engel.

This warm-hearted play had long legs of its own, first as a Broadway hit then on the road and in four movie versions. Teenage or-

phan Judy Abbott is secretly financed by a middle-aged benefactor and years later they fall in love; only then does he reveal his identity. The role of the feisty, likable Judy made Ruth Chatterton a Broadway star but the part was given to Mary Pickford in the 1919 movie and it was ideal for "America's sweetheart." A 1931 talkie with Janet Gaynor as Judy was a resounding hit. Warner Baxter played the benefactor with skill and the rest of the cast was splendid as well. The bare bones of the plot were recycled for the 1935 Shirley Temple vehicle *Curly Top* then two decades later the story was used again for the Fred Astaire film musical called *Daddy Longlegs*. Leslie Caron was a French orphan who is educated in America through the good wishes of benefactor Astaire. The age difference between the two was uncomfortably wide and the logic of the original story was somehow lost. But the film does boast a fine Johnny Mercer score and Astaire never disappoints in the musical numbers.

Damn Yankees

May 5, 1955 (46th Street Theatre), a musical comedy by George Abbott, Douglas Wallop. *Score*: Richard Adler, Jerry Ross. *Cast*: Ray Walston (Applegate), Gwen Verdon (Lola), Stephen Douglass (Joe Hardy), Shannon Bolin, Russ Brown, Rae Allen, Jean Stapleton, Robert Shafer, Nathaniel Frey. *Songs*: Whatever Lola Wants; Heart; Shoeless Joe From Hannibal, Mo.; Two Lost Souls; Near to You; A Little Brains—A Little Talent; Who's Got the Pain? *Director*: George Abbott. *Choreographer*: Bob Fosse. *Producers*: Frederick Brisson, Harold Prince, Robert Griffith. 1,019 performances.

(Warner 1958). *Screenplay*: George Abbott. *Score*: Richard Adler, Jerry Ross. *Cast*: Ray Walston (Applegate), Gwen Verdon (Lola), Tab Hunter (Joe Hardy), Shannon Bolin, Russ Brown, Rae Allen, Jean Stapleton, Robert Shafer, Nathaniel Frey, Bob Fosse. *Songs*: Whatever Lola Wants; Heart; Shoeless Joe From Hannibal, Mo.; Two Lost Souls; A Little Brains—A Little Talent; Who's Got the Pain? *Director-producers*: George Abbott, Stanley Donen. *Choreographer*: Bob Fosse.

Most of the creative talents from the hit musical *The Pajama Game* (qv) were reunited for this musical fantasy about baseball and the devil. Ray Walston shone as the sly, satanic Applegate who gets a baseball fan to sell his soul for a winning season. Gwen Verdon was featured as the devil's helper Lola who tries to seduce the fan before he backs out of the deal. The tuneful Adler and Ross score and Bob Fosse's vivacious dances helped make the show another hit for the team, both this and *The Pajama Game* running over a thousand performances. The Broadway cast (except for Tab Hunter replacing Stephen Douglass as the star baseballer) and staff were used in the film which often feels liked a filmed play but is sometimes delicious all the same. A bonus in the movie version is seeing Fosse himself dance with Verdon in the quirky "Who's Got the Pain?" number.

The Dark Angel

February 10, 1925 (Longacre Theatre), a play by H. B. Trevelyan, Guy Bolton. *Cast*: Patricia Collinge (Kitty Fahenstock), Reginald Mason (Capt. Hilary Trent), John Williams (Gerald Shannon), Stanley Logan, Claud Allister, Elsie Mackay, Auriol Lee. *Producer:* Robert Milton. 63 performances.

(First National 1925). *Screenplay*: Francis Marion. *Cast*: Vilma Banky (Kitty Vane), Ronald Colman (Capt. Alan Trent), Wyndham Standing (Gerald Shannon), Frank Elliott, Charles Lane, Helen Jerome Eddy, Florence Turner. *Director*: George Fitzmaurice. *Producer*: Samuel Goldwyn.

(Goldwyn 1935). *Screenplay*: Lillian Hellman, Mordaunt Shairp. *Cast*: Merle Oberon (Kitty Vane), Fredric March (Alan Trent), Herbert Marshall (Gerald Shannon), Janet Beecher, John Halliday, Henrietta Crosman. *Director*: Sidney Franklin. *Producer*: Samuel Goldwyn.

A melodrama guaranteed to reduce the audience to tears, this play told the weepy tale of Kitty Fahenstock whose fiancé Captain Trent is believed killed in the war. But he is not dead, only blind and he returns to learn that Kitty is engaged to another. Not wanting her to have to deal with his affliction, Trent releases her from their engagement without her ever knowing about his blindness. The play was a moderate success on Broadway but a giant hit on the screen in 1925 with Vilma Banky (in her first American film) and Ronald Colman. A talkie version in 1935 was also popular and featured Merle Oberon, Frederic March, and Herbert Marshall in the love triangle. It may be called a "women's picture" but the acting and production values are so expert it rises above the genre's connotation.

The Dark at the Top of the Stairs

December 5, 1957 (Music Box Theatre), a drama by William Inge. *Cast*: Teresa Wright (Cora Flood), Pat Hingle (Rubin Flood), Eileen Heckart (Lottie), Timmy Everett (Sammy Goldenbaum), Charles Saari, Judith Robinson, Frank Overton, Carl Reindel. *Director*: Elia Kazan. *Producers:* Saint Subber, Elia Kazan. 468 performances.

(Warner 1960). *Screenplay*: Harriet Frank, Irving Ravetch. *Cast*: Dorothy McGuire (Cora Flood), Robert Preston (Rubin Flood), Eve Arden (Lottie), Lee Kinsolving (Sammy Golden), Angela Lansbury, Shirley Knight, Frank Overton, Robert Eyer. *Director*: Delbert Mann. *Producer*: Michael Garrison.

William Inge's look at a Midwestern family in the 1920s dealing with minor and major crises is filled with sharply drawn characters and some adept dialogue. While harness salesman Rubin Flood sees the rising popularity of the automobile as the death knell for his business, his marriage is floundering. Sexual frustration, an occurrence of anti–Semitism, and problems with relatives are added to the tension but the Flood family survives. The talky but lively drama ran over a year on Broadway and in 1960 was made into a faithful and effective movie. The play was opened up somewhat which helped to better recreate the period and place. Robert Preston is quietly compelling as Rubin and he is surrounded by vibrant performances by Dorothy Maguire as his wife, Eva Arden as his sister-in-law, Angela Lansbury as his mistress, and Shirley Knight as his daughter.

Dark Victory

November 7, 1934 (Plymouth Theatre), a drama by George Brewer, Bertram Bloch. *Cast*: Tallulah

Bankhead (Judith Traherne), Earle Larimore (Dr. Frederick Steele), Dwight Fiske, Ann Andrews, Helen Strickland. *Director*: Robert Milton. *Producer:* Alexander McKaig. 51 performances.

(Warner 1939). *Screenplay*: Casey Robinson. *Cast*: Bette Davis (Judith Traherne), George Brent (Dr. Frederick Steele), Humphrey Bogart, Geraldine Fitzgerald, Ronald Reagan, Henry Travers, Cora Witherspoon. *Director*: Edmund Goulding. *Producers*: Hal B. Wallis, David Lewis.

Stolen Hours (United Artists 1963). *Screenplay*: Jessamyn West. *Cast*: Susan Hayward (Laura Pember), Michael Craig (Dr. John Carmody), Diane Baker, Edward Judd, Paul Rogers. *Director*: Daniel Petrie. *Producer*: Denis Holt.

Dark Victory (TV 1976). *Teleplay*: M. Charles Cohen. *Cast*: Elizabeth Montgomery (Katherine Merrill), Anthony Hopkins (Dr. Michael Grant), Michele Lee, Janet MacLachlan, Michael Lerner, Herbert Berghof. *Director*: Robert Butler. *Producer*: Jules Irving.

Audiences never seen to tire of this classic tearjerker yet, ironically, the original Broadway production was not a success. Judith Traherne is cured of a rare disease and joyfully marries the surgeon who saved her. But the illness returns and oncoming blindness is the first symptom that the end is near. The melodrama's final scene is a surefire climax: Judith bids goodbye to her husband as he goes off on a call, pretending she can see him and not letting on that she is blind. Tallulah Bankhead was applauded in the stage production but the play failed to run. The 1939 movie, on the other hand, was one of Bette Davis's biggest hits. Although considered the stuff of cliché today, the film is expertly made and the acting is uniformly effective (though some quibble about Humphrey Bogart's Irish brogue). The British updated the story in 1963 as *Stolen Hours* with Susan Hayward as the dying heroine. The characters seems tired and not convinced of their own sincerity but the Cornish settings are pleasant and the film strikes the right mood at times. A 1976 television remake restored the *Dark Victory* title but not the quality of the Davis movie. Elizabeth Montgomery was the doomed lady and Anthony Hopkins her doctor-lover.

David Harum

October 1, 1900. (Garrick Theatre), a play by R. and M. W. Hitchcock. *Cast*: William H. Crane (David Harum), George S. Probert (John Lenox), Katherine Florence (Mary Blake), Kate Meek (Aunt Polly), William Sampson (Dick Larribee), Eloise Frances Clark, Homer Granville, Frank Burbeck. *Director*: Edward E. Rose. *Producer:* Charles Frohman. 148 performances.

(Famous Players 1915). *Screenplay*: Allan Dwan. *Cast*: William H. Crane (David Harum), Harold Lockwood (John Lenox), May Allison (Mary Blake), Kate Meek (Aunt Polly), Hal Clarendon. *Director*: Allan Dwan. *Producer*: Jesse L. Lasky.

(Fox 1934). *Screenplay*: Walter Woods. *Cast*: Will Rogers (David Harum), Evelyn Venable (Ann), Kent Taylor (John), Louise Dresser (Aunt Polly), Stepin Fetchit, Charles Middleton, Noah Beery. *Director*: James Cruze.

Edward Noyes Wescott's novel about a colorful, rural horse trader was one of the most popular books during the first two decades of the 20th century and, despite its episodic nature, it was turned into a very enjoyable play. Although he is a banker by profession, the small-town raconteur David Harum loves nothing better than buying, selling, and trading horses. In between all his haggling and storytelling he manages to help the romance between two young people, save a widow from the clutches of sharp financiers, and see that a handful of troublesome locals get their comeuppance. Popular comic actor William H. Crane triumphed as Harum on Broadway, on the road, and in revivals for many years. He even made the first movie version of the play, a 1915 silent that captured some of the rustic atmosphere of the piece. A 1934 talkie featured Will Rogers as Harum and the role fit him like a glove. The action of the play was opened up (including an exciting horse race) but the spirit of the book and play were still there.

Dead End

October 28, 1935 (Belasco Theatre), a drama by Sidney Kingsley. *Cast*: Theodore Newton (Gimpty), Joseph Downing (Babyface Martin), Billy Halop (Tommy), Gabriel Dell (T.B.), Martin Gabel (Hunk), Huntz Hall, Charles R. Duncan, Charles Bellin, Marjorie Main. *Director:* Sidney Kingsley. *Producer:* Norman Bel Geddes. 687 performances.

(Goldwyn 1937). *Screenplay:* Lillian Hellman. *Cast:* Humphrey Bogart (Babyface Martin), Sylvia Sidney (Drina), Joel McCrea (Dave), Bill Halop (Tommy), Wendy Barrie, Claire Trevor, Marjorie Main, Huntz Hall, Allen Jenkins, Gabriel Dell, Leo Gorcey. *Director:* William Wyler. *Producer:* Samuel Goldwyn.

The Belasco Theatre overflowed with scenery, characters, and action in this atmospheric melodrama set on a dead end street in Manhattan. Various low-lifes of the neighborhood mix with respectable folks as the ritzy penthouse apartment occupants look down on them from above. There were several plots, from young street hoodlums getting caught stealing from a rich kid to a big-time racketeer getting gunned down by the police when he returns home to visit his mother, and the salty, gutter talk made the dialogue fresh and animated. Norman Bel Geddes's famous setting even included the East River in the orchestra pit where neighborhood boys jumped into the water and swam. The 1937 film opened the action up a bit further but still focused on the street and the characters who lived there. Humphrey Bogart is memorable as the racketeer and there were also admirable performances by Joel McCrea, Sylvia Sidney, and Marjorie Main. The last came from the stage production, as did the boys who were dubbed the Dead End Kids. They were later featured in a series of seven films and, when they were adults, some of the same actors were billed as the Bowery Boys in other movies.

Dear Ruth

December 13, 1944 (Henry Miller's Theatre), a comedy by Norman Krasna. *Cast:* Virginia Gilmore (Ruth Wilkins), John Dall (Lt. William Seawright), Lenore Lonergan (Miriam Wilkins), Phyllis Provah (Edith Wilkins), Howard Smith, Barlett Robinson, Kay Coulter, Richard McCracken. *Director:* Moss Hart. *Producer:* Joseph M. Hyman, Bernard Hart. 683 performances.

(Paramount 1947). *Screenplay:* Arthur Sheekman. *Cast:* Joan Caulfield (Ruth Wilkins), William

Holden (Lt. William Seacroft), Mona Freeman (Miriam Wilkins), Mary Philips (Mrs. Wilkins), Edward Arnold, Billy DeWolfe, Virginia Welles. *Director:* William D. Russell. *Producer:* Paul Jones.

This wartime comedy delighted Broadway audiences for two years and was a staple in community theatres for years. Teenager Miriam Wilkins does her bit for the war effort by writing dozens of letters to different lonely GI's overseas. But she signs her older sister Ruth's name to the letters and encloses a picture of her very attractive sibling (who is engaged to be married). When a young lieutenant on leave comes looking to meet Ruth, complications set in and chaos reigns in the Wilkins household until Miriam comes clean. But by that time Ruth and the serviceman have fallen in love. The escapist entertainment resembled later television sit-coms but as such was highly polished and satisfying. The 1947 movie featured Joan Caulfield as Ruth and William Holden as the confused officer and it was also warmly welcomed by the press and the public. The film was popular enough to spawn two sequels, *Dear Wife* (1949) and *Dear Brat* (1951), but neither had the charm of the original story. Strange-but-true footnote: writer J. D. Salinger saw a movie marquee advertising the 1947 picture and got the name of his hero in *Catcher in the Rye* from the stars' last names: Holden Caulfield.

Death of a Salesman

February 10, 1949 (Morosco Theatre), a drama by Arthur Miller. *Cast:* Lee J. Cobb (Willy Loman), Mildred Dunnock (Linda), Arthur Kennedy (Biff), Cameron Mitchell (Happy), Howard Smith (Charley), Don Keefer, Thomas Chalmers, Alan Hewitt, Winifred Cushing. *Director:* Elia Kazan. *Producers:* Kermit Bloomgarden, Walter Fried. 742 performances. Pulitzer Prize, Tony Award.

(Columbia 1951). *Screenplay:* Arthur Miller, Stanley Roberts. *Cast:* Frederic March (Willy Loman), Mildred Dunnock (Linda), Kevin McCarthy (Biff), Cameron Mitchell (Happy), Howard Smith (Charley), David Albert, Don Keefer, Jesse White. *Director:* Laslo Benedek. *Producer:* Stanley Kramer.

(TV 1985). *Teleplay*: Arthur Miller. Cast: Dustin Hoffman (Willy Loman), Kate Reid (Linda), John Malkovich (Biff), Stephen Lang (Happy), Charles Durning (Charley), Louis Zorich, Jon Polito, David S. Chandler. *Director:* Volker Schlondorff. *Producer:* Robert F. Colesberry.

One of the greatest of all American dramas, Arthur Miller's look at a common man, the salesman Willy Loman who has lived his whole life with the wrong ideals, and raising his plight to the level of tragedy has lost none of its power over the decades. The original production boasted superb performances under Elia Kazan's direction and a famous skeletal setting by Jo Mielziner that peered into the Loman house just as the script dissected the characters. Lee J. Cobb's Willy is considered a hallmark of American acting but he was viewed as a stage and television actor, not a bankable screen star, so Fredric March got to play the salesman on screen, giving what many consider his finest celluloid performance. Also impressive is Kevin McCarthy as the troubled son Biff. Despite some glowing notices, the movie was not very popular. Cobb did get to recreate Willy (again opposite Mildred Dunnock) in an abridged 1966 television version so there is a record of his towering portrayal. *Death of a Salesman* has been revived often on Broadway over the years, one of the most popular productions being a 1984 mounting starring Dustin Hoffman as Willy. The 1985 television version was not a film of the revival (though the cast stayed the same) but a highly expressionistic and cinematic version conceived by German filmmaker Volker Schlondorff. Everything about the small-screen *Death of a Salesman* was controversial, from Hoffman's very Jewish, very hyperkinetic Willy to the unrealistic sets and lighting that reminded viewers that Schlondorff was indeed a German expressionist. A filmed version of the popular 2000 Broadway revival featuring Brian Dennehy as Willy captures some fine performances but visually is flat and stagy.

Deathtrap

February 26, 1978 (Music Box Theatre), a thriller by Ira Levin. Cast: John Wood (Sydney Bruhl), Marian Seldes (Myra Bruhl), Victor Garber (Clifford Anderson), Marian Winters, Richard Woods. *Director*: Robert Moore. *Producers:* Alfred de Liagre, Roger L. Stevens. 1,793 performances.

(Warner 1982). *Screenplay*: Jay Presson Allen. *Cast*: Michael Caine (Sidney Bruhl), Christopher Reeve (Clifford Anderson), Dyan Cannon, Irene Worth, Henry Jones, Joe Silver. *Director*: Sidney Lumet. *Producer*: Burt Harris.

The longest-running thriller in Broadway history, this clever suspense play actually opened to poor reviews but audiences thought otherwise and made it a hit in New York and in little theatres across the country. Mystery writer Sydney Bruehl is suffering a dry spell so when he comes upon a rousing good stage thriller written by an unknown author, he plots to kill the young man and take credit for the play himself. But the whole plot is a charade to frighten Sidney's rich wife into having a heart attack, which she does, leaving Sydney and the young writer as lovers and, eventually, deadly rivals. The melodrama had more gimmicks than true plot twists but it was as chilling as it was funny and remains so when revived. Yet the 1982 screen version is a misfire, rarely scary or amusing. Michael Caine is an appropriately diabolical Sydney but few believed Christopher Reeve as the younger lover-writer. The movie is poorly paced and seems to defeat itself with each endless scene. Again the critics carped but this time audiences agreed with them and the film bombed.

A Delicate Balance

September 22, 1966 (Martin Beck Theatre), a drama by Edward Albee. *Cast*: Hume Cronyn (Tobias), Jessica Tandy (Agnes), Rosemary Murphy (Claire), Marian Seldes (Julia), Henderson Forsythe, Carmen Mathews. *Director*: Alan Schneider. *Producers:* Richard Barr, Clinton Wilder. 132 performances. Pulitzer Prize.

(American Film Theatre 1975). *Screenplay*: Edward Albee. *Cast*: Paul Scofield (Tobias), Katharine Hepburn (Agnes), Kate Reid (Claire), Lee Remick (Julia), Joseph Cotton, Betsy Blair. *Director*: Tony Richardson. *Producer*: Ely A. Landau.

One of Edward Albee's elusive yet fascinating puzzles, the drama on the surface is easy to follow. A late middle-aged couple has a peaceful yet strained relationship which is disturbed by the appearance of their alcoholic relative, often-divorced daughter, and two married friends who are afraid of their own house. The dialogue is both stiff and poetic, the characters both complex and familiar. The play was greeted with caution by the press and with mild curiosity by the public and it was awarded the Pulitzer Prize probably because the committee had botched it the year before and not given Albee the award for his *Who's Afraid of Virginia Woolf?* (qv). The 1976 movie of *A Delicate Balance* was pretty much a filmed play and the static production did little to illuminate the difficult piece. The all-star cast was uneven, though Paul Scofield and Katharine Hepburn as the central couple were outstanding. But even they could not make the film into a lively curiosity. Although the play had often been produced by colleges and regional theatres, it was never an audience favorite. It wasn't until 1996 that a celebrated revival on Broadway managed to present the play as a satisfying theatre experience, finding the humor amid all the cold dark corners of the script.

The Desert Song

November 30, 1926 (Casino Theatre), an operetta by Otto Harbach, Oscar Hammerstein, Frank Mandel. *Score:* Sigmund Romberg, Otto Harbach, Oscar Hammerstein. *Cast:* Vivienne Segal (Margot Bonvalet), Robert Halliday (Pierre Birabou/Red Shadow), Eddie Buzzell, Pearl Regay, William O'Neal. *Songs:* The Desert Song; One Alone; The Riff Song; Romance; It; Let Love Go; French Military Marching Song; I Want a Kiss. *Director:* Arthur Hurley. *Choreographer:* Bobby Connolly. *Producers:* Laurence Schwab, Frank Mandel. 471 performances.

(Warner 1929). *Screenplay:* Harvey Gates. *Score:* Sigmund Romberg, Otto Harbach, Oscar Hammerstein. *Cast:* John Boles (Red Shadow), Carlotta King (Margot), Louise Fazenda, John Miljan, Marie Wells, Johnny Arthur, Myrna Loy, Edward Martindel, Jack Pratt. *Songs:* The Desert Song; One Alone; The Riff Song; Romance; Sabre Song; French Military Marching Song; Then You Will Know. *Director:* Roy Del Ruth.

(Warner 1943). *Screenplay:* Robert Buckner. *Score:* Sigmund Romberg, Otto Harbach, Oscar Hammerstein, etc. *Cast:* Dennis Morgan (Paul Hudson), Irene Manning (Margot), Bruce Cabot, Gene Lockhart, Lynne Overman, Faye Emerson. *Songs:* The Desert Song; One Alone; The Riff Song; Romance; Sabre Song; French Military Marching Song; Long Live the Night; Fifi's Song. *Director:* Robert Florey. *Choreographer:* LeRoy Prinz. *Producer:* Robert Buckner.

(Warner 1953). *Screenplay:* Roland Kibbee. *Score:* Sigmund Romberg, Otto Harbach, Oscar Hammerstein, etc. *Cast:* Gordon MacRae (Paul Bonnard), Kathryn Grayson (Margot Birabeau), Raymond Massey, Steve Cochran, Ray Collins, Dick Wesson, Allyn McLerie. *Songs:* The Desert Song; One Alone; The Riff Song; Romance; French Military Marching Song; Gay Parisienne; Long Live the Night. *Director:* Bruce Humberstone. *Choreographer:* LeRoy Prinz. *Producer:* Rudi Fehr.

While most operettas were set in a fairy tale-like past, this one was inspired by two current events: the recent uprising of the Riffs in French Morocco and the wide popularity of Rudolph Valentino as the romantic desert sheik of the silent screen. The stage libretto told of the mysterious Red Shadow, an outlaw leading the Riff revolt in North Africa. The French noblewoman Magot is in love with the dashing revolutionary without knowing his true identity. It is eventually revealed that he is the supposedly-sniveling son of the governor. It was a grandiose and implausible story but served the lush Sigmund Romberg music well. Hollywood filmed the operetta three times, each time with a slightly different but equally contrived plot. An early talkie in 1929 featured John Boles and Carlotta King as the lovers and, while the story was pure claptrap, they got to sing much of the famous score. A 1943 version turned the tale into a World War Two adventure with the Red Shadow as an American freedom fighter helping to kick the Nazis out of French Morocco. Again much of the score survived. The third version, made during the Cold War years, dropped the Red Shadow moniker fearing that the hero might be labeled a communist.

This version was not only the most feeble plotwise, it also butchered most of the score. All three films failed at the box office but *The Desert Song* is still produced on the stage.

Desire Under the Elms

November 11, 1924 (Greenwich Village Theatre), a drama by Eugene O'Neill. *Cast*: Charles Ellis (Eben Cabot), Mary Morris (Abby Putnam), Walter Huston (Ephraim Cabot), Allen Nagle, Peter Ivins, Walter Abel. *Director*: *Producer*: Provincetown Players. 208 performances.

(Paramount 1958). *Screenplay*: Irwin Shaw. *Cast*: Burl Ives (Ephraim Cabot), Sophia Loren (Anna), Anthony Perkins (Eben Cabot), Frank Overton, Pernell Roberts, Rebecca Welles, Jean Willis, Anne Seymour. *Director*: Delbert Mann. *Producer*: Don Hartman.

Eugene O'Neill's Americanization of the Greek Phardre and Hippolytus legend ended up being more than a cultural adaptation, for the play became an independent form of tragedy of its own. The tough and miserly old Ephraim Cabot marries the young Abbie Putnam for free labor. She and Cabot's son Eben become rivals over who will inherit the farm, then becomes lovers and she gives birth to a child, Ephraim thinking it is his own. When the old man makes the baby his heir, Eben leaves Abbie, so she murders the infant to prove her love. The classic tale makes sense in the stark, unbending New England setting that O'Neill creates so vividly and the characters are realistically drawn. The drama was a success Off Broadway so it transferred to Broadway where it only attracted audiences when the police attempted to close it for indecency. It remains a difficult but demanding play and is occasionally revived. The 1958 movie suffers from a lack of style, wavering from melodramatic hysterics to gritty realism. Burl Ives is appropriately grizzly as Ephraim and Anthony Perkins believably confused as Eben but the heavily accented Sophia Loren is miscast as Abbie, exuding sensuality but no sense of the desperate, driven Abbie.

The Desk Set

October 24, 1955 (Broadhurst Theatre), a comedy by William Marchant. *Cast*: Shirley Booth (Bunny Watson), Byron Sanders (Richard Sumner), Frank Milan (Abe Cutler), Doris Roberts, Joyce Van Patten, Dorothy Blackburn, Elizabeth Wilson, Clarice Blackburn, Anne-Marie Gayer. *Director*: Joseph Fields. *Producers*: Robert Fryer, Lawrence Carr. 296 performances.

(Fox 1957). *Screenplay*: Phoebe and Henry Ephron. *Cast*: Spencer Tracy (Richard Sumner), Katharine Hepburn (Bunny Watson), Gig Young (Mike Cutler), Joan Blondell, Dina Merrill, Sue Randall, Neva Patterson. *Director*: Walter Lang. *Producer*: Henry Ephron.

Although it wasn't called a computer, the center of attention in this breezy comedy is Emmerac, an Electro-Magnetic Memory and Research Arithmetical Calculator that is able to store and retrieve tons of information. The sharp and knowing Bunny Watson and her staff of brainy women comprise the research department in a big corporation but they are to be replaced by Emmerac until the complicated machine goes on the fritz and starts spitting out all the wrong facts. It was a lightweight comedy that became a hit because of Shirley Booth's funny, sly performance as Bunny. When the play was rewritten as a screen vehicle for Spencer Tracy and Katharine Hepburn, it was improved upon in terms of plot and character. On stage Bunny has a romance with a corporate vice president. On screen her love interest is Richard Sumner, the man responsible for installing Emmerac. He and Bunny are friends who become rivals and then lovers, and with the Tracy-Hepburn chemistry each step in the relationship is delightful to watch. They are helped by a first-rate supporting cast (including Dina Merrill in her film debut) and the movie is well paced and well directed, allowing the comedy and romance to compliment each other.

The Desperate Hours

February 10, 1955 (Ethel Barrymore Theatre), a melodrama by Joseph Hayes. *Cast*: Karl Malden (Dan Hilliard), Paul Newman (Glenn Griffin), George Grizzard (Hank Griffin), Nancy Coleman

(Eleanor Hilliard), James Gregory (Jesse Bard), Kendall Clark, Fred Eisley, Judson Pratt, Malcolm Broderick, Patricia Peardon, George Matthews. *Director*: Robert Montgomery. *Producers:* Howard Erskine, Joseph Hayes. 212 performances. Tony Award.

(Paramount 1955). *Screenplay*: Joseph Hayes. *Cast*: Fredric March (Dan Hilliard), Humphrey Bogart (Glenn Griffin), Dewey Martin (Hal Griffin), Martha Scott (Eleanor Hilliard), Arthur Kennedy, Gig Young, Mary Murphy, Richard Eyer, Robert Middleton. *Director-producer*: William Wyler.

(MGM 1990). *Screenplay*: Lawrence Konner, etc. *Cast*: Mickey Rourke (Michael Bosworth), Anthony Hopkins (Tim Cornell), Mimi Rogers (Nora Cornell), Elias Koteas (Wally Bosworth), Lindsay Crouse, Kelly Lynch, David Morse. *Director*: Michael Cimino. *Producers*: Dino De Laurentis, Michael Cimino.

A taut melodrama that kept playgoers at the edge of their seats for six months, Joseph Hayes's play was taken from his novel and it was a powerful adaptation. Three escaped convicts take over the home of an Indianapolis family and one by one are outwitted by those whom they hold captive. The Broadway production boasted a highly proficient cast and a huge set that showed all the major rooms in the Indiana home. An equally fine cast was assembled for the 1955 film and the acting is top notch throughout. But the tension created in the theatre becomes less threatening and less effective on the screen. The theatre audience felt intimidated by the three intruders but we watch them passively in the movie. In the 1990 remake moviegoers laughed as the story was given an overblown and ridiculous makeover. Out of control acting and directing turned the old thriller into a campy melodrama that is memorable for its inanity.

Detective Story

March 23, 1949 (Hudson Theatre), a drama by Sidney Kingsley. *Cast*: Ralph Bellamy (Detective McLeod), Meg Mundy (Mary McLeod), Edward Binns (Detective Gallagher), James Westerfield (Detective Brody), Patrick McVey, Robert Strauss, Harry Worth, Joan Copeland, Warren Stevens, Lee Grant. *Director*: Sidney

Kingsley. *Producers:* Howard Lindsay, Russel Crouse. 581 performances.

(Paramount 1951). *Screenplay*: Robert Wyler, Philip Yordan. *Cast*: Kirk Douglas (Detective James McLeod), Eleanor Parker (Mary McLeod), William Bendix (Detective Brody), Cathy O'Donnell, George Macready, Horace McMahon, Gladys George, Joseph Wiseman, Lee Grant. *Director-producer*: William Wyler.

This unsentimental and almost documentary look at the everyday workings at a city police station is the grandfather of all the cops shows that later appeared on television. In a New York precinct office, the hardboiled Detective McLeod is not above going above the law to get results. This gets him into touchy situations, one of which leads to his death. Much of the fascination with the play was the collection of shoplifters, cops, clerks, and lawyers that paraded through the station, giving the drama a naturalistic feeling of big city goings on, just as playwright Sidney Kingsley had done in his previous *Dead End* (qv). The 1951 screen version also went for a documentary approach, using no music on the soundtrack and filming the cramped police headquarters with almost claustrophobic intensity. The film also features a reputable cast led by Kirk Douglas as McLeod and all of the minor characters glow with individuality.

Dial M for Murder

October 29, 1952 (Plymouth Theatre), a thriller by Frederick Knott. *Cast*: Maurice Evans (Tony Wendice), Gusti Huber (Margot Wendice), Richard Derr (Max Halliday), John Williams (Inspector Hubbard), Anthony Dawson. *Director*: Reginald Denham. *Producer:* James P. Sherwood. 552 performances.

(Warner 1954). *Screenplay*: Frederick Knott. *Cast*: Ray Milland (Tony Wendice), Grace Kelly (Margot Wendice), Robert Cummings (Mark Halliday), John Williams (Inspector Hubbard), Anthony Dawson. *Director-producer*: Alfred Hitchcock.

(TV 1981). *Teleplay*: John Gay. *Cast:* Angie Dickinson (Margot Wendice), Christopher Plummer (Tony Wendice), Anthony Quayle (Inspector Hubbard), Ron Moody, Michael Parks. *Director:* Boris Sagal. *Producer:* Peter Katz.

A Perfect Murder (Warner 1998). *Screenplay*: Patrick Smith Kelly. *Cast*: Michael Douglas (Steven Taylor), Gwyneth Paltrow (Emily Taylor), Viggo Mortensen (David Shaw), David Suchet (Mohamed Karaman), Sarita Chouldhury, Michael P. Moran, Constance Towers. *Director*: Andrew Davis. *Producers*: Anne Kopelson, etc.

Here is a clever thriller that is not so much about who did it as how he did it and will he be caught. Tennis pro Tony Wendice wants to dispose of his wealthy wife so he hires someone to murder her. So that he has an airtight alibi, Tony goes to his club with others and telephones his wife at home; her getting out of bed to answer the phone is the killer's opportunity. But in the struggle, the wife stabs the murderer to death and Tony has to maneuver around an astute police inspector. The tight, gripping little suspense play was a hit on Broadway and also popular with theatre groups across the country. A television version was broadcast the same year the play opened but was little seen. Alfred Hitchcock directed the 1954 movie and, while he gave it a few of his characteristic touches, it pretty much comes across as a staged play. Ray Milland and Grace Kelly were skillful as Tony and his wife but much of the film is stolen by John Williams who plays the inspector (as he had on Broadway). The movie was filmed in 3D, though Hitchcock seems mostly to have ignored its possibilities. Kelly's hand, clutching a pair of scissors to stab her assailant, jumped out at the audience, a cheap effect not worthy of Hitchcock. The movie was popular enough to warrant three more television remakes. A British version was broadcast in 1960 and Laurence Harvey, Diane Cilento, and Hugh O'Brien were starred in a 1967 American production that stuck very close to the original play. In 1981 Christopher Plummer and Angie Dickinson played the married couple in a new adaptation and though it was less stagy than the film it lacked the efficiency and style of Hitchcock's version. The story was remade again as a movie in 1998 and called *A Perfect Murder*. (Dial phones no longer familiar to most of the audience, the original title had to go.) This version made some major changes to the plot, including the twist that the man hired to kill the wife is her lover. Michael Douglas does his snarling best as the husband. Where Maurice Evans, Ray Milland, and others had played Tony as a chilly, unfeeling murderer, Douglas chews the scenery and looks as guilty as they come. His reason for murder is not money but jealousy; he knows his wife has a lover. Gwyneth Paltrow as the wife, a role much expanded on in this film, is as sleek and stylish as Grace Kelly, which is not easy to do. Some critics preferred this juicy melodrama over Hitchcock's reserved and subtle movie.

Diamond Lil

April 9, 1928 (Royale Theatre), a play by Mae West. *Cast*: Mae West (Diamond Lil), Curtis Cooksey (Capt. Cummings), J. Merrill Holmes (Gus Jordan), Ernest Anderson, Raffaella Ottiano, Herbert Duffy. *Director*: Mae West. *Producer:* Jack Linder. 176 performances.

She Done Him Wrong (Paramount 1933). *Screenplay*: Harvey F. Thew, John Bright, Mae West. *Cast*: Mae West (Lady Lou), Cary Grant (Capt. Cummings), Owen Moore (Chick Clark), Gilbert Roland (Serge Stanieff), Noah Berry (Gus Jordan), David Landau, Rafaela Ottiano, Louise Beavers. *Director*: Lowell Sherman. *Producer*: William LeBaron.

Having become infamous in New York for writing and starring in her play *Sex* (1926), Mae West continued to flaunt her comic sexuality in front of the authorities and this, her most successful effort, was no exception. Diamond Lil is the mistress of a gangster who runs a saloon that also serves as a front for the white slavery trade. Never very faithful to the mobster, Lil finds out one of her lovers in a cop in disguise and she rats on him. The policeman closes down the saloon and arrests Lil but she loves him and thinks she might try to reform. Although denounced as trashy melodrama by many, the play was a hit and brought West to the attention of Hollywood. It was filmed as *She Done Him Wrong* in 1933 and, co-written by West, it was her best screen vehicle. The basic plot stayed the same but the dialogue and characterizations were improved. West got to sing a few songs in her distinctive style and her rapport with Cary Grant as the incognito cop crackles with sex and humor. With its excellent production values, the movie makes one wish that other West vehicles were as competently made. She must have thought so too: in 1947 she starred in a revival of *Diamond Lil* on the London stage and in 1949 on Broadway; both were solid hits.

The Diary of Anne Frank

October 5, 1955 (Cort Theatre), a drama by Frances Goodrich, Albert Hackett. *Cast*: Susan Strasberg (Anne Frank), Joseph Schildkraut (Mr. Frank), Gusti Huber (Mrs. Frank), Dennie Moore (Mrs. Van Daan), David Levin (Peter), Lou Jacobi, Jack Gilford. *Director*: Garson Kanin. *Producer:* Kermit Bloomgarden. 717 performances. Pulitzer Prize.

(Paramount 1959). *Screenplay*: Frances Goodrich, Albert Hackett. *Cast*: Millie Perkins (Anne Frank), Joseph Schildkraut (Otto Frank), Shelley Winters (Mrs. Van Daan), Gusti Huber (Mrs. Frank), Richard Beymer (Peter), Ed Wynn, Lou Jacobi, Diane Baker. *Director-producer*: George Stevens.

(TV 1980). *Teleplay*: Frances Goodrich, Albert Hackett. *Cast*: Melissa Gilbert (Anne Frank), Maximilian Schell (Otto Frank), Joan Plowright (Mrs. Frank), Doris Roberts (Mrs. Van Daan), Scott Jacoby (Peter), Clive Revill, James Coco, Melora Marshall. *Director*: Boris Sagal.

Frances Goodrich and Albert Hackett were screenwriters who specializes in comedies so it was surprising when their stage adaptation of Anne Frank's diary was so delicately and sincerely done. While the actual diary only described the fellow Jews in hiding in Amsterdam and related some events, the play was able to present a series of episodes that were constructed like a tight little drama. The real situation being so potent, the authors avoided any sensationalism and allowed the material to speak for itself. The Broadway production featured a gifted cast led by veteran Joseph Schildkraut as Anne's father. The 1959 movie does romanticize the story in spots, trying to turn the tale into a love story of sorts, but it is also beautifully acted. Schildkraut reprised his Mr. Frank but the most memorable performance was by Shelley Winters as the vulgar Mrs. Van Daan. (She won an Oscar for her efforts; the statuette can be seen in the Anne Frank Museum in Amsterdam.) The play has been revived hundreds of times in schools, community theatres, professional theatres, and on and Off Broadway. There have also been many television productions in different countries around the world. In English, a 1967 version featured Diane Davila, Peter Beiger, Viveca Lindfors, Theodore Bikel, Donald Pleasance, and Max Von Sydow (as Mr. Frank); Melissa Gilbert and Maximilian Schell played daughter and father in a 1980 broadcast that also included a very strong supporting cast; and a British-German television production in 1987 featured Katharine Scheslinger as Anne.

Dinner at Eight

October 22, 1932 (Music Box Theatre), a play by George S. Kaufman, Edna Ferber. *Cast*: Ann Andrews (Millicent Jordan), Conway Tearle (Larry Renault), Constance Collier (Carlotta Vance), Paul Harvey (Dan Packard), Judith Wood (Kitty Packard), Malcolm Duncan, Austin Fairman, Olive Wyndham, Marguerite Churchill. *Director*: George S. Kaufman. *Producer:* Sam H. Harris. 232 performances.

(MGM 1933). *Screenplay*: Frances Marion, Herman J. Mankiewicz. *Cast*: Billie Burke (Millicent Jordan), John Barrymore (Larry Renault), Lionel Barrymore (Oliver Jordan), Marie Dressler (Carlotta Vance), Wallace Beery (Dan Packard), Jean Harlow (Kitty Packard), Lee Tracy, Edmund Lowe, Madge Evans. *Director*: George Cukor. *Producer*: David O. Selznick.

(TV 1989). *Teleplay*: Tom Griffin. *Cast*: Lauren Bacall (Carlotta Vance), Charles Durning (Dan Packard), Ellen Greene (Kitty Packard), Marsha Mason (Millicent Jordan), John Mahoney (Oliver Jordan), Harry Hamlin (Larry Renault), Stacy Edwards, Joel Brooks, Ralph Bruneau. *Director*: Ron Lagomarsino. *Producer*: Bridget Terry.

When Millicent Jordan invites a group of people to a dinner party, she has no idea of the drama that lies behind each of her guest's lives. The has-been actor Larry Renault, who has been having an affair with the

Jordan's daughter, sees his chance for a comeback fail so he commits suicide. The gruff businessman Dan Packard is planning to destroy Mr. Jordan's business. Packard's wife Kitty is having an affair with her doctor so she never seems to get well. The flamboyant actress Carlotta Vance is desperate for money and inadvertently helps to ruin the Jordans' shipping firm. The various scenes leading up to the dinner party ranged from the farcical to the tragic and authors George S. Kaufman and Edna Ferber handle both with panache. While the Broadway production was a hit, it was later overshadowed by the all-star Hollywood version in 1933. The multi-scene play easily lent itself to the film medium so it never had to be opened up but the plot was still a bit forced at times, as it was on stage. But it was the performances that counted and some of the screen's biggest stars gave the performance of their careers in the movie. As indelible as the screen version is, there have been three television productions that tried (and mostly failed) to best it. An early television version was broadcast in 1948 with Peggy Wood, Dennis King, Mary Boland and Vicki Cummings among the cast. In 1955, Mary Astor, Everett Sloane, Pat O'Brien, and Mary Beth Hughes led a television cast. And in 1989 another set of stars were assembled to perform the roles still associated with the 1930s legends. Each version only served to point out the weaknesses in the old script and the lack of stars today like Marie Dressler, Jean Harlow, John Barrymore, Wallace Beery, and Billie Burke.

Dinner with Friends

November 4, 1999 (Variety Arts Theatre), a drama by Donald Margulies. *Cast:* Matthew Arkin (Gabe), Lisa Emery (Karen), Julie White (Beth), Kevin Kilner (Tom). *Director:* Daniel Sullivan. *Producers:* Mitchell Maxwell, etc. 654 performances. Pulitzer Prize.

(TV 2001). *Teleplay:* Donald Margulies. *Cast:* Dennis Quaid (Gabe), Andie MacDowell (Karen), Toni Collette (Beth), Greg Kinnear (Tom). *Director:* Norman Jewison. *Producers:* Norman Jewison, Margo Lion, Daryl Roth, etc.

While this Off Broadway drama covered familiar territory (the breakup of a marriage), the point of view was refreshingly original: we see Beth and Tom separate and form new attachments through the eyes of their best friends, the married couple Gabe and Karen. The end of one relationship forces the other couple to re-evaluate and reconsider themselves as old friendships are dissolved. The prize-winning play was small in scope and not ideally suited for the big screen. Yet Margulies' teleplay opened the story up a bit, showed characters only talked about on stage, and tried to be more visual. Ironically it was only the intimate two-character scenes that played as well as in the theatre.

Dr. Cook's Garden

September 25, 1967 (Belasco Theatre), a play by Ira Levin. *Cast:* Burl Ives (Dr. Leonard Cook), Keir Dullea (Dr. Jim Tennyson), Bette Henritze, Lee Sanders, Bob Berger. *Director:* Ira Levin. *Producer:* Saint Subber. 8 performances.

(TV 1971). *Teleplay:* Art Wallace. *Cast:* Bing Crosby (Dr. Leonard Cook), Frank Converse (Jimmy Tennyson), Blythe Danner (Janey Rausch), Helen Stenborg, Barnard Hughes, Staats Cotsworth, Bethel Leslie. *Director:* Ted Post. *Producer:* Bob Markell.

Kindly old Dr. Cook is beloved in his small town as he works in his garden, removing unwanted or defective plants. When a young intern pays him a visit, he discovers the old physician has been killing off defective citizens: the terminally ill, the infirm, the disabled, the troublesome. Dr. Cook attempts to poison the intern to keep him quiet and almost succeeds before he suffers a heart attack and dies. Although the nasty little chiller only lasted a week on Broadway, it was remade for television in 1971 and Bing Crosby got to play Dr. Cook, the most atypical role of his long career. He is quite disarming in the piece and the production, an improvement over the stage script, plays effectively on the small screen.

Dodsworth

February 24, 1934 (Shubert Theatre), a play by Sidney Howard. *Cast*: Walter Huston (Sam

Dodsworth), Fay Bainter (Fran Dodsworth), Nan Sunderland (Edith Cortright), John Williams (Clyde Lockert), Dorothy Raymond (Baroness Von Obersdorf), Kent Smith (Kurt Von Obersdorf), Charles Halton, Harlan Briggs, Leonore Harris, Ethel Jackson. *Director*: Robert B. Sinclair. *Producer:* Max Gordon. 317 performances.

(United Artists 1936). *Screenplay*: Sidney Howard. *Cast*: Walter Huston (Sam Dodsworth), Ruth Chatterton (Fran Dodsworth), Paul Lukas (Arnold Iselin), Mary Astor (Edith Cortright), David Niven (Capt. Clyde Lockert), Maria Ouspenskaya (Baroness Von Obersdorf), Gregory Gaye (Count Von Obersdorf), Odette Myrtil, Spring Byington, Harlan Briggs. *Director*: William Wyler. *Producer*: Samuel Goldwyn.

While many American novels were adapted to the stage in the 1930s, Sidney Howard's version of Sinclair Lewis's book was considered one of the best. The wealthy manufacturer Sam Dodsworth retires from business and goes on a grand tour of Europe with his wife. While there he discovers his wife's many infidelities and he meets a woman more to his liking. Walter Huston's performance as Dodsworth was considered the hit of the season though he was ably supported by Fay Bainter as his careless yet conniving wife. Huston reprised the role in the 1936 film with Ruth Chatterton as his wife and they are the centerpiece of a well-acted, beautifully filmed movie that presents the story in a straightforward, unfussy manner. A television version of the play in 1956 featured the married actors Frederic March and Florence Eldridge as Mr. and Mrs. Dodsworth.

Don't Drink the Water

November 17, 1966. (Morosco Theatre), a comedy by Woody Allen. *Cast*: Lou Jacobi (Walter Hollander), Kay Medford (Marion Hollander), Anthony Roberts (Axel Magee), Anita Gillette (Susan Hollander), Dick Libertini, James Dukas, Gerry Matthews. *Director*: Stanley Praeger. *Producer:* David Merrick. 598 performances.

(AVCO Embassy 1969). *Screenplay*: R. S. Allen, etc. *Cast*: Jackie Gleason (Walter Hollander), Estelle Parsons (Marion Hollander), Ted Bessell (Axel Magee), Joan Delaney (Susan Hollander), Michael Constantine, Howard St. John, Danny

Meehan, Richard Libertini. *Director*: Howard Morris. *Producers*: Charles H. Joffe, Jack Rollins.

(TV 1994). *Teleplay*: Woody Allen. *Cast*: Woody Allen (Walter Hollander), Julie Kavner (Marion Hollander), Michael J. Fox (Axel Magee), Mayim Bialik (Susan Hollander), Josef Sommer, Edward Herrmann, Robert Stanton. *Director*: Woody Allen. *Producer*: Robert Greenhut.

Woody Allen's early, pre-cinema-career comedy runs like an extended vaudeville sketch but the lines are funny and the character types enjoyable. The Hollander family is touring Europe and mistakenly takes photographs in a country behind the Iron Curtain. The authorities pursue them so the family takes refuge in the American Embassy where they spend the rest of the play dealing with incompetent officials as they try to get out of the country. Filled with one-liners that were delivered by a cast of comic veterans, the comedy ran nearly two years and was later a favorite with schools and community groups. The 1969 screen version featured a WASP cast trying to do the Borscht Belt kind of jokes and they fall flat at every turn. Efforts to open up the story and include physical farce were also in vain. The numbing movie was quickly forgotten and twenty-five years later Allen made a television production of the comedy and played the Hollander father himself. Filmed in a studio with few cinematic touches by a bright and capable cast, the play is only intermittently funny. The emphasis in on the verbal humor but too much of the talk is hollow and the material seems to cry out for a live audience.

The Doughgirls

December 30, 1942 (Lyceum Theatre), a comedy by Joseph Fields. *Cast*: Virginia Field (Edna), Arleen Whelan (Vivian), Doris Nolan (Nan), Arlene Francis (Natalia Chodorov), King Calder (Julian Cadman), Reed Brown, Jr., Sydney Grant, William J. Kelly. *Director*: George S. Kaufman. *Producer:* Max Gordon. 671 performances.

(Warner 1944). *Screenplay*: Sam Hellman, etc. *Cast*: Ann Sheridan (Edna), Alexis Smith (Nan), Jane Wyman (Vivian), Eve Arden (Sgt. Natalia

Moskeroff), Jack Carson (Arthur Halstead), John Ridgely (Julian Cadman), Irene Manning, Charles Ruggles, Alan Mowbray, John Alexander. *Director*: James V. Kern. *Producer*: Mark Hellinger.

Three American women and a Russian female sniper all room together in a crowded hotel suite in wartime Washington and the complications come fast and furious. Very popular with Broadway audiences, the comedy was definitely a product of its time and has seen few revivals. Yet the writing was very polished, as was the original cast. A movie was made in 1944 when the material was still topical but Hollywood had to censor parts of the plot. On stage a couple living in sin try to rendezvous at the hotel. On screen the couple is married but they find out their ceremony was illegal. The mostly-women cast is top-notch (Eve Arden as the Russian is particularly risible) and the movie is well paced.

Dream Girl

December 14, 1945 (Coronet Theatre), a comedy by Elmer Rice. *Cast*: Betty Field (Georgina), Wendell Corey (Clark Redfield), Evelyn Varden, William A. Lee, Don Stevens, David Pressman, Sonya Stokowski. *Director*: Elmer Rice. *Producer*: Playwrights' Company. 348 performances.

(Paramount 1948). *Screenplay*: Arthur Sheekman. *Cast*: Betty Hutton (Georgina), Macdonald Carey (Clark Redfield), Patric Knowles, Virginia Field, Walter Abel, Peggy Wood, Carolyn Butler. *Director*: Mitchell Leisen. *Producer*: P. J. Wolfson.

Bookshop manager Georgina is bored with her worklife and her lovelife so she dreams up fantastic situations for herself, often triggered by a word someone says or something she sees looking out her shop window. But her fantasies wane when she meets a book reviewer who offers her happiness in reality. The expressionistic comedy owed a debt of gratitude to James Thurber's story "The Secret Life of Walter Mitty" but the Elmer Rice play had charms of its own, particularly Betty Field as Georgina. The 1948 movie made every mistake possible: the script was changed so that Georgina was a

bored rich socialite, the fantasy sequences were garish and unfunny, and miscast Betty Hutton milked the role like a frantic dairy-maid. Rarely has Rice (or any other playwright) been so abused by Hollywood.

Driving Miss Daisy

April 15, 1987 (Playwrights Horizons), a play by Alfred Uhry. *Cast*: Dana Ivey (Daisy Werthan), Morgan Freeman (Hoke Coleburn), Ray Gill (Boolie Werthan). *Director*: Ron Lagomarsino. *Producer*: Playwrights Horizons. 1,195 performances. Pulitzer Prize.

(Warner 1989). *Screenplay*: Alfred Uhry. *Cast*: Jessica Tandy (Daisy Werthan), Morgan Freeman (Hoke Coleburn), Dan Aykroyd (Boolie Werthan), Patti LuPone, Esther Rolle. *Director*: Bruce Beresford. *Producers*: Richard D. Zanuck, Lili Fini Zanuck. Academy Award.

This character piece about a cranky aging Jewish woman and her illiterate but dignified African American chauffeur was slight even in the little Off Broadway theatre where it played for three years. But the characters were likable and the various casts made them come alive for audiences looking for a life-affirming comedy-drama. The popular 1989 film wisely kept the story simple, only opening it up enough to create the atmosphere of the passing years. It also boasted finely controlled performances (Jessica Tandy won an Oscar) and adept, gimmick-free direction.

DuBarry

December 25, 1901 (Criterion Theatre), a drama by David Belasco. *Cast*: Mrs. Leslie Carter (Jeanette Vaubernier), Hamilton Revelle (Cosse-Brissac), Campbell Gollan (Comte DuBarry), Charles A. Stevenson (Louis XV), Frederick Perry (Duc de Richeleau), Blanche Rice, Ruth Dennis, Henry Weaver, Sr. *Director-producer*: David Belasco. 165 performances.

(George Kleine Pictures 1915). *Screenplay*: Arrigo Frusta. *Cast*: Mrs. Leslie Carter (Jeanette Vaubernier), Hamilton Revelle (Cosse-Brissac), Campbell Gollan (Comte Jean DuBarry), Richard Thornton (Louis XV), Louis Payne. *Director*: Eduardo Bencivenga. *Producer*: George Kleine.

DuBarry, Woman of Passion (United Artists 1930). *Screenplay:* Sam Wood. *Cast:* Norma Talmadge (Jeanette Vaubernier), Conrad Nagel (Cosse-Brissac), William Farnum (Louis XV), Ullrich Haupt, Alison Skipworth, Henry Kolker, Hobart Bosworth. *Director:* Sam Taylor. *Producer:* Joseph M. Schenck.

This historical costume drama, about the pretty milliner who rises through the social ranks of Paris only to be guillotined during the French Revolution, was one of Mrs. Leslie Carter's greatest stage triumphs. Playwright-producer David Belasco created the vehicle especially for her (though he stole much of the text from a French play) and her performance was roundly praised. The elaborate production featured accurate sets, furniture, and costumes of the period as only the finicky Belasco could create and the play ran six months. Carter reprised the role for the camera in 1915 and, though she is far too old for the youthful Jeanette, the silent version is a lavish record of what the original production must have been like. An early talkie was made in 1930, under the more alluring title of *DuBarry, Woman of Passion*, and it starred silent screen star Norma Talmadge. Moviegoers thought it more talk than passion and the film failed, bringing a sad end to Talmadge's screen career. But like the earlier movie, it featured lush scenic design and a thrilling depiction of 18th-century Paris.

DuBarry Was a Lady

December 6, 1939 (46th Street Theatre), a musical comedy by Herbert Fields, B. G. DeSylva. *Score:* Cole Porter. *Cast:* Bert Lahr (Louis Blore/Louis XV), Ethel Merman (May Daly/DuBarry), Betty Grable (Alice Barton), Benny Baker, Charles Walters, Ronald Graham, Kay Sutton. *Songs:* Friendship; Well, Did You Evah?; Katie Went to Haiti; Do I Love You?; But in the Morning, No. *Director:* Edgar MacGregor. *Choreographer:* Robert Alton. *Producer:* B. G. DeSylva. 408 performances.

(MGM 1943). *Screenplay:* Irving Brecher. *Score:* Cole Porter, Ralph Freed, Burton Lane, E. Y. Harburg, Roger Edens, etc. *Cast:* Red Skelton (Louis Blore/Louis XV), Lucille Ball (May Daly/DuBarry), Gene Kelly (Alec Howe/Black

Arrow), Virginia O'Brien (Ginny), Rags Ragland, Zero Mostel, Tommy Dorsey, Dick Haymes, Jo Stafford. *Songs:* Friendship; Katie Went to Haiti; Do I Love You?; No Matter How You Slice It, It's Still Salome; I Love an Esquire Girl; Madame, I Love Your Crepes Suzettes. *Director:* Roy Del Ruth. *Choreographer:* Charles Walters. *Producer:* Arthur Freed.

Two of Broadway's brightest musical comedy stars, Bert Lahr and Ethel Merman, were teamed for this clever Cole Porter musical about a washroom attendant who drinks a Mickey Finn and dreams he is King Louis XV of France. Merman was the nightclub singer in the present and the notorious Du Barry in the fantasy and her "Friendship" duet with Lahr was a highpoint of the evening. Both stars were passed over for the film version, just as much of the Porter score was also cut. Red Skelton and Lucille Ball, who would become two of television's most popular comics years later, played the leading roles and they were less than stellar. The expensive production was more elaborate than fun and even Gene Kelly seems ill at ease as the mock hero. But there is one choice moment: stone-faced Virginia O'Brien singing the interpolated "No Matter How You Slice It, It's Still Salome."

DuBarry, Woman of Passion see *DuBarry*

Dulcy

August 13, 1921 (Frazee Theatre), a comedy by George S. Kaufman, Marc Connelly. *Cast:* Lynn Fontanne (Dulcinea Smith), John Westley (Gordon Smith), Wallis Clark, Norma Lee, Howard Lindsay, Gregory Kelly, Gilbert Douglas. *Director:* Howard Lindsay. *Producers:* George C. Tyler, H. H. Frazee. 246 performances.

(Talmadge Film Co. 1923). *Screenplay:* John Emerson, etc. *Cast:* Constance Talmadge (Dulcy), Jack Mulhall (Gordon), Claude Gillingwater, May Wilson, John Harron, Anne Cornwall. *Director:* Sidney Franklin. *Producer:* Constance Talmadge.

Not So Dumb (MGM 1929). *Screenplay:* Wanda Tuclock, Edwin Justus Mayer. *Cast:* Marion

Davies (Dulcinea Smith), Elliott Nugent (Gordon Smith), Raymond Hackett (Willie Parker), Franklin Pangborn, Julia Faye. *Director:* King Vidor. *Producers:* King Vidor, Marion Davies.

Dulcy (MGM 1940). *Screenplay:* Albert Mannheimer, etc. *Cast:* Ann Sothern (Dulcy Ward), Ian Hunter (Gordon Dale), Roland Young, Reginald Gardiner, Billie Burke, Lynn Carver, Dan Dailey. *Director:* S. Sylvan Simon. *Producer:* Edgar Selwyn.

A scatterbrained but well-meaning young wife tries to help her husband by throwing a dinner party for some of his business contacts but seems to say and do all the wrong things. Yet it turns out her meddling saves the day. This lightweight comedy launched the playwriting careers of George S. Kaufman and Marc Connelly and made Lynn Fontanne a Broadway star. A silent film adaptation starred Constance Talmadge, followed by an early talkie in 1929 called *Not So Dumb* with Marion Davies as Dulcy. Both women saw the allure of the juicy role and helped bankroll their movie vehicles. The Talmadge film lost the witty Kaufman-Connelly dialogue but was still appealing. Davies's vehicle is less successful, the stage dialogue coming across flat and unfunny in the primitive sound system. For some reason Dulcy was not married and she made all her silly efforts on behalf of her boy friend. A 1940 remake, using the title *Dulcy* again, destroyed the play beyond recognition. Ann Sothern played a Chinese orphan (still named Dulcy!) who meddles in the lives of an American family and leaves them all the better for it. The pleasant cast tried in vain to make something of this odd comic bomb.

Dutchman

March 23, 1964 (Cherry Lane Theatre), a play by LeRoi Jones. *Cast:* Robert Hooks (Clay), Jennifer West (Lulu). *Director:* Edward Parone. *Producers:* Richard Barr, etc. 366 performances.

(Dutchman Film Co. 1966). *Screenplay:* Amiri Baraka (aka LeRoi Jones). *Cast:* Shirley Knight (Lula), Al Freeman, Jr. (Clay). *Director:* Anthony Harvey. *Producer:* Eugene Persson.

On a deserted New York subway car, a sexy but psychotic blonde taunts and berates a well-dressed African American youth, then stabs him to death. Amiri Baraka's allegory about white-black relations was the talk of the town during the Civil Rights Movement years and the little drama ran Off Broadway for a year. The 1966 movie was presented realistically so the situation seemed very contrived. But the performances are effective and the talky piece still has its interest.

The Easiest Way

January 19, 1909 (Belasco-Styvesant Theatre), a play by Eugene Walter. *Cast:* Frances Starr (Laura Murdock), Joseph Kilgour (Willard Brockton), Edward G. Robins (John Madison), Laura Nelson Hall (Elfie), William Sampson (Jack Weston), Emma Dunn. *Director-producer:* David Belasco. 157 performances.

(Clara Kimball Young Picture Co. 1917). *Screenplay:* Albert Capellani, Frederick Chapin. *Cast:* Clara Kimball Young (Laura Murdock), Joseph Kilgour (Willard Brockton), Louise Bates (Elfie), Rockliffe Fellowes (John Madison), Cleo Desmond, George Stevens, Frank Kingdom. *Director:* Albert Capellani. *Producer:* Clara Kimball Young.

(MGM 1931). *Screenplay:* Edith Ellis. *Cast:* Constance Bennett (Laura Murdock), Robert Montgomery (John Madison), Adolphe Menjou (William Brockton), Anita Page (Peg), Marjorie Rambeau, F. Farrell MacDonald, Clark Gable, Clara Blandick. *Director:* Jack Conway. *Producer:* Hunt Stromberg.

Laura Murdock is a kept woman, the mistress of a wealthy man, but when she meets the young journalist John Madison and they fall in love she cannot decide whether or not to tell him about her past. But John finds out and breaks their engagement, leaving Laura to take the easiest way: return to her former lover. The play ended with Laura telling her maid to get out her best dress because "I'm going to Rector's [restaurant] to make a hit and to hell with the rest." The lack of a conventional happy ending and Laura's scandalous final comment made the play the talk of the town and Frances Starr's bold performance assured her stardom on Broadway. Some critics applauded the drama's honesty, others condemned it, and audiences came for six months to see for themselves. The 1917 silent movie was able to tell the story as it appeared on stage but Hollywood was more careful a few decades later and the 1931 movie is cleaned up and given a happy ending: Laura finds salvation in a snowstorm on Christmas eve. Constance Bennett is Laura in the latter film and her performance as she is torn between truelove Robert Montgomery and wealthy Adolphe Menjou is impressive. But the laundered film was just another melodrama with a moral.

East Is West

December 25, 1918 (Astor Theatre), a play by Samuel Shipman, John B. Hymer. *Cast*: Fay Bainter (Ming Toy), Forrest Winant (Billy Benson), George Nash (Charlie Yong), Harry Huguenot (Hop-Toy), Lester Lonergan (Lo Sang Kee), Hassard Short, Frank Kemble Cooper, Walter Hart. *Director*: Clifford Brooke. *Producer:* William Harris. 680 performances.

(Talmadge Film Co. 1922). *Screenplay*: Frances Marion. *Cast*: Constance Talmadge (Ming Toy), Edmund Burns (Billy Benson), Warner Oland (Charley Yong), Frank Lanning (Hop-Toy), E. Allyn Warren (Lo Sang Kee), Nick De Ruiz, Nigel Barrie. *Director*: Sidney Franklin. *Producer*: Constance Talmadge.

(Universal 1930). *Screenplay*: Tom Reed. *Cast*: Edward G. Robinson (Charlie Yong), Lupe Velez (Ming Toy), Lew Ayres (Billy Benson), E. Allyn Warren (Lo Sang Kee), Tetsu Komai (Hop-Toy), Henry Kolker, Mary Forbes, Edgar Norton. *Director*: Monta Bell. *Producer*: Carl Laemmle, Jr.

A far-fetched tale filled with contrivances, this play was popular nevertheless because of Fay Bainter's droll performance. She played a Chinese immigrant named Ming Toy who loves an American but everything stands between them, from laws against interracial marriage to a Chinaman who claims her hand by purchase. But all ends happily when it is discovered that Ming was adopted as a baby and is really Spanish. Constance Talmadge played Ming in a 1922 silent film and Lupe Velez portrayed her in the 1930 talkie. Both versions were as preposterous as the play but audiences didn't seem to mind. The most interesting aspect of the 1930 film is Edward G. Robinson, in his first talkie, playing the Asian Charlie

Yong, the Chop Suey king of Chinatown; it is a fearless and politically incorrect performance that is fascinating all the same.

East Lynne

March 23, 1863 (Winter Garden Theatre), a melodrama by Clifton W. Tayleure. *Cast*: Lucille Western (Isabel Mount Severn), A. H. Davenport (Archibald Carlyle), Lawrence Barrett (Sir Francis Levison). c. 20 performances.

(Fox-Biograph 1916). *Screenplay*: Mary Murillo. *Cast*: Theda Bara (Lady Isabel), Ben Deeley (Arch Carlisle), Stuart Holmes (Capt. Livison), William H. Tooker, Claire Whitney, Stanhope Wheatcoft, Eugenie Woodward. *Director*: Bertram Bracken. *Producer*: William Fox.

(Fox 1925). *Screenplay:* Lenore J. Coffee, Emmett J. Flynn. *Cast:* Alma Rubens (Lady Isabel), Lou Tellegen (Francis Levison), Edmund Lowe, Frank Keenan, Marjorie Daw, Leslie Fenton. *Director:* Emmett J. Flynn. *Producer:* William Fox.

(Fox 1931). *Screenplay*: Bradley King, Tom Barry. *Cast*: Ann Harding (Lady Isabella), Clive Brook (Capt. Levison), Conrad Nagal (Robert Caryle), O. P. Heggie, Cecilia Loftus, Beryl Mercer, Flora Sheffield. *Director*: Frank Lloyd.

(TV 1982). *Cast:* Lisa Eichhorn (Lady Isabel), Tim Woodward (Francis Levison), Gemma Craven, Annette Crosbie, Patrick Allen, Jane Asher, Kenneth Connor. *Director:* David Green.

One of the most popular melodramas of the American theatre, this crowd pleaser was based on a novel by Mrs. Henry Wood about the tragic Lady Isabel who leaves her husband and children because she is convinced by a cad that her husband is unfaithful. The cad elopes with Isabel but never marries her so she sinks into a life of decay. A few years later she disguises herself as Madame Vine and returns to the homestead called East Lynne to see her children and gain forgiveness from her husband before she dies. Critics scowled but for over fifty years the play was a staple in repertory companies and touring troupes and was guaranteed to fill houses. It is estimated that over fourteen different movies were made of the play, all of them silent and some of them shorts. Film versions were released in 1902, 1903, 1908, 1910, 1912, two in 1913, 1915 (with Louise

Vale as Isabella), 1921 (with Mabel Ballin), and two in 1922 (with Iris Hoey and Ethel Jerdan). A British film farce called *East Lynne on the Western Front* (1931) was about some soldiers putting on *East Lynne* to relieve the wartime drudgery and a television series in 1976 featured Polly James as Isabel and Christopher Cazenove as Francis Levison.

The Eccentricities of a Nightingale

November 23, 1976 (Morosco Theatre), a play by Tennessee Williams. *Cast*: Betsy Palmer (Alma Winemiller), David Selby (John Buchanan), Shepperd Strudwick, Nan Martin, Grace Carney. *Director*: Edwin Sherin. *Producer*: Gloria Hope Sher. 24 performances.

(TV 1976). *Teleplay*: Tennessee Williams. *Cast*: Blythe Danner (Alma Winemiller), Frank Langella (John Buchanan), Tim O'Connor, Louise Latham, Neva Patterson. *Director-producer*: Glenn Jordan.

Tennessee Williams was never satisfied with the version of his drama *Summer and Smoke* (qv) that was produced on Broadway in 1948 so years later he rewrote the drama as *The Eccentricities of a Nightingale* and it was briefly seen in New York in 1976. The story still concerned the preacher's daughter Alma Winemiller who refutes the sexual advances of the handsome young Dr. Buchanan and years later regrets her decision. The new version has fewer characters and is more tightly constructed. Some critics agreed with Williams that the new play was an improvement over the original but New York audiences were not interested. Over the years the new work has been presented by regional theatres and colleges and more are convinced it is the better work. It certainly seems so judging by the excellent television production made the same year the play was on Broadway. Blythe Danner is extraordinary as the dreamy, regretful Alma, Frank Langella brings a sensual quality to the doctor, and the supporting cast is commendable down to the smallest role.

The Effect of Gamma Rays on Man-in-the-Moon Marigolds

April 7, 1970 (Mercer-O'Casey Theatre), a play by Paul Zindel. *Cast*: Sada Thompson (Beatrice), Pamela Payton-Wright (Tillie), Amy Levitt (Ruth), Judith Lowery, Swoozie Kurtz. *Director*: Melvin Bernhardt. *Producer:* Orin Lehman. 819 performances. Pulitzer Prize.

(Fox 1972). *Screenplay*: Alvin Sargent. *Cast*: Joanne Woodward (Beatrice), Nell Potts (Matilda), Roberta Wallach (Ruth), Judith Lowery, David Spielberg, Richard Venture. *Director-producer*: Paul Newman.

The bitter Beatrice sits in her cluttered home reading real estate ads in the paper and doing her best to ignore her two teenage daughters and the ancient old lady she is paid to care for. When shy daughter Tillie finds out her science project (the play's title) is up for an award, the dysfunctional little family starts to see some hope. Tillie wins the award and Beatrice makes moves toward a change but it is all bluster; her final comment to her daughter is "Tillie, I hate the world." The piece was first written as a television play but playwright Paul Zindel turned it into a theatre piece and it was seen regionally before becoming a surprise hit Off Broadway. Veteran actress Sada Thompson was unanimously saluted for her tough but easily broken Beatrice; the role made her a star. Because of its strong female cast of characters, the drama has always been very popular with schools. The 1972 movie opened the story up, added unnecessary characters and scenes, and generally destroyed the play's intimacy and wistful quality. Joanne Woodward is believably angry and despondent as Beatrice but there is nothing else there. Nell Potts and Roberta Wallach, on the other hand, are remarkable as the very differently troubled daughters.

The Elephant Man

April 19, 1979 (Booth Theatre), a drama by Bernard Pomerance. *Cast*: Kevin Conway (Dr. Frederick Treves), Philip Anglim (John Merrick), Carole Shelley (Mrs. Kendal), Richard

Clarke, I. M. Hobson. *Director*: Jack Hofsiss. *Producers*: Richmond Crinkley, etc. 916 performances. Tony Award.

(EMI/Brooksfilms 1980). *Screenplay*: Christopher de Core, etc. *Cast*: Anthony Hopkins (Dr. Frederick Treves), John Hurt (John Merrick), Anne Bancroft (Mrs. Kendal), John Gielgud, Freddie Jones, Wendy Hiller. *Director*: David Lynch. *Producer*: Stuart Cornfield.

(TV 1982). *Teleplay*: Steve Lawson. *Cast:* Philip Anglim (John Merrick), Kevin Conway (Dr. Frederick Treves), Penny Fuller (Mrs. Kendal), Richard Clarke, Glenn Close, Jarlath Conroy, Rex Everhart, Christopher Hewett. *Director:* Jack Hofsiss. *Producer:* Richmond Crinkley.

The true story of the Victorian Englishman John Merrick, a grossly deformed man taken in by a doctor who discovers his poetic nature and a sharp brain, was given a Brechtian stage adaptation by Bernard Pomerance, an American playwright living in England. After the drama was seen in London it was restaged Off Broadway then transferred to Broadway for a long run. The American production was minimalist in design and presentation and the bizarre tale was told through suggestion and commentary. Merrick, for example, was performed by Philip Anglim with no special makeup or body padding. This allowed the powerful story to be told with elegance and without sensationalism. The 1980 movie used the same title as the play but it was a totally different adaptation of the true story and was presented realistically with plenty of makeup and a lot of melodramatic acting by some very famous players. It wasn't until two years later that the Broadway play was adapted into a television production featuring some of the original cast and creative artists. It is an accurate presentation of the stage drama and as evocative and enthralling as it was in New York.

Elizabeth the Queen

November 3, 1930 (Guild Theatre), a drama by Maxwell Anderson. *Cast*: Lynn Fontanne (Queen Elizabeth), Alfred Lunt (Robert Deveraux, Earl of Essex), Percy Waram (Raleigh), Arthur Hughes (Cecil), Morris Carnovsky (Bacon), Anita Kerry, Phoebe Brand, Whitford Kane. *Di-*

rector: Philip Moeller. *Producer:* Theatre Guild. 147 performances.

The Private Lives of Elizabeth and Essex (Warner 1939). *Screenplay*: Norman Reilly Raine, Aeneas Mackenzie. *Cast*: Bette Davis (Queen Elizabeth), Errol Flynn (Robert Devereaux, Earl of Essex), Olivia De Havilland (Lady Penelope Gray), Donald Crisp (Francis Bacon), Vincent Price (Walter Raleigh), Alan Dale, Henry Stephenson, Henry Daniell, Leo G. Carroll, Nanette Fabray. *Director*: Michael Curtiz. *Producer*: Robert Lord.

Elizabeth the Queen (TV 1968). *Teleplay*: Maxwell Anderson. *Cast*: Judith Anderson (Queen Elizabeth), Charlton Heston (Robert Devereaux, Earl of Essex). *Director-producer*: George Schaefer.

The story of the Virgin Queen and her love-hate affair with Robert Devereaux, the Earl of Essex, was a familiar story that had been presented on stages around the world but Maxwell Anderson's blank-verse version, which was not afraid to change some historical details, was rich in its characterizations and proficient in its dialogue. The famous Lunts starred as Elizabeth and Essex and both were in top form. But the play was also a success with other actors in revival. The 1939 movie gave the tale the more provocative title of *The Private Lives of Elizabeth and Essex* and starred Bette Davis and Errol Flynn as the title characters. It is a lavish, colorful production and Davis is quite accomplished as the Queen but the adaptation misses much of the play's poetic charms and the story ends up being a rousing good melodrama. In 1968 the original play was presented on television with the dissimilar actors Judith Anderson and Charlton Heston as the fated lovers.

Elmer the Great

September 24, 1928 (Lyceum Theatre), a play by Ring Lardner. *Cast*: Walter Huston (Elmer Kane), Nan Sutherland (Nellie Poole), Lida MacMillan (Mrs. Kane), Mark Sullivan (Ben Beeson), Tom Blake (Bull Wade), George Sawyer, Gordon Hicks, Jack Clifford, Edwin Walter, Harold Healy. *Director*: Sam Forrest. *Producer:* George M. Cohan. 40 performances.

Fast Company (Paramount 1929). *Screenplay*: Walton Butterfield. *Cast*: Jack Oakie (Elmer), Evelyn Brent (Evelyn), Richard Gallagher, Sam Hardy,

Arthur Housman, Eugenie Besserer. *Directors*: A. Edward Sutherland, Edwin H. Knopf.

Elmer the Great (Warner 1933). *Screenplay*: Thomas Geraghty. *Cast*: Joe E. Brown (Elmer), Patricia Ellis (Nellie), Frank McHugh (Healy High-Hips), Claire Dodd (Evelyn), Preston Foster, Russell Hopton, Sterling Holloway, Charles C. Wilson. *Director*: Mervyn LeRoy. *Producer*: Ray Griffith.

The Cowboy Quarterback (Warner-First National 1939). *Screenplay*: Fred Niblo, Jr. *Cast*: Bert Wheeler (Harry Lynn), Marie Wilson (Marie Williams), Gloria Dickson, William Demerest, Eddie Foy, Jr. *Director*: Noel M. Smith.

Small-town baseball pitcher Elmer Kane is scouted by a big-time team but he doesn't want to leave Gentryville, Indiana, and his sweetheart Nellie who runs the grocery store where he works off season. Not to stand in his way, Nellie fires Elmer so he goes to New York where he falls into the hands of corruption and gambling until Nellie comes to rescue him. Although Walter Huston was praised for his amusing, heartfelt portrayal of Elmer, the play failed to find an audience and closed a little after a month. But the flop spawned three movie versions and the character of the local yokel baseballer would show up in other films as well. The first screen treatment in 1929 was called *Fast Company* and featured Jack Oakie as Elmer, one of the first of many buffoon characters he would play throughout the 1930s. A 1933 movie, using the play's title, starred Joe E. Brown as Elmer and it was one of his best screen roles. The film is closest to the stage work and made the most satisfying screen version. The venue was switched from baseball to football for the 1939 farce *The Cowboy Quarterback* with Bert Wheeler as the comic hero. Character names and plot details changed from the original play but it was basically the same story.

The Emperor Jones

November 1, 1920 (Neighborhood Playhouse), a drama by Eugene O'Neill. *Cast*: Charles S. Gilpin (Brutus Jones), Jasper Deeter (Smithers), Charles Ellis. *Director:* George Cram Cook. *Producer:* Provincetown Players. 204 performances.

(United Artists 1933). *Screenplay*: DuBose Heyward. *Cast*: Paul Robeson (Brutus Jones), Dudley Digges (Smithers), Frank H. Wilson, Fredi Washington, Ruby Elzy. *Director*: Dudley Murphy. *Producers*: Gifford Cochran, etc.

Eugene O'Neill's expressionistic drama begins realistically as the former Pullman porter Brutus Jones, who rules as emperor of a primitive West Indies island, decides to leave because the natives are getting wise to him. But as Jones runs through the tropical jungle to escape, the play gets less real and more allegorical as images of the past and spirits of the present haunt him until the natives shoot their emperor with a silver bullet. The original production Off Broadway was memorable for its bold, inventive sets by Robert Edmond Jones and the riveting performance by Charles S. Gilpin as Jones. Paul Robeson played the role on the London stage and repeated his unforgettable performance in the 1933 film. The special effects seem primitive by today's standards but the visuals are nonetheless effective. Long popular with academic theatre, the play was presented on television twice: in 1938 with Robert Adams as Jones and in 1955 starring Ossie Davis.

Enter Laughing

March 13, 1963 (Henry Miller Theatre), a comedy by Joseph Stein. *Cast*: Alan Arkin (David Kolowitz), Sylvia Sidney (Mrs. Kolowitz), Marty Greene (Mr. Kolowitz), Vivian Blaine (Angela), Alan Mowbray (Marlowe), Michael J. Pollard (Marvin), Pierre Epstein, Walt Wanderman, Barbara Dana. *Director*: Gene Saks. *Producer:* Morton Gottlieb. 419 performances.

(Columbia 1967). *Screenplay*: Joseph Stein, Carl Reiner. *Cast*: Reni Santoni (David Kolowitz), José Ferrer (Mr. Marlowe), Shelley Winters (Mrs. Kolowitz), Elaine May (Angela), David Opatoshu (Morris Kolowitz), Michael J. Pollard (Marvin), Jack Gilford, Don Rickles, Rob Reiner. *Director*: Carl Reiner. *Producers*: Joseph Stein, Carl Reiner.

Joseph Stein adapted Carl Reiner's autobiographical novel into a sprightly comedy hit and launched the stage career of Alan Arkin. He played the Jewish nerd David

Kolowitz who is slated by his parents to be a pharmacist but he wants to be an actor. After studying with a booze-swilling old teacher and stumbling through a shaky opening night, David is still far from talented but happy all the same. The slight piece was enlivened by its expert cast (Sylvia Sidney and Marty Greene as David's parents were particularly amusing) and firm direction by newcomer Gene Saks. Reiner directed the 1967 movie version of his own story and did not serve himself well. The tale seems drawn out and tiresome and only the likable cast keeps the movie alive. A special actor like Arkin was need to play David but Reni Santori was not it. Yet accomplished performers such as José Ferrer, Shelley Winters, Elaine May, Jack Gilford, and David Opatoshu almost make up for it. The original play was turned into the short-lived Broadway musical *So Long, 174th Street* (1976).

Escape in the Desert see The Petrified Forest

The Eve of St. Mark

October 7, 1942 (Cort Theatre), a drama by Maxwell Anderson. *Cast*: William Prince (Quizz West), Matt Crowley (Deck), Aline MacMahon (Nell), Mary Rolfe (Janet Feller), Grover Burgess, Clifford Carpenter, Edwain Cooper. *Director*: Lem Ward. *Producer:* Playwrights' Company. 305 performances.

(Fox 1944). *Screenplay*: George Seaton. *Cast*: William Eythe (Pvt. Quizz West), Anne Baxter (Janet Feller), Ray Collins (Deckman West), Ruth Nelson (Nell), Michael O'Shea, Vincent Price, Stanley Praeger, Henry Morgan. *Director*: John M. Stahl. *Producer*: William Perlberg.

Maxwell Anderson had co-written *What Price Glory?* (qv), the most successful play about World War One, and this drama was the longest-running work about World War Two to be seen during the war years. Quizz West leaves his family's farm and his sweetheart Janet to enlist in the Army but he seems to appear to her each night in her dreams. So when Quizz is killed in the Philippines, Janet seems to sense it already

and takes the news with stoic resignation. At the end of the drama Quizz's brothers enlist, urged by their father to "Make a new world, boys." While Anderson's earlier work was a condemnation of warfare, this later play is patriotic without being an empty flag waver. All the same, Hollywood didn't like the tragic ending and Quizz lived in the 1944 movie. It is a competently made film and well acted but it ended up being just another wartime propaganda melodrama.

Excess Baggage

December 26, 1927 (Ritz Theatre), a comedy by John McGowan. *Cast*: Eric Dresser (Eddie Kane), Miriam Hopkins (Elsa McCoy), Frank McHugh (Jimmy Dunn), Nace Bonville (Jack Merrill), John H. Dilson (Frank Arnold), Boyd Marshall (Herbert Crammon), Mort Downey, Denton Vane, Maud Blair. *Director*: Melville Burke. *Producer:* Barbour, Crimmins & Bryant. 216 performances.

(MGM 1928). *Screenplay*: Frances Marion, Ralph Spence. *Cast*: William Haines (Eddie Kane), Josephine Dunn (Elsa McCoy), Neely Edwards (Jimmy Dunn), Kathleen Clifford, Greta Granstedt, Ricardo Cortez. *Director*: James Cruze. *Producers*: James Cruze, Julius Hagen.

The vaudeville team of Eddie and Elsa is not really a team at all since he does the juggling and she just stands there looking pretty. Considering herself "excess baggage," Elsa tries the movies and soon is a silent screen star. But in Hollywood Eddie is now the excess baggage, living off of her success. So he returns to vaudeville where she pursues him and two become a true team. While the critics only offered faint praise, the comedy appealed to audiences and it ran nearly a year. The young and popular stage star Miriam Hopkins played Elsa on Broadway but she was passed over for the 1928 silent film which featured William Haines and Josephine Dunn as the couple. Hopkins would make her screen debut two years later and immediately become a Hollywood star as well.

Extremities

December 22, 1982 (Cheryl Crawford Theatre), a play by William Mastrosimone. *Cast*: Susan

Sarandon (Marjorie), James Russo (Raul), Ellen Barkin (Terry), Deborah Hedwall (Patricia). *Director*: Robert Allan Ackerman. *Producers:* Frank Gero, etc. 325 performances.

(Atlantic 1986). *Screenplay*: William Mastrosimone. *Cast*: Farrah Fawcett (Marjorie), James Russo (Joe), Alfre Woodard (Patricia), Diana Scarwid (Terry), Sandy Martin. *Director*: Robert M. Young. *Producers*: George W. Perkins, Burt Sugarman.

A nailbiter that is uncomfortably tense, this problem drama offered no easy solutions to its dilemma. An intruder attempts to rape Marjorie when she is home alone but she manages to spray insect repellent into his face, blinding him enough so she can tie him up. Marjorie's housemates return and urge her to call the police but she questions whether the law will believe her story. Not until Marjorie threatens to kill the intruder does he confess to a series of rapes and the police are called. Since none of the characters were painted in black or white, the drama was all the more disturbing and led to much discussion during its year-long run Off Broadway. The 1986 screen version is also uncomfortable viewing but the acting is not as strong as it had been on the stage and the viewer tends to watch the unpleasant events with little threat or passion.

Eyes of Youth

August 22, 1917 (Maxine Elliott's Theatre), a play by Charles Guernon, Max Marcin. *Cast*: Marjorie Rambeau (Gina Ashling), Charles Abbe, Donald Gallaher, Fay Wallace, Leonard Ide, Ralph Kellerd, Caroline Leonard. *Director*: Lawrence Marston. *Producers:* Al Woods, Shuberts. 414 performances.

(Garson Productions 1919). *Screenplay*: Charles E. Whittaker, Albert Parker. *Cast*: Clara Kimball Young (Gina Ashling), Gareth Hughes, Pauline Starke, Sam Southern, Edmund Lowe, Ralph Lewis. *Director*: Albert Parker. *Producer*: Harry Garson.

Called a "trick melodrama" in the business, this surprisingly successful play had enough sensationalism and mystery to appeal to audiences on Broadway and for several years on the road. When young Gina Ashling consults a fortune teller, he reveals several possibilities for her future: a lonely, deserted schoolteacher, a ballet star with an empty life, an unhappy marriage ending in an ugly court battle, a life of prostitution, and a path he cannot tell her about. Since all of the choices were dramatized, the play offered plenty of theatrics to chew on. But in the end Gina chooses the unknown path and we can only hope is it the right one. The 1919 silent movie was able to handle the flashbacks effectively and pre-code Hollywood allowed the story's more lurid aspects to remain uncensored. But Gina does not choose a path in the film; she goes off and marries the man who loves her and that suffices for a happy ending.

The Faith Healer

January 19, 1910 (Savoy Theatre), a play by William Vaughn Moody. *Cast*: Henry Miller (Ulrich Michaelis), Jessie Bonstelle (Rhoda Williams), Marble Bert (Mary Beeler), Harold Russell (Matthew Beeler), Edward See, Theodore Friebus, Lillian Dix, Laura Hope Crews. *Director-producer:* Henry Miller. 13 performances.

(Famous Players-Lasky 1921). *Screenplay*: Z. Wall Covington, Mrs. William Vaughn Moody. *Cast*: Milton Sills (Michaelis), Ann Forrest (Rhoda Williams), Fountain La Rue (Mary Beeler), Frederick Vroom (Matthew Beeler), Loyola O'Connor, Mae Giraci, John Curry, Adolphe Menjou. *Director*: George Medford.

A small-town faith healer overrides the objections of the local preacher and minister and when he makes a crippled woman walk his powers are recognized. But when he finds out the woman he loves has been the mistress of the doctor, his powers fail him and only her love saves him. Although not a success in its initial engagement, the ambitious character drama slowly gained an audience once it was printed. A silent film version in 1921 plays up the melodramatic and romantic aspects of the story whereas the play had greater themes in mind.

The Fall and Rise of Susan Lenox

June 9, 1919 (44th Street Theatre), a melodrama by George V. Hobart. *Cast*: Alma Tell (Susan Lenox), Perce Benton (Roderick Spencer), Walter Walker (George Warham), Robert T. Haines (Jeb Ferguson), Harry Southard (Sam Wright), Anne Sutherland, Marie Vernon, Paul Stewart. *Producer:* Shuberts.

Susan Lenox: Her Fall and Rise (MGM 1931). *Screenplay*: Leo Gordon, etc. *Cast*: Greta Garbo (Susan Lenox), Clark Gable (Rodney), Jean Hersholt (Ohlin), John Miljan (Burlington), Alan Hale, Hale Hamilton, Hilda Vaughn. *Director-producer*: Robert Z. Leonard.

Illegitimate Susan Lenox is raised by uncaring relatives, seduced and abandoned by a cad, is forced to marry an alcoholic farmer, then runs away to the city where she gets a job in a department store. It is there that she finally meets a man who treats her well and their marriage will seemingly end her series of woes. The melodrama, based on a novel by David Graham Phillips, was a slicker variation of several older plays about innocent women in distress. The difference in this case is that the rural life was the evil one and the city brings hope—the opposite of most 19th century plots. The play was turned into a 1931 talkie vehicle for Greta Garbo and even in such a lurid melodrama she shone as the heroine. The studio cleaned up the story somewhat, making Susan legitimate and running away to the city rather than marrying a brute her father has picked out for her. Clark Gable is the man who saves her and the picture is worth watching to see two of Hollywood's most commanding stars in the same film.

The Fall Guy

March 10, 1925 (Eltinge Theatre), a comedy by James Gleason, George Abbott. *Cast*: Ernest Truex (Johnnie Quinlan), Beatrice Noyes (Bertha Quinlan), Henry Mortimer (Charles Newton), Hartley Power (Frank Herman), Ralph Sipperly (Dan Walsh), Dorothy Peterson, Alf Weinberger, Joseph R. Garry. *Producer:* Shuberts. 177 performances.

(RKO 1930). *Screenplay*: Tim Whelan. *Cast*: Jack Mulhall (Johnnie Quinlan), Mae Clark (Bertha Quinlan), Ned Sparks (Dan Walsh), Pat O'Malley (Charles Newton), Thomas E. Jackson (Nifty Herman), Wynne Gibson, Ann Brody. *Director*: Leslie Pearce. *Producer*: William Sistrom.

Put-upon, out-of-work Johnnie Quinlan needs money to support his wife and sponging relatives so he agrees to deliver a suitcase full of illegal booze to a gang leader. But before he can, Johnnie is mistaken for a drug dealer and soon federal agents and two rival gangs are after him. Beloved comic Ernest Truex gave a nimble performance as Johnnie and the subject matter during the unpopular Prohibition helped make the comedy a success. While still topical, the story was not as appealing to moviegoers and the 1930 film, with Jack Mulhall, was not a hit. It was a sunnier version of the story with Johnnie actually outwitting the mobster Nifty Herman and getting a job as an assistant to the government agent. Years later Bob Hope would build his career playing hapless fall guys like Johnnie in several screen comedies.

Family Business

April 12, 1978 (Astor Place Theatre), a play by Dick Goldberg. *Cast*: Harold Gary (Isaiah Stein), David Garfield (Norman), Richard Greene (Bobby), Joel Polis (Jerry), David Rosenbaum (Phil), Richard Levine. *Director*: John Stix. *Producer:* Honey Waldman. 438 performances.

(TV 1983). *Teleplay*: Dick Goldberg. *Cast*: Milton Berle (Isaiah Stern), Jeff Marcus (Jerry), David Garfield (Norman), Richard Greene (Bobby), David Rosenbaum (Phil), Brian Benben, Julia Meadows. *Director*: John Stix. *Producer*: American Playhouse.

There was much talk and little action in this domestic drama but the characters were vividly drawn and the acting distinguished enough that the play ran Off Broadway for over a year. The aged businessman Isaiah Stein wants to change his will and the way his money will be distributed after he dies so his four sons panic. Old grudges and resentments are brought up and the desperate son Phil threatens the old man so soundly that Isaiah dies of a heart attack while Phil delays in calling an ambulance. After the funeral the four siblings attempt to make amends for the sake of their deceased mother's memory. This modern variation on *The Little Foxes* (qv) even had a similar death scene but much of the writing was uniquely its own. The 1983 television production gave comic Milton Berle a shot at a dramatic role and he holds his own with the younger actors, most of whom had appeared in the original stage play.

The Famous Mrs. Fair

December 22, 1919 (Henry Miller Theatre), a play by James Forbes. *Cast*: Blanche Bates (Nancy Fair), Henry Miller (Mr. Fair), Margalo Gillmore (Sylvia), Jack Devereaux (Alan), Virginia Hammond, Robert Strange. *Producer*: A. L. Erlanger. 343 performances.

(Louis B. Mayer Prod. 1923). *Screenplay*: Frances Marion. *Cast*: Myrtle Stedman (Mrs. Fair), Marguerite de la Motte (Sylvia), Cullen Landis (Alan), Huntley Gordon (Jeffrey Fair), Ward Crane, Carmel Myers, Helen Ferguson. *Director*: Fred Niblo. *Producer*: Louis B. Mayer.

After having been awarded a medal for her service with the Red Cross during World War One, feminist Nancy Fair is offered a lecture tour to talk about the new role of women in society. But Mrs. Fair realizes her weak husband and confused children need her at home so she decides to give up the tour and her feminist ideas. Definitely a product of its time, the play says more about the mores and sentiments of the pre–Roaring Twenties than anything unique about the characters. But the drama was very successful, helped by the show's three stars (Blanche Bates, Henry Miller, and Margalo Gillmore) who were at the peak of their popularity. The 1923 silent movie came out in the flapper era but most audiences still responded favorably to the story and its homespun ideas.

Fanny

Majestic Theatre, 4 November 4, 1954 (Majestic Theatre), a musical play by S. N. Behrman, Joshua Logan. *Score:* Harold Rome. *Cast:* Ezio Pinza (César), Florence Henderson (Fanny Cabinis), William Tabbert (Marius), Walter Slezak (Panisse). *Songs:* Fanny; Be Kind to Your Parents; Restless Heart; Why Be Afraid to Dance?; Welcome Home; Love Is a Very Light Thing. *Director:* Joshua Logan. *Choreographer:* Helen Tamiris. *Producers:* David Merrick, Joshua Logan. 888 performances.

(Warner 1961). *Screenplay:* Julius Epstein. *Cast:* Leslie Caron (Fanny), Horst Buchholz (Marius), Maurice Chevalier (Panisse), Charles Boyer (César), Georgette Anys, Lionel Jeffries, Baccaloni. *Director:* Joshua Logan. *Producer:* Ben Kadish.

An unusual Broadway hit, this evocative musical was based on a trilogy of French films by Marcel Pagnol, consisting of *Marius, Fanny,* and *César,* that told a long and engrossing tale about two lovers in Marsailles who are separated, but the girl is found to be pregnant so she marries an older man. Years later the real father returns and is convinced by his own father to let the child stay with the older man who raised him. Only after time and the death of the surrogate father are the lovers reunited. It was a lot to pack into one evening but the libretto was well crafted and Harold Rome's gentle, intoxicating score gave the piece a Gallic flavor. The show was a surprise hit and ran nearly three years but the bigger surprise came when Hollywood cut all the songs and filmed the story in 1961 as a nonmusical. The cast was first rate but the movie was a plodding affair and, being inferior to the French original and the Broadway musical, served no purpose.

The Fantasticks

May 3, 1960 (Sullivan Street Theatre), a musical fable by Tom Jones. *Score:* Harvey Schmidt, Tom Jones. *Cast:* Jerry Orbach (El Gallo), Kenneth Nelson (Matt), Rita Gardner (Luisa), William Larson, Hugh Thomas. *Songs:* Try to Remember; I Can See It; Soon It's Gonna Rain; Much More; They Were You; Never Say No; It Depends on What You Pay; Round and Round. *Director:* Word Baker. *Producer:* Lore Noto. 17,162 performances.

(United Artists 1995/2000). *Screenplay:* Tom Jones, Harvey Schmidt. *Score:* Harvey Schmidt,

Tom Jones. *Cast:* Jean Louisa Kelly (Luisa), Joseph McIntyre (Matt), Joel Grey, Brad Sullivan, Jonathan Morris, Barnard Hughes, Teller. *Songs:* Try to Remember; I Can See It; Soon It's Gonna Rain; Much More; They Were You; Never Say No; It Depends on What You Pay; Round and Round. *Director:* Michael Ritchie. *Choreographer:* Michael Smuin. *Producers:* Art Schaeffer, etc.

America's longest-running musical has the simplest boy-meets-girl story, but then everything about this charming little show is simple. Under a cardboard moon, the two lovers woo and win each other, but in the second act, under a cardboard sun, reality sets it. Few musicals are as straightforward and beguiling at the same time. The phenomenal success of *The Fantasticks* first Off Broadway then around the world is the stuff of legend. An abridged television version in 1964 featured John Davidson and Susan Watson as the lovers, Stanley Holloway and Bert Lahr as their fathers, and Ricardo Montalban as the bandit El Gallo who brings them all together. It was also a simple production, filmed in a studio. A movie version of the show was discussed and attempted several times before one was made in 1995. The result was so poor that Hollywood kept it on the shelf for five years, then in 2000 gave it a brief and limited release in theatres before it became available on video. It is easy to see why the studio was so reluctant to showcase the film. It is a charmless, dreary affair with lackluster or annoying performances and an oddly disjointed look. Perhaps a satisfying movie of the little Off Broadway wonder was never possible but no one suspected it could be this dismal.

The Farmer Takes a Wife

October 30, 1934 (46th Street Theatre), a comedy by Frank B. Elser, Marc Connelly. *Cast:* June Walker (Molly Larkins), Henry Fonda (Dan Harrow), Gibbs Penrose (Jotham Klore), Herb Williams (Fortune Friendly), Margaret Hamilton (Lucy Gurget), Mary McQuade, Ruth Gillmore, Kate Mayhew, Ralph Briggs. *Director:* Marc Connelly. *Producer:* Max Gordon. 104 performances.

(Fox 1935). *Screenplay:* Edwin Burke. *Cast:* Janet Gaynor (Molly Larkins), Henry Fonda (Dan

Harrow), Charles Bickford (Jotham Klore), Slim Summerville (Fortune Friendly), Margaret Hamilton (Lucy Gurget), Jane Withers, Andy Devine, Roger Imhof, Sig Ruman. *Director:* Victor Fleming. *Producer:* Winfield R. Sheehan.

(Fox 1953). *Screenplay:* Sally Benson, etc. *Score:* Harold Arlen, Dorothy Fields. *Cast:* Betty Grable (Molly Larkins), Dale Robertson (Dan Harrow), John Carroll (Jotham Klore), Eddie Foy, Jr. (Fortune Friendly), Thelma Ritter (Lucy Cashdolar), Charlotte Austin, Kathleen Crowley, Gwen Verdon. *Songs:* We're in Business; On the Erie Canal; Today I Love Everybody; With the Sun Warm Upon Me. *Director:* Henry Levin. *Choreographer:* Jack Cole. *Producer:* Frank P. Rosenberg.

Walter D. Edmonds' novel *Rome Haul*, about romance and rivalry on the Erie Canal in 1850, afforded Henry Fonda his first stage and film hits, playing a reticent but noble character he could portray better than anyone else. The play was a success so Hollywood bought the play and Fonda (it was his first movie) and made an engaging rustic romance featuring Janet Gaynor and the newcomer and peppered it with a cast of character-actor favorites. The 1953 musicalization remained faithful to the play and earlier film but Betty Grable and Dale Robertson failed to set off any sparks and the musical lacked punch. Only a few of the dances bring the movie to life. (Gwen Verdon is easy to spot as a featured dancer.) None of the songs became famous though it is a charming score all the same.

Fast Company see *Elmer the Great*

A Few Good Men

November 15, 1989 (Music Box Theatre), a play by Aaron Sorkin. *Cast:* Tom Hulce (Lt. Daniel Kaffee), Megan Gallagher (Lt. Cmdr. Joanne Galloway), Stephen Lang (Col. Nathan Jessup), Michael Dolan, Victor Love, Arnold Molina, Mark Nelson, Edmond Genest, Robert Hogan, Ted Marcoux, Clark Gregg. *Director:* Don Scardino. *Producers:* David Brown, etc. 497 performances.

(Columbia 1992). *Screenplay:* Aaron Sorkin. *Cast:* Tom Cruise (Lt. Daniel Kaffee), Jack Nicholson

(Col. Nathan Jessup), Demi Moore (Lt. Cmdr. JoAnne Galloway), Kevin Bacon, Keifer Sutherland, Kevin Pollack, James Marshall, J. T. Walsh, Christopher Guest. *Director*: Rob Reiner. *Producers*: David Brown, etc.

The most successful military courtroom drama since *The Caine Mutiny Court-Martial* (qv), this well scripted, ardently acted play was the surprise hit of the season. When a Marine dies suspiciously on the U.S. Military base on Guantánamo Bay in Cuba, the Navy is asked to look into the matter and assigns the young, inexperienced lawyer Lt. Daniel Kaffee to handle the defense of two Marines accused. But the more Kaffee and his assistant Lt. Commander JoAnne Galloway look into the matter they discover a secret code of honor that commanded the defendants to punish the deceased. The command is traced to the base commander Lt. Colonel Jessup who denies the charge at first, then under pressure proudly proclaims he ordered the assault that led to murder. The dialogue sparkled with vitality, the characters were well drawn and fascinating, and the cast was outstanding. Playwright Aaron Sorkin penned the screenplay for the 1992 movie and it was even finer than the stage script with some added twists in the plot and effective use of various locations. But the acting in the film is generally disappointing, the stars either overacting or underplaying their scenes and the best performances coming from supporting players such as Kevin Bacon.

Fiddler on the Roof

September 22, 1964 (Imperial Theatre), a musical play by Joseph Stein. *Score:* Jerry Bock, Sheldon Harnick. *Cast:* Zero Mostel (Teyve), Maria Karnilova (Golde), Bert Convy (Perchick), Austin Pendleton (Motel), Beatrice Arthur (Yente), Joanna Merlin, Julia Migenes, Michael Granger. *Songs:* Matchmaker, Matchmaker; Sunrise, Sunset; If I Were a Rich Man; Far From the Home I Love; Tradition; Do You Love Me?; Now I Have Everything; To Life; Sabbath Prayer; Tevye's Dream. *Director-choreographer:* Jerome Robbins. *Producer:* Harold Prince. 3,242 performances. Tony Award.

(Mirisch/United Artists 1971). *Screenplay:* Joseph Stein. *Score:* Jerry Bock, Sheldon Harnick. *Cast:* Topol (Tevye), Norma Crane (Golde), Leonard Frey (Motel), Molly Picon (Yente), Paul Mann, Rosalind Harris, Michele Marsh, Neva Small, Michael Glaser. *Songs:* Matchmaker, Matchmaker; Sunrise, Sunset; If I Were a Rich Man; Far From the Home I Love; Tradition; Do You Love Me?; To Life; Sabbath Prayer; Tevye's Dream. *Director-producer:* Norman Jewison. *Choreographers:* Tom Abbott, Jerome Robbins.

While most 1960s musical were heavy on glitz and glamour, this quietly affecting piece about the Jewish inhabitants of a small Russian village at the turn of the century was refreshingly intimate and ultimately moving. Jerome Robbins's staging and dances conjured up a folk-like feeling as the warmhearted stories by Sholom Aleichem came to life on stage. The score was just as warm and engaging and the original cast, led by Zero Mostel as the dairyman Tevye, was superb. The film version was faithful to the play, keeping all but two of the songs and retaining all the characters and scenes. It is a leisurely paced movie (it ran 180 minutes when first released, later re-released at 148 minutes) and the performances tend to be on a lower key than on the stage. But it remains one of the most painterly and visually evocative of all movie musicals (it was partially shot on location in Yugoslavia) and often has the look of an old sepia photographs or paintings by Millet. The musical was remade for television in 2005 with Victor Garber as Tevye.

Fifth of July

April 27, 1978 (Circle Theatre), a play by Lanford Wilson. *Cast*: William Hurt (Kenneth Talley), Jonathan Hogan (John), Nancy Snyder (Gwen), Helen Stenborg (Aunt Sally), Jeff Daniels (Jed), Joyce Reehling (June Talley), Amy Wright (Shirley), Danton Stone (Weston Hurley). *Director*: Marshall W. Mason. *Producer:* Circle Repertory Company. 159 performances.

(TV 1982). *Teleplay*: Lanford Wilson. *Cast*: Richard Thomas (Kenneth Talley), Jonathan Hogan (John), Swoozie Kurtz (Gwen), Helen Stenborg (Aunt Sally), Jeff Daniels (Jed), Joyce Reehling (June Talley), Cynthia Nixon (Shirley), Danton Stone (Weston Hurley). *Directors*: Kirk Browning, Marshall W. Mason. *Producer*: Samuel Paul.

With little plot but fascinating characters and vigorous dialogue, this Chekhov-like play (sometimes titled *The Fifth of July*) by Lanford Wilson is one of his most satisfying efforts. The Vietnam vet Kenneth Talley, having lost both his legs in battle, returns to his family's Missouri farmhouse where his male lover, his aged aunt and other relatives, and some old friends from his radical days gather for the Fourth of July holiday weekend. The assembled group is a varied and sometimes oddball lot and the reminiscences and accusations that surface help Kenneth made some decisions about his future. The Off Broadway production featured the Circle Repertory Company's finest actors and some reprised their performances when the play was revived on Broadway in 1980 for a long run. Several of them are also in the laudable 1982 television production which was co-directed by Marshall W. Mason, the Circle director who guided many of Wilson's plays to success over the years. Standouts in the television cast are Richard Thomas as Kenneth and Swoozie Kurtz as the over-sexed, under-enlightened singer Gwen.

Fifty Million Frenchmen

November 27, 1929 (Lyric Theatre), a musical comedy by Herbert Fields. *Score:* Cole Porter. *Cast:* William Gaxton (Peter Forbes), Genevieve Tobin (Looloo Carroll), Helen Broderick (Violet Hildegarde), Evelyn Hoey, Betty Compton, Jack Thompson, Thurston Hall. *Songs:* You Do Something to Me; Find Me a Primitive Man; You've Got That Thing; Paree, What Did You Do to Me?; You Don't Know Paree. *Director:* Monty Woolley. *Choreographer:* Larry Ceballos. *Producer:* E. Ray Goetz. 254 performances.

(Warner 1931). *Screenplay:* Al Boasberg, Joseph Jackson, Eddie Welch. *Score:* Cole Porter. *Cast:* William Gaxton (Jack Forbes), Claudia Dell (Looloo Carroll), Ole Olsen (Simon), Chic Johnson (Peter), Helen Broderick (Violet), John Halliday, Lester Crawford, Evalyn Knapp. *Director:* Lloyd Bacon.

Stock full of more hit songs than any other Cole Porter musical of the 1920s, this spirited show celebrated Paris in both its scenery and its score and was a hit even during the early days of the Depression. An American playboy in Paris poses as a tour guide to win a bet that he can woo a wealthy American socialite without using his money. Of course he falls in love with her for real and audiences got to hear such delectable songs as "Find Me a Primitive Man," "Paree, What Have You Done to Me?" and "You Do Something to Me." Hollywood kept leading man William Gaxton but foolishly tossed out the entire Porter score, filming the show as a comedy with the famous tunes as background music only. One of the brightest Broadway musicals of the decade became one of the most quickly forgotten films of the era. Sadly, the piece was never remade.

Finian's Rainbow

January 10, 1947 (46th Street Theatre), a musical fantasy by E. Y. Harburg, Fred Saidy. *Score:* Burton Lane, E. Y. Harburg. *Cast:* David Wayne (Og), Ella Logan (Sharon McLonergan), Albert Sharpe (Finian McLonergan), Donald Richards (Woody Mahoney), Anita Alverez, Robert Pitkin. *Songs:* How Are Things in Glocca Morra?; Old Devil Moon; Look to the Rainbow; If This Isn't Love; Something Sort of Grandish; When I'm Not Near the Girl I Love; Necessity; When the Idle Poor Become the Idle Rich; The Begat. *Director:* Bretaigne Windust. *Choreographer:* Michael Kidd. *Producers:* Lee Sabinson, William Katzell. 725 performances.

(Warner/Seven Arts 1968). *Screenplay:* E. Y. Harburg, Fred Saidy. *Score:* Burton Lane, E. Y. Harburg. *Cast:* Fred Astaire (Finian McLonergan), Petula Clark (Sharon McLonergan), Tommy Steele (Og), Don Francks (Woody Mahoney), Keenan Wynn, Al Freedman, Jr., Avon Long, Barbara Hancock. *Songs:* How Are Things in Glocca Morra?; Old Devil Moon; Look to the Rainbow; If This Isn't Love; Something Sort of Grandish; When I'm Not Near the Girl I Love; When the Idle Poor Become the Idle Rich; The Begat. *Director:* Francis Ford Coppola. *Choreographers:* Hermes Pan, Fred Astaire. *Producer:* Joseph Landon.

Filled as it is with sly commentary on capitalism, racial inequality, labor relations, poverty, and awakening sexual awareness, it is remarkable that this musical fantasy is so whimsically charming. E. Y. Harburg was the impish librettist and lyricist who was behind the tall tale about an Irishman who steals a leprechaun's pot of gold and buries it near Ft. Knox so that it will grow. Without his gold, the leprechaun is becoming a mortal and discovering lust. The poor sharecroppers are led by a labor organizer to oppose big business while a bigoted Senator is turned black and finds out for himself what it is like to live in the segregated South. But a show that was bound to offend many instead became a surprise hit, helped by its lighthearted approach and superb score. Despite all the *Hit Parade* songs, Hollywood did not consider filming such a potentially explosive story. When the film was finally made, once the Civil Rights movement was in full swing, the issues were still potent and beginning director Francis Ford Coppola did not shy away from them. He also tried to modernize the movie musical form, opening up the action, editing musical numbers in quirky ways, and filming the fantasy both on location and in the studio. Often the effect is delightful, others times it is jarring or just plain confusing. But the uneven movie musical is worth watching for Fred Astaire's musical cinema farewell, a gentle, elegant performance that seems all the more nostalgic when set against the garish 1960s tone throughout.

The Firefly

December 2, 1912 (Lyric Theatre), a comic operetta by Otto Harbach. *Score:* Rudolf Friml, Otto Harbach. *Cast:* Emma Trentini (Nina Corelli), Roy Atwell (Jenkins), Craig Campbell (Jack Travers), Sammy Lee (Pietro), Audrey Maple, Melville Stewart. *Songs:* Giannina Mia; Love Is Like a Firefly; Sympathy; When a Maid Comes Knocking at Your Heart. *Director:* Fred Latham. *Choreographers:* Signor Albertieri, Sammy Lee. *Producer:* Arthur Hammerstein. 120 performances.

(MGM 1937). *Screenplay:* Frances Goodrich, Albert Hackett. *Score:* Rudolf Friml, Herbert Stothart, Otto Harbach, Robert Wright, George Forrest. *Cast:* Jeanette MacDonald (Nina Maria Azara), Allan Jones (Don Diego/Francois Andre), Douglass Dumbrille, Warren William, Billy Gilbert, Henry Daniell, George Zucco. *Songs:* Giannina Mia; The Donkey Serenade; Love Is Like a Firefly; Sympathy; When a Maid Comes Knocking at Your Heart. *Director:* Robert Z. Leonard. *Choreographer:* Albertina Rasch. *Producer:* Hunt Stromberg.

Rudolf Friml's first operetta was a resounding hit in its day and in revival for many years. While the story, about a fledgling singer who disguises herself as a cabin boy on a private yacht and falls in love with a handsome aristocrat before becoming a stage star, was serviceable at best, the musical overflowed with wonderful songs, a few of which became enduring standards. The film version discarded the stage plot completely and Hollywood came up with a new adventure story about a Spanish singer who serves as a spy during the Napoleonic invasion of Europe. Her love interest is a counter-spy who falls in love with her even as he discovers her true identity. It was an implausible tale but not more so than most operettas. The highlights of Friml's score were retained and, as sung by Jeanette MacDonald and Allen Jones, the movie was musically very strong. Yet the hit song of the film was a new one written for Jones: "The Donkey Serenade." He made it his signature number and sang it for the rest of his career.

First Lady

November 26, 1935 (Music Box Theatre), a comedy by Katharine Dayton, George S. Kaufman. *Cast*: Jane Cowl (Lucy Chase Wayne), Stanley Ridges (Stephen Wayne), Lily Cahill (Irene Hibbard), Jessie Busley (Belle Hardwick), Regina Wallace, Ethel Wilson, Rita Vale, Judson Laire, Thomas Findlay. *Director*: George S. Kaufman. *Producer:* Sam H. Harris. 246 performances.

(Warner 1937). *Screenplay:* Rowland Leigh. *Cast*: Kay Francis (Lucy Chase Wayne), Preston Foster (Stephen Wayne), Verree Teasdale (Irene Hibbard), Marjorie Rambeau (Belle Hardwick), Anita Louise, Victor Jory, Walter Connolly, Louise Fazenda. *Director*: Stanley Logan. *Producers*: Hal B. Wallis, Jack L. Warner.

The major players in this witty comedy about Washington politics are two woman, the outspoken society leader Lucy Chase Wayne and her upstart rival, the manipulating Irene Hibbard. The two ladies plot and plan behind each other's backs, funding candidates they favor and digging up dirt on the choice candidates of the other. The dialogue was sprightly, the performers engaging, and audiences flocked to the topical play. Though the wit is somewhat watered down in the 1937 movie, there is still much to enjoy in the well-acted comedy. Kay Francis and Verree Teasdale play the rival madams and they are ably supported by a fine collection of polished character actors.

First Monday in October

October 3, 1978 (Majestic Theatre), a play by Jerome Lawrence, Robert E. Lee. *Cast*: Henry Fonda (Daniel Snow), Jane Alexander (Ruth Loomis), Larry Gates (James Jefferson Crawford), Earl Sydnor (Josiah Clewes), Maurice Copeland (Waldo Thompson), Alexander Reed, Patrick McCullough, Eugene Stuckmann, Tom Stechschulte, John Wardwell, John Newton. *Director*: Edwin Sherin. *Producers:* Kennedy Center, etc. 79 performances.

(Paramount 1981). *Screenplay*: Jerome Lawrence, Robert E. Lee. *Cast*: Walter Matthau (Dan Snow), Jill Clayburgh (Ruth Loomis), Barnard Hughes (Crawford), Jan Sterling, Joshua Bryant, James Stephens, Wiley Harker. *Director*: Ronald Neame. *Producers*: Paul M. Heller, Martha Scott.

The sometimes friendly, sometimes bitter rivalry between the liberal Supreme Court Justice Dan Snow and the conservative judge Ruth Loomis was the subject of this talky comedy-drama that often dealt in clichés but occasionally struck a nerve. Because no woman had yet been appointed to the Supreme Court when the play was produced, it was an interesting premise but one that was never followed up on. Yet the production seemed like pure gold in the capable hands of Henry Fonda and Jane Alexander in the major roles and the play quickly showed a profit during its short run in a large house. By the time the 1981 movie was released, a woman did sit on the Court so the novelty of the idea was gone. So was the masterful interplay between the two characters as Walter Matthau and Jill Clayburgh gave predictable and unexciting performances as the rival judges.

The First Year

October 20, 1920 (Little Theatre), a comedy by Frank Craven. *Cast*: Frank Craven (Tommy Tucker), Roberta Arnold (Grace Livingston), Tim Murphy (Dr. Myron Anderson), Lester Chambers (Dick Loring), William Sampson (Mr. Livingston), Maude Granger (Mrs. Livingston), Leila Bennett, Hale Norcross. *Director*: Mitchell Smith. *Producer:* John Golden. 725 performances.

(Fox 1926). *Screenplay*: Frances Marion. *Cast*: Matt Moore (Tommy Tucker), Katherine Perry (Grace Livingston), Frank Currier (Dr. Livingston), John Patrick (Dick Loring), Frank Cooley, Virginia Madison. *Director*: Frank Borzage.

(Fox 1932). *Screenplay*: Lynn Starling. *Cast*: Janet Gaynor (Grace Livingston), Charles Farrell (Tommy Tucker), Minna Gombell (Mrs. Basstow), George Meeker (Dick Loring), Dudley Digges (Dr. Anderson), Robert McWade (Fred Livingston), Leila Bennett, Henry Kolker. *Director*: William K. Howard.

This domestic little comedy was a big hit in its day and was considered a refreshing look at marital life. When Tommy Tucker finally marries Grave Livingston, their first year of wedded bliss is touch and go as jealousy over a past boy friend and problems in the family business converge on the couple. But Uncle Myron helps straighten things out and the news that Grace is pregnant solidifies the marriage. The 1926 silent movie was a routine adaptation of the likable comedy but the 1932 talkie was a popular star vehicle for the beloved team of Janet Gaynor and Charles Farrell and the story seemed to be tailor made for their particular talents. While the issues in the movie are old hat today, the two stars are still worth watching.

Five Star Final

December 30, 1930 (Cort Theatre), a melodrama by Louis Weitzenkorn. *Cast*: Arthur Byron (Joseph W. Randall), Merle Maddern (Nancy Vorhees-Townsend), Malcolm Townsend (Michael Townsend), Frances Fuller (Jenny), Berton Churchill (Bernard Hinchcliffe), Allen Jenkins, Bruce McFarlane. *Director*: Worthington Miner. *Producer:* A. H. Woods. 175 performances.

(Warner 1931). *Screenplay*: Byron Morgan, Robert Lord. *Cast*: Edward G. Robinson (Joseph W. Randall), Frances Starr (Nancy Vorhees-Townsend), H. B. Warner (Michael Townsend), George E. Stone (Ziggie Feinstein), Boris Karloff (Rev. Isopod), Anthony Bushell, Marian Marsh, Ona Munson, Aline MacMahon. *Director*: Mervyn LeRoy. *Producer*: Hal B. Wallis.

Two Against the World (Warner 1936). *Screenplay:* Michael Jacoby. *Cast:* Humphrey Bogart (Sherry Scott), Beverly Roberts (Alma Ross), Helen MacKellar (Martha Carstairs), Henry O'Neill (Jim Carstairs), Linda Perry (Edith Carstairs), Carlyle Moore, Jr. (Malcolm Sims Jr), Claire Dodd, Virginia Brissac. *Director:* William McGann. *Producer:* Bryan Foy.

A scathing indictment against sensational journalism, this taut melodrama showed the tragic results of irresponsible newspaper reporting. Editor Joseph Randall is ordered by his newspaper's owner to dig up an old story about Nancy Voorhees who had been acquitted for shooting her lover. The story breaks on the day that Nancy and her husband Malcolm are seeing their daughter get married. The scandal is too much for them and the parents commit suicide while Jenny goes to the newspaper office to kill Randall. He has already resigned in disgust but the damage has been done. The 1931 screen version was as powerful as the play and, with top-notch performances by Edward G. Robinson as Randall and by others, the melodrama still packs a wallop. The story was remade in 1936 as *Two Against the World* and was set in a radio station rather than a newspaper. The emphasis of the remake was on reporter Humphrey Bogart and his assistant Beverly Roberts trying to kill the story and, as such, the plot seemed less gripping than in the play and earlier film.

Flamingo Road

March 19, 1946 (Belasco Theatre), a play by Robert and Sally Wilder. *Cast*: Judith Parrish (Lane Ballou), Francis J. Felton (Titus Semple), Lauren Gilbert (Fielding Carlisle), Philip Bourneuf (Dan Curtis), Paul Ford, Will Geer, Frank McNellis, Doris Rich, Bernard Randall. *Director*: José Ruben. *Producer:* Rowland Stebbins. 7 performances.

(Warner 1949). *Screenplay*: Edmund North, Robert Wilder. *Cast*: Joan Crawford (Lane Bellamy), Zachary Scott (Fielding Carlisle), Sydney Greenstreet (Sheriff Titus Semple), David Brian (Dan Reynolds), Gladys George (Lute Mae Sanders), Virginia Huston, Fred Clark. *Director*: Michael Curtiz. *Producer*: Jerry Wald.

Although it was a one-week flop on Broadway, this steamy melodrama inspired a hit movie and a popular television series. The obese, corrupt sheriff Titus Semple has it in for the former cooch dancer Judith Parrish, getting her fired from very job she gets and arresting her falsely as a prostitute. But when Semple tries to frame Dan Curtis for helping defend Judith, that is the last straw. She shoots the sheriff as he sits in his rocking chair on the hotel porch. A newsman, who is sympathetic to Judith and hated Semple, swears to the police that the sheriff's dying words said he was shot by a passing car. Hollywood bought the play as a screen vehicle for Joan Crawford in 1949 and it is one of her best performances: sexy, sullen, vulnerable, and dangerous. Sydney Greenstreet was also cunning as the sheriff with Zachary Scott and David Brian as the two men who help the heroine. A 1980 television movie with Morgan Fairchild and Howard Duff was so popular that it was turned into a series in 1981-82. On the small screen the heroine (called Constance) was the daughter of Sheriff Semple and she was married to the Scott character, Fielding Carlisle.

Flower Drum Song

December 1, 1958 (St. James Theatre), a musical comedy by Joseph Fields, Oscar Hammerstein. *Score:* Richard Rodgers, Oscar Hammerstein. *Cast:* Miyoshi Umeki (Mei Li), Larry Blyden (Sammy Fong), Juanita Hall (Madam Liang), Pat Suzuki (Linda Low), Keye Luke (Wang Chi Yang), Ed Kenny (Wang Ta), Arabella Hong, Jack Soo. *Songs:* I Enjoy Being a Girl; Love, Look Away; You Are Beautiful; Don't Marry Me; A Hundred Million Miracles; I Am Going to Like It Here; Chop Suey; Grant Avenue; Sunday. *Director:* Gene Kelly. *Choreographer:* Carol Haney. *Producers:* Rodgers and Hammerstein. 600 performances.

(Universal 1961). *Screenplay:* Joseph Fields. *Score:*

Richard Rodgers, Oscar Hammerstein. *Cast:* Miyoshi Umeki (Mei Li), Juanita Hall (Madam Liang), Nancy Kwan (Linda Low), Jack Soo (Sammy Fong), James Shigeta (Wang Ta), Benson Fong. *Songs:* I Enjoy Being a Girl; Love, Look Away; You Are Beautiful; Don't Marry Me; A Hundred Million Miracles; I Am Going to Like It Here; Chop Suey; Grant Avenue; Sunday. *Director:* Henry Koster. *Choreographer:* Hermes Pan. *Producers:* Ross Hunter, Joseph Fields.

Rodgers and Hammerstein's only musical comedy is about the generation gap among Chinese-Americans in San Francisco's Chinatown. Despite this unique situation, the plot is rather traditional with two pairs of lovers and a tuneful, lighthearted score. On Broadway the non–Asian Larry Blyden played the comic lead Sammy Fong with ethnic makeup but the film version is cast entirely with Asians, Hollywood's only such musical. All of the songs but one were kept in the movie and repeating their stage roles were Miyoshi Umecki as the young immigrant and Juanita Hall as the sarcastic aunt. Nancy Kwan and James Shigeta shone as the romantic leads but Jack Soo often stole the show as the worldly-wise Sammy. Gene Kelly directed the stage production but not the film; yet helmer Henry Koster and choreographer Hermes Pan managed to keep the movie bright, colorful, and light-footed.

Flying High

March 3, 1930 (Apollo Theatre), a musical comedy by John McGowan, B. G. DeSylva, Lew Brown. *Score:* Ray Henderson, B. G. DeSylva, Lew Brown. *Cast:* Oscar Shaw (Tod Addison), Bert Lahr (Rusty Krause), Kate Smith (Pansy Parks), Grace Brinkley (Eileen Cassidy), Russ Brown, Pearl Osgood. *Songs:* Thank Your Father; Red Hot Chicago; I'll Know Him; Good for You—Bad for Me; Without Love. *Directors:* George White, Edward Clark Lilley. *Choreographer:* Bobby Connolly. *Producer:* George White. 357 performances.

(MGM 1931). *Screenplay:* A. P. Younger. *Score:* Jimmy McHugh, Dorothy Fields, etc. *Cast:* Bert Lahr (Rusty), Charlotte Greenwood (Pansy), Pat O'Brien (Sport), Kathryn Crawford (Eileen), Charles Winninger, Hedda Hopper, Guy Kibbee. *Songs:* Happy Landing; We'll Dance Till Dawn;

Flying High. *Director:* Charles F. Riesner. *Choreographer:* Busby Berkeley. *Producer:* George White.

This screwball musical comedy about the young aviation business featured Bert Lahr as an airplane mechanic who is terrified of flying but wins an air race by mistake; he breaks a distance record because he can't figure out how to land his plane. The DeSylva-Brown-Henderson score was tuneful but not very memorable, yet Lahr's clowning and the able support of Kate Smith as his mail order fiancée helped the show run a year in the dark days of the Depression. Lahr (in his screen debut) was teamed with Charlotte Greenwood for the movie version but the sparks didn't fly, the film often coming across as forced and unfunny. Worth noting are two early production numbers by Busby Berkeley that foreshadow some of his later (and better) work.

Follow the Fleet see Hit the Deck!

Follow Thru

January 9, 1929 (46th Street Theatre), a musical comedy by B. G. DeSylva, Laurence Schwab. *Score:* Ray Henderson, B. D. DeSylva, Lew Brown. *Cast:* Jack Haley (Jack Martin), Zelma O'Neal (Angie Howard), Irene Delroy (Lora Moore), Eleanor Powell (Molly), Madeline Cameron (Ruth Van Horn), John Barker. *Songs:* Button Up Your Overcoat; My Lucky Star; You Wouldn't Fool Me, Would You?; I Want to Be Bad. *Director:* Edgar MacGregor. *Choreographer:* Bobby Connolly. *Producers*: Laurence Schwab, Frank Mandel. 403 performances.

(Paramount 1930). *Screenplay:* Laurence Schwab, Lloyd Corrigan. *Score:* Ray Henderson, B. G. DeSylva, Lew Brown, etc. *Cast:* Nancy Carroll (Lora Moore), Jack Haley (Jack Martin), Charles "Buddy" Rogers (Jerry Downes), Zelma O'Neal (Angie Howard), Eugene Pallette, Thelma Todd. *Songs:* Button Up Your Overcoat; It Must Be You; A Peach of a Pair; I Want to Be Bad; Then I'll Have Time for You. *Directors:* Laurence Schwab, Lloyd Corrigan. *Producers:* Laurence Schwab, Frank Mandel.

A professional golf championship was the setting for this musical comedy by De-

Sylva, Brown, and Henderson who had previously musicalized football in *Good News!* (qv) and boxing in *Hold Everything* (qv). While two rival lady golfers fight over the same man, Jack Haley became a Broadway comic star as a girl-shy millionaire. The delightful score included the standard "Button Up Your Overcoat." Both the song and Haley (in his screen debut) were used in the movie but the magic wasn't there and the dull musical did not please many, despite the presence of the beloved cinema team of Nancy Carroll and "Buddy" Rogers in the leading roles.

Fool for Love

May 26, 1983 (Circle Repertory Theatre), a play by Sam Shepard. *Cast*: Ed Harris (Eddie), Kathy Whitton Baker (May), Dennis Ludlow (Martin), Will Marchetti. *Director*: Sam Shepard. *Producer*: Circle Repertory Company. 1,000 performances.

(Cannon Group 1985). *Screenplay*: Sam Shepard. *Cast*: Sam Shepard (Eddie), Kim Bassinger (May), Harry Dean Stanton, Randy Quaid, Martha Crawford, Louise Egolf. *Director*: Robert Altman. *Producers*: Yoram Globus, Menahem Golan.

Eddie and his half-sister May are lovers, friends, and enemies as they torment and tease each other in a small motel room on the edge of a desert. Sam Shepard's smallest, most compact play is still full of mystery and ambiguity, as seen in the old man sitting on the porch who may or may not be their father. The drama was very popular Off Broadway and then in regional and college theatres. The 1985 film fleshed out some of the details and added a few characters but the aura of mystery was lost in the efficient but realistic direction by Robert Altman. Shepard wrote the screenplay and played Eddie himself but most agreed that the series of actors to essay the role Off Broadway were more interesting.

A Fool There Was

March 24, 1909 (Liberty Theatre), a play by Porter Emerson Browne. *Cast:* Katherine Kaelred (Woman), Robert Hilliard (Husband), Nannette Comstock (Wife), Emily Wurster (Child), Edna Conroy, William Courtleigh, Howard Hull. *Director:* George Marion. *Producer:* Frederick Thompson. 93 performances.

(Fox 1915). *Screenplay*: Roy L. McCardell. *Cast*: Theda Bara (Vamp), Edward José (John Schuyler), Mabel Frenyear (Mrs. Schuyler), Runa Hodges (Child), May Allison, Clifford Bruce, Frank Powell. *Director*: Frank Powell. *Producer*: William Fox.

(Fox 1922). *Screenplay*: Bernard McConville. *Cast*: Estelle Taylor (Gilda Fontaine), Lewis Stone (Mr. Schuyler), Irene Rich (Mrs. Schuyler), Muriel Dana (Muriel Schuyler), Marjorie Daw, Mahlon Hamilton, Wallace MacDonald. *Director*: Emmett J. Flynn.

A lurid melodrama that titillated theatregoers in New York and on the road became a film that was a sensation and introduced the word "vamp" into the popular language of the day. A Wall Streeter, who has been named a diplomat, travels across the Atlantic with his family and on the ocean liner meets the alluring *femme fatale* only identified as the Woman. She so totally conquers the husband that soon he forsakes his family, loses his job, and ends up dying of a heart attack at her feet. While the critics scoffed, Broadway audiences were drawn to the play and it was even more popular on tour. Although the melodrama took the form of a morality tale, the Woman came across as more appealing than cautionary. Her most famous line, often repeated by others later, was "Kiss me, my fool." The first silent screen version introduced Theda Bara to moviegoers. The Woman was now labeled the Vamp (the story was suggested by Kipling's poem "The Vampire") and both Bara and the name stuck. The film was a major hit but when it was remade in 1922 with Estelle Taylor as the seductress it caused few ripples. Although *A Fool There Was* was never filmed as a talkie, the vampire-like Woman and the situation were repeated later in countless "bad girl" pictures.

Forsaking All Others

March 1, 1933 (Times Square Theatre), a comedy by Edward Roberts, Frank Cavett. *Cast*: Tallulah Bankhead (Mary Clay), Anderson Lawlor (Dillon Todd), Millicent Hanley (Constance Barnes),

Fred Keating (Jefferson Tingle), Cora Witherspoon, Ilka Chase, Harlan Briggs, Barbara O'Neil, Donald MacDonald. *Director*: Thomas Mitchell. *Producer:* Arch Selwyn. 110 performances.

(MGM 1934). *Screenplay*: Edward Barry Roberts, Joseph L. Mankiewicz. *Cast*: Robert Montgomery (Dillon Todd), Joan Crawford (Mary Clay), Clark Gable (Jeff Williams), Charles Butterworth (Shempy), Billie Burke (Aunt Paula), Frances Drake, Rosalind Russell. *Director*: W. S. Van Dyke. *Producer*: Bernard H. Hyman.

When Mary Clay is left standing at the altar while her fiancé Dillon Todd runs off with another woman, she vows revenge. She later meets Dillon and his wife at a speakeasy and, in a verbal battle of wits, reduces the wife to tears. Soon Dillon is off to Mexico for a divorce and he proposes again to Mary. She accepts but on the wedding day she leaves him at the altar and weds an old flame of hers. The ridiculous story was enlivened by some facetious dialogue and a roguish performance by Tallulah Bankhead as Mary. The role made her a Broadway star after years of little notice in New York and some success in London. The contrived plot was pretty much dismissed and replaced by a romantic triangle in the 1934 movie which starred Joan Crawford, Clark Gable, and Robert Montgomery. The performances throughout are engaging (Charles Butterworth is particularly amusing) but the material is not what they deserve.

Forty Carats

December 26, 1968 (Morosco Theatre), a comedy by Jay Presson Allen. *Cast*: Julie Harris (Ann Stanley), Marco St. John (Peter Latham), Nancy Marchand (Mrs. Latham), Polly Rowles (Mrs. Margolin), Murray Hamilton (Billy Boylan), Glenda Farrell, Gretchen Corbett, John Cecil Holm. *Director*: Abe Burrows. *Producer:* David Merrick. 780 performances.

(Columbia 1973). *Screenplay*: Leonard Gershe. *Cast*: Liv Ullmann (Ann Stanley), Edward Albert (Peter Latham), Binnie Barnes (Maud Ericson), Gene Kelly (Billy Boylan), Nancy Walker (Mrs. Margolin), Deborah Raffin, Billy Green Bush, Don Porter, Rosemary Murphy. *Director*: Milton Katselas. *Producer*: M. J. Frankovich.

A French comedy by Pierre Barillet and Jean-Pierre Gredy, who had penned the popular *Cactus Flower* (qv), was Americanized by Jay Presson Allen into a Broadway hit that gave Julie Harris a chance to shine, even if her vehicle was far from polished. Forty-year-old Ann Stanley falls in love with her daughter Trina's twenty-two-year old date Peter Latham just as Trina is attracted to Ann's middle-aged beau Eddy. Ann's ex-husband Billy finds both romances very upsetting but Ann's worldly-wise mother knows better and gives both couples her blessing. Although the characters were only types and the dialogue was forced, Harris and her highly competent co-performers were able to gloss over the comedy's many weaknesses. Yet the miscast players in the 1973 movie were not able to hide anything and the questionable play became a dreary and endless film uncomedy. For a play that ran for years on Broadway, revivals have been scarce and it and the movie are pretty much forgotten now.

The Fourposter

October 24, 1951 (Ethel Barrymore Theatre), a play by Jan de Hartog. *Cast*: Jessica Tandy (Agnes), Hume Cronyn (Michael). *Director*: José Ferrer. *Producer:* Playwrights' Company. 632 performances. Tony Award.

(Columbia 1952). *Screenplay*: Allan Scott, Jan de Hartog. *Cast*: Rex Harrison (John Edwards), Lilli Palmer (Abby Edwards). *Directors*: John Hubley, Irving Reis. *Producer*: Stanley Kramer.

Thirty-five years of a marriage are surveyed in a series of scenes set in Michael and Agnes's bedroom with its big fourposter bed. Like any marriage, it is filled with joy, regret, fear, resignation, and contentment, and the universal quality of the play made it a hit in American and several other countries as well. One of the reasons for its success was the remarkable rapport between actors Hume Cronyn and Jessica Tandy (who were married in real life). Rex Harrison and Lilli Palmer (who were also married at the time) starred in the 1952 screen version and they were also quite charming as the couple (now called John and Abby), but the film seems restricted in its small space and the animated sequences that were used to bridge the various scenes struck some as clever, others as irritating. There was a television miniseries based on the play in 1959 in Argentina and a 1964 Australian television version featured Alistair Duncan and Anne Haddy as the couple. The play was also turned into the successful Broadway musical *I Do! I Do!* (1966) starring Robert Preston and Mary Martin.

Foxfire

November 11, 1982 (Ethel Barrymore Theatre), a play by Hume Cronyn, Susan Cooper. *Cast*: Jessica Tandy (Annie Nations), Hume Cronyn (Hector), Keith Carradine (Dillard), Trey Wilson (Prince Carpenter), Katherine Corteze (Holly Burrell), James Greene. *Director*: David Trainer. *Producers*: Robert Lussier, etc. 213 performances.

(TV 1987). *Teleplay*: Susan Cooper. *Cast*: Jessica Tandy (Annie Nations), Hume Cronyn (Hector Nations), John Denver (Dillard), Gary Grubbs (Prince), Harriet Hall (Holly). *Director*: Jud Taylor. *Producer*: Dorothea G. Petrie.

The old Appalachian mountain woman Annie Nations refuses to sell the land her ramshackle cabin sits on because her dead husband Hector often appears to her there and she doesn't want to desert him. Her son Dillard, a popular hillbilly singer, visits Annie and that brings on a series of memories of the past, some pleasant, others not so. In the end Annie decides to let her dead husband lie in peace and she goes off with Dillard to help him with his troubled marriage. While most critics thought the script was more a collection of potent acting scenes than a play, the performances were so proficient that they recommended the production wholeheartedly. Jessica Tandy won a Tony for her tough, vulnerable Annie and she was given strong support by Hume Cronyn as Hector and Keith Carradine as Dillard. A 1987 television version gave Tandy and Cronyn the chance to reprise their stage performances and they were both extraordinary, though the script still disappointed.

Frankie and Johnny see Frankie and Johnny in the Claire de Lune

Frankie and Johnny in the Claire de Lune

October 14, 1987 (Westside Arts Theatre), a play by Terrence McNally. *Cast*: Kathy Bates (Frankie), Kenneth Welsh (Johnny). *Director*: Paul Benedict. *Producers*: Steven Baruch, etc. 533 performances.

Frankie and Johnny (Paramount 1991). *Screenplay*: Terrence McNally. *Cast*: Al Pacino (Johnny), Michelle Pfeiffer (Frankie), Hector Elizondo, Nathan Lane, Kate Nelligan. *Director-producer*: Garry Marshall.

The guarded waitress Frankie and the open, talkative short-order cook Johnny who works with her decide to go on a date and end up making love in her apartment. She is fearful of getting deeply involved but he wants more than a one-night stand. Throughout the night they argue, joke, and open up to each other, ending up in each other's arms watching television. This honest, unsentimental look at two unlikely lovers was one of playwright Terrence McNally's biggest hits and Kathy Bates and Kenneth Welsh were brutally and unflatteringly sincere in their portrayals. The two-actor piece was revived in many regional theatres and a film was made in 1991. Al Pacino managed to be slovenly attractive and likable as Johnny but the ravishing Michelle Pfeiffer could not help but look like a movie star despite all her efforts to appear like an unwanted drudge. Yet the two stars play off each other well and they make the talky, static movie work much of the time.

The Front Page

August 14, 1928 (Times Square Theatre), a comedy by Ben Hecht, Charles MacArthur. *Cast*: Lee Tracy (Hildy Johnson), Osgood Perkins (Walter Burns), George Leach (Earl Williams), Dorothy Stickney (Molly Malloy), Walter Baldwin, George Barbier, Carrie Weller, Claude Cooper,

Frances Fuller. *Director*: George S. Kaufman. *Producer:* Jed Harris. 276 performances.

(Howard Hughes 1931). *Screenplay*: Bartlett Cormack, Charles Lederer. *Cast*: Adolphe Menjou (Walter Burns), Pat O'Brien (Hildy Johnson), Mary Brian (Peggy Grant), George E. Stone (Earl Williams), Mae Clark (Molly Malloy), Edward Everett Horton, Slim Summerville, Walter Catlett, Frank McHugh, Matt Moore. *Director*: Lewis Milestone. *Producers*: Howard Hughes, Lewis Milestone.

His Girl Friday (Columbia 1940). *Screenplay*: Charles Lederer. *Cast*: Cary Grant (Walter Burns), Rosalind Russell (Hildy Johnson), Ralph Bellamy (Bruce Baldwin), Helen Mack (Molly Mally), John Qualen (Earl Williams), Ernest Truex, Gene Lockhart, Clarence Kolb, Porter Hall, Roscoe Karnes, Frank Jenks. *Director-producer*: Howard Hawks.

The Front Page (Universal 1974). *Screenplay*: Billy Wilder, I. A. L. Diamond. *Cast*: Walter Matthau (Walter Burns), Jack Lemmon (Hildy Johnson), Susan Sarandon (Peggy), Austin Pendleton (Earl Williams), Carol Burnett (Molly Malloy), David Wayne, Vincent Gardenia, Charles Durning, Allen Garfield, Herb Edelmann. *Director*: Billy Wilder. *Producer*: Paul Monash.

Arguably the best play ever written about the newspaper profession, this fast-paced, raucous comedy-drama has remained an audience favorite for over seventy years on stage and screen. Reporter Hildy Johnson want to quit his paper and his overbearing boss, Walter Burns, and get married but when the convicted murderer Earl Williams escapes from jail and is holed up somewhere in the Chicago Criminal Courts building, Hildy can't resist a good story and pursues it. Hildy even manages to find the gentle, unassuming Earl and hides him in a rolltop desk in the newsroom until Burns arrives. The two newsmen uncover some juicy information on the corrupt chief of police and the warden and hold them off until the governor pardons Earl. Still determined to quit journalism, Hildy goes off to get married but Burns is just as determined to keep Hildy. He presents him with a gold watch then calls the police to report that "the son of a bitch stole my watch!" As well as many revivals on Broadway and across the country, the play has been made into three films. An early talkie in 1931 featured Pat O'Brien and Adolphe Menjou as Hildy and Burns and it is a merry romp with a masterful cast and razor sharp direction. With very little rewriting the story was remade as *His Girl Friday* in 1940 with Cary Grant as Burns and Rosalind Russell as Hildy. Director Howard Hawks paced the comedy like a chase and the lines fly faster than bullets. Again the whole cast is superb and the effect it that of an inspired free-for-all. Much less satisfying was the 1974 remake (again called *The Front Page*) which boasted a fine cast but somehow lacked the urgency and vitality of the earlier versions. Jack Lemmon and Walter Matthau are ideal as Hildy and Burns but their familiarity seems too obvious and they don't do anything we haven't seen them do better in earlier movies together.

The Fugitive Kind see *Orpheus Descending*

Funny Face

November 22 1927 (Alvin Theatre), a musical comedy by Paul Gerard Smith, Fred Thompson. *Score:* George and Ira Gershwin. *Cast:* Adele Astaire (Frankie), Fred Astaire (Jimmy Reeve), Victor Moore (Herbert), William Kent (Dugsie Gibbs), Allen Kearns (Peter Thurston), Betty Compton, Dorothy Jordan. *Songs:* Funny Face; 'S Wonderful; He Loves and She Loves; High Hat; My One and Only; The Babbitt and the Bromide; Let's Kiss and Make Up. *Director:* Edgar MacGregor. *Choreographer:* Bobby Connolly. *Producers*: Alex A. Aarons, Vinton Freedley. 244 performances.

(Paramount 1957). *Screenplay:* Leonard Gershe. *Score:* George and Ira Gershwin, Roger Edens. *Cast:* Fred Astaire (Dick Avery), Audrey Hepburn (Jo Stockton), Kay Thompson (Maggie Prescott), Michel Auclair, Robert Flemyng, Virginia Gibson. *Songs:* Funny Face; 'S Wonderful; How Long Has This Been Going On?; He Loves and She Loves; Think Pink; Bonjour, Paris!; Clap Yo' Hands; On How to Be Lovely; Let's Kiss and Make Up. *Director:* Stanley Donen. *Choreographers:* Eugene Loring, Fred Astaire. *Producer:* Roger Edens.

A delectable Gershwin brothers's score

and star turns by Adele and Fred Astaire made this Broadway musical a hit despite a hackneyed plot that was cliché-ridden even in its day. Fred played the guardian of three young ladies, including Adele who gets her aviator sweetheart to steal her diary from a safe even as two bumbling crooks are after jewels in the same safe. A terrific supporting cast and expert production numbers did justice to the score. Hollywood didn't get around to filming the show until thirty years later and when they did the entire plot and all the characters were (wisely) tossed away. They did keep Fred Astaire who played a fashion photographer who picks up the intellectual beauty Audrey Hepburn in a Greenwich Village book shop, whisks her off to Paris to make her an internationally famous model, and the two eventually fall in love. The movie is superior in most areas: engaging performances (including a delicious portrayal of a magazine editor by Kay Thompson), lovely Paris locations beautifully photographed, a wry, satirical script, and a memorable score made up of Gershwin gems and new numbers.

Funny Girl

March 26, 1964 (Winter Garden Theatre), a musical comedy by Isobel Lennart. *Score:* Jule Styne, Bob Merrill. *Cast:* Barbra Streisand (Fanny Brice), Sydney Chaplin (Nick Arnstein), Kay Medford (Mrs. Brice), Danny Meehan, Jean Stapleton, Buzz Miller, Larry Fuller. *Songs:* People; Don't Rain on My Parade; The Music That Makes Me Dance; I'm the Greatest Star; You Are Woman; His Love Makes Me Beautiful; I Want to Be Seen With You Tonight; Who Are You Now?; Sadie, Sadie. *Directors:* Garson Kanin, Jerome Robbins. *Choreographer:* Carol Haney. *Producer:* Ray Stark. 1,348 performances.

(Columbia/Rastar 1968). *Screenplay:* Isobel Lennart. *Score:* Jule Styne, Bob Merrill, etc. *Cast:* Barbra Streisand (Fanny Brice), Omar Sharif (Nick Arnstein), Kay Medford (Mrs. Brice), Walter Pidgeon, Tommy Rall, Anne Francis, Mae Questral. *Songs:* People; Don't Rain on My Parade; My Man; I'm the Greatest Star; You Are Woman; His Love Makes Me Beautiful; I'd Rather Be Blue Over You; Sadie, Sadie; Funny Girl. *Director:* William Wyler. *Choreographer:* Herbert Ross. *Producer:* Ray Stark.

Although this musical bio was supposedly about the legendary comedienne Fanny Brice, both the play and the film ended up being showcases for Barbra Streisand. The stage version is a traditional rags-to-riches show biz musical with a noteworthy score by Broadway veterans Jules Styne and Bob Merrill. Although other characters besides Brice had their own songs and scenes, most of these were gone when the show was filmed as a vehicle for Streisand and she carried the impressive-looking period musical effortlessly, establishing herself as a full-fledged movie star in her first outing. Yet sometimes the movie resembles one of Streisand's celebrated one-woman television specials because all the other characters (including Omar Sharif's quiet and understated Nick) fail to register. Much of the stage score was dropped on screen and replaced by period songs that the original Brice had actually sung during her long career. William Wyler's direction is unobtrusive and polished and the film captures the era beautifully.

A Funny Thing Happened on the Way to the Forum

May 8, 1962 (Alvin Theatre), a musical comedy by Burt Shevelove, Larry Gelbart. *Score:* Stephen Sondheim. *Cast:* Zero Mostel (Pseudolus), Jack Gilford (Hysterium), Brian Davies (Hero), David Burns (Senex), John Carradine (Lycus), Preshy Marker (Philia), Ronald Holgate (Miles Gloriosus), Ruth Kobart (Domina), Raymond Walburn. *Songs:* Comedy Tonight; Everybody Ought to Have a Maid; Lovely; I'm Calm; Pretty Little Picture; Love I Hear; Free; Bring Me My Bride; Impossible; That'll Show Him. *Director:* George Abbott. *Choreographer:* Jack Cole. *Producer:* Harold Prince. 964 performances. Tony Award.

(United Artists 1966). *Screenplay:* Melvin Frank, Michael Pertwee. *Score:* Stephen Sondheim. *Cast:* Zero Mostel (Pseudolus), Phil Silvers (Lycus), Jack Gilford (Hysterium), Michael Crawford (Hero), Michael Hordern (Senex), Annette Andre, Buster Keaton, Leon Greene. *Songs:* Comedy Tonight; Everybody Ought to Have a Maid; Lovely; Bring Me My Bride. *Director:* Richard Lester. *Choreographers:* Ethel and George Martin. *Producer:* Melvin Frank.

Stephen Sondheim's first Broadway show in which he wrote both music and lyrics, this musical farce set in ancient Rome was based on plays by Plautus but had plenty of vaudeville and all–American show biz in it. Zero Mostel played the slave who seeks his freedom by helping his young master wed the courtesan that he desires. It is a fast-moving, complicated, and delightful plot, one of the musical theatre's most astute and accomplished. Sondheim's score would not be fully appreciated until years later but songs like the opening "Comedy Tonight" and "Everybody Ought to Have a Maid" were showstoppers from the start. Frequently revived by every kind of theatre group, *Forum* fails to grow stale and rarely fails to please. Most of the stage score was dropped for the screen version and more emphasis was put on the story. Mostel and Jack Gilford got to reprise their stage roles and they got expert support by Phil Silvers and other polished comics. It is an enjoyable film comedy but most of the time it hardy seems like a musical.

Futz!

June 13, 1968 (Theatre de Lys), a play by Rochelle Owens. *Cast*: John Bakos (Cyrus Futz), Sally Kirkland (Narrator), Peter Craig, Fred Forrest, Beth Porter, Seth Allen, Mari-Claire Charba, Victor Lipari, Jerry Cunliffe, Marilyn Roberts. *Director*: Tom O'Horgan. *Producer:* Harlan P. Kleiman. 233 performances.

(Cafe La Mama/Guvnor 1969). *Screenplay*: Rochelle Owens, Joseph Stefano. *Cast*: John Bakos (Cyrub Futz), Seth Allen (Oscar Loop), Sally Kirkland (Merry Lee), Frederick Forrest, Jane Holzer, Beth Porter. *Director*: Tom O'Horgan.

One of the most controversial of all plays of the radical 1960s, this dark satire about a farmer who loves (and has sexual relations with) his pig was more a test to see how far one could go in the theatre rather than much of a commentary on anything. The hot young director Tom O'Horgan staged the bizarre piece in his usual bold and theatrical manner. But when he directed the 1969 screen version his sense of showmanship failed him and the result was an odd but ultimately dull movie.

Gay Divorce

November 29, 1932 (Ethel Barrymore Theatre), a musical comedy by Dwight Taylor. *Score:* Cole Porter. *Cast:* Fred Astaire (Guy Holden), Claire Luce (Mimi Pratt), Luella Gear (Hortense), Erik Rhodes (Tonetti), Betty Starbuck, Eric Blore. *Songs:* Night and Day; After You, Who?; I've Got You on My Mind; How's Your Romance?; Mister and Missus Fitch. *Director:* Howard Lindsay. *Choreographers:* Carl Randall, Barbara Newberry. *Producers*: Dwight Deere Wiman, Tom Weatherly. 248 performances.

The Gay Divorcee (RKO 1934). *Screenplay:* George Marion, Jr., Dorothy Yost, Edward Kaufman. *Score:* Cole Porter, Harry Revel, Mack Gordon, etc. *Cast:* Fred Astaire (Guy Holden), Ginger Rogers (Mimi Glossop), Alice Brady (Hortense Ditherwell), Edward Everett Horton (Egbert Fitzgerald), Erik Rhodes (Tonetti), Betty Grable, Eric Blore, Lillian Miles. *Songs:* Night and Day; The Continental; Don't Let It Bother You; Let's K-nock K-nees; A Needle in a Haystack. *Director:* Mark Sandrich. *Choreographers:* Dave Gould, Hermes Pan, Fred Astaire. *Producer:* Pandro S. Berman.

Fred Astaire's last Broadway musical (and his only one without his sister Adele) was a modern and slightly risqué tale about Mimi who hires a professional correspondent and checks into a hotel with him in order to use adultery as grounds for a divorce. Astaire loves Mimi and is more than happy to be mistaken by her as her correspondent. Cole Porter's score is delectable but the show is most remembered for introducing "Night and Day." Hollywood kept Astaire and the song but softened the divorce aspects of the plot. It was the title that most upset the studios. It wasn't the use of the word "gay"—it would not gain a homosexual connotation until decades later. According to the Hays Office, a divorce cannot be a happy thing. But they reasoned that the woman might be cheerful so the movie was titled *The Gay Divorcee*. With Ginger Rogers as Mimi, Astaire and Rogers were starred together for the first time. (They had only played supporting roles previously.) The twosome did justice to "Night and Day" but the highlight of the film turned out to be the dance number "The Continental," the first song to win an Oscar.

The Gay Divorcee see Gay Divorce

The Gazebo

December 12, 1958 (Lyceum Theatre), a play by Alec Coppel. *Cast*: Walter Slezak (Elliott Nash), Jayne Meadows (Nell Nash), Ruth Gillette (Mrs. Chandler), Ralph Chambers, Don Grusso, Edward Andrews, Richard Posten. *Director*: Jerome Chodorov. *Producer:* Playwrights' Company, Frederick Brisson. 218 performances.

(MGM 1959). *Screenplay*: George Wells. *Cast*: Glenn Ford (Elliott Nash), Debbie Reynolds (Nell Nash), Carl Reiner (Harlow Edison), Mabel Albertson (Mrs. Chandler), John Mc-Giver, Doro Merande, Bert Freed, Martin Landau, Zasu Pitts. *Director*: George Marshall. *Producer*: Lawrence Weingarten.

Mystery writer Elliott Nash shoots the man who is supposedly blackmailing his wife and buries the body beneath a gazebo that is under construction in his yard. But when Nash later sells the house and the new owners decide to take the gazebo down, the body is discovered. Luckily for Nash, it turns out his bullet missed the victim and he died of a heart attack. The contrived comic melodrama, based on a short story by Mary Coppel, was presented in a slick, polished manner and appealed to theatregoers and critics. The 1959 movie turned Nash into a television writer and opened up the tale somewhat but the picture lacks a sense a style, not funny enough to be a comedy nor suspenseful enough to be taken seriously. The stars are proficient enough but it is the supporting players that are more fun.

Gemini

May 21, 1977 (Little Theatre), a comedy by Albert Innaurato. *Cast*: Robert Picardo (Francis Geminiani), Danny Aiello (Fran) Geminiani), Jessica James (Bunny Weinberger), Jonathan Hadary, Reed Birney, Carol Potter, Anne DeSalvo. *Director*: Peter Mark Schiffer. *Producers:* Circle Repertory Company, etc. 1,788 performances.

Happy Birthday, Gemini (United Artists 1980). *Screenplay*: Richard Benner. *Cast*: Alan Rosenberg (Francis Geminiani), Robert Viharo (Nick Geminiani), Madeline Kahn (Bunny Weinberger), Rita Moreno, Sarah Holcomb, Timothy Jenkins, David Marshall Grant. *Director*: Richard Benner. *Producers*: Bruce Calnan, Rupert Hitzig.

When two of his WASP friends from college come to visit Francis Geminiani in his Italian neighborhood home in Philadelphia, both social and sexual complications arise. A broad but believable farce, it was peopled with larger-than-life characters, none more so than the vulgar Jewish neighbor Bunny whose moods go from carefree to suicidal in the same breath. The Off Broadway comedy was so well received by the critics that it moved to a small Broadway house where it stayed for four years. But what was so fiery on stage came across as merely loud and overacted in the 1980 movie. Madeline Kahn does get her laughs as Bunny but much of the cast irritates rather than entertains.

Generation

October 6, 1965 (Morosco Theatre), a comedy by William Goodhart. *Cast*: Henry Fonda (Jim Bolton), Holly Turner (Doris Owen), Richard Jordan (Walter Owen), A. Larry Haines, Don Fellows, Sandy Baron. *Director*: Gene Saks. *Producer:* Frederick Brisson. 299 performances.

(AVCO Embassy 1969). *Screenplay*: William Goodhart. *Cast*: David Janssen (Jim Bolton), Kim Darby (Doris Owen), Peter Duel (Walter Owen), Carl Reiner, Andrew Prine, James Coco, Sam Waterston. *Director*: George Schaefer. *Producer*: Frederick Brisson.

A rather tame comedy about the generation gap, this forgettable play opened during a newspaper strike in New York so playgoers didn't know anything about it than the fact that Henry Fonda was in it so they went. Fonda played an ad executive who visits his newly-wedded daughter in the big city and finds her nine months pregnant and living with an anti-establishment hippie who wants to deliver the baby himself. After a lot of insults tossed back and forth between father-in-law and son-in-law, the daughter goes into a difficult labor and when a doctor is called in to help deliver the baby successfully everyone seems contented for the moment. With a lackluster cast, the 1969 film has little to recommend. It is faithful to the play yet seems more like an unsuccessful sit-com than a real movie.

Gentlemen Prefer Blondes

September 28, 1926 (Times Square Theatre), a comedy by Anita Loos, John Emerson. *Cast*: June Walker (Lorelei Lee), Edna Hibbard (Dorothy Shaw), Arthur S. Ross (Gus Eisman), Frank Morgan (Henry Spofford), G. P. Huntley (Sir Francis Beekman), Grace Hampton, Georges Romain, Adrian Rosley, Will T. Hayes. *Director-producer:* Edgar Selwyn. 199 performances.

(Paramount-Lasky 1928). *Screenplay*: Anita Loos, John Emerson. *Cast*: Ruth Taylor (Lorelei Lee), Alice White (Dorothy Shaw), Ford Sterling (Gus Eisman), Holmes Herbert (Henry Spofford), Mark Swain (Sir Francis Beekman), Emily Fitzroy, Trixie Friganza. *Director*: Malcolm St. Clair. *Producer*: Jesse L. Lasky.

December 8, 1949 (Ziegfeld Theatre), a musical comedy by Joseph Stein, Anita Loos. *Score:* Jule Styne, Leo Robin. *Cast:* Carol Channing (Lorelei Lee), Yvonne Adair (Dorothy Shaw), Jack McCauley (Gus Esmond), Eric Brotherson (Henry Spofford), Rex Evans (Sir Francis Beekman), Alice Pearce, Anita Alverez, George S. Irving. *Songs:* Diamonds Are a Girl's Best Friend; A Little Girl From Little Rock; Bye Bye Baby; Just a Kiss Apart; It's Delightful Down in Chile. *Director:* John C. Wilson. *Choreographer:* Agnes de Mille. *Producers*: Herman Levin, Oliver Smith. 740 performances.

(Fox 1953). *Screenplay:* Charles Lederer. *Score:* Jule Styne, Leo Robin, Hoagy Carmichael, Harold Adamson. *Cast:* Marilyn Monroe (Lorelei Lee), Jane Russell (Dorothy Shaw), Charles Coburn (Sir Francis Beekman), Elliot Reed (Enrie Malone), Tommy Noonan (Gus Esmond), Taylor Holmes. *Songs:* Diamonds Are a Girl's Best Friend; A Little Girl From Little Rock; Ain't There Anyone Here for Love?; Bye Bye Baby; When Love Goes Wrong. *Director:* Howard Hawks. *Choreographer:* Jack Cole. *Producer*: Sol C. Siegel.

Anita Loos's classic comic novel introduced Americans to the wily, funny gold digger Lorelei Lee and she has been making readers and audiences laugh ever since. Loos and John Emerson turned the episodic book into a popular play, concentrating on Lorelei's adventures in Europe with her friend Dorothy. This was turned into a 1928 silent film that failed to please since most of Lorelei's humor was verbal. The 1949 Broadway musical kept the title and much of the plot and added a zesty score by Jule Styne and Leo Robin. The show made Carol Channing a stage star and for the rest of her career there was always a little bit of Lorelei in everything she did. When the musical was filmed in 1953, most of the stage score was dropped and some new numbers were added. While the story remained basically the same, the tale was no longer set in the Roaring Twenties and Marilyn Monroe's Lorelei was more a funny, sexy nightclub singer rather than an ingenious flapper. But the movie musical is immensely entertaining all the same and the humor of the original is still there in spots. Broadway saw a revamped musical version of the story in 1974 called *Lorelei* and again it starred Carol Channing, too old for the character but dazzling all the same. A 1998 television production of the original play featured Barbara Eden as Lorelei and Rita McKenzie as Dorothy.

George Washington Slept Here

October 18, 1940 (Lyceum Theatre), a comedy by George S. Kaufman, Moss Hart. *Cast*: Ernest Truex (Newton Fuller), Jean Dixon (Annabella Fuller), Dudley Digges (Uncle Stanley), Percy Kilbride (Mr. Kimber), Peggy French, Mabel Taliaferro, Ruth Weston, Edward Elliott. *Director*: George S. Kaufman. *Producer:* Sam H. Harris. 173 performances.

(Warner 1942). *Screenplay*: Everett Freeman. *Cast*: Jack Benny (Bill Fuller), Ann Sheridan (Connie Fuller), Charles Coburn (Uncle Stanley), Percy Kilbride (Mr. Kimber), Hattie McDaniel, William Tracy, Joyce Reynolds, Lee Patrick. *Director*: William Keighley. *Producer*: Jerry Wald.

Newton Fuller buys a dilapidated old farm house that claims to have hosted General Washington and he plans to restore it to live in. Other members of the family are less enthused and as problems arise, ranging from a dry well to a prolonged stay by their obnoxious rich uncle, it looks like the whole venture will be a disaster. To add insult to injury, Newton finds out that the uncle is broke and that it was Benedict Arnold, not Washington, who slept in the house. Yet the crafty uncle figures out a way to end the family's squabbling and it looks like a happy ending in the ramshackle homestead. The last of the Kaufman and Hart collaborations, it suffered in comparison to their earlier hits but was entertaining all the same. The Broadway run was modest but the comedy was long a favorite in community theatres. The 1942 screen version was tailored to the talents of radio star Jack Benny but the material did not always fit in with his public persona. In the film it is wife Ann Sheridan who buys the run-down house so most of the comic barbs about its hideous condition are uttered by Benny and the playful antagonism between father and family is gone. A bright spot in the movie is Percy Kilbride as a fatalistic hick contractor, a role he had created in the Broadway production.

Get-Rich-Quick Wallingford

September 19, 1910 (Gaiety Theatre), a comedy by George M. Cohan. *Cast*: Hale Hamilton (J. Rufus Wallingford), Edward Ellis (Blackie Daws), Frances Ring (Fannie Jasper), Grant Mitchell (Edward Lamb), Spencer Charters (Tom Donahue), Purnell Pratt, Frederick Maynard, Ida Lee Caston. *Directors*: George M. Cohan, Sam Forrest. *Producer*: Cohan & Harris. 424 performances.

(Cosmopolitan 1921). *Screenplay*: Luther Reed. *Cast*: Sam Hardy (J. Rufus Wallingford), Norman Kerry (Blackie Daws), Doris Kenyon (Fannie Jasper), Diana Allen (Gertrude Dempsey), Edgar Nelson, Billie Dove, Mac Barnes. *Director*: Frank Borzage.

The New Adventures of Get-Rich-Quick Wallingford (MGM 1931). *Screenplay:* Charles MacArthur. *Cast:* William Haines (Jimmy Wallingford), Jimmy Durante (Clarence Schnozzle), Ernest Torrence (Blackie), Leila Hyams (Dorothy Layton), Guy Kibbe, Hale Hamilton, Clara Blandick. *Director:* Sam Wood.

Con-man J. Rufus Wallingford and his partner Blackie go from town to town cooking up phony business schemes that the local boobs invest in before the two rascals sneak away. But when Rufus sets up a business making carpet tacks in one burg, it is a surprising success. Getting rich legitimately, he decides to marry the sweet Fannie Jasper and settle down. Based on a series of magazine stories by George Randolph Chester, the comedy was written and staged by George M. Cohan and it became his first non-musical hit. Three silent film versions were made: a short in 1915 with Burr McIntosh as Wallingford, in 1916 with Fred Niblo, and in 1921 with Sam Hardy. A 1931 talkie was titled *The New Adventures of Get-Rich-Quick Wallingford* and William Haines was Rufus. All were popular with moviegoers and Wallingford-like con-men would pop up in later plays and films, most memorably *The Music Man* (qv).

Getting Gertie's Garter

August 1, 1921 (Republic Theatre), a farce by Wilson Collison, Avery Hopwood. *Cast*: Hazel Dawn (Gertie), Donald MacDonald (Ken Waldrick), Louis Kimball (Teddy Darling), Dorothy Mackaye (Pattie Walrick), Eleanor Dawn, Ivan Miller. *Director*: Bertram Harrison. *Producer*: A. H. Woods. 120 performances.

(Metropolitan 1927). *Screenplay*: Tay Garnett, McGrew Willis. *Cast*: Marie Prevost (Gertie Darling), Charles Ray (Ken Walrick), Sally Rand (Teddy Darling), Harry Myers, William Orlamond, Fritzi Ridgeway, Franklin Pangborn. *Director*: E. Mason Hopper.

(United Artists 1945). *Screenplay*: Allan Dwan, Karen de Wilf. *Cast*: Marie McDonald (Gertie), Dennis O'Keefe (Ken), Binnie Barnes (Barbara), Barry Sullivan (Ted), J. Carrol Naish. *Director*: Allan Dwan. *Producer*: Edward Small.

Long before Gertie married Teddy Darling she was given a garter with her picture on it from her boy friend Ken Walrick. Now that Ken has married she thinks it best to return the garter before Teddy sees it but doing so leads to all sorts of comic complications. A slight but animated farce, it was a hit in New York and on the road before becoming a favorite in little theatres across the country. Being very physical, the play was ideal for the silents and the 1927 version with Marie Prevost as Gertie was popular. The 1945 remake is also enjoyable with its tight direction and spirited cast.

Getting Out

October 19, 1978 (Marymount Manhattan Theatre), a drama by Marsha Norman. *Cast*: Susan Kingsley (Arlene), Pamela Reed (Arlie), Leo Burmester (Carl), Joan Pape (Ruby), Madeleine Thornton-Sherwood (Mother), Barry Corbin, Kevin Bacon. *Director*: Jon Jory. *Producer:* Phoenix Theatre. 259 performances.

(TV 1994). *Teleplay*: Eugene Corr, Ruth Shapiro. *Cast*: Rebecca De Mornay (Arlene Holsclaw), Amy Dott (Young Arlie), Robert Knepper (Carl), Carole Mitchell-Leon (Ruby), Ellen Burstyn (Mother), Richard Jenkins, Tandy Cronyn, Norm Skaggs. *Director*: John Korty. *Producer*: Dorothea G. Petrie.

When Arlene is released from prison, she is determined to lead a better life but she is haunted by the memory of her vicious teenage self Arlie. Her mother, her former pimp, her jailer who has taken an interest in her, and a helpful neighbor all converge on her life, but eventually Arlene learns how to take care of herself and live with her demons. This powerful, sordid, uncompromising drama was first mounted at the Actors Theatre of Louisville then brought to New York where it enjoyed critical acclaim and a successful run Off Broadway. A television version was made sixteen years later as a vehicle for Rebecca De Mornay as Arlene and Ellen Burstyn as her mother. The teleplay opened up the action somewhat and did a little updating of the play but it proved to be as intense and disturbing as the stage work was in the 1970s.

The Gin Game

October 6, 1977 (John Golden Theatre), a play by D. L. Coburn. *Cast*: Hume Cronyn (Martin Weller), Jessica Tandy (Fonsia Dorsey). *Director*: Mike Nichols. *Producer:* Shuberts. 517 performances. Pulitzer Prize.

(TV 1981). *Teleplay*: D. L. Coburn. *Cast*: *Cast*: Hume Cronyn (Martin Weller), Jessica Tandy (Fonsia Dorsey). *Director*: Mike Nichols. *Producer:* Terry Hughes.

(TV 2003). *Teleplay*: D. L. Coburn. *Cast*: Dick Van Dyke (Weller Martin), Mary Tyler Moore (Fonsia Dorsey). *Director*: Arvin Brown. *Producers*: Monica Levinson, Ellen Krass.

As two residents of a home for the aged play a series of gin rummy games, they reveal their best and worst sides without really changing much because of it. Martin is a cranky, failed businessman while Fonsia is a more optimistic, controlled person. Although she is new to the game, she keeps winning, which only makes Martin more furious at her and the world. Slight to the point of being a non-play, the two-actor piece is a showcase for performers and the team of Cronyn and Tandy were never less than riveting. The couple performed the play for its long run on Broadway, for several months on the road, and in the 1981 television production. Other stars in other companies also shone in the little comedy-drama, most memorably Julie Harris and Charles Durning. A 2003 television version reunited Dick Van Dyke and Mary Tyler Moore and, though they often seemed like older variations of the sit-com characters that everybody loved, there was an unmistakable chemistry still there.

The Gingerbread Lady

December 13, 1970 (Plymouth Theatre), a play by Neil Simon. *Cast*: Maureen Stapleton (Evy Meara), Michael Lombard (Jimmy Perry), Betsy Von Furstenburg (Toby Landau), Ayn Ruymen (Polly Meara), Charlie Siebert (Lou Tanner). *Director*: Robert Moore. *Producer:* Saint Subber. 193 performances.

Only When I Laugh (Columbia 1981). *Screenplay*: Neil Simon. *Cast*: Marsha Mason (Georgia), Kristy McNichol (Polly), James Coco (Jimmy), Joan Hackett (Toby), Ed Moore, John Vargas. *Director*: Glenn Jordan. *Producers*: Roger M. Rothstein, Neil Simon.

Neil Simon's comedy-drama, about the recovering alcoholic singer Evy Meara trying to establish new relationships with her teenage daughter and two of her friends, was more serious than the playwright's fans wanted and, despite a penetrating performance by Maureen Stapleton as Evy, the play had a modest Broadway run. But there is much to admire in the writing and with such a sarcastic, knowing central character as Evy to write for, Simon creates wonderfully funny and disturbing dialogue. Marsha Mason makes valiant efforts in the 1981 film, now called *Only When I Laugh*, but she does not convince as the mother, now called Georgia and an actress rather than a singer. What is worth watching are the fine performances of James Coco as the middle-aged, out-of-work actor Jimmy and Joan Hackett as the frustrated society icon Toby.

Girl Crazy

October 14, 1930 (Alvin Theatre), a musical comedy by Guy Bolton, John McGowan. *Score:* George and Ira Gershwin. *Cast:* Allen Kearns (Danny Churchill), Willie Howard (Gieber Goldfarb), Ginger Rogers (Molly Gray), Ethel Merman (Kate Fothergill), William Kent. Lew Parker. *Songs:* I Got Rhythm; Embraceable You; I'm Bidin' My Time; But Not for Me; Could You Use Me?; Sam and Delilah. *Director:* Alexander Leftwich. *Choreographer:* George Hale. *Producers:* Alex A. Aarons, Vinton Freedley. 272 performances.

(RKO 1932). *Screenplay:* Herman Mankiewicz. *Score:* George and Ira Gershwin. *Cast:* Bert Wheeler (Jimmy Deagan), Robert Woolsey (Slick Foster), Mitzi Green (Tessie), Eddie Quillan, Stanley Fields, Dorothy Lee, Kitty Kelly. *Songs:* I Got Rhythm; Embraceable You; But Not for Me; Could You Use Me?; Sam and Delilah. *Director:* William A. Seiter. *Choreographer:* Busby Berkeley. *Producer:* William LeBaron.

(MGM 1943). *Screenplay:* Fred Finklehoffe. *Score:* George and Ira Gershwin. *Cast:* Mickey Rooney (Danny Churchill), Judy Garland (Ginger Gray), Rags Ragland, Robert Strickland, Tommy Dorsey, Gil Stratton, June Allyson, Nancy Walker. *Songs:* I Got Rhythm; Embraceable You; I'm Bidin' My Time; But Not for Me; Fascinating Rhythm; Could You Use Me?; You've Got What Gets Me. *Directors:* Norman Taurog, Busby Berkeley. *Choreographers:* Charles Walters, Busby Berkeley. *Producer:* Arthur Freed.

When the Boys Meet the Girls (MGM 1965). *Screenplay:* Robert E. Kent. *Score:* George and Ira Gershwin, etc. *Cast:* Harve Presnell (Danny Churchill), Connie Francis (Ginger Gray), Sue Anne Langdon (Tess Rawley), Fred Clark, Frank Faylen, Joby Baker, Louis Armstrong, Liberace.

Songs: I Got Rhythm; Embraceable You; I'm Bidin' My Time, But Not for Me; Treat Me Rough; When the Boys Meet the Girls; Mail Call; Listen People. *Director:* Alvin Ganzer. *Choreographer:* Earl Barton. *Producer:* Sam Katzman.

A Gershwin show loaded with hit songs, this musical comedy told the farcical tale of playboy New Yorker Danny Churchill who is sent to a small Arizona town by his father to manage a theatre and keep him away from predatory females. But Danny falls for the local postmistress, his cab driver from Manhattan stays to become sheriff, and the whole town is soon swinging to Ethel Merman singing "I Got Rhythm." It was her Broadway debut and she was a smash, as was the whole show. The musical was filmed three times and later rewritten into the new-old Broadway hit *Crazy for You* (1992). The first screen version fiddled with the plot (the hero attends college in Arizona), cut some of the score, and was turned into a vehicle for the comedy team of Bert Wheeler and Robert Woolsey. The 1943 film became a vehicle for Mickey Rooney and Judy Garland and, as such, it was highly entertaining. Most of the Gershwin score was reinstated, as was more of the original plot (though the college setting was kept). The cast and the musical numbers are outstanding, making it one of the best in the Rooney-Garland series. Retitled *When the Girls Meet the Boys*, the 1965 remake was a misguided musical that mixed pop songs with five of the Gershwin standards. The new (and feeble) plot revolved around a dude ranch for divorcées and the mostly lackluster cast was unable to breathe any life into the new-old material.

Girl of the Golden West

November 14, 1905 (Belasco Theatre), a play by David Belasco. *Cast:* Blanche Bates (Minnie Falconer), Robert Hilliard (Dick Johnson), Frank Keenan (Jack Rance), Thomas J. McGrane, Clifford Hipple, John W. Cope, Fred Maxwell, J. H. Benrimo, Harriet Sterling. *Director-producer:* David Belasco. 224 performances.

(Lasky Feature Play Co. 1915). *Screenplay:* Cecil

B. DeMille. *Cast*: Mabel Van Buren (Minnie), Theodore Roberts (Jack Rance), House Peters (Ramerrez), Anita King, Sydney Deane, William Elmer. *Director-producer*: Cecil B. DeMille.

(First National 1923). *Screenplay*: Adelaide Heilbron. *Cast*: Sylvia Breamer (Minnie), Russell Simpson (Jack Rance), J. Warren Kerrigan (Ramerrez), Rosemary Theby, Wilfred Lucas, Nelson McDowell. *Director*: Edwin Carewe.

(Warner 1930). *Screenplay*: Waldemar Young. *Cast*: Ann Harding (Minnie), James Rennie (Dick Johnson), Harry Bannister (Jack Rance), Ben Hendricks, Jr., J. Farrell MacDonald. *Director*: John Francis Dillon. *Producer*: Robert North.

(MGM 1938). *Screenplay*: Isobel Dawn, Boyce DeGaw. *Score:* Sigmund Romberg, Gus Kahn. *Cast*: Jeanette MacDonald (Mary Robbins), Nelson Eddy (Ramirez), Walter Pidgeon (Jack Rance), Leo Carrillo (Mosquito), Buddy Ebsen, Olin Howland. *Songs*: The Mariache; Sun-Up to Sun-Down; Shadows on the Moon; The West Ain't Wild Anymore. *Director*: Robert Z. Leonard. *Producer*: William Anthony McGuire.

One of the most thrilling of all of David Belasco's theatrical pieces, this melodrama set in a California mining camp centered on the tough-talking, warm-hearted Minnie who is courted by the sheriff but is in love with the bandit Dick Johnson. In one of the play's most remembered scenes, she hides the wounded Dick in the loft of her cabin while the sheriff and her play a game of poker beneath him. Drops of Dick's blood fall onto the table as Minnie fervently tries to win her sweetheart's freedom. In the end, Minnie and Dick quit the camp and head for new pastures together. Director-producer Belasco devised the naturalistic sets and scenic effects (including a blizzard that shakes the cabin) and they were stunning to behold. Also adding to the Broadway hit was Blanche Bates's zestful performance as Minnie. Two successful silent films, in 1915 and 1923, were made of the play, as well as two talkies. The 1930 movie featured Ann Harding as Minnie and it resembles a standard Western with all the action scenes well presented. A 1938 remake was a musical vehicle for the popular singing team of Jeanette MacDonald and Nelson Eddy and it was one of their less successful efforts. MacDonald is hard to believe as the tom-boyish Minnie

(now called Mary) and her duets with Eddy seem heavy and dreary. The forgettable Sigmund Romberg-Gus Kahn score didn't help, especially when the 1919 Puccini opera version of the story had become so famous in opera houses.

The Glass Menagerie

March 31, 1945 (Playhouse Theatre), a play by Tennessee Williams. *Cast*: Laurette Taylor (Amanda), Eddie Dowling (Tom), Julie Haydon (Laura), Anthony Ross (Jim). *Directors*: Eddie Dowling, Margo Jones. *Producers:* Eddie Dowling, Louis J. Singer. 561 performances.

(Fox 1950). *Screenplay*: Peter Berneis, Tennessee Williams. *Cast*: Gertrude Lawrence (Amanda), Arthur Kennedy (Tom), Jane Wyman (Laura), Kirk Douglas (Jim). *Director*: Irving Rapper. *Producers*: Charles K. Feldman, Jerry Wald.

(TV 1966). *Teleplay*: Tennessee Williams. *Cast*: Shirley Booth (Amanda) Barbara Loden (Laura), Hal Holbrook (Tom) Pat Hingle (Jim). *Director*: Michael Elliott. *Producers*: David Susskind, etc.

(TV 1973). *Teleplay*: Tennessee Williams. *Cast*: Katharine Hepburn (Amanda), Sam Waterston (Tom), Joanna Miles (Laura), Michael Moriarty (Jim). *Director*: Anthony Harvey. *Producer*: David Susskind.

(Cineplex-Odeon 1987). *Screenplay*: Tennessee Williams. *Cast*: Joanne Woodward (Amanda), John Malkovich (Tom), Karen Allen (Laura), James Naughton (Jim). *Director*: Paul Newman. *Producer*: Burt Harris.

Tennessee Williams's first major work is still one of the finest of all American dramas. The delicate memory play about a dysfunctional family during the Depression is both poetic and gritty as it looks at a driven, suffocating mother, her emotionally crippled daughter, her restless son, and the gentleman caller who symbolizes hope for them all. The acclaimed Broadway production launched Williams's career and gave the once-celebrated actress Laurette Taylor a final triumph before her death. Her performance as the mother Amanda Wingfield remains one of the most cherished of all theatre legends. Many renowned actresses have essayed the role over the years on Broadway, on tour, and in regional theatres. The drama is also one of the most produced works in schools and community theatres. Therefore it is puzzling that most film and television productions of *The Glass Menagerie* disappoint. The 1950 movie is very atmospheric but slow-moving and heavy handed. It features an all-star cast and the quartet of major players do competent work. But Gertrude Lawrence only seems to skim the surface of Amanda, Jane Wyman and Kirk Douglas are a little too glossy for the would-be lovers, but Arthur Kennedy captures the moodiness and restlessness of the son Tom beautifully. Two noteworthy television versions also miss the mark but have their merits. Shirley Booth is appropriately slovenly as Amanda in a 1966 production but one cannot find the lost Southern elegance that the woman clings on to. Katharine Hepburn gives a no-nonsense interpretation of Amanda in the 1973 television version but as energized and fascinating as it is, she doesn't convince. Yet both of these small screen productions offered some reputable performances in the other roles. A 1987 movie took a slightly more modern acting approach to the piece and all four of the principals are very skillful without being very effective. It is a competent film and, while there is nothing wrong with it, very little seems better than average.

Glengarry Glen Ross

March 25, 1984 (John Golden Theatre), a play by David Mamet. *Cast:* Joe Mantegna (Richard Roma), Robert Prosky (Shelly Levene), James Tolkan (Dave Moss), J. T. Walsh (John Williamson), Mike Nussbaum (George Aaronow), Lane Smith (James Lingk), Jack Wallace (Baylen). *Director:* Gregory Mosher. *Producers:* Elliott Martin, etc. 378 performances. Pulitzer Prize.

(New Line 1992). *Screenplay:* David Mamet. *Cast:* Jack Lemmon (Shelly Levene), Al Pacino (Ricky Roma), Ed Harris (Dave Moss), Alan Arkin (George Aaronow), Kevin Spacey (John Williamson), Alec Baldwin (Blake), Jonathan Pryce (James Lingk), Bruce Altman (Mr. Spannel). *Director:* James Foley. *Producers:* Jerry Tokofsky, Stephen R. Zupnik.

The cut-throat, crass, manipulative world of high-powered real estate salesmen comes alive in this play that crackles with colorful language and despicable but fascinating characters. As they sell worthless Florida real estate with exotic names like the play's title, the salesmen compete and show no mercy on the battleground of sales. The Broadway production featured a vibrant cast under the astute direction of Gregory Mosher and the play ran a year. Playwright David Mamet made several changes (including an intriguing new major character) in his screenplay for the 1992 movie but the spirit of the original was still there and an outstanding cast made the talky, stagy film exciting.

Godspell

May 17, 1971 (Cherry Lane Theatre), a musical by John-Michael Tebelak. *Score:* Stephen Schwartz. *Cast:* Stephen Nathan (Jesus), David Haskell (John the Baptist/Judas), Sonia Manzano, Johanne Jonas, Jeffrey Mylett, Lamar Alford, Robin Lamont. *Songs:* Day By Day; All for the Best; By My Side; Save the People; All Good Gifts; Turn Back, O Man; We Beseech Thee; Light of the World. *Director:* John-Michael Tebelak. *Producer:* Edgar Lansbury, etc. 2,651 performances.

(Columbia 1973). *Screenplay:* David Greene. *Score:* Stephen Schwartz. *Cast:* Victor Garber (Jesus), David Haskell (John the Baptist/Judas), Robin Lamont, Katie Hanley, Lynn Thigpen, Jeffrey Mylett, Joanne Jonas, Jerry Sroka, Gilmer McCormick, Merrell Jackson. *Songs:* Day By Day; All for the Best; By My Side; Save the People; All Good Gifts; Turn Back, O Man; Beautiful City; Light of the World. *Director:* David Greene. *Choreographer:* Sammy Bayes. *Producer:* Edgar Lansbury.

This surprise Off Broadway hit musical was a loose and joyous piece based on St. Matthew's gospel and was more a celebration than a linear tale. The small and inventive musical used vaudeville, mime, acrobatics, and improvisation to recreate the events and parables of the gospel and Stephen Schwartz's eclectic score ranged from folk and rock to gospel and soft shoe. Few Off Broadway musicals have been filmed and this one, with its cast of ten flower children and little scenery or spectacle, seemed an unlikely screen project. But the movie was cleverly opened up and filmed on location in and around Manhattan, becoming a slaphappy cinematic collage and a forerunner of the later music videos. As on stage, the cast was made up of unknowns (four were from the play) and most of the infectious score was retained. Because it was such a product of its time, much of *Godspell* dates on the screen. But just as the play is still popular, the movie has its own enduring qualities.

Golden Boy

November 4, 1937 (Belasco Theatre), a play by Clifford Odets. *Cast:* Luther Adler (Joe Bonaparte), Morris Carnovsky (Mr. Bonaparte), Frances Farmer (Laura), Art Smith (Tokio), John Garfield (Siggie), Phoebe Brand, Howard Da Silva, Elia Kazan. *Director:* Harold Clurman. *Producer:* Group Theatre. 250 performances.

(Columbia 1939). *Screenplay:* Lewis Meltzer, etc. *Cast:* William Holden (Joe Bonaparte), Lee J. Cobb (Mr. Bonaparte), Barbara Stanwyck (Lorna Moon), Sam Levene (Siggie), Joseph Calleia, Edward Brophy, Beatrice Blinn. *Director:* Rouben Mamoulian. *Producer:* William Perlberg.

Although this boxing melodrama has been spoofed over the years, its gripping story and forceful characters were fresh and stimulating in the late 1930s. Despite the wishes of his father to be a concert violinist, Joe Bonaparte knows the surest way out of the slums is with his fists, so he becomes a prize fighter and enjoys some success until tragedy strikes: he kills a man in the ring and then dies in a car crash with his girl friend. The Group Theatre production featured some of the most interesting stage actors of the day and represented the new American style of acting. The 1939 movie also had an accomplished cast but it was newcomer William Holden as Joe who was most memorable; the part made him a screen star. Director Rouben Mamoulian captured the gritty atmosphere of the story and gave the film a documentary-like sense of realism. Stage revivals of the play were common for several years and in 1962 there was a West German television production with Klaus Kammer as Joe and Hildegarde Knef

as his sweetheart Lorna Moon. In 1964 the material was adapted into a Broadway musical vehicle for Sammy Davis, Jr. which kept the same title but changed its African American hero's name from Joe Bonaparte to Joe Wellington.

Golden Dawn

November 30, 1927 (Hammerstein Theatre), an operetta by Otto Harbach, Oscar Hammerstein. *Score:* Emmerich Kalman, Otto Harbach, Oscar Hammerstein, Herbert Stothart. *Cast:* Lois Hunter (Dawn), Paul Gregory (Steve Allen), Robert Chisholm (Shep Keyes), Marguerita Sylva, Olin Howland, Barbara Newberry, Gil Squires. *Songs:* We Two; Dawn; When I Crack My Whip; My Bwana; Jungle Shadows; Here in the Dark. *Director:* Reginald Hammerstein. *Choreographer:* Dave Bennett. *Producer:* Arthur Hammerstein. 184 performances.

(Warner 1930). *Screenplay:* Walter Anthony. *Score:* Herbert Stothart, Emmerich Kalman, Otto Harbach, Oscar Hammerstein, etc. *Cast:* Vivienne Segal (Dawn), Walter Woolf King (Tom Allen), Noah Berry (Shep Keyes), Lupino Lane (Mr. Pigeon), Alice Gentle, Dick Henderson. *Songs:* My Heart's Love Call; Whip Song; Africa Smiles No More; Dawn; My Bwana; We Too; In a Jungle Bungalow; No More. *Director:* Ray Enright. *Choreographer:* Larry Ceballos.

Even though this operetta was saddled with one of the most inane plots of its eras, it found some success because of the agreeable score. The African princess Dawn is in love with the German-prisoner-of-war Steve but she is pursued by the cruel black overseer. The triangle was resolved when it was discovered that Dawn was really white so she and Steve run off together. This ridiculous tale was retained when the musical was filmed with Vivienne Segal and Walter Woolf King as the lovers and Noah Berry in blackface as the overseer. If it all weren't in such bad taste, the film might have become a camp classic.

Gone Are the Days see Purlie Victorious

Good News!

September 6, 1927 (46th Street Theatre), a musical comedy by Laurence Schwab, B. G. DeSylva. *Score:* Ray Henderson, B. G. DeSylva, Lew Brown. *Cast:* Mary Lawlor (Constance Lane), John Price Jones (Tom Marlowe), Zelma O'Neal (Flo), Gus Shy , Inez Courtney, Shirley Vernon. *Songs:* The Best Things in Life Are Free; Good News; The Varsity Drag; Just Imagine; Lucky in Love; He's a Ladies Man. *Director:* Edgar MacGregor. *Choreographer:* Bobby Connolly. *Producers:* Laurence Schwab, Frank Mandel. 551 performances.

(MGM 1930). *Screenplay:* Frances Marion. *Score:* Ray Henderson, B. G. DeSylva, Lew Brown, etc. *Cast:* Stanley Smith (Tom Malone), Mary Lawlor (Connie Lane), Bessie Love (Dixie O'Day), Cliff Edwards (Pooch Kearney), Lola Lane, Dorothy McNulty (aka Penny Singleton), Thomas Jackson. *Songs:* Good News; The Varsity Drag; Students Are We; If You're Not Kissing Me; Gee But I'd Like to Make You Happy; He's a Ladies Man. *Directors:* Nick Grinde, Edgar MacGregor. *Choreographer:* Sammy Lee.

(MGM 1947). *Screenplay:* Betty Comden, Adolph Green. *Score:* Ray Henderson, B. G. DeSylva, Lew Brown, Roger Edens, etc. *Cast:* June Allyson (Connie Lane), Peter Lawford (Tom Marlowe), Patricia Marshall (Pat McClellan), Joan McCracken (Babe Doolittle), Ray McDonald, Mel Tormé. *Songs:* The Best Things in Life Are Free; Good News; The Varsity Drag; Just Imagine; Pass That Peace Pipe; The French Leson; Lucky in Love; Be a Ladies Man. *Director:* Charles Walters. *Choreographers:* Robert Alton, Charles Walters. *Producer:* Arthur Freed.

One of the Roaring Twenties' biggest Broadway hits, this collegiate musical was filled with all the academic clichés (including the big football game) but was such a funny and tuneful show that it still pleases. The DeSylva-Brown-Henderson score introduced more standards than perhaps any other musical comedy of the decade so it is amazing that Hollywood left out such gems as "The Best Things in Life Are Free" when the show was first filmed in 1930. This version suffered from a lackluster cast and mediocre production values. But the 1947 remake was a major hit that included most of the stage score but also some commendable new songs by Roger Edens and others. The cast is pleasantly likable and the musical numbers this time are showstoppers.

Goodbye Charlie

December 16, 1959 (Lyceum Theatre), a comedy by George Axelrod. *Cast:* Lauren Bacall (Charlie), Sydney Chaplin (George Tracy), Frank Roberts, Sarah Marshall, Michelle Reiner, Dan Frazer, Clinton Anderson. *Director:* George Axelrod. *Producer:* Leland Hayward. 109 performances.

(Fox 1964). *Screenplay:* Harry Kurnitz. *Cast:* Debbie Reynolds (Charlie), Tony Curtis (George Tracy), Pat Boone, Joanna Barnes, Ellen Burstyn, Martin Gabel, Walter Matthau. *Director:* Vincente Minnelli. *Producer:* David Weisbart.

This one-joke comedy managed a modest run thanks to the star appeal and waggish clowning by screen favorite Lauren Bacall in her Broadway debut. When the libertine Charlie is shot dead when found in bed with another man's wife, he is punished by being sent back to earth as an attractive woman so he will learn what it is like to be female and have to deal with men like he was. Bacall's throaty voice and expert comic timing allowed her to bedazzle in the role and as much as the critics disliked the play they praised her. The 1964 film was not so lucky. Debbie Reynolds as the reincarnated Charlie was perky but without the droll sense of humor the part demanded. The adaptation is clumsy, the comic acting strained, and the one-joke plot continues long after it ceased to hold anyone's attention. A television sit-com in 1985 with Suzanne Somers was based on the same premise and the 1991 film *Switch* featured Ellen Barkin as a similarly reincarnated character.

Goodbye, My Fancy

November 17, 1948 (Morosco Theatre), a comedy by Fay Kanin. *Cast:* Madeleine Carroll (Agatha Reed), Shirley Booth (Grace Woods), Sam Wanamaker (Matt Cole), Conrad Nagle (James Merrill), Bethel Leslie (Ginny Merrill), Lillian Foster, George Mitchell. *Director:* Sam Wanamaker. *Producer:* Michael Kanin. 446 performances.

(Warner 1951). *Screenplay:* Ivan Goff, Ben Roberts. *Cast:* Joan Crawford (Agatha Reed), Robert Young (Dr. James Merrill), Frank Lovelov (Matt

Cole), Eve Arden (Woody), Janice Rule (Virginia Merrill), Lurene Tuttle, Ellen Corby. *Director*: Vincent Sherman. *Producer*: Henry Blanke.

A celebrated Congresswoman returns to her alma mater to receive an honorary degree and is reunited with an old flame. But soon the liberal politician is put off by his conservative ways and, after making a few strikes for her cause, goes off to marry another man. While the preach comedy was nothing special, audiences were anxious to see the long-absent movie star Madeleine Carroll so the play ran over a year on Broadway. The 1951 movie toned down the politics and emphasized the love story but Joan Crawford was miscast as the Congresswoman and few sparks were generated by her teaming with Robert Young as the former love of her life.

The Goodbye People

December 3, 1968 (Ethel Barrymore Theatre), a play by Herb Gardner. *Cast*: Milton Berle (Max Silverman), Bob Dishy (Arthur Korman), Brenda Vaccaro (Nancy Scott), Tony Lo Bianco (Michael Silverman), Jess Osuna, Sammy Smith. *Director*: Herb Gardner. *Producers:* Cy Feuer, Ernest Martin. 7 performances.

(Embassy 1984). *Screenplay*: Herb Gardner. *Cast*: Judd Hirsch (Arthur Korman), Martin Balsam (Max Silverman), Pamela Reed (Nancie Scot), Ron Silver, Michael Tucker, Gene Saks. *Director*: Herb Gardner. *Producers*: Mel Howard, David V. Picker.

Although this comedy-drama was a quick flop in New York and also failed when revived on Broadway in 1979, a film version was made but it was so unpromising that it sat on the shelf for years before being released in 1984 and then disappearing again. An elderly Jew decides to come out of retirement and open a fruit juice stand at Coney Island in the middle of winter. His plan was as short-lived as the play and the film version of his story.

Grease

February 14, 1972 (Eden Theatre), a musical comedy by Jim Jacobs, Casey Warren. *Cast:* Barry Bostwick (Danny Zuko), Carole Demas (Sandy Dumbrowski), Adrienne Barbeau (Rizzo), Timothy Myers, Marya Small. *Songs:* Freddy, My Love; Summer Nights; Beauty School Dropout; There Are Worse Things I Could Do; It's Raining on Prom Night; Look At Me, I'm Sandra Dee; Greased Lightnin'; We Go Together. *Director:* Tom Moore. *Choreographer:* Patricia Birch. *Producers:* Kenneth Waissman, Maxine Fox. 3,388 performances.

(Paramount 1978). *Screenplay:* Bronte Woodard. *Score:* Jim Jacobs, Casey Warren, etc. *Cast:* John Travolta (Danny Zuko), Olivia Newton-John (Sandy Alston), Stockard Channing (Rizzo), Didi Conn, Jeff Conaway, Eve Arden, Frankie Avalon, Joan Blondell, Sid Caesar, Lorenzo Lamas. *Songs:* Grease, Freddy, My Love; Summer Nights; Beauty School Dropout; There Are Worse Things I Could Do; Hopelessly Devoted to You; You're the One That I Want; Look At Me, I'm Sandra Dee; Greased Lightnin'; We Go Together. *Director:* Randal Kleiser. *Choreographer:* Patricia Birch. *Producers:* Robert Stigwood, Allan Carr.

A highly popular pastiche of the 1950s, this musical spoof was a lively, carefree entertainment with a pseudo-rock-and-roll score and spirited staging. A surprise hit, it ran on Broadway for eight years and remains today the most oft-produced musical by high schools. The film version was just as successful, eventually becoming the biggest-grossing movie musical of all time, surpassing *The Sound of Music* in money if not in attendance. The film of *Grease* added some actual 1950s songs as well as some new ones that surpassed those heard on the stage. The star appeal of John Travolta and Olivia Newton-John was also a plus. Both play and film remain popular favorites, particularly by audience members too young to know firsthand the period being spoofed.

The Great Divide

October 3, 1906 (Princess Theatre), a play by William Vaughn Moody. *Cast*: Henry Miller (Stephen Ghent), Margaret Anglin (Ruth Jordan), Charles Wyngate (Philip), Laura Hope Crews (Polly), Henry B. Walthall, Charles Gotthold. *Director-producer:* Henry Miller. 238 performances.

(Lubin 1915). *Screenplay*: Anthony Paul Kelly. *Cast*: House Peters (Stephen Ghent), Ethel Clayton

(Ruth Jordan), Hayden Stevenson (Phil Jordan), Marie Sterling, Mary Moore, Warner D. Richmond. *Director*: Edgar Lewis.

(MGM 1925). *Screenplay*: Benjamin Glazer, Waldemar Young. *Cast*: Alice Terry (Ruth Jordan), Conway Tearle (Stephen Ghent), Wallace Beery (Dutch), Huntley Gordon (Philip Jordan), Allan Forrest, George Cooper, Zasu Pitts. *Director*: Reginald Barker. *Producer*: Louis B. Mayer.

(First National 1929). *Screenplay*: Fred Myton, Paul Perez. *Cast*: Dorothy Mackaill (Ruth Jordan), Ian Keith (Stephen Ghent), Myrna Loy (Manuella), Lucien Littlefield (Texas Tommy), Creighton Hale, George Fawcett, Claude Gillingwater. *Director*: Reginald Barker. *Producer*: Robert North.

Though long forgotten now, this early and ambitious American modern drama was one of the first to tackle the major themes that Eugene O'Neill and others would later write about. Ruth Jordan despises her Puritanical upbringing and leaves her native New England to go out West and help her brother in a business venture. But the crude, unsophisticated ways of the prairie also frighten her and she even runs from the man who loves her because he seems too close to the earth. But he follows Ruth to New England and together they try to reconcile the opposing forces within them. The drama's poetry and passionate ideas may seem dated today but the play was nonetheless some sort of milestone in American playwriting and successful enough to tour for over a decade. The silent screen versions in 1915 and 1925 concentrated on the play's plot more than its ideas but both were popular. Wallace Beery's performance as the cruel outlaw Dutch in the latter was one of his first and juiciest screen roles. The 1929 talkie was able to include some of the drama's poetic ideas yet it was still a rousing enough melodrama to become a box office hit.

The Great White Hope

October 3, 1968 (Alvin Theatre), a drama by Howard Sackler. *Cast*: James Earl Jones (Jack Jefferson), Jane Alexander (Ellie Bachman), Lou Gilbert (Goldie), Jimmy Pelham, George Matthews, Marlene Warfield, Jon Cypher, Peter Masterson, Eugene R. Wood, Hector Elizondo. *Director*: Edwin Sherin. *Producer:* Herman Levin. 556 performances. Pulitzer Prize, Tony Award.

(Fox 1970). *Screenplay*: Howard Sackler. *Cast*: James Earl Jones (Jack Jefferson), Jane Alexander (Ellie Bachman), Lou Gilbert (Goldie), Joel Fluellen, Chester Morris, Robert Webber, Marlene Warfield, Hal Holbrook, Moses Gunn. *Director*: Martin Ritt. *Producer*: Lawrence Turman.

The true story of celebrated Negro prizefighter Jack Johnson was brought to the stage in a large, vivacious production with dozens of characters and many cinematic-like scenes. Playwright Howard Sackler called his hero Jack Jefferson and concentrated on his gradual decline and fall from being the heavyweight champion to just another black man defeated by the white race. While the writing was often skillful and the sprawling production very impressive, it was the performances by James Earl Jones as Jefferson and Jane Alexander (in her New York stage debut) as his white mistress that most captivated the critics. Both got to reprise their roles in the 1970 movie and they remain the center of attention. The movie has impressive period details and some of the crowd scenes are exhilarating but it is the more intimate scenes with Jones and Alexander that really count.

Green Pastures

February 26, 1930 (Mansfield Theatre), a fable by Marc Connelly. *Cast*: Richard B. Harrison (Lawd God), Wesley Hill (Gabriel), Tutt Whitney, Daniel L. Haynes, Susie Sutton, Charles H. Moore, Inez Richardson Wilson, Lou Vernon. *Director*: Marc Connelly. *Producer:* Laurence Rivers, Inc. 640 performances. Pulitzer Prize.

(Warner 1936). *Screenplay*: Sheridan Gibney, Marc Connelly. *Cast*: Rex Ingram (De Lawd), Oscar Polk (Gabriel), Eddie Anderson, Frank H. Wilson, George Reed, Abraham Gleaves, Myrtle Anderson, Al Stokes. *Directors*: Marc Connelly, William Keighley. *Producers*: Henry Blake, Jack L. Warner.

(TV 1957). *Teleplay:* Marc Connelly. *Cast:* William Warfield (De Lawd), Earle Hyman, Frederick O'Neal, Eddie Anderson. *Director:* George Schaefer.

Much beloved in its day but scorned as nothing more than stereotypic today, this affection retelling of stories from the Bible with a Negro folklore point of view was a giant hit on Broadway and was able to move audiences to laughter and tears. Non-actor Richard B. Harrison was so imposing as De Lawd that anyone who saw him in the role could ever quite shake his image in their minds. Harrison played De Lawd over 2,000 times throughout his life but never acted professionally in any other play. Unfortunately he did not recreate the role on screen but Rex Ingram in the 1936 movie is pretty impressive in his own right. The film used a variety of cinematic techniques to enhance the presentation of the Biblical stories and the all-black cast is nimble and often moving. If one can get past the dated portrayal of African Americans, the movie still manages to be one of the finest religious films ever made. The original play was adapted for television in 1957 and, on a smaller scale, has its own merits, including some commendable performances.

Grown Ups

December 10, 1981 (Lyceum Theatre), a play by Jules Feiffer. *Cast*: Bob Dishy (Jake), Frances Sternhagen (Helen), Harold Gould (Jack), Kate McGregor-Stewart, Cheryl Giannini, Jennifer Dundas. *Director*: John Madden. *Producers:* Mike Nichols, etc. 83 performances.

(TV 1985). *Teleplay*: Jules Feiffer. *Cast*: Charles Grodin (Jake), Jean Stapleton (Helen), Martin Balsam (Jack), Paddy Campanaro, Marilu Henner, Kerry Segal. *Director*: John Madden. *Producer*: Patrick Whitley.

The cartoonist and social satirist Jules Feiffer dissects the American family in this angry dark comedy that some thought brilliant but others found tiresome. The successful journalist Jake is at the top of his profession and seems happily married but he still feels that he has not grown up, always trying to please his demanding parents and fulfill expectations he cannot achieve. There was comedy and ranting in the play, both of which the expert cast handled with distinction. The original Broadway production only

ran a few months but the play would find more favor in revivals. The 1985 television version featured Charles Grodin and his quiet, seething take on Jake was much different from the bombastic performance Bob Dishy had presented on stage. His supporting cast was excellent and the production resembles the play in look and tone, meaning it continued to divide audiences on its effectiveness.

Guest in the House

February 24, 1942 (Plymouth Theatre), a play by Hagar Wilde, Dale Eunson. *Cast*: Mary Anderson (Evelyn Heath), Leon Ames (Douglas Proctor), Louise Campbell (Ann Proctor), Joan Spenser (Lee Proctor), Katherine Emmet (Aunt Martha), William Prince, J. Robert Breton, Pert Kelton. *Director*: Reginald Denham. *Producers:* Stephen and Paul Ames. 153 performances.

(1944). *Screenplay*: Ketti Frings, André De Toth. *Cast*: Anne Baxter (Evelyn Heath), Ralph Bellamy (Douglas Proctor), Aline MacMahon (Aunt Martha), Ruth Warrick (Ann Proctor), Scott McKay (Dr. Dan Proctor), Marie McDonald, Jerome Cowan, Margaret Hamilton, Percy Kilbride. *Director*: John Brahm. *Producer*: Hunt Stromberg.

The Proctor family takes in their overemotional niece Evelyn and soon she is driving the father to drink, the mother into a nervous breakdown, and the daughter into panic. Only the wise Aunt Martha manages to subdue the wild girl before she totally destroys everyone else. But in calming Evelyn the aunt awakens the girl's worst fears and she drops dead of heart failure. This kind of lurid melodrama demanded first-rate acting and the Broadway production was blessed with some striking performances. The 1944 screen version was also well acted, Anne Baxter making the erratic Evelyn both theatrical and believable. The tricky material is handled well throughout and the film is much more effective than one expects from such a tale.

Guys and Dolls

November 24, 1950 (46th Street Theatre), a musical comedy by Abe Burrows. *Score*: Frank

Loesser. *Cast:* Robert Alda (Sky Masterson), Sam Levene (Nathan Detroit), Isabel Bigley (Sarah Brown), Vivian Blaine (Adelaide), Stubby Kaye, Pat Rooney, Sr., Johnny Silver. *Songs:* Luck Be a Lady Tonight; Adelaide's Lament; If I Were a Bell; A Bushel and a Peck; The Oldest Established; Guys and Dolls; Sit Down, You're Rockin' the Boat; I've Never Been in Love Before; Marry the Man Today; Take Back Your Mink; My Time of Day. *Director:* George S. Kaufman. *Choreographer:* Michael Kidd. *Producers:* Cy Feuer, Ernest Martin. 1,200 performances. Tony Award.

(Goldwyn/MGM 1955). *Screenplay:* Joseph L. Mankiewicz. *Score:* Frank Loesser. *Cast:* Marlon Brando (Sky Masterson), Frank Sinatra (Nathan Detroit), Jean Simmons (Sarah Brown), Vivian Blaine (Adelaide), Stubby Kaye, Robert Keith, Johnny Silver, Sheldon Leonard. *Songs:* Luck Be a Lady Tonight; Adelaide's Lament; If I Were a Bell; The Oldest Established; Guys and Dolls; Sit Down, You're Rockin' the Boat; I've Never Been in Love Before; Marry the Man Today; Take Back Your Mink; Pet Me, Poppa; My Time of Day; Adelaide; A Woman in Love. *Director:* Joseph L. Mankiewicz. *Choreographer:* Michael Kidd. *Producer:* Samuel Goldwyn.

Still one of the funniest and most melodic of Broadway musical comedies, this oft-revived show about gamblers, chorines, and religious rescuers inhabiting a fablized Broadway seems timeless in its appeal. The original production shone in all areas, from Abe Burrows's clever libretto and Frank Loesser's exhilarating score to the vibrant funny performances and Michael Kidd's spirited choreography. Movie producer Samuel Goldwyn paid a record $1 million for the screen rights and then spent another $4 million on the production; it all paid off at the box office but what an oddly unsatisfying movie musical it turned out to be. Non-singers Marlon Brando and Jean Simmons had to handle most of the musical numbers while crooner Frank Sinatra, in the non-singing comic role of gambler Nathan Detroit, saw his part padded with some dull new songs. At least Vivian Blaine got to reprise her hilarious showgirl Adelaide from Broadway and the sets and costumes also recalled the stylized look of the stage original. Because *Guys and Dolls* is such an indestructible show much of the movie still works; but what it might have been!

Gypsy

Broadway Theatre, 21 May 1959 (Broadway Theatre), a musical play by Arthur Laurents. *Score:* Jule Styne, Stephen Sondheim. *Cast:* Ethel Merman (Rose), Jack Klugman (Herbie), Sandra Church (Louise), Maria Karnilova, Paul Wallace, Lane Bradbury, Jacqueline Mayro. *Songs:* Let Me Entertain You; Together; Everything's Coming Up Roses; Some People; Small World; Mr. Goldstone; All I Need is the Girl; If Momma Was Married; You Gotta Have a Gimmick; Rose's Turn; Little Lamb. *Director-choreographer:* Jerome Robbins. *Producers:* David Merrick, Leland Hayward. 702 performances.

(Warner 1962). *Screenplay:* Leonard Spigelgass. *Score:* Jule Styne, Stephen Sondheim. *Cast:* Rosalind Russell (Rose), Karl Malden (Herbie), Natalie Wood (Louise), Paul Wallace, Betty Bruce, Ann Jillian, Faith Dane. *Songs:* Let Me Entertain You; Everything's Coming Up Roses; Some People; Small World; Mr. Goldstone; All I Need is the Girl; If Momma Was Married; You Gotta Have a Gimmick; Rose's Turn; Little Lamb. *Director-producer:* Mervyn LeRoy. *Choreographer:* Robert Tucker.

(TV 1993). *Teleplay:* Arthur Laurents. *Cast:* Bette Midler (Rose), Peter Riegert (Herbie), Cynthia Gibb (Louise), Jennifer Rae Beck, Jeffrey Broadhurst, Christine Ebersole, Linda Hart, Anna McNeely, Andrea Martin, Edward Asner, Michael Jeter. *Songs:* Let Me Entertain You; Together; Everything's Coming Up Roses; Some People; Small World; Mr. Goldstone; All I Need is the Girl; If Momma Was Married; You Gotta Have a Gimmick; Rose's Turn; Little Lamb. *Director-producer:* Emile Ardolino.

Ethel Merman's greatest stage triumph and one of the highpoints of the post-war musical theatre, this backstager about the early life of stripper Gypsy Rose Lee concentrated on her driven stage mother Rose and how she manipulated her children and others in her efforts to realize her own dreams. Arthur Laurents' libretto is unsentimental and unwavering in its portrayal of the characters and the times and the Jule Styne-Stephen Sondheim score is as brilliant as it is uncompromising. Even Merman's staunchest fans could not have anticipated the dramatic power she brought to the role of Rose, a performance filled with sharp humor, bitterness, and guarded vulnerability. The fact that she did not get to recreate her Rose on film is generally considered the greatest *faux pas* in the history of movie musicals. Rosalind Russell was funny in the part but rarely revealed the other levels of emotion going on inside the character. All but one of the stage songs were kept, the script was opened up without being diminished, and the supporting cast was commendable. But the ghost of Merman haunts the picture and it never truly comes to life. Not that other actresses have not done justice to the role. Angela Lansbury, Tyne Daly, and Bernadette Peters are among those who succeeded as Rose on stage. Bette Midler was also outstanding in a 1993 television version that remained very faithful to the original stage work. Like the best interpreters of Rose, Midler found something unique in the character and one can appreciate her performance without missing Merman.

Hair

April 29, 1968 (Biltmore Theatre), a rock musical by Gerome Ragni, James Rado. *Score:* Galt MacDermot, Gerome Ragni, James Rado. *Cast:* Gerome Ragni (Berger), James Rado (Claude), Lynn Kellogg (Sheila), Steve Curry, Melba Moore, Shelley Plimpton, Lamont Washington, Diane Keaton, Sally Eaton. *Songs:* Aquarius; Let the Sunshine In; Good Morning, Starshine; Easy to Be Hard; Hair; Ain't Got No; I've Got Life; Frank Mills. *Director:* Tom O'Horgan. *Choreographer:* Julie Arenel. *Producer:* Michael Butler. 1,750 performances.

(United Artists 1979). *Screenplay:* Michael Weller. *Score:* Galt MacDermot, Gerome Ragni, James Rado. *Cast:* Treat Williams (Berger), John Savage (Claude), Beverly D'Angelo (Sheila), Annie Golden, Don Dacus, Dorsey Wright, Cheryl Banes, Laurie Beechman, Melba Moore, Nell Carter, Charlotte Rae, Nicholas Ray. *Songs:* Aquarius; Let the Sunshine In; Good Morning, Starshine; Easy to Be Hard; Hair; Ain't Got No; I've Got Life; Frank Mills. *Director:* Milos Forman. *Choreographer:* Twyla Tharp. *Producers:* Lester Persky, Michael Butler.

This "American tribal love-rock musical" introduced rock music to Broadway and best represented the way political and social protests were affecting the theatre. The musical is thinly plotted, loose and carefree, and the songs are more commentaries on issues rather than extensions of story or character. Yet *Hair* held together in its own slapdash, electric style and it even found humor and some self-satire in its telling. The show was very popular Off Broadway, then on Broadway and the road and the excellent songs became pop favorites. By the time the 1979 movie version was made the "Age of Aquarius" movement had passed and the film was practically nostalgic in its recreation of the late 1960s. The screenplay took a more linear, traditional approach to the slight story and a few of the characters were more defined but much of the screen version captured the exuberant joy of the original. There was nothing shocking or revolutionary about the scrubbed-up, romanticized film but there is much that is still stirring about *Hair*.

The Hairy Ape

March 9, 1922 (Provincetown Theatre), a play by Eugene O'Neill. *Cast:* Louis Wolheim (Yank), Mary Blair (Mildred Douglas), Harry O'Neill, Harold West, Eleanor Hutchinson. *Producer:* Provincetown Players. 120 performances.

(Jules Levy Productions 1944). *Screenplay:* Robert Hardy Andrews, Decla Dunning. *Cast:* William Bendix (Yank), Susan Hayward (Mildred Douglas), John Loder, Dorothy Comingore, Roman Bohnen, Tom Fadden. *Director:* Alfred Santell. *Producer:* Jules Levy.

The central character in this expressionistic fable is the ape-like Yank, a muscular, hairy man who shovels coal in the bowels of a steamship and never questions his bleak existence until one day a young lady, taking a tour of the ship, sees him and faints at the sight of the beastlike man. The incident forces Yank to re-evaluate his life so he quits his job and goes searching for a place in which he fits in. But the outside world treats him badly as he is scorned, put in jail, and rejected by all. Yank ends up at the zoo and, seeing himself as similar to a caged ape, he goes into the pen where the animal kills him. Eugene O'Neill's bold, experimental work was well received in its original Off Broadway presentation and has been occasionally revived by schools and ambitious theatre groups. The 1944 film turned the innovative piece into a cheap melodrama with Yank seeking revenge on the socialite who referred to him as an ape. Not only is the style and the focus changed, the movie also seems to miss the whole point of the play.

The Happiest Millionaire

November 20, 1956 (Lyceum Theatre), a comedy by Kyle Crichton. *Cast*: Walter Pidgeon (Anthony J. Drexel Biddle), Ruth Matteson (Mrs. Biddle), Martin Ashe, George Grizzard, Ruth White, Joe Bishop, Katharine Raht, Lou Nova, Rocco Bufano, Diana van der Vlis, Don Britton, Dana White. *Directors-producers:* Howard Erskine, Joseph Hayes. 271 performances.

(Disney 1967). *Screenplay:* A. J. Carothers. *Score:* Richard M. and Robert B. Sherman. *Cast*: Fred MacMurray (Anthony J. Drexel Biddle), Greer Garson (Mrs. Biddle), Tommy Steele (John Lawless), Geraldine Page, Gladys Cooper, Hermione Baddeley, Lesley Ann Warren, John Davidson, Paul Peterson, Eddie Hodges. *Songs*: Fortuosity; Valentine Candy; Let's Have a Drink on It; I Believe in This Country; Are We Dancing. *Director*: Norman Tokar *Producer*: Bill Anderson.

A best-selling memoir by Cordelia Drexel Biddle and Kyle Crichton called *My Philadelphia Father* was dramatized by Crichton into a pleasant stage comedy about a delightfully eccentric father who keeps alligators in his Philadelphia mansion and enjoys boxing with his family and guests. The episodic piece was tied together by a romance between his daughter Cordelia and a young heir to a tobacco fortune. Walter Pidgeon was both prankish and endearing in the role of the millionaire Biddle and his nimble performance helped the play run several months. Walt Disney, in the last live-action film he personally supervised, turned the tale into a big, colorful movie musical in 1967 with an eye on repeating the success of his earlier *Mary Poppins* but the long, overproduced, tiresome production was not very popular. Fred MacMurray played Biddle with predictable ease while Tommy Steele, as the family's new British butler, chews the

scenery voraciously in his efforts to inject some life into the project. A few of the Sherman and Sherman songs are pleasant and well staged and the supporting cast is likable enough but the movie grinds to a dead halt so many times that it is a chore to sit through.

Happy Anniversary see The Anniversary Waltz

Happy Birthday, Gemini see Gemini

Happy Birthday, Wanda June

October 7, 1970 (Theatre de Lys), a play by Kurt Vonnegut, Jr. *Cast*: Kevin McCarthy (Harold Ryan), Marsha Mason (Penelope Ryan), Steven Paul (Paul Ryan), Keith Charles (Dr. Norbert Woodley), William Hickey (Looseleaf Harper), Nicolas Coster, Louis Turenne, Ariane Munker, Pamela Saunders. *Director*: Michael J. Kane. *Producer:* Lester M. Goldsmith. 290 performances.

(Columbia 1971). *Screenplay*: Kurt Vonnegut, Jr. *Cast*: Rod Steiger (Harold Ryan), Susannah York (Penelope Ryan), George Grizzard (Dr. Norbert Woodley), Steven Paul (Paul Ryan), William Hickey (Looseleaf Harper), Don Murray, Pamela Ferdin. *Director*: Mark Robson. *Producer*: Lester M. Goldsmith.

Big-game hunter Harold is believed to be dead, killed in the Amazon jungle, so his wife Penelope allows two suitors to woo her so that her son Paul will have a father. But Harold surprises everyone by walking into the house one day, terrorizing and boasting his way back into their lives. Being a crude, mock-heroic figure, Harold taunts Paul into trying to shoot his own father then berates the boy for refusing. Harold also plans a Hemingway-like suicide but when he fails he is emotionally shattered. Pop novelist Kurt Vonnegut, Jr.'s surreal take on Homer's *The Odyssey* met with mixed notices, some finding it a bold satire while others called it a boorish prank, but audiences wanted to see what the popular writer came up with so the play enjoyed a considerable run. The 1971 movie is rather stagy and the performances are more suited to a big theatre than the camera but the film is intermittently amusing and very Vonnegut-like in its ridiculousness. Director Mark Robson didn't take advantage of cinematic techniques which would have helped this very bizarre story.

The Happy Time

January 24, 1950 (Plymouth Theatre), a comedy by Samuel Taylor. *Cast*: Claude Dauphin (Papa), Leona Dana (Mama), Johnny Stewart (Bibi), Edgar Stehli, Richard Hart, Kurt Kasznar, Eva Gabor. *Director*: Robert Lewis. *Producer:* Rodgers and Hammerstein. 614 performances.

(Columbia 1952). *Screenplay*: Earl Felton. *Cast*: Charles Boyer (Jacques Bonnard), Louis Jourdan (Uncle Desmond), Bobby Driscoll (Bibi), Kurt Kasznar, Marsha Hunt, Linda Christian, Marcel Dalio. *Director*: Richard Fleischer. *Producer*: Stanley Kramer.

A gentle domestic comedy that is probably too tame for contemporary audiences, the Samuel Taylor play was much loved in its day and ran for nearly two years on Broadway. In a French Canadian household in the 1920s, the adolescent Bibi is starting to wonder about sex and women and his parents fear that his heavy-drinking uncles will be a bad influence on him. But after a few minor trials and disappointments, Bibi seems ready for manhood. Based on a series of stories by Robert Fontaine, the episodic play was warmhearted and lovingly acted. The 1952 screen version was made with restraint and few Hollywood embellishments were added so it too was a quietly affectionate piece. The cast is generally estimable and the comedy, while very mild, is genuine. The tale was turned into the 1968 musical of the same title with a melodic, understated score by John Kander and Fred Ebb but a brash, overstated production that was not in keeping with the small story.

Harriet Craig see Craig's Wife

Harvey

November 1, 1944 (48th Street Theatre), a comedy by Mary Chase. *Cast*: Frank Fay (Elwood P. Dowd), Josephine Hull (Vita Louise Simmons), Tom Seidel (Dr. Lyman Sanderson), Fred Irving Lewis (Dr. Chumley), Jesse White, Jane van Duser, Dora Clement, John Kirk. *Director*: Anoinette Perry. *Producer:* Brock Pemberton. 1,775 performances. Pulitzer Prize.

(Universal 1950). *Screenplay*: Myles Connolly, etc. *Cast*: James Stewart (Elwood P. Dowd), Josephine Hull (Veta Louise Simmons), Charles Drake (Sanderson), Cecil Kellaway (Dr. Chumley), Peggy Dow, Jesse White, Victoria Horne. *Director*: Henry Koster. *Producer*: John Beck.

(TV 1972). *Teleplay*: Mary Chase. *Cast*: James Stewart (Elwood P. Dowd), Helen Hayes (Vita Louise Simmons), Richard Milligan (Dr. Lyman Sanderson), John McGiver (Dr. Chumley), Jesse White, Fred Gwynne, Arlene Francis, Marian Hailey, Dorothy Blackburn, Madeline Kahn. *Director*: Fiedler Cook.

(TV 1999). *Teleplay*: Joseph Dougherty. *Cast*: Harry Anderson (Elwood P. Dowd), Swoozie Kurtz (Veta Louise Simmons), Jonathan Banks (Dr. Lyman Sanderson), Leslie Nielson (Dr. Chumley), Jim O'Heir, Jessica Hecht, Lynda Boyd, Sheila Moore. *Director*: George Schaefer. *Producer*: Lisa Towers.

This whimsical tale about a pleasant alcoholic who befriends a giant but invisible white rabbit seems an unlikely premise for success but the play is one of the most beloved of all American comedies and has been revived hundreds of times by every kind of theatre group. The original Broadway production boasted a quiet and wry performance by Frank Fay as Elwood P. Dowd but the role is most associated with James Stewart who replaced him on Broadway, starred in the delightful 1950 movie, and again essayed the part in a successful Broadway revival in 1970. Josephine Hull played his flustered sister Veta Louise on stage and screen, as did character actor Jesse White as the hyperactive orderly Wilson. The Broadway production ran for nearly five years and the film was a box office hit as well. Television productions were made in 1972 with Stewart and Helen Hayes (both of whom starred in the 1970 Broadway revival) and in 1999 with Harry Anderson and Swoozie

Kurtz. The latter was less satisfying but even a routine production of *Harvey* is more fun than most plays.

The Hasty Heart

January 3, 1945 (Hudson Theatre), a play by John Patrick. *Cast*: Richard Basehart (Lachlen), Anne Burr (Margaret), John Lund (Yank), Edward Cooper, John Campbell, Victor Chapin, Earl Jones, Douglas Chandler. *Director*: Bretaigne Windust. *Producers:* Howard Lindsay, Russel Crouse. 207 performances.

(Assoc. British Pictures 1949). *Screenplay*: Ranald MacDougall. *Cast*: Richard Todd (Lachlen), Patricia Neal (Sister Parker), Ronald Reagan (Yank), Anthony Nicholls, Howard Marion, Ralph Michael. *Director*: Vincente Sherman. *Producers*: Howard Lindsay, Russel Crouse.

(TV 1983). *Teleplay*: John Patrick. *Cast*: Jesse Furguson (Lachlen), Cheryl Ladd (Margaret), Perry King (Yank), Gregory Harrison. *Director*: Martin M. Speer.

In an army hospital in Burma during World War Two, soldiers from different English-speaking countries are bunked together in a hut and get along with each other very well. But not true for one newcomer, the wounded Scottish lad Lachlen, who is bitter, unfriendly, and even insulting to the others. Over time the inmates and staff manage to break down Lachlen's tough exterior and, even though his wounds are fatal, he starts to appreciate life and other people. The tender comedy-drama avoided sentimentality and obvious clichés as the various nationalities were portrayed with honesty. The play enjoyed a long run on Broadway and was made into a British film in 1949 that wallowed in sentimentality and stilted characterizations. Yet there was still something moving about the piece which was enjoyed my many post-war moviegoers. A 1983 television version featured Gregory Harrison, Perry King, Cheryl Ladd and, as Lachlen, Jesse Furguson.

A Hatful of Rain

November 9, 1955 (Lyceum Theatre), a drama by Michael V. Gazzo. *Cast*: Ben Gazzara (Johnny Pope), Shelley Winters (Celia Pope), Anthony Franciosa (Polo Pope), Frank Silvera, Henry Silva, Harry Guardino, Paul Richards, Christine White. *Director*: Frank Corsaro. *Producer:* Jay Julien. 398 performances.

(Fox 1957). *Screenplay*: Michael V. Gazzo, etc. *Cast*: Don Murray (Johnny Pope), Eva Marie Saint (Celia Pope), Anthony Franciosa (Polo Pope), Lloyd Nolan, Henry Silva, Gerald S. O'Loughlin, William Hickey. *Director*: Fred Zinnemann. *Producer*: Buddy Adler.

(TV 1968). *Teleplay:* Michael V. Gazzo. *Cast*: Sandy Dennis (Celia Pope), Peter Falk (Polo Pope), Michael Parks (Johnny Pope), Don Stroud, Herschel Bernardi, John P. Ryan, Jack Kejhoe. *Director:* John Llewellyn Moxey. *Producer*: David Susskind.

Veteran Johnny Pope became addicted to drugs in the Army hospital but has kept his habit secret from his wife and father. Only his brother Polo knows and he provides money for his brother in order to keep the truth from the family. But Johnny's behavior deteriorates and the drug problem is revealed, the wife vowing to help Johnny break the habit. This early play about a growing post-war problem may have simplified the complexity of the situation but the drama was well acted and struck audiences as penetrating and disturbing. The 1957 film was also very well acted, in particular Anthony Franciosa who played Polo on stage and screen. Filmed with unglamorous realism, the movie still manages to enthrall. A 1969 television version is rather stagy but boasts a fine cast, including Peter Falk as Polo.

Having Wonderful Time

February 20, 1937 (Lyceum Theatre), a comedy by Arthur Kober. *Cast*: Katherine Locke (Teddy Stern), John Garfield (Chick Kessler), Sheldon Leonard (Pinky Aaronson), Philip Van Zandt (Itchy Flexner), Frank Gould, Cornel Wilde, Janet Fox, Muriel Campbell. *Director-producer:* Marc Connelly. 372 performances.

(RKO 1938). *Screenplay*: Morrie Ryskind, etc. *Cast*: Ginger Rogers (Teddy Shaw), Douglas Fairbanks, Jr. (Chick Kirkland), Lee Bowman (Buzzy Armbruster), Red Skelton (Itchy Faulkner), Lucille Ball, Peggy Conklin, Eve Arden,

Dorothea Kent, Donald Meek, Jack Carson. *Director*: Alfred Santell. *Producer*: Pandro S. Berman.

Although they are long gone now, summer camps for Jewish single adults were very common from the 1930s into the 1950s. This popular comedy set in such a camp followed the summer romantic and comic adventures of some New Yorkers in the Berkshires. The characters were all Jewish types familiar to Broadway audiences and the comedy pleased them for nearly a year. The 1938 movie downplayed the Jewishness of the camp (now set in the Catskills) so the humor coming out of WASP mouths often fell flat. More time was spent on the romance between Ginger Rogers and Douglas Fairbanks, Jr. than on the comedy and the film suffered because of it. All the same, there are some agreeable performances and Red Skelton, in his feature film debut, is memorable as the clownish Itchy Faulkner. The original play was turned into the Broadway musical *Wish You Were Here* in 1952 with a bright score by Harold Rome.

Hazel Kirke

February 4, 1880 (Madison Square Theatre), a drama by Steele MacKaye. *Cast*: Effie Ellsler (Hazel Kirke), Eben Plympton (Arthur Carrington), C. W. Couldock (Dunstan Kirke), Mrs. Cecil Rush (Emily Carrington), Dominick Murray, Mrs. Thomas Whiffen, Joseph Frankau, Thomas Whiffen. *Producer:* Steele MacKaye. 486 performances.

(Wharton, Inc. 1916). *Cast*: Pearl White (Hazel Kirke), Riley Hatch (Dunstan Kirke), Allan Murnane (Arthur Carringford), Florence Edney, Bruce McRae, Ceighton Hale, Kate Mayhew, Frances White. *Directors*: Louis J. Gashier, Theodore and Leopold Wharton. *Producers*: Theodore and Leopold Wharton.

When the middle-class Hazel Kirke disobeys her father and marries the aristocratic Arthur Carrington instead of man he has chosen, her father disowns her. The marriage is also looked down on by Arthur's mother who feels her son has wed beneath his station so she tells Hazel lies and torments her until the young wife tries to commit suicide. In the play's climatic scene

Hazel jumps into the water then calls for help. Her now-blind father hears her cries but is helpless to save her so it is Arthur who rescues Hazel. A cut above the melodramas of its day (for example, there was no overt villain), the play was so popular that five road companies were sent out while the Broadway production ran over a year. A 1916 silent film featured Pearl White as Hazel and because she was already famous for her *Perils of Pauline* movies, this one was looked on as just another of her heroine-in-distress flicks when in truth it was much more.

Heads Up!

November 11, 1929 (Alvin Theatre), a musical comedy by John McGowan, Paul Gerard Smith. *Score:* Richard Rodgers, Lorenz Hart. *Cast:* Barbara Newberry (Mary Trumbell), Jack Whiting (Jack Mason), Victor Moore (Skippy Dugan), Betty Starbuck, Ray Bolger, John Hundley, Robert Gleckler, Lew Parker, Janet Velie. *Songs:* A Ship Without a Sail; Why Do You Suppose?; My Man Is on the Make; It Must Be Heaven. *Director-choreographer:* George Hale. *Producers*: Alex A. Aarons, Vinton Freedley. 144 performances.

(Paramount 1930). *Screenplay:* John McGowan, Jack Kirkland. *Score:* Richard Rodgers, Lorenz Hart, Victor Schertzinger. *Cast:* Charles "Buddy" Rogers (Jack Mason), Margaret Breen (Mary Trunbull), Victor Moore (Skippy Dugan), Helen Kane, Helen Carrington, Gene Cowing. *Songs:* A Ship Without a Sail; My Man Is on the Make; If I Knew You Better. *Director:* Victor Schertzinger. *Choreographer:* George Hale.

Here is a Rodgers and Hart musical that was in so much trouble on the road that the show was largely rewritten before opening night. It dealt with a Coast Guard lieutenant who falls for a socialite on a yacht but the story only got interesting when Victor Moore was on stage, playing the ship's cook who is also a crackpot inventor. Most of the songs were dropped for the screen version but Moore was retained and he offers the only bit of fun in the tedious movie.

The Heart of Maryland

October 22, 1895 (Herald Square Theatre), a melodrama by David Belasco. *Cast*: Mrs. Leslie

Carter (Maryland Calvert), Maurice Barrymore (Col. Alan Kendrick), Frank Mordaunt (Gen. Hugh Kendrick), John E. Kellerd (Col. Fulton Thorpe), Edward J. Morgan, Cyril Scott. *Director-producer*: David Belasco. 229 performances.

(Tiffany Film Corp. 1915). *Cast*: Mrs. Leslie Carter (Maryland Calvert), William E. Shay (Col. Alan Kendrick), Matt Snyder (Gen. Hugh Kendrick), J. Farrell MacDonald (Col. Thorpe), Doris Baker, Bert Hadley, Joseph Hazelton, Marcia Moore. *Director*: Herbert Brenon.

(Vitagraph 1921). *Screenplay*: William B. Courtenay. *Cast*: Catherine Calvert (Maryland), Wilbur Crane (Alan Kendrick), Felix Krembs (Col. Thorpe), Henry Hallam (Gen. Kendrick), William Collier, Jr., Ben Lyon, Warner P. Richmond. *Director*: Tom Terriss.

(Warner 1927). *Screenplay*: C. Graham Baker. *Cast*: Dolores Costello (Maryland), Jason Robards, Sr. (Alan Kendrick), Warner P. Richmond (Capt. Thorpe), Erville Alderson (Gen. Kendrick), Carroll Nye, Helen Costello, Paul Kruger. *Director*: Lloyd Bacon.

The Maryland families of Calvert and Kendrick have split apart because one sympathizes with the North during the Civil War while the other is faithful to the South. Maryland Calvert breaks off her engagement with Alan Kendrick but still he sneaks through enemy lines to see his sweetheart. When Alan is captured, Maryland helps him escape by stabbing the vengeful Colonel Thorne with his bayonet. Thorpe orders the church bell to be rung to alert the soldiers of the escape but Maryland climbs the church tower and grabs hold of the clapper, swinging back and forth and silencing the alarm. When Alan returns with Northern troops, Thorpe is captured and Alan and Maryland agree to wed. One of the most exciting melodramas of its day, the gripping play and sensational production put author-producer David Belasco in the front ranks of Broadway artists. He wrote the part of Maryland specifically for Mrs. Leslie Carter and she triumphed in the role. The scene with Carter swinging from the church bell became one of the most vivid of all theatre-going memories. The Broadway production enjoyed a long run and a touring version was a hit for three seasons. Decades later the melodrama was still well known and three silent film versions were made. Carter reprised her Maryland in a highly abridged 1915 movie, followed by one in 1921 with the appropriately named actress Catherine Calvert and in 1927 with Dolores Costello.

Hedwig and the Angry Inch

February 21, 1998 (Jane Street Theatre), a musical by John Cameron Mitchell. *Score*: Stephen Trask. *Cast*: John Cameron Mitchell (Hedwig/Tommy Gnosis), Miriam Shor (Yitzak). *Songs*: Origin of Love; Angry Inch; Wicked Little Town; Tear Me Down. *Director*: Peter Askin. *Choreography*: Jerry Mitchell. *Producers*: Peter Askin, etc. 857 performances.

(New Line 2001). *Screenplay*: John Cameron Mitchell. *Score*: Stephen Trask. *Cast*: John Cameron Mitchell (Hedwig), Andrea Martin (Phyllis Stein), Michael Pitt (Tommy Gnosis), Miriam Shor (Yitzak). *Songs*: Origin of Love; Angry Inch; Wicked Little Town; Tear Me Down. *Director*: John Cameron Mitchell. *Choreographer*: Jerry Mitchell. *Producers*: Mark Tusk, etc.

This Off Broadway cult hit took the form of a concert with Hedwig narrating his/her tale between songs. Young Hansel was born in East Berlin the year the wall goes up and grows into a confused transsexual. He marries an American G.I. to get to the States but has to have a sex change operation to qualify. The operation is botched and Hedwig is left with an inch of undetermined sexual embarrassment. Once in America, she is dumped by the G.I., has an affair with a military brat named Tommy Gnosis who becomes a rock star using Hedwig's songs, then he too abandons her. Left singing rock and roll dirges in third-class dives, Hedwig continues on, searching for a personal and sexual identity. The bewigged, heavily made up Mitchell was amazing, singing the rock score, telling his/her story in a phony German accent, and exuding a strange sensuality that was sexy without knowing which sex it was. The little musical quickly caught on and ran over two years. Mitchell not only wrote and starred in the film but he also directed it, but the movie often gets bogged down in the cinematic tricks and the bizarre storyline is not always clear. People who were only talked about on stage, such as the G.I. and Tommy, were cast and given scenes in the film, yet the characters rarely seemed as interesting as they were when described by Hedwig in a concert setting. But the things that made *Hedwig and the Angry Inch* rock on stage are still there: Stephen Trask's score, the weird concept, and Mitchell's astonishing performance.

The Heidi Chronicles

March 9, 1989 (Plymouth Theatre), a play by Wendy Wasserstein. *Cast*: Joan Allen (Heidi Holland), Boyd Gaines (Peter Patrone), Peter Friedman (Scoop Rosenbaum), Ellen Parker, Anne Lange, Joanne Camp, Cynthia Nixon, Drew McVety. *Director*: Daniel Sullivan. *Producers:* Shuberts, etc. 621 performances. Pulitzer Prize, Tony Award.

(TV 1995). *Teleplay*: Wendy Wasserstein. *Cast*: Jamie Lee Curtis (Heidi Holland), Tom Hulce (Peter Patrone), Peter Friedman (Scoop Rosenbaum), Kim Cantrall, Eve Gordan, Sharon Lawrence, Julie White. *Director*: Paul Bogart. *Producer*: Leanne Moore.

The story of Heidi Holland, from her senior year at a private boarding school through the radical 1960s to her involvement in the women's rights movement in the 1970s and 1980s, provides an interesting chronicle of the history of feminist ideas in modern America. Wendy Wasserstein's comedy-drama is filled with humor, avoid preachiness, and presents a handful of intriguing characters throughout its episodic plot. Joan Allen was widely applauded for her performance as Heidi, as were Boyd Gaines as her homosexual doctor friend Peter and Peter Friedman as her politically-minded boy friend Scoop. The 1995 television production was able to handle the episodic nature of the script well but Jamie Lee Curtis found less in the character of Heidi than was needed. Tom Hulce was engaging as Peter and Friedman got to reprise his Broadway portrayal of Scoop. As faithful as the production is to the play, it still fails to sparkle as the chronicle did on stage.

The Heiress

(September 29, 1947 Biltmore Theatre), a play by Ruth and Augustus Goetz. *Cast*: Wendy Hiller (Catherine Sloper), Basil Rathbone (Dr. Austin Sloper), Peter Cookson (Morris Townsend), Patricia Collinge (Lavinia Penniman), Craig Kelly, Augusta Roeland, Betty Linley. *Director*: Jed Harris. *Producer:* Fred F. Finklehoffe. 410 performances.

(Paramount 1949). *Screenplay*: Ruth and Augustus Goetz. *Cast*: Olivia De Havilland (Catherine Sloper), Ralph Richardson (Dr. Austin Sloper), Montgomery Clift (Morris Townsend), Miriam Hopkins (Lavinia Penniman), Selena Royle, Vanessa Brown, Paul Lees, Ray Collins, Betty Linley. *Director-producer*: William Wyler.

(TV 1961). *Screenplay*: Ruth and Augustus Goetz. *Cast*: Julie Harris (Catherine Sloper), Farley Granger (Morris Townsend), Barry Morse (Dr. Austin Sloper), Muriel Kirkland, David O'Brien, Barbara Robbins, Mary Van Fleet. *Director*: Marc Daniels. *Producer*: CBS.

Henry James's novel *Washington Square*, about a shy spinster who is wooed by a handsome man for her money, was turned into a splendid stage piece by Ruth and Augustus Goetz. When her father objects to the marriage the daughter stands up to him, only to realize the truth so she takes her revenge on the suitor by ignoring his planned elopement. The drama has served as a first-class vehicle for actors, beginning with Wendy Hiller and Basil Rathbone as daughter and father in the original Broadway production. Frequently revived, the play was also filmed with success in 1949 with Olivia De Havilland giving a sterling performance that won her an Oscar. Ralph Richardson and Montgomery Clift as father and suitor were also excellent and the beautifully filmed, atmospheric movie opened the action up without diluting any of the drama. There was also a television version in 1961 that featured Julie Harris in an extraordinary performance. The stagy production values were unimpressive and the supporting cast did not measure up, but Harris is luminous in the part. A British television production in 1969 with Jill Bennett as the spinster featured Vincent Price as her father.

Hello, Dolly!

January 16, 1964 (St. James Theatre), a musical comedy by Michael Stewart. *Score:* Jerry Herman. *Cast:* Carol Channing (Dolly Levi), David Burns (Horace Vandergelder), Charles Nelson Reilly (Cornelius Hackl), Eileen Brennan (Irene Malloy), Jerry Dodge, Sondra Lee. *Songs:* Hello, Dolly!; Put on Your Sunday Clothes; Before the Parade Passes By; It Takes a Woman; So Long, Dearie; It Only Takes a Moment; Ribbons Down My Back; Motherhood; Dancing. *Director-choreographer:* Gower Champion. *Producer:* David Merrick. 2,844 performances. Tony Award.

(Fox 1969). *Screenplay:* Ernest Lehman. *Score:* Jerry Herman. *Cast:* Barbra Streisand (Dolly Levi), Walter Matthau (Horace Vandergelder), Michael Crawford (Cornelius Hackl), Marianne McAndrew (Irene Malloy), Louis Armstrong, Danny Lockin, E. J. Peaker, Tommy Tune, Joyce Ames. *Songs:* Hello, Dolly!; Put on Your Sunday Clothes; Before the Parade Passes By; It Takes a Woman; So Long, Dearie; It Only Takes a Moment; Ribbons Down My Back; Love Is Only Love; Dancing. *Director:* Gene Kelly. *Choreographer:* Michael Kidd. *Producer:* Ernest Lehman.

Probably the happiest musical comedy of the 1960s, this colorful, tuneful show offered a nostalgic recreation of turn-of-the-century New York, Jerry Herman's catchy songs, a tight and funny libretto by Michael Stewart, Gower Champion's parade-like staging and spirited dances, and the cartoon-like Carol Channing as the lovable title matchmaker. The show broke records and remains a favorite with audiences across the country. The film version was the last of the big-budget Hollywood musicals, using talents from the golden days (such as director Gene Kelly and choreographer Michael Kidd) but trying to outdo the old classics in size if not quality. Some of the giant production numbers work, such as the contagious "Put on Your Sunday Clothes" sequence complete with a trainful of singing passengers. Sometimes big was just big, such as the enormous parade with thousands of extras but not too much excitement. The twenty-six-year-old Barbra Streisand was miscast as the middle-aged Dolly but she reinvented the role and just about carried the whole movie with her talent. A highlight that rivals the musicals of old: Streisand's duet version of the title song with Louis Armstrong. *Hello, Dolly!* may be an expensive ($24 million) musical giant that just about bankrupted the old studios but there is much in it that is thrilling to watch.

Hellzapoppin

September 22, 1938 (46th Street Theatre), a musical revue with sketches by Ole Olsen, Chic Johnson. *Score:* Sammy Fain, Charles Tobias, etc. *Cast:* Ole Olsen, Chic Johnson, Barto & Mann, Hal Sherman, Ray Kinney. *Songs:* Fuddle Dee Duddle; It's Time to Say Aloha; Boomps-a-Daisy; Abe Lincoln. *Director:* Edward Duryea Dowling. *Producers:* Olsen and Johnson. 1,404 performances.

(Universal 1941). *Screenplay:* Nat Perrin, Warren Wilson. *Score:* Gene de Paul, Don Raye, etc. *Cast:* Ole Olsen (Olsen), Chic Johnson (Johnson), Robert Paige (Jeff Hunter), Jane Frazee (Kitty Rand), Lewis Howard (Woody Taylor), Martha Raye, Mischa Auer, Hugh Hubert. *Songs:* Watch the Birdie; What Kind of Love Is This?; Heaven for Two; You Were There; Hellzapoppin'; Putting on the Dog; Waiting for the Robert E. Lee. *Director:* H. C. Potter. *Choreographer:* Nick Castle. *Producer:* Jules Levey.

The freak success of the 1930s, this Broadway revue had no stars, no memorable songs, and no spectacle yet it ran over four years in a large theatre. What it did have was the comic chaos of the comedy team of Olson and Johnson, two wacky, far-from-subtle clowns who filled the show with running gags, gunshots, exploding firecrackers, and sirens blaring. The jokes came fast and furious and audiences loved it. Hollywood knew they needed the comedy team for any film version; it also needed some structure. So the studio came up with a bland backstage plot about a millionaire putting on a revue to win the heart of his would-be actress-girl friend. New songs were also added but the only time the picture came to life was when Olson and Johnson did their zany routines which they had perfected after years in vaudeville. Just as the Broadway show was a curiosity, the movie does have its appealing oddity as well.

High Society see The Philadelphia Story

Higher and Higher

April 4, 1940 (Shubert Theatre), a musical comedy by Gladys Hurlbut, Joshua Logan. *Score:* Richard Rodgers, Lorenz Hart. *Cast:* Jack Haley (Zachary Ash), Marta Eggert, (Minnie Sorenson), Shirley Ross (Sandy Moore), Leif Erickson, Lee Dixon, Robert Chisholm, Billie Worth, Hollace Shaw, Robert Rounseville. *Songs:* It Never Entered My Mind; Mornings at Seven; How's Your Health?; Nothing But You; From Another World; Disgustingly Rich; Ev'ry Sunday Afternoon. *Director:* Joshua Logan. *Choreographer:* Robert Alton. *Producer:* Dwight Deere Wiman. 104 performances.

(RKO 1944). *Screenplay:* Jay Dratler, Ralph Spence. *Score:* Jimmy McHugh, Harold Adamson. *Cast:* Frank Sinatra (Frank Sinatra), Jack Haley (Mike), Michele Morgan (Millie), Leon Errol (Cyrus Drake), Victor Borge, Mary Wickes, Barbara Hale, Mel Tormé, Dooley Wilson. *Songs:* A Lovely Way to Spend an Evening; The Music Stopped; I Couldn't Sleep a Wink Last Night; It's a Most Important Affair; I Saw You First; Boccherini's Minuet in Boogie; You're on Your Own. *Director-producer:* Tim Whelan. *Choreographer:* Ernest Matray.

One of Rodgers and Hart's least successful Broadway entries, the musical did offer the lively Jack Haley and the late-blooming standard "It Never Entered My Mind." The plot concerned a group of house servants facing unemployment who try to pass one of the girls off as an heiress. Hollywood bought the show, kept the lame plot, cut all of the stage score, and had Harold Adamson and Jimmy McHugh come up with new songs, some of them sounding quite appealing when sung by Frank Sinatra in his first starring movie role. Bobbysoxer fans of Sinatra made the film a success but there is little in it today to amuse modern audiences.

Hilda Crane

November 1, 1950 (Coronet Theatre), a play by Samson Raphaelson. *Cast:* Jessica Tandy (Hilda Crane), Frank Sundstrom (Prof. Charles Jensen), John Alexander (Henry Ottwell), Evelyn Varden, Eileen Heckart, Madeline King, Richard McMurray. *Director:* Hume Cronyn. *Producer:* Arthur Schwartz. 70 performances.

(Fox 1956). *Screenplay:* Philip Dunne. *Cast:* Jean Simmons (Hilda Crane), Guy Madison (Russell Burns), Jean-Pierre Aumont (Prof. Jacques LeLisle), Judith Evelyn (Stella Crane), Evelyn Varden, Peggy Knudsen, Gregg Palmer. *Director:* Philip Dunne. *Producer:* Herbert B. Swope, Jr.

This small-town melodrama sometimes resembled the soap operas that were starting to appear on television but Jessica Tandy's performance as the title character made the play seem like high drama. Returning from the big city after a failed marriage and failed career, Hilda Crane comes home where she is wooed by two men. When she decides to marry one of them, his mother threatens to expose Hilda's past, yet the strong-willed Hilda is not deterred. But the marriage soon goes badly and Hilda, seeing a dismal future in store, swallows a handful of sleeping pills. Despite a laudable production, the Broadway run was not very long. The movie in 1956 cast Jean Simmons as Hilda and she also brings strength and intrigue to the role. The film is well acted and directed but does not seem much beyond the ordinary.

His Girl Friday see The Front Page

Hit the Deck!

April 25, 1927 (Belasco Theatre), a musical comedy by Herbert Fields. *Score:* Vincent Youmans, Clifford Grey, Leo Robin. *Cast:* Louise Groody (Looloo), Charles King (Bilge Smith), Stella Mayhew, Brian Donlevy, Madeline Cameron, Jack McCauley. *Songs:* Hallelujah; Sometimes I'm Happy; Why, Oh, Why?; Looloo; Join the Navy; Harbor of My Heart. *Director:* Alexander Leftwich. *Choreographer:* Seymour Felix. *Producers:* Lew Fields, Vincent Youmans. 352 performances.

(RKO 1930). *Screenplay:* Luther Reed. *Score:* Vincent Youmans, Clifford Grey, Leo Robin, etc. *Cast:* Jack Oakie (Bilge Smith), Polly Walker (Looloo), Roger Gray, Frank Wood, Harry

Sweet, Marguerita Padula, June Clyde. *Songs:* Hallelujah; Sometimes I'm Happy; Why, Oh, Why?; More Than You Know; I Know That You Know; Keeping Myself for You. *Director:* Luther Reed. *Choreographer:* Pearl Eaton. *Producer:* William LeBaron.

Follow the Fleet (RKO 1936). *Screenplay:* Dwight Taylor, Allan Scott. *Score:* Irving Berlin. *Cast:* Fred Astaire (Bake Baker), Ginger Rogers (Sherry Martin), Randolph Scott (Bilge Smith), Harriet Hilliard (Connie Martin), Lucille Ball, Astrid Allwyn, Joy Hodges, Tony Martin, Betty Grable. *Songs:* Let's Face the Music and Dance; I'm Putting All My Eggs in One Basket; We Saw the Sea; Let Yourself Go; I'd Rather Lead a Band; But Where Are You?; Get Thee Behind Me, Satan. *Director:* Mark Sandrich. *Choreographers:* Hermes Pan, Fred Astaire. *Producer:* Pandro S. Berman.

Hit the Deck! (MGM 1955). *Screenplay:* Sonia Levien, William Ludwig. *Score:* Vincent Youmans, Clifford Grey, Leo Robin, etc. *Cast:* Tony Martin (William Clark), Jane Powell (Susan Smith), Debbie Reynolds (Carol Pace), Vic Damone (Rici Ferrari), Russ Tamblyn (Danny Smith), Walter Pidgeon, Ann Miller, Gene Raymond, Kay Armen, J. Carroll Naish. *Songs:* Hallelujah; Sometimes I'm Happy; More Than You Know; Keeping Myself for You; Why, Oh, Why?; Join the Navy; Ciribiribin. *Director:* Roy Rowland. *Choreographer:* Hermes Pan. *Producer:* Joe Pasternak.

The 1922 comedy *Shore Leave* (qv) was thin on plot but all the same it inspired a movie and a musical which was filmed three times. Cafe owner Looloo loves the sailor Bilge so much that she follows the fleet all the way to China to present him with his own boat that she refurbished with her life's savings. Musicalized on Broadway as *Hit the Deck*, the popular attraction featured a lively, rhythmic score by Vincent Youmans, a likable young cast, and cheerful production numbers. The first movie version cut most of the stage songs but replaced them with new Youmans numbers, two of which were outstanding: "Keeping Myself for You" and "More Than You Know." But despite an early use of color in the film, there was little luster in it. Retitled *Follow the Fleet*, the tale was altered greatly in the 1936 movie and all new songs by Irving Berlin were added; it was one of his best Hollywood scores. A sparkling cast, led by Fred Astaire

and Ginger Rogers, made this version much more enticing and the dancing alone created an outstanding movie musical. Hollywood returned to the original stage score for the 1955 *Hit the Deck* which featured a young and bright cast of MGM players. The plotline was altered to accommodate the new stars and the tale now followed a trio of sailors on leave and the romantic tangles that await them ashore. It remains a highly entertaining movie and captures the joyous fun of its original Broadway ancestor.

Hogan's Goat

November 11, 1965 (St. Clement's Church), a play by William Alfred. *Cast:* Ralph Waite (Matt Stanton), Faye Dunaway (Kathleen Stanton), Tom Ahearne (Edward Quinn), Cliff Gorman (Petey Boyle), Tresa Hughes (Josephine Finn), Conrad Bain, Barnard Hughes, Roland Wood, Michaele Myers, Agnes Young, Grania O'Malley. *Director:* Frederick Rolf. *Producer:* American Place Theatre. 607 performances.

(TV 1971). *Teleplay:* William Alfred. *Cast:* Robert Foxworth (Matt Stanton), Faye Dunaway (Kathleen Stanton), Margaret Linn (Bessie), George Rose (Quinn), Rue McClanahan (Jo Finn), Philip Bosco. *Director-producer:* Glenn Jordan.

Political treachery and dark secrets among Irish immigrants in Brooklyn in the 1890s were the subject of this blank-verse drama that included an array of fiery characters and a top-notch cast to play them. The Off Broadway hit launched the career of Faye Dunaway, who played the common-law wife of a candidate for mayor, and the drama ran nearly two years. The 1971 television version featured a gifted cast as well (including Dunaway, now famous because of the movies) and the studio production has a great deal of atmosphere even though it is far from elaborate.

Hold Everything!

October 10, 1928 (Broadhurst Theatre), a musical comedy by B. G. DeSylva, John McGowan. *Score:* Ray Henderson, B. G. DeSylva, Lew Brown. *Cast:* Jack Whiting (Sonny Jim Brooks), Ona Munson (Sue Burke), Bert Lahr (Gink

Schiner), Betty Compton (Norine Lloyd), Victor Moore (Nosey Bartlett), Nina Olivette, Frank Allworth. *Songs:* You're the Cream in My Coffee; Too Good to Be True; Don't Hold Everything; To Know You Is to Love You. *Choreographers:* Sam Rose, Jack Haskell. *Producers:* Alex A. Aarons, Vincent Freedley. 413 performances.

(Warner 1930). *Screenplay:* Robert Lord. *Score:* Joe Burke, Al Dubin. *Cast:* Joe E. Brown (Gink Schiner), Winnie Lightner (Toots Breen), Georges Carpentier (Georges La Verne), Dorothy Rivier, Sally O'Neil, Edmund Breese. *Songs:* Take It on the Chin; Girls We Remember; Isn't This a Cockeyed World; When Little Red Roses Get the Blues for You; All Alone Together; Physically Fit. *Director:* Roy Del Ruth. *Choreographer:* Larry Ceballos.

Although this musical comedy centered on a professional boxer who gets involved with a socialite, the attention shifted to newcomer Bert Lahr who was hilarious as a punch drunk pug. The DeSylva-Brown-Henderson score was chipper and tuneful, particularly the hit "You're the Cream in My Coffee." Inexplicably the studio passed on the song and Lahr when the musical was made as a vehicle for Joe E. Brown. Musically the movie is uninteresting but as a comedy it has its bright moments.

A Hole in the Head

February 28, 1957 (Plymouth Theatre), a play by Arnold Schulman. *Cast*: Paul Douglas (Sidney), David Burns (Max), Tommy White (Ally), Joyce Van Patten (Shirl), Kay Medford (Sophie), Lee Grant, Tom Pedi, Larry Hart. *Director*: Garson Kanin. *Producer:* Robert Whitehead. 156 performances.

(United Artists 1959). *Screenplay*: Arnold Schulman. *Cast*: Frank Sinatra (Tony Marietta), Edward G. Robinson (Mario), Eddie Hodges (Ally), Carolyn Jones (Shirl), Thelma Ritter (Sophie), Keenan Wynn, Joi Lansing, Connie Sawyer, Dub Taylor. *Director-producer*: Frank Capra.

Widower Sidney owns a cheap Miami Beach motel but business is poor and he hopes to borrow $5000 from his rich, opinionated brother Max. But Max and his equally opinionated wife think Sidney ought to wed a wealthy widow who is interested in him, though Sidney doesn't love her. When the plan falls through, the in-laws try to take Sidney's young son to live with them but the boy elects to stay and stick it out with his dad. The story began as a television play by Arnold Schulman called *The Heart Is a Forgotten Hotel*, then he rewrote it as a play for Broadway where the comedy-drama had a successful run. The 1959 movie was tailored to accommodate movie stars and worked pleasantly as a lightweight vehicle for Frank Sinatra as Sidney and Edward G. Robinson and Thelma Ritter as the in-laws, supported by Carolyn Jones, Eleanor Parker, Keenan Wynn and, as the son, Eddie Hodges. A highlight of the film is Sinatra and Hodges singing "High Hopes" together; the song won the Oscar. In 1968 the story was totally revamped and turned into the Broadway musical *Golden Rainbow*.

Holiday

November 26, 1928 (Plymouth Theatre), a comedy by Philip Barry. *Cast*: Hope Williams (Linda Seaton), Ben Smith (Johnny Case), Dorothy Tree (Julia Seaton), Monroe Owsley (Ned Seaton), Walter Walker, Donald Ogden Stewart, Barbara White. *Director-producer:* Arthur Hopkins. 229 performances.

(Pathé 1930). *Screenplay*: Horace Jackson. *Cast*: Ann Harding (Linda Seaton), Mary Astor (Julia Seaton), Robert Ames (Johnny Case), Edward Everett Horton (Nick Potter), Hedda Hopper (Susan Potter), Monroe Owsley (Ned), William Holden, Mabel Forrest. *Director*: Edward H. Griffith. *Producer*: E. B. Derr.

(Columbia 1938). *Screenplay*: Donald Odgen Stewart. *Cast*: Katharine Hepburn (Linda Seaton), Cary Grant (Johnny Case), Doris Nolan (Julia Seaton), Edward Everett Horton (Nick Potter), Ruth Donnelly (Susan Potter), Lew Ayres (Ned), Henry Kolker, Binnie Barnes. *Director*: George Cukor. *Producer*: Everett Riskin.

The resourceful businessman Johnny Case decides he wants to make a bundle then take off work for some years and enjoy life while he is young. His plan does not go over with his stuffy fiancée Julia and her rich, money-driven family. But Julia's unconventional sister Linda thinks it's a great idea and by the final curtain they go off together. Philip Barry's polished, sportive comedy of manners is as close as the American theatre ever came to the works of Noel Coward, yet there is something uniquely American about the play. The Broadway production was directed and performed with a lighthearted style and had a long run. The first film version was an early talkie in 1930 with Robert Ames as Johnny and Ann Harding and Mary Astor as the two sisters. It is a competent, intelligent movie highlighted by Edward Everett Horton and Hedda Hopper as Johnny's cockeyed married friends, the Potters. But it is the 1938 film that is a cinema classic with Cary Grant as Johnny, Doris Nolan as Julia, and Katharine Hepburn as Linda. All are outstanding, as is Lew Ayres as the somber brother Ned and Horton returning again as Nick Potter. The movie opens the action up enough as to not feel like a play yet the emphasis is placed on the witty dialogue and the tricky relationships between the characters. The Barry play was turned into the failed Broadway musical *Happy New Year* in 1980.

Home of the Brave

December 27, 1945 (Belasco Theatre), a drama by Arthur Laurents. *Cast*: Joseph Pevney (Coney), Russell Hardie (T.J.), Alan Baxter (Mingo), Henry Barnard (Finch), Kendall Clark (Maj. Robinson), Edward Franz (Capt. Bitterger). *Director*: Michael Gordon. *Producer:* Lee Sabinson. 69 performances.

(Screen Plays Corp. 1949). *Screenplay*: Carl Foreman. *Cast*: James Edwards (Peter Moss), Lloyd Bridges (Finch), Steve Brodie (T.J.), Cliff Clark (Colonel), Jeff Corey (Doctor), Douglas Dick, Frank Lovejoy. *Director*: Mark Robson. *Producer*: Stanley Kramer.

This war drama was more psychological than military, though critics praised the few battle scenes in the play for their effectiveness. Private Coen, nicknamed Coney, is hospitalized for paralysis of the legs yet there is no visible wound. The doctors determine the ailment is psychological, caused in battle when his buddy called Coney a "yellow Jew" and Coney wished his pal dead. When the friend is killed, Coney's guilt causes the paralysis. Critics were sharply divided on the play, some extolling it as a brilliant drama, others finding it trite and contrived. War-weary audiences kept away and the production only ran two months. The 1949 screen version was faithful to the play except for one drastic change: Coney was now the African American G.I. Peter Moss and it is a racial slur from a white soldier that sets off the climax of the story. Very daring in its day, the movie seems tame and a bit too pat today but there is still some exceptional acting to enjoy.

The House of Long Shadows see *Seven Keys to Baldpate*

How to Be Very, Very Popular see *She Loves Me Not*

How to Succeed in Business Without Really Trying

October 14, 1961 (46th Street Theatre), a musical comedy by Abe Burrows. *Score:* Frank Loesser. *Cast:* Robert Morse (J. Pierpont Finch), Rudy Vallee (J. B. Biggley), Bonnie Scott (Rosemary), Virginia Martin (Hedy LaRue), Charles Nelson Reilly (Frump), Ruth Kobart, Sammy Smith. *Songs:* I Believe in You; The Company Way; Brotherhood of Man; Rosemary; Grand Old Ivy; A Secretary Is Not a Toy; Paris Original. *Director:* Abe Burrows. *Choreographer:* Bob Fosse. *Producers*: Cy Feuer, Ernest Martin. 1,417 performances. Pulitzer Prize, Tony Award.

(Mirisch/United Artists 1967). *Screenplay:* David Swift. *Score:* Frank Loesser. *Cast:* Robert Morse (J. Pierpont Finch), Rudy Vallee (J. B. Biggley), Michele Lee (Rosemary), Anthony Teague (Frump), Maureen Arthur (Hedy LaRue), Murray Matheson, Sammy Smith, Ruth Kobart. *Songs:* I Believe in You; The Company Way; Brotherhood of Man; Rosemary; Grand Old Ivy; A Secretary Is Not a Toy; Paris Original. *Director-producer:* David Swift. *Choreographers:* Dale Moreda, Bob Fosse.

Perhaps one of the least sentimental of its era's musicals, this satiric look at big business and the precarious ways you can climb to the top of the corporate ladder was refreshingly sly and funny. Robert Morse played the Horatio Alger-like hero with a boyish, grinning charm and oldtime radio crooner Rudy Vallee was appropriately sour as the company's boss. Abe Burrows's libretto is witty and mischievous and the Frank Loesser score echoes that satiric playfulness. Even the show's hit ballad, "I Believe in You," was sung by the hero to himself in the mirror. The movie version is very faithful to the Broadway original, with Morse and others repeating their performances, most of the score is used, and the colorfully garish sets and costumes and Bob Fosse's erratic choreography recreated on the screen. The studio did turn "I Believe in You" into a tearful love song for Michele Lee but for the most part the wry spirit of the original made it to the screen.

Humoresque

February 27, 1923 (Vanderbilt Theatre), a play by Fannie Hurst. *Cast*: Laurette Taylor (Sarah Kantor), Luther Adler (Leon Kantor), Sam Sidman (Abraham Kantor), Lou Sorin (Isador Kantor), Dorothy Burton (Esther Kantor), Frank Manning, Lillian Garrick, Hubert Wilke. *Director*: J. Hartley Manners. 32 performances.

(Cosmopolitan 1920). *Screenplay*: William LeBaron, Frances Marion. *Cast*: Gaston Glass (Leon Kantor), Vera Gordon (Mama Kantor), Alma Rubens (Gina Berg), Ann Wallack (Esther Kantor), Dore Davidson (Abraham Kantor), Sidney Carlyle, Bobby Connolly, Helen Connolly. *Director*: Frank Borzage.

(Warner 1946). *Screenplay*: Zachary Gold, Clifford Odets. *Cast*: Joan Crawford (Helen Wright), John Garfield (Paul Boray), Oscar Levant (Sid Jeffers), J. Carroll Naish (Rudy Boray), Joan Chandler (Gina), Tom D'Andrea, Peggy Knudsen, Ruth Nelson, Craig Stevens. *Director*: Jean Negulesco. *Producer*: Jerry Wald.

Fanny Hurst adapted her heart-wrenching novel into a passionate stage piece about a Jewish immigrant, Sarah Kantor, who struggles so that her son Leon can study the violin and someday become a concert artist. But when Leon grows up he puts aside the violin to join the doughboys going off to France, thereby breaking his mother's heart.

The acclaimed actress Laurette Taylor was extolled by the critics for her performance as Sarah but audiences preferred to see her in light comedies and stayed away, forcing the production to close in a month. Vera Gordon played Sarah in the 1920 silent movie with Gaston Glass as Leon and it also played as sentimental melodrama. But the 1946 talkie reworked the story, concentrated on the adult Leon (now called Paul) and what happens when his talent lets him into the world of high society, and the tragic results that follow. The screenplay is much more intelligent and accomplished than the play and the stage stereotypes become more interesting, especially Joan Crawford as the socialite who loves and destroys Paul, superbly played by John Garfield.

Hurlyburly

June 21, 1984 (Promenade Theatre), a play by David Rabe. *Cast*: William Hurt (Eddie), Christopher Walken (Mickey), Harvey Keitel (Phil), Sigourney Weaver (Darlene), Judith Ivey (Bonnie), Cynthia Nixon (Donna), Jerry Stiller (Artie). *Director*: Mike Nichols. *Producers:* Frederick M. Zollo, etc. 388 performances.

(Storm Entertainment 1998). *Screenplay*: David Rabe. *Cast*: Sean Penn (Eddie), Kevin Spacey (Mickey), Chazz Palminteri (Phil), Robin Wright Penn (Darlene), Meg Ryan (Bonnie), Anna Paquin (Donna), Garry Shandling (Artie). *Director*: Anthony Drazan. *Producers*: Richard N. Gladstein, Davis S. Hamburger.

A pair of sleazy Hollywood casting agents make deals, drift in and out of affairs with women, advise and (indirectly) destroy their hot-tempered actor friend, and even share a teenage prostitute, all in an aimless lifestyle that they consider top of the heap. The unlikable characters were funny in their crudity and interesting in their phony dialogue that sounded like one long con. The cast of movie stars made the play a hot item Off Broadway and then it transferred to Broadway where, with a series of other stars, it enjoyed a long run. By the time the film was made in 1998 the play already seemed like something from the far past and the updated screenplay that took the action all over

L. A. could not hide the stage origins of the piece. An emotive cast of young film stars makes some of the movie worth watching, though one never quite cares about any of them.

I Am a Camera

November 28, 1951 (Empire Theatre), a play by John Van Druten. *Cast*: Julie Harris (Sally Bowles),William Prince (Christopher Isherwood), Olga Fabian (Fraulein Schneider), Martin Brooks (Fritz Wendel), Marian Winters (Natalia Landauer), Edward Andrews, Catherine Willard. *Director*: John Van Druten. *Producer*: Gertrude Macy. 262 performances.

(Romulus Films 1955). *Screenplay*: John Collier. *Cast*: Julie Harris (Sally Bowles), Laurence Harvey (Christopher Isherwood), Shelley Winters (Natalia Landauer), Anton Diffring (Fritz Wendel), Ron Randell, Patrick McGoohan, Lea Seidl, Jack Healy. *Director*: Henry Cornelius. *Producer*: Jack Clayton.

John Van Druten adapted Christopher Isherwood's autobiographical *Berlin Stories* into an intimate comedy-drama. The "camera" was Isherwood himself, a British writer living in Berlin as the Nazi Party is coming to power. He remains objective about the local political situation but not about the flamboyant British cabaret singer Sally Bowles, whom he falls in love with. When she gets pregnant by another man, Isherwood offers to marry her. But married life is not for the hedonistic Sally so she has an abortion and Isherwood leaves Berlin to its fateful future. The centerpiece of the Broadway production was Julie Harris as the irresistible yet irritating Sally and her acclaimed performance allowed the play to run several months. Harris got to reprise her Sally in the 1955 movie and it is perhaps her finest screen performance, joyous, sly, yet pathetic underneath. Laurence Harvey is a bit stiff as Isherwood and the whole film is a little on the stagy side yet it is still a provocative look at a fascinating time and place. The play served as the basis for the musical *Cabaret* (qv).

I Married an Angel

May 11, 1938 (Shubert Theatre), a musical fantasy by Richard Rodgers, Lorenz Hart. *Score:* Richard Rodgers, Lorenz Hart. *Cast:* Dennis King (Count Willy Palaffi), Vera Zorina (Angel), Vivienne Segal (Countess Peggy Palaffi), Walter Slezak, Audrey Christie, Charles Walters. *Songs:* I Married an Angel; Spring Is Here; At the Roxie Music Hall; I'll Tell the Man in the Street. *Director:* Joshua Logan. *Choreographer:* George Balanchine. *Producer:* Dwight Deere Wiman. 338 performances.

(MGM 1942). *Screenplay:* Anita Loos. *Score:* Richard Rodgers, Lorenz Hart, etc. *Cast:* Jeanette MacDonald (Anna Zador/Briggitta), Nelson Eddy (Count Willy Palaffi), Edward Everett Horton (Peter), Binnie Barnes (Peggy Canery), Reginald Owen, Douglass Dumbrille, Janis Carter. *Songs:* I Married an Angel; Spring Is Here; At the Roxie Music Hall; I'll Tell the Man in the Street; Aloha Oe; Now You've Met the Angel; A Twinkle in Your Eye. *Director:* W. S. Van Dyke. *Choreographer:* Ernest Matray. *Producer:* Hunt Stromberg.

A fantasy about a Hungarian count who literally marries an angel, it began as a movie musical by Rodgers and Hart but MGM dropped the project and it arrived first on Broadway. The script used the disguise of fantasy to make some trenchant comments on marriage and sex, with plenty of references to the angel losing her wings once she had enjoyed carnal pleasures. Also, the count's sister revealed many feminine tricks and tactics when she teaches the angel to give up her heavenly ways and learn to lie and flatter to succeed as a woman. The highlight of the show was the irrelevant but delightful "At the Roxie Music Hall" which satirized the giant movie palaces of the era. But that number was dropped, along with all references to sex, when the musical was filmed. Hollywood, always distrustful of fantasy, reset the whole tale as a dream that the Count is experiencing after all his women's problems get the best of him. With Nelson Eddy and Jeanette MacDonald (in their last film together) as the central lovers, the sly musical comedy of the stage came closer to operetta on the screen. It is a curiously unsatisfying film musical, even the standard "Spring Is Here" rewritten by others into a lame love duet.

I Never Sang for My Father

January 25, 1968 (Longacre Theatre), a play by
Robert Anderson. *Cast*: Hal Holbrook (Gene
Garrison), Alan Webb (Tom Garrison), Lillian
Gish (Margaret Garrison), Teresa Wright
(Alice), Sloane Shelton, Matt Crowley, Allan
Frank, Daniel Keyes. *Director*: Alan Schneider.
Producer: Gilbert Cates. 124 performances.

(Columbia 1970). *Screenplay*: Robert Anderson.
Cast: Gene Hackman (Gene Garrison), Melvyn
Douglas (Tom Garrison), Dorothy Stickney
(Margaret Garrison), Estelle Parsons (Alice),
Elizabeth Hubbard, Lovelady Powell, Daniel
Keyes, Conrad Bain. *Director-producer*: Gilbert
Cates.

This domestic drama about a man who
can never quite reconcile himself to his
difficult father was regarded as polished soap
opera by some critics, deeply felt drama by
others. But everyone agreed that the acting
was distinguished, particularly Hal Holbrook and Alan Webb as son and father and
Lillian Gish and Teresa Wright as mother
and daughter. While none of the cast appeared in the 1970 film, it was pretty much
a carbon copy of the play and also divided
critics on its merits. Gene Hackman and
Melvyn Douglas, as son and father, led the
strong cast and they are all commendable,
even if the material tends to depress rather
than exhilarate.

I Ought to Be in Pictures

April 3, 1980 (Eugene O'Neill Theatre), a comedy by Neil Simon. *Cast*: Ron Leibman (Herb),
Dinah Manoff (Libby), Joyce Van Patten (Steffy).
Director: Herbert Ross. *Producer:* Emanuel Azenberg. 324 performances.

(Fox 1982). *Screenplay*: Neil Simon. *Cast*: Walter
Matthau (Herbert Tucker), Dinah Manoff
(Libby), Ann-Margret (Stephanie), Lance Guest.
Director: Herbert Ross. *Producers*: Herbert Ross,
Neil Simon.

An efficient little comedy with a bit of
pathos thrown in, this economical three-
character play entertained audiences for a
year even though it was probably Neil
Simon's thinnest stage work. Spunky teenager Libby travels from Brooklyn to California to break into the movies and be reunited with her estranged father, the screenwriter Herb. She doesn't become a movie
star but she and her slovenly dad become
friends. The small cast did mostly journey-
man's work, though newcomer Dinah Manoff
was refreshing as Libby. She was the only
member of the Broadway cast to be in the
1982 film version and she livened up the movie
considerably. Walter Matthau played her
grumpy father with forgettable familiarity
and the story was opened up some to show
scenes at the studios. But the material is still
slight and is at best modestly amusing.

I Remember Mama

October 19, 1944 (Music Box Theatre), a play by
John van Druten. *Cast*: Mady Christians
(Mama), Joan Tetzel (Katrin), Richard Bishop
(Papa), Oscar Homolka (Uncle Chris), Marlon
Brando, Frances Heflin, Adrienne Gessner, Ellen
Mahar. *Director*: John van Druten. *Producers:*
Rodgers and Hammerstein. 714 performances.

(RKO 1948). *Screenplay*: DeWitt Bodeen. *Cast*:
Irene Dunne (Mama), Barbara Bel Geddes (Ka-
trin), Oscar Homolka (Uncle Chris), Philip Dorn
(Papa), Cedric Hardwicke, Edgar Bergman, Rudy
Vallee, Barbara O'Neill, Florence Bates, Ellen
Corby. *Director*: George Stevens. *Producer*: Har-
riet Parsons.

Kathryn Forbes's poignant memoir
Mama's Bank Account was turned into a
warm if unexciting play that pleased wartime
audiences with its simple honesty and
untheatrical sincerity. Swedish immigrant
Mama is not only raising her children but
keeping her relatives at peace and putting
every extra penny into savings. But it turns
out that the nest egg was a gentle fib to keep
hope in the family so the eldest daughter
Katrin, who wants to be a writer, begins to
put the family's adventures into a book. A
gifted cast in a lovely production made the
play a hit on Broadway and the 1948 screen
version was also a success. Irene Dunne was
Mama and she was surrounded by some vibrant supporting players who breathed the
necessary life into the quiet, nostalgic piece.
Production values in the film are top notch
and the San Francisco setting is used well
throughout. The material resurfaced the

next year as a very popular television series with Peggy Wood as Mama. The show warmed the hearts of American audiences for seven years on the small screen. The original play was turned into the 1979 failed Broadway musical of the same name; it contained Richard Rodgers's last Broadway score.

Icebound

February 10, 1923 (Sam H. Harris Theatre), a play by Owen Davis. *Cast*: Phyllis Povah (Jane Crosby), Edna May Oliver (Hannah), Robert Ames (Ben), Willard Robertson, Eva Condon, Boots Wooster, Lotta Linthicum, Frances Neilson, Charles Henderson. *Director*: Sam Forrest. *Producer:* Sam H. Harris. 170 performances. Pulitzer Prize.

(Famous Players 1924). *Screenplay*: Clara Beranger. *Cast*: Lois Wilson (Jane Crosby), Edna May Oliver (Hannah), Richard Dix (Ben), Helen Dubois, Vera Reynolds, Mary Foy, Ethel Wales. *Director*: William C. de Mille. *Producer*: Jesse L. Lasky.

The Jordan clan in rural Maine is a greedy pack of relatives who are more than anxious for old Mother Jordan to die and they can inherit her money. So they are all pretty furious when Mother Jordan dies and her will leaves everything to a distant cousin Jane, the only family member who tended to the old lady in her final years. All the Jordans are contemptuous of Jane except Ben, the black sheep of the family, and it is Jane's friendship then love that eventually reforms him. The vigorous characters and a first-class cast made this melodrama a critical and popular hit on Broadway. Some of the players appeared in the 1924 silent film as well. The intriguing story and colorful characters played well on the screen and the picture enjoyed some popularity.

The Iceman Cometh

October 9, 1946 (Martin Beck Theatre), a drama by Eugene O'Neill. *Cast*: James Barton (Theodore Hickman), Dudley Digges (Harry Hope), E. G. Marshall (Willie Oban), Carl Benton Reid (Larry Slade), Paul Crabtree (Dan Paritt), Frank Tweddell, Russell Collins, Nicholas Joy, Ruth Gilbert, Jeanne Cagney, Marcella Markham, Michael Wyler, John Marriott. *Director*: Eddie Dowling. *Producer:* Theatre Guild. 136 performances.

(TV 1960). *Teleplay*: Eugene O'Neill. *Cast*: Jason Robards (Theodore Hickman), Farrell Delly (Harry Hope), James Broderick (Willie Oban), Myron McCormick (Larry Slade), Robert Redford (Dan Parritt), Roland Winters, Michael Strong, Hilda Brawner, Ronald Radd, Harrison Dowd. *Director*: Sidney Lumet. *Producers*: Lewis Freedman, Worthington Miner.

(American Film Theatre 1973). *Screenplay*: Thomas Quinn Curtiss. *Cast*: Lee Marvin (Theodore Hickman), Robert Ryan (Larry Slade), Fredric March (Harry Hope), Jeff Bridges (Dan Parritt), Bradford Dillman (Willie Oban), Hildy Brooks, Sorrell Brooke, Moses Gunn, George Voskovec, Martyn Green, Tom Pedi. *Director*: John Frankenheimer. *Producer*: Ely A. Landau.

One of Eugene O'Neill's longest and most densely-packed dramas, the play overflows with interesting characters and some mesmerizing dialogue. The patrons of Harry Hope's grimy waterfront saloon are has-been, misfits, failed professionals, war veterans, and street walkers. They like drinking at the place because it seems like an escape from the real world. But "Hickey," the vivacious traveling salesman Theodore Hickman, encourages them to give up their pipe dreams and make a new start in life. Some of the group tries and fails, then Hickey himself admits that he has murdered his beloved wife and that he is the biggest pipe dreamer of all. Although the play, cast, and production were lauded by the press, playgoers were wary of the difficult piece and it only enjoyed a modest run. An Off Broadway revival in 1956 with Jason Robards as Hickey was sensational and launched his career and brought the play back into prominence. Robards reprised the role in a 1960 television version which boasted an admirable cast, including newcomer Robert Redford, but the play was greatly abridged. A 1973 movie starred Lee Marvin as Hickey and he was not quite up to the part but the supporting cast is very distinguished, including Fredric March (in his last screen role), Robert Ryan, Bradford Dillman, Jeff Bridges, and others. It is a slow, introspective production and no attempts are made to open up the story for the screen yet the power of O'Neill's play comes through.

Idiot's Delight

March 24, 1936 (Shubert Theatre), a comedy by Robert E. Sherwood. *Cast*: Alfred Lunt (Harry Van), Lynn Fontanne (Irene), Barry Thompson (Donald Navadel), Sydney Greenstreet (Dr. Waldersee), Richard Whorf (Quillery), Murray O'Neill (Major), Bretaigne Windust, Jean McIntyre, Francis Compton. *Director-producer:* Theatre Guild. 299 performances. Pulitzer Prize.

(MGM 1939). *Screenplay*: Robert E. Sherwood. *Cast*: Clark Gable (Harry Van), Norma Shearer (Irene Fellara), Charles Coburn (Dr. Waldersee), Burgess Meredith (Quillary), Edward Arnold (Achille Weber), Joseph Schildkraut (Capt. Kirvline), Laura Hope Crews, Skeets Gallagher, Pat Patterson, Fritz Feld. *Director*: Clarence Brown. *Producer*: Hunt Stromberg.

On the eve of a world war, the guests at an Austrian mountain resort await the future with different states of mind. The American hoofer Harry Van is nonplused, especially when he discovers an old flame of his is at the hotel disguised as the Russian countess Irene. Others are more fatalistic about the upcoming crisis and by the final scene bombs are beginning to drop as Harry and Irene celebrate the new world that will result from all this. The dark comedy was filled with wit, gloom, and pungent satire and, as uncomfortable as it was, the play enjoyed a long run, in part because of the popularity of the Lunts who played Harry and Irene. The all-star movie in 1938 managed to keep much of the play's wit but it was more conventional with its lengthy exposition scenes and a happy ending. But the cast shines, particularly Norma Shearer loosening up as Irene and Clark Gable hoofing and smirking as Harry. The story was updated for the failed Broadway musical *Dance a Little Closer* (1983).

If I Were King

October 14, 1901 (Garden Theatre), a play by Justin Huntly McCarthy. *Cast*: E. H. Sothern (Francois Villon), Cecilia Loftus (Katherine de Vaucelles), George W. Wilson (King Louis XI), Suzanne Sheldon (Huguette), Fanny I. Burt, Arthur Lawrence, Norman Conniers, Sydney C. Mather, Charlotte Deane. *Producer*: Daniel Frohman. 56 performances.

(Fox 1920). *Screenplay:* E. Lloyd Sheldon. *Cast*: William Farnum (Francois Villon), Betty Rose Clarke (Katherine de Vaucelles), Fritz Leiber (King Louis XI), Renita Johnson (Huguette), Walter Law, Henry Carvill, Claude Dayton. *Director*: J. Gordon Edwards. *Producer*: William Fox.

(Paramount 1938). *Screenplay:* Preston Sturges. *Cast:* Ronald Colman (Francois Villon), Frances Dee (Katherine de Vaucelles), Basil Rathbone (King Louis XI), Ellen Drew (Huguette), C. V. France, Heather Thatcher, Henry Wilcoxon, Sidney Toler. *Director-producer*: Frank Lloyd.

A swashbuckling romantic adventure of the first order, this dashing vehicle for the celebrated stage star E. H. Sothern told the story of French poet and outlaw Francois Villon who serves as king for a week, during which time he defeats the Burgundians, outwits the real king's soldiers, and woos and weds the aristocratic Katherine de Vaucelles. Although the original Broadway production's run was limited, the melodrama remained popular on the road and in revival for decades. The 1920 silent screen version featured stage star William Farnum as Villon but the role is most remembered for Ronald Colman's dazzling interpretation in the 1938 remake. Both movies were lavish recreations of the period and had high audience appeal. The play served as the basis for the operetta *The Vagabond King* (qv).

I'll Never Forget You see Berkeley Square

I'm Not Rappaport

June 6, 1985 (American Place Theatre), a comedy by Herb Gardner. *Cast*: Judd Hirsch (Nat), Cleavon Little (Midge), Mercedes Ruehl, Gregg Almquist, Jace Alexander, Liann Pattison, Ray Baker. *Director*: Daniel Sullivan. *Producers:* James Walsh, etc. 1,071 performances. Tony Award.

(Greenstreet Films 1996). *Screenplay*: Herb Gardner. *Cast*: Walter Matthau (Nat), Ossie Davis (Midge), Amy Irving, Craig T. Nelson, Boyd Gaines, Martha Plimpton, Guillermo Diaz. *Director*: Herb Gardner. *Producers*: John Penotti, John H. Starke.

Two crusty but determined octogenarians, the Jewish Nat and the African American Midge, spend much of their days sitting together on a park bench in Central Park where they reminisce and complain even as they have to deal with dope peddlers and muggers. The slight comedy-drama provided juicy roles for Judd Hirsch and Cleavon Little and audiences enjoyed their zesty performances (and their replacements) for a few months Off Broadway and then for nearly three years on Broadway. The 1996 movie was not very cinematic and it made the material seem even thinner, but Walter Matthau and Ossie Davis are so compelling as Nat and Midge that one can almost overlook the script's many flaws.

The Impossible Years

October 13, 1965 (Playhouse Theatre), a comedy by Bob Fisher, Arthur Marx. *Cast*: Alan King (Dr. Jack Kingsley), Jane Eliot (Linda), Neva Small (Abbey), Janet Ward (Mrs. Kingsley), Terrence Logan, Bert Convy, Michael Vale. *Director*: Arthur Storch. *Producers:* David Black, Walter A. Hyman. 670 performances.

(MGM 1968). *Screenplay*: George Wells. *Cast*: David Niven (Jonathan Kingsley), Christina Ferrare (Lina), Lola Albright (Alice Kingsley), Don Beddoe, Chad Everett, Ozzie Nelson, Jeff Cooper, John Harding. *Director*: Michael Gordon. *Producer*: Lawrence Weingarten.

Although television had pretty much replaced the theatre when it came to sit-com domestic comedy, this popular play seemed to ignore the trend and ran two years by offering a television comic doing television jokes. Jack Kingsley is a psychologist who is writing a book on dealing with children even though he is having no luck controlling his own. When he discovers that his teenage daughter has lost her virginity, Jack and his wife panic and there are plenty of "virgin" jokes until they discover she is also secretly married to a nice young man. The genera-

tion-gap comedy was generally dismissed by the critics but playgoers came to see Alan King as Jack crack the kind of jokes he usually delivered on the tube. Hollywood foolishly cast an actor instead of a comic in the role in the 1968 film and the jokes fell with a thud. The classy actor David Niven was hopelessly miscast as Jack and the rest of the cast were either dull or incompetent. Both critics and moviegoers were struck by how obscene the film was, even though there was no nudity or blue language. The movie's tastelessness at least differentiated it from most television sit-coms.

In Hollywood with Potash and Perlmutter see Potash and Purlmutter

In Mizzoura

September 4, 1893 (Fifth Avenue Theatre), a play by Augustus Thomas. *Cast*: Nat Goodwin (Sheriff Jim Radburn), Mabel Amber (Kate Vernon), Emmett Corrigan (Robert Travers), Burr McIntosh (Jo Vernon), Jean Clara Walters (Mrs. Vernon), Minnie Dupree (Lisbeth), Arthur Hoops, Emmet Corrigan. *Producer:* Nat Goodwin. 64 performances.

(All-Star 1914). *Cast*: Raymond Bond (Jim Radburn), Harry Blakemore (Col. Bollinger), William Conklin (Travers), Francesca Rotoli (Kate Vernon), Burr McIntosh, Charlotte Lambert. *Director*: Lawrence B. McGill.

(Famous Players-Paramount 1919). *Screenplay*: Beulah Marie Dix. *Cast*: Robert Warwick (Jim Rayburn), Eileen Percy (Kate Vernon), Robert Cain (Travers), Noah Beery (Jo Vernon), Monte Blue (Sam Fowler), Gertrude Short (Lisbeth), Milla Davenport, William H. Brown. *Director*: Hugh Ford. *Producer*: Jesse L. Lasky.

This heartwarming comedy-drama about a rural sheriff with a tender heart was an ideal vehicle for stage comic Nat Goodwin but the play was also popular on the road and in revival for several years with others in the role. Jim Radburn, the kindly sheriff of Bowling Green, Missouri, has been quietly paying for the education of his neighbor's daughter Kate. When Kate returns from boarding school she has no time for Jim, instead running around with a young cad who turns out to be a train robber. Jim helps the crook escape to spare Kate's feelings and only then does she start to see the sheriff in a new, more romantic light. Two silent films were made of the play: in 1914 with Raymond Bond as Jim and in 1919 starring Robert Warwick. A more modern equivalent to the piece might be the television series *The Andy Griffith Show*.

In Old Kentucky

October 23, 1893 (Academy of Music), a play by Charles T. Dazey. *Cast*: Bettina Gerard (Madge Brierly), William Courtleigh (Frank Layson), Burt G. Clark (Col. Sandusky Doolittle), William McVay (Horace Holton), George W. Deyo (Joe Lorey). *Producer*: 160 performances.

(Biograph 1909). *Screenplay*: Stanner E. V. Taylor. *Cast*: Vernon Clarges (Mr. Wilkinson), Kate Bruce (Mrs. Wilkinson), Henry B. Walthall (Robert), Owen Moore, William Butler, Frank Powell, Mack Sennett. *Director-producer*: D. W. Griffith.

(L. B. Mayer Productions 1919). *Screenplay*: Thomas Geraghty. *Cast*: Anita Stewart (Madge Brierly), Mahlon Hamilton (Frank Layson), Edward Coxen (Joe Lorey), Charles Arling (Horace), Edward Connelly (Col. Doolittle), Adele Farrington, Marcia Manon, Frank Duffy. *Director*: Marshall Neilan. *Producer*: Louis B. Mayer.

(MGM 1927). *Screenplay*: Marian Ainslee, Ruth Cummings. *Cast*: James Murray (Jimmy Brierly), Helene Costello (Nancy Holder), Wesley Barry (Skippy Lowery), Dorothy Cumming, Edward Martindel, Stepin Fetchit, Harvey Clark. *Director-producer*: John M. Stahl.

(Fox 1935). *Screenplay*: Sam Hellman, Gladys Lehmann. *Cast*: Will Rogers (Steve Tapley), Bill Robinson (Washington), Dorothy Wilson (Nancy), Russell Hardie (Lee Andrews), Alan Dinehart, Esther Dale, John Ince, Etienne Girardot. *Director*: George Marshall. *Producer*: Edward Butcher.

Madge Brierly is a skilled horsewoman who longs to leave her Kentucky home and the local feuding behind. When the dashing aristocrat Frank Layson comes to town to race his prize runner in the Derby, Madge opposes local prejudice and rides the horse in the race, winning both the Derby and Frank. This simple, straightforward tale became one of the most popular of all 19th century melodramas; it was seen either in New York or on the road for twenty-seven seasons. The story was also made into at least four movies, all of which altered the characters and the details of the plot but always climaxed with the horse race. Silent versions in 1909, 1919, and 1927 were followed by a successful talkie in 1935 featuring Will Rogers in his last screen appearance before his premature death. The family feud in this version is settled by the race and there is a lot of homespun humor in the characters and local atmosphere. Bill Robinson's tapping is also an added delight.

Incident at Vichy

September 3, 1964 (Lincoln Center Theatre), a drama by Arthur Miller. *Cast*: David Wayne (Von Berg), Joseph Wiseman (Leduc), Hal Holbrook (Major), Paul Mann (Marchand), Graham Jarvis (Ferrand), David J. Stewart (Monceau), Will Lee, Alek Primrose, Harold Scott, Michael Strong, James Greene. *Director*: Harold Clurman. *Producer*: Repertory Theatre of Lincoln Center. 99 performances.

(TV 1973). *Teleplay*: Arthur Miller. *Cast*: Richard Jordan (Von Berg), Harris Yulin (Leduc), Andy Robinson (Major), Bert Freed (Marchand), Ed Bakey (Ferrand), Rene Auberjonais (Monceau), William Hanson, Joseph Hindy, Allan Garfield, Barry Primus, Ed Gilbert. *Director*: Stacy Keach.

The issue of moral responsibility is at the center of this Arthur Miller drama that poses many difficult questions for its characters and for its audience. Eight men are picked up by the Nazis in 1942 France and questioned one by one, trying to determine if they are Jews or not. Among the detainees is the Austrian prince Von Berg who despises anti–Semitism yet, as pointed out by the Jewish doctor Leduc, has done nothing to stop it. Although much of the play was a debate of sorts, it was still dramatically viable and the strong all-male cast made for some splendid theatrics. Despite generally favorable notices, the play's run was limited and no film was made. The 1973 television version seemed more stagebound than it needed to be but the cast was uniformly excellent right down to the smallest part. Because of the nature of Miller's inquiry, the play has not dated much and still intrigues.

Indians

October 13, 1969 (Brooks Atkinson Theatre), a play by Arthur Kopit. *Cast*: Stacy Keach (Buffalo Bill), Charles Durning (Ned Buntline), Manu Tupou (Sitting Bull), Sam Waterston, Thomas Aldredge, Ronny Cox, Kevin Conway, George Mitchell, Raul Julia. *Director*: Gene Frankel. *Producers:* Roger L. Stevens, etc. 96 performances.

Buffalo Bill and the Indians (United Artists 1976). *Screenplay*: Alan Rudolph, Robert Altman. *Cast*: Paul Newman (Buffalo Bill), Burt Lancaster (Ned Buntline), Frank Kaquitts (Sitting Bull), Joel Grey, Kevin McCarthy, Harvey Keitel, Geraldine Chaplin, John Considine, Denver Pyle. *Director-producer*: Robert Altman.

Absurdist playwright Arthur Kopit put his passionate ideas about the mistreatment of Native Americans in the form of a Wild West Show with Buffalo Bill as host, narrator, confessor, and sinner. The series of short scenes covered everything from the slaughter of the buffalo to the starvation of the tribes and the drama ended with the cast accusing the audience of genocide. The inflammatory piece met with mixed notices and was called everything from a powerful exposé to simpleminded hysterics. But the vigorous production, headed by Stacy Keach as Buffalo Bill, was very theatrical and stirring. The 1976 movie, retitled *Buffalo Bill and the Indians*, is much more conventional in that a real Wild West Show is going on yet there are dream sequences, flashbacks, and even some hallucinatory scenes. Paul Newman as Bill headed an impressive cast but few of the characters come alive as they discuss rather than do anything. There are some nice Robert Altman touches (he co-wrote the script as well as directed) and there are some moments of ironic humor not found in the play, but despite its potent subject it remains a curiously uninvolving film.

Indiscreet see *Kind Sir*

Inherit the Wind

April 21, 1955 (National Theatre), a play by Jerome Lawrence, Robert E. Lee. *Cast:* Paul Muni (Henry Drummond), Ed Begley (Matthew Harrison Brady), Tony Randall (E. K. Hornbeck), Karl Light (Bertram Cates), Bethel Leslie, Staats Cotsworth, Muriel Kirkland, Louis Hector, James Maloney. *Director-Producer:* Herman Shumlin. 806 performances.

(United Artists-Lomitas 1960). *Screenplay:* Nedrick Young, Harold Jacob Smith. *Cast:* Spencer Tracy (Henry Drummond), Fredric March (Matthew Harrison Brady), Gene Kelly (E. K. Hornbeck), Dick York (Bertram Cates), Harry Morgan, Donna Anderson, Claude Akins, Elliott Reid, Paul Hartman. *Director-Producer:* Stanley Kramer.

(TV 1988). *Teleplay:* John Gay. *Cast:* Jason Robards (Henry Drummond), Kirk Douglas (Matthew Harrison Brady), Darren McGavin (E. K. Hornbeck), Kyle Secor (Bertram Cates), John Harkins, Jean Simmons, Michael Ensign, Megan Follows. *Director:* David Greene. *Producer:* Robert Papazian, Jr.

(TV 1999). *Teleplay:* Nedrick Young, Harold Jacob Smith. *Cast:* Jack Lemmon (Henry Drummond), George C. Scott (Matthew Harrison Brady), Beau Bridges (E. K. Hornbeck), Tom Everett Scott (Bertram Cates), Piper Laurie, John Cullum, Kathryn Morris, Russ Tamblyn. *Director:* Daniel Petrie. *Producer:* Dennis Bishop.

The 1925 Scopes trial, in which a Tennessee teacher is brought to trial for teaching Darwin's ideas of evolution in his classroom, was turned into an exciting courtroom drama with the characters's names changed but some of the trial transcript used as dialogue. The crusty, homespun Clarence Darrow-like Henry Drummond defends the teacher while the righteous Matthew Harrison Brady, the play's version of William Jennings Bryant, attacks the irreligious ideas of evolution using a literal interpretation of the Bible as his reference point. The teacher is found guilty but Brady dies and Drummond is left questioning how man continues to try and understand God. Paul Muni and Ed Begley were in top form as Drummond and Brady on Broadway and the large cast included several other noteworthy performances, in particular Tony Randall as the sour journalist E. K. Hornbeck. The 1960 film was also performed with a flourish, even if some of the acting was more on a theatrical level than one more appropriate for the camera. Spencer Tracy's Drummond was down to earth and solid but Fredric March's Brady had more than a touch of a villain's snarl in it. There were also three television versions of the play. Begley got to reprise his Brady in a 1965 production with Melvyn Douglas as Drummond, and Kirk Douglas and Jason Robards essayed Brady and Drummond in a 1988 broadcast. George C. Scott starred as Drummond in a 1996 Broadway revival of the play and then played Brady in a 1999 television version with Jack Lemmon as Drummond. The play was long a favorite with school and community theatres and recent revivals have shown the script still to be very lively.

The Innocents

February 1, 1950 (Playhouse Theatre), a drama by William Archibald. *Cast:* Beatrice Straight (Miss Giddens), Isobel Elsom (Mrs. Grose), Iris Mann (Flora), David Cole (Miles). *Director:* Peter Glenville. *Producer:* Peter Cookson. 141 performances.

(Fox 1961). *Screenplay:* Truman Capote, William Archibald. *Cast:* Deborah Kerr (Miss Giddens), Megs Jenkins (Mrs. Grose), Martin Stephens (Miles), Pamela Franklin (Flors), Peter Wyngarde, Michael Redgrave. *Director-Producer:* Jack Clayton.

Henry James's novel *The Turn of the Screw*, about two children haunted by the ghosts of their past governess and her lover, was turned into a riveting stage thriller that boasted a memorably atmospheric setting by Jo Mielziner and compelling performance by Beatrice Straight as the new governess who discovers the hair-raising situation too late to stop tragedy. The 1961 movie starred Deborah Kerr as the governess and added a very Freudian ending in which she kisses the dead boy on the lips. The whole thing would seem very silly except that the production values are impressive and the film creates the images of the ghosts better than on stage.

The play has received occasional revivals but James's original book has been made into television productions in 1959, 1974, 1982, 1990, and 1999, and into movies in 1992, 1994, and 2004, making it one of the most filmed of all ghost stories.

Irene

November 18, 1919 (Vanderbilt Theatre), a musical comedy by James Montgomery. *Score:* Harry Tierney, Joseph McCarthy. *Cast:* Edith Day (Irene O'Dare), Walter Regan (Donald Marshall), Bobbie Watson (Madame Lucy), John Litel, Dorothy Walters, Eva Puck. *Songs:* Alice Blue Gown; Castle of Dreams; Irene; The Last Part of Ev'ry Party; Skyrocket. *Director-choreographer:* Edward Royce. *Producers:* Carle Carlton, Joseph McCarthy. 670 performances.

(RKO 1940). *Screenplay:* Alice Duer Miller. *Score:* Harry Tierney, Joseph McCarthy. *Cast:* Anna Neagle (Irene O'Dare), Ray Milland (Donald Marshall), Roland Young (Mr. Smith), May Robson (Granny O'Dare), Billie Burke, Alan Marshall, Arthur Treacher, Marsha Hunt, Ethel Griffies, Doris Nolan. *Songs:* Alice Blue Gown; Castle of Dreams; You've Got Me Out on a Limb; Irene; There's Something in the Air; Sweet Vermosa Brown. *Director-Producer:* Herbert Wilcox. *Choreographer:* Aida Broadbent.

One of the most perennially beloved Cinderella musicals, it centers on the spunky, working class Irish gal Irene who goes to a Long Island mansion to sew cushions, is passed off as a socialite, and ends up marrying a young millionaire. This early variation of the *My Fair Lady* story was the most popular Broadway musical of the 1920s and a 1926 silent film version was also a hit, even without the score and its two standards: "Alice Blue Gown" and the title number. Hollywood wanted to make a talkie version with Fred Astaire and Ginger Rogers in the late 1930s but the team thought the material dated. It was but that didn't stop the studio from making it with Anna Neagle and Ray Milland in the leading roles. Neagle oozes with charm and, despite her limited singing and dancing talents, makes the corny romance work. Audiences, facing the prospect of World War Two, found the escapist piece charming and the film was a success.

Is Zat So?

January 5, 1925 (39th Street Theatre), a comedy by James Gleason, Richard Tabor. *Cast:* James Gleason (Hap Hurley), Robert Armstrong (Chick Cowan), Sidney Riggs (C. Clinton Blackburn), John C. King (Robert Parker), Marie Chambers (Susan Blackburn Parker), Victor Morley, Jo Wallace, Marjorie Crossland. *Producer:* Earl Boothe. 618 performances.

(Fox 1927). *Screenplay:* Philip Klein. *Cast:* Edmund Lowe (Hap Hurley), George O'Brien (Chick Cowan), Douglas Fairbanks, Jr. (C. Clifton Blackburn), Cyril Chadwick (Robert Parker), Doris Lloyd (Sue Parker), Katherine Perry, Diane Ellis, Richard Maitland. *Director:* Alfred E. Green. *Producer:* William Fox.

This rough and tumble farce is about a man of means who hires a boxer and his manager to train him to stand up to his brother-in-law. He has the two men assume the identity of butler and footman in his mansion and the ill-equipped lugs get everyone into all kinds of comic complications before the brother-in-law is found out. The incongruous comedy delighted Broadway audiences for nearly two years and secured James Gleason's fame as a playwright and actor. The 1927 silent film starred Edmund Lowe, George O'Brien, and Douglas Fairbanks, Jr. and was able to successfully capture the stage mayhem on screen.

It Pays to Advertise

September 8, 1914 (Cohan Theatre), a farce by Roi Cooper Megrue, Walter Hackett. *Cast:* John W. Cope (Cyrus Martin), Grant Mitchell (Rodney Martin), Ruth Shepley (Mary Grayson), Will Deming (Ambrose Peale), Louise Drew, Kenneth Hill, Harry Driscole. *Director:* Sam Forrest. *Producer:* Cohan & Harris. 399 performances.

(Famous Players 1919). *Screenplay:* Elmer Harris. *Cast:* Frank Currier (Cyrus Martin), Bryant Washburn (Rodney Martin), Lois Wilson (Mary Grayson), Walter Heirs (Ambrose Peale), Clarence Geldart, Julia Faye, Guy Oliver. *Director:* Donald Crisp. *Producer:* Jesse L. Lasky.

(Paramount 1931). *Screenplay:* Arthur Kober, Ethel Goherty. *Cast:* Norman Foster (Rodney Martin), Carole Lombard (Mary Grayson), Skeets Gallagher (Ambrose Peale), Eugene Pallette (Cyrus Martin), Louise Brooks (Thelma Temple), Lucien Littlefield, Judith Wood, Morgan Wallace. *Director:* Frank Tuttle.

Soap fortune heir Rodney Martin is not interested in the family's suds business even though his fiancée wants him to follow in his father's footsteps. But Rodney turns away from both fiancée and father and starts a rival soap company that manufactures Number 13 Soap, the product that is "unlucky for dirt." But the new company has spent all its money on advertising and has none left to make the soap once the orders come in, so dad puts in the extra money, father and son become partners, and Rodney gets his girl back. The raucous farce ran over a year and was filmed twice: a 1919 silent version and a 1931 talkie. The latter is still enjoyable to watch, particularly for the supporting performances by Louise Brooks and newcomer Carole Lombard.

Jake's Women

March 24, 1992 (Neil Simon Theatre), a play by Neil Simon. *Cast:* Alan Alda (Jake), Brenda Vaccaro (Karen), Joyce Van Patten (Edith), Helen Shaver (Maggie), Kate Burton (Julie), Talia Balsam (Sheila), Genia Michaela, Tracy Pollan. *Director:* Gene Saks. *Producer:* Emanuel Azenberg. 245 performances.

(TV 1976). *Teleplay:* Neil Simon. *Cast:* Alan Alda (Jake), Anne Archer (Maggie), Lolita Davidovich (Sheila), Julie Kavner (Karen), Mira Sorvino (Julie), Joyce Van Patten (Edith), Kimberly Williams. *Director-Producer:* Glenn Jordan.

When novelist Jake watches his second wife walk out on him, he conjures up memories of all the woman in his life, hoping that they will provide some consolation. His first wife, daughter, sister, analyst, and new girl friend all appear either in reality or in Jake's imagination but they can offer no answers to his difficult questions. Critics generally dismissed the script but praised the cast, headed by Alan Alda as Jake. Alda reprised the role in the abridged television version in 1996 and only his charm makes the production noteworthy. As on stage, the actresses in the play are far more interesting than the women in Jake's life.

Janie

September 10, 1942 (Henry Miller Theatre), a comedy by Josephine Bentham, Herschel Williams. *Cast:* Gwen Anderson (Janie Colburn), Herbert Evers (Pvt. Dick Lawrence), Frank Amy (Scooper Nolan), Maurice Manson, Clare Foley, Howard St. John, Betty Breckenridge. *Director:* Antoinette Perry. *Producer:* Brock Pemberton. 642 performances.

(Warner 1944). *Screenplay:* Charles Hoffman, Agnes Christine Johnson. *Cast:* Joyce Reynolds (Janie Conway), Robert Hutton (Pfc. Dick Lawrence), Edward Arnold (Charles Conway), Ann Harding, Alan Hale, Robert Benchley, Clare Foley, Hattie McDaniel. *Director:* Michael Curtiz. *Producers*: Alex Gottlieb, Brock Pemberton.

Teenager Janie Colburn seems to forget all about her boy friend Scooper when an Army private shows an interest in her. But when all his Army buddies converge on the Colburn house and throw a wild party in the parents's absence, Janie realizes she prefers Scooper. This slight but agreeable comedy was ideal escapist entertainment for wartime audiences and the play overrode weak reviews and ran nearly two years. The 1944 film version was similarly lightweight and was similarly enjoyed by moviegoers. The next year a sequel, *Janie Gets Married*, was made with most of the same cast members.

The Jazz Singer

September 14, 1925 (Fulton Theatre), a play by Samson Raphaelson. *Cast:* George Jessel (Jack Robin né Jakie Rabinowitz), Howard Lang (Cantor Rabinowitz), Dorothy Raymond (Sarah Rabinowitz), Phoebe Foster (May Dale), Sam Jaffe, Robert Russell, Paul Byron. *Director:* Albert Lewis. *Producers*: Al Lewis, Max Gordon, Sam H. Harris. 303 performances.

(Warner 1927). *Screenplay:* Alfred A. Cohn. *Score:* Irving Berlin, etc. *Cast:* Al Jolson (Jack Robin né Jakie Rabinowitz), May McAvoy (May Dale), Warner Oland (Cantor Rabinowitz), Eugenie Besserer (Sarah Rabinowitz), Bobby Gordon, William Demarest. *Songs:* Blue Skies; Toot Toot Tootsie; My Gal Sal; My Mammy; Mother of Mine, I Still Have You. *Director:* Alan Croslan. *Producer:* Darryl F. Zanuck.

(Warner 1952). *Screenplay:* Frank Davis, etc. *Score:* various. *Cast:* Danny Thomas (Jerry Golding), Peggy Lee (Judy Lane), Mildred Dunnock (Mrs. Golding), Edward Franz (Cantor Golding), Alex Gerry, Harold Gordon, Justin Smith, Anitra Stevens. *Songs:* Just One of Those Things; This Is a Very Special Day' Lover; Birth of the Blues; I'll String Along With You; Breezin' Along With the Breeze; If I Could Be With You; Living the Life I Love. *Director:* Michael Curtiz. *Producer:* Louis F. Edelman.

(EMI 1980). *Screenplay:* Herbert Baker, Stephen H. Foreman. *Score:* Neil Diamond, etc. *Cast:* Neil Diamond (Yussel Rabinovitch), Laurence Olivier (Cantor Rabinovitch), Lucie Arnaz (Molly Bell), Caitlin Adams (Rivka Rabinovitch), Frank Ajaye, Paul Nicholas, Sully Boyar. *Songs:* America; You Baby Baby; Love on the Rocks; Hello Again; Amazed and Confused; Louise; Summer Love. *Director:* Richard Fleischer. *Producer:* Jerry Leider.

Hollywood's first talkie started as a non-musical play on Broadway about a cantor's son who wishes to go into show business. He turns his back on his religion and family but, when his father is on his deathbed, the son returns to make amends and sing in the synagogue service. George Jessel shone as the repentant son and the sentimental melodrama ran nearly a year. Warner Brothers bought the script and Jessel for a silent film version but when he heard that parts of the movie were to have sound, Jessel demanded more money. Instead the studio went with Al Jolson and, because he was Broadway's biggest singing sensation, the play was rewritten so that Jolson could sing a few numbers. The movie was still silent except for the songs but when Jolson ad-libbed a few lines to his mother in between verses of a song, the movies talked for the first time and audiences loved it. As primitive as this early film is, there is much in it that still enthralls. The depiction of Manhattan's Lower East Side, the backstage scenes, and Jolson's performance all remain fascinating to watch. Warners remade the piece in 1952 with Danny Thomas as the cantor's son and it was inferior in all aspects. The script seemed even more sentimental this time and Thomas lacked charisma and the ability to sing the old standards effectively. Only Peggy Lee, as his girl friend Judy, had worthwhile moments, mostly when singing. The old story was given a new twist when *The Jazz Singer* was remade in 1980 with Neil Diamond as a cantor's son who becomes a rock star. Although the writing aimed to be hip, it was a rather tired, contrived story that built up the role of the father for Laurence Olivier. Diamond had the star quality to make the story work but Olivier gave what is generally considered his most embarrassingly poor film performance. Still, the newest version captured the times and proved that there was still life in the familiar tale.

Jeffrey

March 6, 1993 (Minetta Lane Theatre), a play by Paul Rudnick. *Cast:* John Michael Higgins (Jeffrey), Tom Hewitt (Steve), Edward Hibbert (Sterling), Bryan Batt (Darius), Richard Poe, Harriet Harris, Patrick Kerr, Darryl Theirse. *Director:* Christopher Ashley. *Producers*: Thomas Viertel, etc. 365 performances.

(Workin' Man Films-Booking Office 1995). *Screenplay:* Paul Rudnick. *Cast:* Steven Weber (Jeffrey), Michael T. Weiss (Steve), Patrick Stewart (Sterling), Bryan Batt (Darius), Robert Klein, Christine Baranski, Sigourney Weaver, Kathy Najimy, Nathan Lane. *Director:* Christopher Ashley. *Producers*: Mark Balsam, etc.

While most gay plays during the 1990s dealt with the AIDS epidemic with anger, bitterness, or pathos, this comedy tried to look at the comic side of being gay and living during a plague. The Paul Rudnick comedy could easily have been in poor taste but instead it was a joyous affirmation of life. Gay actor-waiter Jeffrey decides the only way to survive the epidemic is to remain celibate, even though his friends tease him about his plans. But when Jeffrey meets Steve, who is HIV positive, he forgets his scheme and embraces life. Some of the characters were no more than stereotypes but Rudnick's hilarious dialogue saved the day. The Off Broadway play ran a year, much longer than most serious works about AIDS. The plot was opened up somewhat for the 1995 movie which was filled with gifted comic actors and some, such as Patrick Stewart, who were rarely given the chance to do comedy. The weakness of the plotting is more evident on screen but the one-liners are still zingers.

Jezebel

December 19, 1933 (Ethel Barrymore Theatre), a drama by Owen Davis. *Cast:* Miriam Hopkins (Julie Kendrick), Reed Brown, Jr. (Preston Kendrick), Owen Davis, Jr. (Ted Kendrick), Leo Curley, Cora Witherspoon, Lew Payton, Frederic Worlock. *Director:* Guthrie McClintic. *Producers*: Katharine Cornell, Guthrie McClintic. 32 performances.

(Warner-First National 1938). *Screenplay:* Clements Ripley, etc. *Cast:* Bette Davis (Julie Madison), Henry Fonda (Preston Dillard), George Brent (Buck Cantrell), Fay Bainter (Aunt Belle), Margaret Lindsay, Donald Crisp, Richard Cromwell, Henry O'Neil, Spring Byington. *Director-producer:* William Wyler.

This tale of a selfish Southern belle who bewitches men with her charm predates the popular book *Gone with the Wind* but when the movie version of *Jezebel* was released, audiences saw it as a copy of the more famous book. In 1953, Julie Kendrick returns home to Louisiana from Europe to find that her beau has married someone else. So she takes her revenge by flirting with several men, destroying engagements, and even getting two men to fight a duel over her. Soon Julie is being called Jezebel and is shunned by all decent society. But when the yellow fever epidemic strikes, she unselfishly volunteers to nurse the sick and eventually is forgiven. Miriam Hopkins shone as Julie on Broadway and the period sets and costumes were highly praised, but the play only lasted a month. Hollywood bought the property as a vehicle for Bette Davis and her vicious, charming Jezebel won her an Oscar. The film of *Gone with the Wind* was still in preproduction at the time but comparisons were inevitable. But *Jezebel* has its own merits and much of the movie is still compelling.

Joan of Lorraine

November 18, 1946 (Alvin Theatre), a play by Maxwell Anderson. *Cast:* Ingrid Bergman

(Joan/Mary Grey), Sam Wanamaker (Inquisitor/Jimmy Masters), Romney Brent (Dauphin/ Les Ward), Kevin McCarthy (Dunois/Long), Berry Kroeger (Alain Chartier/Sheppard), Roger De Koven, Joseph Wiseman, Gilmore Bush, Martin Rudy, Charles Ellis. *Director:* Margo Jones. *Producer:* Playwrights' Company. 199 performances.

Joan of Arc (RKO 1948). *Screenplay:* Andrew Solt, Maxwell Anderson. *Cast:* Ingrid Bergman (Joan), Francis L. Sullivan (Pierre Cauchon), J. Carroll Naish (Luxembourg), José Ferrer (Dauphin), Ward Bond (La Hire), Shepperd Strudwick, Gene Lockhart, John Emery, Leif Erickson, Cecil Kellaway. *Director:* Victor Fleming. *Producer:* Walter Wanger.

On a bare stage some actors rehearse a play about Joan of Arc and the actress Mary Grey argues and discusses Joan's character with the director. Joan's story comes to life in the scenes rehearsed and by the end both the audience and Mary come closer to understanding the mysterious saint. Audiences and critics did not give Maxwell Anderson's script as much attention as they did the Hollywood star Ingrid Bergman who returned to the Broadway stage after a long absence. Bergman was luminous in the double roles, as she was in the 1948 film version called *Joan of Arc*, though the part of Mary Grey was dropped and the plot only concerned the last few years of Joan's life. The spectacular battle scenes alternated with numbing talk in lavish settings until nothing in the film survived save a few performances. Although Anderson contributed to the screenplay, the movie seems more like a travesty of the stage work and audiences did not crowd the movie theatres as playgoers had made the play a hit in New York.

John Loves Mary

February 4, 1947 (Booth Theatre), a comedy by Norman Krasna. *Cast:* William Prince (John), Nina Foch (Mary), Tom Ewell (Fred Taylor), Max Showalter, Loring Smith, Ann Mason, Ralph Chambers, Pamela Gordon. *Director:* Joshua Logan. *Producers*: Rodgers and Hammerstein. 423 performances.

(Warner 1949). *Screenplay:* Henry and Phoebe Ephron. *Cast:* Ronald Reagan (John Lawrence),

Patricia Neal (Mary McKinley), Jack Carson (Fred Taylor), Wayne Morris, Edward Arnold, Virginia Field, Katharine Alexander, Paul Harvey. *Director:* David Butler. *Producer:* Jerry Wald.

A contrived but merry post-war comedy, the plot was certainly questionable but the play was highly entertaining all the same. Returning vet John has married an English girl so that she can come to America and be with her G.I. sweetheart. But John really loves Mary, a Senator's daughter. Since he cannot marry Mary until he divorces his English wife and he won't say that he is already married, the complications pile up before all is resolved. The 1949 screen version was a close copy of the stage script and, though it made no more logical sense, it also was amusing. Of particular interest is Patricia Neal, in her screen debut, as Mary.

Johnny Belinda

September 18, 1940 (Belasco Theatre), a drama by Elmer Harris. *Cast:* Helen Craig (Belinda Harris), Horace McNally (Dr. Jack Davidson), Willard Parker (Locky McCormick), Louis Hector (Black McDonald), William Chambers, Bram Nossen, Jane Bancroft, Edward Craig. *Director-producer:* Harry Wagstaff Gribble. 321 performances.

(Warner 1948). *Screenplay:* Allan Vincent. *Cast:* Jane Wyman (Delinda McDonald), Lew Ayres (Dr. Robert Richardson), Charles Bickford (Black McDonald), Agnes Moorehead (Aggie McDonald), Stephen McNally (Locky McCormick), Jan Sterling (Stella McCormick), Rosalind Ivan, Dan Seymour, Alan Napier. *Director:* Jean Negulesco.

While most critics dismissed this lurid melodrama as nothing but cheap theatrics, audiences made it a hit on Broadway and on the screen. In a small Canadian village, the deaf mute Belinda is scorned by her family and raped by the local ruffian. Only the new town doctor treats her with pity and teaches her sign language. When Belinda gives birth, the ruffian tries to take the baby away from her. Belinda kills the brute and at the trial is defended by the doctor who has grown to love her. She is acquitted and the two are united in marriage. The script called for some fervent acting and the Broadway production was well performed, led by Helen Craig as Belinda. When Jane Wyman played the role in the 1948 movie she won the Oscar. The rest of the film cast is also commendable and the torrid story was presented on screen with few changes, making the film very progressive for its day. Another plus is the excellent production values with the Canadian fishing village beautifully recreated. Two television versions were also made of the tale: in 1967 with Mia Farrow and in 1982 with Rosanna Arquette.

Jumbo

November 16, 1935 (Hippodrome Theatre), a musical comedy by Ben Hecht, Charles MacArthur. *Score:* Richard Rodgers, Lorenz Hart. *Cast:* Jimmy Durante (Claudius B. Bowers), Donald Novis (Matt Mulligan, Jr.), Gloria Grafton (Mickey Considine), A. P. Kaye, George Watts. *Songs:* The Most Beautiful Girl in the World; My Romance; Little Girl Blue; Over and Over Again; The Circus Is on Parade. *Directors:* John Murray Anderson, George Abbott. *Choreographer:* Allan K. Foster. *Producer:* Billy Rose. 233 performances.

(MGM 1962). *Screenplay:* Sidney Sheldon. *Score:* Richard Rodgers, Lorenz Hart, Roger Edens. *Cast:* Jimmy Durante (Pop Wonder), Doris Day (Kitty Wonder), Martha Raye (Lulu), Stephan Boyd (Sam Rawlins), Dean Jagger, Grady Sutton. *Songs:* The Most Beautiful Girl in the World; My Romance; This Can't Be Love; Little Girl Blue; Over and Over Again; The Circus Is on Parade; Sawdust, Spangles and Dreams. *Director:* Charles Walters. *Choreographer:* Busby Berkeley. *Producers:* Joe Pasternak, Martin Melcher.

Remembered as the biggest Broadway show ever produced, this circus musical opened at the 5,200-seat Hippodrome Theatre which was set up like a gigantic bigtop and featured so much scenery that even the title elephant sometimes got lost in the shuffle. The story concerned two rival circus troupes and the romance that develops between the son of one owner and the daughter of the other. The Rodgers and Hart score offered a few hit songs and George Abbott, in his directing debut, managed to stage the mammoth production with efficiency. Rarely

revived, the musical was not filmed until twenty-seven years later and Hollywood matched the original's spectacle in size if not class. Only five songs from the stage score remained but Jimmy Durante, who was in the Broadway version, returned to play one of the circus owners. All of the cast is very personable and make the movie worth sitting through.

June Moon

October 9, 1929 (Broadhurst Theatre), a comedy by Ring Lardner, George S. Kaufman. *Cast:* Norman Foster (Fred M. Stevens), Linda Watkins (Edna Baker), Jean Dixon (Lucille Sears), Harry Rosenthal (Maxie Schwartz), Frank Otto, Lee Patrick, Florence D. Rice, Philip Loeb. *Director: Producer:* Sam H. Harris. 273 performances.

(Paramount 1931). *Screenplay:* Vincent Lawrence. *Cast:* Jack Oakie (Fred M. Stevens), Frances Dee (Edna Baker), Wynne Gibson (Lucille Sears), Harry Akst (Maxie Schwartz), June MacCloy (Eileen Fletcher), Ernest Wood (Paul Sears), Sam Hardy, Harold Waldridge. *Director:* A. Edward Sutherland.

(TV 1974). *Teleplay:* Burt Shevelove. *Cast:* Tom Fitzsimmons (Fred M. Stevens), Barbara Dana (Edna Baker), Jack Cassidy (Paul Sears), Estelle Parsons (Lucille Sears), Stephen Sondheim (Maxie Schwartz), Susan Sarandon (Eileen Fletcher), Kevin McCarthy, Austin Pendleton, Lee Meredith, Beatrice Colen. *Directors:* Kirk Browning, Burt Shevelove. *Producer:* Bo Goldman.

Naive Fred Stevens comes to New York to become a songwriter and, teaming up with a veteran songster, writes the hit ditty "June Moon." Soon Fred is being seduced by a vampire-like gold digger but before he weds her the smart aleck pianist Maxie sets Fred straight and sends him back to the sweet girl who loves him. The bright, caustic comedy satirized Tin Pan Alley and rags-to-riches stories and was filled with the kind of wisecracking dialogue only humorists Ring Lardner and George S. Kaufman could write. The 1931 movie featured Jack Oakie as Fred and retained much of the play's humor if not its sharp satire. The story was remade in 1937 as *Blonde Trouble* but most of the songwriting jokes were dropped to concentrate on the gold digging plot. A 1974 television production edited the play somewhat and eliminated a few characters but it captured the witty, carefree style of the original. The cast was outstanding, from Tom Fitzsimmons's gullible Fred to Austin Pendleton as a hyperactive songwriter. Another interesting aspect of the production is the appearance of Broadway songwriter Stephen Sondheim giving a droll performance as Maxie.

Junior Miss

November 18, 1941 (Lyceum Theatre), a comedy by Jerome Chodorov, Joseph Fields. *Cast:* Patricia Peardon (Judy Graves), Phillip Ober (Harry Graves), Francesca Bruning (Ellen), Alexander Kirkland (Uncle Willis), Lenore Lonergan (Fluffy Adams), Matt Briggs, Barbara Robbins, Joan Newton, John Cushman. *Director:* Moss Hart. *Producer:* Max Gordon. 710 performances.

(Fox 1945). *Screenplay:* George Seaton. *Cast:* Peggy Ann Gardner (Judy Graves), Allyn Joslyn (Harry Graves), Faye Marlowe (Ellen), Stephen Dunne (Uncle Willis), Barbara Adams (Fluffy Adams), Mona Freeman, Sylvia Field, Stanley Praeger, John Alexander. *Director:* George Seaton. *Producer:* William Perlberg.

A series of short stories by Sally Benson in *The New Yorker* were adapted into a breezy domestic comedy that wartime audiences embraced for over two years. Teenager Judy Graves has such an overactive imagination that she believes her father is having an affair and that her uncle is a former crook. When she and her friend Fluffy act on these assumptions, a series on comic complications arise, each made worst when the two girls come up with new ways to try and fix things. By the end of the play Judy has lost interest in imagining things and finds that boys are much more interesting. Broadway had trouble casting plays once the war was in full swing so a play like this, which utilized youngsters and elderly character actors, was ideal. The comedy was also a favorite with theatre groups across the country long after the war ended. The 1945 movie was a faithful adaptation of the play and it also was popular with audiences. While much of it seems naive and obvious today, the movie is

an accurate record of the comic tone favored by the public at the time.

K-2

March 30, 1983 (Brooks Atkinson Theatre), a play by Patrick Meyers. *Cast:* Jeffrey De Munn (Taylor), Jay Patterson (Harold). *Director:* Terry Schreiber. *Producers:* Mary K. Frank, Cynthia Wood. 85 performances.

K 2: The Ultimate High (Paramount/Miramax 1992). *Screenplay:* Patrick Meyers, Scott Roberts. *Cast:* Michael Biehn (Taylor), Matt Craven (Harold), Raymond J. Barry (Claiborne), Hiroshi Fujioka (Takane Shimuzu), Luca Bercovici (Dallas Woolf), Julia Nickson, Patricia Charbonneau, Jamal Shah. *Director:* Franc Roddam. *Producers:* Melvyn J. Estrin, etc.

Near the summit of K2, the world's second highest mountain, two American climbers are stranded. One has broken his leg and the other struggles in vain to lower his companion down to safety. After a small avalanche buries some of their equipment, the wounded climber faces his fate and convinces the other to return to civilization. The most talked about aspect of the gripping drama was Ming Cho Lee's amazing scenic design, a three-story wall of ice that was realistic yet suggested something mythic in its shape and texture. The two-character play managed a modest run on Broadway but its technical difficulties allowed for few revivals. The 1992 British film was partially filmed on the real K2 but, for all its magnificent scenery, the movie is rather dull after its opening action sequence. Several characters and scenes were added in the flashbacks but the only interesting story was up on the mountain.

Key Exchange

July 14, 1981 (Orpheum Theatre), a play by Kevin Wade. *Cast:* Mark Blum (Michael), Brooke Adams (Lisa), Ben Masters (Philip). *Director:* Barnet Kellman. *Producers:* Frank Gero, etc. 352 performances.

(Fox 1985). *Screenplay:* Paul Kurta, Kevin Scott. *Cast:* Brooke Adams (Lisa), Ben Masters (Philip), Daniel Stern (Michael), Nancy Mette

(April), Danny Aiello (Carabello), Tony Roberts, Rex Robbins, Holland Taylor, Seth Allen, Bill Smitrovich. *Director:* Barnet Kellman. *Producers:* Paul Kurta, Mitchell Maxwell.

This intimate comedy-drama, about three Manhattan friends who meet on Sundays to ride their bicycles in Central Park, intrigued and amused Off Broadway audiences for a year. The cycling jaunts framed the plot which dealt with the newlywed Michael's growing awareness of his wife infidelity and a romantic relationship between Philip and Lisa that is trying to find enough commitment for them to exchange keys to each other's apartment. The three-character play was opened up for the 1985 movie and several characters and locations were added but, except for some pleasant footage of New York City, little was gained in the process. Brooke Adams and Ben Masters, the Lisa and Philip from the stage production, also appeared in the film and they are very agreeable, as is Daniel Stern as the neurotic Michael.

Key Largo

November 27, 1939 (Ethel Barrymore Theatre), a drama by Maxwell Anderson. *Cast:* Paul Muni (King McCloud), José Ferrer (Victor d'Alcala), Uta Hagen (Alegre d'Alcala), Frederic Tozere (Murillo), Ralph Theodore, Ruth March, Karl Malden, Harold Johnsrud. *Director:* Guthrie McClintic. *Producer:* Playwrights' Company. 105 performances.

(Warner 1948). *Screenplay:* Richard Brooks, John Huston. *Cast:* Humphrey Bogart (Frank McCloud), Edward G. Robinson (Johnny Rocco), Lauren Bacall (Nora Temple), Claire Trevor (Gaye Dawn), Thomas Gomez, Jay Silverheels, Marc Lawrence. *Director:* John Huston. *Producer:* Jerry Wald.

Some gangsters terrorize a Florida family but King McCloud, a bitter and disillusioned veteran from the Spanish civil war, appears on the scene and sacrifices himself to save the family. McCloud also managed to keep two innocent Native Americans from being framed by a local sheriff for a murder the gangsters committed. The drama offered riveting characters and much talk about the

war and personal responsibility. Some critics applauded the ideas presented, others found it preachy. But audience came to see the powerhouse cast headed by film star Paul Muni as McCloud. Humphrey Bogart played McCloud in the 1948 film and he was surrounded by several excellent supporting players, including Edward G. Robinson as the head gangster and Claire Trevor as his boozy mistress. The movie is better plotted and more exciting than the play even though it still pretty much takes place in one house on the Keys. Director John Huston builds the story to a climax that was also an improvement over the stage production.

Kid Boots

December 31, 1923 (Earl Carroll Theatre), a musical comedy by William Anthony McGuire, Otto Harbach. *Score:* Harry Tierney, Joseph McCarthy, etc. *Cast:* Eddie Cantor (Kid Boots), Ethelind Terry (Carmen Mendoza), Mary Eaton (Polly), Beth Beri, Harland Dixon, Marie Callahan, Harry Short. *Songs:* Keep Your Eye on The Ball; Let's Do and Say We Didn't; I'm in My Glory; Dinah; In the Rough. *Director:* Edgar Royce. *Producer:* Florenz Ziegfeld. 479 performances.

(Famous Players-Paramount 1926). *Screenplay:* George Marion, Jr., etc. *Cast:* Eddie Cantor (Kid Boots), Clara Bow (Clara McCoy), Billie Dove (Eleanore Belmore), Natalie Kingston (Carmen Mendoza), Lawrence Gray, Malcolm Waite, Harry Von Meter. *Director:* Frank Tuttle. *Producer:* B. P. Schulberg.

A merry musical vehicle for Eddie Cantor, this farcical show centered on golf and Prohibition. Caddie Cantor sells crooked golf balls as well as illegal hooch but when one of his balls is used in a championship, comic complications follow. The score was mediocre (except for the interpolated "Dinah") and the plot negligible but Cantor's fans kept the show running on Broadway for well over a year. Cantor reprised his role in the 1926 silent movie that, having lost the songs, played up the physical comedy. Cantor's clowning is still very enjoyable and the appearance of sassy Clara Bow adds to the fun.

Kind Lady

April 23, 1935 (Booth Theatre), a play by Jerome Chodorov. *Cast:* Grace George (Mary Herries), Henry Daniell (Henry Abbott), Irby Marsall (Lucy Weston), Florence Briton (Phyllis Glenning), Justine Chase (Ada Abbott), Alan Bunce (Peter Santard), Thomas Chambers, Francis Compton, Barbara Shields, Elfrida Derwent. *Director:* H. C. Potter. *Producers:* Potter & Haight. 102 performances.

(MGM 1935). *Screenplay:* Bernard Schubert. *Cast:* Aline MacMahon (Mary Herries), Basil Rathbone (Henry Abbott), Mary Carlisle (Phyllis), Frank Alberton (Peter Santard), Dudley Digges (Mr. Edwards), Doris Lloyd (Lucy Weston), Donald Meek. *Director:* George B. Seitz. *Producer:* Lucien Hubbard.

(MGM 1951). *Screenplay:* Charles Bennett, Jerry Davis, Jerome Chodorov. *Cast:* Ethel Barrymore (Mary Herries), Maurice Evans (Henry Elcott), Angela Lansbury (Mrs. Edwards), Keenan Wynn (Mr. Edwards), Betsy Blair (Ada Elcott), John Williams (Mr. Foster), Doris Lloyd (Rose). *Director:* John Sturges. *Producer:* Armand Deutsch.

Without a murder or murderer in sight, this thriller still managed to enthrall Broadway audiences with its everyday but diabolical story. The aged Mary Herries invites the kindly gentleman Henry Abbott in for tea on Christmas eve and before long he and his family take over the house, turn away Mary's friends saying she has gone abroad, are selling her art collection to live on, and keep Mary a virtual prisoner in her own home. Only when she can get the attention of a banker friend is she rescued. The melodrama, based on a Hugh Walpole story, was intriguing and disturbing because the way Henry insinuates his way into Mary's life is done in such a believable manner. The Broadway production was further enlivened by the return of stage favorite Grace George as Mary. The 1935 movie featured Aline MacMahon as Mary and Basil Rathbone as Henry and both played up the melodramatics of the piece so the story was less convincing. But the 1951 remake was more subtly done and, consequently, more effective. Ethel Barrymore was Mary and Maurice Evans was Henry and there are memorable supporting performances by Angela Lansbury, John Williams, and Keenan Wynn.

Kind Sir

November 4, 1953 (Alvin Theatre), a comedy by Norman Krasna. *Cast:* Mary Martin (Jane Kimball), Charles Boyer (Philip Clair), Dorothy Stickney (Margaret Munson), Frank Conroy (Alfred Munson), Margalo Gillmore, Robert Ross. *Director-producer:* Joshua Logan. 166 performances.

Indiscreet (Warner 1958). *Screenplay:* Norman Krasna. *Cast:* Cary Grant (Philip Adams), Ingrid Bergman (Anne Kalman), Cecil Parker (Alfred Munson), Phyllis Calvert (Margaret Munson), David Kossoff, Megs Jenkins. *Director:* Stanley Donen. *Producer:* Stanley Donen.

Mary Martin and Charles Boyer were the attraction in this pleasant romantic comedy about two far-from-young lovers. Actress Jane Kimball and diplomat Philip Clair have fallen in love but he says he is already married so the two settle for an extended affair. But when Jane finds out that Philip is not married and he only said it to avoid commitment, she is furious and vows revenge. But Philip has grown to love her so much that he gives up the ruse and proposes. The simplistic plot was punctuated by animated dialogue and a lovely production. The 1958 screen version was given the more provocative title *Indiscreet* and the stars were the mature Ingrid Bergman and Cary Grant. Both give superlative comic performances: subtle, charming, and magnetic. The story is nicely opened up to include several locations but the cast size is the same so the emphasis remains on the engaging characters and the breezy dialogue.

The King and I

March 29, 1951 (St. James Theatre), a musical play by Oscar Hammerstein. *Score:* Richard Rodgers, Oscar Hammerstein. *Cast:* Gertrude Lawrence (Anna Leonowens), Yul Brynner (King), Doretta Morrow (Tuptim), Dorothy Sarnoff (Lady Thiang), Larry Douglas. *Songs:* Shall We Dance?; Getting to Know You; Hello Young Lovers; We Kiss in a Shadow; Something Wonderful; I Whistle a Happy Tune; I Have Dreamed; A Puzzlement; My Lord and Master. *Director:* John Van Druten. *Choreographer:* Jerome Robbins. *Producers:* Rodgers and Hammerstein. 1,246 performances. Tony Award.

(Fox 1956). *Screenplay:* Ernest Lehman. *Score:* Richard Rodgers, Oscar Hammerstein. *Cast:* Deborah Kerr (Anna Leonowens), Yul Brynner (King), Rita Moreno (Tuptim), Martin Benson, Terry Saunders, Rex Thompson. *Songs:* Shall We Dance?; Getting to Know You; Hello Young Lovers; We Kiss in a Shadow; Something Wonderful; I Whistle a Happy Tune; A Puzzlement. *Director:* Walter Lang. *Choreographer:* Jerome Robbins. *Producer:* Charles Brackett.

Rodgers and Hammerstein's most "foreign" of musicals, this engrossing tale about the rivalry and hidden affection between a powerful Siamese king and the plucky Englishwoman sent to teach his children is a masterful work. Oscar Hammerstein's libretto handles the tricky relationship well and uses it to echo ideas about East and West, male and female, old ways and new ideas. The intoxicating score sounds Asian without ever leaving the familiar flavor of Broadway. The original production boasted two legendary performances: Gertrude Lawrence as sly Anna and Yul Brynner as the commanding King. Lawrence died during the run of the show and Deborah Kerr played Anna on the screen. Her singing is dubbed but it doesn't detract from a firm, beguiling performance. Even better, Brynner got to recreate his stage portrayal in the film and it is a vibrant, dangerous performance. With its evocative sets and costumes, recreated Jerome Robbins choreography, and nearly intact score, this remains the finest of all the Rodgers and Hammerstein movie musicals. A dreadful animated version of the musical was made by Disney in 1999 and aimed at children. With its abbreviated score, talking animals, miscalculated plot changes (the teenage prince is now a handsome stud in love with Tuptim), and annoying treatment of the characters, this embarrassment was disliked by all and the studio quickly withdrew it from movie houses.

King of Hearts

April 1, 1954 (Lyceum Theatre), a comedy by Jean Kerr, Eleanor Brooke. *Cast:* Donald Cook (Larry Larkin), Cloris Leachman (Dunreath Henry), Jackie Cooper (Francis X. Dignan), Rex Thompson, Carl Low, David Lewis, John Drew Dev-

ereaux. *Director:* Walter Kerr. *Producer:* Elaine Perry. 279 performances.

That Certain Feeling (Paramount 1956). *Screenplay:* William Altman, etc. *Cast:* Bob Hope (Francis X. Dignan), Eva Marie Saint (Dunreath Henry), George Sanders (Larry Larkin), Pearl Bailey (Gussie), Jerry Mathers, Al Capp, David Lewis. *Director-producers:* Norman Panama, Melvin Frank.

Egotistical cartoonist Larry Larkin thinks he is in love with his secretary Dunreath because she hangs on his every word. But when Larry hires the ghost cartoonist Francis X. Dignan to help him, Dunreath shifts her affections from Larry to Francis, who just happens to be her ex-husband. While not as polished as Jean Kerr's later comedies, the play has its fair share of laughs and interesting characters. The likable cast also helped and the comedy ran several months. Hollywood changed the title to *That Certain Feeling* so that Larry's housekeeper Pearly Bailey could sing the Gershwin song of the title in the 1956 movie. Bob Hope was starred (and miscast) as Francis with George Sanders and Eva Marie Saint in better form as Larry and Dunreath. But the only one who seems to have any fun with the story is Bailey who acts as a matchmaker to get Saint and Hope back together.

Kismet

December 25, 1911 (Knickerbocker Theatre), a play by Edward Knoblauch. *Cast:* Otis Skinner (Hajj), Hamilton Revelle (Wazir Mansur), Fred Eric (Caliph Abdullah), Rita Jolivet (Marsinah), Sheridan Block (Sheik Jawan), Amelia Barleon, Eleanor Gordon. *Director:* Harrison Grey Fiske. *Producers:* Charles Frohman, etc. 184 performances.

(Waldorf 1920). *Screenplay:* Charles E. Whittaker. *Cast:* Otis Skinner (Hajj), Rosemary Theby (Kut-al-Kulub), Elinor Fair (Marsinah), Marguerite Comot, Nicholas Dunaew. *Director:* Louis J. Gasnier.

(First National 1930). *Screenplay:* Howard Estabrook. *Cast:* Otis Skinner (Hajj), Loretta Young (Marsinah), David Manners (Caliph Abdallah), Sidney Blackmer (Wazir Mansur), Mary Duncan (Zaleekha). *Director:* John Francis Dillon. *Producer:* Robert North.

(MGM 1944). *Screenplay:* John Meehan. *Cast:* Ronald Colman (Hafiz), Marlene Dietrich (Jamille), James Craig (Caliph), Edward Arnold (Vizier Mansur), Joy Page (Marsinah), Hugh Hubert, Harry Davenport, Florence Bates, Hobart Cavanaugh. *Director:* William Dieterle. *Producer:* Everett Riskin.

December 3, 1953 (Ziegfeld Theatre), a musical comedy by Charles Lederer, Luther Davis. *Score:* Alexander Borodin, Robert Wright, George Forrest. *Cast:* Alfred Drake (Hajj), Doretta Morrow (Marsinah), Richard Kiley (Caliph), Joan Diener (LaLume), Henry Calvin, Steve Reeves. *Songs:* Stranger in Paradise; Baubles, Bangles and Beads; And This Is My Beloved; Night of My Nights; Sands of Time. *Director:* Albert Marre. *Choreographer:* Jack Cole. *Producers*: Charles Lederer, Edwin Lester. 583 performances. Tony Award.

(MGM 1955). *Screenplay:* Charles Lederer, Luther Davis. *Score:* Alexander Borodin, Robert Wright, George Forrest. *Cast:* Howard Keel (Hajj), Ann Blyth (Marsinah), Vic Damone (Caliph), Dolores Gray (Lalume), Monty Woolley (Omar), Sebastian Cabot (Wazir), Mike Mazurki, Jay C. Flippen. *Songs:* Stranger in Paradise; Baubles, Bangles and Beads; And This Is My Beloved; Night of My Nights; Sands of Time. *Director:* Vincente Minnelli. *Choreographer:* Jack Cole. *Producer:* Arthur Freed.

A first-rate adventure romance, this popular comedy-drama was stage actor Otis Skinner's greatest triumph and he returned to the work throughout his career. He played Hajj, a poet-beggar in old Baghdad who gets into all kinds of scrapes and escapades, from killing an evil Sheik, escaping from prison, rescuing his daughter from a harem, and outwitting the Wazir. The American playwright Edward Knoblauch couldn't get a Broadway producer to do the play so it was first presented in London. But when it was done in New York it was an immediate hit and often revived. Skinner recreated his Hajj in the 1920 silent screen version and in the 1930 talkie. In all, over a dozen movies were made from the story, several of them shorts or in foreign languages. Perhaps the most entertaining is the 1944 movie with Ronald Colman as Hajj and Marlene Dietrich, Edward Arnold, Hugh Herbert, Florence Bates, and others lending support. Some of the scenes drag but the production values are reputable and much of the stage's swagger

and playfulness remains. The familiar tale was given a new lease on life when the songwriting team of Robert Wright and George Forrest turned *Kismet* into a Broadway musical using the exotic and flowing melodies of Alexander Borodin. The larger than-life-characters were effectively musicalized and the score even produced two *Hit Parade* songs: "Baubles, Bangles and Beads" and "Stranger in Paradise." Because the musical was a hit both in New York and London, Hollywood filmed it and gave the work lush sets and costumes. But the score was so truncated that the movie failed to please as a musical and the plot so watered down that it missed being a satisfying adventure. Only Sebastian Cabot's wily Wazir comes close to the playfulness of the earlier versions. A television version of the musical was made in 1967 with Anna Maria Alberghetti, George Chakiris, and José Ferrer.

Kiss and Tell

March 17, 1943 (Biltmore Theatre), a comedy by F. Hugh Herbert. *Cast:* Judith Parrish (Mildred Pringle), Richard Widmark (Lt. Lenny Archer), Joan Caulfield (Corliss Archer), Robert White, Tommy Lewis, Jessie Royce Landis, Robert Keith, John Harvey. *Director-producer:* George Abbott. 957 performances.

(Columbia 1945). *Screenplay:* F. Hugh Herbert. *Cast:* Shirley Temple (Corliss Archer), Walter Abel (Harry Archer), Katharine Alexander (Janet Archer), Virginia Welles (Mildred Pringle), Jerome Courtland (Dexter Franklin), Robert Benchley, Porter Hall, Edna Holland, Tom Tully. *Director:* Richard Wallace. *Producer:* George Abbott.

Because the Archer and Pringle families do not get along with each other, Mildred Pringle keeps her elopement with Lenny Archer a secret, even after she gets pregnant. Mildred visits her obstetrician with her friend Corliss Archer (who is in on the secret) but Mrs. Pringle only sees Corliss come out of the office so rumors that Corliss is pregnant start to circulate. The comic confusions only resolve themselves when Lenny becomes a war hero and he and Mildred tell the truth about their marriage. The comedy was more technique than heart as the contrived plot struggled along in spite of itself but the play provided much-needed wartime comic relief and was a giant hit. The 1945 film starred a grown-up Shirley Temple as Corliss and, while some were shocked to even think of the former curly top pregnant out of wedlock, it was one of her better adult vehicles. The plot from the stage stayed pretty much the same so the film was considered a bit racy at times. But Temple and the spirited supporting cast helped make the movie a success so a sequel, *A Kiss for Corliss*, was made in 1949 with Temple as Corliss in love with an older man. The dull and unfunny comedy was a box office bomb and Temple retired from the screen.

Kiss Me, Kate

December 30, 1948 (New Century Theatre), a musical comedy by Bella and Samuel Spewack. *Score:* Cole Porter. *Cast:* Alfred Drake (Fred Graham/Petruchio), Patricia Morison (Lili Vanessi/Kate), Lisa Kirk (Lois Lane/Bianca), Harold Lang (Bill Calhoun/Lucentio), Jack Diamond, Harry Clark, Annabelle Hill, Lorenzo Fuller. *Songs:* Wunderbar; So in Love; Another Op'nin', Another Show; Too Darn Hot; Brush Up Your Shakespeare; Always True to You in My Fashion; I Hate Men; Where Is the Life That Late I Led?; Were Thine That Special Face. *Director:* John C. Wilson. *Choreographer:* Hanya Holm. *Producers:* Saint Subber, Lemuel Ayers. 1,070 performances. Tony Award.

(MGM 1953). *Screenplay:* Dorothy Kingsley. *Score:* Cole Porter. *Cast:* Howard Keel (Fred Graham/Petruchio), Kathryn Grayson (Lilli Vanessi/Kate), Ann Miller (Lois Lane/Bianca), Tommy Rall (Bill Calhoun/Lucentio), Keenan Wynn, James Whitmore. *Songs:* Wunderbar; So in Love; From This Moment On; Too Darn Hot; Brush Up Your Shakespeare; Always True to You in My Fashion; I Hate Men; Where Is the Life That Late I Led?; Were Thine That Special Face. *Director:* George Sidney. *Choreographers:* Hermes Pan, Bob Fosse. *Producer:* Jack Cummings.

Cole Porter's greatest triumph is a delicious blending of psuedo–Elizabethan period piece and contemporary backstage panache as a troupe of players perform a musical version of Shakespeare's *The Taming of the Shrew*. The clever libretto manages to tell both the onstage tale as well as the backstage story equally well and Porter devised two scores to fill out both plots. The show ran twice as long as any previous Porter musical and it remains a favorite in revival. The movie version faithfully kept the whole score (and even added the delightful "From This Moment On") but tinkered with the script a bit, particularly in the early portions. But the best of *Kiss Me, Kate* comes across on the screen. There is one irritating intrusion: the studio filmed the musical in 3-D and awkwardly had objects and the players being flung out to the camera at times. The 3-D fad quickly passed and the movie was re-released in a traditional format, but one is still stuck with those flying plates and Howard Keel inexplicably delivering "Where Is the Life That Late I Led?" on a runway jetting out into the audience. A television version in 1968, with Robert Goulet and Carol Lawrence as the battling couple, was greatly abridged but was still enjoyable for the most part.

Kiss the Boys Goodbye

September 28, 1938 (Henry Miller Theatre), a comedy by Clare Boothe. *Cast:* Helen Claire (Cindy Lou Bethany), Millard Mitchell (Lloyd Lloyd), Philip Ober (Horace Rand), Sheldon Leonard (Herbert Z. Harner), Hugh Marlowe (Top Rumson), Benay Venuta (Myra Stanhope), Wyman Holmes, John Alexander, Edwin Nicander. *Director:* Antoinette Perry. *Producer:* Brock Pemberton. 286 performances.

(Paramount 1941). *Screenplay:* Dwight Taylor, Harry Tugend. *Score:* Frank Loesser, Victor Schertzinger. *Cast:* Mary Martin (Cindy Lou Bethany), Don Ameche (Lloyd Lloyd), Oscar Levant (Dick Rayburn), Virginia Dale (Gwen Abbott), Barbara Jo Allen (Myra Stanhope), Raymond Walburn (Top Rumson), Elizabeth Patterson, Jerome Cowan, Connee Boswell, Eddie Anderson. *Songs:* That's How I Got My Start; Sand in My Shoes; Find Yourself a Melody; Kiss the Boys Goodbye. *Director:* Victor Schertzinger. *Producers:* William LeBaron, Paul Jones.

While not nearly as caustic as *The Women*, Boothe's other popular satire had plenty of punch in it on stage as she spoofed the current mania over the filming of *Gone With the Wind*. The demure Southern belle Cindy Lou gets the role when she throws a temper tantrum but loses it when she shoots the movie producer who tries to seduce her. Hollywood was the butt of most of the jokes, which always pleased theatregoers. But the film softened the script and turned the piece into a musical, affording Mary Martin a chance to show off her singing and comic talents. Connee Boswell also shines in delivering the film's hit song "Sand in My Shoes." The satire lost in the screen version was somewhat replaced by the musical numbers. The movie was quickly forgotten and the play has been unjustly neglected.

Knickerbocker Holiday

October 19, 1938 (Ethel Barrymore Theatre), a musical comedy by Maxwell Anderson. *Score:* Kurt Weill, Maxwell Anderson. *Cast:* Walter Huston (Pieter Stuyvesant), Ray Middleton (Washington Irving), Jeanne Madden (Tina Tienhoven), Richard Kollmar (Brom Broeck), Robert Rounseville, Howard Freeman. *Songs:* September Song; How Can You Tell an American?; It Never Was You; There's Nowhere to Go But Up. *Director:* Joshua Logan. *Choreographers*: Carl Randall, Edwin Denby. *Producer:* Playwrights' Company. 168 performances.

(United Artists 1944). *Screenplay:* David Boehm, Rowland Leigh, Harold Goldman. *Score:* Kurt Weill, Maxwell Anderson, etc. *Cast:* Charles Coburn (Pieter Stuyvesant), Nelson Eddy (Brom Broeck), Constance Dowling (Tina Tienhoven), Johnnie "Scat" Davis, Richard Hale, Shelley Winters, Ernest Cossart, Otto Kruger. *Songs:* September Song; There's Nowhere to Go But Up; Love Has Made This Such a Lovely Day; Holiday; One More Smile. *Director-producer:* Harry Joe Brown.

Maxwell Anderson's politically charged libretto about governor Pieter Stuyvesant in 1647 New Amsterdam was a thinly disguised attack against FDR whose growing power during the Depression alarmed some Americans. Yet the sting was softened by the fact that Walter Huston was a charming, lovable despot and his singing of the haunting "September Song" became one of the musical theatre's fondest memories. Nonetheless,

most Americans approved of Roosevelt and the play had limited appeal. By the time the film was made in 1944, FDR was at the peak of his popularity and the watered-down screen version only concentrated on a feeble romantic triangle rather than politics. Surprisingly, movie favorite Huston was passed over for Charles Coburn as Stuyvesant and he was the most interesting aspect of the film. Most of the Anderson-Weill score was dropped for new songs, but the "September Song" remained. Both play and film are largely forgotten now but that song continues to haunt.

Lady, Be Good!

December 1, 1924 (Liberty Theatre), a musical comedy by Guy Bolton, Fred Thompson. *Score:* George and Ira Gershwin. *Cast:* Adele Astaire (Susie Trevor), Fred Astaire (Dick Trevor), Walter Catlett (J. Watterson Watkins), Alan Edwards, Cliff Edwards, Kathlene Martyn. *Songs:* Fascinating Rhythm; Oh, Lady, Be Good!; Hang Onto Me; So Am I; The Half of It Dear Blues; Little Jazz Bird. *Director:* Felix Edwardes. *Choreographer:* Sammy Lee. *Producers:* Alex A. Aarons, Vinton Freedley. 330 performances.

(MGM 1941). *Screenplay:* Jack McGowan, Kay Van Riper, John McClain. *Score:* George and Ira Gershwin, Jerome Kern, Oscar Hammerstein, etc. *Cast:* Ann Sothern (Dixie Donegan Crane), Robert Young (Eddie Crane), Eleanor Powell (Marilyn Marsh), Lionel Barrymore (Judge Murdock), John Carroll, Red Skelton, Dan Dailey. *Songs:* Fascinating Rhythm; The Last Time I Saw Paris; Oh, Lady Be Good!; You'll Never Know; Your Words and My Music. *Director:* Norman Z. McLeod. *Choreographer:* Busby Berkeley. *Producer:* Arthur Freed.

This innovative, jazz-influenced musical marked the first Broadway show scored by the Gershwin brothers and the first starring appearance by Adele and Fred Astaire. The storyline followed a vaudeville brother-sister act on the outs and how her posing as a Spanish countess gets them involved with both complications and romance. But it was the vibrant Gershwin score and the stars's infectious dancing that made the show such a hit. Hollywood made a silent version of the tale in 1928 featuring Jack Mulhall,

Dorothy Mackaill, and John Miljan, and a sound remake thirteen years later. But, aside from two tunes from the Broadway score, little remained of the original stage work. The new plot was a dreary affair about the on and off relationship of two married songwriters and the movie only came to life when Eleanor Powell tapped and Ann Sothern sang the poignant "The Last Time I Saw Paris."

Lady in the Dark

January 23, 1941 (Alvin Theatre), a musical comedy by Moss Hart. *Score:* Kurt Weill, Ira Gershwin. *Cast:* Gertrude Lawrence (Liza Elliott), Macdonald Carey (Charley Johnson), Danny Kaye (Russell Paxton), Victor Mature (Randy Curtis), Bert Lytell (Kendall Nesbitt). *Songs:* My Ship; The Saga of Jennie; Tschaikowsky; This Is New; Girl of the Moment. *Directors:* Hassard Short, Moss Hart. *Choreographer:* Albertina Rasch. *Producer:* Sam H. Harris. 467 performances.

(Paramount 1944). *Screenplay:* Frances Goodrich, Albert Hackett. *Score:* Kurt Weill, Ira Gershwin, etc. *Cast:* Ginger Rogers (Liza Elliott), Ray Milland (Charley Johnson), Warner Baxter (Kendall Nesbitt), Jon Hall (Randy Curtis), Barry Sullivan, Mischa Auer. *Songs:* The Saga of Jenny; Girl of the Moment; One Life to Live; This Is New; Dream Lover. *Director:* Mitchell Leisen. *Choreographer:* Billy Daniels. *Producer:* B. G. DeSylva.

One of the most innovative musicals of the 1940s, this play with songs broke several conventions as it told its story of fashion magazine editor Liza Elliott who seeks psychiatric help because she finds she is having trouble making any decisions of late. All of the production numbers occurred in dream sequences prompted by the psychiatrist and the characters in Liza's real life appeared in various guises in her fantasies. Moss Hart wrote the clever script and Kurt Weill and Ira Gershwin provided the distinguished score. One of the main reason's for the musical's popularity was the star turn by beloved favorite Gertrude Lawrence as Liza and the show also made a star of Danny Kaye who demonstrated his comic prowess in the rapid-fire delivery of the song "Tschaikowsky." Lawrence was no movie

star so the screen version was headed by Ginger Rogers as Liza. Kaye and his song were also cut along with most of the score, including the haunting ballad "My Ship" which was the unifying link in the Broadway musical. Although the color dream sequences were done up elaborately and expensively, most of the movie was flat and ineffective. The expressionistic original was ideal material for a vibrant cinematic treatment; instead the movie was just another mindless star vehicle.

Lakeboat

February 23, 1982 (Goodman Theatre—Chicago), a play by David Mamet. *Cast*: Ron Dean (Dale), Robert Knepper, Bruce Jarchow, Mike Nussbaum, Robert Scogin, Dennis Kennedy, Jack Wallace, Nathan Davis. *Director*: Gregory Mosher. *Producer:* Goodman Theatre. 26 performances.

(Panorama 2001). *Screenplay*: David Mamet. *Cast*: Tony Mamet (Dale Katzman), Charles Durning, Peter Falk, Denis Leary, Andy Garcia, Robert Forster, J. J. Johnston, Jack Wallace, George Wendt. *Director*: Joe Mantegna. *Producers*: Eric R. Epperson, etc.

Although it has never received a major New York production, this atmospheric slice-of-life drama was David Mamet's first produced play and it foreshadows his later, more mature work. Ivy League grad student Dale Katzman gets a summer job as cook aboard a commercial freighter that sails the Great Lakes. The crew is a colorful, low-brow gang of "lifers" who are as irreverent and salty as their talk. There is little plot but during a series of vignettes Dale gradually finds much to admire about the crude but solid men. After being presented as a one-act in Vermont, Mamet expanded the piece and it was produced at a handful of regional theatres. Many years later he adapted and opened up the drama for a 2001 film with his younger brother Tony Mamet playing Dale. It is a rather stagnant movie plotwise but the performances, including some star turns by celebrities, are riveting and the potent Mamet stage dialogue remains in scatological full force.

The Last Mile

February 13, 1930 (Sam H. Harris Theatre), a drama by John Wexley. *Cast*: Spencer Tracy (John Mears), George Leach (Eddie Werner), Howard Phillips (Fred Mayor), James Bell (Richard Walters), Hal Norcross, Ernest Whitman. *Director*: Chester Erskin. *Producer:* Herman Shumlin. 285 performances.

(K-B-S 1932). *Screenplay*: Seton I. Miller. *Cast*: Preston Foster (Killer Mears), Howard Phillips (Richard Walters), George E. Stone (Berg), Noel Madison (D'Amoro), Alan Roscoe, Paul Fix. *Director-producer*: Samuel Bischoff.

(United Artists 1959). *Screenplay*: Seton I. Miller, Milton Subotsky. *Cast*: Mickey Rooney (Killer Mears), Clifford David (Richard Walters), Don Barry (Drake), Harry Millard, Michael Constantine, Frank Conroy, Alan Bunce, Leon Janney. *Director*: Howard W. Koch. *Producer*: Max Rosenberg.

One of the most explosive of prison dramas, this tense story of a mutiny on death row of a state penitentiary was disturbing to audiences used to stereotypic portrayals of criminals. The mutiny is led by the impassioned John Mears who kills a guard coming to deliver an inmate his last meal. Although they know the plan must ultimately fail, the prisoners are so bitter they follow Mears's lead and take over parts of the facility until Mears is gunned down. Among the highlights of the powerful production was a vivid performance by Spencer Tracy as Mears, his first major Broadway role. The notoriety won Tracy a Hollywood contract and he would only return to the New York stage one more time fifteen years later. Oddly, the 1932 movie did not include Tracy and Mears was played by Preston Foster. The picture is more melodramatic than the play and it builds in suspense to a penetrating climax. The adult Mickey Rooney attempted to change his image and played Mears in the 1959 remake which was also very potent. Rooney's hysterical breakdown before his execution is nightmarish in its intensity and brutal honesty.

The Last of Mrs. Lincoln

December 12, 1972 (ANTA Theatre), a play by James Prideaux. *Cast*: Julie Harris (Mary Lincoln), David Rounds (Robert Lincoln), Ralph Clanton (Ninian Edwards), Maureen Anderman (Mary Harlan), Tobias Haller, Leora Dana, Kate Wilkinson, Brian Farrell. *Director*: George Schaefer. *Producers:* Richard Barr, etc. 63 performances.

(TV 1976). *Teleplay*: James Prideaux. *Cast*: Julie Harris (Mary Lincoln), Michael Cristofer (Robert Lincoln), Patrick Duffy, John Furlong, Robby Benson. *Director-producer*: George Schaefer.

During the eighteen years after the assassination of Lincoln, his wife Mary traveled from place to place trying to make a home but was suspected by many of being a Confederate sympathizer. Her pension is reduced, her young son Tad dies, and her elder son Robert commits her to a mental asylum. It was a sad tale and, as told in this episodic drama, there seemed little reason to tell it. But Julie Harris's performance as Mary Todd Lincoln was widely cherished as she turned the character into a complex, desperate, yet brave woman. Even though Harris won the Tony Award, the play only lasted two months. Fortunately she reprised her performance in a 1976 television production. Much of the cast seems stiff and uncomfortable in the period piece and the abridged plotting is not any better than the stage script but, again, Harris makes it all worthwhile.

The Last of the Red Hot Lovers

December 28, 1969 (Eugene O'Neill Theatre), a comedy by Neil Simon. *Cast*: James Coco (Barney Cashman), Linda Lavin (Elaine Navazio), Marcia Rodd (Bobbi Michele), Doris Roberts (Jeanette Fisher). *Director*: Robert Moore. *Producer:* Saint Subber. 706 performances.

(Paramount 1972). *Screenplay*: Neil Simon. *Cast*: Alan Arkin (Barney Cashman), Sally Kellerman (Elaine), Renee Taylor (Jeanette), Paula Prentiss (Bobbi Michele), Sandy Salson, Frank Loverde, Bella Bruck. *Director*: Gene Saks. *Producer*: Howard W. Koch.

Fish restaurant owner Barney Cashman has had a "nice" life but he wants to put some color in his waning years so he sets out to have an extramarital affair. His three attempts are all dismal failures, none of the relationships are consummated, and Barney is left with a better appreciation of his wife and his dull life. James Coco played Barney with sparkling comic desperation and the role made him a Broadway star. The three would-be lovers were deftly played by Linda Lavin as the cold Elaine, Marcia Rodd as the bubble-headed Bobbi, and Doris Roberts as the depressing Jeanette. While Barney's misadventures were predictable, the recurring comic details and the hilarious dialogue made the play highly entertaining. The comedy ran over two years on Broadway and also found success on the road, in dinner theatres, and with community groups. Where it failed miserably was on the screen. Alan Arkin was miscast as Barney in the 1972 film and his idea of comedy was to scream at each of the three ladies. Sally Kellerman, Paula Prentiss, and Renee Taylor fared somewhat better in the roles but the pedestrian direction made the piece look more stagnant than any play.

The Late George Apley

November 21, 1944 (Lyceum Theatre), a comedy by John P. Marquand, George S. Kaufman. *Cast*: Leo G. Carroll (George Apley), Joan Chandler (Eleanor), Reynolds Evans (Horatio Willing), Margaret Philips (Agnes Willing), John Conway (Howard Boulder), David McKay, Janet Beecher, Catherine Proctor. *Director*: George S. Kaufman. *Producer:* Max Gordon. 385 performances.

(Fox 1947). *Screenplay*: Philip Dunne. *Cast*: Ronald Colman (George Apley), Peggy Cummins (Eleanor), Vanessa Brown (Agnes Willing), Richard Haydn (Horatio Willing), Charles Russell (Howard Boulder), Edna Best, Mildred Natwick, Richard Ney. *Director*: Joseph L. Mankiewicz. *Producer*: Fred Kohlmar.

John P. Marquand's novel, about a stuffy Boston Brahmin and his difficulty with anything that threatens his quiet, conservative life, was adapted into an episodic comedy that amused audiences in its own gentle way. George Apley sees his children doing such horrifying things such as date a Yalie or go into business. Yet when George dies his son seems to fall into his father's manner and it looks like the old lifestyle will continue on. Leo G. Carroll was unanimously lauded for his dry, precise performance as George and the genteel comedy pleased enough to run a year. But such soft-spoken satire doesn't sit as well with movie-goers and the faithful 1947 film struck most reviewers as dull. Yet Ronald Colman makes an impressive effort to tone down his charisma to play George and his supporting cast is first rate.

Laughter on the 23rd Floor

November 22, 1993 (Richard Rodgers Theatre), a play by Neil Simon. *Cast*: Nathan Lane (Max Prince), Lewis J. Stadlen (Milt), Mark-Linn Baker (Val), Randy Graff (Carol), Stephen Mailer (Lucas), John Slattery (Kenny), Ron Orbach (Ira), J. K. Simmons (Brian), Betty Schram (Helen). *Director*: Jerry Zaks. *Producers:* Emanuel Azenberg, Leonard Soloway. 320 performances.

(TV 2001). *Teleplay*: Neil Simon. *Cast*: Nathan Lane (Max Prince), Mark Linn-Baker (Val Skotsky), Saul Rubinek (Ira Stone), Dan Castellaneta (Milt Fields), Richard Portnow (Harry Prince), Sherry Miller (Faye), Ardon Best, Victor Garber, Colin Fox, Frank Proctor. *Director*: Richard Benjamin. *Producer*: Jeffrey Lampert.

The Sid Caesar-like television comic Max Prince pops pills, puts his fist through walls, and generally is always on the verge of a nervous breakdown as he and his writers try to come up with a show each week. Adding to Max's worries are meddling sponsors, the McCarthy witch hunt hearings, and requests by the network to "dumb down" his show for the masses. Neil Simon's semi-autobiographical play was filled with one-liners but was basically a bitter, angry work and not the laughfest most theatregoers wanted. Nathan Lane was perhaps too convincing as Max because it was difficult to like him or his performance. The supporting cast was estimable and, their characters being less neurotic, easier to enjoy. Mixed notices aside, the play ran a year on Broadway. Simon did some rewriting for the 2001 television production and director Richard Benjamin handled the material better because the new version was a vast improvement over the stage production. Lane was again Max but this time his harsh qualities were balanced with his fearful interior and Simon's new scenes allowed those qualities to come through. The play is opened up nicely for the small screen and again the supporting players are very proficient. If this production had played on Broadway it would have run much longer.

Leah Kleschna

December 12, 1904. (Manhattan Theatre), a drama by C. M. S. McLellan. *Cast*: Minnie Maddern Fiske (Leah Kleschna), John Mason (Paul Sylvaine), George Arliss (Raoul Berton), William B. Mack (Schram), Emily Stevens (Claire Berton), Charles Cartwright, Etienne Giradot, Edward Donnelly. *Director*: Harrison Fiske. *Producers:* Minnie Maddern Fiske, Harrison Fiske. 131 performances.

(Famous Players 1913). *Screenplay*: C. M. S. McLellan. *Cast*: Carlotta Nillson (Leah Kleschna), House Peters (Paul Sylvaine), Hal Clarendon (Kleschna), Alexander Gaden, Frank H. Crane. *Director*: J. Searle Dawley. *Producer*: Daniel Frohman.

One of the most popular of the "crook" plays at the turn of the century, this melodrama provided a fertile vehicle for the celebrated Mrs. Fiske who usually attacked more highbrow roles. Leah Kleschna is a thief who steals at her father's command. But when she attempts to purloin some jewels at the home of Paul Sylvaine, Leah recognizes him as the man who had once saved her life during a shipwreck. She doesn't go through with the theft but is accused all the same when the villainous Raoul Berton takes the goods and casts suspicion on Leah. By the final curtain Leah is cleared and she even ends up in the arms of Paul. Splendid performances by Fiske, John Mason, and George Arliss helped make the melodrama a hit in New York and on the road but the story was dated by the end of World War One and the play was rarely revived afterwards. A silent film version in 1913 featured Carlotta Nillson as Leah and the melodramatic romance was ideal for moviegoers looking for a rousing good story.

Leathernecking see Present Arms

Lemon Sky

May 17, 1970 (Playhouse Theatre), a play by Lanford Wilson. *Cast*: Christopher Walken (Alan), Charles Durning (Douglas), Bonnie Bartlett, Steven Paul, Kathryn Bauman, Lee McCain, Willie Rook. *Director*: Warren Enters. *Producers:* Haila Stoddard, etc. 17 performances.

(TV 1988). *Teleplay*: Lanford Wilson. *Cast*: Kevin Bacon (Alan), Tom Atkins (Douglas), Lindsay Crouse (Ronnie), Kyra Sedgwick (Carol), Welker White, Casey Affleck, Peter MacEwan. *Director*: Jan Egleson. *Producer*: Marcus Viscidi.

Teenager Alan visits the California home of his estranged father and his new family and they seem to get along so well that Alan considers staying. But eventually old wounds are reopened and Alan realizes what the reality of his father means and decides to live away from him. One of playwright Lanford Wilson's earliest works, this domestic drama was rich in characterization and interesting talk but lean on plot. Although a handful of critics recognized a promising talent, the Off Broadway production closed in two weeks. The play would be re-evaluated after Wilson became well known and in 1985 a superb revival in New York led to a new appreciation of the work. The 1988 television production, with Kevin Bacon as Alan, was beautifully preformed and directed though the play does not compare favorably to Wilson's later works.

Lenny

May 26, 1971 (Brooks Atkinson Theatre), a play by Julian Barry. *Cast*: Cliff Gorman (Lenny Bruce), Jane House (Rusty), Joe Silver, Paul Lieber, Erica Yohn, Jody Oliver, Bill Smith, Robert Weil. *Director*: Tom O'Horgan. *Producers:* Jules Fisher, etc. 455 performances.

(United Artists 1974). *Screenplay*: Julian Berry. *Cast*: Dustin Hoffman (Jenny Bruce), Valerie Perrine (Honey Bruce), Jan Miner (Sally Marr), Stanley Beck, Frankie Man, Gary Morton. *Director*: Bob Fosse. *Producer*: Marvin Worth.

This surrealistic play based on "the life and words of Lenny Bruce" was not so much a biography of the controversial stand-up comic as it was an expressionistic celebration of his persona. Moving from nightclub routines to bizarre dream sequences induced by drugs, Lenny relives his short, tragic life while he is surrounded by giant puppets, voices, and monologues by those who knew him. Both critics and audiences were not so sure about the hyperactive production, but they all extolled Cliff Gorman giving the performance of his career as Lenny. Gorman won the Tony Award but was overlooked by the studios for the 1974 film version, wishing to use a more bankable star. Dustin Hoffman was electric in the role but the production was a far cry from the stage original. Director Bob Fosse filmed the story more as a straightforward biopic but used a gritty, documentary approach to the material. Stunningly photographed in black and white, the movie had a distinctive look and texture that was right in keeping with Hoffman's brutal, uncompromising performance.

Let Us Be Gay

February 21, 1929 (Little Theatre), a comedy by Rachel Crothers. *Cast*: Francine Larrimore (Kitty Brown), Charlotte Granville (Mrs. Bouncy Bouccicault), Warren William (Bob Brown), Rita Vale (Deidre Lessing), Ross Alexander, Gilbert Douglas, George Wright, Jr., Adele Klaer. *Director*: Rachel Crothers. *Producer*: John Golden. 363 performances.

(MGM 1930). *Screenplay*: Frances Marion. *Cast*: Norma Shearer (Kitty Brown), Marie Dressler (Mrs. Bouncy Bouccicault), Rod La Rocque (Bob Brown), Gilbert Emery (Townley), Hedda Hopper (Madge Livingston), Raymond Hackett, Sally Eilers, Tyrell Davis. *Director-producer*: Robert Z. Leonard.

When Kitty and Bob Brown quickly divorce, they go their separate ways. But three years later they are thrown together when Bob is dating a granddaughter of one of Kitty's elderly friends. Kitty is asked to break up the relationship but she refuses. Regardless, she and Bob end up back together. Rachel Crothers's usual insight into

women and what lies beneath the clichés is in evidence in this light but observant comedy that ran a year on Broadway. The play also became a favorite of summer stock and community theatres for many years after. The 1930 movie boasted a stellar cast and was reset in Paris so that the romantic aspects of the comedy could be heightened. It is an engaging film but, like its title, long out of date and a bit too thin for modern tastes.

Let's Do It Again see *The Awful Truth*

Let's Face It!

October 29, 1941 (Imperial Theatre), a musical comedy by Herbert and Dorothy Fields. *Score*: Cole Porter. *Cast*: Danny Kaye (Jerry Walker), Eve Arden (Maggie Watson), Benny Baker (Frankie Burns), Vivian Vance (Nancy Collister), Mary Jane Walsh (Winnie Potter), Nanette Fabray, Edith Meiser, Jack Williams. *Songs*: Ace in the Hole; Farming; Melody in 4-F; Let's Not Talk About Love; Ev'rything I Love. *Director*: Edgar MacGregor. *Choreographer*: Charles Walters. *Producer*: Vinton Freedley. 547 performances.

(Paramount 1943). *Screenplay*: Harry Tugend. *Score*: Cole Porter, etc. *Cast*: Bob Hope (Jerry Walker), Betty Hutton (Winnie Potter), Eve Arden (Maggie Watson), Phyllis Povah (Nancy Collister), ZaSu Pitts, Dave Willock, Cully Richards. *Songs*: Let's Not Talk About Love; Let's Face It!; Who Did? I Did. *Director*: Sidney Lanfield. *Producer*: Fred Kohlmar.

This wartime musical, about three jealous wives who take up with a trio of servicemen to avenge their husbands, was a funny and topical show, based on the comedy *Cradle Snatchers* (qv), that boasted lively performances and a tuneful Cole Porter score. Danny Kaye, in his first starring Broadway role, was particularly entertaining with his fast-talking renditions of "Farming" and "Melody in 4-F" (the second number written by his wife Sylvia Fine). The 1943 screen version was fashioned into a vehicle for Bob Hope in Kaye's role and the stage plot was made more convoluted by having the hero outwit a German submarine and his fiancée running a ladies' health camp. Only two Porter songs were used and not much other music was added so the film played more like a goofy wartime comedy than a musical.

A Life in the Theatre

October 20, 1977 (Theatre de Lys), a play by David Mamet. *Cast*: Ellis Rabb (Robert), Peter Evans (John). *Director*: Gerald Gutierrez. *Producer:* Jane Harmon. 288 performances.

(TV 1993). *Teleplay*: David Mamet. *Cast*: Jack Lemmon (Robert), Matthew Broderick (John). *Director*: Gregory Mosher. *Producers*: Thomas A. Bliss, Patricia Wolff.

Perhaps David Mamet's least typical work, this intimate two-character play about two actors who perform together in a series of productions was lightweight, simple, and even a bit affectionate. We see the two men, the elder, experienced Robert and the younger, eager John, before and after performances and sometimes in the middle of acting in clichéd plays. Their conversation is often sparse and cryptic but usually very funny and knowing. The Off Broadway production was simple but elegantly directed and the performances by veteran Ellis Rabb and newcomer Peter Evans were precise and charming. After many revivals in regional theatres, the little play was adapted for television in 1993 with realistic settings and major stars for the cast. Matthew Broderick is appropriately unpolished and earnest as John but Jack Lemmon's Robert is too theatrical and too emphatic. He tries so hard that sometimes Broderick seems more like the more experienced performer.

Life with Father

November 8, 1939 (Empire Theatre), a comedy by Howard Lindsay, Russel Crouse. *Cast*: Howard Lindsay (Father), Dorothy Stickney (Vinnie), John Drew Devereaux (Clarence), Teresa Wright (Mary), Richard Simon, Raymond Roe, Ruth Hammond, Richard Sterling, Larry Robinson, Katherine Bard. *Director*: Bretaigne Windust. *Producer:* Oscar Serlin. 3,224 performances.

(Warner 1947). *Screenplay*: Donald Ogden Stewart. *Cast*: William Powell (Father), Irene Dunne (Mother), Jimmy Lydon (Clarence Day, Jr.), Elizabeth Taylor (Mary), Edmund Gwenn, ZaSu Pitts, Martin Milner, Emma Dunn, Johnny Calkins, Moroni Olsen. *Director*: Michael Curtiz. *Producer*: Robert Buckner.

Clarence Day's stories in *The New Yorker* about his stern father and dithering mother were turned into a comedy classic that broke the record for the longest-running non-musical in New York, a record that has never been bested. The play is mostly episodic as Father has his disagreements and frustrations with all of his family members, particularly over the issue of his being baptized after all these years. But, as usual, Father loses the battle and goes off to church complaining "I'm going to be baptized, damn it!" Co-author Howard Lindsay played Father in the original cast and he brought a stuffy, silliness to the role while Dorothy Stickney was hilarious as the illogical but sensible mother. The 1947 screen version featured risible performances by William Powell as Father and Irene Dunne as Mother, with enjoyable support from Edmund Gwenn, Elizabeth Taylor, Jimmy Lydon, and others. The period decor is as bright as a musical and the costumes are perhaps more Hollywood than turn-of-the-century New York but the movie has its charms even if it moves along too slowly at times. Unfortunately the censorship code would not let Father bellow his famous exit line. A television series based on the play ran from 1953 to 1955 with Leon Ames as Father.

Lightnin'

August 26, 1918 (Gaiety Theatre), a play by Winchell Smith, Frank Bacon. *Cast*: Frank Bacon (Lightnin' Bill Jones), Ralph Morgan (John Marvin), Jessie Pringle (Mrs. Jones), Beatrice Nichols (Millie), Paul Stanton (Raymond Thomas), Harry Davenport (Rodney Harper), George Thompson, Jane Oaker. *Producers:* John Golden, Winchell Smith. 1,291 performances.

(Fox 1925). *Screenplay*: Frances Marion. *Cast*: Jay Hunt (Lightnin' Bill Jones), Wallace MacDonald (John Marvin), Richard Travers (Raymond Thomas), J. Farrell MacDonald, Otis Harlan, Edythe Chapman. *Director*: John Ford.

(Fox 1930). *Screenplay*: Sonya Levien, S N. Behrman. *Cast*: Will Rogers (Lightnin' Bill Jones), Louise Dresser (Mary Jones), Joel McCrea (John Marvin), Helen Cohan (Millie), Jason Robards, Sr., Luke Cosgrave. *Director*: Henry King. *Producers*: John Golden, Henry King.

Lightnin' Bill Jones and his wife own a hotel that straddles the California-Nevada border and a painted line runs down the middle of the lobby to tell you which state you are in. This comes in handy for those needing an out-of-state divorce or a quick getaway across the state line. In fact, the talkative boozer Jones has used it for that purpose himself. But Mrs. Jones is fed up with Lightnin's behavior and it takes all his powers to keep her from divorcing him and, at the same time, help out a young speculator with whom he has become friends. The waggish plot was entertaining but the highlight of the play was the character of the crafty, seemingly slow-witted Lightnin', an American original played by co-author Frank Bacon. His performance was so acclaimed that the producers feared the production would only work with Bacon in it. But *Lightnin'* was a hit on the road and ran on Broadway for nearly four years, a record at the time. Bacon played the title character 2,000 times in various productions but died in 1922 so the first screen version featured Jay Hunt as Lightnin' Jones. Since the character's humor was vocal rather than physical, the silent film was only mildly interesting. But the 1930 movie, in which Will Rogers made his talkie debut as Lightnin', has all the folksy flavor and rural humor of the play. Rogers is ideally cast in the part and his slow but beautifully-timed delivery is an American classic of sorts. The film also has a notable supporting cast and fine production values. The play is rarely revived today but the character of Lightnin' Bill Jones is still with us in many variations.

Li'l Abner

November 15, 1956 (St. James Theatre), a musical comedy by Norman Panama, Melvin Frank. *Score*: Gene de Paul, Johnny Mercer. *Cast*: Peter Palmer (Abner Yokum), Edith Adams (Daisy Mae), Stubby Kaye (Marryin' Sam), Charlotte Rae (Mammy Yokum), Howard St. John (Gen. Bullmoose), Tina Louise (Appassionata von Climax), Julie Newmar, Grover Dale. *Songs:* Namely You; Jubilation T. Cornpone; If I Had My Druthers; Rag Offen the Bush; The Country's in the Very Best of Hands. *Director-choreographer:* Michael Kidd. *Producers:* Norman Panama, Melvin Frank, Michael Kidd. 693 performances.

(Panama 1959). *Screenplay:* Norman Panama, Melvin Frank. *Score:* Gene de Paul, Johnny Mercer. *Cast:* Peter Palmer (Abner Yokum), Leslie Parrish (Daisy Mae), Stubby Kaye (Marryin' Sam), Joe E. Marks (Pappy Yokum), Stella Stevens (Appassionata von Climax), Howard St. John (Gen. Bullmoose), Billie Hayes, Julie Newmar. *Songs:* Namely You; Jubilation T. Cornpone; If I Had My Druthers; Rag Offen the Bush; The Country's in the Very Best of Hands. *Director:* Melvin Frank *Choreographers:* Michael Kidd, Dee Dee Woods. *Producers*: Norman Panama, Melvin Frank.

The popular Al Capp comic strip, known for its potent political flavor, lost much of its bite when turned into a Broadway musical but the cartoonish show was very successful and is still revived. The silly plot, about the U. S. Government trying to use Dogpath, U.S.A. as a bomb test site because it is such a worthless place, included many of the famous characters, from the dim-witted Abner and his forever hopeful sweetheart Daisy Mae to the greedy General Bullmoose and his assistant, the oversexed Appassionata von Climax. The score was as vivacious as Michael Kidd's fast-paced direction and choreography. The movie version is a very faithful reproduction of the original, even using the cartoon-like sets from the Broadway production. Most of the score and just about all of the stage cast appear in the film. Stealing much of the movie is Stubby Kaye as the rotund Marryin' Sam. Another highlight is Kidd's two raucous production numbers: "(Don't That Take the) Rag Offen the Bush" and the "Sadie Hawkins' Day" ballet.

Lily Dale

November 20, 1986 (Samuel Beckett Theatre), a play by Horton Foote. *Cast*: Molly Ringwald

(Lily Dale Robedaux), Greg Zittel (Pete Daven-
port), Don Bloomfield (Horace Robedaux), Julie
Heberlein, Johnny Kline, Jane Welch, Cullen
Johnson. *Director*: William Alderson. *Producer:* J.
R. Productions. 112 performances.

(TV 1996). *Teleplay*: Horton Foote. *Cast*: Mary
Stuart Masterson (Lily Dale), Sam Shepard (Pete
Davenport), Tim Guinee (Horace Robedaux),
Stockard Channing (Corella), John Slattery, Jean
Stapleton. *Director*: Peter Masterson. *Producer*:
John Thomas Lenox.

A complex brother-sister relationship
is explored in this delicate domestic drama
set in Texas early in the 20th century. When
the father of Horace and Lily Dale Robedaux dies, their mother remarries and moves
to another town with Lily Dale and her
stepfather while Horace remains behind to
work as a clerk in a dry goods store. When
he visits the family, Horace discovers that
his stepfather is spoiling Lily Dale and dis-
paraging the name of their real father. Horace catches malaria and stays with the family to recuperate and this gives the siblings
time to thrash out their resentments and ex-
orcise some demons of the past. Like all of
playwright Horton Foote's works, the play
was lean on plot but rich in characterization
and naturalistic dialogue. The drama enjoyed a healthy run Off Broadway and was
made into a television production in 1996
with Foote on the soundtrack as narrator.
The acting is uneven but the production values are very evocative of the period.

The Lion in Winter

March 3, 1966 (Ambassador Theatre), a play by
James Goldman. *Cast*: Robert Preston (King
Henry II), Rosemary Harris (Queen Eleanor),
James Rado (Richard), Christopher Walken
(Philip), Bruce Scott (John), Dennis Cooney
(Geoffrey), Suzanne Grossman (Alais). *Director*:
Noel Willman. *Producers:* Eugene V. Wolsk, etc.
92 performances.

(Avco-Embassy 1968). *Screenplay*: James Goldman. *Cast*: Peter O'Toole (Henry II), Katharine
Hepburn (Eleanor of Aquitaine), Anthony Hopkins (Richard), John Castle (Geoffrey), Timothy
Dalton (King Philip), Nigel Terry (John), Jane
Merrow (Alais). *Director*: Anthony Harvey. *Producer*: Martin Poll.

Although King Henry II of England
has imprisoned his wife, Eleanor of Aquitaine,
because she keeps raising civil wars against
him, he lets her out for the Christmas holiday and the two of them argue over which
of their three sons will be the next king. The
verbal battle of wits results in a lot of emotional bloodshed and nothing is agreed upon
when Eleanor is sent back to prison. Filled
with vicious dialogue and engrossing characters, the play was unique in its use of history and comedy together. The critics were
highly complimentary, especially for Robert
Preston and Rosemary Harris as the quarreling royal couple, but audiences were not
interested and the Broadway production
only ran a few months. The 1968 movie, on
the other hand, was popular and led to many
revivals of the original play. Peter O'Toole
and Katherine Hepburn as the king and queen
made an extraordinary team, their timing
and verbal rapport nothing short of miracu-
lous. There were also solid performances by
John Castle and Anthony Hopkins (his feature film debut). The precise direction, a
first-rate screenplay that opened the action
up, and the skillful recreation of medieval castle life were among the movies other assets.

The Little Foxes

February 15, 1939 (National Theatre), a play by
Lillian Hellman. *Cast*: Tallulah Bankhead (Regina
Giddens), Charles Dingle (Ben), Patricia
Collinge (Birdie), Frank Conroy (Horace Gid-
dens), Carl Benton Reid (Oscar), Dan Duryea
(Leo), Florence Williams (Alexandra), Lee
Baker, Abbie Mitchell, John Marriott. *Director-
producer*: Herman Shumlin. 410 performances.

(RKO-Goldwyn 1941). *Screenplay*: Lillian Hell-
man, Dorothy Parker, etc. *Cast*: Bette Davis
(Regina Giddens), Herbert Marshall (Horace
Giddens), Teresa Wright (Alexandra Giddens),
Dan Duryea (Leo Hubbard), Patricia Collinge
(Birdie), Richard Carlson, Charles Dingle. *Di-
rector*: William Wyler. *Producer*: Samuel Gold-
wyn.

There has probably never been a more
greedy, rapacious bunch than the Hubbards,
a Southern family of some wealth who claw
at each other to make more money out of

the late Reconstruction. Brothers Ben and Oscar tend to stick together but are not above cheating the other, while the cunning Regina, not willing to be left out, goes so far as to let her husband die of a heart attack in front of her without calling for help so that he will not live to interfere with her plans. The two innocents in this hate-filled brood are the abused alcoholic Birdie and Regina's young daughter Alexandra; the first is resigned to an empty life while the second manages to get away from the family. Tallulah Bankhead triumphed as Regina yet the entire cast was outstanding and the Broadway production was skillfully staged and designed. Generally considered Lillian Hellman's finest work, the melodrama is tightly constructed and the characters are three-dimensional monsters rather than types. The play is regularly revived and the 1941 screen version remains a film classic. Hellman's screenplay is thought by many to be even better than the stage script. The action is opened up, some telling scenes are added, and the story is condensed in such a way that it builds beautifully. Bette Davis gives one of her most memorable performances as Regina and she is surrounded by a superior cast, including Teresa Wright as Alexandra and Dan Duryea and Patricia Collinge from the Broadway production, all making their screen debuts. Hellman later wrote a prequel to the story called *Another Part of the Forest* (qv) and the original play was turned into the opera *Regina* by Marc Blitzstein in 1949.

Little Johnny Jones

Liberty Theatre, 7 November 1904 (Liberty Theatre), a musical comedy by George M. Cohan. *Score:* George M. Cohan. *Cast:* George M. Cohan (Johnny Jones), Jerry Cohan (Anthony Anstey), Ethel Levey (Goldie Gates), Donald Brian (Henry Hapgood), Helen Cohan, Sam J. Ryan. *Songs:* The Yankee Doodle Boy; Give My Regards to Broadway; Life's a Funny Proposition After All.; They're All My Friends; A Girl I Know. *Director:* George M. Cohan. *Producer:* Sam H. Harris. 52 performances.

(Warner/First National 1929). *Screenplay:* Adelaide Heilbron. *Score:* George M. Cohan, etc. *Cast:* Eddie Buzzell (Johnny Jones), Alice Day

(Mary Baker), Robert Edeson, Edna Murphy. *Songs:* The Yankee Doodle Boy; Give My Regards to Broadway; Painting the Clouds With Sunshine; Go Find Somebody to Love; My Paradise. *Director:* Mervyn LeRoy.

The show that launched George M. Cohan's Broadway career also ushered in a new kind of slangy, cocky American kind of musical comedy. American jockey Johnny Jones goes to England to ride in the Derby but is falsely accused of throwing the race by some racketeers. Johnny not only clears his name but, back in the States, rescues his sweetheart from the same villains. It was Cohan's show all around and his vivacious performance and his hit songs quickly became the stuff of legend. In 1923 a silent movie version was made with Johnny Hines as Jones, then six years later a talkie remake was released with comic Eddie Buzzell as the jockey. It seemed foolhardy to film *Little Johnny Jones* without Cohan but Buzzell is surprisingly fresh and funny in the role. The movie itself seemed to lumber along awkwardly and only two songs from the Broadway score were used. Cohan never had much luck with movies (except for the wonderful biopic of his life, *Yankee Doodle Dandy*), but one wishes that his Johnny Jones had been better preserved on film.

Little Murders

April 25, 1967 (Broadhurst Theatre), a play by Jules Feiffer. *Cast:* Barbara Cook (Patsy), Heywood Hale Broun (Carol Newquist), Ruth White (Marjorie), Elliott Gould (Alfred Chamberlain), David Steinberg, Richard Schaal, Phil Leeds. *Director:* George L. Sherman. *Producer:* Alexander Cohen. 7 performances.

(Fox 1971). *Screenplay:* Jules Feiffer. *Cast:* Elliott Gould (Alfred Chamberlain), Marcia Rodd (Patsy Newquist), Vincent Gardenia (Mr. Newquist), Elizabeth Wilson (Mrs. Newquist), Jon Korkes, John Randolph, Alan Arkin, Lou Jacobi, Doris Roberts, Donald Sutherland. *Director:* Alan Arkin. *Producer:* Jack Brodsky.

Jules Feiffer's dark comedy centers on the Newquist family who are living in a big city during a string of sniper killings. While the family tries to keep the outside world out of sight and mind, daughter Patsy brings home her nerdy fiancé Alfred who has learned to tune out and ignore all the craziness about. Patsy is just getting Alfred to open up when she is killed by a stray bullet. But Alfred moves in with the family and, by the end of the play, he and Mr. Newquist and the effeminate son are shooting people from their living room window, laughing and happy to be part of the real world. Mixed notices and a wary public forced the Broadway production to close in a week but a 1968 New York revival ran a year and led to numerous regional productions. The 1971 movie boasted a noteworthy cast (including Elliot Gould reprising his Alfred from the original production) but director Alan Arkin could not find a way to make the tricky material work on screen. Ironically, Arkin's supporting performance as a hyperactive police officer is one of the film's few genuinely funny moments.

Little Nellie Kelly

November 13, 1922 (Liberty Theatre), a musical comedy by George M. Cohan. *Score:* George M. Cohan. *Cast:* Elizabeth Hines (Nellie Kelly), Charles King (Jerry Conroy), Robert Pitkin (Francois DeVere), Arthur Deagon (Capt. John Kelly), Georgia Caine, Frank Parker, Barrett Greenwood, Jack Oakie. *Songs:* Nellie Kelly, I Love You; You Remind Me of My Mother; Till Good Luck Comes Rolling Along; The Voice in My Heart. *Director-producer:* George M. Cohan. *Choreographer:* Julian Mitchell. 276 performances.

(MGM 1940). *Screenplay:* Jack McGowan. *Score:* George M. Cohan, Roger Edens, etc. *Cast:* Judy Garland (Nellie Kelly/Little Nellie), George Murphy (Jerry Kelly), Charles Winninger (Michael Noonan), Douglas MacPhail, Arthur Shields, Rita Page. *Songs:* Nellie Kelly, I Love You; It's a Great Day for the Irish; Singin' in the Rain; Danny Boy; A Pretty Girl Milking Her Cow. *Director:* Norman Taurog. *Producer:* Arthur Freed.

One of George M. Cohan's last but most popular Broadway shows, this sentimental musical comedy about a policeman's daughter who must choose between a slick businessman and an honest Irish lad was very similar to the kind of tale Cohan had offered twenty years earlier. But the score was tuneful (especially "Nelly Kelly, I Love You"), the cast was appealing, and the old-fashioned show was a hit on Broadway (where it ran longer than any other Cohan musical) and in London. The screen version made major changes in the plot with Judy Garland playing Nellie in Ireland, marrying against her father's wishes, traveling to America, and dying in childbirth. Years pass and the second Nellie (also played by Garland) grows up to fall in love against her grandfather's wishes but eventually wins the old man over. It was Garland's first solo star feature and also her first adult role and she rose to the occasion beautifully. Only the title song was kept from the stage score but Garland got to sing a string of standards, including a vibrant rendition of "Singin' in the Rain." The movie's sentimentality and patriotism are laid on a bit thick but it is a surprisingly effective film.

A Little Night Music

February 25 1973 (Shubert Theatre), a comic operetta by Hugh Wheeler. *Score:* Stephen Sondheim. *Cast:* Len Cariou (Fredrik Egerman), Glynis Johns (Desirée Armfeldt), Hermione Gingold (Mme. Armfeldt), Patricia Elliott (Charlotte Malcolm), Victoria Mallory (Anne Egerman), Mark Lambert (Henrik Egerman), Laurence Guittard (Carl-Magnus Malcolm), D. Jamin-Bartlett. *Songs:* Send in the Clowns; Now-Later-Soon; The Miller's Son; A Weekend in the Country; You Must Meet My Wife; Remember?; The Glamorous Life; Liaisons; Every Day a Little Death; It Would Have Been Wonderful. *Director-producer:* Harold Prince. *Choreographer:* Patricia Birch. 600 performances. Tony Award.

(Sascha-Wein-New World 1978). *Screenplay:* Hugh Wheeler. *Score:* Stephen Sondheim. *Cast:* Elizabeth Taylor (Desirée Armfeldt), Len Cariou (Fredrik Egerman), Hermione Gingold (Mme. Armfeldt), Lesley-Ann Down (Anne Egerman), Diana Rigg (Charlotte Malcolm), Laurence Guittard (Carl-Magnus Malcolm), Chloe Franks. *Songs:* Send in the Clowns; Now-Later-Soon; A Weekend in the Country; You Must Meet My Wife; Remember?; The Glamorous Life; Liaisons; Every Day a Little Death; Love Takes Time; The Letter Song. *Director:* Harold Prince. *Choreographer:* Patricia Birch. *Producer:* Elliott Kastner.

This adult, sophisticated musical proved that the operetta form was far from dead. Based on the Ingmar Berman movie *Smiles of a Summer Night* (1955), the plot was a series of love triangles among the Swedish upper class, all of them finding romance and foolishness during the short summer night. Stephen Sondheim's score was a waltzing marvel filled with more wit and subtext that the old operetta form was used to and the production by Harold Prince was one of the loveliest Broadway had ever seen. But turning the musical back into a film was not an easy task and the jumbled and botched movie that resulted was a sad curiosity. Perhaps to avoid comparison with the Bergman film, the screen musical was set in Austria, to no good effect. Elizabeth Taylor, as the worldly-wise actress Desirée, floundered in both her singing and acting but the rest of the cast (including a few from the Broadway production) was fine. The fact that none came off looking very well was more the fault of the filmmakers than the performers. One of Broadway's finest works became an embarrassing cinematic flop.

Little Shop of Horrors

July 27, 1982 (Orpheum Theatre), a musical comedy by Howard Ashman. *Score:* Alan Menken, Howard Ashman. *Cast:* Lee Wilkof (Seymour Krelbourn), Ellen Greene (Audrey), Hy Anzell, Franc Luz. *Songs:* Little Shop of Horrors; Somewhere That's Green; Suddenly Seymour; Grow for Me; Skid Row; Feed Me; Dentist. *Director:* Howard Ashman. *Choreographer:* Edie Cowan. *Producers:* David Geffen, Cameron Mackintosh, WPA Theatre. 2,209 performances.

(Geffen 1986). *Screenplay:* Howard Ashman. *Score:* Alan Menken, Howard Ashman. *Cast:* Rick Moranis (Seymour Krelbourn), Ellen Greene (Audrey), Vincent Gardenia, Steve Martin. *Songs:* Little Shop of Horrors; Somewhere That's Green; Suddenly Seymour; Grow for Me; Skid Row; Feed Me; Dentist; Mean Green Mother from Outer Space. *Director:* Frank Oz. *Choreographer:* Pat Garrett. *Producer:* David Geffen.

The long-running Off Broadway musical spoof was a vast improvement over the low-budget 1960 sci-fi movie it was based on. The story of a nerd who finds popularity and even fame because of his man-eating plant was comic book in nature and style and the Menken-Ashman score captured the sounds of the early 1960s cleverly and accurately. While the characters were still cartoonish, they had heart and what could have been a mindless spoof was thoroughly entertaining. Even the fatalistic ending, with the blood-thirty plant devouring the major characters and then taking over the world, was in keeping with the genre. The film is very faithful to the original and most of the performances retain the wacky charm of the stage work. The ending was changed to a happier one, only hinting that the plant will return to wreck havoc once again. While the special effects on screen are superior to those Off Broadway, one misses the corny theatrics that made the plant come to life on stage.

London Suite

April 9, 1995 (Union Square Theatre), a play by Neil Simon. *Cast:* Paxton Whitehead (Billy/Sidney/Dr. McMerlin), Carole Shelley (Mrs. Semple/Diana. Mrs. Sitgood), Kate Burton (Lauren/Grace/Annie), Jeffrey Jones, Brooks Ashmanskas. *Director:* Daniel Sullivan. *Producers:* Emanuel Azenberg, Leonard Soloway. 169 performances.

(TV 1996). *Teleplay:* Neil Simon. *Cast:* Kelsey Grammer (Sidney Nichols), Patricia Clarkson (Diana Nichols), Madeline Kahn (Sharon Semple), Kristen Johnston (Grace Chapman), Jonathan Silverman, Richard Mulligan, Michael Richards, Julia Louis-Dreyfus, Julie Haggerty. *Director:* Jay Sandrich. *Producer:* Greg Smith.

Four different set of occupants of a luxury suite in a London hotel are viewed in four playlets, just as in Neil Simon's earlier *Plaza Suite* (qv) and *California Suite* (qv). But this was the weakest entry of the three and even in a small Off Broadway house the play struggled to run a few months. Of the four stories, the most interesting one involved two characters that Simon introduced in *California Suite*: the movie actress Diana and her bisexual husband Sidney. The couple have separated but are reunited at the hotel when he asks her for money for his male lover dying of cancer. The 1996 television version fared somewhat better because

Simon wrote the teleplay with all four stories told at the same time, cutting from one hotel room to another. They were still mostly routine tales but they seemed more interesting when viewed in pieces. The cast, made up mostly of television stars, was uneven but there were moments in which some of them shone.

Lonelyhearts see Miss Lonelyhearts

Long Day's Journey Into Night

November 7, 1956 (Helen Hayes Theatre), a drama by Eugene O'Neill. *Cast*: Fredric March (James Tyrone), Florence Eldridge (Mary), Jason Robards (Jamie), Bradford Dillman (Edmund). *Director*: José Quintero. *Producers:* Leigh Connell, etc. 390 performances. Pulitzer Prize, Tony Award.

(Embassy 1962). *Screenplay*: Eugene O'Neill. *Cast*: Katharine Hepburn (Mary Tyrone), Ralph Richardson (James Tyrone, Sr.), Jason Robards (James Tyrone, Jr.), Dean Stockwell (Edmund Tyrone), Jeanne Barr. *Director*: Sidney Lumet. *Producer*: Ely Landau.

(TV 1973). *Teleplay*: Eugene O'Neill. *Cast*: Laurence Olivier (James Tyrone, Sr.), Constance Cummings (Mary Tyrone), Dennis Quilley (James Tyrone, Jr.), Ronald Pickup (Edmund Tyrone), Maureen Lipman. *Directors*: Michael Blakemore, Peter Wood. *Producer*: Cecil Clarke.

(TV 1987). *Teleplay*: Eugene O'Neill. *Cast*: Jack Lemmon (James Tyrone), Bethel Leslie (Mary Tyrone), Peter Gallagher (Edmund Tyrone), Kevin Spacey (James Tyrone, Jr.). *Director*: Jonathan Miller.

During the course of one day, we see the Tyrone family unravel and sink into deep despair as the past catches up with them. The once-famous actor James Tyrone is now a miserly father with a failed marriage and failed career. His elder son Jamie is a libertine who is becoming an alcoholic while the younger son Edmund finds out that his consumption has returned and he must go into a sanitarium. The news so upsets his mother,

the former society beauty Mary, that she returns to her morphine habit and is so drugged by the middle of the night that she thinks she is a young girl again. Eugene O'Neill's most autobiographical work and arguably his greatest play, the long, intimate, and devastating drama was produced on Broadway three years after his death, though he had stipulated in his will that the producers should wait twenty-five years. Fredric March and Florence Eldridge's performances as James and Mary were greatly admired, as was Bradford Dillman as Edmund. But the surprise of the production was Jason Robards's portrayal of Jamie. The play was a critical hit but a modest box office success and it would be revived frequently in theatres across the country. The 1962 film allowed Robards to reprise his performance and he was never less than compelling. Ralph Richardson played James, Dean Stockwell was Edmund and, in a daring piece of casting, Katharine Hepburn essayed Mary. The movie actress usually played strong, independent women, so her weak, self-delusional Mary was as surprising as it was indelible. Because of the four-hour length of the play, the movie was greatly abridged but the unhurried, precise direction covers any awkwardness that the cutting may have caused. A television version in 1973 featured Laurence Olivier as James with Constance Cummings as Mary and Dennis Quilley and Ronald Pickup as the sons. It is a rather stagy and slow production but the performances are so strong that there is much to appreciate. A second television production, based on a stage revival in London and New York, starred Jack Lemmon as James with Bethel Leslie as Mary and the sons played by Kevin Spacey and Peter Gallagher. Director Jonathan Miller solved the problem of length somewhat by having the dialogue move swiftly and with plenty of overlapping. Some thought this made the text more conversational, others thought it ruined O'Neill's poetic prose. The television version is also very stagy but it moves along and there is an intriguing rapport between Spacey and Gallagher. Also from a stage revival is the 1996 television production from the Stratford Festival in Canada. Although there is no audience present, it is pretty much a filming of the stage production. William Hutt and Martha Henry give affecting performances as James and Mary.

The Long Voyage Home

November 3, 1924 (Playwrights' Theatre), a one-act drama by Eugene O'Neill. *Cast*: Walter Abel (Ole Olson), Lawrence Cecil (Driscoll), Walter Kingsford (Cocky), E. J. Ballantine (Smitty), Stanley Howlett, Louise Bradley, Jeannie Begg. *Producer*: Provincetown Players. 105 performances.

(Argosy 1940). *Screenplay*: Dudley Nichols. *Cast*: John Wayne (Ole Olsen), Thomas Mitchell (Driscoll), Barry Fitzgerald (Cocky), Ian Hunter (Smitty), John Qualen (Axel Swanson), Wilfred Lawson, Ward Bond, Mildred Natwick. *Director*: John Ford. *Producers*: John Ford, Walter Wanger.

Crew members of the S. S. *Glencairn* go ashore to drink at a ramshackle bar on the London waterfront where they celebrate the end of Ole Olson's career at sea. He is determined to return to his Swedish homeland and live on land. But Olson is slipped a drugged drink and after he passes out he is shanghaied to Cape Horn, sailing on a vessel that has a reputation for being the "worst ship dat sail the sea." The one-act drama was first produced in 1917 by the Provincetown Players. The play was revived with three other O'Neill one-acts in 1924 under the title S. S. *Glencairn*. The 1940 movie version of *The Long Voyage Home* used incidents from the other plays in the screenplay but mostly focused on Olson's misadventure. Beautifully photographed and directed, the slow, atmospheric film has the poetic quality of a foreign import and the acting is understated and hypnotic. John Wayne, in a very atypical role, plays Olson and he is surprisingly gentle and wistful in the part. It is a unique and unforgettable film.

A Loss of Roses

November 29, 1959 (Eugene O'Neill Theatre), a play by William Inge. *Cast*: Carol Haney (Lila Green), Warren Beatty (Kenny), Betty Field (Helen Baird), Michael J. Pollard (Jelly), James O'Rear, Joan Morgan, Margaret Braidwood, Robert Webber. *Director*: Daniel Mann. *Producer*: Saint Subber, Lester Osterman. 25 performances.

The Stripper (Fox 1963). *Screenplay*: Meade Roberts. *Cast*: Joanne Woodward (Lila Green), Richard Beymer (Kenny), Claire Trevor (Helen Baird), Carol Lynley, Louis Nye, Robert Webber, Gypsy Rose Lee, Michael J. Pollard. *Director*: Franklin J. Schaffner. *Producer*: Jerry Wald.

Teenager Kenny Baird is very close to his widowed mother but when Lila Green, a friend of Mrs. Baird's who now works performing in cheap blue movies, visits them in their small Midwest town she comes between mother and son. Kenny and Lila have a one-night stand but the next day he is so harsh to her that Lila tries to commit suicide. In the end Kenny leaves town in search of understanding his confused feelings for his mother and Lila. Although the cast was commended (particularly newcomer Warren Beatty as Kenny), the play failed to find favor with either critics or playgoers and it closed in a few weeks. But Hollywood bought the property all the same, hoping to find the same success that playwright William Inge's other works had enjoyed on screen. In the 1963 movie Lila and the title was changed to *The Stripper*, though the story was pretty much the same so any moviegoers hoping for anything salacious were greatly disappointed. Joanne Woodward is very affecting as Lila but Richard Beymer is a one-dimensional Kenny so there is no chemistry to be found in any of their scenes together. The rest of the cast does an admirable job and there is even a cameo by Gypsy Rose Lee as an aging stripper.

Lost in the Stars

October 30, 1949 (Music Box Theatre), a musical play by Maxwell Anderson. *Score:* Kurt Weill, Maxwell Anderson. *Cast:* Todd Duncan (Stephen Kumalo), Leslie Banks (James Jarvis), Inez Matthews (Irina), Warren Coleman, Julian Mayfield. *Songs:* Trouble Man; Lost in the Stars; Cry the Beloved Country; Stay Well; Train to Johannesburg; Thousands of Miles. *Director:* Rouben Mamoulian. *Producer:* Playwrights' Company. 273 performances.

(American Film Theatre 1972). *Screenplay:* Alfred Hayes. *Score:* Kurt Weill, Maxwell Anderson.

Cast: Brock Peters (Stephen Kumalo), Paul Rogers (James Jarvis), Melba Moore (Irina), Clifton Davis, Raymond St. Jacques, Paula Kelly, Alan Weeks, Jitu Cumbuka. *Songs:* Trouble Man; Lost in the Stars; Cry the Beloved Country; Bird of Paradise; Train to Johannesburg. *Director:* Daniel Mann. *Choreographer:* Paula Kelly. *Producer:* Ely Landau.

One of the most ambitious musical undertakings of the 1940s, this powerful musical drama was based on *Cry the Beloved Country*, Alan Paton's novel about racial strife in South Africa. When the black preacher Stephen Kumalo leaves his village to find his dissipated son in Johannesburg, his faith is sorely tested. His white neighbor Jarvis seems to have all the advantages, yet both men are tied in unity by the death of their sons. The Weill-Anderson score soared with passion and pain and Todd Duncan's portrayal of Kumalo was inspiring. The difficult musical was filmed thirteen years later by the independent American Film Theatre but, honorable intentions aside, it is a pedestrian movie that seems stagebound, even though it was partially filmed on location in Jamaica. Brock Peters as Kumalo is the movie's saving grace and his rendition of the title song is memorable.

Lost in Yonkers

February 21, 1991 (Richard Rodgers Theatre), a play by Neil Simon. *Cast:* Irene Worth (Grandma Kurnitz), Mercedes Ruehl (Bella), Kevin Spacey (Louis), Jamie Marsh (Jay), Danny Gerard (Arty), Mark Blum, Lauren Klein. *Director:* Gene Saks. *Producer:* Emanuel Azenberg. 780 performances. Pulitzer Prize, Tony Award.

(Columbia-Rastar 1993). *Screenplay:* Neil Simon. *Cast:* Irene Worth (Grandma Kurnitz), Mercedes Ruehl (Bella Kurnitz), Richard Dreyfuss (Uncle Louie), Brad Stoll, Mike Damus, David Strathairn. *Director:* Martha Coolidge. *Producer:* Ray Stark, etc.

Widower Eddie Kurnitz is in debt so during the Depression he leaves his two young sons in the care of his mother in Yonkers while he goes on the road as a salesman. Grandma Kurnitz is a cold, nasty penny pincher who torments the boys and her grown but simple-minded daughter Bella. But when Bella starts to date a moviehouse usher who is also mentally challenged, she finds the strength at last to stand up to her mother. Critics proclaimed the bittersweet play was among Neil Simon's best and it ran on Broadway for over two years. The splendid production featured a superior cast, particularly Irene Worth as Grandma and Mercedes Ruehl, both of whom won Tony Awards and appeared in the 1993 screen version. As rewarding as it is to see these two memorable performances preserved on film, the movie itself is a major disappointment. Simon rewrote the script to build up the minor role of Uncle Louie, a small-time hood who comes to visit. Kevin Spacey played him in the Broadway production (and also won a Tony) but Richard Dreyfuss turned Louis into a star turn that not only threw the story off balance but injected a crude, easy kind of humor that was nor worthy of the play. Poorly directed, the movie seems stagy, artificial, and endless. One of Simon's finest plays became one of his most dismal films.

Louisiana Purchase

Imperial Theatre, 28 May 1940 (Imperial Theatre), a musical comedy by Morrie Ryskind, B. G. DeSylva. *Score:* Irving Berlin. *Cast:* William Gaxton (Jim Taylor), Victor Moore (Sen. Oliver P. Loganberry), Vera Zorina (Marina Van Linden), Irene Bordoni (Mme. Bordelaise), Carol Bruce, Nick Long, Jr. *Songs:* It's a Lovely Day Tomorrow; Louisiana Purchase; What Chance Have I?; You're Lonely and I'm Lonely; Fools Fall in Love; Outside of That I Love You. *Director:* Edgar MacGregor. *Choreographer:* George Balanchine. *Producer:* B. G. DeSylva. 444 performances.

(Paramount 1942). *Screenplay:* Jerome Chodorov, Herbert Fields. *Score:* Irving Berlin. *Cast:* Bob Hope (Jim Taylor), Victor Moore (Sen. Oliver P. Loganberry), Vera Zorina (Marina Von Minden), Irene Bordoni (Madame Bordelaise), Dona Drake, Andrew Tombes, Ray Walburn, Maxie Rosenbloom. *Songs:* It's a Lovely Day Tomorrow; Louisiana Purchase; You're Lonely and I'm Lonely; Take a Letter to Paramount Pictures. *Director:* Irving Cummings. *Producer:* B. G. DeSylva.

Irving Berlin wrote one of his finest scores for this political satire about a corrupt

New Orleans company being investigated by a bumbling U. S. senator. Victor Moore was in rare form as the squeaky-clean politician, William Gaxton was the slippery business-man, and Irene Bordoni and Vera Zorina were the *femme fatale*s hired to put the senator in a compromising position. It was high flying fun filled with wit in the script and the score and gave Berlin his biggest Broadway hit to date. With only three songs and one dance number, the screen version hardly felt like a musical at all. Bob Hope played Gaxton's part and Moore, Bordoni, and Zorina repeated their stage roles. But much of the comedy falls flat and the movie is only of mild interest.

Love! Valour! Compassion!

February 14, 1995 (Walter Kerr Theatre), a play by Terrence McNally. *Cast*: Stephen Bogardus (Gregory Mitchell), Nathan Lane (Buzz Hauser), Anthony Heald (Perry Sellars), John Benjamin Hickey (Arthur Pape), John Glover (John/James Jeckyll), Justin Kirk (Bobby Brahms), Randy Becker (Ramon Fornos). *Director*: Joe Mantello. *Producers:* Manhattan Theatre Club, etc. 249 performances. Tony Award.

(Krost-Chapin 1997). *Screenplay*: Terrence McNally. *Cast*: Jason Alexander (Buzz Hauser), Stephen Spinella (Perry Sellars), John Glover (John & James Jeckyll), Stephen Bogardus (Gregory Mitchell), John Benjamin Hickey (Arthur Pape), Justin Kirk (Bobby Brahms), Randy Becker (Ramon Fornos). *Director*: Joe Mantello. *Producers*: Barry Krost, Doug Chapin.

Broadway choreographer Gregory Mitchell invites a group of his gay friends to his upstate New York farm for the Memorial Day, Fourth of July, and Labor Day weekends and during each holiday we see relationships created, destroyed, and strengthened. The plotless, jokey play was filled with colorful characters and pungent dialogue, further brightened by an exceptional cast. Nathan Lane was particularly funny as the screaming-queen costume designer Buzz and John Glover impressed playing twin brothers with very different personalities. The comedy-drama was so popular Off Broadway that it moved to Broadway for a long run. All of the cast and

creative team reunited for the 1997 movie except Lane who was replaced by Jason Alexander but the magic of the stage production was lost somewhere along the way. Alexander is very weak, which took the comic core out of the piece, but even the others seem less defined in the realistic scenery and unimaginative direction.

Lovely Mary see Mrs. Wiggs of the Cabbage Patch

Lovely to Look At see Roberta

Lovers and Other Strangers

September 18, 1968 (Brooks Atkinson Theatre), a quartet of comic one-acts by Renee Taylor, Joseph Bologna. *Cast*: Renee Taylor (Wilma), Richard Castellano (Frank), Helen Verbit (Bea), Bobby Alto (Richy), Zohra Lampert (Brenda), Candy Azzara, Mariclare Costello, Ron Carey, Marvin Lichterman, Gerald O'Loughlin. *Director*: Charles Grodin. *Producer:* Stephanie Sills. 69 performances.

(ABC Films 1970). *Screenplay*: Joseph Bologna, Renee Taylor, David Zelag Goodman. *Cast*: Beatrice Arthur (Bea), Bonnie Bedelia (Susan), Richard Castellano (Frank), Michael Brandon (Mike), Gig Young (Hal), Bob Dishy (Jerry), Harry Guardino, Anne Jackson, Diane Keaton, Cloris Leachman, Marian Hailey, Anne Meara, Joseph Hindy. *Director*: Cy Howard. *Producer*: David Susskind.

The short playlets that comprised this anthology program were more like blackout sketches with their stereotypic characters, contrived situations, and sit-com humor. Only one of them seemed to go beyond the obvious: two middle-aged parents try to talk their son and daughter-in-law from giving up on the rocky marriage. There was honest comedy in the piece and Richard Castellano was very droll as the quietly resigned father. Reviews were not favorable and the play closed after nine weeks but Hollywood picked up the property and the co-play-wrights fashioned it into a more conventional comedy built around that one satisfying sketch. While some of the characters, situations, and even lines from the other three playlets were kept, the new screenplay was a tightly constructed comedy revolving around a wedding. The parents are now trying to throw a wedding even as they try to save a marriage and the plot was further complicated by the ladies' man Hal looking for fulfillment but willing to settle for sex. Castellano returned to play the father and he was cleverly matched with Bea Arthur as his wife. Other noteworthy performances were given by Gig Young as Hal, Anne Jackson, Michael Brandon, Diane Keaton, and others. A lame evening of theatre was turned into a cinema gem.

Luv

November 11, 1964 (Booth Theatre), a comedy by Murray Schisgal. *Cast*: Alan Arkin (Harry Berlin), Anne Jackson (Ellen Manville), Eli Wallach (Milt Manville). *Director*: Mike Nichols. *Producer:* Claire Nichtern. 901 performances.

(Columbia 1967). *Screenplay*: Elliott Baker. *Cast*: Jack Lemmon (Harry Berlin), Peter Falk (Milt Manville), Elaine May (Ellen Manville), Nina Wayne (Linda), Eddie Mayehoff, Paul Hartman, Alan DeWitt, Severn Darden. *Director*: Clive Donner. *Producer*: Martin Manulis.

This three-character absurdist farce was set on a lonely bridge that resembled the landscape of one of Samuel Beckett's mysterious works yet the humor was often vaudeville in tone and the comedy was a surprise hit. Destitute Harry Berlin is about to jump off the bridge and end it all when his old buddy Milt Manville walks by, convinces him that life is worth living, and even does some matchmaking between his wife Ellen and Harry so that he can get a divorce and wed his young girl friend. When Harry meets Ellen, they hit it off and everything seems to go according to Milt's plan. But months later Harry and Ellen are miserable married to each other and Milt is unhappy with his new life as well. Ellen and Milt attempt to push Harry off the bridge but Milt ends up in the water instead. All the same, the couple is reconciled and Harry is left

more destitute than before. Mike Nichols directed the oddball comedy with panache and the three performers had just the right kind of craziness to pull off these outrageous characters. A movie version would be problematic because there was a kind of surrealism to the play. But the 1967 film played it as a conventional comedy and opened up the action so that the story seemed more illogical than funny. Inspired comic actors Jack Lemmon, Peter Falk, and Elaine May struggled in vain yet each gave an embarrassingly impotent performance. The added characters and scenes did nothing to help the situation.

M. Butterfly

March 20, 1988 (Eugene O'Neill Theatre), a play by David Henry Hwang. *Cast*: John Lithgow (René Gallimard), B. D. Wong (Song Liling), John Getz, Lori Tan Chinn, George N. Martin. *Director*: John Dexter. *Producers:* Stuart Ostrow, David Geffen. 777 performances. Tony Award.

(Geffen-Miranda 1993). *Screenplay*: David Henry Hwang. *Cast*: Jeremy Irons (René Gallimard), John Lone (Song Liling), Barbara Sukowa, Shizuko, Ian Richardson, Annabel Leventon. *Director*: David Cronenberg. *Producer*: Gabriella Martinelli.

The French diplomat René Gallimard, who loves Puccini's *Madama Butterfly* and dreams of having a woman like Cio-Cio-San, has a long affair with a beautiful actress from the Peking Opera while stationed in China. But it turns out the actress is a man and a spy and Gallimard is imprisoned as an accessory to the Communists. Gallimard argues that he never knew the truth because he was so caught up in the fantasy of his "feminine ideal." Dressing up like Cio-Cio-San, Gallimard commits suicide just as his beloved character did. Aside from its intriguing story (which was based on an actual incident), the play was filled with penetrating ideas about East and West and the roles of men and women. John Lithgow was saluted for his heartfelt portrayal of Gallimard while newcomer B. D. Wong was outstanding as the actress-spy. Also commendable was the ingenious staging and theatrical scenery. The

Broadway production was showered with awards and ran two years so there was much interest in a movie version. When one was released in 1993 the result was so disappointing that the studios let it quietly disappear. On stage, Gallimard addressed the audience from his jail cell and scenes sprung up from his memory. But the film took a more conventional form of plotting and the story turned into a bizarre but ultimately dull soap opera. Jeremy Irons and John Lone make valiant attempts at Gallimard and the spy but both performances are unconvincing and sometimes downright silly.

Madame Butterfly

March 5, 1900 (Herald Square Theatre), a drama by David Belasco, John Luther Long. *Cast*: Blanche Bates (Cho-Cho-San), Frank Worthing (Lt. Pinkerton), Claude Gillingwater (Mr. Sharpless), Mary Barker (Suzuki), Katherine Black, Albert Bruning, E. P. Wilkes. *Director-producer*: David Belasco. 24 performances.

(Famous Players 1915). *Cast*: Mary Pickford (Cho-Cho-San), Marshall Neilan (Lt. Pinkerton), Olive West (Suzuki), Jane Hall, Lawrence Wood, Caroline Harris, William T. Carleton, David Burton. *Director*: Sidney Olcott.

(Paramount 1932). *Screenplay*: Josephine Lovett, John Moncure March. *Cast*: Sylvia Sidney (Cho-Cho-San), Cary Grant (Lt. Pinkerton), Louise Carter (Suzuki), Charles Ruggles, Irving Pichel, Helen Jerome Eddy, Edmund Breese. *Director*: Marion Gering. *Producer*: B. P. Schulberg.

The Japanese geisha Cho-Cho-San fell in love with the American naval Lieutenant Pinkerton and they wed in a Japanese ceremony before he shipped out. When he returns years later and Cho-Cho-San discovers that he has remarried, she commits suicide. Puccini's celebrated 1904 opera was based on David Belasco's play, a short afterpiece that telescoped all the events of the story into two brief scenes. Blanche Bates was applauded for her performance of Cho-Cho-San but the play itself was not a hit. Yet the production was stunning, particularly a famous scene in which the lighting changed as Cho-Cho-San waited for the dawn and news of her husband, and the beautiful story

was told with simple and poignant passion. A 1915 silent screen version starred Mary Pickford as Cho-Cho-San but it was not the kind of role moviegoers wanted to see "America's sweetheart" play so it was not popular. The 1932 talkie updated the story but it is so stiff and formal the plot seems more old fashioned that it really was. Sylvia Sidney and Cary Grant played the lovers and both are impressive without being totally convincing. There are at least a dozen film and television versions of Puccini's *Madama Butterfly* as well.

The Magnificent Yankee

January 22, 1946 (Royale Theatre), a play by Emmet Lavery. *Cast*: Louis Calhern (Oliver Wendell Holmes), Dorothy Gish (Fanny Holmes), Edgar Barrier (Justice Brandeis), Sherling Oliver (Owen Wister), William Roerick, Philip Truex, Fleming Ward, Christopher Marvin. *Director-producer*: Arthur Hopkins. 160 performances.

(MGM 1950). *Screenplay*: Emmet Lavery. *Cast*: Louis Calhern (Oliver Wendell Holmes), Ann Harding (Fanny Holmes), Eduard Franz (Judge Louis Brandeis), Philip Ober (Owen Wister/Narrator), Edith Evanson, Richard Anderson, Jimmy Lyndon. *Director*: John Sturges. *Producer*: Armand Deutsch.

This bio-drama about the life and career of Supreme Court Justice Oliver Wendell Holmes was episodic and each scene was mildly interesting or charming rather than compelling but the gifted cast made the play a success. Louis Calhern was subtle and warm as Holmes and Dorothy Gish was more than competent in the rather thankless role of his wife Fanny. Calhern played Holmes on Broadway, on the road, and reprised his performance for the 1950 movie but Gish was replaced by Ann Harding. They and the rest of the cast turn in affecting performances even if the characters and the story have little dramatic punch. A 1965 television version of the play starring Alfred Lunt and Lynn Fontanne is more interesting because it is one of the very few film records of the famous Lunts and their remarkable stage chemsistry.

A Majority of One

February 16, 1959 (Shubert Theatre), a comedy by Leonard Spigelgass. *Cast*: Gertrude Berg (Mrs. Jacoby), Cedric Hardwicke (Koichi Asano), Ina Balin, Michael Tolan, Mae Questel, Kanna Ishii, Marc Marno, Barnard Hughes. *Director*: Dore Schary. *Producers:* Theatre Guild, Dore Schary. 556 performances.

(Warner 1961). *Screenplay*: Leonard Spigelgass. *Cast*: Rosalind Russell (Mrs. Jacoby), Alec Guinness (Koichi Asano), Ray Danton, Madlyn Rhue, Mae Questel, Marc Marno, Gary Vinson. *Director-producer*: Mervyn LeRoy.

The unlikely friendship between a Japanese businessman and a Jewish housewife from Brooklyn made this comedy unusual and disarmingly charming. The two meet on board a ship and, although she lost a son in the Pacific in World War Two and he lost his daughter at Hiroshima, the couple slowly overcome their prejudices and start to understand each other. The Broadway production ran nearly two years, helped by the performances of radio star Gertrude Berg and classy British actor Cedric Hardwicke whose acting styles were as different as their characters. The 1961 film lost most of the play's warmth and featured harsh and overblown performances by Rosalind Russell and Alec Guinness. The direction is as stagy as the acting and the movie seems to go nowhere.

The Male Animal

January 9, 1940 (Cort Theatre), a comedy by James Thurber, Elliot Nugent. *Cast*: Elliot Nugent (Tommy Turner), Ruth Matteson (Ellen), Leon Ames (Joe Ferguson), Gene Tierney (Patricia Stanley), Don Defore, Richard Beckhard, Ivan Simpson. *Director-producer:* Herman Shumlin. 243 performances.

(Warner 1942). *Screenplay*: Julius J. Epstein, Philip G. Epstein, etc. *Cast*: Henry Fonda (Tommy Turner), Olivia De Havilland (Ellen Turner), Jack Carson (Joe Ferguson), Joan Leslie (Patricia Stanley), Eugene Pallette, Herbert Anderson, Hattie McDaniel. *Director*: Elliott Nugent. *Producer*: Hal B. Wallis.

She's Working Her Way Through College (Warner 1952). *Screenplay*: Peter Milne. *Score:* Vernon Duke, Sammy Cahn, etc. *Cast*: Virginia Mayo (Angela Gardner), Ronald Reagan (Prof. John Palmer), Phyllis Thaxter (Helen Palmer), Don Defore (Shep Slade), Gene Nelson (Don Weston), Patrice Wymore, Roland Winters, Raymond Greenleaf. *Songs:* Give 'Em What They Want; The Stuff That Dreams Are Made Of; With Plenty of Money and You; She's Working Her Way Through College. *Director:* H. Bruce Humberstone. *Choreographer*: LeRoy Prinz. *Producers*: William Jacobs, Herman Shumlin.

Just as college professor Tommy Turner is getting into trouble because he read an anarchist's letter in class, an old flame of his wife Ellen, the former football hero Joe Ferguson, returns to town and starts to flirt with her. Matters are only set right after Tommy and Joe get drunk together and fight it out in a harmless brawl. The pleasant comedy pleased both critics and playgoers, ran for several months, and enjoyed a number of professional and amateur revivals over the years. The 1942 movie featured Henry Fonda and Olivia De Havilland as the Turners and Jack Carson as Joe, and all three are in top comic form. The play is opened up enough to include a satiric sports rally and some atmospheric campus locations. The basic story was retained for the 1952 film musical *She's Working Her Way Through College* but the emphasis was on a burlesque star who decides to go academic and ruffles the life of a staid professor. Some enjoyable production numbers aside, the movie is more tacky than funny and few of the performances rise above average. Yet the film was popular enough to warrant a sequel, *She's Back on Broadway* (1953). A 1958 television version of the original play starred Andy Griffith as Tommy and a British television production featured Lee Montague.

Mame

May 24, 1966 (Winter Garden Theatre), a musical comedy by Jerome Lawrence, Robert E. Lee. *Score:* Jerry Herman. *Cast:* Angela Lansbury (Mame Dennis), Beatrice Arthur (Vera Charles), Jane Connell (Agnes Gooch), Charles Braswell (Beauregard Burnside), Frankie Michaels, Jerry Lanning. *Songs:* Mame; If He Walked Into My Life Today; We Need a Little Christmas; Bosom

Buddies; My Best Girl; Open a New Window; It's Today; That's How Young I Feel. *Director:* Gene Saks. *Choreographer:* Onna White. *Producers*: Robert Fryer, etc. 1,508 performances.

(Warner 1974). *Screenplay:* Paul Zindel. *Score:* Jerry Herman. *Cast:* Lucille Ball (Mame Dennis), Beatrice Arthur (Vera Charles), Robert Preston (Beauregard Burnside), Jane Connell (Agnes Gooch), Bruce Davison, John McGiver, Kirby Furlong, Doria Cook, Joyce Van Patten. *Songs:* Mame; If He Walked Into My Life Today; We Need a Little Christmas; Bosom Buddies; My Best Girl; Open a New Window; It's Today; Loving You. *Director:* Gene Saks. *Choreographer:* Onna White. *Producers*: Robert Fryer, James Cresson.

Auntie Mame (qv) had found success as a book, play, and film, so it was not surprising that the irresistible aunt showed up in a Broadway musical. The woman is a one-person show in herself and Angela Lansbury surprised and delighted audiences and critics with her singing-dancing talents and her warm and carefree interpretation. Jerry Herman provided a tuneful score and the Broadway production glistened with professional know how. What is so surprising is how amateur the movie version turned out. Here was a vehicle that cried out to be filmed yet the movie musical is stagy and contrived. Much blame has been put on the miscast, overage Lucille Ball as Mame and her performance is often painful to behold. But the movie around her isn't much better. Even as it remained faithful to the stage hit, the film seems clueless as to what makes the material work. Yet both were directed by theatre veteran Gene Saks; it was his first film, which proves the two media are not quite the same.

Man of La Mancha

November 22, 1965 (ANTA Theatre), a musical play by Dale Wasserman. *Score:* Mitch Leigh, Joe Darion. *Cast:* Richard Kiley (Cervantes/Don Quixote), Joan Diener (Aldonza), Irving Jacobson (Sancho Panza), Robert Rounseville (Padre), Ray Middleton (Innkeeper), Jon Cypher. *Songs:* The Impossible Dream; To Each His Dulcinea; Man of La Mancha; Dulcinea; What Does He Want of Me?; I Really Like Him; I'm Only Thinking of Him; Little Bird, Little Bird. *Direc-tor:* Albert Marre. *Choreographer:* Jack Cole. *Producers:* Albert W. Selden, Hal James. 2,328 performances. Tony Award.

(United Artists 1972). *Screenplay:* Dale Wasserman. *Score:* Mitch Leigh, Joe Darion. *Cast:* Peter O'Toole (Cervantes/Don Quixote), Sophia Loren (Aldonza), James Coco (Sancho Panza), Harry Andrews (Innkeeper), John Castle, Brian Blessed, Julie Gregg, Ian Richardson. *Songs:* The Impossible Dream; To Each His Dulcinea; Man of La Mancha; Dulcinea; I Really Like Him; I'm Only Thinking of Him; Little Bird, Little Bird. *Director-producer:* Arthur Hiller. *Choreographer:* Gillian Lynne.

Cervantes's epic work *Don Quixote* was efficiently adapted for the musical stage by turning the tale of a demented knight errant into a play-within-a-play performed by Cervantes and his fellow prisoners of the Spanish Inquisition. The premise worked well on stage, letting the audience imagine all the places and adventures that Quixote and his sidekick Pancho experience. Richard Kiley played both author and his character creation and with a series of lyrical ballads to sing the musical was both lofty and moving. The literal movie version, played in a realistic prison and then against a bleak landscape, came across more dreary than enlightening and the cast of non-singers diminished the score considerably. Peter O'-Toole valiantly sings his dialogue but when he comes to the songs he seems tentative and weak. Sophia Loren as the sluttish Aldonza is also fine until she has to sing and her power evaporates right before our eyes. The movie is oddly unsatisfying and rarely even feels like a musical.

The Man Who Came to Dinner

October 16, 1939 (Music Box Theatre), a comedy by George S. Kaufman, Moss Hart. *Cast*: Monty Woolley (Sheridan Whiteside), Edith Atwater (Maggie Cutler), Theodore Newton (Bert Jefferson), Carol Goodner (Lorraine Sheldon), David Burns (Banjo), Mary Wickes (Miss Preen), John Hoysradt, Virginia Hammond, George Lessey, Ruth Vivian. *Director*: George S. Kaufman. *Producer:* Sam H. Harris. 739 performances.

(Warner–First National 1942). *Screenplay*: Julius J. Epstein, Philip G. Epstein. *Cast*: Monty Woolley (Sheridan Whiteside), Bette Davis (Maggie Cutler), Richard Travis (Bert Jefferson), Jimmy Durante (Banjo), Ann Sheridan (Lorraine Sheldon), Mary Wickes (Nurse Preen), Billie Burke, Grant Mitchell, Reginald Gardiner, George Barbier. *Director*: William Keighley. *Producer*: Jerry Wald.

Although it is filled with 1930s references that are lost on some audiences today, this American comedy classic is still highly entertaining and is frequently revived by professional, community, and school groups. When the eccentric, demanding radio personality Sheridan Whiteside slips and falls on the ice and must convalesce in the Stanley residence in a small Ohio town, he drives everyone in the household crazy with his commands, international friends, and interfering in the lives of others. The comedy employs some delightful plot twists and the large cast of characters includes some hilarious people. Playwrights George S. Kaufman and Moss Hart based Whiteside on their equally pompous friend Alexander Woollcott and Monty Woolley played him with aplomb on stage and in the 1942 movie. Both versions were very popular, with Kaufman himself staging the raucous Broadway production and the film well paced and brimming with wonderful character actors. A 1947 British television production featured Frank Pettingwell as Sheridan, in 1954 Woolley reprised his performance once again in an abridged American television broadcast, and Orson Welles essayed the title role in a 1972 television version. Also noteworthy is a Broadway revival starring Nathan Lane that was broadcast live on television in 2000. The original play was turned into the unsuccessful Broadway musical *Sherry!* in 1967.

Margin for Error

November 3, 1939 (Plymouth Theatre), a play by Clare Boothe. *Cast*: Otto Preminger (Karl Baumer), Elspeth Eric (Sophia Baumer), Sam Levene (Moe Finklestein), Bramwell Fletcher (Baron Alvenstor), Matt Briggs, Leif Erickson, Bert Lytell. *Director*: Otto Preminger. *Producers*:

Richard Aldrich, Richard Myers. 264 performances.

(Fox 1943). *Screenplay*: Lillie Hayward, Samuel Fuller. *Cast*: Otto Preminger (Karl Baumer), Joan Bennett (Sophia Baumer), Milton Berle (Moe Finklestein), Carl Esmond (Baron Max von Alvenstor), Howard Freeman, Poldi Dur. *Director*: Otto Preminger. *Producer*: Ralph Dietrich.

This melodrama with plenty of comic relief was the first anti–Nazi play to reach Broadway and parts of the work have the wit found in Clare Boothe's earlier *The Women* (qv). The German consul in New York is the racist, anti–American Karl Baumer who rants and raves when he finds out the police officer assigned to protect him, Moe Finklestein, is Jewish. As hard as Finklestein tries to safe guard the official, Baumer is poisoned, stabbed, and shot. (When the police captain hears of it, he asks Finklestein, "Did it kill him?") Finklestein finds out who the murderers are but turns a blind eye and lets them escape. German director Otto Preminger played Baumer and a young Sam Levene was masterful as Finklestein. Preminger also directed and acted in the 1943 movie but, perhaps because America was deep in the war by then, much of the humor was gone and the film often played like a standard whodunit. Milton Berle was Finklestein but the role did not suit his particular comic talents.

The Marriage-Go-Round

October 29, 1958 (Plymouth Theatre), a play by Leslie Stevens. *Cast*: Charles Boyer (Paul Delville), Claudette Colbert (Mrs. Delville), Julie Newmar (Katrin Sveg), Edmond Ryan (Ross Barnett). *Director*: Joseph Anthony. *Producer:* Paul Gregory. 431 performances.

(Fox 1961). *Screenplay*: Leslie Stevens. *Cast*: Susan Hayward (Mrs. Delville), James Mason (Paul Delville), Julie Newmar (Katrin Sveg), Robert Paige (Dr. Ross Barnett), June Clayworth, Joe Kirkland, Jr., Mary Patton. *Director*: Walter Lang. *Producer*: Leslie Stevens.

Paul Deville is an anthropology professor and his wife is dean of women and they seem happily married until a sexy Swedish exchange students asks Paul to father her baby.

Raging with jealousy and revenge, the wife attempts an affair with another professor. But she doesn't go through with it and neither does Paul take up the blonde's offer so all ends happily. This slight comedy ran over a year thanks to the star presence of Charles Boyer and Claudette Colbert as the couple. The 1961 movie suffers from miscasting and a tendency to wallow in its pretend salaciousness. James Mason and Susan Hayward have no grasp of the light comic touch needed but Julie Newmar, who had played the Swedish student on stage, reprises her comfortably amusing performance on the screen.

Marvin's Room

December 5, 1991 (Playwrights Horizons), a play by Scott McPherson. *Cast*: Laura Esterman (Bessie), Lisa Emery (Lee), Alice Drummond (Ruth), Mark Rosenthal (Hank), Karl Maschek, Tim Monsion, Tom Aulino. *Director*: David Petrarca. *Producer:* Playwrights Horizons. 214 performances.

(Tribeca 1996). *Screenplay*: Scott McPherson. *Cast*: Diane Keaton (Bessie), Meryl Streep (Lee), Leonardo DiCaprio (Hank), Hume Cronyn (Marvin), Gwen Verdon (Ruth), Robert De Niro, Hal Scardino. *Director*: Jerry Zaks. *Producers*: Robert De Niro, etc.

Bessie cares for her invalid father and crippled aunt without help from anyone else but when she is diagnosed with leukemia and needs a family member with compatible bone marrow, Bessie contacts her estranged sister Lee. The reunion is awkward and Lee's two troubled children do not take an immediate liking to their sick relatives. But even though none of the relations have the right kind of marrow, Bess is optimistic and an understanding is reached with her sister. The somber subject matter didn't keep the play from being funny and inspiring at times and it ran several months Off Broadway. The 1996 screen version was given an all-star cast and directed with tenderness and buoyancy. Although it was not a popular hit, the film was well received by the press and remains as a faithful yet cinematic record of the play. Playwright Scott McPherson was widely cheered as a promising find but he died of AIDS soon after completing the screenplay.

Mary Mary

March 8, 1961 (Helen Hayes Theatre), a comedy by Jean Kerr. *Cast*: Barbara Bel Geddes (Mary McKellaway), Barry Nelson (Bob McKellaway), Michael Rennie (Dirk Winston), Betsy von Furstenberg, John Cromwell. *Director*: Joseph Anthony. *Producer:* Roger L. Stevens. 1,572 performances.

(Warner 1963). *Screenplay*: Richard Breen. *Cast*: Debbie Reynolds (Mary McKellaway), Barry Nelson (Bob McKellaway), Michael Rennie (Dirk Winston), Diane McBain, Hiram Sherman. *Director-producer*: Mervyn LeRoy.

One of Broadway's longest-running comedies, this Jean Kerr play turned a familiar story into something fresh with her sparkling dialogue. Bob and Mary McKellaway are divorced and each is dating a new partner but when they are thrown together to clear up some tax disputes the old magic returns. Barbara Bel Geddes, often lauded for her serious roles, was a surprising delight as the caustic Mary and her supporting cast played the boulevard comedy with lightweight style. Debbie Reynolds is appropriately perky as Mary in the 1963 film and Barry Nelson and Michael Rennie reprise their stage roles, but the movie is awkwardly stagy and flat in its timing. At least some of Kerr's merry dialogue is there to enjoy.

Mary of Scotland

November 27, 1933 (Alvin Theatre), a drama by Maxwell Anderson. *Cast*: Helen Hayes (Mary Stuart), Helen Menken (Queen Elizabeth), Philip Merivale (Earl of Bothwell), George Couclouris (Lord Burghley), Stanley Ridges, Leonard Willey, Wilton Graff. *Director*: Theresa Helburn. *Producer:* Theatre Guild. 248 performances.

(RKO 1936). *Screenplay*: Dudley Nichols. *Cast*: Katharine Hepburn (Mary Stuart), Fredric March (Earl of Bothwell), Florence Eldridge (Elizabeth Tudor), Douglas Watson, John Carradine, Robert Barrat, Gavin Muir. *Director*: John Ford. *Producer*: Pandro S. Berman.

Maxwell Anderson took a few liberties with history in this period drama about the rivalry between Queen Elizabeth and her sister Mary, such as a terrific scene between the two queens when in reality they never met each other. Helen Hayes and Helen Menken were equally enthralling as the sisters and the handsome production also boasted a strong supporting cast. The Broadway production was generally commended and it ran several months. The 1936 screen version, on the other hand, was mostly panned, did poor business, and star Katharine Hepburn was labeled box office poison. It is a lavish and atmospheric film but the characters seem lifeless, even Hepburn only showing some spirit on occasion.

Mass Appeal

April 22, 1980 (Manhattan Theatre Club Downstage), a play by Bill C. Davis. *Cast*: Milo O'Shea (Fr. Tim Farley), Eric Roberts (Mark Dolson). *Director*: Geraldine Fitzgerald. *Producer:* Manhattan Theatre Club. 104 performances.

(Jalem 1984). *Screenplay*: *Cast*: Jack Lemmon (Fr. Tim Farley), Zeljko Ivanek (Mark Dolson), Charles Durning, Louise Latham, Alice Hirson, Helene Heigh, Sharee Gregory. *Director*: Glenn Jordan. *Producers*: David Foster, Lawrence Turman.

This sentimental two-hander was a modest hit Off Broadway but was very popular regionally where the inexpensive production values were appealing. The congenial old pastor, Fr. Tim Farley, believes in comfort for himself and his congregation so his sermons are pleasant talks with nothing very disturbing in them. But the young seminarian Mark, who is assigned to the parish as part of his training, is radical and inflammatory and his sermons upset the conservative churchgoers. When Mark goes too far and the diocese expels him, Tim vainly comes to his defense and changes his own lackadaisical ways. Two vibrant performances was all the comedy-drama needed and many actors tackled the roles across the country. Jack Lemmon and Zeljko Ivanek make a nice contrasting pair in the 1984 film but the opening up of the material is artificial and the issues at hand seem rather humdrum in the easily forgettable movie.

The Matchmaker

December 5, 1955 (Royale Theatre), a farce by Thornton Wilder. *Cast*: Ruth Gordon (Dolly Levi), Loring Smith (Horace Vandergelder), Arthur Hill (Cornelius Hackl), Eileen Herlie (Mrs. Molloy), Robert Morse (Barnaby Tucker), Rosamund Greenwood (Minnie Fay), Esme Church, Patrick McAlinney, Alexander Davion, Prunella Scales. *Director*: Tyrone Guthrie. *Producers:* Theatre Guild, David Merrick. 486 performances.

(Paramount 1958). *Screenplay*: John Michael Hayes. *Cast*: Shirley Booth (Dolly Levi), Paul Ford (Horace Vandergelder), Anthony Perkins (Cornelius Hackl), Shirley MacLaine (Irene Malloy), Robert Morse (Barnaby Tucker), Perry Wilson (Minnie Fay), Wallace Ford, Joe Scanlon, Gavin Gordon. *Director*: Joseph Anthony. *Producer*: Don Hartman.

The now-familiar story, about the Jewish matchmaker Dolly Levi and all the fuss she causes when she arranges romances for both her clients and herself, has roots in neoclassic French and turn-of-the-century Austrian theatre, but Thornton Wilder's zesty version is very American in temperament as well as locale and character. The Broadway production was filled with seasoned performers, such as Ruth Gordon, and up-and-coming talents, like Arthur Hill and Robert Morse, and was dashingly directed by Tyrone Guthrie. The 1958 movie, on the other hand, tends to plod along not like a farce but a period slideshow. The cast is mostly enjoyable and the decor is commendable but the spirit of Wilder's play is gone. The story would resurface as the musical *Hello, Dolly!* (qv).

Maybe It's Love see *Saturday's Child*

Maytime

August 16, 1917 (Shubert Theatre), an operetta by Rida Johnson Young. *Score:* Sigmund Romberg, Rida Johnson Young. *Cast:* Peggy Wood (Ottilie Van Zandt), Charles Purcell (Richard Wayne), William Norris (Matthew Van Zandt), Maude Odell, Ralph Herbert, Gertrude Vanderbilt.

Songs: Will You Remember?; The Road to Paradise; Jump Jim Crow; Dancing Will Keep You Young. *Director:* Edward Temple. *Choreographer:* Allan K. Foster. *Producers:* Shuberts. 492 performances.

(MGM 1937). *Screenplay:* Noel Langley. *Score:* Sigmund Romberg, Rida Johnson Young, Herbert Stothart, Robert Wright, George Forrest, etc. *Cast:* Jeanette MacDonald (Marcia Mirnay), Nelson Eddy (Paul Allison), John Barrymore (Nicolai Nazaroff), Herman Bing, Harry Davenport, Billy Gilbert, Lynne Carver, Tom Brown, Leonid Kinskey, Walter Kingsford. *Songs:* Will You Remember?; Ham and Eggs; Carry Me Back to Old Virginny. *Director:* Robert Z. Leonard. *Producer:* Hunt Stromberg.

This ambitious operetta has a storyline that extended over three generations and, as melodramatic as the tale may seem, it is less contrived and more sincere than most samples of the genre. The wealthy New Yorker Ottilie loves the working-class Richard but obeys her father and marries a rich man instead. As the years pass, her fortunes fall and his rise. Richard, still in love with her, helps the destitute Ottilie but the two die of old age without ever getting together again. Years later the two grandchildren of their marriages fall in love with each other in the same garden where their ancestors wooed and, because the new generation was played by the same actors as the older one, the love between Otillie and Richard seemed to blossom again. Sigmund Romberg's score boasted two major hit songs, "Will You Remember?" and "The Road to Paradise," which helped the operetta become a favorite during World War One. The movie version kept only the title and one song, rewriting the story into an obvious melodrama about an aging opera singer who looks back to the lost love of her youth and how her Svengali-like husband murdered him when he came back into her life. Jeanette MacDonald and Nelson Eddy, the reigning king and queen of Hollywood operettas, played the lovers and John Barrymore was corny but effective as the jealous husband. But much of the movie is clumsy and contrived and the Romberg score is not there to save it.

The Member of the Wedding

January 5, 1950 (Empire Theatre), a play by Carson McCullers. *Cast:* Julie Harris (Frankie Addams), Ethel Waters (Berenice Sadie Brown), Brandon De Wilde (John Henry West), James Holden, Janet De Gore, William Hansen, Margaret Barker. *Director:* Harold Clurman. *Producers:* Robert Whitehead, etc. 501 performances.

(Columbia 1952). *Screenplay:* Edna Anhalt, Edward Anhalt. *Cast:* Julie Harris (Frankie Addams), Ethel Waters (Berenice Sadie Brown), Brandon De Wilde (John Henry), Arthur Franz, Nancy Gates, William Hansen. *Director:* Fred Zinnemann. *Producer:* Stanley Kramer.

(TV 1982). *Teleplay:* Carson McCullers. *Cast:* Pearl Bailey (Berenice Sadie Brown), Dana Hill (Frankie Addams), Benjamin Berouny (John Henry), Howard E. Rollins, Jr., Dwier Brown. *Director:* Delbert Mann.

(TV 1997). *Teleplay:* David W. Rintels. *Cast:* Anna Paquin (Frankie Addams), Alfre Woodard (Berenice Sadie Brown), Corey Dunn (John Henry), Enrico Colantoni, Anne Tremko, Matt McGrath. *Director:* Fielder Cook. *Producer:* David W. Rintels.

The lonely but talkative tomboy Frankie Addams is ignored by her widowed father and grows up in a small Southern town befriending their African American cook Berenice and the young John Henry from next door. Frankie comes alive when she is asked to be a member of her elder brother's wedding party but is crushed when she realizes they will leave her behind when they travel afar after the ceremony. When John Henry dies of meningitis and Berenice gets married again and moves away, Frankie is alone but the promise of an adolescent romance gives her hope. Carson McCullers adapted her novel for the stage and it overflowed with warmth and unforgettable characters. The young Julie Harris became a stage star with her fervent Frankie and veteran singer-actress Ethel Waters gave one of her last and best performances as Berenice. Both women, as well as Brandon De Wilde as John Henry, got to recreate their roles in the 1952 movie and all three are extraordinary. No effort is made to open up the story and it is a very static piece cinematically. But the camera captures the indelible characters

and that is enough. In 1982 a television production with Pearl Bailey as Berenice was
broadcast live. The play was remade for television in 1997 with Alfre Woodard as a noteworthy Berenice and Anna Paquin overacting as Frankie.

A Memory of Two Mondays

September 29, 1955. (Coronet Theatre), a one-
act play by Arthur Miller. *Cast*: Leo Penn (Bert),
Biff McGuire (Kenneth), Eileen Heckart
(Agnes), Van Heflin (Larry), Jack Warden
(Frank), Russell Collins, Gloria Marlowe, J. Car-
roll Naish, Richard Davalos. *Director*: Martin
Ritt. *Producers:* Kermit Bloomgarden, etc. 149
performances.

(TV 1974). *Teleplay*: Arthur Miller. *Cast*:
Kristoffer Tabori (Bert), Dan Hamilton (Ken-
neth), Estelle Parsons (Agnes), George Grizzard
(Larry), Tony Lo Bianco (Frank), Jack Warden,
Barnard Hughes, Harvey Keitel, Catherine
Burns. J. D. Cannon. *Director*: Paul Bogart. *Pro-
ducer*: Jacqueline Bubbin.

This very atypical Arthur Miller work
is a quiet, understated memory play about a
youth named Bert who works in a warehouse
to earn enough money to go to college. The
characters that surround him range from a
failed poet to lecherous boys but all are recalled with a wistful kind of affection. The
Chekhov-like work was first presented as
part of a double bill with *A View From the
Bridge* (qv) and is rarely revived because it
calls for many actors for such a short play.
But it remains a distinctive and beautifully
written little drama. An expert cast was featured in the 1974 television production
which captured the leisurely but engrossing
charm of the play.

Men in White

September 26, 1933 (Broadhurst Theatre), a
drama by Sidney Kingsley. *Cast*: Alexander Kirkland (George Ferguson), Margaret Barker (Laura
Hudson), Phoebe Brand (Barbara Dennin), Art
Smith (Mr. Hudson), Morris Carnovsky (Dr.
Levine), Sanford Meisner, Russell Collins,
Luther Adler, Ruth Nelson, Alan Baxter. *Director*: Lee Strasberg. *Producer:* Group Theatre. 351
performances. Pulitzer Prize.

(MGM 1934). *Screenplay*: Waldemar Young. *Cast*:
Clark Gable (George Ferguson), Myrna Loy
(Laura Hudson), Jean Hersholt (Dr. Hockberg),
Elizabeth Allen (Barbara Denham), Otto Kruger
(Dr. Levine), C. Henry Gordon, Russell Hardie,
Wallace Ford, Henry B. Walthall. *Director*:
Richard Boleslawski. *Producer*: Monta Bell.

The idealistic young intern George
Ferguson is torn by his sense of dignity and
his fiancée's pushing him to accept easy ad-
vancements through her connections. But
George has an affair with a nurse who dies
during an abortion operation so the dis-
traught medical man leaves his fiancée to
finish his studies in Vienna. After decades of
hospital films and television shows, it is
difficult to understand how unique this
drama about the medical profession was.
Critics carped about the soap opera story
but the scenes in the operating room and the
medical jargon fascinated playgoers for a
year. Clark Gable played George in the 1934
movie and Myra Loy was the socialite he
was engaged to. Both turn in respectable
performances, as do a handful of accomplished character actors, but the film rarely
rises above slick melodrama. All the same, it
was very successful at the box office and inspired a slew of doctors dramas that would
continue into television years later.

Merton of the Movies

November 13, 1922 (Cort Theatre), a comedy by
George S. Kaufman, Marc Connelly. *Cast*: Glenn
Hunter (Merton Gill), Florence Nash (Flips
Montague), Gladys Feldman (Beulah Baxter),
Edwin Maxwell (Sigmund Rosenblatt), Edward
M. Favor, J. K. Murray, A. Romaine Callender,
W. H. Seniro. *Director*: Hugh Ford. *Producers:*
George Tyler, Hugh Ford. 398 performances.

(Famous Players 1924). *Screenplay*: Walter Woods.
Cast: Glenn Hunter (Merton Gill), Viola Dana
(Flips Montague), Charles Sellon (Pete Gashwiler),
Sadie Gordon (Mrs. Gashwiler), Gale Henry,
Luke Cosgrave. *Director-producer*: James Cruze.

Make Me a Star (Paramount 1932). *Screenplay:*
Sam Wintz, etc. *Cast*: Sturat Erwin (Merton
Gill), Joan Blondell (Flips Montague), ZaSu
Pitts (Mrs. Scudder), Ben Turpin, Florence
Roberts. *Director:* William Beaudine. *Producer:*
Lloyd Sheldon.

(MGM 1947). *Screenplay*: Lou Breslow, George Wells. *Cast*: Red Skelton (Merton Gill), Virginia O'Brien (Phyllis Montague), Gloria Grahame (Beuah Baxter), Leon Ames, Alan Mowbray, Charles D. Brown. *Director*: Robert Alton. *Producer*: Albert Lewis.

A series of stories in the *Saturday Evening Post* by Harry Leon Wilson was turned into a slapstick hit by George S. Kaufman and Marc Connelly that ran a year, was a favorite in community theatres, and was filmed three times. General store clerk Merton Gill loves the flickers so much he leaves his small Illinois hometown and goes to Hollywood where he runs up against deception and crass moviemakers who destroy his illusions about Tinsel Town. But when Merton is cast in a comedy short he plays it seriously and is so funny that he becomes a movie star. One of the earliest and best Broadway satires about Hollywood, the play was first filmed as a silent in 1924 with Glenn Hunter reprising his daffy Merton from the stage. A farcical 1932 talkie, retitled *Make Me a Star*, cast Stuart Erwin as the bumbling hero and he was both funny and endearing in the part. The movie was well paced and well cast, including guest appearances by such stars as Tallulah Bankhead, Gary Cooper, Claudette Colbert, and Maurice Chevalier. Red Skelton played Merton in the 1947 remake (which used the play's title) but the humor was pretty strained by then and his performance is more energetic than amusing, more calculated than sincere.

Mexican Hayride

January 28, 1944 (Winter Garden Theatre), a musical comedy by Herbert and Dorothy Fields. *Score*: Cole Porter. *Cast*: Bobby Clark (Joe Bascom), June Havoc (Montana), Wilbur Evans (David Winthrop), George Givot (Lombo Campos), Luba Malina, Edith Meiser, Paul Haakon, Corinna Mura. *Songs*: I Love You; There Must Be Someone for Me; Sing to Me, Guitar; Count Your Blessings; Abracadabra. *Directors*: Hassard Short, John Kennedy. *Choreographer*: Paul Haakon. *Producer*: Michael Todd. 481 performances.

(Universal 1948). *Screenplay*: Oscar Brodney, John Grant. *Cast*: Bud Abbott (Harry Lambert), Lou Costello (Joe Bascom), Virginia Grey (Montana), Luba Malina, John Hubbard, Pedro de Cordoba, Tom Powers, Fritz Feld. *Director*: Charles Barton. *Producer*: Robert Arthur.

This lighthearted musical romp was an escapist wartime amusement that ran on the strength of its comic star Bobby Clark, though he was given able support by a farcical script and some memorable Cole Porter songs. Clark played a numbers racketeer on the lam who goes to Mexico where he takes on various disguises, from a matador to a mariachi flute player to an Indian squaw. Hollywood cut all the songs and made the movie a non-singing vehicle for Bud Abbott and Lou Costello, the two of them getting into the scrapes that Clark had encountered on the stage. As an Abbott and Costello comedy, the picture has its moments; as a recreation of the original musical, it is a total bust.

Middle of the Night

February 8, 1956 (ANTA Theatre), a play by Paddy Chayevsky. *Cast*: Edward G. Robinson (Manufacturer), Gena Rowlands (Girl), June Walker (Mother), Anne Jackson (Daughter), Martin Balsam (Son-in-Law), Lee Philips, Joan Chambers, Nancy Pollock, Betty Walker. *Director-producer*: Joshua Logan. 477 performances.

(Columbia 1959). *Screenplay*: Paddy Chayevsky. *Cast*: Fredric March (Jerry Kingsley), Kim Novak (Betty Preisser), Martin Balsam (Jack), Effie Afton, Anna Berger, Rudy Bond, Joan Copeland. *Director*: Delbert Mann. *Producer*: George Justin.

Paddy Chayevsky wrote this domestic drama as a television play but it was produced on Broadway where it was called everything from a subtle and penetrating character study to bland soap opera. But everyone agreed that Edward G. Robinson gave a profoundly moving performance so the play ran over a year. He played a middle-aged, widowed manufacturer who falls in love with his secretary, a much younger divorcée. The families on both sides oppose the relationship but the couple eventually wins out. Fredric March was commendable as the manufacturer in the 1959 film version but co-star Kim Novak was less than compelling. The movie is slowly paced but directed with taste and insight and the New York City locations add to the story.

The Milk Train Doesn't Stop Here Anymore

January 16, 1963 (Morosco Theatre), a play by Tennessee Williams. *Cast*: Hermione Baddeley (Flora Goforth), Mildred Dunnock (Vera Ridgeway Condotti), Paul Roebling (Chris Flanders), Maria Tucci (Angelina), Clyde Ventura, Ann Williams. *Director*: Herbert Machiz. *Producer*: Roger L. Stevens. 69 performances.

Boom (Universal 1968). *Screenplay*: Tennessee Williams. *Cast*: Elizabeth Taylor (Flora Goforth), Richard Burton (Chris Flanders), Noel Coward (Witch of Capri), Joanna Shimkus, Romolo Valli, Michael Dunn, Veronica Wells, Fernando Piazza. *Director*: Joseph Losey. *Producers*: John Heyman, Norman Priggen.

The oft-widowed millionairess Flora Goforth is dying of cancer in her Italian villa and dictating her memoirs to a tape recorder when a handsome young poet enters, calls himself the Angel of Death, and tries to seduce her. But Flora thinks he is just an opportunist and sends him on his way, only to regret it later. The highly symbolic play was one of Tennessee Williams's less successful efforts and only managed to intrigue playgoers for two months. The next year the odd play was rewritten by the playwright and revived on Broadway with Tallulah Bankhead; it was deemed even less satisfactory and quickly closed, bringing Bankhead's long stage career to an anti-climatic end. Williams again did some rewriting for the 1968 movie version, retitled *Boom!*, but the basic story was the same except that the decaying Fora is now a middle-aged but still-ravishing Elizabeth Taylor and the poet was not a young man but the quickly-aging Richard Burton. Noel Coward was featured in the rewritten role of the Witch of Capri but the trio of stars could create no sparks on the screen or at the box office. It is a curiously misconceived film, further muddled by Joseph Losey's offbeat direction. But the scenery in Sardinia and Rome is spectacular and there is a fine supporting performance by Joanna Shimkus.

The Miracle Worker

October 19, 1959 (Playhouse Theatre), a play by William Gibson. *Cast*: Anne Bancroft (Anne Sullivan), Patty Duke (Helen Keller), Patricia Neal (Kate Keller), Torin Thatcher (Capt. Keller), James Congdon, Michael Constantine. *Director*: Arthur Penn. *Producer:* Fred Coe. 700 performances. Tony Award.

(Playfilm 1962). *Screenplay*: William Gibson. *Cast*: Anne Bancroft (Anne Sullivan), Patty Duke (Helen Keller), Inga Swenson (Kate Keller), Victor Jory (Capt. Keller), Andrew Prine, Kathleen Comegys. *Director*: Arthur Penn. *Producer*: Fred Coe.

(TV 1979). *Teleplay*: *Cast*: Patty Duke (Anne Sullivan), Melissa Gilbert (Helen Keller), Diana Muldaur (Kate Keller), Charles Siebert (Capt. Keller), Stanley Wells, Anne Seymour, Hilda Haynes, Titos Vandis. *Director*: Paul Aaron. *Producer*: Fred Coe.

(TV 2000). *Teleplay*: Monte Merrick. *Cast*: Alison Elliott (Anne Sullivan), Hallie Kate Eisenberg (Helen Keller), Kate Greenhouse (Kate Keller), Davis Strathairn (Capt. Keller), Lucas Black, Damir Andrei, Patricia Gage. *Director*: Nadia Tass. *Producer*: Suzy Beugen.

This fascinating true story, about the blind-deaf-mute child Helen Keller and how she was finally reached by her teacher Annie Sullivan, was originally written as a television play and was broadcast on *Playhouse 90* in 1959 with Patty McCormack as Helen and Teresa Wright as Annie. Author William Gibson reworked it for the stage and, with Patty Duke and Anne Bancrost as pupil and teacher, it was a hit on Broadway in 1959. Both actresses got to reprise their Tony Award-winning performances in the 1962 screen version, both winning Oscars as well. It is a stark, shadowy black and white film that often resembles a documentary but it is no less emotionally potent because of that. The play remains one of the most-often produced dramas in schools and community theatres and there have been a number of New York revivals as well. The grown-up Patty Duke played Annie in the 1978 television production with Melissa Gilbert as Helen, and Alison Elliott and Hallie Kate Eisenberg were teacher and pupil in a largely-rewritten Disney version in 2000.

Both small screen productions had their merits but seemed to emphasize the melodramatics of the plot over the more subtle aspects of the characters.

Miss Brewster's Millions see Brewster's Millions

Miss Firecracker see The Miss Firecracker Contest

The Miss Firecracker Contest

May 1, 1984 (Manhattan Theatre Club UpStage), a play by Beth Henley. *Cast*: Holly Hunter (Carnelle Scott), Mark Linn-Baker (Delmount Williams), Belita Moreno (Popeye Jackson), Patricia Richardson, Margo Martindale, Budge Threlkeld. *Director*: Stephen Tobolowsky. *Producer*: Manhattan Theatre Club. 244 performances.

Miss Firecracker (Guadalupe 1989). *Screenplay*: Beth Henley. *Cast*: Holly Hunter (Carnelle Scott), Mary Steenburgen (Elain Rutledge), Tim Robbins (Delmount Williams), Alfre Woodard (Popeye Jackson), Scott Glenn, Veanne Cox. *Director*: Thomas Schlamme. *Producer*: Fred Berner.

Even though Carnelle Scott is called "Miss Hot Tamale" behind her back because of her tarnished reputation, she hopes to win the Miss Firecracker Contest held in her small Mississippi town each year. For the talent section of the competition she practices twirling the baton to the "Star Spangled Banner" while firecrackers explode. But her dreams are dashed when she flubs the act and realizes she has got to stop trying so hard "t' belong." The comedy was punctuated with some deliciously wacky characters, such as the seamstress Popeye Jackson who hears through her eye balls ever since someone mistakenly put ear drops in her eyes when she was a child. Holly Hunter as Carnelle led the farcical cast and the well-received comedy had a limited three-month run Off Broadway, then returned the next season for another three months. Hunter reprised her performance in the 1989 movie, the title shortened to *Miss Firecracker*, and it

is a sprightly portrayal filled with vivacity and pathos. The supporting cast is also first-rate and playwright Beth Henley adapted her play for the screen with a comfortable kind of lunacy. The mad-ball film was well received by the critics but never caught on with the public.

Miss Lonelyhearts

October 3, 1957 (Music Box Theatre), a play by Howard Teichmann. *Cast*: Pat O'Brien (William Spain), Fritz Weaver (Boy), Ruth Warrick (Mary Spain), Irene Daily, Henderson Forsythe, William Hickey, Anne Meara, Maurice Ellis, Pippa Scott, Marian Reardon, Jo Anna March. *Director*: Alan Schneider. *Producer:* Lester Osterman, Alfred R. Glancy, Jr. 12 performances.

Lonelyhearts (United Artists 1958). *Screenplay*: Dore Schary. *Cast*: Montgomery Clift (Adam White), Robert Ryan (William Shrike), Myrna Loy (Florence Shrike), Maureen Stapleton (Fay Doyle), Dolores Hart, Jackie Coogan, Mike Kellin. *Director*: Vincent J. Donehue. *Producer*: Dore Schary.

Miss Lonelyhearts (TV 1983). *Teleplay*: Michael Dinner, Robert Bailey. *Cast*: Eric Roberts (Miss Lonelyhearts), Arthur Hill (Willy Shrike), Conchata Ferrell (Faye Doyle), John P. Ryan, Sally Kemp, Gregory Itzin, Martina Deignan, Jackie Earle Haley. *Director*: Michael Dinner. *Producers*: Lydia Woodard, Michael Dinner.

Nathaniel West's somber novel about an advice columnist was adapted into a poignant but fatalistic little drama that quickly closed. The "Miss Lonelyhearts" column in a big city newspaper is being written by the rookie reporter who doesn't take his job seriously at first but is soon caught up in the lonely lives of his correspondents. He becomes interested in one woman so much that he throws off his girl friend and begins an affair with her, only to be shot by her jealous husband. Despite its failure on Broadway, the drama was filmed as *Lonelyhearts* in 1958 and it too is rather depressing even though the studio insisted on a happy ending. Montgomery Clift is dark and troubled as the columnist and there are also noteworthy performances by Robert Ryan, Myrna Loy, Maureen Stapleton (in her film debut), and others. The moody piece is not for everyone's tastes but the talent is there. A television version in 1983, titled *Miss Lonelyhearts*, featured Eric Roberts as the columnist and it was closer to the novella and the play. The downbeat ending was restored and, as in the other versions, the supporting cast is estimable. Also of interest is the fine 1933 film *Advice to the Lovelorn* based on West's book and starring Lee Tracy as the columnist. Made twenty-five years before the stage adaptation, it nonetheless contains many similarities.

Miss Lulu Bett

December 27, 1920 (Belmont Theatre), a play by Zona Gale. *Cast*: Carroll McComas (Lulu Bett), Brigham Royce (Ninian), William E. Holden (Dwight Deacon), Catherine Calhoun Doucet (Ina), Louise Closer Hale, Jack Bohn, Willard Robertson. *Director-producer:* Brock Pemberton. 201 performances. Pulitzer Prize.

(Famous Players 1921). *Screenplay*: Clara Beranger. *Cast*: Lois Wilson (Lulu Bett), Clarence Burton (Ninian Deacon), Milton Sills (Neil Cornish), Theodore Roberts (Dwight Deacon), Helen Ferguson, Mae Giraci, Taylor Graves. *Director*: William C. de Mille. *Producer*: Adolph Zukor.

Zona Gale adapted her own popular novel about Midwestern life into a prize-winning drama and, though some critics denounced the melodrama, theatregoers were caught up in the story. Spinster Lulu Bett is no better than a servant in the home of her sister Ina and brother-in-law Dwight but her life changes when Dwight's brother Ninian comes to visit and he flirts with her. Lulu takes the attention seriously and begins to blossom. Dwight plays along with his brother's teasing and unwittingly weds the two in a civil ceremony. A happy ending is delayed when Dwight tells Lulu that Ninian is already married but it turns out he is a widower now so all is well. The contrived drama allowed Carroll McComas to shine as Lulu and it proved to be the non-musical role of her career. A silent film version of the play was made in 1921 with Lois Wilson as Lulu and again the public responded to the rural romance.

Miss Sadie Thompson see *Rain*

Mr. Music see *Accent on Youth*

Mister Roberts

February 18, 1948 (Alvin Theatre), a play by Thomas Heggen, Joshua Logan. *Cast*: Henry Fonda (Lt. Doug Roberts), David Wayne (Ensign Pulver), William Harrigan (Captain), Robert Keith (Doc), Jocelyn Brando, Rusty Lane, Joe Marr, Ralph Meeker, Steven Hill, Karl Lucas. *Director*: Joshua Logan. *Producer:* Leland Hayward. 1,157 performances. Tony Award.

(Warner 1955). *Screenplay*: Joshua Logan, Frank Nugent. *Cast*: Henry Fonda (Lt. Doug Roberts), James Cagney (Capt. Morton), William Powell (Doc), Jack Lemmon (Ensign Pulver), Betsy Palmer, Ward Bond, Philip Carey, Nick Adams, Perry Lopez, Harry Carey, Jr., Ken Curtis. *Directors*: John Ford, Mervyn LeRoy. *Producer*: Leland Hayward.

(TV 1984). *Teleplay*: Joshua Logan, Thomas Heggen. *Cast*: Robert Hayes (Lt. Doug Roberts), Kevin Bacon (Ensign Pulver), Charles Durning (Captain), Howard Hesseman (Doc), Raye Birk, Marilou Henner, Charley Lang, Christopher Murray, Joe Pantoliano. *Director*: Melvin Bernhardt.

One of the finest plays about World War Two, this comedy-drama was not about warfare but about the drudgery of life on a cargo ship that supplies the forces in the Pacific. Captain Morton runs his ship with an iron hand but Lieutenant Roberts acts as a buffer between the captain and the crew. After some adventures and misadventures that pit the Captain against Roberts, the latter finally gets transferred to the battlelines where he is killed. News of the beloved Roberts's death spurs the weak-willed Ensign Pulver to stand up to the Captain. Based on Thomas Heggen's book, the play was a critical and popular success and Henry Fonda's performance as Roberts was widely acclaimed. He got to reprise the role in the faithful 1955 movie which also starred James Cagney as the Captain, William Powell (in his last film) as the ship's doctor, and Jack

Lemmon as Pulver. The story opened up naturally for the screen and was as successful as the Broadway play. An uninspired sequel, *Ensign Pulver*, was made in 1965 with Robert Walker, Jr. in the Lemmon role and in 1965 there was a television series with Roger Smith as Roberts. The original play was remade for television in 1984 with a laudable cast but it could not compare favorably with the Fonda versions.

Mr. Sycamore

November 13, 1942 (Guild Theatre), a comedy by Ketti Frings. *Cast*: Stuart Erwin (John Gwilt), Enid Markey (Estelle Benlow), Lillian Gish (Jane Gwilt), Russell Collins (Rev. Dr. Doody), Otto Hulett, Leona Powers. *Director*: Lester Vail. *Producer*: Theatre Guild. 19 performances.

(Capricorn 1975). *Screenplay*: Pancho Kohner. *Cast*: Jason Robards (John Gwilt), Sandy Dennis (Jane Gwilt), Jean Simmons (Estelle Benbow), Mark Miller, Jerome Thor. *Director-producer*: Pancho Kohner.

This must be the most oddball entry in this book. Mailman John Gwilt is so disgusted with life that he decides he'd rather be a tree. His loving wife Jane helps him dig a hole in the backyard and, taking off his shoes and socks, John plants his feet in the dirt. Neighbors mock him but Jane brings John a chair to make him comfortable and food to eat until he takes root. John gets discouraged and almost gives up the idea but one day he turns into an actual tree so Jane spends the rest of her days sitting in its shade and chatting with the transformed John. Ketti Frings adapted Robert Ayre's story for the stage and the prestigious Theatre Guild produced it, though it only lasted a few weeks. As bizarre as the play is, it is even more bizarre that thirty-three years later the piece was rediscovered and made into a movie. Jason Robards played John in the 1975 film with Sandy Dennis as his wife and Jean Simmons as the local librarian who gives John the idea when she reads a poem to him. Despite the stars attached to the project, the movie seems to have disappeared without anyone much noticing it. But it is available for viewing and it is a curiosity, to

say the least. Neither funny enough to be a comedy nor reasonable enough to be taken serious, the allegorical tale is a real puzzle, and not a puzzle easy to sit through.

Mogambo see *Red Dust*

The Moon Is Blue

March 8, 1951 (Henry Miller Theatre), a comedy by F. Hugh Herbert. *Cast*: Barbara Bel Geddes (Patty O'Neill), Barry Nelson (Donald Gresham), Donald Cook (David Slater), Ralph Dunn. *Director*: Otto Preminger. *Producers*: Richard Aldrich, etc. 924 performances.

(United Artists 1953). *Screenplay*: F. Hugh Herbert. *Cast*: William Holden (Donald Gresham), Maggie McNamara (Patty O'Neill), David Niven (David Slater), Tom Tully, Dawn Addams, Fortunio Bonanova, Gregory Ratoff. *Director-producer*: Otto Preminger.

When architect Donald Gresham and open-minded Patty O'Neill meet on the observation deck of the Empire State Building, they fall instantly in love (and lust) but others try to ruin the relationship until the lovers triumph by the final curtain. Few comedies of the 1950s were less substantial but few ran as long. The young and amiable cast were endorsed by the press even if the play was considered in poor taste by some. The 1953 film was also criticized for its loose morals and flippant use of words like "virgin' and "mistress" (the Production Code refused to give its approval) but it also was very popular. William Holden and Maggie McNamara played the lovers and David Niven was among the characters complicating the situation. It is a stagnant film version and hopelessly dated today but at the time the story and the outspoken characters were considered rather racy. Director Otto Preminger made a German-language version of the play at the same time he was helming the American one.

The Mound Builders

February 2, 1975 (Triplex Theatre), a play by Lanford Wilson. *Cast*: Jonathan Hogan (Dan

Loggins), Trish Hawkins (Jean Loggins), Tanya Berezin (Delia Eriksen), John Strasberg (Chad Jasker), Robert Thirkield, Stephanie Gordon. *Director*: Marshall W. Mason. *Producer:* Circle Repertory Company. 29 performances.

(TV 1976). *Teleplay*: Lanford Wilson. *Cast*: Ken Marshall (Dan Loggins), Tanya Berezin (Delia Eriksen), Trish Hawkins (Jean Loggins), Brad Dourif (Chad Jasker). *Directors*: Ken Campbell, Marshall W. Mason. *Producer*: Ken Campbell.

On an archeological dig in rural Illinois, a college professor and his associates and family members work by day exploring a prehistoric civilization while at night personalities clash and temperaments run high. A local farm boy grows attached to an archeologist's wife and when he discovers that the couple is expecting a baby, the boy goes berserk and destroys the dig, the husband, and himself. An early Lanford Wilson play that was seen in a limited Off Off Broadway run, the character study has slowly found revivals over the years. A 1976 television production was beautifully acted but was studio bound when it needed some more exteriors to help show the complete story.

Mourning Becomes Electra

October 26, 1931 (Guild Theatre), a trilogy by Eugene O'Neill. *Cast*: Alla Nazimova (Christine Mannon), Alice Brady (Lavinia Mannon), Earle Larrimore (Orin Mannon), Lee Baker (Gen. Ezra Mannon), Thomas Chambers (Capt. Adam Brant), Philip Foster, Thomasa Chakmers. *Director*: Philip Moeller. *Producer:* Theatre Guild. 157 performances.

(RKO 1947). *Screenplay*: Dudley Nichols. *Cast*: Rosalind Russell (Lavinia Mannon), Katina Paxinou (Christine Mannon), Michael Redgrave (Orin Mannon), Raymond Massey (Gen. Ezra Mannon), Leo Genn, Kirk Douglas. *Director-producer*: Dudley Nichols.

(TV 1978). *Teleplay:* Eugene O'Neill, Kenneth Cavander. *Cast:* Joan Hackett (Christine), Roberta Maxwell (Lavinia), Bruce Davison (Orin), Josef Sommer (Gen. Mannon), Jeffrey DeMunn (Adam Brant). *Director:* Nick Havinga. *Producers:* Jac Venza, Ann Blumenthal.

Eugene O'Neill's most ambitious of his completed works, this trilogy of plays ran over five hours (it was performed in one day with a dinner break) and retold the Greek *Oresteia* legend in American terms. General Mannon returns from the Civil War to his New England home where he is murdered by his wife Christine and her lover Adam Brant. The general's daughter Lavinia convinces her brother Orin to avenge their father's death so the two of them kill Brant, thereby causing Christine to commit suicide. But the guilt is too much for Orin who also kills himself leaving Lavinia to shut herself up in the family home as punishment for her many sins. O'Neill added several Freudian touches to the old tale (Lavinia seems to have an unnatural affection for both her father and Brant just as Orin questions his motherlove for Christine) and keeps the characters and dialogue on a more realistic level than the Greeks had used. The Broadway production was simply but elegantly staged, the cast was quite distinguished, and the unlikely commercial offering was a success. Obviously much of the text had to be cut for a screen version and the 1947 movie, running close to three hours, was a bit choppy at times. But more distracting was the slow, talky, and uncinematic way the story was told. Rosalind Russell was cast against type as the mournful Lavinia and audiences didn't quite buy it, but Katina Paxinou, Michael Redgrave, Raymond Massey, and some others are commendable even if their New England accents are all over the map. When the movie bombed at the box office the studio cut it and re-released it, losing even more money. The difficult play has seen few revivals but some have been memorable, such as a 1972 Broadway production with Colleen Dewhurst and Pamela Payton-Wright that was remounted for television. The text is well edited and the acting is so accomplished that the story seems very convincing and the characters quite involving. Also noteworthy is a five-part television miniseries of the play in 1978, edited by Greek translator-scholar Kenneth Cavander. This is the most complete film record and it also has a masterful cast, particularly Roberta Maxwell as Lavinia.

Mrs. Wiggs of the Cabbage Patch

September 3, 1904 (Savoy Theatre), a comedy by Anne Crawford Flexner. *Cast*: Madge Carr Cook (Mrs. Wiggs), Mabel Taliaferro (Lovey Mary), Thurston Hall (Mr. Bob), Argyle Campbell (Billy), Nora Shelby (Lucy), Oscar Eagle (Mr. Wiggs), Argyle Campbell, William T. Hodge. *Director*: Oscar Eagle. *Producer:* Liebler &. Co. 150 performances.

(California 1914). *Screenplay*: Anne Crawford Flexner. *Cast*: Blanche Chapman (Mrs. Wiggs), Beatriz Michelena (Lovey Mary), House Peters (Bob), Andrew Robson (Mr. Wiggs), La Belle Carmen, Belle Bennett, William Pike. *Director*: Harold Entwhistle. *Producer*: George Middleton.

(Famous Players 1919). *Screenplay*: Eve Unsll. *Cast*: Mary Carr (Mrs. Wiggs), Marguerite Clark (Lovey Mary), Gareth Hughes (Billy), Vivian Ogden, Gladys Valerie. *Director*: Hugh Ford.

Lovey Mary (MGM 1926). *Screenplay*: Agnes Christine Johnston, Charles Maigne. *Cast*: Mary Alden (Mrs. Wiggs), Bessie Love (Lovey Mary), William Haines (Billy), Vivian Ogden, Martha Mattox, Jackie Coombs. *Director*: King Baggot.

Mrs. Wiggs of the Cabbage Patch (Paramount 1934). *Screenplay*: William Slavens McNut, Jane Storm. *Cast*: Pauline Lord (Mrs. Wiggs), W. C. Fields (C. Ellsworth Stubbins), ZaSu Pitts, Evelyn Venable, Kent Taylor, Charles Middleton. *Director*: Norman Taurog. *Producer*: Douglas MacLean.

Mrs. Wiggs of the Cabbage Patch (Paramount 1942). *Screenplay*: Doris Anderson. *Cast*: Fay Bainter (Mrs. Wiggs), Hugh Herbert (Marcus Throckmorton), Carolyn Lee, Barbara Jo Allen, Barbara Britton, Betty Brewer. *Director*: Ralph Murphy. *Producers*: Ralph Murphy, Sol C. Siegel.

Alice Hegan Rice's stories about the good-hearted Mrs. Wiggs was adapted into one of the most beloved stage works of the early 20th century. Although she is the abandoned mother of several children and can hardly make ends meet, the optimistic Mrs. Wiggs spends her days helping others. She brings a couple together, finds a loving mate for her grown son in the person of the orphan Lovey Mary, and even takes back her dissolute alcoholic husband when he returns one day. Madge Carr Cook played Mrs. Wiggs in the successful Broadway production and the role was forever after identified with her as she continued to perform it for years. The comedy itself went on for years with many touring productions. There have been at least five screen versions of the tale, including silent films in 1914 with Blanche Chapman as Mrs. Wiggs, in 1919 with Mary Carr, and a 1926 version called *Lovey Mary* in which Mary Alden was Mrs. Wiggs and Bessie Love was the orphan of the title. The 1934 talkie was superbly made and still fascinates with its almost surreal view of the Depression. The great stage actress Pauline Lord makes one of her few screen appearances as Mrs. Wiggs and W. C. Fields shines as the bumptious suitor to neighbor ZaSu Pitts. The 1942 remake also has much to recommend, including a fine performance by Fay Bainter as Mrs. Wiggs. The plot changes considerably in all of these screen versions as different episodes from the stories are used. But at the center of every film is the kindly Mrs. Wiggs.

Murder at the Vanities

September 12, 1933 (New Amsterdam Theatre), a musical mystery by Earl Carroll, Rufus King. *Score*: Richard Myers, Edward Heyman, etc. *Cast*: Pauline Moore (Liane Ware), James Rennie (Inspector Ellery), Beryl Wallace (Hope Carol), Naomi Ray (Miss Jones), Billy House (Walter Buck), Jean Adair (Madame Tanqueray), Lisa Gilbert, Bela Lugosi, Olga Baclanova, Woods Miller. *Songs*: Sweet Madness; Me For You Forever; Fans; You Love Me; Virgins Wrapped in Cellophane. *Director-producer:* Earl Carroll. *Choreographer:* Chester Hale. 207 performances.

(Paramount 1934). *Screenplay:* Carey Wilson, Joseph Gollomb, Sam Hellman. *Score:* Arthur Johnston, Sam Coslow. *Cast:* Carl Brisson (Eric Lander), Kitty Carlisle (Ann Ware), Jack Oakie (Jack Ellery), Victor McLaglen (Lt. Bill Murdock), Dorothy Stickney (Norma Watson), Gertrude Michael, Donald Meek, Gail Patrick, Duke Ellington and his Orchestra. *Songs:* Cocktails for Two; Live and Love Tonight; Where Do They Come From Now?; Sweet Marijuana; Lovely One. *Director:* Mitchell Leisen. *Choreographers:* Larry Ceballos, LeRoy Prinz. *Producer:* E. Lloyd Sheldon.

Producer Earl Carroll hoped to resurrect the age of the lavish revues by presenting this musical mystery with its plot backstage of a glittering Broadway revue. The eye-popping production numbers had little to do with the story, which was a whodunit about a chorus girl who is murdered in her dressing room. (The understudy's mother did it.) Not quite satisfying as either a revue or book show, *Murder at the Vanities* nevertheless ran out the season. On screen the murder plot seemed secondary for the movie only came to life with the production numbers. The Broadway version had a forgettable score by several songsmiths but the film offered a better set of tunes by Sam Coslow and Arthur Johnson, in particular the popular "Cocktails for Two."

Music in the Air

November 8, 1932 (Alvin Theatre), an operetta by Oscar Hammerstein. *Score:* Jerome Kern, Oscar Hammerstein. *Cast:* Katherine Carrington (Sieglinde Lessing), Al Shean (Dr. Walther Lessing), Walter Slezak (Karl Reder), Natalie Hall (Frieda Hatzfeld), Reinald Werrenrath (Cornelius), Tullio Carminati (Bruno Mahler), Nicholas Joy, Marjorie Main. *Songs:* I've Told Ev'ry Little Star; There's a Hill Beyond a Hill; The Song Is You; In Egern on the Tegern See; And Love Was Born; We Belong Together; I'm Alone; I Am So Eager; One More Dance. *Directors:* Jerome Kern, Oscar Hammerstein. *Producer:* Peggy Fears. 342 performances.

(Fox 1934). *Screenplay:* Howard Young, Billy Wilder. *Score:* Jerome Kern, Oscar Hammerstein. *Cast:* John Boles (Bruno Mahler), Gloria Swanson (Frieda Hatzfeld), Al Shean (Dr. Walther Lessing), June Lang (Sieglinde Lessing), Douglass Montgomery, Reginald Owen, Joseph Cawthorn, Fuzzy Knight, Marjorie Main. *Songs:* I've Told Ev'ry Little Star; There's a Hill Beyond a Hill; We Belong Together; I'm Alone; I Am So Eager; One More Dance. *Director:* Joe May. *Choreographer:* Jack Donohue. *Producer*: Erich Pommer.

Although the Depression pretty much killed off operetta on Broadway, musicals such as this lovely piece managed to find success by calling themselves something else. Yet the Jerome Kern-Oscar Hammerstein score overflows with rhapsodic music that nostalgically recalls the operettas of the past. Two Bavarian sweethearts hike from their little village to Munich with her father who has written a song called "I've Told Ev'ry Little Star." They hope to interest a publisher but instead they get caught up in the politics of the music business and a temperamental opera singer. In the end the threesome happily return to their rural home. The movie version placed more emphasis on the opera diva, played with panache by Gloria Swanson, but generally followed the Broadway libretto. Sadly, four of the lyrical stage songs were cut so the film does not quite have the musical flow of the original.

The Music Man

December 19, 1957 (Majestic Theatre), a musical comedy by Meredith Willson, Franklin Lacey. *Score:* Meredith Willson. *Cast:* Robert Preston (Harold Hill), Barbara Cook (Marian Paroo), David Burns (Mayor Shinn), Iggie Wolfington (Marcellus), Pert Kelton (Mrs. Paroo), Eddie Hodges, Buffalo Bills. *Songs:* Till There Was You; Seventy-Six Trombones; Goodnight, My Someone; Marian the Librarian; Trouble; Rock Island; Lida Rose; It's You; My White Knight; Shipoopi; Gary, Indiana. *Director:* Morton Da Costa. *Choreographer:* Onna White. *Producer:* Kermit Bloomgarden. 1,375 performances. Tony Award.

(Warner 1962). *Screenplay:* Marian Hargrove. *Score:* Meredith Willson. *Cast:* Robert Preston (Harold Hill), Shirley Jones (Marian Paroo), Buddy Hackett (Marcellus), Paul Ford (Mayor Shinn), Hermione Gingold (Mrs. Shinn), Pert Kelton (Mrs. Paroo), Ronnie Howard, Buffalo Bills. *Songs:* Till There Was You; Seventy-Six Trombones; Goodnight, My Someone; Marian the Librarian; Trouble; Rock Island; Lida Rose; Being in Love; Shipoopi; Gary, Indiana. *Director-producer:* Morton Da Costa. *Choreographer:* Onna White.

(TV 2003). *Teleplay:* Sally Robinson. *Score:* Meredith Willson. *Cast:* Matthew Broderick (Harold Hill), Kristin Chenoweth (Marian Paroo), David Aaron Baker (Marcellus), Victor Garber (Mayor Shinn), Molly Shannon (Mrs. Shinn), Debra Monk (Mrs. Paroo), Clyde Alves, Cameron Monaghan, Cameron Asams. *Songs:* Till There Was You; Seventy-Six Trombones; Goodnight, My Someone; Marian the Librarian; Trouble; Rock Island; Lida Rose; My White Knight; Shipoopi; Gary, Indiana. *Director:* Jeff Bleckner. *Choreographer:* Kathleen Marshall. *Producer:* John M. Eckert.

A funny, satiric, yet affectionate look back at life in a small Iowa town at the turn of the century, this musical comedy was filled with surprises: a con man for the principal male, a smart and knowing heroine, and a score filled with marches, barbershop quartets, rhythm numbers, contrapuntal duets, and other kinds of music not usually heard in a 1950s musical. Meredith Willson wrote the score as well as the libretto which was filled with daffy, lovable supporting characters. Robert Preston, in his first major musical role, was the production's biggest surprise and his performance quickly became the stuff of Broadway legend. He is just as vital in the faithful screen version, and all the characters come to life in the expert movie. The whole stage score, save one song and one reworked number, was kept and the film opened up the action is a way that seemed natural in a musical comedy world. Even the new ending, with Harold Hill's pipe dream of a band materializing before us, seems to be in the spirit of the original; few Broadway shows were filmed as well as *The Music Man*. A 2003 television version was even more faithful to the stage work, retaining all of the songs, but it was a misfire. Matthew Broderick was a charming but not very magnetic Harold and talented Kristin Chenoweth was hopelessly miscast, being physically, vocally, and temperamentally wrong for Marian. The supporting cast members varied from competent to tiresome and most of the comedy in the musical was missing. This production did have excellent sets and costumes and was photographed in dusty, sepia-like tones, but that is not what *The Music Man* is all about.

My Fair Lady

March 15, 1956 (Mark Hellinger Theatre), a musical comedy by Alan Jay Lerner. *Score:* Frederick Loewe, Alan Jay Lerner. *Cast:* Rex Harrison (Henry Higgins), Julie Andrews (Eliza Doolittle), Stanley Holloway (Alfred P. Doolittle), Robert Coote (Col. Pickering), John Michael King, Cathleen Nesbit. *Songs:* I've Grown Accustomed to Her Face; I Could Have Danced All Night; On the Street Where You Live; Wouldn't It Be Loverly?; Get Me to The Church on Time;

The Rain in Spain; Show Me; A Hymn to Him; Without You. *Director:* Moss Hart. *Choreographer:* Hanya Holm. *Producer:* Herman Levin. 2,717 performances. Tony Award.

(Warner 1964). *Screenplay:* Alan Jay Lerner. *Score:* Frederick Loewe, Alan Jay Lerner. *Cast:* Rex Harrison (Henry Higgins), Audrey Hepburn (Eliza Doolittle), Stanley Holloway (Alfred P. Doolittle), Wilfred Hyde-White (Col. Pickering), Jeremy Brett, Gladys Cooper, Theodore Bikel. *Songs:* I've Grown Accustomed to Her Face; I Could Have Danced All Night; On the Street Where You Live; Wouldn't It Be Loverly?; Get Me to The Church on Time; The Rain in Spain; Show Me; A Hymn to Him; Without You. *Director:* George Cukor. *Choreographer:* Hermes Pan. *Producer:* Jack L. Warner. Academy Award.

Considered by many as the greatest of all Broadway musicals, it is certainly the most literate. Alan Jay Lerner's libretto and lyrics flow brilliantly from George Bernard Shaw's drawing room comedy *Pygmalion* and Frederick Loewe's music moves from the comic to the romantic to the rowdy. The musical is so well known now that one forgets how unlikely a show it was. It is very British, is mostly talk, has little dance, and the love story is muted to the point of near invisibility. Yet *My Fair Lady* turned out to be the most successful musical up to that point and remains a favorite in revival. Warner Brothers paid a record $5.5 million for the screen rights and foolishly tried to get Cary Grant to play the phonetics teacher Henry Higgins. Luckily Rex Harrison got to recreate the role on screen, even if he sometimes seems a bit old and too tired for the part. Julie Andrews was a luminous Eliza Doolittle on stage but, never having made a movie before, was passed over for Audrey Hepburn whose singing had to be dubbed. Her flower girl is a little suspect but Hepburn glows as the lady that Eliza becomes. Every character, scene, and song from the stage work was retained for the film but the faithfulness is sometimes defeated by sluggish scenes, costumes that seem more fashion show than period decor, and an elegant but frequently lifeless sense of style. The movie is a competent, pedestrian version of a dazzling musical play.

My Sister Eileen

December 26, 1940 (Biltmore Theatre), a comedy by Joseph Fields, Jerome Chodorov. *Cast*: Shirley Booth (Ruth Sherwood), Jo Ann Sayers (Eileen Sherwood), Gordon Jones, Morris Carnovsky, Richard Quine, Bruce MacFarlane, William Post, Jr. *Director*: George S. Kaufman. *Producer:* Max Gordon. 864 performances.

(Columbia 1942). *Screenplay*: Joseph Fields, Jerome Chodorov. *Cast*: Rosalind Russell (Ruth Sherwood), Janet Blair (Eileen Sherwood), Brian Aherne, George Tobias, Allyn Joslyn. *Director*: Alexander Hall. *Producer*: Max Gordon.

(Columbia 1955). *Screenplay*: Blake Edwards, Richard Quine. *Score*: Jule Styne, Leo Robin. *Cast*: Betty Garrett (Ruth Sherwood), Janet Leigh (Eileen Sherwood), Jack Lemmon, Bob Fosse, Kurt Kasznar, Tommy Rall, Dick York. *Songs*: Give Me a Band and My Baby; It's Bigger Than You and Me; This Is Greenwich Village; There's Nothing Like Love. *Director*: Richard Quine. *Choreographer:* Bob Fosse. *Producer*: Fred Kohlmar.

Ruth McKenney's stories in *The New Yorker*, about two sisters from Ohio trying to find love and careers in Manhattan, was smartly adapted into a Broadway comedy that found success on stage, screen, and in musical form. Shirley Booth played the wisecracking sister Ruth who hopes to be a writer while Jo Ann Sayers was the prettier sister Eileen who has no trouble finding male admirers. The episodic play chronicles their misadventures until both find success in their work and in love.

The well-received Broadway production ran nearly three years and was filmed in 1942 with Rosalind Russell and Janet Blair. The wise-cracking Ruth was tailor-made for Russell and she gave one of her funniest performances, which she later repeated in the musical *Wonderful Town* (qv). It is a slaphappy movie, playfully performed, and well paced. Using the same title, the 1955 remake was a musical with Betty Garrett and Janet Leigh as Ruth and Eileen and supporting help by Jack Lemmon, Bob Fosse, Tommy Rall, and others. The Jule Styne-Leo Robin score is not very memorable but some of the production numbers are, especially as choreographed and danced by Fosse. It is also interesting to see Lemmon in a singing role. While not as funny as its non-musical origins, the film is enjoyable enough. In 1960 the stories were turned into a television series with Elaine Stritch as Ruth and Shirley Bonne as Eileen.

My Sweet Charlie

December 6, 1966 (Longacre Theatre), a play by David Westheimer. *Cast*: Bonnie Bedalia (Marlene Chambers), Louis Gossett (Charles Roberts), Sarah Cunningham, John Randolph, Gar Wood, David Tabor. *Director*: Howard Da Silva. *Producer:* Bob Banner. 31 performances.

(TV 1970). *Teleplay*: Richard Levinson, William Link. *Cast*: Patty Duke (Marlene Chambers), Al Freeman, Jr. (Charles Roberts), Ford Rainey, William Hardy, Chris Wilson, Noble Willingham. *Director*: Lamont Johnson. *Producers*: Richard Levinson, William Link.

The African American lawyer Charles Roberts goes South for a Civil Rights demonstration and accidentally kills a redneck who attacks him. Charles flees and finds refuge in a deserted shack, only to learn that the uneducated, unwed, and very pregnant Marlene Chambers is hiding there from her white-trash family. Despite her prejudices against blacks, Marlene slowly accepts Charles and the two form a friendship so deep that he gives himself up to the police in order to get a doctor for Marlene during her difficult labor. Although both the play and the performances were enthusiastically admired by the press, the little drama could not find an audience and closed in a month. A 1970 television production starred Patty Duke as Marlene with Al Freeman, Jr. as Charles and both were exceptional in the very contrasting roles.

Native Son

March 24, 1941 (St. James Theatre), a drama by Paul Green, Richard Wright. *Cast*: Canada Lee (Bigger Thomas), Philip Bourneuf (Buckley), Anne Burr (Mary Dalton), Ray Collins (Paul Max), Joseph Pevney (Jan Erlone), Evelyn Ellis (Hannah Thomas), Rena Mitchell (Clara), Everett Sloane (Britten), Helen Martin, Nell

Harrison, Erskine Sanford. *Director:* Orson Welles. *Producers:* Orson Welles, John Houseman. 114 performances.

(SACI 1950). *Screenplay:* Pierre Chenal. *Cast:* Richard Wright (Bigger Thomas), Gloria Madison (Bessie Mears), Willa Pearl Curtis (Mrs. Thomas), Nicholas Joy, Ruth Robert, Charles Cane, George D. Greene. *Director:* Pierre Chenal. *Producer:* James Prades.

(Cinecom 1986). *Screenplay:* Richard Wesley. *Cast:* Victor Love (Bigger Thomas), Matt Dillon (Jan), Oprah Winfrey (Mrs. Thomas), Elizabeth McGovern (Mary Dalton), Geraldine Page, Akosua Busia, Carroll Baker, John McMartin, Art Evans. *Director:* Jerrold Freedman. *Producer:* Richard Wesley.

An early and still potent story about race relations, Richard Wright's novel was adapted by Paul Green into a powerful stage drama. The troubled African American youth Bigger Thomas gets a job as chauffeur for a rich white family but when he accidentally kills the daughter, he burns her body in the basement furnace and flees the house. Bigger is caught, found guilty at his trial, and only while waiting execution does he come to understand his role in helping his people. The Broadway production was directed with skill by Orson Welles and Canada Lee was outstanding as Bigger. But despite some rave notices, the play failed to run. The author Wright played Bigger himself in the 1950 screen version which seems to have been made on the cheap (box office prospects for a black film at the time being weak) and the acting is more stilted than moving. The 1986 remake has much better production values and several stars in the cast but it never adds up to anything more than an interesting melodrama. The eloquent anger of the novel and play are missing and the story is more a cautionary tale than a cry of pain.

Naughty Marietta

November 7, 1910 (New York Theatre), an operetta by Rida Johnson Young. *Score:* Victor Herbert, Rida Johnson Young. *Cast:* Emma Trentini (Marietta d'Altena), Orville Harrold (Capt. Dick Warrington), Marie Duchene (Adah), Edward

Martindel (Etienne Grandet), Peggy Wood. *Songs:* Italian Street Song; Ah! Sweet Mystery of Life; Tramp! Tramp! Tramp!; I'm Falling in Love With Someone; 'Neath the Southern Moon. *Director:* Jacques Coini. *Choreography:* Pauline Verhoeven. *Producer:* Oscar Hammerstein I. 136 performances.

(MGM 1935). *Screenplay:* John Lee Mahin, Frances Goodrich, Albert Hackett. *Score:* Victor Herbert, Rida Johnson Young. *Cast:* Jeanette MacDonald (Marietta d'Altena), Nelson Eddy (Capt. Dick Warrington), Frank Morgan (Gov. Gaspard d'Annard), Elsa Lanchester (Mme. d'Annard), Douglass Dumbrille, Marjorie Main, Joseph Cawthorn, Akim Tamiroff, Cecilia Parker. *Songs:* Italian Street Song; Ah! Sweet Mystery of Life; Tramp! Tramp! Tramp!; I'm Falling in Love With Someone; Chansonette; 'Neath the Southern Moon. *Director:* W. S. Van Dyke. *Choreography:* Chester Hale. *Producer:* Hunt Stromberg.

Considered Victor Herbert's masterpiece, the operetta is very demanding musically (he wrote it for an opera company) but thrilling when well sung. Marietta flees from an unwanted marriage in France and goes to New Orleans in the 1780s where she ends up in the arms of a captain in the Rangers. Songs such as "Ah, Sweet Mystery of Life" are the stuff of parody today but during the golden age of American operetta they were giant hits. The 1935 movie version featured Jeanette MacDonald and Nelson Eddy in their first teaming. Both the pair and the film were so popular that a series of seven more such vehicles for the duo followed and Hollywood enjoyed a decade of operetta successes. The screen version altered the plot somewhat (Marietta was now a French aristocrat disguised as a street singer) but the highlights of the score remained and the stars did justice to the music. Interestingly, the success of the movie made Herbert's work popular in Europe for the first time, a decade after his death.

Never Too Late

November 27, 1962 (Playhouse Theatre), a comedy by Sumner Arthur Long. *Cast:* Paul Ford (Harry Lambert), Maureen O'Sullivan (Edith Lambert), Orson Bean (Charlie), Connie Stevens, Fran Sharon, Leona Maricle, John Alexander. *Director:* George Abbott. *Producers:*

Elliott Martin, Daniel Hollywood. 1,007 performances.

(Warner 1965). *Screenplay*: Sumner Arthur Long. *Cast*: Paul Ford (Harry Lambert), Maureen O'-Sullivan (Edith Lambert), Jim Hutton (Charlie Clinton), Lloyd Nolan, Connie Stevens, Jane Wyatt, Henry Jones, Timothy Hutton. *Director*: Bud Yorkin. *Producer*: Norman Lear.

When a late-middle-aged couple finds they are expecting a baby it plays havoc on their grown children, the in-laws and relatives, but mostly with the flabbergasted father-to-be. The thin plot was enhanced by some sprightly dialogue but the initial success of the play was credited to Paul Ford's hilarious performance as the father. Yet the comedy continued to run on Broadway long after Ford left it and community groups revived it for years. The 1965 film retained Ford and Maureen O'Sullivan, who had played the expectant mother on Broadway, and they are both delightful even when the supporting cast is overacting and the direction is wooden.

The New Adventures of Get-Rich-Quick Wallingford see Get-Rich-Quick Wallingford

The New Moon

Imperial Theatre, 19 September 1928 (Imperial Theatre), an operetta by Oscar Hammerstein, Frank Mandel, Laurence Schwab. *Score:* Sigmund Romberg, Oscar Hammerstein. *Cast:* Evelyn Herbert (Marianne Misson), Robert Halliday (Robert Misson), William O'Neal (Philippe), Gus Shy (Alexander), Marie Callahan, Max Figman. *Songs:* One Kiss; Softly, As in a Morning Sunrise; Stouthearted Men; Lover, Come Back to Me; Wanting You; Marianne. *Director:* Edgar MacGregor. *Choreographer:* Bobby Connolly. *Producers:* Laurence Schwab, Frank Mandel. 509 performances.

New Moon (MGM 1930). *Screenplay:* Sylvia Thalberg, Frank Butler. *Score:* Sigmund Romberg, Oscar Hammerstein. *Cast:* Grace Moore (Princess Tanya Strogoff), Lawrence Tibbett (Lt. Michael Petroff), Adolphe Menjou (Boris Strogoff), Gus Shy (Poykin), Roland Young, Emily Fitzroy. *Songs:* One Kiss; Stouthearted Men; Lover, Come Back to Me; Wanting You; Marianne. *Director:* Jack Conway.

New Moon (MGM 1940). *Screenplay:* Jacques Deval, Robert Arthur. *Score:* Sigmund Romberg, Oscar Hammerstein. *Cast:* Jeanette MacDonald (Marianne de Beaumanior), Nelson Eddy (Charles), Mary Boland (Valerie de Rossac), George Zucco (Vicomte Ribaud), Richard Purcell (Alexander), Grant Mitchell, H. B. Warner. *Songs:* One Kiss; Softly, As in a Morning Sunrise; Stouthearted Men; Lover, Come Back to Me; Wanting You; Marianne. *Director-producer:* Robert Z. Leonard. *Choreographer:* Val Raset.

Considered the last of the great American operettas, *The New Moon* opened right before the Depression which pretty much killed off the genre on Broadway. Set in French New Orleans in the final days before the French Revolution, the plot centered on the French aristocrat Robert Misson who disguises himself as a common bondsman and escapes to the New World where he falls in love with the high-born lady Marianne. Although he is captured, Mission and his "Stouthearted Men" escape to an island where they set up a utopian society. When news of the storming of the Bastille arrives, all social barriers fall apart and the lovers are united. While hardly a plausible story, it played well on stage with the luscious Sigmund Romberg score. The first film version dropped the title's "the" and reset the tale in Russia with a love triangle between an aristocratic lady, a dashing lieutenant, and a conniving government official. It made less sense than the stage libretto but with opera singers Grace Moore and Lawrence Tibbitt singing much of the lovely score it proved to be very entertaining. The 1940 movie returned to the original plot for the most part and Jeanette MacDonald and Nelson Eddy added the film to their list of musical triumphs.

Nice People

March 2, 1921 (Klaw Theatre), a play by Rachel Crothers. *Cast*: Katharine Cornell (Eileen Baxter Jones), Tallulah Bankhead (Hallie Livingston), Francine Larrimore (Teddy Gloucester), Hugh Huntley (Scottie Wilbur), Robert Ames (Billy Wade), Guy Milham, Frederick Perry, Merle

Maddern. *Director*: Rachel Crothers. *Producer*: Sam H. Harris. 247 performances.

(Famous Players 1922). *Screenplay*: Clara Beranger. *Cast*: Eve Sothern (Eileen Baxter), Julia Faye (Hallie Livingston), Wallace Reid (Billy Wade), Bebe Daniels (Teddy Gloucester), Conrad Nagel (Scotty White), Claire McDowell, Edward Martindel, Bertram Johns. *Director*: William C. de Mille. *Producer*: Adolph Zukor.

Teddy Gloucester and her flapper girl friends are enjoying the new freedom of the Roaring Twenties but when she goes off with the wild Scottie Wilbur and they end up in a country cottage one night, Teddy's reputation is only saved by the arrival of a stranded motorist. He turns out to be the straitlaced Billy Wade, so when Teddy falls in love with him and they wed, the others lament that Teddy's flapper days are over. A dated but insightful look at the attitudes of the 1920s, the comedy was actually thought-provoking and audiences gave it a long run. The silent 1922 film starred Bebe Daniels as Teddy and it too was popular. By the time the talkies arrived, this kind of exposé on the youth of the era was already on the way out.

The Nigger

December 4, 1909 (New Theatre), a drama by Edward Sheldon. *Cast*: Guy Bates Post (Philip Morrow), Annie Russell (Georgiana), Ben Johnson (Clifton Noyes), Beverly Sitgreaves (Jinny), Pedro de Cordoba, Howard Kyle, Lee Baker, William McVey. In repertory.

(Fox 1915). *Screenplay*: Edgar Lewis. *Cast*: William Farnum (Philip Marlowe), Claire Whitney (Georgiana Boyd), George De Carlton, Henry Armetta. *Director*: Edgar Lewis.

The Southern governor Philip Morrow keeps advocating laws that secure white supremacy but when he discovers that he is the grandson of a black slave, Morrow is forced to look at the situation differently. With the encouragement of his fiancée, he reveals his background to the voters even though he knows it will greatly hinder his re-election. The melodrama handled the touchy subject matter boldly and, like its abrupt title, the play met the issues head on. The Broadway production was esteemed by most of the press (though African Americans and some whites objected to the title) and it was popular enough to warrant two road companies. The 1915 silent movie starred the stage star William Farnum as Morrow and the romance between he and his fiancée was emphasized over the social questions in the play.

'night, Mother

March 31, 1983 (John Golden Theatre), a play by Marsha Norman. *Cast*: Kathy Bates (Jessie), Anne Pitoniak (Thelma Cates). *Director*: Tom Moore. *Producers*: Shuberts, etc. 388 performances. Pulitzer Prize.

(Universal 1986). *Screenplay*: Marsha Norman. *Cast*: Sissy Spacek (Jessie Cates), Anne Bancroft (Thelma Cates), Ed Berke (Dawson), Carol Robbins (Loretta), Jennifer Roosendahl, Michael Kenworthy, Sari Walker. *Director*: Tom Moore. *Producers*: Alan Greisman, Aaron Spelling.

Jessie Cates is divorced, epileptic, and unhappy. She lives with her mother in an isolated rural home and sees only a bleak future for herself. So after much thought she calmly tells her mother that she is going to kill herself with her late father's gun. For ninety minutes the mother pleads with Jessie and tries to change her mind but her daughter's arguments are unemotional and rational and she goes through with her plan. The uninterrupted play was very tense as the audience watched the clock on the wall tell real time and the action edged closer and closer to the suicide. The superior cast (the role made Kathy Bates a stage star) and precise direction kept the drama from becoming a maudlin gimmick. Despite its unlikely box office appeal, the production ran over a year and the two-character play was produced by regional theatres across the country. The 1986 movie featured movie stars Sissy Spacek as Jessie and Anne Bancroft as her mother and both were is top form. Other characters were added and the play was somewhat opened up, but it only served to dilute the tension of the stage work. The film was as uncompromising as the play but somehow it didn't create the same kind of emotional pull.

Night of January 16

September 16, 1935 (Ambassador Theatre), a play by Ayn Rand. *Cast*: Doris Nolan (Karen André), Edmund Breese (D. A. Flint), Robert Shayne (D. A. Stevens), Walter Pidgeon (Guts Regan) Leo Kennedy, Calvin Thomas, Verna Hillie, Harry Short, Clyde Fillmore. *Director:* John Hayden. *Producer:* A. H. Woods. 232 performances.

The Night of January 16 (Paramount 1941). *Screenplay*: Robert Pirash, Delmer Daves. *Cast*: Ellen Drew (Kit Lane), Robert Preston (Steve Van Rungle), Nils Asther (Bjorn Faulkner), Donald Douglas (Attorney Polk), Margaret Hayes (Nancy Wakefield), Clarence Kolb, Rod Cameron, Alice White. *Director*: William Clemens. *Producer*: Sol C. Siegel.

This courtroom suspense drama was different from others in that Ayn Rand wrote two endings, depending on whether the jury voted guilty or not guilty. That jury consisted of audience members selected before the play began who sat on stage in the jurors's seats. The murder trial itself was not very unique: a young woman is accused of murdering her millionaire lover. The prosecution argues that she found out that he was marrying another but the defendant reveals that the man is alive and in South America and that someone else was murdered in his place. Critics berated the melodrama but audiences enjoyed the gimmick so the play ran several months. The 1941 screen version could not select a jury and provide alternate endings so the plot was reworked to become a triangle between the millionaire, his secretary-lover, and a young sailor who loves her and helps defend her when she is accused of murder. It is interesting to see a young Robert Preston play the sailor but otherwise it is a routine melodrama.

The Night of the Iguana

December 28, 1961 (Royale Theatre), a play by Tennessee Williams. *Cast*: Patrick O'Neal (Rev. Shannon), Bette Davis (Maxine Faulk), Margaret Leighton (Hannah Jelkes), Alan Webb (Nonno), Patricia Roe, Lane Bradbury, Louis Guss. *Director*: Frank Corsaro. *Producer:* Charles Bowden. 316 performances.

(MGM 1964). *Screenplay*: Anthony Veiller, John Huston. *Cast*: Richard Burton (Rev. T. Shannon), Ava Gardner (Maxine Faulk), Deborah Kerr (Hannah Jelkes), Sue Lyon (Charlotte Goodall), Grayson Hall (Judith Fellowes), Cyril Delavanti (Nonno), James Ward, Mary Boylan. *Director*: John Huston. *Producers*: Ray Stark, John Huston.

Tennessee Williams's last Broadway hit was set in a run-down Mexican resort where a group of tourists gather, bringing their neuroses, loneliness, and lust with them. The defrocked reverend Shannon is now a tour guide who brings his charges to the place so he can continue an old affair with the salty-mouthed proprietress Maxine. But while there Shannon is drawn to the spinster artist Hannah Jelkes who is traveling with her semi-senile poet father. The relationship remains unconsummated, the old man dies, Hannah moves on, and Shannon remains to entertain Maxine with sexual favors. The superior cast, including Margaret Leighton as Hannah and Bette Davis as Maxine, was beautifully directed and the uneven drama was very affecting. The 1964 screen version starred Richard Burton as Shannon with Deborah Kerr and Ava Gardner as Hannah and Maxine; all give very different kinds of performances but the chemistry works. John Huston's direction is efficient and gets to the point, though much of the poetic quality of the play seems to have disappeared. A little-seen 2001 British film remake featured Jeremy Irons as Shannon.

Night Watch

February 28, 1972 (Morosco Theatre), a thriller by Lucille Fletcher. *Cast*: Joan Hackett (Elaine Wheeler), Len Cariou (John Wheeler), Elaine Kerr (Blanche Cooke), Keene Curtis, Barbara Carson, Rudy Bond, Martin Shakar, William Kiehl. *Director*: Fred Coe. *Producers:* George W. George, Barnard S. Straus. 121 performances.

(AVCO Embassy 1973). *Screenplay*: Tony Williamson. *Cast*: Elizabeth Taylor (Ellen Wheeler), Laurence Harvey (John Wheeler), Billie Whitelaw (Sarah Cooke), Robert Lang, Tony Britton, Bill Dean, Michael Danvers. *Director*: Brian G. Hutton. *Producers*: George W. George, Martin Poll, Barnard Straus.

Elaine Wheeler suffers from insomnia so late one night she sees a dead body in the empty apartment across the courtyard of her Manhattan townhouse. Although her husband John is convinced it is all in her mind, the police are called and no body is found. The same thing happens a few days later when Elaine claims to see the body of a woman in the same apartment. When the police discover nothing again, John makes plans to have his wife committed. Then Elaine learns that John has a mistress and that the two of them are setting up the fake bodies in order to put Elaine away and live off her money. So she gets the two of them to the empty apartment, shoots them, then calmly calls the police knowing they will not come. The tidy little thriller entertained Broadway audiences for a few months then became a movie in 1973 with Elizabeth Taylor as the heroine. But Taylor was so crazed from the first frame that even the audience felt the wife should be put away whether she was seeing bodies or not. Also, opening up the action for the movie added little to the story except to dilute it. Despite a few cheap shocks, there is not many thrills in this thriller.

No No Nanette

September 16, 1925 (Globe Theatre), a musical comedy by Otto Harbach, Frank Mandel. *Score:* Vincent Youmans, Otto Harbach, Irving Caesar. *Cast:* Louise Groody (Nanette), Charles Winninger (Jimmy Smith), Wellington Cross (Billy Early), Josephine Whittell (Lucille Early), Georgia O'Ramey (Pauline), Mary Lawlor, John Barker. *Songs:* Tea for Two; I Want to Be Happy; No No Nanette; Too Many Rings Around Rosie; Where Has My Hubby Gone? Blues; You Can Dance With Any Girl at All. *Director:* H. H. Frazee. *Choreographer:* Sammy Lee. *Producers:* Herbert Clayton, Jack Waller. 321 performances.

(First National 1930). *Screenplay:* Howard Emmett Rogers. *Score:* Vincent Youmans, Otto Harbach, Irving Caesar, etc. *Cast:* Bernice Claire (Nanette), Alexander Gray (Tom Trainer), Bert Roach (Bill Early), Lilyan Tashman (Lucille Early), ZaSu Pitts (Pauline), Louise Fazenda, Lucien Littlefield. *Songs:* Tea for Two; I Want to Be Happy; No No Nanette; Dance of the Wooden Shoes; As Long as I'm With You; Dancing to Heaven. *Director:* Clarence Badger. *Choreographer:* Larry Ceballos. *Producer:* Ned Marin.

(RKO 1940). *Screenplay:* Ken Englund. *Score:* *Cast:* Anna Neagle (Nanette), Richard Carlson (Tom), Victor Mature (William), Roland Young (Mr. Smith), ZaSu Pitts (Pauline), Helen Broderick, Tamara, Eve Arden, Billy Gilbert. *Songs:* Tea for Two; I Want to Be Happy; No No Nanette; Where Has My Hubby Gone? Blues; Take a Little One-Step. *Director-producer:* Herbert Wilcox. *Choreographer:* Larry Ceballos.

The quintessential Roaring Twenties musical, about a Bible salesman who gets into a compromising position with three ladies he's helped out financially, captures all the zest and silliness of the era. Songs such as "Tea for Two" and "I Want to Be Happy" have an idiotic kind of happiness that only could be found on Broadway at this time. The old show found new life on Broadway in the 1970s and since then has remained in the repertory of revived musicals. The first movie version was faithful to the original in plot and characters but much of Vincent Youmans's score was cut and newer, duller songs added. The score also suffered in the 1940 remake in which more time was spent on the story and some of the famous songs were reduced to background music. In many ways *No No Nanette* only works as live theatre; its contagious qualities require a theatre audience.

No Time for Comedy

April 17, 1939 (Ethel Barrymore Theatre), a play by S. N. Behrman. *Cast:* Katharine Cornell (Linda Esterbrook), Laurence Olivier (Gaylord Esterbrook), Margalo Gillmore (Amanda Smith), Robert Flemyng, John Williams. *Director:* Guthrie McClintic. *Producer:* Playwrights' Company. 185 performances.

(Warner–First National 1940). *Screenplay:* Julius J. Epstein, Philip G. Epstein. *Cast:* James Stewart (Gaylord Esterbrook). Rosalind Russell (Linda Esterbrook), Genevieve Tobin (Amanda Swift), Charles Ruggles (Philo Swift), Allyn Joslyn, Clarence Kolb. *Director:* William Keighley. *Producer:* Jack L. Warner.

S. N. Behrman, a comic playwright who never had as much luck with his dramas, wrote this high-style comedy of manners about a playwright who has had success with farce and wants to write something more serious. Gaylord Esterbrook pens funny parts for his actress-wife Linda so she is not at all pleased at his new interest in tragedy. But the crafty Amanda Smith likes the idea and likes Gaylord and the two plan to run away together until he decides on a happier, comedy ending: he returns to his wife. Behrman's scintillating dialogue and Katherine Cornell and Laurence Oliver's droll performances as Linda and Gaylord made the Broadway production a critical and popular hit. But major changes were made to the plot in the 1940 movie in which elegant Gaylord became down-home James Stewart and sleek Linda became wisecracking Rosalind Russell. Even so, it was more sophisticated fun than most romantic comedies and everyone in the cast is enjoyable.

No Time for Sergeants

October 20, 1955 (Alvin Theatre), a comedy by Ira Levin. *Cast*: Andy Griffith (Will Stockdale), Myron McCormick (Sgt. King), Roddy Mc-Dowell (Ben Whiteledge), Robert Webber, Floyd Buckley, Don Knotts, Maree Dow, Ed Peck, Rex Everhart. *Director*: Morton Da Costa. *Producer:* Maurice Evans. 796 performances.

(Warner 1958). *Screenplay*: John Lee Mahin. *Cast*: Andy Griffith (Will Stockdale), Myron Mc-Cormick (Sgt. King), Nick Adams (Ben Whiteledge), Murray Hamilton, Howard Smith, Will Hutchins, Sydney Smith, James Millhollin, Don Knotts. *Director*: Mervyn LeRoy. *Producers*: Mervyn LeRoy, Alex Segal.

Mac Hyman's comic novel about military life was adapted into a television play on the *U. S. Steel Hour* in 1955 and then into a ludicrous stage comedy that ran two years on Broadway and made a star of Andy Griffith. The naive, optimistic hillbilly Will Stockdale drives the gruff Sergeant King up the wall. The more awful the sergeant treats the Air Force recruit, the more Will smiles and talks. The sergeant hopes to transfer Will to another camp and even gives him the answers to the classification test but Will puts the right answers to the wrong questions. Sgt. King is finally satisfied when a plane carrying Will is lost in an atomic testing ground. But Will survives and shows up

at the ceremony honoring his memory with a medal; the Air Force gives him a second medal to silence him. Griffith likable performance was the core of the comedy but the supporting cast was first-rate and the production was well staged. Griffith played Will in the 1958 film version, along side Myron McCormick who reprised his Sgt. King, and the stage work opened up nicely for the screen. Some critics complained that the movie played more like a sit-com and, sure enough, it was turned into one in 1964 with Sammy Jackson as Will.

Norman ... Is That You?

February 19, 1970 (Lyceum Theatre), a comedy by Ron Clark, Sam Bobrick. *Cast*: Lou Jacobi (Ben Chambers), Maureen Stapleton (Beatrice Chambers), Martin Huston (Norman Chambers), Walter Willison, Dorothy Emmerson. *Director*: George Abbott. *Producer:* Harold D. Cohen. 12 performances.

(MGM 1976). *Screenplay*: George Schlatter. *Cast*: Redd Foxx (Ben Chambers), Pearl Bailey (Beatrice Chambers), Michael Warren (Norman Chambers), Dennis Dugan, Tamara Dobson, Vernee Watson, Jayne Meadows, Wayland Flowers. *Director-producer*: George Schlatter.

The Ohio dry-cleaning mogul Ben Chambers finds out his wife has run off with his brother so he goes to New York to get sympathy from his son Norman. But Norman is living in a homosexual love nest with boyfriend Garson, which upsets his father to no end. Ben tries to "cure" Norman by hiring a prostitute but it doesn't work. After plenty of gay jokes (many of them in poor taste), Norman is drafted, Ben's wife returns to him, and the two bring Garson home with them. Critics denounced the comedy almost as much as gay rights groups did and the show closed within two weeks. But Hollywood bought the property for African American comedian Redd Foxx who played Ben opposite Pearl Bailey as his wife and Michael Warren as Norman. Although efforts were made to give the material an African American tone, it was still an offensive comedy that pleased no one.

Not So Dumb see Dulcy

Nuts

April 28, 1980 (Biltmore Theatre), a play by Tom Topor. *Cast*: Anne Twomey (Claudia Faith Draper), Lenka Peterson (Rose Kirk), Hansford Rowe (Arthur Kirk), Richard Zobel, Gregory Abels, Paul Stolarsky. *Director*: Stephen Zuckerman. *Producers:* Stevie Phillips, etc. 96 performances.

(Warner-Barwood 1987). *Screenplay*: Tom Topor, Alvin Sargent, etc. *Cast*: Barbra Streisand (Claudia Draper), Richard Dreyfuss (Aaron Levinsky), Maureen Stapleton (Rose Kirk), Karl Malden (Arthur Kirk), Eli Wallach, Robert Webber, James Whitmore, Leslie Nielsen. *Director*: Martin Ritt. *Producer*: Barbra Streisand.

Mental patient Claudia, a girl from a rich family who prefers to work as a prostitute, stands trial before a judge at Bellevue Hospital to determine if she was sane when she stabbed one of her clients. Claudia admits to the crime but fights the doctors's decision that she is "nuts." Her arguments are forceful and rational, even though she is quite unconventional in her way of expressing herself. When her mother and stepfather are brought forward as witnesses we begin to see Claudia's sexually abusive home life and her views on sex as power. In the end, Claudia wins her right to be tried before a jury as a sane woman. The drama had no action to speak of but the dialogue was gripping and the performances were forceful, particularly Ann Twomey as Claudia. Barbra Streisand bought the rights as a screen vehicle for herself and her performance in the 1987 film is very skillful. The all-star supporting cast is also impressive but several of the characters seem to slip into clichés. The play is opened up awkwardly and most scenes negate the information given in later scenes so the whole thing seems to be carelessly thrown together.

The Odd Couple

March 10, 1965 (Plymouth Theatre), a comedy by Neil Simon. *Cast*: Walter Matthau (Oscar Madison), Art Carney (Felix Ungar), Nathaniel Frey, Paul Dooley, Carole Shelley, Monica Evans, Sidney Armus, John Fiedler. *Director*: Mike Nichols. *Producer:* Saint Subber. 964 performances.

(Paramount 1968). *Screenplay*: Neil Simon. *Cast*: Jack Lemmon (Felix Ungar), Walter Matthau (Oscar Madison), John Fiedler, David Sheiner, Herb Edelman, Larry Haines, Monica Evans, Carole Shelley. *Director*: Gene Saks. *Producer*: Howard W. Koch.

Neil Simon's third play, about two mismatched divorced men sharing the same Manhattan apartment with farcical results, remains one of his most produced works and is arguably his best comedy. The Broadway production starred Art Carney as the neatnik Felix and Walter Matthau as the slob Oscar, under the precise direction of Mike Nichols. Matthau reprised the role in the very popular 1968 film with screen partner Jack Lemmon as Felix and the rapport between the two was masterful. The movie opens up the story comfortably and is well directed; one of the better stage-to-screen transitions of a Simon work. A highly successful television series based on the comedy starred Tony Randall as Felix and Jack Klugman as Oscar and Simon wrote a female version of the work for Broadway in 1985; it was far less satisfying than the original but was a favorite on Broadway and in community theatres all the same. Simon also penned a movie sequel, *The Odd Couple II*, in 1998 with Lemmon and Matthau that was a critical and box office dud.

Of Mice and Men

November 23, 1937 (Music Box Theatre), a play by John Steinbeck. *Cast*: Broderick Crawford (Lennie), Wallace Ford (George), Sam Byrd (Curley), Claire Luce (Curley's Wife), Leigh Whipper, Will Geer, Walter Baldwin. *Director*: George S. Kaufman. *Producer:* Sam H. Harris. 207 performances.

(United Artists 1939). *Screenplay*: Eugene Solow. *Cast*: Burgess Meredith (George), Lon Chaney, Jr. (Lennie), Betty Field (Curley's Wife), Bob Steele (Curley), Charles Bickford, Roman Bohnen, Noah Berry, Jr. *Director-producer*: Lewis Milestone.

(TV 1981). *Teleplay*: Eugene Solow, E. Nick Alexander. *Cast*: Robert Blake (George), Randy Quaid (Lennie), Ted Neeley (Curley), Cassie Yates (Mae), Mitch Ryan, Lew Ayres, Pat Hingle, Whitman Mayo. *Director*: Reza Badiyi. *Producers*: Robert Blake, etc.

(MGM 1992). *Screenplay*: Horton Foote. *Cast*: John Malkovich (Lennie), Gary Sinise (George), Casey Siemaszko (Curley), Sherilyn Fenn (Curley's Wife), Ray Walston, John Terry. *Director*: Gary Sinise. *Producers*: Russell Smith, Gary Sinise.

John Steinbeck turned his novella into a powerful stage drama that has continued to move audiences in various stage revivals and film and television versions. The half-witted but gentle-natured Lenny and the scheming George move from one migrant farm to another doing field work until Lenny gets in trouble and they have to move on. But when Lenny accidentally strangles a cowboy's wife, George knows there is no escape so he shoots Lenny before a lynch mob finds him. The Broadway production was beautifully directed by George S. Kaufman, mostly known for staging comedies and musicals, and audiences responded to the compelling drama. The faithful 1939 movie featured Burgess Meredith as George and silent film star Lon Chaney, Jr. as Lenny and both were excellent. A television version in 1970 had an unusual cast: the articulate English Nicol Williamson as Lenny, the urban-styled George Segal as George, and sex kitten Joey Heatherton as the murdered wife. All make valiant efforts but are difficult to believe. Somewhat more satisfying is a 1981 television production with Randy Quaid as Lenny and Robert Blake as George. But the finest adaptation was the one Horton Foote wrote for the 1992 movie that Gary Sinise directed and in which he played George. John Malkovich was Lenny and the two actors, who had acted together on stage many times, had an electric rapport. The film is also beautifully photographed and captured the locale better than any of the previous versions.

Officer 666

January 29, 1912 (Gaiety Theatre), a farce by Augustin MacHugh. *Cast*: Wallace Eddinger (Tra-

vers Gladwin), Ruth Maycliffe (Helen Burton), Francis D. McGinn (Officer 666), George Nash, Charles K. Gerard, Camilla Crume. *Producer*: Cohan & Harris. 291 performances.

(Kleine 1914). *Screenplay*: Augustin MacHugh. *Cast*: Howard Estabrook (Travers Gladwin), Lois Burnett (Helen Burton), Dan Moyles (Officer 666), Harold Howard, Sydney Seaward, Makoto Inokuchi, Ada Neville, Della Connor. *Director*: Frank Powell. *Producer*: George Kleine.

(Goldwyn 1920). *Screenplay*: Gerald C. Duffy. *Cast*: Tom Moore (Travers Gladwyn), Jean Calhoun (Helen), Harry Dunkinson (Officer 666), Jerome Patrick, Raymond Hatton. *Director*: Harry Beaumont. *Producer*: Samuel Goldwyn.

When the aristocratic Travers Gladwin returns from Europe, he finds that someone is trying to steal his girl friend and his celebrated art collection. So he disguises himself as a police officer and investigates himself, setting off all kinds of comic complications (including getting arrested for trying to steal his own paintings) before the happy ending. The popular farce was very physical and ideal for silent movies. A 1914 version featured Howard Estabrook as Travers and Tom Moore played him in the 1920 remake. Both were successful so it is curious that no talking picture was ever made of the play.

Oh Dad, Poor Dad, Mamma's Hung You in the Closet and I'm Feelin' So Sad

February 26, 1962 (Phoenix Theatre), a play by Arthur Kopit. *Cast*: Jo Van Fleet (Madame Rosepettle), Austin Pendleton (Jonathan), Barbara Harris (Rosalie), Tony Lo Bianco. *Director*: Jerome Robbins. *Producers:* T. Edward Hambleton, etc. 454 performances.

(Paramount 1967). *Screenplay*: Ian Bernard. *Cast*: Rosalind Russell (Madame Rosepettle), Robert Morse (Jonathan), Barbara Harris (Rosalie), Hugh Griffith, Jonathan Winters, Lionel Jeffries. *Directors*: Richard Quine, Alexander Mackendrick. *Producer*: Richard Quine.

The flamboyant, smothering Madame Rosepettle and her stuttering, neurotic son Jonathan arrive for a vacation in a Caribbean hotel and are confronted by the "babysitter"

Rosalie, a high-class prostitute who has an eye on the son. But when she tries to seduce him, Jonathan smothers her to death and Mama has to scold him. The absurdist comedy was the talk of Off Broadway and brought recognition to playwright Arthur Kopit. Perhaps nothing is more difficult to put on the big screen than absurdism but the 1967 ignored the genre altogether and presented the tale as a dark farce. In the play, Mama brings the stuffed corpse of her husband with her wherever she goes; thus, the long, descriptive title. But in the film, the father becomes a major character as Jonathan Winters speak from the dead in silly still photographs and urges his son Robert Morse to pursue Rosalie, played by Barbara Harris who originated the role on stage. Rosalind Russell does her familiar *grande dame* act as Madame Rosepettle but rarely is she very funny. The film also has a happy ending with Morse and Harris romantically united so the last vestiges of absurdism are erased. Because of Winters's eccentric comic delivery, there are some laughs in the film but mostly it is just odd.

Oh Men! Oh Women!

December 17, 1953 (Henry Miller Theatre), a comedy by Edward Chodorov. *Cast*: Franchot Tone (Alan Coles), Betsy von Furstenberg (Myra Hagerman), Anne Jackson (Mildred Turner), Gig Young (Arthur Turner), Larry Blyden, Henry Sharp. *Director*: Edward Chodorov. *Producer*: Cheryl Crawford. 382 performances.

(Fox 1957). *Screenplay*: Nunnally Johnson. *Cast*: Ginger Rogers (Mildred Turner), David Niven (Alan Coles), Dan Dailey (Arthur Turner), Barbara Rush (Myra Hagerman), Tony Randall (Cobbler), Natalie Schafer, Franklin Pangborn. *Director-producer*: Nunnally Johnson.

Psychoanalyst Alan Coles thinks he is in control of his emotions but when he finds out that his fiancée has been sleeping around and that a movie star is her latest flame, Alan has to do some quick self-analysis to secure a happy ending. While the critics dismissed the comedy as a slim vehicle for some expert performances (in particular Anne Jackson in her breakthrough role as an overwrought pa-

tient), audiences were more forgiving and kept the show on the boards for a year. The stars were also likable in the 1957 film though the comedy seemed even more strained on the big screen and the sex farce often fell flat. Moviegoers were not as forgiving and the picture quickly faded away.

Oklahoma!

March 31, 1943 (St. James Theatre), a musical play by Oscar Hammerstein. *Score*: Richard Rodgers, Oscar Hammerstein. *Cast*: Alfred Drake (Curly) McLain), Joan Roberts (Laurey Williams), Bette Garde (Aunt Eller), Celeste Holm (Ado Annie), Joseph Buloff (Ali Hakim), Howard Da Silva (Jud Fry), Lee Dixon (Will Parker), Joan McCracken. *Songs*: Oh, What A Beautiful Mornin'; The Surrey With the Fringe on Top; People Will Say We're in Love; Oklahoma; I Cain't Say No; Kansas City; Many a New Day; Pore Jud; Out of My Dreams; All er Nothin'; Lonely Room; The Farmer and the Cowman. *Director*: Rouben Mamoulian. *Choreographer*: Agnes de Mille. *Producer*: Theatre Guild. 2,212 performances.

(Magna/Fox 1955). *Screenplay*: Sonia Levien, William Ludwig. *Score*: Richard Rodgers, Oscar Hammerstein. *Cast*: Gordon MacRae (Curly McLain), Shirley Jones (Laurey Williams), Charlotte Greenwood (Aunt Eller), Gloria Graham (Ado Annie), Eddie Albert (Ali Hakim), Gene Nelson (Will Parker), Rod Steiger (Jud Fry). *Songs*: Oh, What A Beautiful Mornin'; The Surrey With the Fringe on Top; People Will Say We're in Love; Oklahoma; I Cain't Say No; Kansas City; Many a New Day; Pore Jud; Out of My Dreams; All er Nothin'; The Farmer and the Cowman. *Director*: Fred Zinnemann. *Choreographer*: Agnes de Mille. *Producer*: Arthur Hornblow, Jr.

The history of the American Broadway musical can be divided into two epochs: before and after *Oklahoma!* This first Rodgers and Hammerstein collaboration brought the integrated musical to light, with every character, song, plot development, and even dance all coordinated into an exhilarating whole. The simple tale of a cowboy and a farmhand fighting over who gets to take a prairie girl to a picnic becomes an American icon of sorts in *Oklahoma!* The songs are overflowing with vitality and honesty and the characters, little more than types, are practically mythic. The original Broadway production was the most successful musical up to that time and Rodgers and Hammerstein would not allow a movie version to be made until the long run had ended. When the film was made a dozen years later, the team maintained strict control over the project. It shows, for the result is very true to the original (only three songs were cut), very long (145 minutes), and rather tame. The production values are noteworthy and the cast commendable but there is something missing in this bright, earnest movie. Looking at it today one would never suspect that *Oklahoma!* started a revolution in the American musical theatre. All the same, it is an enjoyable, if uninspired, movie. Much more accomplished was a British television filming of a 1999 London stage revival of *Oklahoma!* that was broadcast in the States in 2003.

Old Acquaintance

December 23, 1940 (Morosco Theatre), a comedy by John Van Druten. *Cast*: Jane Cowl (Katherine Markham), Peggy Wood (Mildred Watson Drake), Adele Longmire (Deirdre), Kent Smith (Rudd Kendall), Hunter Gardner, Edna West. *Director*: Auriol Lee. *Producer:* Dwight Deere Wiman. 170 performances.

(Warner 1943). *Screenplay*: John Van Druten, Lenore J. Coffee. *Cast*: Bette Davis (Katherine Marlowe), Miriam Hopkins (Mildred Watson Drake), Gig Young (Rudd Kendall), Dolores Moran (Deirdre Drake), John Loder, Philip Reed. *Director*: Vincent Sherman. *Producer*: Henry Blanke.

Rich and Famous. (MGM 1981). *Screenplay*: Gerald Ayres. *Cast*: Jacqueline Bissett (Liz Hamilton), Candice Bergen (Merry Noel Blake.), David Selby, Meg Ryan, Steven Hill, Hart Bochner, Matt Lattanzi. *Director*: George Cukor. *Producer*: William Allyn.

Author Katherine Markham writes critically acclaimed books that sell few copies while Mildred Watson pens trashy novels that become bestsellers. The two women are friends from way back and usually can reconcile their differences but when Midred's daughter attempts to steal away

Katherine's latest love interest, the friendship is sorely tested. The beloved stage stars Jane Cowl and Peggy Wood were the prime attraction in this character comedy and both were so extolled by the critics that the play had a profitable run. Hollywood stars Bette Davis and Miriam Hopkins faced off in the 1943 movie and the fireworks that resulted made the film a hit. The screen adaptation opened the story up to show the twenty-year friendship of the two writers and the screenplay is an improvement over the play. The 1981 remake, titled *Rich and Famous*, also showed the pair over the course of many years but so many details in the story were changed that it hardly resembles the earlier versions. Jacqueline Bisset and Candice Bergen were the writer-friends; the former seemed to take the whole tale too seriously but Bergen gives a juicy, unrestrained comic performances as a Southern housewife-turn-novelist who tries to grab happiness by its throat. Sadly, it was the last movie directed by veteran George Cukor and not at all up to his past work.

The Old Maid

January 7, 1935 (Empire Theatre), a play by Zoe Atkins. *Cast*: Judith Anderson (Delia Ralston), Helen Menken (Charlotte Lovell), Margaret Anderson (Tina), John Cromwell, George Nash, Mary Ricard. *Director*: Guthrie McClintic. *Producer:* Harry Moses. 305 performances. Pulitzer Prize.

(Warner 1939). *Screenplay*: Casey Robinson. *Cast*: Bette Davis (Charlotte Lovell), Miriam Hopkins (Delia Lovell Ralston), George Brent (Lt. Clem Spender), Jane Bryan, Donald Crisp. Louise Fazenda, James Stephenson. *Director*: Edmund Goulding. *Producer*: Henry Blanke.

When the spinster Charlotte Lovell has an illegitimate baby girl, her married cousin Delia agrees to raise the child as her own and avoid scandal. The child Tina grows up loving her supposed mother and barely tolerating her maiden aunt. Only on Tina's wedding day does Charlotte make an attempt to tell her the truth but she finds she can't. The sentimental melodrama was adapted from a novel by Edith Wharton and was considered a soppy version of the book. The critics were even more disdainful when the play won that year's Pulitzer Prize over better contenders. But the Broadway production boasted splendid performances by Judith Anderson and Helen Menken and managed to run almost a year. Bette Davis was Charlotte and Miriam Hopkins played Delia in the 1939 screen version that was highly polished and beautifully presented. The two stars shone together, raising the soap operaish tale to a fine art. It remains one of the best, as they called it then, "women's picture" to come out of Hollywood in the 1930s.

Oleanna

October 25, 1992 (Orpheum Theatre), a play by David Mamet. *Cast*: William H. Macy (John), Rebecca Pidgeon (Carol). *Director*: David Mamet. *Producers:* Frederick Zollo, etc. 513 performances.

(Goldwyn 1994). *Screenplay*: David Mamet. *Cast*: William H. Macy (John), Debra Eisenstadt (Carol), Scott Zigler. *Director*: David Mamet. *Producers*: Sarah Green, Patricia Wolff.

One of the most heatedly discussed plays of the early 1990s was this two-character drama about sexual harassment. College student Carol is having trouble in a course so she goes to her distracted, pedantic professor John for help. He suggests private tutorials and she interprets this as harassment and, encouraged by a feminist group, presses charges. The more John tries to reason with Carol, the worse the situation becomes until he becomes so angry he throws her to the floor and actually becomes what she accused him of. The provocative play left it up to the audience to determine who (if anyone) was guilty and playgoers argued about it for nearly two years. The 1994 movie made no attempt to open up the action and the two-character scenes seemed contrived on the big screen, just as the acting was deemed simplistic and melodramatic. Instead of causing controversy, the film just quietly faded away.

On a Clear Day You Can See Forever

October 17, 1965 (Mark Hellinger), a musical comedy by Alan Jay Lerner. *Score:* Burton Lane, Alan Jay Lerner. *Cast:* Barbara Harris (Daisy Gamble/Melinda), John Cullum (Dr. Mark Bruckner), William Daniels (Warren Smith), Clifford David, Titos Vandis. *Songs:* On a Clear Day You Can See Forever; Come Back to Me; Hurry! It's Lovely Up Here; On the S. S. Bernard Cohn; What Did I Have That I Don't Have?; Melinda; Wait Till We're Sixty-Five; She Wasn't You. *Director:* Robert Lewis. *Choreographer:* Herbert Ross. *Producer*: Alan Jay Lerner. 280 performances.

(Paramount 1970). *Screenplay:* Alan Jay Lerner. *Score:* Burton Lane, Alan Jay Lerner. *Cast:* Barbra Streisand (Daisy Gamble/Melinda), Yves Montand (Dr. Marc Chabot), Larry Blyden (Warren Smith), Bob Newhart, Simon Oakland, Jack Nicholson, John Richardson. *Songs:* On a Clear Day You Can See Forever; Come Back to Me; Hurry! It's Lovely Up Here; Love With All the Trimmings; Go to Sleep; What Did I Have That I Don't Have?; Melinda; He Wasn't You. *Director:* Vincente Minnelli. *Producer:* Howard W. Koch.

This charming musical about ESP and reincarnation had a problematic script but an intriguing premise and the score by Alan Jay Lerner and Burton Lane was filled with wonderful songs which were delivered with style by Barbara Harris and John Cullum. Chain-smoking Daisy Gamble goes to a psychiatrist to hypnotize her into giving up cigarettes but under the trance she reveals a former life as Melinda, a *femme fatale* back in Regency England. Daisy falls for the doctor but he loves Melinda and librettist Lerner came up with a new angle on the romantic triangle. The script did not resolve itself satisfactorily so Lerner made several changes when he wrote the screenplay for the 1970 film version. He added more scenes in the 18th century flashbacks, cut half of the songs and added new ones, and rewrote the end, hinting that Daisy and the doctor will get together in some future life. It wasn't much of an improvement over the stage plot but with Barbra Streisand as Daisy much of the film worked better than one would suspect. The rest of the cast is rather unimpressive, including a muted performance by Yves Montand as the psychiatrist and Jack Nicholson as Daisy's half-brother (whose role was cut to only one scene by the studio). But it is a beautiful-looking movie and Streisand is in top comic form.

On Borrowed Time

February 3, 1938 (Longacre Theatre), a play by Paul Osborn. *Cast*: Dudley Digges (Gramps Northrup), Frank Conroy (Mr. Brink), Jean Adair (Aunt Dementia), Dorothy Stickney (Nellie), Peter Miner (Pud), Clyde Franklin, Margaret O'Donnell, Richard Sterling, Clyde Franklin. *Director*: Joshua Logan. *Producer:* Dwight Deere Wiman. 321 performances.

(MGM 1939). *Screenplay*: Alice D. G. Miller, etc. *Cast*: Lionel Barrymore (Gramps), Cedric Hardwicke (Mr. Brink), Bobs Watson (Pud), Beulah Bondi (Nellie), Una Merkel, Nat Pendleton, Henry Travers. *Director*: Harold S. Bucquet. *Producer*: Sidney Franklin.

Lawrence Edward Watkin's allegorical novel, about an old man who faces the angel of Death and chases him up an apple tree, was turned into a delightful stage fantasy that pleased playgoers for a year. Character actor favorite Dudley Digges played Gramps who fights off death until his young grandson falls from the tree and dies. Only then will Gramps give in to Mr. Brink (as the angel is called) so that he can be with the boy. Highly sentimental yet droll in a satirical way, the play became a favorite in community theatres and schools. Lionel Barrymore played Gramps to Cedric Hardwicke's Mr. Brink in the 1939 movie which handled the comedy, fantasy, and sentiment very well. For the screen, Mr. Bink was able to appear and disappear at will. The dreamy quality of the film is still impressive and the tale is rather poignant if one gives into the premise.

On Golden Pond

February 28, 1979 (New Apollo Theatre), a play by Ernest Thompson. *Cast*: Tom Aldredge (Norman Thayer), Frances Sternhagen (Ethel Thayer), Barbara Andres (Chelsea Thayer Wayne), Ronn Carroll, Stan Lachow, Mark Bendo. *Director*: Craig Anderson. *Producers:* Arthur Cantor, Greer Garson. 156 performances.

(Universal 1981). *Screenplay*: Ernest Thompson. *Cast*: Henry Fonda (Norman Thayer), Katharine Hepburn (Ethel Thayer), Jane Fonda (Chelsea), Dabney Coleman (Bill Ray), Doug McKeon, William Lanteau. *Director*: Mark Rydell. *Producer*: Bruce Gilbert.

(TV 2001). *Teleplay*: Ernest Thompson. *Cast*: Julie Andrews (Ethel Thayer), Christopher Plummer (Norman Thayer), Glenne Headly (Chelsea), Sam Robards (Bill Ray), Will Rothhaar, Brett Cullen. *Director*: Ernest Thompson. *Producer*: Samuel Paul.

First seen Off Broadway then on Broadway in a small, intimate production, this warm-hearted comedy-drama was unpretentious in its plot and characters and was all the more affecting because of it. The elderly couple Norman and Ethel Thayer have been spending their summers at their Maine cottage for years but he is now eighty years old and they wonder how much longer they can continue. The episodic plot dealt with the couple's grown daughter visiting with her new husband and stepson and the way crotchety old Norman slowly befriends the boy. The characters were drawn with affection and the pleasant play left a lump in the playgoer's throat. The 1981 movie, on the other hand, was a manufactured soap opera that telegraphed its emotions and transformed the little play into a star-studded melodrama. The screenplay built up the role of the daughter so that Jane Fonda had more to do and a series of clichés were added to guarantee the feel-good picture's appeal. Henry Fonda, in his last film, does not convince as the hypercritical Norman but he does have a certain glow about him that is endearing. He also seems to have a nice rapport with Katharine Hepburn as Ethel and some of their scenes are genuine. The movie was extremely popular (both Fonda and Hepburn won Oscars) but not the swan song those two stars deserved. A 2001 television production of the play was built on a gimmick: the couple was played by Julie Andrews and Christopher Plummer, reunited for the first time since *The Sound of Music* thirty-six years before. The two stars are also the only reason to see this tired remake, for they seem to have a sincerity of affection for each other that outshines their romancing in the previous blockbuster.

On the Town

December 28, 1944 (Adelphi Theatre), a musical comedy by Betty Comden, Adolph Green. *Score:* Leonard Bernstein, Betty Comden, Adolph Green. *Cast:* John Battles (Gabey), Betty Comden (Claire de Loon), Adolph Green (Ozzie), Nancy Walker (Brunhilde Esterhazy), Sono Osato (Ivy Smith), Cris Alexander (Chip Offenbloch), Alice Pearce (Lucy Schmeeler), Ray Harrison, Allyn Ann McLerie. *Songs:* New York, New York; Some Other Time; Lucky to Be Me; Lonely Town; Come Up to My Place; I Get Carried Away; Ya Got Me. *Director:* George Abbott. *Choreographer:* Jerome Robbins. *Producers:* Oliver Smith, Paul Feigay. 463 performances.

(MGM 1949). *Screenplay:* Betty Comden, Adolph Green. *Score:* Leonard Bernstein, Betty Comden, Adolph Green, Roger Edens. *Cast:* Gene Kelly (Gabey), Frank Sinatra (Chip), Vera-Ellen (Ivy Smith), Jules Munshin (Ozzie), Ann Miller (Claire Huddessen), Betty Garrett (Hildy), Alice Pearce (Lucy Schmeeler), Florence Bates. *Songs:* New York, New York; Come Up to My Place; Count on Me; Prehistoric Man; Main Street; On the Town. *Director-choreographers:* Gene Kelly, Stanley Donen. *Producer:* Arthur Freed.

Besides being a smash musical comedy hit, this dance-emphasis show was the first Broadway effort of songwriters Leonard Bernstein, Betty Comden, and Adolph Green and choreographer Jerome Robbins. The plot, about three sailors on 24-hour leave in New York City, was routine but it afforded its creators the opportunity to display their considerable musical and dancing talents. Because of the long modern ballet sections, the musical is not frequently revived. But when it is the results can be enthralling. Hollywood producer Arthur Freed admitted he did not like Bernstein's quirky, unpredictable music so when the studio bought the screen rights he cut all but three of the stage songs. Comden and Green collaborated with Roger Edens on some new ones and, although some were staged with panache, none matched the quality of Bern-

stein's. The film does boast a dynamite cast and adventurous location shooting; it was the first movie musical to extensively use the real New York City, not a studio recreation. Robbins's recreated choreography is also one of the film's many pluses.

On Trial

August 19, 1914 (Candler Theatre), a drama by Elmer Rice. *Cast:* Frederick Perry (Robert Strickland), Mary Ryan (Mrs. Strickland), Frederick Truesdale (Gerald Trask), J. Wallace Clinton, William Walcott, Helen Lackaye, Hans Robert, Gardner Crane. *Director:* Sam Forrest. *Producers:* George M. Cohan, Sam H. Harris, Arthur Hopkins. 365 performances.

(Essenay 1917). *Screenplay:* James Young. *Cast:* Sidney Ainsworth (Robert Strickland), Barbara Castleton (Mrs. Strickland), James Young (Gerald Trask), Mary McAllister (Doris Strickland), Corene Uzzell, Patrick Calhoun, John Cossar. *Director:* James Young.

(Warner 1928). *Screenplay:* Robert Lord, Max Pollock. *Cast:* Bert Lytell (Robert Strickland), Lois Wilson (May Strickland), Holmes Herbert (Gerald Trask), Pauline Frederick, Richard Tucker, Jason Robards, Sr., Franklin Pangborn. *Director:* Archie Mayo.

(Warner 1939). *Screenplay:* Don Ryan. *Cast:* John Litel (Robert Strickland), Margaret Lindsay (Mae Strickland), James Stephenson (Gerald Trask), Janet Chapman (Doris Strickland), Edward Norris (Arbuckle), Nedda Harrigan, William B. Davidson, Sidney Bracey. *Director:* Terry O. Morse. *Producer:* Bryan Foy.

Robert Strickland is accused of murdering Gerald Trask, a man he owed $10,000 to. But during the trial several secrets are revealed (such as Trask's past affair with Strickland's wife and some money stolen by a secretary) so the defendant is acquitted. The drama is famous for being the first to show the entire trial process on stage and for using flashbacks to illustrate the testimonies. It was a unique piece of melodrama in its day and playgoers allowed it to run a year. A 1917 silent movie was very faithful to the play, though flashbacks on the screen were not so unusual. An early talkie version in 1928 featured Bert Lytell as Strickland and it too stuck pretty closely to the play. But the

1939 remake fiddled with the plot (Strickland murders Trask because he is his wife's lover) and, since flashbacks were then old hat, there was not much to enjoy in the talky piece.

On Your Toes

April 11, 1936 (Imperial Theatre), a musical comedy by George Abbott, Richard Rodgers, Lorenz Hart. *Score:* Richard Rodgers, Lorenz Hart. *Cast:* Ray Bolger (Junior Dolan), Tamara Geva (Vera Barnova), Luella Gear (Peggy Porterfield), Monty Woolley (Sergei Alexandrovitch), Doris Carson (Frankie Frayne), David Morris, Robert Sidney. *Songs:* There's a Small Hotel; On Your Toes; Glad to Be Unhappy; Quiet Night; Too Good for the Average Man; It's Got to Be Love; The Heart Is Quicker Than the Eye. *Directors:* Worthington Miner, George Abbott. *Choreographer:* George Balanchine. *Producer:* Dwight Deere Wiman. 315 performances.

(Warner/First National 1939). *Screenplay:* Jerry Wald, Richard Macaulay. *Cast:* Eddie Albert (Phil Dolan), Vera Zorina (Vera Barnova), James Gleason, Alan Hale, Frank McHugh, Leonid Kinskey, Donald O'Connor, Gloria Dickson, Queenie Smith. *Director:* Ray Enright. *Choreographer:* George Balanchine. *Producer:* Robert Lord.

One of the most innovative musicals of the 1930s, this Rodgers and Hart show used dance in ways not previously seen. The plot centered on the rivalry between American jazz dancers and a Russian ballet troupe with romances and triangles developing between the two groups. Ray Bolger became a top-flight star as the music teacher who ends up dancing the central role in the "Slaughter on Tenth Avenue" ballet. Choreographer George Balanchine's extended dance sequences were highly praised and the songs included some future standards. Still difficult to revive because of its great dance demands, *On Your Toes* continues to enthrall when it is presented on occasion. Hollywood hired Balanchine for the movie version but ended up sabotaging the Broadway hit by cutting all the songs and reducing them to background music. The slight but fun libretto was turned into a dull tale about music teacher Eddie Albert being mistaken for a traitor and without songs to interrupt it the film was more tiresome than entertaining. Even the dancing disappoints and not until the movie bio *Words and Music* (1948) was the famous ballet brought to life on screen.

Once in a Lifetime

September 24, 1930 (Music Box Theatre), a comedy by George S. Kaufman, Moss Hart. *Cast:* Grant Mills (Jerry Hyland), Jean Dixon (May Daniels), Hugh O'Connell (George Lewis), Charles Halton (Herman Glogauer), Lawrence Vail (George S. Kaufman), Sally Phipps (Susan Walker), Leona Maricle, Louis Cruger, Frances E. Brandt, William McFadden. *Director:* George S. Kaufman. *Producer:* Sam H. Harris. 406 performances.

(Universal 1932). *Screenplay:* Seton I. Miller. *Cast:* Jack Oakie (George Lewis), Russell Hopton (Jerry Hyland), Aline MacMahon (May Daniels), Gregory Ratoff (Herman Glogauer), Sidney Fox, Louise Fazenda, ZaSu Pitts. *Director:* Russell Mack. *Producer:* Carl Laemmle, Jr.

This first collaboration between George S. Kaufman and Moss Hart is a daffy farce about Hollywood and the panic that set in when talkies came in. New Yorkers George, Jerry, and May go out to Tinsel Town and pass themselves off as speech specialists who can teach the silent stars how to speak well on screen. The dim-witted George goes even further, becoming a director who is so incompetent that the cockeyed movie he makes is called a masterpiece by the critics and he is named an executive at the studio. The slaphappy satire about the movies ran over a year on Broadway and launched the new writing team's career. The 1932 screen version is also risible with fast-paced direction and an animated cast, particularly Jack Oakie as the blundering George and Gregory Ratoff as the egomaniac head of the studio.

Once More, with Feeling

October 21, 1958 (National Theatre), a comedy by Harry Kurnitz. *Cast:* Joseph Cotton (Victor Fabian), Arlene Francis (Dolly Fabian), Walter

Matthau (Maxwell Archer), Frank Milan, Paul E. Richards, Rex Williams, Leon Belasco, Ralph Bunker. *Director*: George Axelrod. *Producers:* Martin Gabel, Henry Margolis. 263 performances.

(Columbia 1960). *Screenplay*: Harry Kurnitz. *Cast*: Yul Brynner (Victor Fabian), Kay Kendall (Dolly Fabian), Gregory Ratoff (Maxwell Archer), Geoffrey Toone (Dr. Hilliard), Maxwell Shaw, Mervyn Jones, Martin Benson, Harry Lockart. *Director-producer*: Stanley Donen.

A waning symphony orchestra conductor is reunited with his concert singer ex-wife and old grudges and then old sparks are rekindled. The predictable, lightweight comedy managed a healthy run because of its agreeable stars, Joseph Cotten and Arlene Francis. But for many the highlight of the evening was Walter Matthau as the self-deprecating manger who brings the two temperamental artists together. The 1960 movie is able to better capture the concert world than on the stage but the comedy is strained and poorly directed, and the slowly-paced film often goes flat. In her last screen appearance, Kay Kendall still has zest in her delivery and it is interesting to see Yul Brynner in a comedy.

Once Upon a Mattress

May 11, 1959 (Phoenix Theatre), a musical comedy by Jay Thompson, Dean Fuller, Marshall Barer. *Score*: Mary Rodgers, Marshall Barer. *Cast*: Carol Burnett (Princess Winifred), Joseph Bova (Prince Dauntless), Jack Gilford (King Sextimus), Jane White (Queen Agravaine), Harry Snow (Minstrel), Anne Jones, Matt Mattox. *Songs*: Shy; Many Moons Ago; Happily Ever After; In a Little While; Sensitivity; Very Soft Shoes. *Director*: George Abbott. *Choreographer*: Joe Layton. *Producers*: T. Edward Hambleton, etc. 460 performances.

(TV 1971). *Teleplay*: Jay Thompson, Dean Fuller, Marshall Barer. *Score*: Mary Rodgers, Marshall Barer. *Cast*: Carol Burnett (Princess Winifred), Ken Berry (Prince Dauntless), Jack Gilford (King Sextimus), Jane White (Queen Agravaine), Bernadette Peters (Lady Larken), Wally Cox (Jester). *Songs*: Shy; Many Moons Ago; Happily Ever After; In a Little While; Sensitivity; Very Soft Shoes. *Directors:* Ron Field, Dave Powers.

This sassy musical version of *The Princess and the Pea* fairy tale launched the career of Carol Burnett who played the daffy Princess Winifred who comes to marry the mama's boy Prince Dauntless. The script fills out the simple tale with a secondary romantic couple, a nostalgic jester, a mute king, and a harridan of a queen. The merry plot and the tuneful songs were enjoyable but it was Burnett who made the musical tick. The Off Broadway production moved to Broadway where it had a healthy run and the musical comedy was presented by schools and community theatre groups for decades. Some of the original cast members, including Burnett, were reunited for a 1971 television production of the show. Even with its modest production values, the musical still charmed and Burnett's raucous performance was preserved on film.

One Flew Over the Cuckoo's Nest

November 13, 1963 (Cort Theatre), a play by Dale Wasserman. *Cast*: Kirk Douglas (Randle P. McMurphy), Ed Ames (Chief Bromden), Joan Tetzel (Nurse Ratched), Gene Wilder (Billy Bibbit), William Daniels (Dale Harding), Gerald S. O'Loughlin, Al Nesor, Malcolm Atterbury, William Gleason. *Director*: Alex Segal. *Producer:* David Merrick, Edward Lewis. 82 performances.

(United Artists 1975). *Screenplay*: Bo Goldman, Lawrence Hauben. *Cast*: Jack Nicholson (Randle P. McMurphy), Will Sampson (Chief Bromden), Louise Fletcher (Nurse Ratched), William Redfield, Michael Berryman, Brad Dourif, Alonzo Brown, Scatman Crothers, Peter Brocco. *Director*: Milos Forman. *Producers*: Michael Douglas, Saul Zaentz. Academy Award.

Ken Kesey's cult-favorite novel, about the rascally Randle Patrick McMurphy who enters an insane asylum, brings hope to the inmates, and then is destroyed by the evil Nurse Ratched, was adapted for the stage by Dale Wasserman who allowed the mute Chief Bromden to narrative events (as he often did in the book) through a series of voiceovers. It was a theatrical way to handle the tricky story and retained Kesey's wry point of view. Kirk Douglas was vivacious as McMurphy but the drama failed to run very long on Broadway. A 1971 Off Broadway revival, on the other hand, was very well received and ran over 1,000 performances. It was the success of this production that prompted the studio to go ahead with the 1975 film version that was such a hit. The Chief's commentary was cut so the movie was much more conventional in its plotting but the superb cast, the comfortable opening up of the story, and the expert direction all combined to make an outstanding film drama.

One More Tomorrow see The Animal Kingdom

One Sunday Afternoon

February 15, 1933 (Little Theatre), a play by James S. Hagan. *Cast*: Lloyd Nolan (Biff Grimes), Rankin Mansfield (Hugo Barnstead), Mary Holsman (Virginia Brush), Janet Young, Francesca Bruning, Ernst Robert, Bryon Shores. *Director*: Leo Bulgakov. *Producers:* Leo Peters, Leslie Spiller. 322 performances.

(Paramount 1933). *Screenplay*: Grover Jones, William Slavens McNutt. *Cast*: Gary Cooper (Biff Grimes), Neil Hamilton (Hugo Barnstead), Fay Wray (Virginia Brush), Roscoe Karnes, Jane Darwell, Frances Fuller, Clara Blandick. *Director*: Stephen Roberts. *Producer*: Louis D. Lighton.

The Strawberry Blonde (Warner 1941). *Screenplay*: Julius J. Epstein, Philip P. Epstein. *Cast*: James Cagney (Biff Grimes), Olivia De Havilland (Ann Lind Grimes), Rita Hayworth (Virginia Brush), Jack Carson (Hugo Barnstead), Alan Hale, George Tobias, Una O'Connor *Director*: Raoul Walsh. *Producer*: Hal B. Wallis.

One Sunday Afternoon (Warner 1948). *Screenplay*: Robert L. Richards. *Score*: Ralph Blane, etc. *Cast*: Dennis Morgan (Biff Grimes), Don Defore (Hugo Barnstead), Janis Paige (Virginia Brush), Dorothy Malone (Amy Lind), Ben Blue, Dorothy Ford, Oscar O'Shea, Alan Hale, Jr. *Songs*: Some Day; Girls Were Made to Take Care of the Boys; Johnny and Lucille; One Sunday Afternoon; In My Merry Oldsmobile; Daisy Bell. *Director*: Raoul Walsh. *Choreographer*: LeRoy Prinz. *Producer*: Jerry Wald.

Many years ago Hugo Barnstead stole Biff Grimes's girl friend Virginia and framed Grimes so that he unjustly went to prison. Now Grimes is a dentist and Barnstead comes to have a tooth extracted. Grimes plans to kill him with an overdose of gas but seeing what a broken man Barnstead is and how unhappy his marriage to Virginia turned, the happily married Grimes decides to let him live; but he extracts the tooth without the use of any gas. The sly story intrigued playgoers for a year on Broadway and was later filmed three times. The 1933 version starred Gary Cooper as Grimes and it opened up the action to show past events. The youthful Cooper is very effective, as are the period decor and atmospheric touches. The dark corners of the story were deleted for the 1941 remake called *The Strawberry Blonde* but is still a first-rate comedy that is also rich in period detail. James Cagney is charismatic as ever as Grimes and there are lovely supporting performances by Rita Hayworth and Olivia De Havilland as the two women in his life. Hollywood remade the story as a musical in 1948, now called *One Sunday Afternoon* again, but the magic was gone. The slow-paced film offered routine performances and some pleasant but forgettable songs (except for a few period standards thrown in for authenticity) but mostly it was an unexciting remake.

One Third of a Nation

January 17, 1938 (Adelphi Theatre), a "living newspaper" by Arthur Arent. *Cast*: Charles Dill, Roy Le May, Nat Loesberg, Charles Deigham, May Ritchie, Jennie Wren, John Pote. *Director*: Lem Ward. *Producers:* Philip Barber, Federal Theatre Project. 124 performances.

(Paramount 1939). *Screenplay*: Dudley Murphy, Oliver H. P. Garrett. *Cast*: Sylvia Sidney (Mary Rogers), Leif Erickson (Peter Cortlant), Myron McCormick (Sam Moon), Hiram Sherman, Sidney Lumet. *Director*: Dudley Murphy. *Producer*: Harold Orlob.

This powerful stage documentary, about the history of residential living in America, concluded with a bleak, angry view of current tenement life in major cites and argued for government-subsidized housing. The most famous of the "living newspaper" series presented by the Federal Theatre Project, the controversial play featured a four-story stage setting by Howard Bay that teemed with crowded apartments and people living in squalor. There was a story tying the events together but the documentary approach of the series was more interested in facts. (The title came from FDR's speech about one third of the population living in poverty.) The 1939 movie defeated much of the play's purpose by adding a romantic story about a shopgirl who tries to bring reform to her neighborhood and finds love along the way. The movie is well acted and the depiction of the tenement is effective as only a film can do but the social aspects of the piece are secondary.

One Touch of Venus

October 7, 1943 (Imperial Theatre), a musical fantasy by S. J. Perelman, Ogden Nash. *Score:* Kurt Weill, Ogden Nash. *Cast:* Mary Martin (Venus), Kenny Baker (Rodney Hatch), John Boles (Whitelaw Savory), Paula Lawrence (Molly Grant), Teddy Hart, Ruth Bond, Sono Osato, Harry Clark. *Songs:* Speak Low; That's Him; I'm a Stranger Here Myself; Foolish Heart; The Trouble With Women; How Much I Love You; West Wind. *Director:* Elia Kazan. *Choreographer:* Agnes de Mille. *Producers:* Cheryl Crawford, John Wildberg. 567 performances.

(Universal 1948). *Screenplay:* Harry Kurnitz, Frank Tashlin. *Score:* Kurt Weill, Ogden Nash. *Cast:* Ava Gardner (Venus), Robert Walker (Eddie Hatch), Dick Haymes (Joe Grant), Tom Conway (Whitfield Savory), Eve Arden, Olga San Juan, Sara Allgood. *Songs:* Speak Low; That's Him; The Trouble With Women; Don't Look Now But My Heart Is Showing. *Director:* William A. Seiter. *Choreographer:* Billy Daniels. *Producer:* Lester Cowan.

Mary Martin's first starring role on Broadway allowed her to play a goddess with that unique blend of innocence and suggestion that was unique to her. A statue of Venus comes to life in modern times and falls for a timid barber before she realizes that the life of a wife in the suburbs is not for her so she returns to stone. It was a wry, clever script by humorists S. J. Perelman and Odgen Nash and the delectable songs were

by Nash and Kurt Weill. Martin shone in the title role and was admirably supported by Kenny Baker as the barber and a slick production that featured some nimble Agnes de Mille ballets. The screen version cut Martin, the ballets, and all of the stage score but two songs so the result was a mildly humorous fantasy with a lot of talk that was lacking the wit of the original. Robert Walker was a dull barber and Ava Gardner as Venus ended up posing like a contemporary model and trying to act ethereal. A unique Broadway musical became a uniquely numb movie. A television version in 1955 with Janet Blair and Russell Nype was broadcast live from Dallas.

The Only Game in Town

May 20, 1968 (Broadhurst Theatre), a play by Frank D. Gilroy. *Cast:* Barry Nelson (Joe Grady), Tammy Grimes (Fran Walker), Leo Genn (Thomas Lockwood). *Director:* Barry Nelson. *Producer:* Edgar Lansbury. 16 performances.

(Fox 1970). *Screenplay:* Frank D. Gilroy. *Cast:* Elizabeth Taylor (Fran Walker), Warren Beatty (Joe Grady), Charles Braswell (Lockwood), Hank Henry, Olga Valéry. *Director:* George Stevens. *Producer:* Fred Kohlmar.

Las Vegas piano player Joe Grady has gambled most of his savings away by the time he meets the show girl Fran Walker and falls in love. But Fran is waiting for her wealthy lover Thomas Lockwood to get a divorce; by the time he does, Fran is also in love with Joe and turns Lockwood down. Joe gambles his remaining savings at the tables and, after getting down to ten dollars, parlays it into a small fortune for he and Fran to get married with. The storyline was far from enthralling but the three characters were well-drawn and acted with skill by Barry Nelson, Tammy Grimes, and Leo Genn. The three-handed little drama only lasted two weeks on Broadway. Nevertheless, Hollywood bought the property and starred Elizabeth Taylor and Warren Beatty in the 1970 screen version. Because the movie was filmed in a Paris studio, one doesn't get the feeling of Las Vegas, just as one doesn't totally buy the love story with Taylor obviously much older than Beatty and everyone pretending not to notice. It was director George Stevens's last film and not an appropriate finale to his long career.

Only When I Laugh see *The Gingerbread Lady*

The Opposite Sex see *The Women*

Orphans

May 7, 1985 (Westside Arts Theatre), a play by Lyle Kessler. *Cast*: Kevin Anderson (Phillip), Terry Kinney (Treat), John Mahoney (Harold). *Director*: Gary Sinise. *Producers:* Steppenwolf Theatre Company, etc. 285 performances.

(Lorimar 1987). *Screenplay*: Lyle Kessler. *Cast*: Albert Finney (Harold), Matthew Modine (Treat), Kevin Anderson (Phillip), John Kellogg, Anthony Heald, Elizabeth Parrish, Novella Nelson. *Director*: Alan J. Pakula. *Producers*: Alan J. Pakula, Susan Solt.

The petty crook Treat and his dim-witted brother Philip bring the drunk businessman Harold to their North Philadelphia row house with the intention of robbing him. But Harold is wanted by the mob and needs a hideout so he takes over the household, becomes a father figure to the two dysfunctional brothers, and the threesome find camaraderie together. The Off Broadway play (previously seen in Chicago) developed a cult following and ran for months before the drama was picked up by adventurous theatre groups across the country. When the three-actor piece was filmed in 1987, a few other characters were added but it remained an intimate but stagy movie that is noteworthy for its fervent acting. Albert Finney, as the manipulating Harold, is particularly impressive.

Orpheus Descending

March 21, 1957 (Martin Beck Theatre), a play by Tennessee Williams. *Cast*: Maureen Stapleton (Lady Torrance), Cliff Robertson (Val Xavier), Crahan Denton, Lois Smith, Robert Webber, Joanna Roos. *Director*: Harold Clurman. *Producer:* Robert Whitehead. 68 performances.

The Fugitive Kind (United Artists 1959). *Screenplay*: Meade Roberts. *Cast*: Marlon Brando (Val Xavier), Anna Magnani (Lady Torrance), Joanne Woodward, Maureen Stapleton, Victor Jory, *Director*: Sidney Lumet. *Producers*: Martin Jurow, Richard Shepherd.

Orpheus Descending (TV 1990). *Teleplay*: Peter Hall. *Cast*: Vanessa Redgrave (Lady Torrance), Kevin Anderson (Val Xavier), Brad Sullivan, Manning Redwood, Sloane Shelton, Patti Allison. *Director*: Peter Hall. *Producer*: George Manasse.

When the handsome young drifter Val Xavier comes to a small Southern town, he attracts the attentions of several oversexed women, including the lonely Lady Torrence whom he comforts until her jealous husband shoots her and, with his KKK friends, castrates Val. The highly symbolic play puzzled both critics and playgoers but all agreed that Maureen Stapleton was riveting as the erratically desperate Lady. This was a revised version of Tennessee Williams' earlier drama *Battle of Angels* which had closed on the road. The new version only lasted two months on Broadway but would be revived by ambitious theatre groups. The 1959 movie was titled *The Fugitive Kind* and it told the same story in a rather realistic manner so that it all seemed more oddball than mystical. Marlon Brando was Val to Anna Magnani's Lady and a stranger combination of acting styles has rarely been seen. A popular London stage revival of *Orpheus Descending* was turned into a 1990 television version starring Vanessa Redgrave as Lady and a gifted supporting cast met her in the smoky, unrealistic production that may not have been logical but at least was mesmerizing.

Other People's Money

February 16, 1989 (Minetta Lane Theatre), a play by Jerry Sterner. *Cast*: Kevin Conway (Lawrence Garfinkle), Mercedes Ruehl (Kate Sullivan), Arch Johnson (Andrew Jorgenson), William Coles, Scotty Bloch. *Director*: Gloria Muzio. *Producers:* Jeffrey Ash, Susan Quint Gallin. 990 performances.

(Warner 1991). *Screenplay*: Alvin Sargent. *Cast*: Danny DeVito (Lawrence Garfield), Penelope Ann Miller (Kate Sullivan), Gregory Peck (Andrew Jorgenson), Piper Laurie, Dean Jones. *Director*: Norman Jewison. *Producers*: Norman Jewison, Ric Kidney.

The corporate raider Lawrence Garfinkle is notoriously known as "Larry the Liquidator" for his talent for buying companies, destroying them, and making a huge profit in the process. When he attacks the New England Wire and Cable Company, the chairman Andrew Jorgenson hires the smart corporate lawyer Kate Sullivan to save them. But Garfinkle outwits her at every turn, the company is lost, and Kate and Garfinkle end up as unlikely lovers. The funny, insightful play made its financial subject matter fascinating and the characters were all vividly presented by a fine cast. The Off Broadway production ran three years, followed by many regional productions. The irascible but lovable television actor Danny DeVito was cast as Garfinkle in the 1991 film and he captured the comedy in the piece even if the ruthless side of the character was more talked about than seen. He was pitted against noble Gregory Peck (in his last substantial screen role) as the chairman filled with integrity if nor money smarts. Penelope Ann Miller was an attractive but strong-willed Kate and there were commendable supporting performances by Piper Laurie and Dean Jones. The screenplay provided a happy ending for the tale (the company still is taken over but comes back as a manufacturer of fiber optics) but it was well thought out and satisfying, even if the sting of the play was gone.

Our Town

February 4, 1938 (Henry Miller Theatre), a play by Thornton Wilder. *Cast*: Frank Craven (Stage Manager), Martha Scott (Emily Webb), John Craven (George Gibbs), Jay Fassett (Dr. Gibbs), Thomas W. Ross (Mr. Webb), Evelyn Varden (Mrs. Gibbs), Helen Carew (Mrs. Webb), Philip Coolidge (Simon Stimson), Doro Merande, Marilyn Erskine, Tom Fadden. *Director-producer*: Jed Harris. 336 performances. Pulitzer Prize.

(United Artists 1940). *Screenplay*: Harry Chandlee, Frank Craven. *Cast*: William Holden (George Gibbs), Martha Scott (Emily Webb), Thomas Mitchell (Dr, Gibbs), Fay Bainter (Mrs. Gibbs), Guy Kibbee (Mr. Webb), Beulah Bondi (Mrs. Webb), Frank Craven (Stage Manager, etc.). *Director*: Sam Wood. *Producer*: Sol Lesser.

(TV 1977). *Teleplay*: Thornton Wilder. *Cast*: Hal Holbrook (Stage Manager), Robby Benson (George Gibbs), Glynis O'Connor (Emily Webb), Ned Beatty, Barbara Bel Geddes, Sada Thompson, Ronny Cox. *Director-producer*: George Schaefer.

Thornton Wilder's classic work, about living, loving and dying in a small New Hampshire town, is the most produced non-musical play in America with hundreds of revivals in all kinds of theatres each year. It is one of the most poetic, thought-provoking of all plays and time only seems to have strengthened its power. *Our Town* is a highly expressionistic piece, played on a bare stage, so film and television versions are not easy. But some very effective ones have been made over the years and will continue to be made. The 1940 movie takes a realistic approach to the play, recreating the town in detail and presenting the scenes with warm details. The afterlife scenes are done in the form of a dream, which is a simplistic way out of the dilemma, and the play's ending has been changed: Emily does not die in childbirth but only dreams she did. That trite conclusion aside, it is a beautifully made movie with poignant performances throughout, particularly Martha Scott as Emily and Frank Craven in the greatly-reduced role of the Stage Manager. (Both had played the same parts in the original Broadway production.) The play was musicalized in a 1955 television version with Frank Sinatra as the Stage Manager singing the popular ditty "Love and Marriage." The stage script was severely abridged but there was still some of the charm of the original to be enjoyed. Most other television productions were based on stage revivals. Hal Holbrook headed the cast of a 1977 broadcast that included such seasoned actors as Barbara Bel Geddes, Ned Beatty, and Sada Thompson. Spalding Gray was the Stage Manager in a

Lincoln Center revival that was filmed for television in 1989 and Paul Newman, who had appeared as a youth in the 1955 musical broadcast, played the Stage Manager in a Broadway revival that was shown on television in 2003. The quality varied from one version to another (as well as within each production) but all were faithful to the play and, thereby, had glorious moments to offer.

Outward Bound

January 7, 1924 (Ritz Theatre), a play by Sutton Vane. *Cast*: Alfred Lunt (Mr. Prior), Margalo Gillmore (Ann), Leslie Howard (Henry), Dudley Digges (Rev. Thompson), J. M. Kerrigan (Scrubby), Charlotte Granville, Eugene Powers, Lyonel Watts, Beryl Mercer. *Producer:* William Harris, Jr. 144 performances.

(Warner 1930). *Screenplay*: J. Grubb Alexander. *Cast*: Leslie Howard (Tom Prior), Douglas Fairbanks, Jr. (Henry), Dudley Digges (Rev. Thompson), Helen Chandler (Ann), Beryl Mercer, Alec B. Francis, Montagu Love. *Director*: Robert Milton. *Producer*: Jack L. Warner.

Between Two Worlds (Warner 1944). *Screenplay*: Daniel Fuchs. *Cast*: John Garfield (Tom Prior), Paul Henreid (Henry), Eleanor Parker (Ann), Sydney Greenstreet (Rev. Thompson), Edmund Gwenn, George Tobias, George Coulousis, Sara Allgood, Dennis King. *Director*: Edward A. Blatt. *Producer*: Mark Hellinger.

A ship carrying recently dead characters sails through the sea of afterlife as an Examiner decides where each passenger will spend eternity. The allegorical fantasy was interesting enough but it was the brilliant cast that let the drama run several months. Alfred Lunt was particularly splendid as the hard-drinking Mr. Prior, as were Leslie Howard and Margalo Gillmore as a pair of suicidal lovers who are given a chance to return to life. Howard played Mr. Prior in the 1930 movie and Dudley Digges played the Examiner as he had on Broadway. It is a primitive talkie and lacks theatrical flare but several of the performances are notable, such as Douglas Fairbanks, Jr. and Helen Chandler as the lovers. The 1944 remake, titled *Between Two Worlds*, was updated (the passengers are mostly air raid victims) and took

place on an elegant ocean liner but the talky movie was only mildly interesting. Again, it is the cast that makes it worthwhile, particularly Sydney Greenstreet as the Examiner. A 1999 television series also called *Outward Bound* used the same premise as the play but little else.

The Owl and the Pussycat

November 18, 1964 (ANTA Theatre), a comedy by Bill Manhoff. *Cast*: Diana Sands (Doris), Alan Alda (Felix Sherman). *Director*: Arthur Storch. *Producers:* Philip Rose, etc. 427 performances.

(Columbia 1970). *Screenplay*: Buck Henry. *Cast*: Barbra Streisand (Doris), George Segal (Felix), Robert Klein, Allen Garfield, Roz Kelly. *Director*: Herbert Ross. *Producer*: Ray Stark.

The prostitute Doris is kicked out of her apartment when a neighbor complains to the landlord so she barges in on the complainer, the introverted bookworm Felix Sherman, demanding that he put her up for the night, and the unlikely couple eventually hit it off. The two-actor comedy was thin in plot but the characters were enjoyable so playgoers ignored the critics and kept the play on the boards for over a year. The Broadway production broke tradition, of sorts, by casting the African American Diana Sands as Doris when it was written for a white actress. She was quite alluring and funny and a perfect foil for Alan Alda's Felix. The 1970 film starred Barbra Streisand and George Segal and they were not only very amusing but they created some glowing chemistry together. Screenwriter Buck Henry opened the action up a bit but the movie still came down to duet scenes, most of which played nicely.

Paid see Within the Law

Paint Your Wagon

November 12, 1951 (Shubert Theatre), a musical comedy by Alan Jay Lerner. *Score:* Frederick Loewe, Alan Jay Lerner. *Cast:* James Barton (Ben Rumson), Olga San Juan (Jennifer Rumson),

Tony Bavaar (Julio), James Mitchell, Kay Medford. *Songs:* They Call the Wind Maria; I Talk to the Trees; I Still See Elisa; Wand'rin' Star; What's Going on Here?; Another Autumn. *Director:* Daniel Mann. *Choreographer:* Agnes de Mille. *Producer:* Cheryl Crawford. 289 performances.

(Paramount 1969). *Screenplay:* Alan Jay Lerner. *Score:* Frederick Loewe, Alan Jay Lerner, André Previn. *Cast:* Lee Marvin (Ben Rumson), Clint Eastwood (Pardner Newel), Jean Seberg (Elizabeth), Harve Presnell, Ray Walston. *Songs:* They Call the Wind Maria; I Talk to the Trees; I Still See Elisa; Wand'rin' Star; The First Thing You Know; Gold Fever; A Million Miles Away Behind the Door. *Director:* Joshua Logan. *Choreographer:* Jack Baker. *Producer:* Alan Jay Lerner.

Lerner and Loewe's first musical after their break-out hit *Brigadoon* was this very different tale about a prospector, the widow Ben Rumson, and his daughter Jennifer who strike gold in 1853 California, find wealth and, in her case, love, then watch their fortune dissolve as the lode dries up. It was a raucous musical but a sweetly sentimental one as well; Ben dies at the end and Jennifer settles down with her Mexican sweetheart. The show was a modest success and two of the songs, "They Call the Wind Maria" and "I Talk to the Trees," were bestsellers. When Lerner rewrote his libretto and produced the movie version eighteen years later he destroyed any charm the piece had and settled for non-singing Western stars in a ridiculous plot about a frontier *menage a trois.* Gone was the daughter, the Mexican, and Ben's passing away. Instead there were lots of scenes with prospectors tramping in the mud and plenty of jokes about sex. Even the lovely score sounded sour on the screen. A favorite bad movie with its own cult following, *Paint Your Wagon* was a financial and critical bomb that was both puzzling and fascinating to behold.

Painting Churches

November 22, 1983 (Lamb's Theatre), a play by Tina Howe. *Cast*: Elizabeth McGovern (Margaret Church), Marian Seldes (Fanny Church), George N. Martin (Gardner Church). *Director*: Carole Rothman. *Producers*: Elizabeth I. McCann, etc. 206 performances.

The Portrait (TV 1993). *Teleplay*: Lynn Roth. *Cast*: Gregory Peck (Gardner Church), Lauren Bacall (Fanny Church), Cecilia Peck (Margaret Church), Paul McCrane, William Prince, Donna Mitchell, Joyce O'Connor. *Director*: Arthur Penn. *Producer*: Philip Kleinbart.

Artist Margaret Church visits her Boston home to paint a portrait of her parents, the aging poet Gardner and his frustrated wife Fanny. While working on the painting, old wounds and new revelations surface and Margaret has a better understanding of her parents by the time the portrait is finished. The-three-actor piece was admired by the press and the intimate, well-acted Off Broadway production ran six months. The play was opened up considerably for the 1993 television production and the casting of major stars tended to inflate the quiet little drama into something momentous. But it is a tenderly directed drama and Gregory Peck and Lauren Bacall are in fine form as the parents, as is newcomer Cecilia Peck as their daughter.

The Pajama Game

May 13, 1954 (St. James Theatre), a musical comedy by George Abbott, Richard Bissell. *Score:* Richard Adler, Jerry Ross. *Cast:* John Raitt (Sid Sorokin), Janis Paige (Babe Williams), Eddie Foy, Jr. (Hines), Carol Haney (Gladys), Reta Shaw, Stanley Praeger. *Songs:* Hey, There; Hernando's Hideaway; Steam Heat; I'm Not at All in Love; Once a Year Day; Seven and a Half Cents. *Director:* George Abbott. *Choreographer:* Bob Fosse. *Producers:* Frederick Brisson, Harold Prince, Robert E. Griffith. 1,063 performances. Tony Award.

(Warner 1957). *Screenplay:* George Abbott, Richard Bissell. *Score:* Richard Adler, Jerry Ross. *Cast:* John Raitt (Sid Sorokin), Doris Day (Babe Williams), Eddie Foy, Jr. (Hines), Carol Haney (Gladys), Reta Shaw, Barbara Nichols. *Songs:* Hey, There; Hernando's Hideaway; Steam Heat; I'm Not at All in Love; Once a Year Day; Seven-and-a-Half Cents. *Director-producers:* George Abbott, Stanley Donen. *Choreographer:* Bob Fosse.

George Abbott was the veteran director and co-librettist for this musical about labor relations in a pajama factory but the show is more famous as bringing to light producer Harold Prince, songwriters Richard Adler and Jerry Ross, and choreographer Bob Fosse. Almost all of the stage cast and crew were retained for the film version which feels rather stagy at times but is enjoyable all the same. Doris Day, replacing Janis Paige as the labor organizer, is particularly fine in the screen version. The tuneful score also transferred to the screen pretty much intact and it remains one of Broadway's happiest. Of particular interest in the movie are Fosse's sprightly production numbers.

Pal Joey

December 25, 1940 (Ethel Barrymore Theatre), a musical comedy by John O'Hara. *Score:* Richard Rodgers, Lorenz Hart. *Cast:* Gene Kelly (Joey Evans), Vivienne Segal (Vera Simpson), Leila Ernst (Linda English), June Havoc (Gladys Bumps), Jean Casto, Jack Durant, Van Johnson. *Songs:* Bewitched; I Could Write a Book; You Mustn't Kick It Around; Den of Iniquity; Take Him; Zip; That Terrific Rainbow. *Director-producer:* George Abbott. *Choreographer:* Robert Alton. 374 performances.

(Columbia 1957). *Screenplay:* Dorothy Kingsley. *Score:* Richard Rodgers, Lorenz Hart. *Cast:* Frank Sinatra (Joey Evans), Rita Hayworth (Vera Simpson), Kim Novak (Linda English), Barbara Nichols, Bobby Sherwood, Hank Henry. *Songs:* Bewitched; I Could Write a Book; Zip; That Terrific Rainbow; My Funny Valentine; The Lady Is a Tramp; There's a Small Hotel. *Director:* George Sidney. *Choreographer:* Hermes Pan. *Producer:* Fred Kohlmar.

One would think that by the late 1950s Hollywood would not be worrying about sanitizing Broadway musicals but this ground-breaking show was scrubbed so clean that it only daintily resembled the play that had opened seventeen years earlier. John O'Hara's libretto is a masterpiece of unsentimentality. His character creation, the third-rate hoofer Joey Evans, is the musical theatre's first anti-hero as he uses women for his own advancement and has no desire to reform or change. The adult musical annoyed some critics but audiences found the tough-as-nails show fascinating. The Rodgers and Hart score was just as uncom-

promising and the way it was worked into the script foreshadowed the later integrated Broadway musical. Hollywood bought the screen rights but didn't seriously consider filming *Pal Joey* until a popular stage revival in 1952 proved the piece to still have some appeal. While Gene Kelly (in his last Broadway appearance) was a dancing heel, Frank Sinatra was a singing one and he captured the seedy aspect of the character on screen. But the script was laundered until it was unrecognizable, much of the score was cut, and Rodgers and Hart songs from other shows were added even though they did not have the flavor of this work. Rita Hayworth, as the rich dame Joey uses, is in fine form but Kim Novak, as one of Joey's innocent conquests, is hopelessly lost in both her singing and acting. What might have become a hard-hitting film classic like *Cabaret* instead was a second-rate *Cover Girl*.

Panama Hattie

October 30, 1940 (46th Street Theatre), a musical comedy by Herbert Fields, B. G. DeSylva. *Score:* Cole Porter. *Cast:* Ethel Merman (Hattie Maloney), Joan Carroll (Geraldine Bullett), James Dunn (Nick Bullett), Betty Hutton (Florrie), Rags Ragland, Pat Harrington, Arthur Treacher, Frank Hyers, June Allyson. *Songs:* Let's Be Buddies; I've Still Got My Health; Make It Another Old-Fashioned, Please; I'm Throwing a Ball Tonight; My Mother Would Love You. *Director:* Edgar MacGregor. *Choreographer:* Robert Alton. *Producer:* B. G. DeSylva. 501 performances.

(MGM 1942). *Screenplay:* Jack McGowan, Wilkie Mahoney. *Score:* Cole Porter, etc. *Cast:* Ann Sothern (Hattie Maloney), Jackie Horner (Geraldine Bullet), Virginia O'Brien (Flo Foster), Red Skelton (Red), Rags Ragland, Lena Horne, Marsha Hunt, Dan Dailey, Alan Mowbray. *Songs:* Let's Be Buddies; I've Still Got My Health; Make It Another Old-Fashioned, Please; Just One of Those Things; The Son of a Gun Who Picks on Uncle Sam; Hattie From Panama; Good Neighbors. *Director:* Norman Z. McLeod. *Choreographer:* Danny Dare. *Producer:* Arthur Freed.

This slick but enjoyable vehicle for Ethel Merman featured a lively Cole Porter score that showed off the star's considerable talents. Merman played a nightclub owner in

Panama City who can only win the heart of her millionaire beau if she can befriend his young daughter. She does and both the star and the show were hits. Hollywood didn't much care for Merman and gave the role to Ann Sothern for the screen version. But without the beloved Broadway belter the material looked pretty weak, especially when rewritten so that Hattie was now outwitting the Nazis. Some of the Porter songs were mixed with those by others but it didn't matter; the film was a quick and deserved failure.

Paris

October 8, 1928 (Music Box Theatre), a musical comedy by Martin Brown. *Score:* Cole Porter, Walter Kollo, E. Ray Goetz, etc. *Cast:* Irene Bordoni (Vivienne Rolland), Arthur Margetson (Guy Pennell), Louise Closser Hale (Cora Sabbot), Erik Kalkhurst (Andrew Sabbot), Elizabeth Chester, Irving Aaronson and His Commanders. *Songs:* Let's Do It!; Two Little Babes in the Wood; Don't Look at Me That Way; The Land of Going to Be; Paris; An' Furthermore. *Director:* W. H. Gilmore. *Producer:* Gilbert Miller. 195 performances.

(First National 1929). *Screenplay:* Hope Lorning. *Score:* Al Bryan, Ed Ward. *Cast:* Irene Bordoni (Vivienne Rolland), Jack Buchanan (Guy Pennell), Louise Closer Hale (Cora Sabbot), Jason Robards, Sr. (Andrew Sabbot), Margaret Fielding, ZaSu Pitts. *Songs:* Miss Wonderful; Paris; I Wonder What Is Really on His Mind; Crystal Girl; Somebody Mighty Like You. *Director-producer:* Clarence Badger. *Choreographer:* Larry Cebellos.

The Broadway show in which Cole Porter first found recognition, this frothy musical about a Parisian beauty who pursues the son of a strait-laced New Englander introduced the standard "Let's Do It (Let's Fall in Love)." Irene Bordoni shone as the amorous French lady and Hollywood introduced her to moviegoers when she recreated the role on the screen. But the entire Porter stage score was dropped and replaced by a new forgettable one and the film only comes to life when Bordoni is highlighted.

Paris Bound

December 27, 1927 (Music Box Theatre), a comedy by Philip Barry. *Cast:* Madge Kennedy (Mary Hutton), Donn Cook (Jim Hutton), Mary Murray (Noel Farley), Donald Macdonald (Richard Parrish), Hope Williams (Fanny Shipman), Gilbert Emery, Ellen Southbrook. *Director-producer:* Arthur Hopkins. 234 performances.

(Pathé 1929). *Screenplay:* Horace Jackson. *Cast:* Ann Harding (Mary Hutton), Fredric March (Jim Hutton), Carmelita Geraghty (Noel Farley), Ilka Chase (Fanny Shipman), Leslie Fenton (Richard Parrish), George Irving, Charlotte Walker. *Director:* Edward H. Griffith. *Producer:* Arthur Hopkins.

On the day that Mary and Jim Hutton get married, his divorced father warns the couple to pay no attention to an occasional straying of the other or it will destroy their marriage. After six years of marital happiness, Mary finds out that Jim has had an affair and she plans to leave him. But Mary recalls her father-in-law's words and, realizing that Jim turned a blind eye to her own flirtation with a young composer, she decides to live and let live. Playwright Philip Barry, perhaps the finest writer of comedies of American manners, made this predictable plot into shimmering magic with insightful characterization and bright dialogue. An early talkie version of the comedy featured Ann Harding and Fredric March with a primitive soundtrack that was actually lost for many years. When it was rediscovered and restored, it revealed delightful dialogue exchanges between the two young stars and a movie that some consider an overlooked gem. But there is little question that the camera work is static and the direction less than inspired. All the same, there is much to recommend in this knowing comedy.

Parlor, Bedroom and Bath

December 24, 1917 (Republic Theatre), a farce by C. W. Bell, Mark Swan. *Cast:* John Cumberland (Reggie Irving), Sydney Shields (Angelica Irving), Florence Moore, Francine Larrimore, Helen Menken. *Director:* Bertram Harrison. *Producer:* A. H. Woods. 232 performances.

(Metro 1920). *Screenplay:* June Mathis, A. P. Younger. *Cast:* Eugene Pallette (Reggie Irving), Kathleen Kirkham (Angelica Irving), Ruth Stonehouse, Charles West, Dorothy Wallace. *Director:* Edward Dillon.

(MGM 1931). *Screenplay*: Richard Schayer, Robert E. Hopkins. *Cast*: Buster Keaton (Reginald Irving), Dorothy Christy (Angelica Irving), Charlotte Greenwood, Reginald Denny, Cliff Edwards. *Director*: Edward Sedgwick. *Producer*: Buster Keaton.

Shy, introverted Reggie Irving is married to Angelica who is convinced that her husband has had a scandalously lurid past. Sweet Reggie hates to disappoint her so he writes loves letters to himself, signs them "Tootles," and allows Angie to discover them. He even goes so far as to arrange to be caught in a hotel room with another woman, but the plan goes berserk when several women arrive as well as a jealous husband. By the final curtain, all is straightened out and Angie is very impressed. This knockabout farce was a hit on Broadway and was filmed twice. A 1920 silent movie featured the beloved character actor Eugene Pallette as Reggie and, being mostly physical comedy, it played well on screen. But when the great physical comic Buster Keaton played Reggie in a 1931 talkie remake, the film flopped. It is a slow-paced, clumsy comedy and Keaton's special talents are not in evidence. In fact, he is overshadowed by the lively supporting cast. The movie made it clear that Keaton's career disintegrated with the coming of sound.

Partners Again see *Potash and Perlmutter*

Peck's Bad Boy

March 10, 1884 (Comedy Theatre), a play by Charles Pidgin. *Cast*: William Carroll (Henry Peck), Mollie Fuller (Jimmy), Florence Bates. 40 performances.

(Lesser 1921). *Screenplay*: Sam Wood. *Cast*: Jackie Coogan (Henry Peck), James Corrigan (George Peck), Doris May (Letty), Wheeler Oakman (Dr. Martin), Lillian Leighton, Raymond Hatton. *Director*: Sam Wood. *Producer*: Irving M. Lesser.

(Fox 1934). *Screenplay*: Marguerite Roberts, Bernard Schubert. *Cast*: Thomas Meighan (Henry Peck), Jackie Cooper (Bill Peck), Jackie

Searl (Horace Clay), Dorothy Peterson, O. P. Heggie, Charles E. Evans. *Director*: Edward F. Cline. *Producer*: Sol Lesser.

The mischievous youth Henry Peck is known all over town for creating mayhem wherever he goes with his two young chums. Henry never means any harm but accidents always seem to happen. Peck's comic misadventures first appeared in a series of stories by George Peck and were adapted into a stage farce that remained popular for over thirty years. The comedy was particularly successful on the road and many famous stars, such as George M. Cohan, got their start playing Henry. The 1921 silent version featured the popular child star Jackie Coogan as Henry and the 1934 talkie starred the boy-actor favorite Jackie Cooper as Peck (now with the first name of Bill). Both films were popular, just as the similar *Dennis the Menace* comic strip and television series were two generations later. A 1938 sequel called *Peck's Bad Boy with the Circus* was made in 1938 with Tommy Kelly as the title character.

Peck's Bad Boy with the Circus see *Peck's Bad Boy*

Peg 'o My Heart

December 20, 1912. (Cort Theatre), a comedy by J. Hartley Manners. *Cast*: Laurette Taylor (Margaret), Emily Melville (Mrs. Chichester), H. Reeves Smith (Jerry), Christine Norman, Reginald Mason, Hassard Short. *Director*: J. Hartley Manners. *Producer:* Oliver Morosco. 603 performances.

(Metro 1922). *Screenplay*: Mary O'Hara. *Cast*: Laurette Taylor (Margaret), Mahlon Hamilton (Gerald), Vera Lewis (Mrs. Chichester), Ethel Grey Terry, Russell Simpson, Nigel Bruce, Lionel Belmore. *Director*: King Vidor. *Producer*: J. Hartley Manners.

(MGM 1933). *Screenplay*: Frances Marion, Frank R. Adams. *Cast*: Marion Davies (Margaret), Irene Browne (Mrs. Chichester), Onslow Stevens (Jerry), Juliette Compton, J. Farrell MacDonald. *Director-producer*: Robert Z. Leonard.

The haughty but bankrupt Chichester family must take in their orphaned relative

Margaret if they wish to receive an annuity from an uncle's will. But Peg is a scruffy Irish girl who says what she thinks so the family are rather cold to her. Despite this, Peg manages to help the Chichesters avoid disaster on more than one occasion. She slowly wins their affection and even ends up marrying a rich farmer. One of the most beloved plays of the period, it was a huge hit on Broadway (where it broke the record for the longest-running play) and on the road where touring productions entertained audiences for several years. The original New York mounting made a star of Laurette Taylor whose Peg was acclaimed for its warmth and comedy. An abridged silent film version in 1919 featured Wanda Hawley as Peg then Taylor got to reprise her performance in the 1922 remake. Even without hearing the dialogue, Taylor's performance bubbles with spirit. The 1933 talkie starred Marion Davies as Peg and she also was a vivacious presence on the screen, even doing a zesty little song and dance at one point. The production values and supporting cast are all fine but the story seems dated in this version and modern audiences need to view it with patience.

The Perfect Marriage

October 26, 1944 (Ethel Barrymore Theatre), a comedy by Samson Raphaelson. *Cast*: Miriam Hopkins (Jenny Williams), Victor Jory (Dale Williams), Helen Flint (Mabel Manning), James Todd (Addison Manning), Martha Sleeper (Gloria Endicott), Joyce Van Patten, Evelyn Davis. *Director*: Samson Raphaelson. *Producer*: Cheryl Crawford. 92 performances.

(Paramount 1946). *Screenplay*: Leonard Spigelgass. *Cast*: Loretta Young (Maggie Williams), David Niven (Dale Williams), Eddie Albert (Gil Cummins), Rita Johnson (Mabel Manning), Charles Ruggles, Virginia Field, ZaSu Pitts. *Director*: Lewis Allen. *Producer*: Hal B. Wallis.

Dale and Jenny Williams have been happily married for ten years yet each feels the magic is gone. They consider extramarital affairs and even divorce before concluding that they can make their current marriage special. This uneventful, mildly amusing comedy only survived on Broadway for three months on the strength of its stars, Miriam Hopkins and Victor Jory, who gave droll and likable performances. Loretta Young and David Niven were the questioning couple in the 1946 film in which the issues were less subtle and the comedy broader. All the same, it is a lackluster movie that depends on its stars and amusing supporting cast.

A Perfect Murder see Dial M for Murder

Period of Adjustment

November 10, 1960 (Helen Hayes Theatre), a comedy by Tennessee Williams. *Cast*: James Daly (Ralph Bates), Robert Webber (George Haverstick), Barbara Baxley (Isabel Haverstick), Rosemary Murphy (Dorothea Bates), Helen Martin (Susie), Lester Mack, Nancy R. Pollack. *Director*: George Roy Hill. *Producer:* Cheryl Crawford. 132 performances.

(MGM 1962). *Screenplay*: Isobel Lennart. *Cast*: Anthony Franciosa (Ralph Baitz), Jane Fonda (Isabel Haverstick), Jim Hutton (George Haverstick), Lois Nettleton (Dorothea Baitz), John McGiver, Mabel Albertson, Jack Albertson. *Director*: George Roy Hill. *Producer*: Lawrence Weingarten.

Two couples face crisis in this, Tennessee Williams's only comedy. Ralph's wife has taken their child and gone back to her parents because she is tired of his paying more attention to television and drinking beer than to her. Ralph's old pal George shows up on his wedding night, seeking male companionship and avoiding getting intimate with his own wife. Both wives converge on the scene and, after much name calling and apologies, the two couples are happily reunited. The comedy of manners was strained at times but the proficient young cast were engaging and the play had a profitable run. The 1962 screen version featured some of Hollywood's brightest up-and-coming talents and all four give delightful performances that are sometimes as touching as they are funny. The one-set play is awkwardly opened up and the direction is stagy but there is still much to enjoy.

The Petrified Forest

January 7, 1935 (Broadhurst Theatre), a drama by Robert Sherwood. *Cast*: Leslie Howard (Alan Squire), Peggy Conklin (Gabby Maple), Humphrey Bogart (Duke Mantee), Charles Dow Clark (Gramp Maple), Blanche Sweet, Pobert Porterfield, Walter Vonnegut, Frank Milan, Robert Hudson, John Alexander. *Director*: Arthur Hopkins. *Producer:* Gilbert Miller. 197 performances.

(Warner 1936). *Screenplay*: Charles Kenyon, Delmer Daves. *Cast*: Leslie Howard (Alan Squire), Bette Davis (Gabby Maple), Humphrey Bogart (Duke Mantee), Charley Grapewin (Gramp), Genevieve Tobin, Dick Foran, Joe Sawyer, Porter Hall. *Director*: Archie Mayo. *Producer*: Hal B. Wallis.

Escape in the Desert (Warner 1945). *Screenplay:* Thomas Job. *Cast*: Philip Dorn (Philip Artveld), Helmut Dantine (Capt. Becker), Alan Hale (Dr. Orville Tedder), Jean Sullivan (Jane), Irene Manning, Samuel S. Hinds. *Director*: Edward A. Blatt. *Producer:* Alex Gottlieb.

At a gas station-lunch room on the edge of a petrified forest in Arizona, gangster Duke Mantee and his gang arrive and take over the place as their hideout from the police. Eating at the diner is the disillusioned poet Alan Squire who sees a brighter future for the world in the person of the owner's daughter Gabby who dreams of studying art in Paris. Squire signs his life insurance policy over to Gabby and then goads Duke into killing him. The drama was as suspenseful as it was poetic and each of the characters was vividly presented. The Broadway production starred Leslie Howard as Squire and when he went to Hollywood to make the 1936 movie he insisted newcomer Humphrey Bogart repeat his Duke for the cameras. The role made Bogart a star, though it did typecast him as mobsters for a while. The faithful screen adaptation doesn't handle the philosophical aspects of the play very well but the melodrama is first-rate and the performances are penetrating. A 1945 remake called *Escape in the Desert* borrows plot elements but changes the ending and the point of the story. Escaped Nazi prisoners-of-war, instead of gangsters, take over a Nevada desert hotel but an American flyer drops in and saves the day. It is a contrived and flat wartime propaganda adventure with nothing original to say. An abridged television version of *The Petrified Forest* in 1955 allowed Humphrey Bogart to play Duke once again and he was joined by Henry Fonda as Squire and Lauren Bacall as Gabby.

The Philadelphia Story

March 28, 1939 (Shubert Theatre), a comedy by Philip Barry. *Cast*: Katharine Hepburn (Tracy Lord), Joseph Cotton (C. K. Dexter Haven), Van Heflin (Mike Connor), Shirley Booth (Liz Imbrie), Frank Fenton (George Kittredge), Vera Allen (Margaret Lord), Lenore Lonergan (Dinah Lord), Nicholas Joy, Forrest Orr. *Director*: Robert B. Sinclair. *Producer:* Theatre Guild. 417 performances.

(MGM 1940). *Screenplay*: David Ogden Stewart. *Cast*: Katharine Hepburn (Tracy Lord), Cary Grant (C. K. Dexter Haven), James Stewart (Mike Connor), Ruth Hussey (Liz Imbrie), John Howard (George Kittredge), Mary Nash (Margaret Lord), Virginia Weidler (Dinah Lord), Roland Young, John Halliday, Henry Daniell. *Director*: Robert B. Sinclair. *Producer*: Joseph L. Mankiewicz.

High Society (MGM 1956). *Screenplay*: John Patrick. *Score*: Cole Porter. *Cast*: Grace Kelly (Tracy Lord), Bing Crosby (C. K. Dexter Haven), Frank Sinatra (Mike Connor), Celeste Holm (Liz Imbrie), John Lund, Louis Calhern, Sidney Blackmer, Louis Armstrong. *Songs:* True Love; You're Sensational; Well, Did You Evah?; Now You Has Jazz; Who Wants to Be a Millionaire. *Director-choreographer*: Charles Walters. *Producer*: Sol C. Siegel.

The Philadelphia Mainliner Tracy Lord was once married to C. Dexter Haven but divorced him and now plans to marry the stuffy George Kitteredge. Dexter shows up the day before the wedding, still in love with Tracy, and she is finding herself attracted to the down-to-earth journalist Mike Connor who is covering the wedding. But when Tracy gets drunk the night before the ceremony and goes swimming in the nude with Mike, her fiancé breaks off the engagement. In the sober daylight, Tracy and Mike part as friends and she happily agrees to remarry Dexter. Philip Barry wrote the witty comedy of manners with Hepburn in mind and she triumphed as Tracy on Broadway and in the 1940 screen version. In both cases she had sensational co-stars, adept supporting casts, and graceful direction. The movie simplifies the stage plot somewhat and eliminates a few characters, but the romantic trio remains the focal point and the comedy still soars. The story was musicalized in the 1956 film *High Society* and there are enough differences that one can enjoy the new version for itself. The setting was moved to Newport where Dexter is throwing a jazz festival; this allowed Louis Armstrong to make a memorable guest appearance. Cole Porter wrote the scintillating score and the romantic trio of Grace Kelly, Bing Crosby, and Frank Sinatra was pure magic. Much of Barry's wit is lost in the movie musical but it more than makes up for it with lyrical charm. Three television versions of *The Philadelphia Story* were made in the 1950s: an early broadcast in 1950 with Barbara Bel Geddes as Tracy, a 1954 production with Dorothy McGuire, and in 1959 with Diana Lynn.

The Piano Lesson

April 16, 1990. (Walter Kerr Theatre), a play by August Wilson. *Cast*: Charles S. Dutton (Boy Willie), S. Epatha Merkerson (Berniece), Rocky Carroll (Lyman), Tommy Hollis (Avery), Carl Gordon (Doaker), Lou Myers (Wining Boy), Apryl R. Foster (Maretha), Lisa Gay Hamilton (Grace). *Director*: Lloyd Richards. *Producers:* Yale Repertory Theatre, etc. 329 performances. Pulitzer Prize.

(TV 1995). *Teleplay*: August Wilson. *Cast*: Charles S. Dutton (Boy Willie), Alfre Woodard (Berniece), Courtney B. Vance (Lyman), Tommy Hollis (Avery), Carl Gordon (Doaker), Lou Myers (Wining Boy), Rosalyn Coleman (Grace), Zelda Harris (Maretha). *Director*: Lloyd Richards. *Producers*: Brent Shields, August Wilson.

During the Depression the African American Boy Willie drives from Mississippi to his sister's house in Pittsburgh to convince her to sell the family piano so that he can buy farmland with his share. But the piano has been in the family for years and is covered with carvings made by their slave ancestors so she won't sell it. When Boy Willie tries to move it out of the house against her wishes, a strange and haunting force materializes and only by the sister's playing of a hymn on the piano is Boy Willie saved from destruction. The most mystic and arguably the most poetic of August Wilson's works, the drama was both fascinating and moving. Some of the Broadway cast and creative staff were involved in the faithful 1995 television production, including Charles S. Dutton's electric performance as Boy Willie. The play is only opened up a bit for the screen but the lively production rarely feels stagebound.

Picnic

February 19, 1953 (Music Box Theatre), a play by William Inge. *Cast*: Janice Rule (Madge), Kim Stanley (Millie), Ralph Meeker (Hal Carter), Eileen Heckart (Rosemary), Peggy Conklin (Mrs. Owens), Paul Newman, Arthur O'Connell. *Director*: Joshua Logan. *Producer:* Theatre Guild, Joshua Logan. 477 performances. Pulitzer Prize.

(Columbia 1955). *Screenplay*: Daniel Taradash. *Cast*: William Holden (Hal Carter), Kim Novak (Madge Owens), Betty Field (Flo Owens), Susan Strasberg (Millie Owens), Cliff Robertson (Alan), Rosalind Russell (Rosemary), Arthur O'Connell. *Director*: Joshua Logan. *Producer*: Fred Kohlmar.

(TV 1986). *Teleplay*: William Inge *Cast*: Gregory Harrison (Hal Carter), Jennifer Jason Leigh (Madge Owens), Michael Learned (Rosemary), Rue McClanahan (Flo Owens), Dana Hill, Timothy Shelton, Dick Van Patten. *Director*: Marshall W. Mason. *Producers*: Roger Berlind, Gregory Harrison.

(TV 2000). *Teleplay*: Shelley Evans. *Cast*: Josh Brolin (Hal Carter), Gretchen Mol (Madge Owens), Bonnie Bedelia (Flo Owens), Mary Steenburgen (Rosemary), Ben Caswell, Chad Morgan, Jay O. Sanders. *Director*: Ivan Passer. *Producer*: Bruce Hickey.

Some residents of a small Kansas town make big changes in their lives during the Labor Day holiday when the drifter Hal Carter shows up. He steals his old pal's fiancée Madge away from him, breaks the teenage heart of her sister Millie, and even goads the spinster Rosemary into getting her long-time suitor to marry her. William Inge's drama was casual on the surface but was seething with frustration and sexual desire underneath and made for a captivating play. Only Arthur O'Connell, as the middle-aged suitor, reprised his stage role in the 1955 film and his is one of the few performances that is not overwrought on the screen. William Holden was too old for Hal but used his sexual energy well, Kim Novak was a simple-minded Madge, and Rosalind Russell played Rosemary like a vaudeville trouper. Joshua Logan, in his movie directing debut, seems to have lost all the subtlety he brought to his staging of the Broadway production and the movie plods along clumsily. In its day the film was considered a daring, sensual look at the dark side of rural America; today it only interests one perfunctorily. television productions of the play in 1986 and 2000 each boasted some impressive acting and both come closer to Inge's original than the movie.

The Pirate

November 25, 1942 (Martin Beck Theatre), a play by S. N. Behrman. *Cast*: Alfred Lunt (Serafin), Lynn Fontanne (Manuela), Alan Reed (Pedro Vargas), Walter Mosby (Don Bolo), Clarence Derwent, Lea Penman, Estelle Winwood, Maurice Ellis. *Directors*: Alfred Lunt, John C. Wilson. *Producer:* Playwrights' Company. 177 performances.

(MGM 1948). *Screenplay*: Frances Goodrich, Albert Hackett. *Score:* Cole Porter. *Cast*: Judy Garland (Manuela), Gene Kelly (Serafin), Walter Slezak (Don Pedro Vargas), Gladys Cooper, Reginald Owen, Nicholas Brothers, George Zucco. *Songs:* Be a Clown; Niña; Mack the Black; You Could Do No Wrong; Love of My Life. *Director*: Vincente Minnelli. *Choreographers:* Gene Kelly, Robert Alton. *Producer*: Arthur Freed.

When the actor Serafin and his band of strolling players come to town, the mayor Don Vargas refuses to give them a license to perform until Serafin recognizes Vargas as the pirate Macoco whom the authorities are looking for. Serafin then woos and wins Vargas's lovely wife Manuela and hypnotizes her into giving away her husband's true identity. Vargas goes to jail and Serafin gets Manuela. The swashbuckling romance was frequently satirical and the way that the Lunts played Serafin and Manuela was high-styled farce. Hollywood musicalized the comedy in 1948 and turned it into a broad slapstick vehicle for Gene Kelly and Judy Garland who played Serafin and Manuela to Walter Slezak's mayor. The simplified screenplay made Manuela an unmarried maid who suspects that Serafin is Macoco and little that followed made logical sense. But the story was presented as a high-pitched fairy tale with oversized acting and bright Caribbean costumes and sets. Cole Porter wrote the disappointing score which played second fiddle to the athletic dancing and Douglas Fairbanks-like stunts. The odd musical failed at the box office but has been better appreciated over the years for its bright spots, such as Kelly and the Nicholas Brothers performing "Be a Clown."

Play It Again, Sam

February 12, 1969 (Broadhurst Theatre), a comedy by Woody Allen. *Cast*: Woody Allen (Allen Felix), Diane Keaton (Linda), Anthony Roberts (Dick), Jerry Lacy (Bogart), Barbara Brownell. *Director*: Joseph Hardy. *Producers:* David Merrick, etc. 453 performances.

(Paramount 1972). *Screenplay*: Woody Allen. *Cast*: Woody Allen (Allan Felix), Diane Keaton (Linda), Tony Roberts (Dick), Jerry Lacy (Bogart), Susan Anspach. *Director*: Herbert Ross. *Producer*: Arthur P. Jacobs.

Nebbish film critic Allen Felix tries to enter the dating game after his wife leaves him but fails with every woman except his best friend's wife. He is coached along the way by the specter of Humphrey Bogart and in the end nobly gives up the dame just as Bogy did in *Casablanca*. Up-and-coming comic Woody Allen wrote the comedy for himself and it was a comfortable fit for the actor and his anti-hero persona. All of the major cast members from the successful Broadway production appeared in the 1972 film and, as directed by Herbert Ross, it is a conventional romantic comedy rather than a cunning Woody Allen movie. All the same, the faithful screen version is opened up efficiently and the cast is as enjoyable as they were on stage.

Plaza Suite

February 14, 1968 (Plymouth Theatre), a comedy by Neil Simon. *Cast*: George C. Scott (Sam/Jesse/Roy), Maureen Stapleton (Karen/Muriel/Norma), Claudette Nevins, Bob Balaban. *Director*: Mike Nichols. *Producer:* Saint Subber. 1,097 performances.

(Paramount 1971). *Screenplay*: Neil Simon. *Cast*: Walter Matthau (Sam/Jesse/Roy), Maureen Stapleton (Karen), Barbara Harris (Muriel), Lee Grant (Norma), Louise Sorel. *Director*: Arthur Hiller. *Producer*: Howard W. Koch.

(TV 1987). *Screenplay*: Neil Simon. *Cast*: Carol Burnett (Karen/Muriel/Norma), Dabney Coleman (Jesse), Richard Crenna (Roy), Hal Holbrook (Sam), Beth Maitland. *Directors*: Roger Beatty, Kenny Solms. *Producer*: George Sunga.

George C. Scott and Maureen Stapleton, who had built their reputation with serious vehicles, played three different couples who check into the Plaza Hotel in New York in this three-play comedy and dazzled the critics and public with their deft handling of the diverse characters. The first duet concerns a married couple whose marriage is in danger, the second playlet shows how a sly movie producer uses his fame to seduce an old high school sweetheart, and the final offering is a door-slamming farce in which one door doesn't slam because the bride has locked herself in the bathroom while her raving parents try to coax her out. The Broadway production, directed with razor-sharp precision by Mike Nichols, ran nearly three years and (unhappily) inspired playwright Neil Simon to pen three more hotel suite comedies. The 1971 movie of *Plaza Suite* starred Walter Matthau as all three males but cast three different actresses as his co-stars. Maureen Stapleton reprised the worried wife from the stage while Barbara Harris and Lee Grant appeared in the later two episodes. The theatricality of the play is lost in the flatly-directed film but the performances are still effective and the final

farce sequence is well-timed. A 1987 television production reversed the movie's approach and starred Carol Burnett as three women but gave her different male co-stars. Burnett's versatility carries the comedy but most of play dissolves into sit-com antics and too much of the production is mediocre.

The Pleasure of His Company

October 22, 1958 (Longacre Theatre), a comedy by Samuel A. Taylor and Cornelia Otis Skinner. *Cast*: Dolores Hart (Jessica Poole), Cyril Ritchard (Biddeford Poole), Cornelia Otis Skinner (Katherine Dougherty), George Peppard (Roger Henderson), Walter Abel (Jim Dougherty), Charlie Ruggles (Mackenzie Savage), Jerry Fujikawa. *Director*: Cyril Ritchard. *Producers:* Frederick Brisson, Playwrights' Company. 474 performances.

(Paramount 1961). *Screenplay*: Samuel A. Taylor. *Cast*: Debbie Reynolds (Jessica Poole), Fred Astaire (Biddeford Poole), Lilli Palmer (Katharine Dougherty), Tab Hunter (Roger Henderson), Gary Merrill (James Dougherty), Charles Ruggles (Mackenzie Savage), Harold Fong, Elvia Allman. *Director*: George Seaton. *Producer*: William Perlberg.

On the eve of her wedding to the strait-laced Roger Henderson, Jessica Poole receives an unexpected visit from her estranged father, the oft-married playboy Biddeford Poole. His eccentric yet life-affirming ways make Jessica reconsider her future and in the end he persuades her to postpone the wedding for a year and travel the world with him. This intelligent comedy of manners was thinly plotted but the characters were well drawn and the radiant cast made the production a sublime delight. Cyril Ritchard, who also directed, was in top form as Biddeford and his performance helped the play run well over a year. Fred Astaire essayed the dandy Biddeford in the 1961 movie and it is a wry, genteel performance but lacking in the panache to give the story its drive. The rest of the cast also does well but the whole comic style of the play is diluted to the point that it seems nothing much happens on the screen.

Polly of the Circus

December 23, 1907 (Liberty Theatre), a play by
Margaret Mayo. *Cast*: Mabel Taliaferro (Polly),
Malcolm Williams (Rev. John Douglas), J. B.
Hollis, Herbert Ayling, James Cherry, Guy
Nichols. *Director*: Winchell Smith. *Producer*:
Frederick Thompson. 160 performances.

(Goldwyn 1917). *Screenplay*: Adrian Gil-Spear,
Emmett C. Hall. *Cast*: Mae Marsh (Polly), Vernon Steele (Rev. John Douglas), Charles Eldridge, Wellington A. Playter, George S. Trimble, Lucille La Verne. *Directors*: Edwin L.
Hollywood, Charles Horan. *Producer*: Samuel
Goldwyn.

(MGM-Cosmopolitan 1932). *Screenplay*: Carey
Wilson. *Cast*: Marion Davies (Polly), Clark Gable
(Rev. John Hartley), C. Aubrey Smith, Raymond
Hatton, David Landau, Ruth Selwyn. *Director*:
Alfred Santell. *Producer*: Marion Davies.

When the circus bareback rider Polly is
injured in a fall, she is taken to the home of
the Reverend John Douglas and the two fall
in love. But Polly feels a marriage to a circus
performer would harm his reputation so she
leaves, only to be pursued and won over by
John. The romantic comedy was spiced up
with circus acts so audiences got a touch of
spectacle as well as romance, allowing the
play to enjoy a long run. Silent screen star
Mae Marsh played Polly in the 1917 movie
and this first Samuel Goldwyn production
was filled with spectacle, including a rousing
horse race and plenty of circus footage. The
film was popular enough that the story was
remade in 1932 as a vehicle for Marion Davies.
Polly is a trapeze artist in this version and
Clark Gable is the minister she loves; both
seem miscast and neither comes across as
very convincing. The movie has atmosphere
but too few laughs and not much chemistry.

Polly with a Past

September 6, 1917 (Belasco Theatre), a comedy by
George Middleton, Guy Bolton. *Cast*: Ina Claire
(Polly), Herbert Yost (Rex Van Zile), Ann
Meredith (Myrtle Davis), Cyril Scott (Harry
Richardson), George Stuart Christie (Clay Col-
lum), H. Reeves-Smith, William Sampson,
Thomas Reynolds. *Director-producer*: David Be-
lasco. 315 performances.

(Metro 1920). *Screenplay*: June Mathis, Arthur
Zellner. *Cast*: Ina Claire (Polly), Ralph Graves
(Rex Van Zile), Louiszita Valentine (Myrtle
Davis), Harry Benham (Clay Collum), Marie
Wainwright, Myra Brooks, Frank Currier. *Direc-
tor*: Leander De Cordova.

Since the woman he loves seems to
only care about needy people, Rex Van Zile
decides to put on the appearance of a destitute womanizer to attract her affection. His
friends help with the ruse and pair him up
with Polly, a sweet girl from Ohio who
dreams of a concert career. Polly pretends to
be a French vamp and does her job so well
that she and Rex fall in love. In addition to
being a hit comedy, the production made Ina
Claire, who played Polly, into one of the theatre's favorite high comediennes. Claire
reprised her performance in the 1920 silent
movie, which was hardly the venue for showing off her expert comic delivery of dialogue.
But her vivaciousness still came through and
the film was as success.

Porgy and Bess

October 10, 1935 (Alvin Theatre), a folk opera by
DuBose Heyward. *Score:* George and Ira Gersh-
win, DuBose Heyward. *Cast:* Todd Duncan
(Porgy), Anne Brown (Bess), John W. Bubbles
(Sportin' Life), Warren Coleman (Crown), Abbie
Mitchell (Clara), Ruby Elzy (Serena), Georgette
Harvey, Edward Matthews. *Songs:* Summertime;
Bess, You Is My Woman Now; I Got Plenty o'
Nuttin'; It Ain't Necessarily So; My Man's Gone
Now; A Woman Is a Sometime Thing; I Loves
You, Porgy; There's a Boat Dat Leavin' for Soon
New York; I'm on My Way. *Director:* Rouben
Mamoulian. *Producer:* Theatre Guild. 124 per-
formances.

(Columbia/Goldwyn 1959). *Screenplay:* N.
Richard Nash. *Score:* George and Ira Gershwin,
DuBose Heyward. *Cast:* Sidney Poitier (Porgy),
Dorothy Dandridge (Bess), Sammy Davis, Jr.
(Sportin' Life), Brock Peters (Crown), Pearl Bai-
ley (Maria), Ruth Attaway (Serena), Diahann
Carroll (Clara), Leslie Scott. *Songs:* Summertime;
Bess, You Is My Woman Now; I Got Plenty o'
Nuttin'; It Ain't Necessarily So; My Man's Gone
Now; A Woman Is a Sometime Thing; I Loves
You, Porgy; There's a Boat Dat Leavin' for Soon
New York; I'm on My Way. *Director:* Otto Pre-
minger. *Choreographer:* Hermes Pan. *Producer:*
Samuel Goldwyn.

Although this acclaimed folk opera was a financial failure in its initial run on Broadway, over the years the work has been accepted as an American classic and is frequently revived in theatres and opera houses around the world. The tale of the fallen woman Bess and the cripple Porgy who loves her is dramatically sound and much more affecting than most opera plots. George Gershwin's music and the lyrics by his brother Ira and Dubose Heyward remain among the finest in musical theatre. It took several years before Hollywood attempted to make a movie of *Porgy and Bess*, and it only happened because independent producer Samuel Goldwyn was behind the project. While it is not the definitive production of the piece, it has much to recommend. Most of the actors were dubbed by opera singers so the singing is high in quality even if it sometimes does not seem to match the performers on the screen. And the score is highly abridged, which bothers Gershwin and opera purists. But for the most part the movie is quite involving and effective. The folk opera has also appeared on television a few times, but always in live or filmed broadcasts of opera or theatre productions.

The Portrait see *Painting Churches*

The Postman Always Rings Twice

February 25, 1936 (Lyceum Theatre), a drama by James M. Cain. *Cast*: Richard Barthelmess (Frank Chambers), Mary Philips (Cora Papadakis), Joseph Greenwald (Nick Papadakis), Dudley Clements, Charles Halton. *Director*: Robert Sinclair. *Producer:* Jack Curtis. 72 performances.

(MGM 1946). *Screenplay*: Harry Ruskin, Niven Busch. *Cast*: Lana Turner (Cora Smith), John Garfield (Frank Chambers), Cecil Kellaway (Nick Smith), Hume Cronyn (Arthur Keats), Leon Ames (Kyle Sackett), Audrey Totter, Alan Reed. *Director*: Tay Garnett. *Producer*: Carey Wilson.

(1981). *Screenplay*: David Mamet. *Cast*: Jack Nicholson (Frank Chambers), Jessica Lange (Cora Papadakis), John Colicos (Nick Papadakis), Michael Lerner (Mr. Katz), John P. Ryan (Kennedy), Anjelica Huston (Madge), William Traylor, Thomas Hill. *Director*: Bob Rafelson. *Producers*: Charles Mulehill, Bob Rafelson.

James M. Cain's potboiler of a novel, about a bored housewife who has a steamy affair with a drifter, was sold to the movies but was deemed too sensational to get by the censors. Not only was the lovemaking rather graphic but the two lovers kill off the husband and nearly get away with it. Cain adapted the tale into a play but it met with mixed notices, was criticized for its lack of passion, and closed in two months. While Hollywood was afraid of the property, France wasn't and film versions were released in 1939 as *Le Dernier Tourant* and in 1942 as *Ossessione*. When MGM finally filmed the story in 1946, the result was a sensation. Lana Turner, formerly cast as perky ingenues, was an erotic *femme fatale* often dressed all in white and exuding sex through subtext. She was matched in her seething passion by John Garfield as her lover. The script managed to suggest all of the book's sensuality with hardly a bare shoulder and the film remains surprisingly erotic for modern viewing. The 1981 remake was able to show everything suggested in the earlier movie but it was awkwardly uninvolving and rather dull, even when the lovers used the kitchen table for one of their many copulation scenes. Some faulted the cold and distant David Mamet screenplay but most found no chemistry between Jack Nicholson and Jessica Lange.

Potash and Perlmutter

August 16, 1913 (Cohan Theatre), a comedy by Montague Glass. *Cast*: Alexander Carr (Mawruss Perlmutter), Barney Bernard (Abe Potash), Louise Dresser (Ruth Snyder), Joseph Kilgour (Feldman), Albert Parker (Boris Andrieff), Marguerite Anderson (Irma), Stanley Jessup, Elita Proctor Otis, Marguerite Anderson. *Director*: Hugh Ford. *Producer:* A. H. Woods. 441 performances.

(Goldwyn 1923). *Screenplay*: Frances Marion. *Cast*: Alexander Carr (Morris Perlmutter), Barney

Bernard (Abe Potash), Ben Lyon (Boris Andrieff), Hope Sutherland (Irma),Vera Gordon, Edouard Durand, Martha Mansfield. *Director*: Clarence G. Badger. *Producer*: Samuel Goldwyn.

In Hollywood With Potash and Perlmutter Goldwyn 1924). *Screenplay:* Frances Marion. *Cast:* George Sidney (Abe Potash), Alexander Carr (Morris Perlmutter), Vera Gordon (Rosie Potash), Betty Blythe, Belle Bennett, Peggy Shaw, Anders Randolf. *Director:* Alfred E. Green. *Producer:* Samuel Goldwyn.

Partners Again (Goldwyn 1926). *Screenplay*: Frances Marion. *Cast:* George Sidney (Abe Potash), Alexander Carr (Mawruss Perlmutter), Betty Jewel (Hattie Potash), Allan Forrest, Robert Schable, Lillian Elliott. *Director:* Henry King. *Producer:* Samuel Goldwyn.

Partners Potash and Perlmutter in the garment trade are always arguing with each other but when one of their employees, a suspected criminal, runs off and the partners are out of the $20,000 they posted for bail, the two stop fighting and put their heads together to save the business. Based on a series of stories by Montague Glass in the *Saturday Evening Post*, the play was a major Broadway hit and spawned some stage sequels. It was also made into three successful silent films, which is interesting since most of the comedy in the plays is dialect humor. Alexander Carr played Perlmutter on Broadway and all three films; George Sidney partnered with him in two of the screen adaptations. While the plots and titles changed from film to film, the focus was always on the quarreling partners and their slapstick manners.

Prelude to a Kiss

March 14, 1990 (Circle Theatre), a play by Craig Lucas. *Cast*: Alec Baldwin (Peter), Mary-Louise Parker (Rita), Barnard Hughes (Old Man), Debra Monk, Larry Bryggman, Joyce Reehling, L. Peter Callender, John Dossett, Craig Brockhorn, Michael Warren Powell. *Director*: Norman René. *Producer:* Circle Repertory Company. 473 performances.

(Fox 1992). *Screenplay*: Craig Lucas. *Cast*: Alec Baldwin (Peter), Meg Ryan (Rita), Sydney Walker (Old Man), Kathy Bates, Debra Monk, Ned Beatty, Patty Duke, Stanley Tucci, Richard

Riehle. *Director*: Norman René. *Producers*: Michael Gruskoff, Michael I. Levy.

During a wedding reception, an old man comes up to the bride and gives her a kiss of congratulations. From that point on the new wife's personality changes: she has lost her energy and always is forgetting things. The young husband seeks out the old man and finds that the senior citizen is vibrant and full of life. The wife and old man have exchanged personalities with that fateful kiss. But the old man is dying of cancer and the husband's faithful tending of him in his wife's body is so sincere that the spell is reversed and the couple are reunited. The odd but effective comedy fantasy was a hit Off Broadway so it transferred to Broadway where it ran over a year. Alec Baldwin, who had played the husband in the original Off Broadway cast, reprised the role in the 1992 faithful screen adaptation. Although it is well directed and the cast is commendable, the fantasy elements seem harder to swallow in the realistic movie than on the stage. More a curiosity than a heartfelt experience, the movie was not widely popular.

Present Arms

April 26, 1928 (Mansfield Theatre), a musical comedy by Herbert Fields. *Score:* Richard Rodgers, Lorenz Hart. *Cast:* Charles King (Chick Evans), Flora LeBreton (Lady Delphine), Busby Berkeley (Douglas Atwell), Joyce Babour (Edna Stevens), Franker Wood (Frank Derryberry), Fuller Mellish, Jr., Gaile Beverley. *Songs:* You Took Advantage of Me; A Kiss for Cinderella; Blue Ocean Blues; Do I Hear You Saying "I Love You?" *Director:* Alexander Leftwich. *Choreographer:* Busby Berkeley. *Producer*: Lew Fields. 155 performances.

Leathernecking (RKO 1939). *Screenplay:* Jane Murtin. *Score:* Richard Rodgers, Lorenz Hart, etc. *Cast:* Irene Dunne (Delphine Witherspoon), Ken Murray (Frank), Lilyan Tashman (Edna), Eddie Foy, Jr. (Chick Evans), Benny Rubin, Fred Santley, Ned Sparks, Louise Fazenda. *Songs:* You Took Advantage of Me; A Kiss for Cinderella; All My Life; Shake It Off and Smile; Careless Kisses; Evening Star. *Director:* Edward Cline. *Choreographer:* Pearl Eaton. *Producer:* Louis Sarecky.

This minor effort by Rodgers and Hart

still managed a decent run on Broadway and introduced the standard "You Took Advantage of Me." A Marine poses as a captain in order to win the heart of an aristocratic lady in Hawaii but, of course, he is found out. Yet he proves himself during a daring rescue at sea and wins her in the end. All but two of the songs were cut for the movie version that was retitled *Leathernecking* and the plot was beefed up with some clowning by comics Benny Rubin and Eddie Foy, Jr. Numbers by other songwriters were added but the Rodgers and Hart standard was still the highlight of the rather mediocre film that hardly seemed like a musical at all. Worth noting: Irene Dunne made her movie debut as the Honolulu socialite.

The Price

February 7, 1968 (Morosco Theatre), a play by Arthur Miller. *Cast*: Pat Hingle (Victor Franz), Arthur Kennedy (Walter Franz), Kate Reid (Esther Franz), Harold Gray (Gregory Solomon). *Director*: Ulu Grosbard. *Producer:* Robert Whitehead. 429 performances.

(TV 1971). *Teleplay*: Arthur Miller. *Cast*: George C. Scott (Victor Franz), Barry Sullivan (Walter Franz), Colleen Dewhurst (Esther Franz), David Burns (Gregory Solomon). *Director*: Fielder Cook. *Producer*: David Susskind.

During the Depression, Victor Franz stayed with his suddenly-broke family and cared for his parents while his brother Walter left and took care of himself. Years later the two estranged brothers meet when the family's furniture is to be sold off. Walter is now a successful doctor while Victor is a city policeman who struggles with his wife Esther to make ends meet. Recriminations about the past surface, as do revelations that sober both men and lead to a tentative understanding. One of the highlights of the drama is the elderly, philosophical furniture dealer Gregory Solomon, one of the most lively and colorful characters Arthur Miller ever created. The four-character piece was an acting tour de force and overcame mixed notices to run over a year on Broadway, Miller's last hit. A 1971 television production also boasted superb performances, some of them considered even more accomplished than the stage cast. George C. Scott and Colleen Dewhurst make a formidable couple, Barry Sullivan is a lighter but effective Walter, and comic character actor David Burns is exceptional as Solomon, his last role before his death that same year. Since the whole play takes place in an attic filled with furniture, the claustrophobic nature of the video version is appropriate and striking.

The Prisoner of Second Avenue

November 11, 1971 (Eugene O'Neill Theatre), a play by Neil Simon. *Cast*: Peter Falk (Mel Edison), Lee Grant (Edna Edison), Vincent Gardenia (Harry Edison), Florence Stanley, Tresa Hughes, Dena Dietrich. *Director*: Mike Nichols. *Producer:* Saint Subber. 780 performances.

(Warner 1975). *Screenplay*: Neil Simon. *Cast*: Jack Lemmon (Mel Edison), Anne Bancroft (Edna Edison), Gene Saks (Harry Edison), Elizabeth Wilson, Florence Stanley. *Director-producer*: Melvin Frank.

New Yorkers Mel and Edna Edison put up with the hundreds of inconveniences that come with living in the big city but when Mel loses his job due to downsizing and their apartment is robbed, the strain is too much and Mel starts to crack. Edna finds work to help pay the bills but when she begins to share Mel's paranoia about the city, the two learn they must band together in order to survive. Perhaps Neil Simon's sharpest and most uncomfortable comedy, the play had a dark undertone and the hilarious oneliners had a sting to them. Regardless, Broadway audiences embraced the production with its winning cast and it ran over two years. But the miscalculated 1975 screen version could not find the gray area between comedy and tragedy and the story and characters were tiresome and depressing. What seemed like a guaranteed cast was poorly directed, everyone shouted at everyone else, and the effect was numbing.

The Private Lives of Elizabeth and Essex see Elizabeth the Queen

Psycho Beach Party

July 20, 1987 (Players Theatre), a comedy by Charles Busch. *Cast*: Charles Busch (Chicklet), Ralph Buckley (Kanaka), Arnie Kolodner (Star Cat), Michael Belanger (Marvel Ann), Theresa Marlowe (Bettina Barnes), Becky London (Berdine), Andy Halliday (Provoloney), Judith Hansen (Dee Dee), Robert Carey (Yo-To), Mike Leitheed, Meghan Robinson. *Director-producer*: Kenneth Elliott. 344 performances.

(New Oz 2000). *Screenplay*: Charles Busch. *Cast*: Lauren Ambrose (Chicklet), Thomas Gibson (Kanaka), Nicholas Brendon (Star Cat), Charles Busch (Capt. Monica Stark), Kimberley Davies, Matt Keeslar, Beth Broderick. *Director*: Robert Lee King. *Producers*: Virginia Biddle, etc.

Malibou teenager Chicklet Forrest hangs out with the surfing crowd and has a big crush on the wipeout hunk Star Cat. But Chicklet also suffers from multiple personality disorder, sometimes thinking she is a black supermarket cashier, other times a radio talk host, and even a power-hungry vamp. Luckily Star Cat was a psychology major in college and he is able to cure her at the climatic luau. Charles Busch's broad spoof of 1960s beach blanket movies was made even more outrageous by his playing Chicklet himself in drag. The risible Off Off Broadway production attracted a wide audience and ran a year. The 2000 movie bowed to convention by casting a female as Chicklet, which didn't hurt the comedy, but the plot was expanded to include spoofs on 1970s slasher films and the satire was diluted. There are still eccentrically amusing moments but the long, over-stuffed film runs out of steam long before it is over.

Purlie Victorious

September 28, 1961 (Cort Theatre), a comedy by Ossie Davis. *Cast*: Ossie Davis (Purlie Victorious), Sorrell Brooke (Cap'n Cotchipee), Alan Alda (Charley), Ruby Dee (Lutiebelle), Godfrey Cambridge (Gitlow), Helen Martin, Beah Richards. *Director*: Howard Da Silva. *Producer*: Philip Rose. 261 performances.

Gone Are the Days (Hammer 1963). *Screenplay*: Ossie Davis. *Cast*: Ossie Davis (Purlie Victorious), Sorrell Brooke (Cap'n Cotchipee), Ruby Dee (Lutiebelle), Alan Alda (Charley), Godfrey Cambridge (Gitlow), Beah Richards, Hilda Haynes. *Director*: Nicholas Webster. *Producers*: Brock Peters, Nicholas Webster.

This satiric look at the ways and prejudices of the old South was far ahead of its time yet it is still a very funny and telling piece of writing. The African American preacher Purlie Victorious returns to his Southern hometown with the hopes of rebuilding the old church and teaching his people pride in themselves. But he is up against the old bigot Cap'n Cotchipee who owns most of the land and is trying to put the church out of business. Yet with the help of the Cap'n's liberal son Charley and the love of his sweetheart Lutiebelle, Purlie is victorious after all. The Broadway production boasted a superb cast and was able to let playgoers laugh at both white and black stereotypes while making its point. The 1963 film version was titled *Gone Are the Days* and, though its production budget was obviously skimpy, the satire survived and the cast (many of them from the stage production) were first-rate. The play was made into the popular Broadway musical *Purlie* in 1970.

The Racket

November 22, 1927 (Ambassador Theatre), a melodrama by Bartlett Cormack. *Cast*: John Cromwell (Capt. McQuigg), Marian Coakley (Irene Hayes), Edward G. Robinson (Unidentified Man), Willard Robertson (Pratt), Romaine Callender (Welch), Norman Foster (Dave Ames), Hugh O'Connell, Harry English, G. Pat Collins, Ralph Adams. *Producer*: Alexander McKaig. 119 performances.

(Hughes 1928). *Screenplay*: Eddie Adams. *Cast*: Thomas Meighan (Capt. McQuigg), Marie Prevost (Irene Hayes), Louis Wolheim (Nick Scarsi), George E. Stone (Joe Scarsi), John Darrow (Ames), Richard Skeets Gallagher (Miller), Lee Morgan, Lucien Priva. *Director*: Lewis Milestone. *Producer*: Howard Hughes.

(RKO 1951). *Screenplay*: William Wister, W. R. Burnett. *Cast*: Robert Mitchum (Capt. Thomas McQuigg), Lizbeth Scott (Irene Hayes), Robert Ryan (Mike Scanlon), William Talman (Bob Johnson), Ray Collins (D.A. Mortimer X. Welch), Joyce Mackenzie (Mary McQuigg), Robert Hutton, Virginia Huston. *Director*: John Cromwell. *Producer*: Edmund Grainger.

One of the best police dramas of its era, the play concerned an honest cop, Captain McQuigg, who is demoted to an outlying station because he didn't play into the hands of dishonest officials on the take. But when McQuigg is pitted against the gangland boss Nick Scarsi, he outwits him and the corrupt system. As Scarsi, Edward G. Robinson played his first (and last) gangster on the stage; he was soon whisked off to Hollywood where he excelled in playing mobsters, though he didn't appear in either film version of *The Racket*. The 1928 silent movie abridged the stage script considerably but kept to the spirit of the original. The 1951 remake took advantage of America's fascination with the current Kefauver crime hearings on television and updated the story, changing some names and details. Just as Robinson, in the secondary role of the gangster kingpin, stole the play, the tough-faced Louis Wolheim was the highlight of the silent film and Robert Ryan was in particularly fine form as the same character in the remake. Interesting footnote: John Cromwell, a popular actor who became a Hollywood director, played McQuigg on stage and many years later directed the movie remake.

Raffles, the Amateur Cracksman

October 27, 1903 (Princess Theatre), a play by E. W. Hornung, Eugene Presbrey. *Cast*: Kyrle Bellew (A. J. Raffles), E. M. Holland (Capt. Bedford), Frank Connor (Lord Crowley), Frank Roberts (Lord Amersteth), Clara Blandick, Frank McCormack, Staton Elliott. *Director*: Eugene Presbrey. *Producer:* Liebler & Co. 168 performances.

(Hyclass 1917). *Screenplay*: Anthony Kelly. *Cast*: John Barrymore (A. J. Raffles), Dudley Hill (Crowley), H. Cooper Cliffe (Amersteth), Chris-

tine Mayo, Frank Morgan. *Director*: George Irving. *Producer*: Lawrence Weber.

(Universal 1925). *Screenplay*: Harvey F. Thew. *Cast*: House Peters (A. J. Raffles), Fred Esmelton (Capt. Bedford), Walter Long, Hedda Hopper. *Director*: King Baggot.

(Goldwyn 1930). *Screenplay*: Sidney Howard. *Cast*: Ronald Colman (A. J. Raffles), Frances Dade, Kay Francis, David Torrence, Bramwell Fletcher. *Director*: George Fitzmaurice. *Producer*: Samuel Goldwyn.

(Goldwyn 1940). *Screenplay*: John Van Druten, etc. *Cast*: David Niven (A. J. Raffles), Olivia De Havilland, Dame May Whitty, Dudley Digges, Douglas Watton, E. E. Clive. *Director*: Sam Wood. *Producer*: Samuel Goldwyn.

(TV 1975). *Teleplay*: Eugene Wiley Presbrey, E. W. Hornung. *Cast*: Anthony Valentine (A. J. Raffles), James Maxwell, Christopher Strauli. *Director*: Christopher Hodson. *Producer*: Peter Willes.

A. J. Raffles, the gentleman jewel thief, was first introduced to the public in a series of stories by E. W. Hornung, who co-wrote the popular stage version. The educated, debonair Raffles plans to steal a lord's ancestral jewels but he will not stoop to accepting the amorous advances made by the lord's wife and daughter. The amateur sleuth Captain Bedford pursues Raffles but when the culprit returns the precious stones and escapes, Bedford is glad. In addition to its successful Broadway run, the comedy-thriller was a sensation on the road for years. Five silent screen versions were made, as well as four talkies and a television production. The plots may have varied but always in the limelight was the chivalrous cracksman Raffles. Screen cowboy star Gilbert "Bronco Billy" Anderson was the first to play Raffles on screen, in a 1905 film that was a highly abridged adaptation of the play. He played it again in a longer 1908 movie, followed by such notable Raffleses as John Barrymore in 1917, Ford Sterling in 1921, and House Peters in 1925. Ronald Colman was the first talking Raffles in a 1930 movie that is generally considered the best of the lot. Colman exudes charm and his supporting players are elegant foils for him. The 1940 remake was practically a scene-by-scene copy of the 1930 film with David Niven as the Cracksman. Despite Niven's suave performance and some gifted co-stars, this version lacks some of the grace of the Colman movie. Among the other screen adaptations are sequels and prequels, a noteworthy Spanish-language film in 1958, and a British television production in 1975 with Anthony Valentine as Raffles.

Rain

November 7, 1922 (Maxine Elliott Theatre), a play by John Colton, Clemence Randolph. *Cast*: Jeanne Eagels (Sadie Thompson), Robert Kelly (Rev. Davidson), Rapley Holmes, Emma Wilcox, Fritz Williams, Shirley King, Catharine Brooke. *Director*: John D. Williams. *Producer:* Sam H. Harris. 648 performances.

Sadie Thompson (United Artists 1928). *Screenplay*: Raoul Walsh, C. Gardner Sullivan. *Cast*: Gloria Swanson (Sadie Thompson), Lionel Barrymore (Rev. Davidson), Raoul Walsh, Blanche Frederici, Charles Lane, Florence Midgley. *Director-producer*: Raoul Walsh.

Rain (United Artists 1932). *Screenplay*: Maxwell Anderson. *Cast*: Joan Crawford (Sadie Thompson), Walter Huston (Rev. Davidson), Fred Howard, Ben Hendrick, Jr., William Gargan. *Director*: Lewis Milestone. *Producer*: Joseph M. Schenck.

Miss Sadie Thompson (Columbia 1953). *Screenplay*: Harry Kleiner. *Cast*: Rita Hayworth (Sadie Thompson), José Ferrer (Rev. Davidson), Aldo Ray, Russell Collins, Charles Bronson. *Director*: Curtis Bernhardt. *Producer*: Jerry Wald.

The William Somerset Maugham story of the sultry Sadie Thompson has been a favorite on stage and screen, primarily because it gives an actress the opportunity to play one of juiciest of bad girl roles. At a hotel in Pago Pago, two very different people are staying as guests: the blunt prostitute Sadie on the lam and the Puritanical minister Alfred Davidson come to bring religion to the natives. The two confront each other fervently but Davidson is also sexually attracted to Sadie so after he succumbs to her seducing ways he commits suicide. The sensational aspects of the story made the Broadway production the talk of the town but it was Jeanne Eagels's passionate performance

that was most significant. The first screen version of the story was the 1928 silent movie titled *Sadie Thompson* with Gloria Swanson as the streetwalker and Lionel Barrymore as the minister. Swanson was no newcomer when it came to playing vamps but she was more fascinating in this film than perhaps any other pre-sound vehicle. Barrymore is also very proficient and the film (some of which has been lost) is still striking. The first talkie in 1932 used the play title and starred Joan Crawford and Walter Huston as the rival characters but it was not a box office hit. The sound quality is uneven but the performances are first-rate and the movie is filmed creatively, playing up the claustrophobia and sexual tension between the two characters as they are cooped up together indoors while it rains endlessly outside. The 1953 remake, now called *Miss Sadie Thompson*, was a 3D movie featuring Rita Hayworth as Sadie, this time a nightclub singer so that she can sing some songs, and José Ferrer as Davidson. Both stars are vibrant and the old tale still seems to percolate. The play was turned into the unsuccessful Broadway musical *Sadie Thompson* in 1944 with June Havoc in the title role.

The Rainmaker

October 28, 1954 (Cort Theatre), a play by N. Richard Nash. *Cast*: Geraldine Page (Lizzie Curry), Darren McGavin (Starbuck), Cameron Prud'homme (H. C. Curry), Richard Coogan (File), Joseph Sullivan (Noah Curry), Albert Salmi (Jim Curry), Tom Flatley Reynolds. *Director*: Joseph Anthony. *Producer:* Ethel Linder Reiner. 124 performances.

(Paramount 1956). *Screenplay*: N. Richard Nash. *Cast*: Katharine Hepburn (Lizzie Curry), Burt Lancaster (Starbuck), Wendell Corey (File), Cameron Prud'homme (H. C. Curry), Lloyd Bridges (Noah Curry), Earl Holliman (Jim Curry), Wallace Ford, Yvonne Lime. *Director*: Joseph Anthony. *Producer*: Hal B. Wallis.

(TV 1982). *Teleplay*: N. Richard Nash. *Cast*: Tuesday Weld (Lizzie Curry), Tommy Lee Jones (Starbuck), Lonny Chapman, James Cromwell, William Kent. *Director*: John Frankenheimer. *Producer*: Marcia Govons.

A drought threatens the Curry's Kansas farm and spinster daughter Lizzie Curry is quickly becoming an old maid. To solve both problems comes the dashing con man Bill Starbuck who promises to bring rain for $100 and woos the practical Lizzie with his fancy talk and wild ideas. She doesn't believe his talk or his ability to bring rain but she falls for him anyway and by the time rain does start to fall Lizzie has found enough self confidence that she no longer needs Starbuck. The earthy yet poetic comedy-drama was applauded for its strong cast and engaging characters, particularly Geraldine Page as the strong-willed but tender-hearted Lizzie. Katharine Hepburn brought a streak of New England Puritanism to the role and, as an older spinster than Page, revealed a desperation under her no-nonsense exterior. Her lovely performance is matched by Burt Lancaster's fiery Starbuck, all bluster but with Lancaster's charisma it is appealing bluster. The movie tends to be a bit stagy and not enough use is made of the locations; those exteriors that are there look rather fake. But the supporting cast is excellent and the spirit of the play comes through. A 1982 television production boasted an expert performance by Tommy Lee Jones as Starbuck but much of the rest is mediocre. The play was turned into the Broadway musical *110 in the Shade* in 1963.

A Raisin in the Sun

March 11, 1959 (Ethel Barrymore Theatre), a drama by Lorraine Hansberry. *Cast:* Claudia MacNeill (Lena Younger), Sidney Poitier (Walter Lee Younger), Ruby Dee (Ruth Younger), Diana Sands (Beneatha), Louis Gossett, Ivan Dixon, Glynn Turman, John Fielder, Lonne Elder III, Douglas Turner Ward. *Director:* Lloyd Richards. *Producers:* Philip Rose, David J. Cogan. 530 performances.

(Paman/Doris 1961). *Screenplay:* Lorraine Hansberry. *Cast:* Claudia MacNeill (Lena Younger), Sidney Poitier (Walter Lee Younger), Ruby Dee (Ruth Younger), Diana Sands (Beneatha), Louis Gossett, Ivan Dixon, John Fielder, Stephen Perry, Roy Glenn. *Director:* Daniel Petrie. *Producers:* Philip Rose, David Susskind.

(TV 1989). *Teleplay:* Lorraine Hansberry. *Cast:*

Esther Rolle (Lena Younger), Danny Glover (Walter Lee Younger), Starletta DuPois (Ruth), Kim Yancey, Kimble Joyner, Stephen Henderson, Lou Ferguson, John Fiedler. *Director:* Bill Duke. *Producers:* Toni Livingston, Jaki Brown.

A landmark in American drama, this play about an African American family trying to rise above their Chicago slum existence has remained potent longer than any other stage work on the subject. The domestic drama ran nearly two years and has since been revived hundreds of times in theatres across the country. The faithful 1961 movie retained most of the Broadway cast and it is an impressive ensemble. Many of the players would go on to notable careers but for MacNeill her searing, no-nonsense portrayal of the family matriarch was the crowning achievement of her career. The play was set entirely in the Younger's small tenement apartment but film director Petrie, with his extensive background in helming television dramas, kept the action lively while rarely opening up the play. A 1989 television version, with Esther Rolle as Lena and Danny Glover as Walter Lee, was a studio filming of the play and boasted some estimable performances as well. The play was turned into the musical *Raisin* in 1973.

The Ramblers

September 20, 1926 (Lyric Theatre), a musical comedy by Bert Kalmar, Harry Ruby, Guy Bolton. *Score:* Bert Kalmar, Harry Ruby. *Cast:* Bobby Clark (Professor Cunningham), Paul McCullough (Sparrow), Marie Saxon (Ruth Chester), William E. Browning (Black Pedro), Jack Whiting (Billy Shannon), William Sully, Ruth Tester, Georgia O'Ramey. *Songs:* All Alone Monday; You Smiled at Me; Any Little Tune; Like You Do; You Must—We Won't; California Skies. *Director:* John Harwood. *Choreographer:* Sammy Lee. *Producer:* Philip Goodman. 289 performances.

The Cuckoos (RKO 1930). *Screenplay:* Cyrus Wood. *Score:* Bert Kalmar, Harry Ruby, etc. *Cast:* Bert Wheeler (Sparrow), Robert Woolsey (Prof. Bird), June Clyde (Ruth), Dorothy Lee (Anita), Hugh Trevor (Billy), Mitchell Lewis, Ivan Lebedeff, Jobyna Howland. *Songs:* All Alone Monday; I Love You So Much; Knock Knees; Looking for the Limelight in Your Eyes; Dancing the Devil Away; If I Were a Traveling Salesman. *Director:*

Paul Sloane. *Choreographer:* Pearl Eaton. *Producer:* Louis Sarecky.

The traveling spiritualist-medium Dr. Cunningham and his assistant Sparrow are fakes but it doesn't seem to matter to their customers in hick towns. When the pair stumble onto a film crew making a Western in the desert, they get involved with the unit and hilarious misadventures follow. This musical vehicle for the comic team of Bobby Clark and Paul McCullough was a hit even though the plot and score were unexceptional. But the clowning by Clark and McCullough was farcical brilliance and nothing else seemed to matter. In 1930 the comedy team of Bert Wheeler and Robert Woolsey was starred in the early talkie version, retitled *The Cuckoos.* The team again played phony fortune tellers but in the movie they get involved with gypsies and a kidnapped heroine. Several songs were interpolated into the score but the music was secondary to the slapstick.

ness, An Old Straw Hat, Parade of the Wooden Soldiers. *Director:* Allan Dwan. *Choreographer:* Nick Castle. *Producer:* Darryl F. Zanuck.

Kate Douglas Wiggin's best-selling book, about a ten-year-old orphan who comes to live with her crotchety Aunt Miranda and changes the lives of everyone she meets, was turned into one of the few plays of the era that was popular with children. The Broadway production was a hit but the warm comedy-drama was even more successful on the road. Mary Pickford was the first to play Rebecca on screen and she is ideally cast in the 1921 silent movie. The first talkie version in 1932 featured Marian Nixon as Rebecca and it is more competent that inspired, yet it also was a box office hit. The 1938 remake was turned into a musical vehicle for Shirley Temple whose Rebecca becomes a radio star. The rural charm was gone, as was most of the original plot, but the little moppet entertained Depression-era audiences with zest and the film became one of her biggest hits.

Rebecca of Sunnybrook Farm

October 3, 1910 (Republic Theatre), a play by Kate Douglas Wiggin, Charlotte Thompson. *Cast:* Edith Taliaferro (Rebecca Rowena Randall), Marie L. Day, (Aunt Miranda), Archie Boyd (Jeremiah Cobb), Eliza Glassford (Jane), Ralph Kellerd (Adam Ladd), Lorraine Frost, Ada Deaves, Ernest Truex. *Director:* Lawrence Marston. *Producer:* Klaw & Erlanger. 216 performances.

(Pickford 1917). *Screenplay:* Frances Marion. *Cast:* Mary Pickford (Rebecca Randall), Helen Jerome Eddy (Hannah Randall), Charles Ogle (Cobb), Eugene O'Brien (Adam Ladd), Marjorie Daw, Mayme Kelso. *Director:* Marshall Neilan. *Producer:* Mary Pickford.

(Fox 1932). *Screenplay:* Sonya Levien. *Cast:* Marian Nixon (Rebecca), Alphonse Ethier (Cobb), Ralph Bellamy (Dr. Ladd), Alan Hale, Josephine Crowell. *Director:* Alfred Santell.

(Fox 1938). *Screenplay:* Don Ettlinger, Karl Tunberg. *Score:* Mack Gordon, Harry Revel, etc. *Cast:* Shirley Temple (Rebecca Winstead), Helen Westley (Aunt Miranda), Jack Haley (Orville Smithers), Randolph Scott (Tony Kent), Bill Robinson, Gloria Stuart, Slim Summerville, Phyllis Brooks. *Songs:* Come Get Your Happi-

Red Dust

January 2, 1928 (Daly's Theatre), a play by Wilson Collison. *Cast:* Sydney Shields (Van Tene), Curtis Cooksey (Lucien Fourville), Leonard Mudie (Jacques Guidon), Lenore Meyrick-Sorsby (Maurice Chauvenet), Jerome Collamore, Leo Curley. *Director:* Ira Hards. *Producer:* Hugo W. Romberg. 8 performances.

(MGM 1932). *Screenplay:* John Lee Mahin. *Cast:* Clark Gable (Denny Carson), Jean Harlow (Vantine Jefferson), Gene Raymond (Gary Willis), Mary Astor (Babs Willis), Donald Crisp (Guidon), Tully Marshall, Forrester Harvey. *Director-producer:* Victor Fleming.

Mogambo (MGM 1953). *Screenplay:* John Lee Mahin. *Cast:* Clark Gable (Victor Marswell), Ava Gardner (Honey Bear Kelly), Grace Kelly (Linda Nordley), Donald Sinden (Donald Nordley), Philip Stainton, Eric Pohlmann, Laurence Naismith. *Director:* John Ford. *Producer:* Sam Zimbalist.

Although it only lasted a week on Broadway, this torrid melodrama was turned into two very successful films. On an Indonesian plantation, the fiery peasant Van Tene is always getting into trouble because of her stubbornness and high-minded ways. When she kills the overseer who attempted to whip her, plantation owner Lucien Fourville can no longer overlook the problem of Van Tene. But when a neighbor goes berserk and attempts to kill Fourville, it is Van Tene who saves him, getting his thanks and a marriage proposal as well. The preposterous tale was changed considerably for the 1932 film in which Clark Gable played a plantation owner who gets involved with two women, the funny floozie Jean Harlow and Mary Astor, the prim wife of his engineer. There was a lot of tropic heat and lust implied and the movie was a sensation because of its sex appeal and its stars. Gable also starred in the 1953 remake titled *Mogambo* in which he played a white hunter in Africa who has romantic flings with American chorine Ava Gardner and Grace Kelly as the wife of a British archeologist. The passion was not as steamy in Kenya as it was in Indochina and just as much footage was spent on the jungle animals as on the characters but the movie was still a lively jaunt and did very well at the box office.

Redwood Curtain

March 30, 1993 (Brooks Atkinson Theatre), a play by Lanford Wilson. *Cast*: Jeff Daniels (Lyman), Sung Yun Cho (Geri), Debra Monk (Geneva). *Director*: Marshall W. Mason. *Producers:* Robert Cole, etc. 40 performances.

(TV 1995). *Teleplay*: Ed Namzug. *Cast*: Lea Salonga (Geri Riordan), John Lithgow (Laird Riordan), Jeff Daniels (Lyman Fellers), Debra Monk (Geneva), Catherine Hicks. *Director*: John Korty. *Producers*: Robert Christiansen, Rick Rosenberg.

In the dark, brooding redwood forests of Northern California, the homeless Vietnam vet Lyman is being shadowed by the Amerasian teenager Geri who believes that he could tell her something about her real father, a G.I. now dead. Although her wisecracking Aunt Geneva urges her not pursue it, Geri continues on until Lyman is forced to tell her the truth: the man who adopted her was the real father but he kept it secret

as he slowly drank himself to death. Lanford Wilson's three-actor play had sparkling dialogue and touches of mysticism (Geri is somewhat clairvoyant), but critics rejected the drama and it only ran on Broadway for a few weeks. The 1995 television production opened up the story, turning the dead father (played by John Lithgow) into the central character and showing many scenes in the past. Jeff Daniels and Debra Monk reprised their expert Broadway performances and Lea Salonga as Geri was also very proficient.

Remains to Be Seen

October 3, 1951 (Morosco Theatre), a comedy by Howard Lindsay, Russel Crouse. *Cast*: Howard Lindsay (Benjamin Goodman), Janis Paige (Jody Revere), Warner Anderson (Dr. Gresham), Jackie Cooper (Waldo Walton), Madeleine Morka (Valeska Chauvel), Kirk Brown, Harry Shaw Lowe, Frank Campanella, Paul Lipson. *Director*: Bretaigne Windust. *Producer:* Leland Hayward. 199 performances.

(MGM 1953). *Screenplay*: Sidney Shelton. *Cast*: Louis Calhern (Benjamin Goodman), June Allyson (Jody Revere), John Beal (Dr. Glenson), Van Johnson (Waldo Williams), Angela Lansbury (Valeska Chauvel), Dorothy Dandridge, Sammy White, Barry Kelley, Paul Harvey. *Director*: Don Weis. *Producer:* Arthur Hornblow, Jr.

This thriller had more laughs than chills and more plot twists that logic but it managed a healthy Broadway run on the strength of its cast. When a famous anti-pornography crusader is found dead in his apartment, a doctor cites the cause of death as an overdose of insulin. But the undertaker spots a knife stuck in the man when he comes to collect the body so everyone, including the doctor, the deceased's niece, and the building's janitor, sets out to solve the mystery. It turns out the Japanese butler did it, though he only stuck the knife in the already dead body so that the police would find out who poisoned the man. The all-star cast for the 1953 screen version gave risible performances and seemed to mock the ridiculous plotting going on all around them. It is a slick if stagy adaptation and enjoyable in a modest way.

The Remarkable Mr. Pennypacker

December 30, 1953 (Coronet Theatre), a comedy by Liam O'Brien. *Cast*: Burgess Meredith (Pa Pennypacker), Martha Scott (Ma Pennypacker), Una Merkel (Aunt Jane), Glenn Anders, Michael Wager, Thomas Chalmers, Joel Crothers, William Lanteau. *Director*: Alan Schneider. *Producers:* Robert Whitehead, Roger L. Stevens. 221 performances.

(Fox 1959). *Screenplay*: Walter Reisch. *Cast*: Clifton Webb (Pa Pennypacker), Dorothy McGuire (Ma Pennypacker), Jill St. John, Charles Coburn, Ron Ely, Ray Stricklyn, David Nelson. *Director*: Henry Levin. *Producer*: Charles Brackett.

Horace Pennypacker is a model citizen of the 1890s, a pleasant neighbor, a well-dressed gentleman, and even an advocate of liberal causes such as allowing George Bernard Shaw to come to America to lecture. He is so affable that he has a wife and children in Philadelphia and another spouse and family in nearby Delaware (seventeen kids in all) and is a good father in both households. But when one of his Delaware daughters gets engaged to a minister's son, the truth comes out and Pa Pennypacker cannot understand what all the fuss is about. The comedy ends with his Delaware family deciding they like Pa so much they'll keep him, even as he departs for Philadelphia to see what his other family thinks. The whimsical comedy was given an elaborate production and featured a large, gifted cast on Broadway; even though it ran several months the expensive production lost money. The 1959 movie had a perfect Pa with Clifton Webb but the film was poorly directed and the light ridiculousness of the play became too heavy-handed and pedestrian on the screen.

The Return of Peter Grimm

October 17, 1911 (Belasco Theatre), a play by David Belasco. *Cast*: David Warfield (Peter Grimm), Janet Dunbar (Katrien), John Sainpolis (Frederick), Joseph Brennan (Dr. MacPherson), Percy Helton (William), Thomas Meighan,

Tony Bevan. *Director-producer:* David Belasco. 231 performances.

(Fox 1926). *Screenplay*: Bradley King. *Cast*: Alec B. Francis (Peter Grimm), Janet Gaynor (Catherine), John Roache (Frederick Grimm), Richard Walling, Lionel Belmore, Elizabeth Patterson. *Director*: Victor Schertzinger.

(RKO 1935). *Screenplay*: Frances Edward Faragoh. *Cast*: Lionel Barrymore (Peter Grimm), Helen Mack (Catherine), Edward Ellis, Donald Meek, George P. Breakston. *Director*: George Nichols, Jr., Victor Schertzinger. *Producer*: Kenneth Macgowan.

Before the aged Peter Grimm died, he made a compact with his friend Dr. MacPherson that whomever of them should die first will make an attempt to return to earth and get a message to the other. But when Peter returns no one can see him except Wilhelm, the sickly little son of the housekeeper. Peter realizes that a marriage he arranged for his ward cannot take place because her fiancé is Wilhelm's father. He uses the boy to tell the others the truth, but in doing so Wilhelm dies and Peter accompanies him to the afterlife. As sentimental as it was mysterious, the drama was very moving and the fine performances, particularly character actor favorite David Warfield as Peter, were memorable. The play, written, directed, and produced by David Belasco, was a success on Broadway, on the road, and back in New York in 1921, and Warfield devoted years to playing the title role. The 1926 silent screen version is a faithful adaptation but is more melodramatic than necessary. Alec B. Francis played Peter and Janet Gaynor shone as the ward. The acting was uneven in the 1935 talkie with Lionel Barrymore as Peter and a supporting cast that included Helen Mack and Donald Meek. The director seemed unsure how to film the fantasy-melodrama and some sections are played for comedy, others for poignancy.

Reunion in Vienna

November 16, 1931 (Martin Beck Theatre), a comedy by Robert Sherwood. *Cast*: Alfred Lunt (Rudolf), Lynn Fontanne (Elena Krug), Minor Watson (Anton), Cynthia Townsend, Virginia

Chauvenet, Edward Fielding, Lloyd Nolan. *Director*: Worthington Miner. *Producer:* Theatre Guild. 264 performances.

(MGM 1933). *Screenplay*: Ernest Vajda, Claudine West. *Cast*: John Barrymore (Rudolf), Diana Wynyard (Elena), Frank Morgan (Anton), Henry Travers, May Robson, Eduardo Ciannelli, Una Merkel. *Director*: Sidney Franklin.

Although Anton and Elena Krug are happily married, he knows that she cannot get the memory of her lost love Prince Rudolf out of her head. Since the collapse of the Austro-Hungarian Empire, Rudolf is in exile and forced to drive a taxi cab. But a reunion of old aristocratic friends is to take place in Vienna and Anton urges Elena to go and see Rudolf again, hoping the reality of him will break the spell. She is reunited with the prince and the old flame is enkindled for a while, then Elena willingly returns to Anton. The sparkling dialogue and the Lunts's mastery of language and nuance made this comedy one of their most cherished successes. Frank Morgan played Anton in the 1933 film and he captured the high style of the piece, as did John Barrymore who was in top form as Rudolf. But Diana Wynyard disappoints and the unimaginative adaptation and direction make the talky movie drag along, offering only limited enjoyment.

Rich and Famous see *Old Acquaintance*

Rio Rita

February 2, 1927 (Ziegfeld Theatre), an operetta by Guy Bolton, Fred Thompson. *Score:* Harry Tierney, Joseph McCarthy. *Cast:* Ethelind Terry (Rio Rita), J. Harold Murray (Jim), Bert Wheeler (Chick Bean), Robert Woolsey (Ed Lovett), Ada May (Dolly), Vincent Serrano, Walter Petrie. *Songs:* Rio Rita; The Ranger's Song; If You're in Love You'll Waltz; The Kinkajou; Following the Sun Around. *Director:* John Harwood. *Choreographers:* Sammy Lee, Albertina Rasch. *Producer:* Florenz Ziegfeld. 494 performances.

(RKO 1929). *Screenplay:* Russell Mack, Luther Reed. *Score:* Harry Tierney, Joseph McCarthy.

Cast: Bebe Daniels (Rita Ferguson), John Boles (Jim), Bert Wheeler (Chick Bean), Robert Woolsey (Ed Lovett), Don Alvarado, Eva Rosita, George Renavent. *Songs:* Rio Rita; The Ranger's Song; If You're in Love You'll Waltz; River Song; The Kinkajou; You're Always in My Arms; Poor Fool. *Director:* Luther Reed. *Choreographer:* Pearl Eaton. *Producer:* William LeBaron.

(MGM 1942). *Screenplay:* Richard Connell, Gladys Lehman. *Score:* Harry Tierney, Joseph McCarthy, etc. *Cast:* Bud Abbott (Doc), Lou Costello (Wishy Dunn), Kathryn Grayson (Rita Winslow), John Carroll (Ricardo Montera), Patricia Dane, Tom Conway, Barry Nelson. *Songs:* Rio Rita; The Ranger's Song; Long Before You Came Along; Brazilian Dance. *Director:* S. Sylvan Simon. *Producer:* Pandro S. Berman.

Trying to cash in on the popularity of *The Desert Song*, this operetta was set in the American and Mexican desert bordering the Rio Grande and told the story of the notorious bank robber Kinkajou who is terrorizing the nearby Texas towns. The lovers were a Texas Ranger, who is hunting the Kinkajou, and the Mexican senorita Rita, and the villain turned out to be a Mexican general in disguise. The robust operetta was a major stage hit and the first Broadway musical to be filmed as a talkie. Bert Woolsey and Robert Wheeler, the featured comics on stage, were retained for the film, thereby inaugurating their long screen career together. While the early musical movie was rather stagy and clumsy, it pleased when the comics took over or when Bebe Daniels and John Boles sang the lovely duets. The 1942 remake dropped all but two of the stage songs and turned the operetta into a comic vehicle for Abbott and Costello.

Rip Van Winkle

September 3, 1866 (Olympic Theatre), a play by Dion Boucicault. *Cast:* Joseph Jefferson (Rip Van Winkle), Mrs. Saunders (Gretchen), Marie Le Brun (Meenie). 35 performances.

(B. A. Rolfe 1914). *Screenplay:* Frederick Story. *Cast*: Thomas Jefferson (Rip Van Winkle), Clarette Clare (Gretchen), Daisy Robinson (Meenie), Harry Blakemore, Wallace Scott. *Producer*: Edwin Middleton.

(Climax 1914). *Screenplay*: Fred Storey. *Cast*: Fred

Storey (Rip Van Winkle), Ella Brandon (Gretchen), Martin Stuart, Maitland Stapley. *Director*: Stuart Kinder.

(Lascelle 1921). *Screenplay*: Agnes Parsons. *Cast*: Thomas Jefferson (Rip Van Winkle), Milla Davenport (Gretchen), Daisy Robinson (Meenie), Pietro Sosso. *Director-producer*: Ward Lascelle.

Washington Irving's timeless tale, about the ne'er-do-well tippler who falls asleep in the Catskill Mountains for years then returns home where no one recognizes him, became one of the most popular theatre pieces of the 19th century and would remain on the boards for decades of the next century as well. Stage adaptations of the story go back to before the Civil War but it was an 1866 version written for the celebrated character actor Joseph Jefferson that was the most successful; Jefferson played Rip Van Winkle on and off for over fifty years and reprised the role on film in 1903 and 1914. In all, there were over ten movie versions of the tale, most of them silent and many with altered titles such as *In the Haunts of Rip Van Winkle* or *Rip Van Winkle Badly Ripped*. Among the notable screen versions was one in 1921 starring Jefferson's son, Thomas Jefferson, and animated adaptations in 1934 and 1978.

The Ritz

January 20, 1975 (Longacre Theatre), a farce by Terrence McNally. *Cast*: Jack Weston (Gaetano Proclo), Rita Moreno (Googie Gomez), Stephen Collins (Michael Brick), Jerry Stiller (Carmine Vespucci), F. Murray Abraham (Chris), Paul B. Price, Ruth Jaroslow. *Director*: Robert Drivas. *Producer:* Adela Holzer. 400 performances.

(Warner 1976). *Screenplay*: Terrence McNally. *Cast*: Jack Weston (Gaetano Proclo), Rita Moreno (Googie Gomez), Treat Williams (Michael Brick), Jerry Stiller (Carmine Vespucci), F. Murray Abraham (Chris), Paul B. Price, Kaye Ballard. *Director*: Richard Lester. *Producer*: Denis O'Dell.

When Gaetano Proclo is on the run from his gangster brother-in-law, he takes refuge in a Manhattan steam bath, not realizing it caters exclusively to homosexuals. Proclo is pursued by various gay amours, a

policeman in disguise, and even the Hispanic singer Googie Gomez who thinks he is a theatrical producer. Except for its up-to-date locale, the play was reminiscent of traditional door-slamming farces of the past. The characters were outrageous, the plotting complex and tangled, and the dialogue incongruously fun. The Broadway production ran over a year and most of the cast and creative talents involved appeared in the uproarious 1976 movie that was directed at slapstick speed. The play enjoyed a few revivals until the AIDS epidemic in the 1980s and the sexual abandon of the gay bath houses was over. A British television series based on the farce appeared briefly in 1987.

The River Niger

March 27, 1973 (Brooks Atkinson Theatre), a drama by Joseph A. Walker. *Cast*: Douglas Turner Ward (Johnny Williams), Les Roberts (Jeff), Frances Foster (Grandma Wilhelmina), Graham Brown (Dr. Dudley Stanton), Roxie Roker, Neville Richen, Charles Weldon. *Director*: Douglas Turner Ward. *Producer:* Negro Ensemble Company. 280 performances. Tony Award.

(Asanti 1976). *Teleplay*: Joseph A. Walker. *Cast*: James Earl Jones (Johnny Williams), Glynn Turman (Jeff), Cecily Tyson (Mattie), Louis Gossett, Jr., Jonelle Allen, Roger E. Mosley. *Director*: Krishna Shah. *Producers*: Sidney Beckermann, Isaac L. Jones.

The African American house painter Johnny Williams is a poet at heart and the pride of his life is his son Jeff who is a lieutenant in the Air Force. But when Jeff quits the military and gets sucked back into his old black militant gang, Johnny goes on a bender. A cop is murdered and Jeff is shot when the gang attempts to blow up a police station. Johnny finishes his poem then takes the blame for the cop killing so that his son can live. The passionate, poetic drama was a success Off Broadway and then transferred to Broadway for a healthy run. The 1976 film featured some of the finest African American actors of the day and they are all very effective in the taut, well-directed movie that opened up the action but still took time to develop the characters.

Roberta

November 18, 1933 (New Amsterdam Theatre), a musical comedy by Otto Harbach. *Score:* Jerome Kern, Otto Harbach. *Cast:* Bob Hope (Huckleberry Haines), Tamara (Stephanie), Lyda Roberti (Clementina Scharwenka), Fay Templeton (Aunt Minnie), George Murphy, Sydney Greenstreet, Ray Middleton, Fred MacMurray. *Songs:* Smoke Gets in Your Eyes; Yesterdays; The Touch of Your Hand; Let's Begin; I'll Be Hard to Handle; You're Devastating; Something Had to Happen. *Director:* Hassard Short. *Choreographer:* José Limon. *Producer:* Max Gordon. 295 performances.

(RKO 1935). *Screenplay:* Jane Murfin, Stan Mintz, Glen Tryon, Allan Scott. *Score:* Jerome Kern, Otto Harbach, Dorothy Fields. *Cast:* Fred Astaire (Huckleberry Haines), Irene Dunne (Stephanie), Ginger Rogers (Lizzie Gatz), Randolph Scott (John Kent), Helen Westley (Aunt Minnie), Victor Varconi, Lucille Ball. *Songs:* Smoke Gets in Your Eyes; Yesterdays; Lovely to Look At; I Won't Dance; Let's Begin; I'll Be Hard to Handle. *Director:* William A. Seiter. *Choreographers:* Hermes Pan, Fred Astaire. *Producer:* Pandro S. Berman.

Lovely to Look At (MGM 1952). *Screenplay:* George Wells, Harry Ruby. *Score:* Jerome Kern, Otto Harbach, Dorothy Fields. *Cast:* Kathryn Grayson (Stephanie), Howard Keel (Tony Naylor), Red Skelton (Al Marsh), Marge Champion (Clarisse), Gower Champion (Jerry Ralby), Zsa Zsa Gabor, Kurt Kasznar. *Songs:* Smoke Gets in Your Eyes; Lovely to Look At; I Won't Dance; I'll Be Hard to Handle; You're Devastating; The Touch of Your Hand. *Directors:* Mervyn LeRoy, Vincente Minnelli. *Choreographer:* Hermes Pan. *Producer:* Jack Cummings.

Here is a case of a hit song saving a show. The Jerome Kern musical was generally criticized for its contrived plot and, despite a glowing score, the musical floundered at the box office. Then the show's ballad "Smoke Get in Your Eyes" was played on the radio and was so popular that audiences kept the musical on the boards for a profitable run. When American footballer inherits his aunt's Paris dress shop, he and his pals head for France where he falls for the shop assistant who is really a Russian princess in disguise. Bob Hope was quite entertaining as the sidekick Huckleberry Haines and the role was built up for the first movie version that featured Fred Astaire in the part. The plot was slightly altered for the screen but it wasn't much of an improvement over the stage libretto. Yet there is much to enjoy in *Roberta*: Astaire and Ginger Rogers comically squabbling together in song and dance, Irene Dunne's smooth rendition of the ballads, and the lovely Kern songs, some from the stage and others written for the screen. The most popular of these new entries was "Lovely to Look At" which served as the title for the 1952 remake. Lacking the charm of the earlier film, this bright and polished version also changed the plot but it still was the weak link in the piece. More Kern songs were added and many of them were given expert renditions by the capable cast. Anne Miller's "I'll Be Hard to Handle" was particularly fine and Marge and Gower Champion were at their best in "I Won't Dance." Both movie versions were popular; not bad for coming from a Broadway show that barely made it. A greatly abridged television version in 1958 allowed Hope to reprise his stage performance on the small screen. Anna Maria Alberghetti, Howard Keel, and Janis Paige were also featured in the broadcast.

Romance

February 10, 1913 (Maxine Elliott Theatre), a play by Edward Sheldon. *Cast:* Doris Keane (Margherita Cavallini), William Courtenay (Bishop Armstrong), George Le Soir (Harry Putnam), A. E. Anson (Cornelius Van Tuyl), Gladys Wynne (Susan Van Tuyl), William Raymond, Louise Seymour, Paul Gordon, Grace Henderson. 160 performances.

(Griffith 1920). *Screenplay:* Wells Hastings. *Cast:* Doris Keane (Madame Cavallini), Basil Sydney (Armstrong), Norman Trevor (Cornelius Van Tuyl), Betty Rose Clarke (Susan Van Tuyl), Gilda Varesi, A. J. Herbert, Amelia Summerville, John Davidson. *Director:* Chester Withey. *Producer:* D. W. Griffith.

(MGM 1930). *Screenplay:* Edwin Justus Mayer, Bess Meredyth. *Cast:* Greta Garbo (Rita Cavallini), Gavin Gordon (Tom Armstrong), Lewis Stone (Cornelius Van Tuyl), Florence Lake (Susan Van Tuyl), Elliott Nugent, Clara Blandick, Henry Armetta. *Director-producer:* Clarence Brown.

One of the most popular stage love stories of the 1910s, this melodrama went back in time to illustrate the long-lasting effects of true love. When Bishop Armstrong is told by his grandson that he is in love with an artist, the old man tells the youth about his past romance with the opera diva Margherita Cavallini. As a young cleric he fell in love with her and was willing to throw over his career to be with her. But Margherita realized the union would ruin him so she walked out on him. After his grandson departs, the bishop reads in the newspaper of the death of Margherita and he is left with his memories, some faded violets, and her handkerchief. Doris Keane was a sensation as Margherita (she played nothing else for many years) and the play was popular in New York, on the road, and in revivals for much of the decade. Keane recreated her performance in the 1920 silent film and Basil Sydney was the bishop. A 1930 talkie starred Greta Garbo and although it is a clumsily-made melodrama, Gavin Gordon is weak as Armstrong, and Garbo is not at her best, the story is still affecting. A Broadway musical version of the play, titled *My Romance*, failed in 1948 despite a fine score by Sigmund Romberg.

Romantic Comedy

November 8, 1979 (Ethel Barrymore Theatre), a comedy by Bernard Slade. *Cast*: Anthony Perkins (Jason Carmichael), Mia Farrow (Phoebe Craddock), Greg Mullavey (Leo Janowitz), Holly Palance, Deborah May, Carole Cook. *Director*: Joseph Hardy. *Producer*: Morton Gottlieb. 396 performances.

(MGM-UA 1983). *Screenplay*: Bernard Slade. *Cast*: Dudley Moore (Jason Carmichael), Mary Steenburgen (Phoebe Craddock), Ron Leibman (Leo), Frances Sternhagen, Janet Eilber, Robyn Douglass. *Director*: Arthur Hiller. *Producers*: Morton Gottlieb, Walter Mirisch.

On the day that debonair playwright Jason Carmichael is to get married, he meets the awkward young writer Phoebe Craddock who is to collaborate with him. Over the years the twosome write some hits and flops, Jason's marriage falls apart, and Phoebe throws over her fiancé to finally wed Jason. This slick, contrived, and unconvincing

comedy was mostly panned by the critics but star appearances by Anthony Perkins (who had a brief nude scene) and Mia Farrow as the odd lovers allowed the play to run a year. The 1983 movie boasted amusing performances by its stars, Dudley Moore and Mary Steenburgen, but they could not save the faithful but tedious film version and it was a box office failure. The admirable supporting cast is wasted on undeveloped characters and the plodding direction results in a piece that is neither romantic nor comic.

Room Service

May 19, 1937 (Cort Theatre), a farce by John Murray, Allen Boretz. *Cast*: Sam Levene (Gordon Miller), Eddie Albert (Leo Davis), Philip Loeb (Harry Binion), Cliff Dunstan (Joseph Gribble), Teddy Hart, Margaret Mullen, Betty Field, Donald MacBride. *Director-producer*: George Abbott. 500 performances.

(RKO 1938). *Screenplay*: Morrie Ryskind. *Cast*: Groucho Marx (Gordon Miller), Frank Albertson (Leo Davis), Chico Marx (Harry Binion), Lucille Ball, Ann Miller, Harpo Marx, Donald MacBride, Cliff Dunstan, Philip Loeb. *Director*: William A. Seiter. *Producer*: George Abbott.

Step Lively (RKO 1944). *Screenplay*: Warren Duff, Peter Milne. *Score:* Jule Styne, Sammy Cahn. *Cast*: Frank Sinatra (Glen Russell), George Murphy (Gordon Miller), Adolphe Menjou (Wagner), Gloria DeHaven, Eugene Pallette, Walter Slezak, Ann Jeffries, Grant Mitchell. *Songs:* Some Other Time; Come Out, Come Out, Wherever You Are; As Long As There's Music; And Then You Kissed Me. *Director*: Tim Whalen. Choreographer: Ernst Matray. *Producer*: Robert Fellows.

Small-time theatrical producer Gordon Miller is short on cash and cannot open his play on Broadway. In fact, funds are so low he cannot even pay the hotel bill where the company is lodged. So he has the playwright pretend to be deathly ill so that the management won't kick them all out and even goes so far as to announce the playwright's death and funeral to stall for time. One of the most contrived yet delightful of all American farces, the comedy maintains its energy with a cast full of hilarious characters. Sam Levene, as the producer, and Eddie Albert, as the playwright, headed the Broadway company which ran a year and a half, followed by many regional productions. The 1938 movie was rewritten to serve as a vehicle for the Marx Brothers and it is sometimes an uncomfortable fit, the famous clowns having to play characters somewhat removed from their vaudeville creations. Running at a furious pace with rapid one-liners hammered out by the cast, the movie is more noisy than funny and the supporting cast is very uneven. It is one of the few Marx Brothers musicals that does not stop for songs, yet the 1944 remake was a musical called *Step Lively* with a score by Jule Styne and Sammy Cahn. The songs didn't exactly help the pace but when sung by Frank Sinatra, then at the peak of his popularity, audiences didn't complain. Sinatra played the playwright, George Murphy was the producer, and they were surrounded by a first-class cast of character actors. The property may have changed from a frantic farce to a romantic musical comedy but it was enjoyable all the same.

Rosalie

January 10, 1928 (New Amsterdam Theatre), a musical comedy by William Anthony McGuire, Guy Bolton. *Score:* George and Ira Gershwin, Sigmund Romberg, P. G. Wodehouse. *Cast:* Marilyn Miller (Rosalie), Jack Donahue (Bill Delroy), Frank Morgan (King Cyril), Margaret Dale (Queen), Bobbe Arnst, Oliver McLennan. *Songs:* How Long Has This Been Going On?; Say So!; West Point Song; Oh, Gee! Oh, Joy!; Ev'rybody Knows I Love Somebody. *Director:* William Anthony McGuire. *Choreographers:* Seymour Felix, Michel Fokine. *Producer:* Florenz Ziegfeld. 335 performances.

(MGM 1937). *Screenplay:* William Anthony McGuire. *Score:* Cole Porter. *Cast:* Eleanor Powell (Rosalie), Nelson Eddy (Dick Thorpe), Frank Morgan (King Fredrick), Ray Bolger (Bill Delroy), Ilona Massey (Countess Brenda), Billy Gilbert, Edna May Oliver, Reginald Owen, George Zucco, William Demarest. *Songs:* In the Still of the Night; Rosalie; Who Knows?; I've a Strange New Rhythm in My Heart; Spring Love Is in The Air. *Director:* W. S. Van Dyke. *Choreographer:* Albertina Rasch. *Producer:* William Anthony McGuire.

No other Marilyn Miller vehicle had such a contrived plot as this musical that ran on the strength of its effervescent star. Princess Rosalie of Romanza loves a West Point cadet but since he is a commoner they cannot wed until her father renounces the throne and the lovers are equals. Producer Ziegfeld had some of the top songwriters of the day contribute to the score but all that mattered was Miller singing and dancing her way into the hearts of Broadway audiences. The screen version featured tap dancer Eleanor Powell as Rosalie and she was backed by such an expensive, ornate, overpopulated production that it's a wonder she came off looking as good as she did. The plot got more ridiculous in the movie, the princess now attending an American college and falling for student Nelson Eddy who returns with Rosalie to her homeland where he puts down a revolution and becomes king. The stage score was pretty much discarded by Hollywood but some of the new numbers were expert, especially Cole Porter's "In the Still of the Night."

Rose-Marie

September 2, 1924 (Imperial Theatre), an operetta by Otto Harbach, Oscar Hammerstein. *Score:* Rudolf Friml, Herbert Stothart, Otto Harbach, Oscar Hammerstein. *Cast:* Mary Ellis (Rose-Marie La Flamme), Dennis King (Jim Kenyon), William Kent (Hard-Boiled Herman), Dorothy Mackaye (Lady Jane), Eduardo Ciannelli (Sgt. Malone), Pearl Regay (Wanda), Arthur Deagon. *Songs:* Indian Love Call; The Mounties; Rose-Marie; Totem Tom-Tom; The Door of Her Dreams; Why Shouldn't We? *Director:* Paul Dickey. *Choreographer:* David Bennett. *Producer:* Arthur Hammerstein. 557 performances.

Rose Marie (MGM 1936). *Screenplay:* Frances Goodrich, Albert Hackett, Alice Duer Miller. *Score:* Rudolf Friml, Herbert Stothart, Otto Harbach, Oscar Hammerstein, etc. *Cast:* Jeanette MacDonald (Marie de Flor), Nelson Eddy (Sgt. Bruce), Reginald Owen (Myerson), James Stewart (John Flower), Allan Jones, Una O'Connor, Alan Mowbray, David Niven, Herman Bing, George Regas, Gilda Gray. *Songs:* Indian Love Call; The Mounties; Rose-Marie; Diana; Totem Tom-Tom; Some of These Days; Pardon Me, Madame. *Director:* W. S. Van Dyke. *Choreographer:* Chester Hale. *Producer:* Hunt Stromberg.

Rose Marie (MGM 1954). *Screenplay:* Ronald Millar, George Froeschel. *Score:* Rudolf Friml, Herbert

Stothart, Otto Harbach, Oscar Hammerstein, Paul Francis Webster, etc. *Cast:* Ann Blyth (Rose Marie Lemaitre), Howard Keel (Capt. Mike Malone), Fernando Lamas (James Severn Duval), Bert Lahr (Barney McCorkle), Marjorie Main, Ray Collins. *Songs:* Indian Love Call; The Mounties; Rose-Marie; I'm a Mountie Who Never Got His Man; Totem Tom-Tom; The Right Place for a Girl; Free to Be Free. *Director-producer:* Mervyn LeRoy. *Choreographer:* Busby Berkeley.

On Broadway, on the road, and in Europe, this operetta was the most successful musical of the decade and retained its popularity for years. The plot is rather intricate, particularly for an operetta, and often the songs are tied closely to the story. In the Canadian Rockies, singer Rose-Marie loves a fur trapper who is unjustly accused of murder. The various subplots interweave until the true villain is unmasked and the loves are united to the strains of the echoing "Indian Love Call." Arguably Rudolf Friml's greatest score, it was also a triumph for librettist-lyricists Oscar Hammerstein and Otto Harbach who made great strides toward a musical play. The first movie version, featuring Jeanette MacDonald and Nelson Eddy, simplified the story and eliminated most of the stage's secondary characters. Rose Marie (Hollywood eliminated the hyphen) was now an opera singer who goes into the wilds to help her brother, an escaped convict who actually is a murderer. Eddy played the mounted policeman who is searching for the escapee and falls in love with Rose Marie during the pursuit. With MacDonald and Eddy currently the screen's favorite singing duo, the movie was a major hit and it still pleases. The 1954 film version boasted a colorful widescreen depiction of the Rockies but little else measured up to the earlier movie. The plot was a mixture of the stage libretto and the 1936 screenplay without being as cohesive as either. But there is one bonus to be found in this later version: Bert Lahr as a comic policeman singing "The Mountie Who Never Got His Man."

The Rose of the Rancho

November 27, 1906 (Belasco Theatre), a play by David Belasco, Richard Walton Tully. *Cast:*

Frances Starr (Juanita), Charles Richman (Kearney), John W. Cope (Kinkaid), A. Hamilton Revelle, Frank Losee, William Elliott. *Director-producer:* David Belasco. 327 performances.

(Lasky 1914). *Screenplay:* Cecil B. DeMille. *Cast:* Bessie Barriscale (Juanita), Jack W. Johnston (Kearney), Dick La Reno (Kincaid), Monroe Salisbury, James Neill, Sydney Deane. *Director-producer:* Cecil B. DeMille.

(Paramount 1936). *Screenplay:* Charles Brackett, etc. *Score:* Ralph Rainger, Leo Robin. *Cast:* Gladys Swarthout (Rosita), John Boles (Kearney), Charles Bickford (Kincaid), Willie Howard, Herb Williams, Grace Bradley, H. B. Warner. *Songs:* If I Should Lose You; Thunder Over the Prairie; Little Rose of the Rancho; Got a Girl in Cal-i-for-ni-ay; Where Is My Love. *Director:* Marion Gering. *Producer:* William LeBaron.

David Belasco's exciting melodrama set in Spanish California was overflowing with scenery, costumes, intrigue, and romance, though the plot was unoriginal and the characters were familiar types. The young American Kearney is sent by the government to investigate the seizure of Spanish territory and falls for beautiful Juanita of an old Spanish family. The villainous Kinkaid tries to pin the raids on Kearney but in the end he is cleared and Juanita is his. The popular Frances Starr was one of the attractions of the Broadway production, which ran a year and then toured with success. A silent screen version in 1914 featured Bessie Barriscale as Juanita and opera singer Gladys Swarthout played the heroine, now called Rosita, in the 1936 musical remake. The plot was livened up a bit for the musical, Rosita also being the person who is leading the raids. John Boles discovers her identity and falls in love despite the doings of the villain played by Charles Bickford. It is an odd movie as it moves from operetta to adventure to low comedy, best displayed by the antics of Willie Howard as a Jewish cowboy. Swarthout only made a few film musicals but judging by her sparkling presence in this one she ought to have done more.

The Rose Tattoo

February 3, 1951 (Martin Beck Theatre), a play by Tennessee Williams. *Cast:* Maureen Stapleton

(Serafina Rosa), Eli Wallach (Alvaro), Phyllis Love (Rosa), Don Murray (Jack Hunter), Rossana San Marco, Nancy Franklin, Robert Carricart, Daisy Belmore. *Director:* Daniel Mann. *Producer:* Cheryl Crawford. 306 performances. Tony Award.

(Paramount 1955). *Screenplay:* Hal Kanter, Tennessee Williams. *Cast:* Anna Magnani (Serafina Rosa), Burt Lancaster (Alvaro), Maria Pavan (Rosa), Ben Cooper (Jack Hunter), Virginia Grey, Jo Van Fleet. *Director:* Daniel Mann. *Producer:* Hal B. Wallis.

The Sicilian American seamstress Serafina Rosa keeps the memory of her dead truck-driver husband alive, even though he was less than faithful to her in life. But when another truck driver, the warm and optimistic Alvaro Mangiacavallo, enters her life she finally submits to true happiness and even encourages her daughter to go to the young sailor she loves. Tennessee Williams wrote the complex role of Serafina with Anna Magnani in mind but she didn't wish to play it on stage so Maureen Stapleton was given one of her best parts and gave an unforgettable performance. Eli Wallach was also striking as Alvaro and the Broadway production glowed with passion and optimism, a rarity for a Williams work. Magnani did play Serafina in the 1955 movie and it was a more fiery performance, almost too big for the screen. But the overpowering portrayal was impressive enough that Magnani won an Oscar. Burt Lancaster shone as Alvara and the supporting cast and production values were first rate. The play was opened up nicely on the screen and the stunning camera work captured the Gulf Coast atmosphere effectively.

The Round Up

August 26, 1907 (New Amsterdam Theatre), a drama by Edmund Day. *Cast:* Wright Kramer (Dick Lane), Orme Caldara (Jack Payson), Maclyn Arbuckle (Sheriff Slim Hoover), Florence Rockwell (Echo Allen), Joseph Lothian, Elmer Grandin, H. S. Northrup. *Directors:* Joseph Brooks, etc. *Producer:* Klaw & Erlanger. 155 performances.

The Round-Up (Famous Players 1920). *Screenplay:* Tom Forman. *Cast:* Irving Cummings (Dick Lane), Roscoe Arbuckle (Slim Hoover), Mabel Julienne (Echo Allen), Tom Forman, Jean Acker. *Director:* George Melford.

The Roundup (Paramount 1941). *Screenplay:* Edmund Day. *Cast:* Richard Dix (Steve), Don Wilson (Slim), Patricia Morison (Janet), Preston Foster, Ruth Donnelly, Betty Brewer. *Director:* Lesley Selander. *Producers:* Joseph W. Engel, Harry Sherman.

When Jack Payson stole his girl from him and married her, Dick Lane heads out West and works as a mining engineer in dangerous territory to forget his past. But Payson feels guilty so he goes to the desert looking for his friend to ask forgiveness. The two men barely meet before Apaches raid the encampment and the old pals fight side by side together, forgetting past grievances. Lane is killed in the attack and Payson returns home with a less-guilty conscience. As thrilling as the melodrama was, it was the comic relief supplied by rotund comic actor Maclyn Arbuckle as Sheriff Slim Hoover that was most fondly remembered. Another Arbuckle, Rosoe "Fatty" Arbuckle, played Slim in the 1920 silent film and using location shooting it made for an action-packed Western. The 1941 remake was also a standard Western with a bit of romance thrown in. The woman in question was never seen in the play but there was plenty of her to give relief from the action scenes in this version.

Roxie Hart see Chicago

The Royal Family

December 28, 1927 (Selwyn Theatre), a comedy by George S. Kaufman, Edna Ferber. *Cast:* Ann Andrews (Julie Cavendish), Haidee Wright (Fanny Cavendish), Otto Kruger (Tony), Jefferson De Angelis (Oscar Wolfe), Orlando Daly, Sylvia Field, Catherine Calhoun-Doucet, Roger Pryor, Joseph King. *Director:* David Burton. *Producer:* Jed Harris. 343 performances.

The Royal Family of Broadway (Paramount 1930). *Screenplay:* Herman Mankiewicz, Gertrude Purcell. *Cast:* Ina Claire (Julie Cavendish), Fredric March (Tony Cavendish), Henrietta Crosman (Fanny Cavendish), Arnold Korff (Oscar Wolfe), Mary Brien, Frank Conroy, Charles Starrett. *Director:* George Cukor, Cyril Gardner.

The Cavendish family of theatre actors has more than its fair share of eccentrics and colorful personalities. Fanny Cavendish, the grand dame of the brood, is getting too old to perform on stage but she will not admit it. Her daughter Julie is toying with giving up the profession and marrying a banker, while Fanny's son Tony is a movie star who is always in the papers because of one scandal or another. Other relatives and hangers-on populate the Cavendish household while the producer Oscar Wolfe tries to keep the insane family on track. The comedy satirized the theatre profession in general and the Drew-Barrymore family specifically. Audiences enjoyed the in-jokes and the vivacious cast for a year but over time the play fell out of favor and not until a glorious Broadway revival in 1976 did the comedy become popular again in regional theatres. The 1930 film, titled *The Royal Family of Broadway* so it would not be mistaken as a period historical piece, is an early talkie with primitive production values but the cast is lively and the dialogue is still piquant. Newcomer Fredric March is particularly fun as the flamboyant Tony and it is intriguing to see the theatre greats Ina Claire and Henrietta Crosman in one of their rare film appearances. A television version in 1954 starred a much older March with Claudette Colbert and Helen Hayes in the cast.

The Royal Family of Broadway see The Royal Family

The Runner Stumbles

May 18, 1976 (Little Theatre), a play by Milan Stitt. *Cast*: Stephen Joyce (Fr. Rivard), Nancy Donohue (Sister Rita), Sloane Shelton (Mrs. Shandig), Morrie Piersol, Joseph Mathewson, Craig Richard Nelson, James Noble. *Director*: Austin Pendleton. *Producers:* Wayne Adams, Willard Morgan. 191 performances.

(Fox 1979). *Screenplay*: Milan Stitt. *Cast*: Dick Van Dyke (Fr. Rivard), Kathleen Quinlan (Sister Rita), Maureen Stapleton (Mrs. Shandig), Ray

Bolger, Tammy Grimes, Beau Bridges, John Procaccino. *Director*: Stanley Kramer. *Producers*: Melvin Simon, Mario Iscovich.

In 1911, the Michigan priest Fr. Rivard is brought to trial for murdering the nun Sister Rita. But in flashback scenes we see that the radical priest and the free-thinking nun had fallen in love and that she was killed by the suspicious housekeeper who feared a scandal. Although based on a real case, the melodrama was far from convincing with it trite plotting and one-dimensional characters. But the play, first seen in regional theatre and Off Broadway, managed a modest run on Broadway and was later produced by many schools and community theatre groups. While the play was sometimes made palatable by commendable actors, the 1979 movie was mostly panned for the stiff and hollow performances by some usually gifted stars. The ponderous direction and pretentious approach to the material didn't help the situation much.

Sabrina see Sabrina Fair

Sabrina Fair

November 11, 1953 (National Theatre), a play by Samuel Taylor. *Cast*: Margaret Sullivan (Sabrina), Joseph Cotten (Linus Larrabee, Jr.), Scott McKay (David Larrabee), Russell Collins (Fairchild), John Cromwell, Cathleen Nesbitt, Luella Gear. *Director*: H. C. Potter. *Producer*: Playwrights' Company. 318 performances.

Sabrina (Paramount 1954). *Screenplay*: Billy Wilder, Samuel Taylor, Ernest Lehman. *Cast*: Audrey Hepburn (Sabrina), Humphrey Bogart (Linus Larrabee), William Holden (David Larrabee), John Williams (Fairchild), Walter Hampden, Martha Hyer, Francis X. Bushman. *Director-producer*: Billy Wilder.

Sabrina (Paramount 1995). *Screenplay*: Barbara Benedek, David Rayfiel. *Cast*: Julia Ormond (Sabrina), Harrison Ford (Linus Larrabee), Greg Kinnear (David Larrabee), John Wood (Fairchild), Nancy Marchand, Richard Crenna, Angie Dickinson, Lauren Holly, Dana Ivey. *Director*: Sydney Pollack. *Producers*: Scott Rudin, Sydney Pollack.

The chauffeur's daughter Sabrina Fairchild returns from Paris and is reunited with the two men whom she has known since childhood: the reckless, fun-loving David Larrabee and his staid, businessman brother Linus. David pursues her but it is Linus she prefers and after time he loosens up enough to admit that he lovers her too. The breezy romantic comedy was intelligently written and acted with charm by stars Margaret Sullivan and Joseph Cotten, running nearly a year on Broadway. The 1954 screen version, retitled *Sabrina*, also featured stars but not necessarily in roles audiences were used to seeing them in. Audrey Hepburn was a captivating Sabrina and true to type but good guy William Holden played the playboy cad David while anti-hero rebel Humphrey Bogart was the conventional, nerdy even, Linus. Yet all three give nimble performances and the well-directed comedy glows with delight. The 1995 remake did not seem to trust its stars because the movie is padded with pretty Paris locations, more jokes than in the original, and a few plot twists about money and business deals to help beef up its entertainment value. The acting is competent but nothing special and the comedy is not very memorable.

Sadie Thompson see Rain

Sailor, Beware!

September 28, 1933 (Lyceum Theatre), a comedy by Kenyon Nicholson, Charles Robinson. *Cast:* Bruce MacFarlane (Chester Jones), Audrey Christie (Billie Jackson), Edward Craven, Horace MacMahon, George Heller, Ross Hertz, Bradford Hatton, Ann Winthrop. *Director:* Kenyon Nicholson. *Producer:* Courtney Burr. 500 performances.

(Paramount 1952). *Screenplay:* Elwood Ullman, etc. *Cast:* Dean Martin (Al Crowthers), Jerry Lewis (Melvin Jones), Corinne Calvet, Marion Marshall, Robert Strauss, Leif Erickson, Don Wilson, Vince Edwards. *Director:* Hal Walker. *Producer:* Hal B. Wallis.

Billie "Stonewall" Jackson, the cold-hearted hostess at a nightclub in the Canal Zone, is a tough nut to crack but a bunch of sailors make a bet that their favorite ladies'

man, Chester "Dynamite" Jones, can win her heart while the girls at the club bet that he can't. Both Dynamite and Stonewall are as true as their names and only after all bets are called off does Billie admit her affections for Chester. The large, rowdy Broadway production was a long-run hit in the depths of the Depression and gave character actress Audrey Christie the best leading role of her career. A film version of the play was not made until 1951 and it bore little resemblance to the original other than the title and the Navy setting. The comedy was a vehicle for Dean Martin and Jerry Lewis and followed the duo's naval careers from the day they are inducted to their involvement with a farcical boxing match on base. It is one of the better Martin and Lewis films but totally lacking in the kind of vigorous 1930s humor that made the play distinctive.

Sally

December 21, 1920 (New Amsterdam Theatre), a musical comedy by Guy Bolton. *Score:* Jerome Kern, Clifford Grey, B. G. DeSylva, P. G. Wodehouse, etc. *Cast:* Marilyn Miller (Sally Green), Leon Errol (Connie), Walter Catlett (Otis Hooper), Mary Hay (Rosalind Rafferty), Irving Fisher (Blair Farquar), Stanley Ridges. *Songs:* Look for the Silver Lining; Wild Rose; Whip-Poor-Will; Sally; The Church 'Round the Corner; The Lorelei. *Director-choreographer:* Edward Royce. *Producer:* Florenz Ziegfeld. 570 performances.

(Warner/First National 1929). *Screenplay:* Walldemar Young. *Score:* Jerome Kern, Clifford Grey, B. G. DeSylva, etc. *Cast:* Marilyn Miller (Sally), Alexander Gray (Blair Farquar), Joe E. Brown (Connie), T. Roy Barnes (Otis Hooper), Pert Kelton, Ford Sterling, Maude Turner Gordon. *Songs:* Look for the Silver Lining; Sally; All I Want to Do Do Do Is Dance; Walking Off Those Balkan Blues; What Will I Do Without You? *Director:* John Francis Dillon. *Choreographer:* Larry Ceballos.

The preeminent Cinderella musical of the 1920s, this vehicle for Marilyn Miller was musical comedy escapism at its best. The orphan Sally washes dishes in a Greenwich Village eatery and dreams of becoming a *Follies* star. Of course she becomes one, thanks to the help of an ex–Duke, a wily agent, and a handsome young millionaire who falls in love with her. The Jerome Kern score and producer Ziegfeld's opulent production values were first class but the show really came down to Miller who lit up Broadway in a series of similar hit vehicles. A silent film version of the tale was made in 1925 with Colleen Moore as the heroine, then Miller got to reprise her Sally in a 1930 talkie. The production is overstuffed with scenery and extras but amidst it all one can get a glimpse of the kind of excitement Miller created on stage. In some ways the camera does not take to the perky singer-dancer but there are moments worth catching all the same.

Salomy Jane

January 19, 1907 (Liberty Theatre), a play by Paul Armstrong. *Cast*: Eleanor Robson (Salomy), H. B. Warner, Earle Brown, Holbrook Blinn, Reuben Fax, Donald Gallagher. *Director*: Hugh Ford. *Producer:* Liebler & Co. 122 performances.

(Liebler 1914). *Screenplay*: Paul Armstrong. *Cast*: Beatriz Michelena (Salomy), House Peters, Harold Entwhistle, Loretta Ephran, Clara Beyes, Clarence Arpur. *Directors*: Lucius Henderson, William Nigh. *Producer*: Alexander E. Beyfuss.

(Famous Players 1923). *Screenplay*: Waldemar Young. *Cast*: Jacqueline Logan (Salomy), George Fawcett, Maurice Flynn, William B. Davidson, Charles Ogle, Billy Quirk. *Director*: George Melford.

Bret Harte's story "Salomy Jane's Kiss" was adapted into a thrilling melodrama that enthralled playgoers on Broadway and on the road with its gripping plot and Western setting. Salomy Jane is being pestered by an unwanted suitor but her beau will do nothing about it. When the suitor molests her, Salomy vows to take revenge but the culprit is shot by a horse thief on the run from the law. The fugitive tells Salomy he killed the man for personal reasons but she is so thankful she helps him escape the posse, the two of them running off together. Eleanor Robson and H. B. Warner were the stars of the long-running Broadway production but the

melodrama was just as popular in road companies with other players. Two silent film versions were made of the play: a 1914 movie with Beatriz Michelena and House Peters as the central couple and a 1923 remake with Jacqueline Logan and George Fawcett in the leads. Both versions took advantage of location shooting and helped insure that the best venue for Westerns was the screen and not the stage.

Same Time, Next Year

March 13, 1975 (Brooks Atkinson Theatre), a comedy by Bernard Slade. *Cast*: Ellen Burstyn (Doris), Charles Grodin (George). *Director*: Gene Saks. *Producers:* Morton Gottlieb, etc. 1,453 performances.

(Universal 1978). *Screenplay*: Bernard Slade. *Cast*: Ellen Burstyn (Doris), Alan Alda (George), Ivan Bonar, Bernie Kuby. *Director*: Robert Mulligan. *Producers*: Morton Gottlieb, Walter Mirisch.

For one weekend each year George and Doris meet and have an illicit rendezvous at a hotel, unbeknownst to their spouses whom they say they still love. This goes on for twenty-five years as the love affair turns into a friendship (with sex). The implausible, economic little comedy, with a series of likable stars, enjoyed one of the longest Broadway runs of the decade and toured successfully as well. Ellen Burstyn reprised her Doris in the 1978 movie with Alan Alda as George and, like the best of the many actors who had essayed the roles, they were much more accomplished than the writing.

Saturday's Children

January 26, 1927 (Booth Theatre), a comedy by Maxwell Anderson. *Cast*: Ruth Gordon (Bobby Halevy), Roger Pryor (Rims O'Neill), Ruth Hammond, Richard Barbee, Beulah Bondi, Frederick Perry, Lucia Moore. *Director*: Guthrie McClintic. *Producer:* Actor's Theatre, Inc. 167 performances.

(Morosco 1929). *Screenplay*: Forrest Halsey, Paul Perez. *Cast*: Corinne Griffith (Bobby), Grant Withers (Rims), Alma Tell (Florrie), Lucien Littlefield (Willie), Albert Conti. *Director*: Gregory La Cava. *Producer*: Walter Morosco.

Maybe It's Love (First National 1935). *Screenplay:* Lawrence Hazard. *Cast:* Ross Alexander (Rims O'Neill), Gloria Stuart (Bobby Halevy), Frank McHugh, Ruth Donnelly, Henry Travers, Helen Lowell, Joseph Cawthorne. *Director:* William McGann. *Producer:* Harry Joe Brown.

Saturday's Children (Warner 1940). *Screenplay*: Julius J. Epstein, Philip G. Epstein. *Cast*: Anne Shirley (Bobby Halevy), Roscoe Karnes (Willie Sands), John Garfield (Rims), Claude Rains, Lee Patrick, Dennis Moore. *Director*: Vincent Sherman. *Producer*: Jack L. Warner.

When Bobby Halevy marries Rims O'Neill, she thinks her wildest dreams of happiness have come true. But married life with its financial problems and interfering relatives is more a nightmare than a dream so Bobby runs away and takes a room in a boarding house for women only. But Rims still loves her, climbs a fire escape to get to her room, and convinces her to return and together they will try to keep love in their marriage. The gentle comedy was rich in characterization rather than jokes and the fine cast (particularly Ruth Gordon as Bobby) played the piece for sincerity and everyday truth. A 1929 silent movie, with Corinne Griffith and Grant Withers, was popular enough that the story was remade as *Maybe It's Love* in 1935. The talkie opened up the story, showing the humorous courtship of Bobby and Rims and adding characters to fill out the story. It is still a very enjoyable movie and the cast is top flight. But the 1940 remake, using the original play title, seems a bit tired and the comedy is more competent than inspired. Again the cast is expert with John Garfield and Ann Shirley as the couple and some splendid supporting players as the parents.

Search and Destroy

February 26, 1992 (Circle in the Square Theatre), a play by Howard Korder. *Cast*: Griffin Dunne (Martin Mirkheim), Stephen McHattie (Dr. Waxling), Gregory Simmons (Roger), T. G. Waites (Robert), Keith Szarabajka (Kim), Jane Fleiss, Paul Guilfoyle, Arnold Molina. *Director*: David Chambers. *Producer:* Circle in the Square Theatre. 46 performances.

(Nu Image 1995). *Screenplay*: Michael Almereyda.

Cast: Griffin Dunne (Martin Mirkheim), Dennis Hopper (Dr. Waxling), David Thornton (Rob), Christopher Walken (Kim), Robert Knepper, Martin Scorcese, Rosanna Arquette, Jason Ferraro. *Director*: David Salle. *Producers*: Ruth Charny, etc.

The ambitious but callous Martin Mirkheim owes over a million dollars in back taxes so he decides to make a movie based on a best-selling inspirational novel written by a television evangelist. Mirkheim goes on a journey of self discovery to find the author, bullying and blackmailing his way, only to find the motivational guru as selfish and mercenary as himself. This dark view of the American dream was told in several short, pointed scenes which some found penetrating and others thought tiresome. The multi-scened play seemed ideal for the screen but the 1995 movie is disjointed and fails to build to any sort of climax so it seems long and pointless. Griffin Dunne reprised his stage performance as Mirkheim and he was joined by some of Hollywood's edgiest actors, such as Dennis Hopper, Christopher Walken, and Rosana Arquette. All are fascinating to watch even as the film falls apart in front of you.

The Search for Signs of Intelligent Life in the Universe

September 26, 1985 (Plymouth Theatre), a play by Jane Wagner. *Cast*: Lily Tomlin. *Director*: Jane Wagner. *Producers:* Lily Tomlin, Jane Wagner, etc. 398 performances.

(TV 1991). *Teleplay*: Jane Wagner. *Cast*: Lily Tomlin. *Director*: John Bailey. *Producer*: Paula Mazur.

Lily Tomlin's one-woman Broadway show was much more than a stand-up comedy act or collection of wacky characters. Jane Wagner wrote a thought-provoking yet hilarious play in which Tomlin performed all the characters without makeup or costume changes. The different women, of various ages and walks of life, were each vividly drawn and many overlapped into each other's stories with an almost Dickensian feeling of plotting. The 1991 television production allowed Tomlin to portray each character with a distinct look by adding hair, costume, and location changes. Also, using camera tricks she was able to do scenes with more than one character at a time. While it was thrilling to see her make these transitions theatrically in the theatre, it was nearly as enjoyable to see them handled differently on the small screen.

Secret Service

October 5, 1896 (Garrick Theatre), a melodrama by William Gillette. *Cast*: William Gillette (Lewis Dumont), Amy Bushy (Edith Varney), Campbell Gollan (Benton Arrelsford), Joseph Brennan (Gen. Randolph), H. D. James, M. L. Alsop, Louis Duval, William B. Smith. *Producer:* Charles Frohman. 176 performances.

(Famous Players 1919). *Screenplay*: Beulah Marie Dix. *Cast*: Robert Warwick (Lewis Dumont), Wanda Hawley (Edith Varney), Theodore Roberts (Gen. Randolph), Edythe Chapman, Raymond Hatton. *Director*: Hugh Ford.

(RKO 1931). *Screenplay*: Bernard Schubert. *Cast*: Richard Dix (Lewis Dumont), Shirley Grey (Edith Varney), Harold Kinney, William Post, Jr., Nance O'Neil. *Director*: J. Walter Ruben. *Producer*: William LeBaron.

One of the theatre's best plays about the Civil War, this melodrama was about spies and counter spies that operated behind the scenes during the war. The Northern spy Lewis Dumont poses as the Confederate Captain Thorpe and goes to Richmond to infiltrate the command headquarters. While there he falls in love with Edith Varney who eventually suspects his true identity and offers to help Dumont escape when a Confederate official uncovers the truth. Dumont refuses her help, revokes an order that would cause a disaster for the South, and is arrested. Edith confesses her love and promises to wait for him to get out of prison. William Gillette wrote the taut, well-constructed drama and played Dumont on Broadway, on the road, and in revival for many years. The 1919 silent screen version simplified the intricate plot and played up the adventure aspects of the play while the 1931 talkie was so slowly paced that the melodrama turned into a dull romance with the spy intrigue lost in the background. The play has enjoyed some notable revivals on stage and one of them was remade for television in 1977 with John Lithgow as Dumont and Meryl Streep as Edith. The production is studio bound but sharply directed and the excitement of the play comes through.

Send Me No Flowers

December 5, 1960 (Brooks Atkinson Theatre), a comedy by Norman Barasch, Carroll Moore. *Cast*: David Wayne (George Kimball), Nancy Olson (Judy Kimball), Richard McMurray, Frank Merlin, Peter Turgeon, Michael Miguel O'Brien, Heywood Hale Broun, Judy Carroll. *Director*: James Dyas. *Producers:* Courtney Burr, Edward Spector. 40 performances.

(United Artists 1964). *Screenplay*: Julius Epstein. *Cast*: Rock Hudson (George Kimball), Doris Day (Judy Kimball), Tony Randall (Arnold Nash), Paul Lynde (Mr. Atkins), Hal March (Winston Burr), Edward Andrews, Patricia Barry, Clive Clerk. *Director*: Norman Jewison. *Producer*: Harry Keller.

When hypochondriac George Kimball overhears his doctor talking about a terminal patient of his, the frantic George assumes it is he who is dying and panics, while his wife mistakes his odd behavior as signs of an extramarital affair. By the time George finds out he is not dying, enough complications have been set rolling to guarantee some laughs. While David Wayne was complimented on his zesty performance as George, there was little else to recommend and the play folded after a few weeks. Hollywood bought the property for the screen's biggest box office duo, Doris Day and Rock Hudson, and the plot was expanded to make the wife an equally important character. Tony Randall shines as the friend ordered by George to find a new husband for the widow-to-be and Paul Lynde steals the show as a cemetery plot salesman. Otherwise there are long sections of ennui between the laughs.

Seven Keys to Baldpate

September 22, 1913 (Astor Theatre), a comedy by George M. Cohan. *Cast*: Wallace Eddinger

(William Hallowell Magee), Edgar Halstead (Elijah Quimby), Purnell B. Prat (John Bland), Gail Kane (Myra Thornhill), Martin L. Alsop (Jim Cargan), Margaret Green (Mary Norton), Carlton Macy (Jiggs Kennedy), Claude Brooke, Roy Fairchilds. *Director*: George M. Cohan. *Producers:* George M. Cohan, Sam H. Harris. 320 performances.

(Artcraft 1917). *Screenplay*: George M. Cohan. *Cast*: George M. Cohan (George Washington Magee), Anna Q. Nilsson, Hedda Hopper, Armand Cortes, Joseph W. Smiley, Corene Uzzell. *Director*: Hugh Ford.

(Famous Players 1925). *Screenplay*: Wade Boteler, etc. *Cast*: Douglas MacLean (William Magee), Edith Roberts, Crawford Kent, Anders Eandolf, Ned Sparks, Willie Oelamond. *Director*: Fred C. Newmeyer. *Producer*: Douglas MacLean.

(RKO 1929). *Screenplay*: Jane Murfin. *Cast*: Richard Dix (William Magee), DeWitt Jennings, Miriam Seegar, Arthur Hoyt, Harvey Clark, Joe Herbert. *Director*: Reginald Baker. *Producer*: Louis Sarecky.

(RKO 1935). *Screenplay*: Anthony Veiller, Wallace Smith. *Cast*: Gene Raymond (Mr. Magee), Margaret Callahan, Eric Blore, Grant Mitchell, Moroni Olsen. *Directors*: William Hamilton, Edward Killy. *Producer*: William Sistrom.

(RKO 1947). *Screenplay*: Lee Loeb. *Cast*: Philip Terry (Kenneth Magee), Jacqueline White, Eduardo Ciannelli, Margaret Lindsay, Arthur Shields. *Director*: Lew Landers. *Producer*: Herman Schlom.

The House of the Long Shadows (Cannon 1983). *Screenplay*: Michael Armstrong. *Cast*: Desi Arnaz, Jr. (Kenneth Magee), Vincent Price, Christopher Lee, Peter Cushing, John Carradine, Richard Todd, Sheila Keith. *Director*: Pete Walker. *Producer*: Jenny Craven, etc.

One of George M. Cohan's greatest non-musical hits, this comic melodrama was a resounding success on Broadway, on the road, and for decades a favorite with summer stock and community theatre groups. Writer William Hallowell Magee makes a bet with a summer hotel owner that he can write a book in twenty-four hours so the proprietor lets Magee use his inn Baldpate which is boarded up for the winter. But when Magee starts to write he is interrupted by a variety of characters, from a gun-toting crook on the lam to a pretty female reporter to a mil-

lionaire trying to make a deal. By the end of the twenty-four hours Magee has finished his story. But were the interruptions a joke played on him by the owner or were they the characters Magee was writing about? At least eight movies were made from the tongue-in-cheek thriller, including a 1916 Australian film, a 1917 version in which Cohan himself played the hero (called George Washington Magee in the screenplay), and an early talkie in 1929 with Richard Dix as the writer. In this last there was no bet and Magee goes to Baldpate to finish his manuscript on time so that he can afford to wed his fiancée. The 1935 movie, with Gene Raymond as Magee, eliminated the ironic trick ending and so it seemed to fade away rather than conclude. But the supporting cast was lively and offered the only bright spots in the movie. Much more enjoyable is the 1947 remake with Phillip Terry as the writer, which is faithful to the play yet doesn't seem too stagebound. Much of the humor was replaced with true horror in *House of the Long Shadows*, a 1983 British film that was another variation on the haunted house genre. There was even an early television production of the play broadcast in 1947.

The Seven Year Itch

November 20, 1952 (Fulton Theatre), a comedy by George Axelrod. *Cast*: Tom Ewell (Richard Sherman), Vanessa Brown (Girl), Neva Patterson, Johnny Klein, Marilyn Clark. *Director*: John Gerstad. *Producers:* Courtney Burr, Elliott Nugent. 1,141 performances.

(Fox 1955). *Screenplay*: Billy Wilder, George Axelrod. *Cast*: Tom Ewell (Richard Sherman), Marilyn Monroe (Girl), Evelyn Keyes, Sonny Tufts, Robert Strauss, Oscar Homolka. *Director*: Billy Wilder. *Producers*: Charles K. Feldman, Billy Wilder.

With his wife and kids away at a summer resort, urban publisher Richard Sherman's wild imagination turns to fantasies about infidelity, dreams that become more vivid when he is attracted to his beautiful neighbor upstairs. But Richard's fantasies are held in check and he remains faithful. Despite the comedy's thin plot and the Broadway production's lack of stars, the show was a surprise hit that ran three years. Tom Ewell was droll yet familiar as Richard and the role made him a star. He reprised his performance in the 1955 movie but all the attention went to Marilyn Monroe in the smaller part of the girl upstairs. The movie is well paced and still very enjoyable, even though it may seem awfully tame by today's standards. Yet the sight of Monroe standing over a subway vent as her skirt billows up around her remains one of the sexiest of all cinema images.

1776

46th Street Theatre, 16 March 1969 (46th Street Theatre), a musical play by Peter Stone. *Score:* Sherman Edwards. *Cast:* William Daniels (John Adams), Howard Da Silva (Benjamin Franklin), Ken Howard (Thomas Jefferson), Paul Hecht (John Dickinson), Clifford David (Edward Rutledge), Virginia Vestoff (Abigail Adams), Ron Holgate (Richard Henry Lee), Betty Buckley (Martha Jefferson). *Songs:* Sit Down, John; Molasses to Rum; Momma Look Sharp; But Mr. Adams; He Plays the Violin; Cool, Cool Considerate Men; Is Anybody There?; The Egg. *Director:* Peter Hunt. *Choreographer:* Onna White. *Producer:* Stuart Ostrow. 1,217 performances. Tony Award.

(Columbia 1972). *Screenplay:* Peter Stone. *Score:* Sherman Edwards. *Cast:* William Daniels (John Adams), Howard Da Silva (Benjamin Franklin), Ken Howard (Thomas Jefferson), Donald Madden (John Dickinson), Virginia Vestoff (Abigail Adams), Ron Holgate (Richard Henry Lee), Blythe Danner (Martha Jefferson), John Cullum (Edward Rutledge) Ray Middleton. *Songs:* Sit Down, John; Molasses to Rum; Momma Look Sharp; But Mr. Adams; He Plays the Violin; Is Anybody There?; The Egg. *Director:* Peter Hunt. *Choreographer:* Onna White. *Producer:* Jack L. Warner.

An unlikely musical hit with its mostly-male cast, lack of romance, and literate historical libretto, *1776* managed to be engaging and entertaining thanks to the superior book by Peter Stone. A show about the debates leading up to the ratifying and signing of the Declaration of Independence would have to have a talky libretto, and this

one had long sections without music, but the talk was fun and fascinating and the songs by Sherman Edwards were accessible enough that the musical became a long-run hit. The director, most of the Broadway cast, and just about the entire score were retained for the 1972 film version but it rarely captures the spirit of the original. The action on stage was primarily confined to the interior of Independence Hall but the movie awkwardly tries to open up the story by forcing characters to romp about outside or to film the debates with obvious camera movements and distracting cross fades or track shots. But the film has its enjoyable moments and it does preserve a handful of expert performances.

Seventh Heaven

October 30, 1922 (Booth Theatre), a play by Austin Strong. *Cast*: Helen Menken (Diane), George Gaul (Chico), Frank Morgan (Brissac), Marion Kirby (Nana), Hubert Druce, Fred Holloway, Beatrice Noyes. *Director-producer:* John Golden. 704 performances.

(Fox 1927). *Screenplay*: Benjamin Glazer. *Cast*: Janet Gaynor (Diane), Charles Farrell (Chico), Ben Bard (Col. Brissac), Albert Gran, David Butler, Marie Mosquini. *Director*: Frank Borzage. *Producer*: William Fox.

(Fox 1937). *Screenplay*: Melvin Baker. *Cast*: Simone Simon (Diane), James Stewart (Chico), Jean Hersholt, Gregory Ratoff, Gale Sondergaard, J. Edward Bromberg. *Director*: Henry King. *Producer*: Darryl F. Zanuck.

Diane is forced by her sister to work as a streetwalker until she is rescued by the sewer cleaner Chico who gives her a place to stay in his seventh floor walkup. When Chico goes to war, Diane promises to remain faithful and works in a munitions factory waiting for his return. But she later hears Chico has been killed and she eventually falls into a romance with Brissac. Chico returns from the front alive but blind and, since he cannot see the other man in Diane's life, the pair are reunited without incrimination. One of the most popular of all tearjerkers, the melodrama ran two years on Broadway and was hit on the road as well.

The 1927 silent movie is a sentimental classic starring the popular screen team of Janet Gaynor and Charles Farrell. It is beautifully shot and directed and its dreamy look was copied by many other later films. Gaynor is particularly moving and she won the first Oscar for Best Actress for her performance. The 1937 remake palls in comparison though the talkie does have impressive production credits. Simone Simon is a poignant Diane but James Stewart is an unconvincing Frenchman and his Chico seems uncomfortable.

Sexual Perversity in Chicago

June 16, 1976 (Cherry Lane Theatre), a play by David Mamet. *Cast*: Peter Riegert (Danny), F. Murray Abraham (Bernie), Jane Anderson (Deborah), Gina Rogers (Joan). *Director*: Albert Takazauckas. *Producers:* Lawrence Goossen, Jeffrey Wachtel. 273 performances.

About Last Night (TriStar 1986). *Screenplay*: Tim Kazurinsky, Denise DeClue. *Cast*: Rob Lowe (Danny), Demi Moore (Debbie), James Belushi (Bernie), Elizabeth Perkins (Joan), George DiCenzo, Michael Alldredge. *Director*: Edward Zwick. *Producers*: Jason Brett, Stuart Oken.

David Mamet's first success was a long one-act that consisted of a series of short scenes in which four characters commented on their sexual thoughts and fell in and out of relationships. It was Mamet's rhythmic and scatological dialogue that was more important than any character development and the play was like a jazzy quartet of words. After its popular Off Broadway run the play was given dozens of productions in regional theatres and colleges. The 1986 film version, titled *About Last Night*, retained the four characters and sections of their jive-like banter but was more interested in telling a conventional story about a failed romance. Except for Jim Belushi's hip performance as the chauvinistic Bernie, the acting in weak but Rob Lowe and Demi Moore were considered sex symbols at the time so their many nude scenes helped make the film popular.

The Shadow Box

March 31, 1977 (Morosco Theatre), a play by Michael Cristofer. *Cast*: Laurence Luckinbill (Brian), Simon Oakland (Joe) Geraldine Fitzgerald (Felicity), Patricia Elliott (Beverly), Mandy Patinkin (Mark), Joyce Ebert (Maggie), Rose Gregorio (Agnes), Josef Sommer, Vincent Stewart. *Director*: Gordon Davidson. *Producers:* Lester Osterman, etc. 315 performances. Pulitzer Prize, Tony Award.

(TV 1980). *Teleplay*: Michael Cristofer. *Cast*: Christopher Plummer (Brian), James Broderick (Joe), Sylvia Sidney (Felicity), Joanne Woodward (Beverly), Ben Masters (Mark), Valerie Harper (Maggie), Melinda Dillon (Agnes), John Considine, Curtiss Marlowe. *Director*: Paul Newman. *Producers*: Jill Marti, Susan Kendall Newman.

At a hospice for the terminally ill, three patients and their families and friends look at death with anger, fear, understanding, and ultimately resignation. The plotless drama nevertheless had very vivid characters and there was some humor amidst all the emotional scenes. The sterling cast, incisive direction, and an evocative setting under huge redwood trees made for a distinguished production. The play had been a success in regional theatre before coming to Broadway where it won all the major awards and ran a year. Many amateur productions followed but the studios passed on filming the play as a feature film, assuming such a dark subject would be box office poison. Instead it was made into a television play in 1980 with a prominent cast who gave beautifully restrained performances. Far from a disease-of-the-week television movie, the production was understated and all the more powerful because of it.

The Shanghai Gesture

February 1, 1926 (Martin Beck Theatre), a melodrama by John Colton. *Cast*: Mary Duncan (Poppy), Florence Reed (Mother Goddam), McKay Morris (Sir Guy Charteris), Cyril Keightley, Henry Warwick, Eva Leonard Boyne, William Worthington. *Director*: Guthrie McClintic. *Producer:* A. H. Woods. 331 performances.

(Pressburger 1941). *Screenplay*: Jules Furthman, etc. *Cast*: Gene Tierney (Poppy), Ona Munson

(Mother Gin Sling), Walter Huston (Sir Guy Charteris), Victor Mature (Dr. Omar), Phyllis Brooks, Albert Basserman, Maria Ouspenskaya, Eric Blore. *Director*: Josef von Sternberg. *Producer*: Arnold Pressburger.

Mother Goddam, the proprietor of a Shanghai brothel, has never forgotten the British businessman Guy Charteris. She was once in love with him and Guy promised to marry her but he left her for an English girl and sold Mother into white slavery. Years later, Charteris visits the brothel and Mother gets her revenge by selling the sweet young girl Poppy to white slavers then explaining that she was Charteris's illegitimate daughter. When Poppy later returns to the brothel as a dope fiend, Mother strangles her to death. While the critics castigated the lurid melodrama, audiences were curious enough to let the Broadway production run a year. Whether it was trash or not, everyone agreed that Florence Reed's Mother Goddam was one of the most chilling characters they could recall. Hollywood had to do a lot of pruning and rewriting to allow a film version to be made that would pass the Hays Code and the 1941 movie is so bowdlerized that often it makes no sense. The brothel was turned into a gambling casino and Poppy is a good-hearted girl that can't hold her liquor. The acting is so fevered that it borders on camp and the decadence seen on the screen, which was so startling in its day, comes across as a rather dull office party today. The film has a cult following of sorts and it remains an immensely enjoyable bad movie.

She Done Him Wrong see Diamond Lil

She Loves Me Not

November 20, 1933 (46th Street Theatre), a comedy by Howard Lindsay. *Cast*: John Beal (Paul Lawton), Polly Walters (Curley Flagg), Burgess Meredith (Buzz Jones), Philip Ober, Florence Rice, Charles O. Brown, Harry Bellaver, Ralph J. Locke. *Director*: Howard Lindsay. *Producers*: Dwight Deere Wiman, Tom Weatherly. 360 performances.

(Paramount 1934). *Screenplay*: Benjamin Glazer. *Score*: Johnny Burke, Sam Coslow, Mark Gordon, etc. *Cast*: Bing Crosby (Paul Lawton), Miriam Hopkins (Curley Flagg), Kitty Carlisle (Midge Mercer), Edward Nugent (Buzz Jones), Henry Stephenson, Warner Hymer, Lynne Overman. *Songs*: Cocktails for Two; Love in Bloom; Straight From the Shoulder; After All, You're All I'm After. *Director*: Elliott Nugent. *Producer*: Benjamin Glazer.

True to the Army (Paramount 1942). *Screenplay:* Art Arthur, Val Burton. *Score:* Frank Loesser, Ralph Rainger, Leo Robin, etc. *Cast:* Judy Canova (Daisy Hawkins), Allan Jones (Pvt. Stephen Chandler), Ann Miller (Vicki Marlow), Jerry Colonna (Pinky Fothergill), Clarence Kolb, Edward Pawley, William Demarest. *Songs:* In the Army; Need I Speak; Jitterbug's Lullaby; Wacky for Khaki; Swing in Line; Love in Bloom; I Can't Give You Anything But Love. *Director:* Albert S. Rogell. *Producer:* Sol C. Siegel.

How to Be Very, Very Popular (Fox 1955). *Screenplay*: Nunnally Johnson. *Cast:* Betty Grable (Stormy Tornado), Sheree North (Curley Flagg), Robert Cummings (Fillmore Wedgewood), Charles Coburn (Dr. Tweed), Fred Clark, Alice Pearce, Orson Bean, Tommy Noonan. *Director-producer*: Nunnally Johnson.

This raucous collegiate farce made no logical sense but the plot moved so fast and the characters were so energetic that few seemed to notice. After she witnesses a gangland murder, nightclub chorine Curley Flagg hides from the questioning police in the Princeton dorm room of Paul Lawton. He and his buddies cut Curley's hair and disguise her as a man, saying she is Paul's brother. Somehow Hollywood gets interested in the youthful-looking man and before you know it press agents and film crews invade the campus and all hell breaks loose. Of all the comic players in the cast, audiences and critics singled out newcomer Burgess Meredith who portrayed Paul's friend Buzz Jones. The 1934 screen adaptation was a musical vehicle for Bing Crosby and it stuck to the stage plot pretty closely, adding some delightful songs and introducing the standard "Love in Bloom." Crosby was college student Paul and Mirian Hopkins, in one of her funniest performances, was Curley. They were surrounded by a playful supporting cast and, with its expert direction and top-notch production values, the movie is still a winner. The 1942 remake, titled *True to the Army*, was also a musical but now set in the military with Judy Canova disguised as a man in uniform. The plotting was more obvious and less funny this time but the cast was highly entertaining, particularly Allan Jones and Ann Miller as the romantic pair. The score was mostly forgettable (except for a replay of "Love in Bloom" and some other older favorites) and the production numbers seem forced. Hollywood returned to the same plot one more time in 1955 with *How to Be Very, Very Popular*, a vehicle for Betty Grable in which she and fellow belly dancer Sheree North are on the lam and hide in a college fraternity. Things progressed predictably from there with a few songs thrown in. Oddly, the highlight of the film was North's exuberant rendition of "Shake, Rattle and Roll" and not Grable's numbers; the gal with the million dollar legs saw the writing on the wall and retired from the screen after this film.

She's Working Her Way Through College see The Mail Animal

Sherlock Holmes

November 6, 1899 (Garrick Theatre), a play by William Gillette. *Cast*: William Gillette (Sherlock Holmes), George Wessells (Prof. Moriarity), Katherine Florence (Alice Faulkner), Judith Berolde (Madge Larrabee), Ralph Delmore (James Larrabee), Bruce McRae (Dr. Watson), Henry McArdle (Billy), Reuben Fax, George Honey. *Producer*: Charles Frohman. 256 performances.

(Essanay 1916). *Screenplay*: H. S. Sheldon. *Cast*: William Gillette (Sherlock Holmes), Ernest Maupain (Prof. Moriarity), Marjorie Kay (Alice), Edward Fielding (Dr. Watson), Stewart Robbins. *Director*: Arthur Berthelet.

(Goldwyn 1922). *Screenplay*: Earle Browne, Marion Fairfax. *Cast*: John Barrymore (Sherlock Holmes), Gustav von Seyffertitz (Prof. Moriarity), Carol Dempster (Alice), Roland Young (Dr. Watson), Louis Wolheim. *Director*: Albert Parker. *Producer*: F. J. Godsol.

(Fox 1932). *Screenplay*: Bertram Millhauser. *Cast*: Clive Brook (Sherlock Holmes), Ernest Torrence (Prof. Moriarity), Miriam Jordan (Alice), Reginald Owen (Dr. Watson), Herbert Mundin. *Director-producer*: William K. Howard.

Of all the stage adaptations of Arthur Conan Doyle's celebrated sleuth, this version by William Gillette was the most popular and Gillette's performance as Holmes was considered the finest portrayal of the character. (Gillette continued to play Holmes for the last thirty-five years of his life.) The plot centered on some stolen letters used for blackmail and the crime trail led to Professor Moriarty who imprisons Holmes in a gas works. But the sleuth escapes and, in very un–Doyle-like fashion, falls in love with his female client. Of the dozens of Sherlock Holmes movies, at least five are based on the play. Gillette himself played Holmes in a 1916 film and John Barrymore essayed the role in the 1922 version, both silent films. An early talkie in 1932 featured Clive Brook as the sleuth but the movie was inexplicably set in contemporary London so the Victorian flavor of the story was lost. Basil Rathbone would later become the most famous screen Holmes, though none of his movies were directly based on the play. A 1982 French television production did return to Gillette's script and the original play is still revived in theatres on occasion.

Shinbone Alley

April 13, 1957 (Broadway Theatre), a musical comedy by Mel Brooks, Joe Darion. *Score:* George Kleinsinger, Joe Darion. *Cast*: Eddie Bracken (archy), Eartha Kitt (mehitabel), Ross Martin (Broadway), George S. Irving (Big Bill), Gwen Harmon, Erik Rhodes, Allegra Kent, Jacques D'Amboise. *Songs*: Shinbone Alley; Flotsam and Jetsam; Toujours Gai; A Woman Wouldn't Be a Woman; Come to Mee-ow; Way Down Blues; True Romance. *Choreographer*: Rod Alexander. *Producer*: Peter Lawrence. 49 performances.

(Allied Artists 1971). *Screenplay:* Mel Brooks, Joe Darion. *Score:* George Kleinsinger, Joe Darion. *Voices:* Eddie Bracken (archy), Carol Channing (mehitabel), Alan Reed (Big Bill), Ken Sansom (Byron Kane), John Carradine (Tyrone T. Tattersall), Hall Smith. *Songs:* Flotsam and Jetsam;

Toujours Gai; A Woman Wouldn't Be a Woman; Cheerio My Deario. *Director:* John D. Wilson. *Producers:* Preston M. Fleet, John D. Wilson.

Don Marquis's clever *archy and mehitabel* stories, about a poetry-writing cockroach who bangs out his poems on lower case typewriter keys and his sweetheart Mehitabel the cat, were turned into a tuneful but unsatisfying musical with little plot and a lot of humans pretending to be animals. Eddie Bracken had his moments as the lovesick archy and Eartha Kitt was seductive as ever as the feline heroine but it wasn't enough to allow the Broadway production to run longer than a few weeks. The musical was turned into a much more enjoyable animated film in 1971 with Bracken supplying the voice for archy and Carol Channing croaking her funniest sounds as mehitabel. The movie is well animated, the songs are playful, and the tone is rather sassy and obviously for adults. Because the film did not appeal to kids, it failed at the box office.

Shore Acres

October 30, 1893 (Fifth Avenue Theatre), a play by James A. Herne. *Cast:* James A. Herne (Uncle Nat), Charles G. Craig (Martin), Katherine Grey (Helen), David M. Murray, Fred Johnson, Helen Gould, Franklin Garland. *Producer:* James A. Herne. 244 performances.

(All Star 1914). *Screenplay:* Louis Reeves Harrison, Augustus E. Thomas. *Cast:* Charles A. Stevenson (Nat Berry), Riley Hatch (Martin), Violet Horner (Helen), Gladys Fairbanks, Edward Connelly. *Director:* John H. Pratt.

(Screen Classics 1920). *Screenplay:* Arthur J. Zellner. *Cast:* Edward Connelly (Nat Berry), Frank Brownlee (Martin), Alice Lake (Helen), Joseph Kilgour, Robert Walker. *Director-producer:* Rex Ingram.

Kindly old Uncle Nat has always been taken advantage of. His villainous brother Martin stole his fiancée years ago and then took all of the family property, leaving Nat to live in a lighthouse. When Martin's daughter Helen wishes to wed a man her father doesn't approve of, Nat helps her and her beau elope aboard ship but the vessel is floundering and heading toward the rocks.

Martin finds out about the elopement and refuses to light the beacon to save them so Nat must wrestle his brother to the ground and secure the light. The play was considered much more sophisticated than most melodramas of the day and, except for the evil Martin, it avoided character stereotypes. After playing successfully in Boston, the play was a hit on Broadway and on the road. Two silent screen versions of the tale were made in 1914 and 1920 and both took advantage of the shipwreck spoken of in the play and made it the climatic action scene. Edward Connelly, who played a supporting role in the 1914 film, graduated to the leading role of Uncle Nat in the remake six years later.

Shore Leave

August 8, 1922 (Lyceum Theatre), a comedy by Hubert Osborne. *Cast:* Frances Starr (Connie Martin), James Rennie (Bilge Smith), Nick Long (Bimby), Thomas E. Jackson, Reginald Barlow, Schuyler Ladd, Audrey Baird. *Director-producer:* David Belasco. 151 performances.

(Inspiration 1925). *Screenplay:* Josephine Lovett. *Cast:* Richard Barthelmess (Bilge Smith), Dorothy MacKaill (Connie Martin), Ted MacNamara, Nick Long, Marie Shotwell. *Director:* John S. Robertson.

New England spinster Connie Martin falls in love with the sailor Bilge Smith when he is on shore leave and when he departs Connie puts all her saving together and buys a small freighter to fix up so Bilge can be captain of his own ship when he returns. But when Bilge does come back he refuses to accept the gift and says he will not live off of a woman's earnings. So Connie wills the boat to their children yet to come and Bilge agrees. The comedy was a success due to the effervescent presence of Frances Starr as Connie and David Belasco's lavish production that recreated both land and sea locales. The 1925 silent movie also boasted several impressive settings but needed a star of the magnitude of Starr to pull it off. Dorothy MacKaill played Connie but more interesting was Richard Barthelmess as Bilge. Today the play is mainly remembered as the source material for the musical *Hit the Deck* (qv).

Short Eyes

February 28, 1974 (Public Theatre), a play by Miguel Pinero. *Cast*: William Carden (Clark Davis), Joseph Carberry (Longshoe Murphy), Tito Goya (Cupcakes Mercado), J. J. Johnson, Kenny Steward, Ben Jefferson, Bimbo. *Director*: Marvin Felix. *Producer*: Public Theatre. 54 performances.

(New Cinema 1977). *Screenplay*: Miguel Pinero. *Cast*: Bruce Davison (Clark Davis), Joseph Carberry (Longshoe Murphy), Don Blakely, Keith Davis, Tony Di Benedetto. *Director*: Robert M. Young. *Producers*: Lewis Harris, Robert M. Young.

When the inmates of a detention center discover that the new inmate Clark Davis is a child molester, they taunt and abuse him, for even among criminals he is looked down upon. The tension grows and in an argument one convict slits Davis's throat and kills him. All the inmates swear to the authorities that they saw nothing; then they learn that Davis was wrongly accused and was innocent. The devastating little drama was a hit Off Off Broadway where producer Joe Papp saw it and transferred it to his theatre for a successful run. The 1977 movie was shot in an actual prison and was filled with a raw and documentary look but it did not diminish the theatrical power of the piece. The acting is uncompromisingly harsh and utterly believable.

Show Boat

December 27, 1927 (Ziegfeld Theatre), a musical play by Oscar Hammerstein. *Score:* Jerome Kern, Oscar Hammerstein. *Cast:* Norma Terris (Magnolia Hawks), Howard Marsh (Gaylord Ravenal), Charles Winninger (Capn Andy Hawks), Helen Morgan (Julie La Verne), Jules Bledsoe (Joe), Edna May Oliver (Parthy Hawks), Eva Puck (Ellie May Chipley), Sammy White (Frank Shultz), Tess Gardella (Queenie). *Songs:* Ol' Man River; Make Believe; Can't Help Lovin' Dat Man; You Are Love; Bill; Why Do I Love You?; Life Upon the Wicked Stage. *Directors:* Zeke Colvan, Oscar Hammerstein. *Choreographer:* Sammy Lee. *Producer:* Florenz Ziegfeld. 572 performances.

(Universal (1929). *Screenplay:* Charles Kenyon. *Score:* Jerome Kern, Oscar Hammerstein, etc. *Cast:* Laura La Plante (Magnolia Hawks), Joseph Schildkraut (Gaylord Ravenal), Alma Rubens (Julie La Verne), Otis Harlan (Capn Andy Hawks), Emily Fitzroy (Parthy Hawks), Stepin Fetchit (Joe), Elise Bartlett, Jack McDonald, Jules Bledsoe (voice only). *Songs:* Ol' Man River; Can't Help Lovin' Dat Man; Bill; The Lonesome Road; Deep River; Here Comes That Show Boat; Down South. *Director:* Harry Pollard. *Producer:* Carl Laemmle.

(Universal 1936). *Screenplay:* Oscar Hammerstein. *Score:* Jerome Kern, Oscar Hammerstein. *Cast:* Irene Dunne (Magnolia Hawks), Allan Jones (Gaylord Ravenal), Helen Morgan (Julie La Verne), Charles Winninger (Capn Andy Hawks), Paul Robeson (Joe), Helen Westley (Parthy Hawks), Queenie Smith (Ellie), Sammy White (Frank Shultz), Hattie McDaniel (Queenie), Donald Cook, Harry Barris. *Songs:* Ol' Man River; Make Believe; Can't Help Lovin' Dat Man; You Are Love; Bill; I Have the Room Above Her; Where's the Mate for Me?; Ah Still Suits Me. *Director:* James Whale. *Choreographer:* LeRoy Prinz. *Producer:* Carl Laemmle, Jr.

(MGM 1951). *Screenplay:* John Lee Mahin. *Score:* Jerome Kern, Oscar Hammerstein. *Cast:* Kathryn Grayson (Magnolia Hawks), Howard Keel (Gaylord Ravenal), Ava Gardner (Julie La Verne), Joe E. Brown (Capn Andy Hawks), William Warfield (Joe), Agnes Moorehead (Parthy Hawks), Marge Champion (Ellie), Gower Champion (Frank Shultz), Robert Sterling. *Songs:* Ol' Man River; Make Believe; Can't Help Lovin' Dat Man; You Are Love; Bill; Why Do I Love You?; Life Upon the Wicked Stage; I Might Fall Back on You. *Director:* George Sidney. *Choreographer:* Robert Alton. *Producer:* Arthur Freed.

The Broadway musical's first and most enduring masterpiece, the landmark operetta opened up the possibilities for the musical form and introduced the musical play. Oscar Hammerstein adapted Edna Ferber's long novel for the stage and came up with the most ambitious libretto the American theatre had yet experienced. The epic tale of a family whose lives and fortunes revolve around a show boat on the Mississippi was punctuated with Jerome Kern's celebrated score, the most significant yet heard on a New York stage. The original production was a resounding hit, followed by many revivals over the years. The show was filmed three times and each version has its virtues. A silent movie version of Ferber's book was being completed just as the musical opened on Broadway. The studio added some sound scenes, put a lot of Negro spirituals in the background, and even had some members of the stage cast sing highlights of the score during an eighteen-minute prologue. It was an odd and disjointed film and was not a success with the public. But the 1936 remake was. Helen Morgan and Charles Winninger got to recreate their stage performances and were matched in quality by Irene Dunne, Allan Jones, Paul Robeson and others. The movie tinkers with the last section of the plot and concludes the action in a New York theatre rather than back at the show boat, a device that helped unify the sprawling tale on stage. Yet this *Show Boat* excels in almost every aspect and remains one of Hollywood's finest movie musicals. But as good as it was it wasn't in color so MGM remade the piece in 1951 with its top singing stars. Although it pales in comparison, there is much to recommend in the color version. The production values are top-notch and even the altered final scenes seem to work well on screen. The film was a hit and, because it was shown on television for years, this is the version most moviegoers are familiar with. But slowly audiences have rediscovered the brilliance of the 1936 movie classic.

The Show-Off

February 5, 1924 (Playhouse Theatre), a comedy by George Kelly. *Cast*: Louis Bartels (Aubrey Piper), Helen Lowell (Mrs. Fisher), Regina Wallace (Amy), Juliette Crosby, Lee Tracy, Gus D'Ennery. *Director*: George Kelly. *Producer:* Stewart & French, Inc. 571 performances.

(Famous Players 1926). *Screenplay*: Pierre Collings. *Cast*: Ford Sterling (Aubrey Piper), Claire McDowell (Mom Fisher), Lois Wilson (Amy), Gregory Kelly, Louise Brooks, Charles Goodrich. *Director-producer*: Malcolm St. Clair.

(MGM 1934). *Screenplay*: Herman J. Mankiewicz. *Cast*: Spencer Tracy (Aubrey Piper), Clara Blandick (Mrs. Fisher), Madge Evans (Amy), Lois Wilson, Grant Mitchell, Henry Wadsworth. *Director*: Charles Reisner. *Producer*: Lucien Hubbard.

(MGM 1946). *Screenplay*: George Wells. *Cast*: Red Skelton (Aubrey Piper), Marjorie Main (Mrs. Fisher), Marilyn Maxwell (Amy), Virginia

O'Brien, Eddie Anderson, Leon Ames, George Cleveland. *Director*: Harry Beaumont. *Producer*: Albert Lewis.

Philadelphian Aubrey Piper dresses fancy and talks big but usually he's out of work and his schemes always seem to fall through. His wife Amy sticks by him but his mother-in-law never misses an opportunity to speak her mind about the show-off. Yet Aubrey proves that he is more than bluff when he arranges for Amy's brother to get a huge sum of money for a rust-proofing invention that he has patented. This beloved American comedy classic finds its humor in the truthful characters rather than plot or witty dialogue and it has remain a favorite with all kinds of theatre groups. The 1926 silent movie featured Ford Sterling as Aubrey and Claire McDowell as the acerbic Mrs. Fisher with Louise Brooks noticeable as the inventor's girl friend. The 1934 talkie gave Spencer Tracy his first important role and his charming, giddy Aubrey made him a screen star. Clara Blandick was a droll Mrs. Fisher and the rest of the cast was admirable, though the film suffered from low production values. The 1946 remake starred Red Skelton as Aubrey and the comic manages to keep his clowning within the confines of the character, giving one of his more subdued performances. Marjorie Main and Marilyn Maxwell played Mrs. Fisher and Amy but it's often Virginia O'Brien who steals the show playing a minor role.

The Shrike

January 15, 1952 (Cort Theatre), a drama by Joseph Kramm. *Cast*: José Ferrer (Jim Downs), Judith Evelyn (Ann), Somer Alberg (Dr. Schlesinger), Edward Platt (Harry Downs), Isabel Bonner (Dr. Barrow), Will Lee, Stephen Elliott, Martin Newman, Philip Huston. *Director-producer:* José Ferrer. 161 performances. Pulitzer Prize.

(Universal 1955). *Screenplay*: Ketti Frings. *Cast*: José Ferrer (Jim Downs), June Allyson (Ann), Joy Page, Kendall Clark, Isabel Bonner, Edward Platt, Mary Bell. *Director*: José Ferrer. *Producer*: Aaron Rosenberg.

When the failed theatre director Jim Downs tries to commit suicide and fails, he is sent to a psychiatric hospital for help. But his estranged wife Ann gains legal control of him and turns the doctors against him. She is very jealous of the young woman Jim had been seeing so Ann agrees to his release only if he returns to her. With no alternate, he agrees. The play was a triumph for José Ferrer who gave a brilliant performance as Jim and directed the Broadway production as well. He repeated both chores in the 1955 movie (though he had never directed a film before) but his acting was deemed more satisfying than his slow-paced direction of the drama. The screenplay extended the story somewhat, showing in more detail how Ann had driven Jim to his breakdown, yet much of the film is talky and less than gripping. Cast against type, smiling June Allyson plays the cruel, manipulative Ann and it is an interesting if not totally convincing performance.

Silent Night, Lonely Night

December 3, 1959 (Morosco Theatre), a play by Robert Anderson. *Cast*: Barbara Bel Geddes (Katherine), Henry Fonda (John), Lois Nettleton (Janet), Eda Heinemann (Mae), Bill Berger, Peter de Vise. *Director*: Peter Glenville. *Producer*: Playwrights' Company. 124 performances.

(TV 1969). *Teleplay*: John Vlahos. *Cast*: Lloyd Bridges (John), Shirley Jones (Katherine), Carrie Snodgrass (Janet), Lynn Carlin, Robert Lipton, Cloris Leachman. *Director*: Daniel Petrie. *Producer*: Jack Farren.

This quiet, intimate little drama lacked excitement but with stars Henry Fonda and Barbara Bel Geddes in the leading roles, the Broadway production managed to run a few months. Katherine is staying at an inn near her son's boarding school. John is at the same inn so he can visit his wife who is in a nearby mental institution. The two meet on Christmas eve and share a night of confession, pity, and lovemaking, only to part the next day and go their separate ways. The 1969 television production also depended on stars, in this case Lloyd Bridges taking a break from his television work and Shirley Jones taking a break from musicals. Both give sincere, heartfelt performances but, despite some flashbacks to dramatize past events, there are few sparks and nothing much to remember about the production.

Silk Stockings

February, 24, 1955 (Imperial Theatre), a musical comedy by George S. Kaufman, Leueen McGrath, Abe Burrows. *Score*: Cole Porter. *Cast*: Hildegarde Neff (Ninotchka), Don Ameche (Steve Canfield), George Tobias (Commissar), Gretchen Wyler (Janice Dayton), Leon Belasco (Brankov), Henry Lascoe (Ivanov), David Opatoshu (Bibinski). *Songs*: All of You; Paris Loves Lovers; It's a Chemical Reaction, That's All; Without Love; The Red Blues; Too Bad; Stereophonic Sound. *Director*: Cy Feuer. *Choreographer*: Eugene Loring. *Producers*: Cy Feuer, Ernest Martin. 478 performances.

(MGM 1957). *Screenplay*: Leonard Gershe, Leonard Spiegelgass. *Score*: Cole Porter. *Cast*: Fred Astaire (Steve Canfield), Cyd Charisse (Ninotchka), Janis Paige (Peggy Dainton), Peter Lorre (Brankov), George Tobias (Commissar), Jules Munshin (Bibinski), Joseph Buloff (Ivanov), Wim Sonneveld, Barrie Chase, Belita. *Songs*: All of You; Paris Loves Lovers; It's a Chemical Reaction, That's All; Without Love; Fated to Be Mated; The Red Blues; Too Bad; Stereophonic Sound. *Director*: Rouben Mamoulian. *Choreographers*: Eugene Loring, Hermes Pan, Fred Astaire. *Producer*: Arthur Freed.

Cole Porter's last stage score was filled with entertaining songs but the troubled libretto, worked on by various hands, was problematic and never captured the high-flying joy of the 1939 film *Ninotchka* on which the musical was based. Talent agent Steve Canfield tries to convince a Russian composer to write a film score so Soviet official Ninotchka arrives in Paris to lay down the law, only to be seduced by the romantic city and Steve's charms. The Broadway show opened to mixed notices but managed a very healthy run. For the film, Steve was turned into a dancing Hollywood producer so that Astaire and Charisse could have some extended dance sequences. These numbers remain the most satisfying aspect of the movie, though some of the comic supporting performances are delightful. Director Mamoulian filmed the whole musical on a soundstage and it never captured the

Parisan flavor found in other 1950s Paris-set musicals such as *Funny Face* (1957) and *Gigi* (1958). Most of Porter's score made it to the screen but the singing (Charisse was dubbed) was always secondary to the dancing.

The Silver Cord

December 20, 1926 (John Golden Theatre), a play by Sidney Howard. *Cast*: Laura Hope Crews (Mrs. Phelps), Earle Larrimore (Robert), Margalo Gillmore (Hester), Eliot Cabot (David), Elizabeth Risdon (Christine). *Director*: John Cromwell. *Producer:* Theatre Guild. 112 performances.

(RKO 1933). *Screenplay*: Jane Murfin. *Cast*: Laura Hope Crews (Mrs. Phelps), Joel McCrea (David), Eric Linden (Robert), Irene Dunne (Christine), Frances Dee. *Director*: John Cromwell. *Producer*: Pandro S. Berman.

Mrs. Phelps is so obsessed about hanging onto her two grown sons that she plots to destroy the wedding engagement of one and the marriage of the other. She succeeds in driving the fiancée to suicide but the daughter-in-law stands up to Mrs. Phelps, tells her to her face the kind of pathological monster she is, then gives her husband the strength to cut loose from his mother's "silver cord" that is strangling them all. The drama was uncomfortably realistic and avoided the melodramatics that might have weakened the argument. Mrs. Phelps was considered one of the most disturbing of characters and Laura Hope Crews's portrayal, with sweetness and tears masking her diabolical nature, was masterful. Crews reprised the role in the very faithful 1933 film which seemed a bit stilted and artificial because there was nothing very cinematic about the movie. Nonetheless, all of the performances are first-rate (especially up-and-coming Irene Dunne as the daughter-in-law) and the power of the play manages to come through in spots. The drama was remake as a television production in 1951 with Judith Anderson as the domineering Mrs. Phelps.

Simpatico

November 14, 1994 (Public Theatre), a play by Sam Shepard. *Cast*: Ed Harris (Carter), Fred Ward (Vinnie), Beverly D'Angelo (Rosie), James Gammon (Simms), Marcia Gay Harden (Cecilia), Welker White (Kelly). *Director*: Sam Shepard. *Producer:* New York Shakespeare Festival. 40 performances.

(Kingsgate, etc. 1999). *Screenplay*: Matthew Warchus, David Nichols. *Cast*: Nick Nolte (Vincent), Jeff Bridges (Lyle Carter), Sharon Stone (Rosie), Albert Finney (Sims), Catherine Keener (Cecilia), Shawn Hatosy, Kimberly Williams. *Director*: Matthew Warchus. *Producers*: Chuck Binder, etc.

Years ago two hucksters pulled off a horse racing swindle that toppled the career of a local commissioner. One of the men now wants to go public with the scam, the other doesn't. Even the ex-commissioner is content to let the past rest so nothing happens and the guilt remains. The long, talky drama was considered one of Sam Shepard's less interesting works but a film was made in 1999 all the same and it too was generally dismissed. But both the stage and screen versions boasted some laudable acting, particularly Albert Finney as the commissioner in the movie.

Sister Mary Ignatius Explains It All for You

October 14, 1981 (Playwrights Horizons Theatre), a comedy by Christopher Durang. *Cast*: Elizabeth Franz (Sr. Mary Ignatius), Mark Stefan, Timothy Landfield, Polly Draper, Mary Catherine Wright, Jeff Brooks. *Director*: Jerry Zaks. *Producer:* Playwrights Horizons. 947 performances.

Sister Mary Explains It All (TV 2001). *Teleplay*: Christopher Durang. *Cast*: Diane Keaton (Sr. Mary Ignatius), Jennifer Tilly, Wallace Langham, Brian Benben, Laura San Giacomo, Max Morrow, Martin Mull. *Director*: Marshall Brickman. *Producer*: Ronald M. Bozman.

Comic playwright Christopher Durang splashed onto the theatre scene with this one-act farce that was presented as part of a double bill Off Broadway for a long run. An aging but still sharp nun, who has long taught at Our Lady of Perpetual Sorrows Catholic School for years, lectures to an audience of adults about church dogma and answers questions that the attendees have written for her on index cards. Sr. Ignatius is very traditional in her confirmed beliefs and when some of her former students, now totally messed up from her teachings, appear and confront her, the nun has no problem scolding, insulting, and even shooting them. The outrageous little sketch was so hilarious because there was an element of truth in both the character and the extreme doctrines she advocated. The 2001 television production, with the abbreviated title of *Sister Mary Explains It All,* misjudges the line between realism and satire and the comedy is forced and offensive in a way the play never was. Diane Keaton makes a valiant stab at playing the obsessed nun but little of it works.

Six Cylinder Love

August 25, 1921 (Sam H. Harris Theatre), a comedy by William Anthony McGuire. *Cast*: Ernest Truex (Gilbert Sterling), June Walker (Marilyn Sterling), Donald Meek (Richard Burton), Eleanor Gordon (Geraldine Burton), Berton Churchill (Mr. Stapleton), Hedda Hopper (Margaret Rogers), Howard Hull Gibson, Betty Linley, Calvin Thomas. *Director*: Sam Forrest. *Producer:* Sam H. Harris. 430 performances.

(Fox 1923). *Screenplay*: Carl Stearns Clancy. *Cast*: Ernest Truex (Gilbert Sterling), Florence Eldridge (Marilyn Sterling), Donald Meek (Richard Burton), Maude Hill (Geraldine Burton), Berton Churchill (Stapleton), Marjorie Milton (Margaret Rogers), Ralph Sipperly, Harold Mann, Ann McKittnick. *Director*: Elner Clifton. *Producer*: William Fox.

(Fox 1931). *Screenplay*: William M. Conselman, Norman Houston. *Cast*: Loren Raker (Gilbert Sterling), Sidney Fox (Marilyn Sterling), William Collier, Sr. (Richard Burton), Spencer Tracy (William Donroy), Edward Everett Horton (Monty Winston), Una Merkel (Margaret Rogers), William Holden, Ruth Warren. *Director*: Thomas Freeland. *Producer*: William Fox.

Having your own automobile is such a status symbol that the newlyweds Richard and Geraldine Burton purchase a six-cylinder beauty. But the young couple soon finds that they are living far beyond their means and need to sell the auto to save them from bankruptcy. Their neighbors Gilbert and Marilyn Sterling, another pair of newly-weds, buy the car from them but soon they too are in debt and Gilbert nearly gets fired when his boss sees such extravagances as the six-cylinder car. So the Sterlings sell the car and spend the money on baby items for their new arrival. The broad, merry farce was very topical (and very popular) in its day and Ernest Truex's animated performance as Gilbert was roundly cheered. He reprised the role in the 1923 silent film with the young Florence Eldridge as his wife. The 1931 talkie featured some future stars in its supporting cast. Both movies opened up the action and handled the physical farce better than the character comedy.

Six Degrees of Separation

November 8, 1990 (Mitzi E. Newhouse Theatre), a play by John Guare. *Cast*: Stockard Channing (Ouisa), James McDaniel (Paul), John Cunningham (Flan), Kelly Bishop, Peter Maloney, John Cameron Mitchell, Mari Nelson, Robert Duncan McNeil. *Director*: Jerry Zaks. *Producer:* Lincoln Center Theatre. 641 performances.

(MGM 1993). *Screenplay*: John Guare. *Cast*: Stockard Channing (Ouisa), Will Smith (Paul), Donald Sutherland (Flan), Ian McKellen, Mary Beth Hurt, Bruce Davison, Heather Graham, Eric Thal, Anthony Rapp, Anthony Michael Hall. *Director*: Fred Schepisi. *Producers*: Armor Milchan, Fred Schepisi.

While the sophisticated Manhattan couple Flan and Ouisa Kittredge are entertaining a businessman, a beaten and bloody African American youth stumbles into their swank apartment claiming to be a friend of their children at college. He says he was mugged and went to the nearest safe place. The Kittredges take the boy in for the night and learn he is Paul, the son of movie actor Sidney Poitier. Paul charms them and even cooks up a splendid dinner as he talks about literature, art, and their children. But when Ouisa discovers Paul in bed with a male hustler and kicks them both out, the Kittredges start to find out that the youth is a con man who knows neither Poitier nor their kids. Paul pulls the same scam on some of their other friends and he even bilks a struggling young couple out of all their savings before he is picked up by the police. Despite their efforts to trace what happened to Paul, the Kittredges lose sight of him and are left wondering about the vibrant youth who managed to bring some life and pain into their smug and self-satisfied existence. One of the finest plays of the decade, the Off Broadway production (which later moved to Broadway) was directed and acted to perfection, Stockard Channing's bewildered, desperate Ouisa getting the most applause. Since several of the characters spoke directly to the audience and the plot did not always follow a chronological pattern, the play was not an easy one to adapt to the screen. But playwright John Guare managed to retell the story in cinematic terms and the drama plays almost as well in the 1993 film. Channing reprises her Ouisa and it remains a brilliant, unforgettable performance.

Skylark

October 11, 1939 (Morosco Theatre), a comedy by Samson Raphaelson. *Cast*: Gertrude Lawrence (Lydia Kenyon), Donald Cook (Tony Kenyon), Glenn Anders (Bill Blake), Vivian Vance (Mrs. Valentine), Gertrude Bryan (Charlotte Franklin), Walter Gilbert (George Gorell), William David, Robert Burton. *Director*: Samson Raphaelson. *Producer:* John Golden. 256 performances.

(Paramount 1941). *Screenplay*: Zion Myers, Allan Scott. *Cast*: Claudette Colbert (Lydia Kenyon), Ray Milland (Tony Kenyon), Brian Aherne (Jim Blake), Mona Barrie (Charlotte Gorell), Ernest Cossart, Binnie Barnes, Grant Mitchell, Walter Abel. *Director-producer*: Mark Sandrich.

Bored with her workaholic husband Tony, Lydia Kenyon has a fling with the lawyer Bill Blake which angers the wealthy Mrs. Valentine who has a yen for Bill herself. Mrs. Valentine sees that Tony loses his job and Lydia feels so bad she returns to him, vowing to adopt a baby and give her a more fulfilled life. The strained comedy of manners appeared to be more sparkling than it actually was thanks to the luminous performance by Gertrude Lawrence as Lydia so the play ran several months. The screenplay for the 1941 movie stays close to the play's plot and again it is the quality of the stars

that is responsible for what fun there is to be had. Claudette Colbert was Lydia with Ray Milland as her husband and Brian Aherne as the other man. The movie is well directed and has a sleek, appealing sheen to it but underneath not all that much is going on.

A Slight Case of Murder

September 11, 1935 (48th Street Theatre), a comedy by Damon Runyon, Howard Lindsay. *Cast*: John Harrington (Remy Marco), Phyllis Welch (Mary Marco), Georgia Caine (Nora Marco), Harry Levian (Sad Sam), Lawrence Grossmith (Theodore Whitelaw), James La Curto (Lefty), John Griggs, Roy Le May, Clyde Veaux, Percy Moore, Eleanor Brent. *Director-producer:* Howard Lindsay. 69 performances.

(Warner 1938). *Screenplay*: Earl Baldwin, Joseph Schrank. *Cast*: Edward G. Robinson (Remy Marco), Jane Bryan (Mary Marco), Allen Jenkins (Mike), Ruth Donnelly (Nora Marco), Willard Parker (Dick Whitehead), John Litel, Edward Brophy, Paul Harvey, Margaret Hamilton. *Director*: Lloyd Bacon. *Producer*: Samuel Bischoff.

Former bootlegger Remy Marco rents a house in Saratoga for the racing season and discovers four armored-truck robbers lying dead in the living room. Marco has his cronies dump each body on the porch of a neighbor who has snubbed him, then finds out there is a huge reward on the robbers's heads. Marco and his gang collect the bodies, put them in the closet, then call the police. When the crooks refuse to come out of the closet with their hands up, the state trooper fires a machine gun at the door, the bodies are collected, and Marco gets the reward. The broad farce had some of the Damon Runyon flavor but most of it was considered a noisy, silly play and it only ran a few months. The 1938 movie improved upon the plot by adding some funny characters and details and the film had a consistent style for the risible dark comedy. The cast was uniformly excellent but the real treat of the movie was Edward G. Robinson who got to play a comic variation of the gangster character that had made him famous.

Smilin' Through

December 30, 1919 (Broadhurst Theatre), a play by Allan Langdon Martin. *Cast*: Jane Cowl (Moonyeen/Kathleen Dungannon), Orme Caldera (Jeremiah/Kenneth Wayne), Henry Stephenson (John Carteret), Philip Tong, Lalive Brownell, Ethelbert D. Hales. *Director*: Priestly Morrison. *Producers:* Selwyns. 175 performances.

(Talmadge 1922). *Screenplay*: James Ashmore Creelman, Sidney Franklin. *Cast*: Norma Talmadge (Kathleen/Moonyeen), Harrison Ford (Jeremiah/Kenneth Wayne), Wyndham Standing (John Carteret), Alec B. Francis, Glenn Hunter. *Director*: Sidney Franklin. *Producer*: Norma Talmadge.

(MGM 1932). *Screenplay*: James B. Fagan, etc. *Cast*: Norma Shearer (Kathleen/Moonyeen), Frederic March (Jeremy/Kenneth Wayne), Leslie Howard (John Carteret), O. P. Heggie, Ralph Forbes. *Director*: Sidney Franklin. *Producer*: Albert Lewin.

(MGM 1941). *Screenplay*: Donald Ogden Stewart, etc. *Cast*: Jeanette MacDonald (Kathleen/Moonyeen), Gene Raymond (Jeremy/Kenneth Wayne), Brian Aherne (John Carteret), Ian Hunter, Frances Robinson, Patrick O'Moore. *Director*: Frank Borzage. *Producer*: Victor Saville.

One of the most beloved tearjerkers of its era, this romantic melodrama alternated from the present to the past as it moved between one generation and another. On the wedding day of Moonyeen and John Carteret, Moonyeen's rejected suitor Jeremiah Wayne bursts onto the ceremony and attempts to shoot John. Instead he kills Moonyeen by mistake and she dies in John's arms. Two generations later, the Cartert and Wayne families still carry their distrust and hatred for each other and it stands in the way of two young lovers. But the elderly John realizes that the sins of the past should not harm those that follow so he relents, allows his niece Kathleen to marry a Wayne, and is left in the garden explaining it all to the ghost of Moonyeen. While some critics carped, audience accepted the sentimental romance and applauded the star Jane Cowl who played Moonyeen and Kathleen and, under a pen name, wrote the play. Silent screen star Norma Talmadge bought the property and produced the 1922 movie version with herself as Moonyeen and Kathleen. It was an ideal vehicle for her and the film was popular. The very successful 1932 talkie was even better with Norma Shearer in the double role and Leslie Howard and Fredric March as the men in her characters' lives. The sentiment runs thick throughout the movie but it is so well presented and played with such conviction that the melodrama glows. The 1942 remake, on the other hand, seems artificial and the emotions are more manufactured than sincere. Jeanette MacDonald, who got to sing a few songs, and co-stars Gene Raymond and Brian Aherne were adequate but something was missing. Perhaps the old weepie had outlived its day. The failed 1932 Broadway musical *Through the Years* was based on the original play.

A Soldier's Play

November 20, 1981 (Theatre Four), a play by Charles Fuller. *Cast*: Adolph Caesar (Sgt. Vernon C. Waters), Charles Brown (Capt. Richard Davenport), Denzel Washington ((Pfc. Melvin Peterson), Samuel L. Jackson (Pvt. Louis Henson), Peter Friedman, Brent Jennings, Larry Riley, James Pickens, Jr., Eugene Lee, Steven A. Jones, Cotter Smith, Stephen Zettler. *Director*: Douglas Turner Ward. *Producer:* Negro Ensemble Company. 468 performances. Pulitzer Prize.

A Soldier's Story (Columbia 1984). *Screenplay*: Charles Fuller. *Cast*: Adolph Caesar (Sgt. Vernon C. Waters), Howard E. Rollins, Jr.(Capt. Richard Davenport), Denzel Washington ((Pfc. Melvin Peterson), William Allen Young (Pvt. Louis Henson), Art Evans, David Alan Grier, David Harris, Robert Townsend, Patti LaBelle, Larry Riley, Trey Wilson. *Director*: Norman Jewison. *Producers*: Ronald L. Schwary, Norman Jewison.

At a Louisiana Army base during World War Two, an African American sergeant is shot dead and the Klan is thought to be responsible. But when the crime is investigated by a black captain, he uncovers racial hatred among the African American soldiers and discovers that the murderer was one of them. Avoiding stereotypes and easy solutions, the drama was both engrossing and thought provoking. A superb cast and precise direction helped the play run over a year. The 1984 film, retitled *A Soldier's Story*, allowed Adolph Caesar and Denzel Washington, as the sergeant and his murderer, to recreate their stage roles on screen and both were extraordinary; it was the crowning achievement for veteran Caesar and the first important role for Washington. The play contained several flashbacks so the movie opened up effectively for the screen, aided by expert direction and a fine supporting cast.

A Soldier's Story see *A Soldier's Play*

The Solid Gold Cadillac

November 5, 1953 (Belasco Theatre), a comedy by Howard Teichmann, George S. Kaufman. *Cast*: Josephine Hull (Laura Partridge), Loring Smith (Edward l. McKeever), Geoffrey Lumb, Wendell K. Philips, Reynolds Evans, Mary Welch. *Director*: George S. Kaufman. *Producer*: Max Gordon. 526 performances.

(Columbia 1956). *Screenplay*: Abe Burrows. *Cast*: Judy Holliday, Paul Douglas (Edward L. McKeever), Fred Clark, John Williams, Hiram Sherman, Ray Collins, Arthur O'Connell, George Burns (narrator). *Director*: Richard Quine. *Producer*: Fred Kohlmar.

Laura Partridge is a kindly old lady who shows up at a stockholders' meeting and starts asking innocent questions that make the executives nervous. So to shut her up, they hire Laura to respond to letters from stockholders. Her responses are so chatty and friendly that by the time the next stockholders' meeting comes around, Laura has enough proxy votes to take over the company. While the situation was promising and the characters amusing, it was the performance by Josephine Hull as Laura that made the play work. Sadly, it was the beloved character actress's final stage appearance; it was also the last Broadway play by co-author George S. Kaufman and producer Max Gordon. The 1956 movie cast another kind of star as Laura: the young, perky, smart-dumb blonde Judy Holliday. The script was rewritten to fit her but the humor of an unprepos-

sessing senior citizen frightening company executives was lost with a younger Laura. A romance was even suggested between Laura and one of the CEOs. But the film has its merits and Holliday is always worth watching.

Something for the Boys

January 7, 1943 (Alvin Theatre), a musical comedy by Herbert and Dorothy Fields. *Score*: Cole Porter. *Cast*: Ethel Merman (Blossom Hart), Bill Johnson (Sgt Rocky Fulton), Betty Garrett (Mary-Frances), Paula Lawrence (Chiquita Hart), Allen Jenkins (Harry Hart), Betty Bruce (Betty-Jean), Jed Prouty (Roger Calhoun), Anita Alverez, Bill Callahan, William Lynn. *Songs*: Hey, Good Lookin'; By the Mississinewah; Could It Be You?; He's a Right Guy; I'm in Love With a Soldier Boy; Something for the Boys; The Leader of a Big Time Band. *Directors*: Hassard Short, Herbert Fields. *Choreographer*: Jack Cole. *Producer*: Michael Todd. 422 performances.

(Fox 1944). *Screenplay*: Robert Ellis, Helen Logan, Frank Gabrielson. *Score:* Jimmy McHugh, Harold Adamson, Cole Porter. *Cast*: Carmen Miranda (Chiquita Hart), Vivian Blaine (Blossom Hart), Phil Silvers (Harry Hart), Perry Como (Sgt. Laddie Green), Michael O'Shea (Sgt. Rocky Fulton), Sheila Ryan, Roger Clark, Thurston Hall. *Songs*: Something for the Boys; I'm in the Middle of Nowhere; Wouldn't It Be Nice?; Boom Brachee; I Wish We Didn't Have to Say Goodnight; Samba Boogie. *Director*: Lewis Seiler. *Choreographer*: Nick Castle. *Producer*: Irving Starr.

One of Cole Porter's lesser scores and a ridiculous plot hindered this silly wartime musical but the show ran on the strength of its star, Ethel Merman. She played a defense plant worker whose dental fillings were able to pick up distress signals from airplanes in trouble. The movie version dropped all the Porter songs except the title number and passed on Merman as well, but kept much of the stupid storyline. Vivian Blaine was given the enviable position of trying to fill Merman's shoes but the film was stolen by Carmen Miranda in a supporting role. The movie is musically unimpressive but as a comedy it has its entertainment value.

Song of Norway

August 21, 1944 (Imperial Theatre), an operetta by Milton Lazaras. *Score:* Edvard Grieg, Robert Wright, George Forrest. *Cast:* Lawrence Brooks (Edvard Grieg), Irra Petina (Louisa Giovanni), Helena Bliss (Nina Hagerup), Robert Shafer (Rikard Nordraak), Sig Arno (Count Peppi Le Loup), Alexandra Danilova, Ivy Scott. *Songs:* Strange Music; Hill of Dreams; Now!; Midsummer's Eve; I Love You; Freddy and His Fiddle; Three Loves. *Directors:* Edwin Lester, Charles K. Freedman. *Choreographer:* George Balanchine. *Producer:* Edwin Lester. 860 performances.

(ABC 1970). *Screenplay:* Virginia and Andrew Stone. *Score:* Edvard Grieg, Robert Wright, George Forrest. *Cast:* Toralv Maurstadt (Edvard Grieg), Florence Henderson (Nina Grieg), Harry Secombe (Bjoersen), Frank Poretta (Richard Nordraak), Robert Morley (Berg), Edward G. Robinson, Oscar Homolka. *Songs:* Strange Music; Hill of Dreams; I Love You; Freddy and His Fiddle; In the Hall of the Mountain King; Hand in Hand. *Director:* Andrew Stone. *Choreographer:* Lee Theodore. *Producers:* Virginia and Andrew Stone.

One of a handful of 1940s musicals that used classical music for its score, this operetta about the life of Norwegian composer Edvard Grieg was weak in plot but quite satisfying when the famous music was given lyrics by the team of Robert Wright and George Forrest. Hollywood wasn't interested in filming the work until after the success of the movie *The Sound of Music*. Hoping that the Norwegian fiords would do for the film what the Alps did for the other tuner, the musical emphasized scenery over character and plot, both of which were embarrassingly sentimental and mundane. Even the vibrant Grieg melodies were only effective when used as background to the lush scenery. This film flop has the distinction of being the most expensive (and the last) movie operetta.

Song of the Flame

December 30, 1925 (44th Street Theatre), an operetta by Oscar Hammerstein, Otto Harbach. *Score:* George Gershwin, Herbert Stothart, Oscar Hammerstein, Otto Harbach. *Cast:* Tessa Kosta (Aniuta), Guy Robertson (Prince Volodya), Greek Evans (Konstantin), Dorothy Mackaye (Grusha), Hugh Cameron, Ula Sharon, Bernard Gorcey. *Songs:* Song of the Flame; The Cossack Love Song; Far Away; Midnight Bells; Woman's Work Is Never Done; Wander Away. *Director:* Frank Reicher. *Choreographer:* Jack Haskell. *Producer:* Arthur Hammerstein. 219 performances.

(First National 1930). *Screenplay:* Gordon Rigby. *Score:* George Gershwin, Herbert Stothart, Oscar Hammerstein, Otto Harbach, etc. *Cast:* Bernice Claire (Aniuta), Alexander Gray (Prince Volodya), Noah Berry (Konstantin), Alice Gentle (Natasha), Bert Roach (Count Boros), Inez Courtney, Shep Camp, Ivan Linow. *Songs:* Song of the Flame; The Cossack Love Song; When Love Calls; One Little Drink; Petrograd; Liberty Song; Passing Fancy. *Director:* Alan Crosland. *Choreographer:* Jack Haskell.

A very atypical work for composer George Gershwin, this operetta was a passionate piece set in Czarist Russia with the aristocratic Aniuta disguising herself as a peasant in a flaming red dress and leading the serfs in revolt. She is loved by a prince who is unaware of her secret identity and only after the fall of the Romanovs do the two meet in Paris and find happiness together. Although the score was a curiosity at best, the show was popular enough to run out the season and to be filmed in 1930. The early talkie is impressive in its attempts to use color in certain scenes and at one point opens up to a widescreen format. But it remains musically uninteresting, a sure sign of failure in an operetta.

The Sound of Music

November 16, 1959 (Lunt-Fontanne Theatre), a musical play by Howard Lindsay, Russel Crouse. *Score:* Richard Rodgers, Oscar Hammerstein. *Cast:* Mary Martin (Maria Rainer), Theodore Bikel (Capt. Georg Von Trapp), Patricia Neway (Mother Abbess), Kurt Kasznar (Max Detweiler), Marian Marlowe (Else Schroeder), Lauri Peters, Brian Davies. *Songs:* The Sound of Music; My Favorite Things; Durham; Climb Every Mountain; Edelweiss; Sixteen Going on Seventeen; The Lonely Gathered; How Can Love Survive?; So Long, Farewell; No Way to Stop It. *Director:* Vincent J. Donehue. *Choreographer:* Joe Layton. *Producers:* Rodgers and Hammerstein, Leland Hayward, Richard Halliday. 1,443 performances. Tony Award.

(Fox 1965). *Screenplay:* Ernest Lehman. *Score:*

Richard Rodgers, Oscar Hammerstein. *Cast:* Julie Andrews (Maria Rainer), Christopher Plummer (Capt. Von Trapp), Peggy Wood (Mother Abbess), Eleanor Parker (Baroness), Richard Haydn (Max Detweiler), Carmen Carr. *Songs:* The Sound of Music; My Favorite Things; Durham; Climb Every Mountain; Edelweiss; Sixteen Going on Seventeen; The Lonely Gathered; I Have Confidence in Me; So Long, Farewell; Something Good. *Director-producer:* Robert Wise. *Choreographers:* Marc Beaux, Dee Dee Wood. Academy Award.

This final collaboration by Rodgers and Hammerstein has gained a reputation over the years for being a cute, cheery musical play about how kids, nuns, music, and love can beat the Nazis. Yet the original stage musical has some bite to it and political issues are always close to the surface. The stern, patriotic Captain will not bend to the Germans; he breaks off his engagement to a baroness because she disagrees with him on this point. There were even two sarcastic, adult songs in the play: "How Can Love Survive" and "No Way to Stop It." But both of these and all the politics were dropped in the hugely successful film version. (His growing love for the governess Maria makes the Captain drop the baroness in the screenplay.) The children and the scenery are given more screen time and it is all so competently done that no one missed the fact that the film version wasn't about much of anything. Yet there is plenty to admire in the movie which is still the screen musical seen by more people than any other. The performances are first-rate with Julie Andrews keeping the whole picture in perspective by being engaging even in her naivete. The songs may have been shuffled around a bit in the film but it is for the better, just as the two new numbers are welcome improvements. Most of all, *The Sound of Music* on screen feels like a movie and not a filmed stage work. It uses all of the joyous cinematic techniques available and blends them with the original tale to become first-class entertainment.

South Pacific

April 7, 1949 (Majestic Theatre), a musical play by Oscar Hammerstein, Joshua Logan. *Score:*

Richard Rodgers, Oscar Hammerstein. *Cast:* Mary Martin (Nellie Forbush), Ezio Pinza (Emile de Becque), Juanita Hall (Bloody Mary), Myron McCormick (Luther Billis), William Tabbert (Lt. Joe Cable), Betta St. John (Liat). *Songs:* Some Enchanted Evening; There Is Nothin' Like a Dame; Bali Ha'i; Younger Than Springtime; This Nearly Was Mine; Happy Talk; I'm Gonna Wash That Man Right Outa My Hair; Honey Bun; You've Got to Be Carefully Taught; A Wonderful Guy; A Cockeyed Optimist. *Director:* Joshua Logan. *Producers:* Rodgers and Hammerstein, Leland Hayward, Joshua Logan. 1,925 performances. Pulitzer Prize, Tony Award.

(Magna/Fox 1958). *Screenplay:* Paul Osborn. *Score:* Richard Rodgers, Oscar Hammerstein. *Cast:* Mitzi Gaynor (Nellie Forbush), Rossano Brazzi (Emile de Becque), John Kerr (Lt. Joe Cable), Ray Walston (Luther Billis), Juanita Hall (Bloody Mary), France Nuyen (Liat). *Songs:* Some Enchanted Evening; There Is Nothin' Like a Dame; Bali Ha'i; Younger Than Springtime; This Nearly Was Mine; Happy Talk; I'm Gonna Wash That Man Right Outa My Hair; Honey Bun; You've Got to Be Carefully Taught; A Wonderful Guy; A Cockeyed Optimist; My Girl Back Home. *Director:* Joshua Logan. *Choreographer:* LeRoy Prinz. *Producer:* Buddy Adler.

(TV 2001). *Teleplay:* Lawrence D. Cohen. *Cast:* Glenn Close (Nellie Forbush), Rade Serbedzija (Emile de Becque), Harry Connick, Jr. (Lt. Joe Cable), Lori Tan Chinn (Bloody Mary), Robert Pastorelli (Luther Billis), Natalia Jackson, Jack Thompson. *Songs:* Some Enchanted Evening; There Is Nothin' Like a Dame; Bali Ha'i; Younger Than Springtime; This Nearly Was Mine; Happy Talk; I'm Gonna Wash That Man Right Outa My Hair; Honey Bun; You've Got to Be Carefully Taught; A Wonderful Guy; A Cockeyed Optimist. *Director:* Richard Pearce. *Producer:* Christine A. Scani.

This very adult musical had a very unlikely love story (the young American nurse Nellie Forbush and the mature French planter Emile de Becque), an unlikely setting (behind the scenes of World War Two), and an unlikely theme (inner prejudice separates the lovers, not external forces). The libretto is intelligent and daring and the Rodgers and Hammerstein score provides memorable Broadway tunes as well as exotic-sounding Pacific islands numbers. The show was written with Mary Martin and Ezio Pinza in mind but has found success with other players in many revivals across the country. The movie version was very faithful in some ways (the entire score was retained) but the script meanders with some lifeless scenes and the long film drags in many spots. The performances are more competent than enthralling and the lovely location scenery is marred by some distracting color filters that are used indiscriminately during several of the songs. This is a film best enjoyed by those who have never experienced a first-class stage production of the musical. The 2001 television production seemed hellbent on being different: a classy, high-mannered Glenn Close as Nellie, scruffy tenor Rade Serbedzija for Emile, and a swinging Harry Connick, Jr. playing Joe. Scripts changes were not for the better and the story seemed unusually dour with the comedy so misplaced. But the score was retained pretty much intact and Lori Tan Chinn was a mean-spirited, almost dangerous Bloody Mary as opposed to the usual cute Polynesian grandma type.

Spring Is Here

March 11, 1929 (Alvin Theatre), a musical comedy by Owen Davis. *Score:* Richard Rodgers, Lorenz Hart. *Cast:* Glenn Hunter (Terry Clayton), Lillian Taiz (Betty Braley), Charles Ruggles (Peter Braley), John Hundley (Stacy Hayden), Inez Courtney (Mary Jane), Joyce Barbour, Dick Keene, Lew Parker. *Songs:* With a Song in My Heart; Spring Is Here (in Person); Yours Sincerely; Baby's Awake Now; Red Hot Trumpet; Why Can't I? *Director:* Alexander Leftwich. *Choreographer:* Bobby Connolly. *Producers:* Alex A. Aarons, Vinton Freedley. 104 performances.

(First National 1930). *Screenplay:* James A. Starr. *Score:* Richard Rodgers, Lorenz Hart, etc. *Cast:* Bernice Claire (Betty Braley), Lawrence Gray (Steve Alden), Alexander Gray (Terry Clayton), Ford Sterling (Peter Braley), Louise Fazenda (Emily Braley), Inez Courtney (Mary Jane Braley), Frank Albertson, Natalie Moorhead. *Songs:* With a Song in My Heart; Spring Is Here in Person; Yours Sincerely; I Married an Angel; Rich Man, Poor Man; Baby's Awake Now; Cryin' for the Carolinas; Have a Little Faith in Me. *Director:* John Francis Dillon.

This second-rate Rodgers and Hart musical managed to squeak by as a hit because of its noteworthy score, in particular the standard "With a Song in My Heart." The story, about a socialite who plans to elope with one man only to end up in the arms of another, was routine at best and Inez Courtney as the heroine's sister was the only interesting character in the show. She was retained for the film version and was sensational singing "Baby's Awake Now" and "Rich Man, Poor Man." But much of the rest of the score was cut for the screen and there is little to recommend in the movie. The title song was not the famous standard but the earlier, less accomplished "Spring Is Here (in Person)."

The Squaw Man

October 23, 1905 (Wallack's Theatre), a play by Edwin Milton Royle. *Cast:* William Faversham (Capt. James Wynnegate), Mabel Morrison (Nat-u-ritch), Selene Johnson (Lady Diana), William S. Hart (Cash Hawkins), Theodore Roberts (Taby-wana), George Fawcett, C. A. Carlton, Evelyn Wright. *Directors:* Edwin Milton Royle, William Faversham. *Producer:* Liebler & Co. 222 performances.

(Lasky 1914). *Screenplay:* Cecil B. DeMille, Oscar Apfel. *Cast:* Dustin Farnum (Capt. James Wynnegate), Red Wing (Nat-u-Rich), Winifred Kingston (Lady Diana), William Elmer (Cash Hawkins), Monroe Salisbury. *Directors:* Oscar Apfel, Cecil B. DeMille. *Producers:* Jesse L. Lasky, Cecil B. DeMille.

(Lasky 1918). *Screenplay:* Beulah Marie Dix. *Cast:* Elliott Dexter (Capt. Jim Wynnegate), Ann Little (Naturich), Katherine McDonald (Diana), Jack Holt (Cash Hawkins), Theodore Roberts. *Director-producer:* Cecil B. DeMille.

(MGM 1931). *Screenplay:* Lenore J. Coffee, etc. *Cast:* Warner Baxter (Jim Wingate), Lupe Velez (Naturich), Eleanor Boardman (Diana), Charles Bickford (Cash Hawkins), Roland Young, Paul Cavanaugh. *Director-producer:* Cecil B. DeMille.

This classic Western tale is a slight variation of the *Madame Butterfly* tale written five years before. The British Captain James Wynnegate is a married man but so in love with Lady Diana that when he learns she stole money from a charity he emigrates to America so that it will look like he was the culprit. Wynnegate goes out West where he falls in love with the Native American Nat-u-ritch who saved his life so they marry and have a son. But when Diana seeks out Wynnegate to tell that his name is cleared and that he has inherited a title, Nat-u-ritch commits suicide so that she will not be in the way of her husband and their son. The melodrama was a hit on Broadway and on the road where it toured for two decades. The 1914 screen version is considered a silent classic with its six-reel length and stunning use of desert locations; one of the first important films to be made in California. The movie also launched the career of director Cecil B. DeMille. In 1917 a sequel titled *The Squaw Man's Son* was released, then de Mille directed a remake of the original story in 1918. It was also successful, though not as popular and influential as the earlier version. The 1931 talkie (also by de Mille) boasted top stars Warner Baxter and Lupe Velez and again the locations were impressive but the now-familiar story did not intrigue audiences and the movie failed. All the same, there is much to admire in this version, including some acting that manages to avoid the obvious and approaches the characters sincerely. The original play was turned into the unsuccessful Broadway musical *The White Eagle* in 1927.

Stage Door

October 22, 1936 (Music Box Theatre), a play by George S. Kaufman, Edna Ferber. *Cast*: Margaret Sullavan (Terry Randall), Onslow Stevens (David Kingsley), Richard Kendrick (Keith Burgess), Frances Fuller (Kaye Hamilton), Phyllis Brooks (Jean Maitland), Jane Buchanan (Linda Shaw), Priestly Morrison, Lee Patrick, Mary Wickes, Tom Ewell. *Director*: George S. Kaufman. *Producer:* Sam H. Harris. 159 performances.

(RKO 1937). *Screenplay*: Morrie Ryskind, Anthony Veiller. *Cast*: Katharine Hepburn (Terry Randall), Adolphe Menjou (Anthony Powell), Kaye Hamilton (Andrea Leeds), Ginger Rogers (Jean Maitland), , Gail Patrick (Linda Shaw), Lucille Ball, Eve Arden, Ann Miller, Constance Collier, Jack Carson. *Director*: Gregory La Cava. *Producer*: Pandro S. Berman.

The residents of a boarding house called the Footlights Club are young, strug-

gling actresses hoping to make it on Broadway. One of them forsakes the stage for the screen, another commits suicide when she is fired from a production, but Terry Randall makes it by staying true to her dreams. The play mixed melodrama with wisecracking comedy and the varied array of characters made for lively theatre. Margaret Sullavan was starred as Terry and the cast was filled with young talent, some of whom, like the residents of the Club, would become famous. The same could be said of the 1937 film which featured Katharine Hepburn as Terry and Ginger Rogers as her smart-aleck rival Jean but offered early glimpses of Lucille Ball, Ann Miller, and Eve Arden. In many ways the movie is more satisfying than the play: the plotting is stronger, the balance between comedy and pathos well handled, and the story opens up nicely outside of the Club. Audiences in 1937 were fascinated by the behind-the-scenes look at the theatre and the film still appeals today for much the same reason. A 1955 television version of the play featured Diana Lynn (as Terry), Rhonda Fleming, Peggy Ann Garner, and Nota Talbot.

Stalag 17

May 8, 1951 (48th Street Theatre), a play by Donald Bevan, Edmund Trzcinski. *Cast*: John Ericson (Sefton), Laurence Hugo (Price), Lothar Rewalt (Col. Shultz), Robert Strauss (Stosh), Harvey Lembeck (Harry Shapiro), Robert Shawley (Herb Gordon), Arthur Walsh (Duke), Frank Maxwell (Hoffman), Douglas Henderson (McCarthy), Garry Davis (Red-Dog), Richard Poston, Mark Roberts, Eric Fleming, William Pierson, Frank Campanella. *Director-producer:* José Ferrer. 472 performances.

(Paramount 1953). *Screenplay*: Billy Wilder. *Cast*: William Holden (Sefton), Don Taylor (Skylar Dunbar), Otto Preminger (Col. von Scherbach), Peter Graves (Price), Sig Ruman (Sgt. Schulz), Harvey Lembeck (Harry Shapiro), Neville Brand (Duke), Robert Strauss (Stosh), Gil Stratton, Jr., Richard Erdman. *Director-producer*: Billy Wilder.

All of the American prisoners in the Nazi Stalag 17 have a sense on camaraderie except the loner Sefton so when the guards discover an escape plan everyone suspects

Sefton is the informer. But it is Sefton who eventually finds out the real informer and sets it up so that the Nazis gun down their own man. Written by two former prisoners of war, the drama was accurate, compelling, and even humorous at times. The 1953 screen version is probably the best POW film ever made as it also mixes comedy and tragedy and looks at prisoners of war without reverence or cliché. The play was opened up masterfully by Billy Wilder who also directed the tricky piece with flair and honesty. The acting throughout is remarkable: William Holden won an Oscar for his Sefton but he is matched all the way by the impressive ensemble. The humor was mostly provided by Richard Strauss and Harvey Lembeck, reprising their stage performances as two prisoners whose stress leads them into wacky comedics. The play has been cited as the source material for the popular television series *Hogan's Heroes* (1965–1971) though they only share a similar locale and not plot, characters, or tone.

The Star-Spangled Girl

December 21, 1966 (Plymouth Theatre), a comedy by Neil Simon. *Cast*: Anthony Perkins (Andy Hobart), Richard Benjamin (Norman Cornell), Connie Stevens (Sophie Rauschmeyer). *Director*: George Axelrod. *Producer:* Saint Subber. 261 performances.

(Paramount 1971). *Screenplay*: Arnold Margolin, Jim Parker. *Cast*: Sandy Duncan (Amy Cooper), Tony Roberts (Andy Hobart), Todd Susman (Norman Cornell), Elizabeth Allen, Artie Lewis. *Director*: Jerry Paris. *Producer*: Howard W. Koch.

Considered by Neil Simon and most everybody else as the playwright's weakest effort, the economical three-character comedy was a financial success on Broadway and it continues to be produced by groups looking for a cheap, non-demanding theatre piece. San Francisco radicals Andy Hobart and Norman Cornell try to make ends meet as they publish the protest magazine *Fallout*. But the duo's friendship is threatened when Norman falls in love with their new all–American neighbor Sophie Rauschmeyer and she is attracted to Andy. The one-liners

were sometimes forced, sometimes inspired, but the characters were as unconvincing as the hippie milieu that Simon tried in vain to create. Most critics agreed that Anthony Perkins and Richard Benjamin were an amusing duo while Connie Stevens was less appreciated. But everyone seemed to concur that the performances in the 1971 movie were as poor as the script. Directed as a broad shouting match, the comedy was a loud embarrassment that quickly disappeared.

State of the Union

November 14, 1945 (Hudson Theatre), a comedy by Howard Lindsay, Russel Crouse. *Cast*: Ralph Bellamy (Grant Matthews), Ruth Hussey (Mary Matthews), Kay Johnson (Kay Thorndyke), Minor Watson, Myron McCormick, Herbert Heyes, G. Albert Smith, Maidel Turner. *Director*: Bretaigne Windust. *Producer:* Leland Hayward. 765 performances. Pulitzer Prize.

(Liberty-MGM 1948). *Screenplay*: Myles Connolly, Anthony Veiller. *Cast*: Spencer Tracy (Grant Matthews), Katharine Hepburn (Mary Matthews), Angela Lansbury (Kay Thorndyke), Van Johnson, Adolphe Menjou, Lewis Stone, Margaret Hamilton, Raymond Walburn. *Director-producer*: Frank Capra.

The Republicans, desperate to get a man in the White House, approach the idealistic businessman Grant Matthews to run for the Presidency and he is supported by the wealthy publisher Kay Thorndyke who, rumor has it, is having an affair with him. But Grant's strong-willed wife Mary must be an active part of the campaign and it takes some convincing before she agrees to play along. But in the end Grant's conscience and not his wife convince him to be honest with himself. He withdraws from the race, gives up Kay, and returns to his wife. The comedy was intelligently written and given a first-class production with a talented cast so it ran two years and won the Pulitzer Prize. The large number of characters and the complicated production demands keep the play from frequent revivals but it remains one of the better theatre pieces about politics. Although the 1948 film was made as a vehicle for the popular team of Spencer

Tracy and Katharine Hepburn, it is an accurate adaptation of the play with the role of Mary enlarged somewhat so that the duo had a few more scenes together. But Tracy and Hepburn are not the only show in town; the entire cast is commendable with particularly fine work from Angela Lansbury as Kay and Van Johnson as the campaign manager. Only the ending gets a bit sentimental, a trademark of director Frank Capra, but mostly it is a superior film. A 1954 television version of the play starred Joseph Cotten, Nina Foch, and Margaret Sullavan.

Steambath

June 30, 1970 (Truck & Warehouse Theatre), a comedy by Bruce Jay Friedman. *Cast*: Anthony Perkins (Tandy), Hector Elizondo (Attendant), Annie Rachel (Meredith), Conrad Bain, Babor Morea, Marvin Lichterman, Mitchell Jason. *Director*: Anthony Perkins. *Producer:* Ivor David Balding. 128 performances.

(TV 1973). *Teleplay*: Bruce Jay Friedman. *Cast*: Bill Bixby (Tandy), José Perez (Attendant), Herb Edelman (Bieberman), Valerie Perrine (Meredith), Stephen Elliott (Oldtimer), Biff Elliott (Flanders), Shirley Kirkus, Kenneth Mars, Peter Kastner. *Director*: Burt Brinckerhoff. *Producer*: Norman Lloyd.

In this dark, comic allegory, purgatory is a steambath where the recently dead wait and where God is a Puerto Rican attendant who keeps the place clean in between deciding the fate of the world. The outrageous comedy had its serious side as well, such as the main character Tandy's long monologue at the end in which he tries to justify his life to God and himself. But mostly the play was an outspoken, politically incorrect farce. The Off Broadway production had so many pre-opening problems that director Anthony Perkins ended up playing Tandy himself. His performance and the rest of the cast were better reviewed than the play but magazine writer Bruce Jay Friedman's off-the-wall humor appealed to enough that the play ran four months. The 1973 television production made few changes, keeping the action in the steambath and allowing Bill Bixby to deliver Tandy's final plea as on stage. The talented

cast is worth watching even if the play has limited appeal. A television series based on the comedy ran only six episodes in 1983.

Steel Magnolias

June 19, 1987 (Lucille Lortel Theatre), a play by Robert Harling. *Cast*: Margo Martindale (Truvy), Rosemary Prinz (M'Lynn), Betsey Aidem (Shelby), Kate Wilkinson, Constance Shulman, Mary Fogarty. *Director*: Pamela Berlin. *Producers:* Kyle Renick, WPA Theatre. 1,126 performances.

(Columbia 1989). *Screenplay*: Robert Harling. *Cast*: Sally Field (M'Lynn), Julia Roberts (Shelby), Dolly Parton (Truvy), Olympia Dukakis, Shirley MacLaine, Daryl Hannah, Tom Skerritt, Sam Shepard. *Director*: Herbert Ross. *Producer*: Ray Stark.

In a series of scenes at Truvy's beauty salon in a small Southern town, we meet a handful of women whose lives and personalities are unveiled over the period of a few years, in particular the diabetic Shelby who weds, has a child, and then dies in the course of the play. The Off Broadway comedy-drama was a surprise hit, running over three years and later revived by hundreds of regional theatres and schools. One of the joys of the unpretentious little play was the way the whole community, male and female, was created through the gossip and jokes of the women at Truvy's. This was all lost in the 1989 film which opened up the action, added male characters only discussed in the play, and showed events that had been far more interesting when comically described by the women on stage. The all-star cast varied in quality and most of the vivid characters became broad stereotypes on screen. All the same, the movie was widely popular and encouraged more amateur productions on the play.

Step Lively see Room Service

Sticks and Bones

November 7, 1971 (Public Theatre), a drama by David Rabe. *Cast*: Tom Aldredge (Ozzie), Elizabeth Wilson (Harriet), David Selby (David), Cliff De Young (Rick), Hector Elias, Asa Gim, Charles Siebert. *Director*: Jeff Bleckner. *Producer*: Joe Papp. 366 performances. Tony Award.

(TV 1973). *Teleplay*: Robert Downey, Sr. *Cast*: Tom Aldredge (Ozzie), Anne Jackson (Harriet), Alan Cauldwell (David), Cliff De Young (Rick), Joe Fields, Asa Gim, Stanley Levine, Ron Nealy, Brad Sullivan. *Director*: Robert Downey, Sr. *Producer*: Joe Papp.

When the Vietnam vet David returns to his white-bread, all–American family blind and emotionally numb from his war experiences, he is looked on as an embarrassment by his parents Ozzie and Harriet, who live by empty platitudes, and his younger brother Rick, who encourages him to commit suicide and even offers him a razor to slit his wrists. Since David can only see the Vietnamese girl that he loved and lost, he gives into Rick's suggestion and kills himself as the family looks on with relief and satisfaction. One of the most harrowing of all anti-war plays of the period, David Rabe's drama made him famous when its Off Broadway production was successfully moved to Broadway. The acting was roundly praised, even if many critics and spectators had difficulty with the disturbing play itself. When it was remade for television in 1973 with most of the stage cast, much controversy surrounded its broadcast and many stations across the country refused to carry it. Because of the theatrical nature of the piece, the play came across more preachy on the small screen and the absence of Elizabeth Wilson's sterling performance as Harriet threw off the balance of the drama. The play has not dated well but in its time it was compelling and not to be forgotten.

Stolen Hours see Dark Victory

Strange Interlude

January 30, 1928 (John Golden Theatre), a drama by Eugene O'Neill. *Cast*: Lynn Fontanne (Nina Leeds), Glenn Anders (Dr. Edmund Darrell), Tom Powers (Charles Marsden), Earle Larrimore

(Sam), Helen Westley (Mrs. Evans), Philip Leigh, Charles Walters, John J. Burns, Ethel Westley. *Director*: Philip Moeller. *Producer:* Theatre Guild. 426 performances. Pulitzer Prize.

(MGM 1932). *Screenplay*: Bess Meredyth, C. Gardner Sullivan. *Cast*: Norma Shearer (Nina Leeds), Clark Gable (Ned Darrell), Ralph Morgan (Charlie Marsden), Alexander Kirkland (Sam), May Robson (Mrs. Evans), Maureen O'-Sullivan, Robert Young, Henry B. Walthall. *Director*: Robert Z. Leonard.

(TV 1987). *Teleplay*: Robert Enders. *Cast*: Glenda Jackson (Nina Leeds), David Dukes (Dr. Ned Darrell), Edward Petherbridge (Charlies Marsden), Ken Howard (Sam), Rosemary Harris (Mrs. Evans), José Ferrer, Kenneth Branagh, Julie Eccles, Elizabeth Kelly. *Director*: Herbert Wise. *Producer*: Robert Enders.

Nina Leeds has always been able to control the men around her, including her professor-father, her naive husband, her doctor-lover, and her son by that doctor. But late in life Nina ends up with the old family friend Charlie and it seems she no longer cares to manipulate those around her. The nine-act drama (it ran over four hours and was presented with a dinner break) was distinguished by Eugene O'Neill's use of interior monologues that stopped the action while the characters expressed their thoughts aloud. This very Freudian device made the melodramatic plot more fascinating and allowed the playwright to develop characters with the depth of a novelist. The play was the talk of the town, in no small part because of its controversial subject matter at times (including insanity, infidelity, and abortion), and Lynn Fontanne and the rest of the cast were roundly praised. The 1932 film version ran half as long as the play but managed to cover most of the plot and some of the interior thoughts as well, much easier to do on screen than on stage. Norma Shearer lacks the strength of character for Nina but Clark Gable is splendid as the doctor and the supporting players throughout are estimable. More surprising, the play's adult issues made it to the screen and the film was a breakthrough of sorts for what could be discussed in a movie. All the same, the film was a box office disappointment. Revivals of the play have been rare but a

London production that traveled to Broadway was remade for television in 1987 with an American-British cast. Glenda Jackson is a brilliant Nina, quietly controlling all around her yet never deriving much happiness for it, and she is surrounded by such talents as Rosemary Harris, David Dukes, Edward Petherbridge, José Ferrer, and a young Kenneth Branaugh. Longer than the movie yet shorted than the original play, the television production is probably the ideal length to appreciate this oddball masterpiece.

The Strawberry Blonde see *One Sunday Afternoon*

Streamers

April 21, 1976 (Mitzi E. Newhouse Theatre), a drama by David Rabe. *Cast*: Paul Rudd (Billy), Terry Alexander (Roger), Peter Evans (Ritchie), Dorian Harwood (Carlyle), Kenneth McMillan, Dolph Sweet, Michael Kell. *Director*: Mike Nichols. *Producer:* New York Shakespeare Festival. 478 performances.

(Streamers Intn'l 1983). *Screenplay*: David Rabe. *Cast*: Matthew Modine (Billy), David Alan Grier (Roger), Mitchell Lichenstein (Richie), Michael Wright (Carlyle), Guy Boyd, George Dzundza. *Director*: Robert Altman. *Producers*: Robert Altman, Nick Mileti.

America's nightmarish confusion over the war in Vietnam and with racial problems at home are all telescoped into this intimate drama set in an Army barracks. The young recruits, uncertain of where they will be sent for duty, create friendships and make enemies as in the outside world and all ends in bloodshed when a black militant goes on a rampage and blindly kills one of the white soldiers. David Rabe's powerful drama was grisly in its realistic dialogue and action and its effect was overwhelming in the smaller space of an Off Broadway theatre. Director Robert Altman aimed for that kind of claustrophobia in the 1983 screen version but it only seemed to emphasize the theatrics of the piece. The acting is mostly fine but the movie becomes overwhelming in a different way, the performances so in-your-face that one starts to observe them dispassionately.

Street Scene

January 10, 1929 (Playhouse Theatre), a play by Elmer Rice. *Cast*: Mary Servoss (Anna Maurrant), Robert Kelly (Frank Maurrant), Erin O'Brien-Moore (Rose), Horace Braham (Sam Kaplan), Glenn Coulter (Harry Easter), Joseph Baird, Russell Griffin, Beulah Bondi, Leo Bulgakov, Eleanor Wesselhoeft, Hilda Bruce. *Director*: Elmer Rice. *Producer:* William A. Brady. 601 performances. Pulitzer Prize.

(Goldwyn/United Artists 1931). *Screenplay*: Elmer Rice. *Cast*: Estelle Taylor (Mrs. Maurrant), Sylvia Sidney (Rose), William Collier, Jr. (Sam Kaplan), Walter Miller (Harry Easter), David Landau, Beulah Bondi, Mat McHugh, Max Montor, T. H. Manning. *Director*: King Vidor. *Producer*: Samuel Goldwyn.

The residents of a brownstone apartment building are viewed from the street in this engrossing drama that moved from comedy to romance to tragedy. The young Rose is attracted to her neighbor Sam Kaplan but is being courted by the flashy Harry Easter who would set her up in her own place uptown and further her acting career. Rose's mother is having an affair with the milkman and when her husband finds out about it, he kills his wife. Rose is left to raise her younger brother and decides to do without the help of either Sam or Harry. Surrounding this basic plot were a dozen or so characters whose lives were seen in glimpses and bits of talk. This rich panorama of a play was a critical and financial success, running nearly two years and securing the reputation of playwright Elmer Rice. The 1931 movie used a lot of moving camera work and zooming in and out of windows to capture the flavor of the neighborhood and for the most part it was very effective. While the play had a poetic feeling, the film has a harsher, more realistic one. Some of the performances are first-rate, others border on stereotypes. All in all it is a dated but still fascinating movie melodrama. The original play was turned into a Broadway musical-opera with the same title in 1947.

A Streetcar Named Desire

December 3, 1947 (Ethel Barrymore Theatre), a play by Tennessee Williams. *Cast*: Jessica Tandy (Blanche DuBois), Marlon Brando (Stanley Kowalski), Kim Hunter (Stella Kowalski), Karl Malden (Harold Mitchell), Peg Hillias, Rudy Bond, Vito Christi. *Director*: Elia Kazan. *Producer:* Irene M. Selznick. 855 performances. Pulitzer Prize.

(Warner 1951). *Screenplay*: Oscar Sand, Tennessee Williams. *Cast*: Vivien Leigh (Blanche Dubois), Marlon Brando (Stanley Kowalski), Kim Hunter (Stella), Karl Malden (Harold Mitchell), Rudy Bond, Nick Dennis, Peg Hillias. *Director*: Elia Kazan. *Producer*: Charles K. Feldman.

(TV 1984). *Teleplay*: Oscar Sand. *Cast*: Ann-Margret (Blanche Dubois), Treat Williams (Stanley Kowalski), Beverly D'Angelo (Stella), Randy Quaid (Harold Mitchell), Erica Yohn, Rafael Campos, Ric Mancini. *Director*: John Erman. *Producer*: Marc Trabulus.

(TV 1995). *Teleplay*: Tennessee Williams. *Cast*: Jessica Lange (Blanche Dubois), Alec Baldwin (Stanley Kowalski), Diane Lane (Stella), John Goodman (Harold Mitchell), Frederick Coffin, Carlos Gomez, Rondi Reed. *Director*: Glenn Jordan.

The faded Southern belle Blanche DuBois comes to the New Orleans apartment of her sister Stella and brother-in-law Stanley Kowalski and a battle between the weak, delicate past and the cruel, realistic present ensues. Before all is done, Stanley destroys Blanche's illusions about herself and she slips into insanity. Perhaps Tennessee Williams's most complex, disturbing, and poetic work, the play is open to many different interpretations. There have been monstrous Stanleys as well as sluttish Blanches and the characters continue to fascinate. Jessica Tandy and Marlon Brando originated the roles on Broadway and few have surpassed them. Kim Hunter and Karl Malden were Stella and "Mitch" and they have never been better. Elia Kazan directed the drama on an unrealistic setting that suggested the French Quarter rather than literally recreated it. Hundreds of revivals over the years on Broadway and in regional, community, and academic theatres continue to explore this marvelous, difficult play.

Brando, Hunter, and Malden appeared in the 1951 screen version which Kazan also directed. It moves from gritty realism in the apartment to shadowy and even surreal scenes outside the Kowalski home. The movie is very atmospheric in both moods but it is the acting that counts in any production of *A Streetcar Named Desire* and the movie doesn't disappoint. Vivien Leigh's Blanche measures up to the three stage performers and rarely has so much electricity between actors been captured on film. The television productions of 1984 and 1995 were often less impressive but each has its merits and one can appreciate the performances in proportion to how much one agrees with the actors's or director's interpretations of the characters.

Strictly Dishonorable

September 18, 1929 (Avon Theatre), a comedy by Preston Sturges. *Cast*: Tullio Carminati (Count Di Ruvo), Muriel Kirkland (Isabelle Parry), Carl Anthony (Judge Dempsey), Louis Jean Heydt (Henry Greene), William Ricciardi, Edward J. McNamara. *Directors*: Brock Pemberton, Antoinette Perry. *Producer:* Brock Pemberton. 557 performances.

(Universal 1931). *Screenplay*: Gladys Lehman. *Cast*: Paul Lukas (Count Di Ruvo), Sidney Fox (Isabelle Perry), Lewis Stone (Judge Dempsey), George Meeker (Henry Greene), William Ricciardi, Sidney Toler. *Director*: John M. Stahl. *Producers*: Carl Laemmle, Jr., John M. Stahl.

(MGM 1951). *Screenplay*: Melvin Frank, Norman Panama. *Cast*: Ezio Pinza (Count Augustino), Janet Leigh (Isabelle Perry), Gale Robbins, Millard Mitchell, Maria Palmer, Esther Minciotti. *Director-producers*: Melvin Frank, Norman Panama.

Years before filmmaker Preston Sturges presented a string of unique film comedies in the 1940s he wrote this Broadway hit about an innocent Southern girl and a rakish Italian opera singer who meet for an illicit tryst but instead fall in love. The comedy is less screwball than Sturges's later work and has a warmth even as there is an element of madness in the characters. A 1931 screen version maintained the sass and feeling of danger from the play and Paul Lukas was enchanting as the would-be seducer. The 1951 remake was tamer and more sentimental with real opera star Ezio Pinza no more alarming than a kindly grandfather; his film career never took off. Inexplicably, the well-written play is rarely revived.

Strike Up the Band

January 14, 1930 (Times Square Theatre), a musical comedy by Morrie Ryskind. *Score:* George and Ira Gershwin. *Cast:* Bobby Clark (Col. Holmes), Paul McCullough (Gideon), Blanche Ring (Grace Draper), Doris Carson (Anne Draper), Jerry Goff, Dudley Clements. *Songs:* Strike Up the Band; I've Got a Crush on You; Soon; I Mean to Say; Mademoiselle in New Rochelle. *Director:* Alexander Leftwich. *Choreographer:* George Hale. *Producer:* Edgar Selwyn. 191 performances.

(MGM 1940). *Screenplay:* John Monks, Jr., Fred Finklehoffe. *Score:* George and Ira Gershwin, Roger Edens, etc. *Cast:* Mickey Rooney (Jimmy Connors), Judy Garland (Mary Holden), June Preisser (Barbara Frances Morgan), Paul Whiteman, William Tracy, Ann Shoemaker, Larry Nunn. *Songs:* Strike Up the Band; Our Love Affair; Nobody; Do the La Conga; The Drummer Boy. *Director-choreographer:* Busby Berkeley. *Producer:* Arthur Freed.

George S. Kaufman's original script for this musical satire, about a war with Switzerland over tariffs on Swiss cheese, was too abrasive for audiences and the show closed on the road. Rewritten and softened by Morrie Ryskind, the musical became a farcical dream about a war over Swiss chocolate and this time it was a hit. With a real war starting in Europe, Hollywood threw out the entire stage script (which was somewhat understandable) and all the Gershwin songs except the title number (which is harder to understand) and turned the film into another entry in a series of Rooney-Garland "let's put on a show" musicals, this one very strong on patriotism. (The song "Strike Up the Band" is a mock anthem but in the film it is presented like a war-bond rally.) As such, it is a highly enjoyable movie musical because of Busby Berkeley's expert staging of the musical numbers. But a dev-

ilishly funny satire was lost in the transition, not to mention the song standard "I've Got a Crush on You."

The Stripper see A Loss of Roses

The Student Prince of Heidelberg

December 2, 1924 (Jolson's 59th Street Theatre), an operetta by Dorothy Donnelly. *Score:* Sigmund Romberg, Dorothy Donnelly. *Cast:* Howard Marsh (Karl Franz), Ilse Marvenga (Kathie), George Hassell (Lutz), Greek Evans (Dr. Engel), Roberta Beatty. *Songs:* Deep in My Heart, Dear; Golden Days; Drinking Song; Serenade; Just We Two; Come, Boys, Let's All Be Gay, Boys. *Director:* J. C. Huffman. *Choreographer:* Max Scheck. *Producers:* Shuberts. 608 performances.

The Student Prince in Old Heidelberg (MGM 1927). *Screenplay:* Marian Ainslee, Ruth Cummings. *Cast:* Ramon Navarro (Prince Karl Heinrich), Norma Shearer (Kathi), Jean Hersholt (Dr. Fredrich Juttner). *Director-producer:* Ernest Lubitsch.

The Student Prince (MGM 1954). *Screenplay:* Sonia Levien, William Ludwig. *Score:* Sigmund Romberg, Nicholas Brodszky, Dorothy Donnelly, Paul Francis Webster. *Cast:* Edmund Purdom (Karl Franz; singing dubbed by Mario Lanza), Ann Blyth (Kathie), Louis Calhern (King of Karlsbery), Edmund Gwenn (Dr. Engel), S. Z. Sakall (Joseph Ruden), John Williams (Lutz), Evelyn Varden. *Songs:* Deep in My Heart, Dear; Golden Days; The Drinking Song; Serenade; I Walk With God; Beloved; Summertime in Heidelberg; Come, Boys, Let's All Be Gay, Boys. *Director:* Richard Thorpe. *Producer:* Joe Pasternak.

One of the most beloved (and revived) of all American operettas, this bittersweet musical can still be performed effectively for modern audiences. German Prince Karl goes to college at Heidelberg and falls in love with the waitress Kathie. But when his father dies, Karl must return to the palace and marry the princess betrothed to him so the lovers tearfully part. The show was unusual with its sad ending and, instead of a chorus line of girls, featured a rousing men's chorus who sang such lively numbers as the "Drinking Song." All of Sigmund Romberg's music is outstanding, from the passionate duets to the carefree numbers to a lovely, unforgettable "Serenade." The operetta was so popular a silent film version was released in 1927 and it too was a sensation; even without the intoxicating score the story had great appeal to audiences. Although the stage work was revived regularly, no sound film version was made until 1954. Mario Lanza was slated to play the prince but only his voice was heard in the finished movie. Kathryn Grayson is a spirited Kathie but the dubbed Edmund Purdom as Karl is as stiff as he is handsome and no sparks are created. But the movie has much of the Romberg score and the playful supporting players help make up for the disappointing central love story.

The Subject Was Roses

May 25, 1964 (Royale Theatre), a play by Frank D. Gilroy. *Cast*: Jack Albertson (John Cleary), Irene Daily (Nettie Cleary), Martin Sheen (Timmy Cleary). *Director*: Ulu Grosbard. *Producer:* Edgar Lansbury. 832 performances. Pulitzer Prize, Tony Award.

(MGM 1968). *Screenplay*: Frank D. Gilroy. *Cast*: Patricia Neal (Nettie Cleary), Jack Albertson (John Cleary), Martin Sheen (Timmy Cleary), Don Saxon, Elaine Williams, Grant Gordon. *Director*: Ulu Grosbard. *Producer*: Edgar Lansbury.

When their son Timmy returns from the war, his parents are overjoyed but within two days the marriage's many problems are revealed and the son decides to move on. The slim, actionless three-character drama managed a long run because it won several awards and its cast was outstanding. Comic Jack Albertson gave a surprisingly effective performance as the father, Irene Dailey was applauded as the mother, and newcomer Martin Sheen launched his career with his striking interpretation of Timmy. Albertson and Sheen reprised their roles in the 1951 movie and they were joined by Patricia Neal who gave a penetrating performance as the mother. The cast is almost enough to make one overlook their slight vehicle that was filmed with attention on little else but the actors.

The Substance of Fire

March 17, 1991 (Playwrights Horizons), a play Jon Robin Baitz. *Cast*: Ron Rifkin (Isaac Geldhart), Patrick Breen (Martin), Sarah Jessica Parker (Sarah), Jon Tenney (Aaron), Maria Tucci. *Director*: Daniel Sullivan. *Producer:* Playwrights Horizons. 120 performances.

(Miramax 1996). *Screenplay*: Jon Robin Baitz. *Cast*: Ron Rifkin (Isaac Geldhart), Tony Goldwyn (Aaron), Timothy Hutton (Martin), Sarah Jessica Parker (Sarah), Lee Grant, Elizabeth Franz, Eric Bogosian, Tom McDermott. *Director*: Daniel Sullivan. *Producers*: Randy Finch, etc.

Isaac Geldhart, a refugee from Nazi Germany, runs a small publishing company that puts out important books that rarely show a profit. His son Aaron thinks that his latest effort, a multi-volume work about Nazi medical experiments, will ruin the family business so he convinces his brother and sister to help him buy the old man out. Forced into retirement, Isaac grows so eccentric that his children plan to have him committed until Isaac convinces a social worker that he is indeed sane. The drama was intelligently written, the characters were both complex and intriguing, and the acting roundly lauded. Some of the stage cast and the same director were used in the 1996 movie which was very faithful to the play and beautifully performed. Ron Rifkin was especially notable as the difficult, struggling Isaac.

SubUrbia

May 22, 1994 (Mitzi E. Newhouse Theatre), a play by Eric Bogosian. *Cast*: Steve Zahn (Buff), Josh Hamilton (Jeff), Tim Guinee (Tim), Wendy Hoops (Bee-Bee), Zak Orth (Pony), Martha Plimpton (Sooze), Samia Shoaib (Pakeeza), Firdous E. Bamji (Norman Chaudry), Babette Renee Props (Erica). *Director*: Robert Falls. *Producer:* Lincoln Center Theatre. 113 performances.

(Castle Rock 1996). *Screenplay*: Eric Bogosian. *Cast*: Steve Zahn (Buff), Giovanni Ribisi (Jeff), Nicky Katt (Tim), Dina Spybey (Bee-Bee), Jayce Bartok (Pony), Amie Carey (Sooze), Samia Shoaib (Pakeeza), Parker Posey (Erica), Ajay Naidu. *Director*: Richard Linklater. *Producer*: Anne Walker-McBay.

In the convenience-store parking lot of a suburban community, the aimless youth gather to joke, partake of drugs, and try to pick up sexual partners. One night the rock star Buff, who was raised in the neighborhood, returns and the raucous gathering turns violent. Some critics thought the plotless drama a powerful portrait of disillusioned young Americans while others dismissed it as sensational and contrived. But the acting by a mostly unknown cast was generally applauded, as it was in the accurate 1996 film which featured few known actors. The action is limited to the parking lot and therefore rather confining at times but the performances are what count.

Suddenly, Last Summer

January 7, 1958 (York Theatre), a play by Tennessee Williams. *Cast*: Hortense Alden (Mrs. Venable), Anne Meacham (Catherine), Robert Lansing (Dr. Cukrowicz), Donna Cameron, Eleanor Phelps, Nanon-Kiam. *Director*: Robert Soule. *Producers:* John C. Wilson, Warner Le Roy. c.165 performances.

(Columbia 1959). *Screenplay*: Gore Vidal, Tennessee Williams. *Cast*: Katharine Hepburn (Mrs. Venable), Elizabeth Taylor (Catherine), Montgomery Clift (Dr. Cukrowicz), Albert Dekker, Mercedes McCambridge. *Director*: Joseph L. Mankiewicz. *Producer*: Sam Spiegel.

(TV 1993). *Teleplay:* Tennessee Williams. *Cast:* Maggie Smith (Violet Venable), Natasha Richardson (Catherine), Rob Lowe (Dr. Cukrowicz), Gillian Raine, Richard E. Grant. *Director:* Richard Eyre. *Producer:* Simon Curtis.

The wealthy, aging Mrs. Venable is trying to have her mentally disturbed niece Catherine given a lobotomy but the doctor who examines her discovers why: the aunt doesn't want Catherine to tell anyone what happened to her son last summer. He was a homosexual who used his attractive cousin to lure men but his plan went wrong when visiting a tropical isle where the native boys killed and cannibalized him. The lurid but fascinating one-act play was part of an Off Broadway double bill called *Garden District* and the sensational little drama was much talked about and ran several months. The 1959 film expanded the story by showing in flashback what Catherine described to the doctor on stage but the final revelation was so cleaned up for the screen that it was ambiguous as to what actually happened. The all-star cast made the talky movie more interesting. While Montgomery Clift seems lost in the thankless role of the doctor, Katharine Hepburn and Elizabeth Taylor plunge into the juicy roles with vigor. A British television production in 1993 starred Maggie Smith and Natasha Richardson as Mrs. Venable and her niece and both are splendid. The production is studio bound and longer than the movie but the two actresses make all the talk exciting.

Summer and Smoke

October 6, 1948 (Music Box Theatre), a play by Tennessee Williams. *Cast*: Margaret Phillips (Alma Winemiller), Tod Andrews (Dr. John Buchanan), Raymond Van Sickle (Rev. Winemiller), Marga Ann Deighton (Mrs. Winemiller), Ray Walston, Anne Jackson, Earl Montgomery, Betty Green Little, Monica Boyer. *Director-producer:* Margo Jones. 100 performances.

(Wallis 1961). *Screenplay*: Meade Roberts, James Poe. *Cast*: Laurence Harvey (John Buchanan, Jr.), Geraldine Page (Alma Winemiller), Rita Moreno, Una Merkel, John McIntyre, Lee Patrick, Thomas Gomez, Pamela Tiffin, Earl Holiman. *Director*: Peter Glenville. *Producer*: Hal B. Wallis.

The high-principled Alma Winemiller is the daughter of a minister and far above the sensual flirtations of the handsome John Buchanan next door. But as time passes, John becomes a doctor and moves to a higher plane while the frustrated Alma sinks until she becomes a prostitute picking up traveling salesmen in the park. The original Broadway production met with mixed notices and ran a few months but a distinguished Off Broadway revival in 1952 with Geraldine Page as Alma was a hit and put both the play and Off Broadway on the map. Page reprised the role in the 1961 film with Laurence Harvey as John. The decor is atmospheric and there is a torrid, sexually-charged feeling in the air but too often the movie is all poetic talk delivered into space. A 1972 television production featured Lee Remick and David Hedison as Alma and John.

Summer Holiday see Ah, Wilderness

Summertime see The Time of the Cuckoo

Summertree

March 3, 1968 (Forum Theatre), a play by Ron Cowen. *Cast*: David Birney (Young Man), Blythe Danner (Girl), Philip Sterling (Father), Priscilla Pointer (Mother), Tom Fuccello. *Director*: David Pressman. *Producer:* Repertory Theatre of Lincoln Center. 127 performances.

(Bryna 1971). *Screenplay*: Edward Hume, Stephen Yafa. *Cast*: Michael Douglas (Jerry), Jack Warden (Herb), Brenda Vaccaro (Vanetta), Barbara Bel Geddes (Ruth), Kirk Callaway, Bill Vint. *Director*: Anthony Newley. *Producer*: Kirk Douglas.

A young man dies in combat in Vietnam and in a series of flashbacks we piece together his life and his relationships with his parents and girl friend. The intimate Off Broadway drama struck a nerve with audiences in the late 1960s and the play was a success in New York and in many colleges and regional theatres. Although the 1971 film boasted some fine performances by a commendable cast, the slight drama seemed even thinner on the screen and was very tame compared to the more explosive plays and films that were being written about the effects of the war.

Sunday in New York

November 29, 1961 (Cort Theatre), a play by Norman Krasna. *Cast*: Pat Stanley (Eileen Taylor), Conrad Janis (Adam Taylor), Robert Redford (Mike Mitchell), Sondra Lee, Pat Harrington, Sr., Ron Nicholas. *Director*: Garson Kanin. *Producer:* David Merrick. 188 performances.

(MGM 1963). *Screenplay*: Norman Krasna. *Cast*:

Jane Fonda (Eileen Tyler), Cliff Robertson (Adam Tyler), Rod Taylor (Mike Mitchell), Robert Culp, Jo Morrow, Jim Backus, Peter Nero. *Director*: Peter Tewksbury. *Producer*: Everett Freeman.

The virginal Eileen Taylor is appalled at her fiancé's suggestion that they sleep together before the wedding so she goes to New York to visit her brother Adam who assures her that she did the right thing. But it turns out Adam has women in and out of his bed all the time so when Eileen meets the attractive Mike Mitchell on a bus, she tries not to be so prudish. After some complications, including the arrival of her fiancé when Mike is in his bathrobe, Eileen and Mike end up together. The silly comedy was just risqué enough for playgoers on the brink of the sexual revolution and the play ran several months. The 1963 screen version is an improvement over the play as Eileen (played with spirit by Jane Fonda) makes a more logical transition as she discovers New York, life, and love all at the same time. The Manhattan locations enhance the story and the cast is so enjoyable that the outdated comedy still pleases.

Sunny

September 22, 1925 (New Amsterdam Theatre), a musical comedy by Otto Harbach, Oscar Hammerstein. *Score:* Jerome Kern, Otto Harbach, Oscar Hammerstein. *Cast:* Marilyn Miller (Sunny Peters), Jack Donahue (Jim Deming), Mary Hay (Weenie Winters), Clifton Webb (Harold Harcourt Wendell-Wendell), Joseph Cawthorn, Cliff Edwards, Paul Frawley, Pert Kelton. *Songs:* Who?; Sunny; D'Ye Love Me?; Let's Say Goodnight Till It's Morning; Two Little Bluebirds. *Director:* Hassard Short. *Choreographer:* Julian Mitchell. *Producer:* Charles B. Dillingham. 516 performances.

(Warner/First National 1930). *Screenplay:* Humphrey Pearson, Henry McCarty. *Score:* Jerome Kern, Otto Harbach, Oscar Hammerstein. *Cast:* Marilyn Miller (Sunny Peters), Joe Donahue (Jim Denning), Lawrence Gray (Tom Warren), O.P. Heggie (Mr. Peters), Inez Courtney (Weenie), Barbara Bedford. *Songs:* Who?; Sunny; D'Ye Love Me?; I Was Alone; Two Little Bluebirds. *Director:* William A. Seiter. *Choreographer:* Theodore Kosloff.

(RKO 1941). *Screenplay:* Sig Herzig. *Score: Cast:* Anna Neagle (Sunny Sullivan), John Carroll (Larry Warren), Ray Bolger (Bunny Billings), Edward Everett Horton (Henry Bates), Grace Hartman (Juliet Runnymeade), Paul Hartman (Egghead), Helen Westley (Aunt Barbara), Benny Rubin, Frieda Inescort, Muggins Davies. *Songs:* Who?; Sunny; D'Ye Love Me?; Two Little Bluebirds. *Director:* Herbert Wilcox. *Choreographers:* Aida Broadbent, Leon Leonidoff. *Producer:* Herbert Wilcox.

A Broadway musical vehicle for stage star Marilyn Miller, this disjointed tale of Sunny Peters, an English bareback rider in the circus who falls in love with an American, didn't seem to know where it was going. Sunny stows aboard a ship heading to America to be near her sweetheart but must marry another U.S. citizen in order to enter the country and win her man. The delightful Jerome Kern score certainly helped but it was Miller who carried the show. Never completely at ease on the screen, the star got to repeat her performance before the cameras and it is probably her best celluloid appearance. Much of the stage score survived the transition and the movie still manages to please. A 1941 remake with Anna Neagle as Sunny seems more old fashioned and contrived than the earlier movie. Neagle lacks the necessary panache to carry the film, though the Kern songs and Ray Bolger in a supporting role are worth the effort.

Sunrise at Campobello

January 30, 1958 (Cort Theatre), a play by Dore Schary. *Cast:* Ralph Bellamy (Franklin D. Roosevelt), Mary Fickett (Eleanor), Henry Jones (Louis McHenry Howe), Alan Bunce (Gov. Alfred E. Smith), Anne Seymour, Mary Welch, Roni Dengel, James Bonnet, Kenneth Kakos, James Earl Jones. *Director:* Vincent J. Donehue. *Producer:* Theatre Guild, Dore Schary. 556 performances. Tony Award.

(Warner 1960). *Screenplay:* Dore Schary. *Cast:* Ralph Bellamy (Franklin D. Roosevelt), Greer Garson (Eleanor), Alan Bunce (Gov. Alfred E. Smith), Hume Cronyn (Louis McHenry Howe), Jean Hagen, Ann Shoemaker, Tim Considine, Zins Bethune. *Director:* Vincent J. Donehue. *Producer:* Dore Schary.

This biographic drama was not so concerned with Franklin D. Roosevelt's political career as with his struggle to overcome the effects of polio and continue his life in public office. Much of the play is about FDR's family and friends who encourage him to fight the crippling effects of the disease and by the final scene he is nominating Al Smith at the 1924 Democratic convention. Tastefully written and far from mawkish or romanticized, the play was one of the first to deal with a handicapped person without sentimentality. Ralph Bellamy was a charismatic FDR and the supporting cast was also excellent. A few of them joined Bellamy for the 1960 movie which is filmed unimaginatively but allows the acting to shine. Greer Garson and Hume Cronyn are particularly reputable as wife Eleanor and longtime associate Louis McHenry Howe.

The Sunshine Boys

December 20, 1972 (Broadhurst Theatre), a comedy by Neil Simon. *Cast:* Jack Albertson (Willie Clark), Sam Levene (Al Lewis), Lewis J. Stadlen (Ben Silverman), Minnie Gentry. *Director:* Alan Arkin. *Producers:* Emanuel Azenberg, Eugene V. Wolsk. 538 performances.

(MGM 1975). *Screenplay:* Neil Simon. *Cast:* Walter Matthau (Willie Clark), George Burns (Al Lewis), Richard Benjamin (Ben Clark), Lee Meredith, Carol DeLuise, Rosetta LeNoire. *Director:* Herbert Ross. *Producer:* Ray Stark.

(TV 1995). *Teleplay:* Neil Simon. *Cast:* Woody Allen (Al Lewis), Peter Falk (Willie Clark), Michael McKean (Ben), Liev Schreiber, Edie Falco, Sarah Jessica Parker. *Director-producer:* John Erman.

Although comics Willie Clark and Al Lewis were a famous comedy team in the days of vaudeville, they have not spoken to each other in years. When Willie's nephew arranges for the two to perform together once again on a television special, the old animosties come out and soon the duo is bickering so heatedly that Willies suffers a heart attack. Slowly recovering, Willie decides to quit show business and go the Actors' Home where, it turns out, Al is also headed. Neil Simon wrote many hilarious one-liners in the old-time style and they were appropriate for the two old comics. But he also wrote some touching, honest moments as well and the play was thoroughly engaging. Veterans Jack Albertson and Sam Levene shone as the vaudeville pair, both in their comic routines and in their character scenes, and the well-received production was Simon's tenth consecutive box office hit. Jack Benny and Walter Matthau were slated for the movie version but when Benny died George Burns stepped in and played Al, giving a wonderfully subdued performance that won him the Oscar and began his second movie career. Matthau is obviously not of Burns's generation and is made up to look older; the makeup is real enough but his hammy overplaying and shouting is as irritating as it is unconvincing. A similar inconsistency was found in the 1995 television production in which Woody Allen gave a subdued and very un–Allen-like performance as Al while Peter Falk chewed the scenery maliciously as Willie.

Susan and God

October 7, 1937 (Plymouth Theatre), a play by Rachel Crothers. *Cast*: Gertrude Lawrence (Susan Trexel), Paul McGrath (Barrie Trexel), Vera Allen (Irene Burroughs), Douglas Gilmore (Michael O'Hara), Nancy Kelly (Blossom), Edith Atwater, Fred Leslie, David Byrne. *Director*: Rachel Crothers. *Producer:* John Golden. 288 performances.

(MGM 1940). *Screenplay*: Anita Loos. *Cast*: Joan Crawford (Susan Trexel), Frederic March (Barrie Trexel), Rose Hobart (Irene Burroughs), Bruce Cabot (Michael O'Hara), Ruth Hussey, John Carroll, Rita Hayworth, Nigel Bruce, Constance Collier. *Director*: George Cukor. *Producer*: Hunt Stromberg.

Susan Trexel finds religion and drives her friends, husband, and daughter to distraction by trying to reform all of their lives. But by the end Susan realizes that faith comes within and not meddling in the lives of others. The intelligent comedy-drama was Rachel Crothers's last play and typical of her thoughtful, telling kind of writing. Gertrude Lawrence was radiant as Susan

and was the main reason the play ran several months. Since Hollywood rarely made films dealing with God in the contemporary world, it is surprising that the 1940 screen version was produced and that it was so true to the play. The vampy Joan Crawford was an unlikely choice for Susan but her performance pleases, as do all of the expert cast members. It is a movie of its time yet is unlike movies of the period.

Susan Lenox: Her Fall and Rise see The Fall and Rise of Susan Lenox

Sweet Adeline

September 3, 1929 (Hammerstein's Theatre), a musical play by Oscar Hammerstein. *Score:* Jerome Kern, Oscar Hammerstein. *Cast:* Helen Morgan (Addie), Charles Butterworth (Ruppert Day), Irene Franklin (Lulu Ward), Robert Chisholm (James Day), Violet Carlson, Max Hoffman, Jr. *Songs:* Why Was I Born?; Here I Am; Don't Ever Leave Me; A Girl Is on Your Mind; 'Twas Not So Long Ago. *Director:* Reginald Hammerstein. *Choreographer:* Danny Dare. *Producer:* Arthur Hammerstein. 234 performances.

(Warner 1935). *Screenplay:* Erwin Gelsey. *Score:* Jerome Kern, Oscar Hammerstein. *Cast:* Irene Dunne (Addie Schmidt), Donald Woods (Sid Barrett), Hugh Hubert (Rupert Rockingham), Ned Sparks (Dan Herzig), Joseph Cawthorn (Oscar Schmidt), Wini Shaw, Louis Calhern, Phil Regan. *Songs:* Why Was I Born?; Here I Am; Don't Ever Leave Me; 'Twas Not So Long Ago; We Were So Young. *Director:* Mervyn LeRoy. *Choreographer:* Bobby Connolly. *Producer:* Edward Chodorov.

After her success in the original *Show Boat*, torch singer Helen Morgan was featured in this Broadway vehicle that was tailored to her specific talents. Adeline is a beer hall waitress who becomes a singing star but along the way she experiences enough romantic heartbreak that she was able to sing such torchy hits as "Don't Ever Leave Me" and "Why Was I Born?" from experience. All of the Jerome Kern-Oscar Hammerstein score was memorable and the show, opening right before the stock market crash, managed a decent run despite the Depression. Because of her alcohol problem and bouts with depression, Morgan was considered too risky for a Hollywood leading role so Irene Dunne played Adeline on screen. It is a competent performance but lacks the desperation and edgey quality that only Morgan could convey. Much of the score and script was retained but the movie failed to ignite.

Sweet Bird of Youth

March 10, 1959 (Martin Beck Theatre), a play by Tennessee Williams. *Cast*: Geraldine Page (Princess Kosmonopolis), Paul Newman (Chance Wayne), Sidney Blackmer (Boss Finley), Diana Hyland (Heavenly Finley), Rip Torn (Tom Junior), Madeleine Sherwood (Miss Lucy), Logan Ramsey, John Napier, Martine Bartlett, Bruce Dern, Monica May. *Director*: Elia Kazan. *Producer:* Cheryl Crawford. 375 performances.

(MGM 1962). *Screenplay*: Richard Brooks. *Cast*: Paul Newman (Chance Wayne), Geraldine Page (Princess Kosmonopolis), Ed Begley (Boss Finley), Shirley Knight (Heavenly Finley), Rip Torn (Tom Finley), Madeleine Sherwood (Miss Lucy), Mildred Dunnock, Philip Abbott. *Director*: Richard Brooks. *Producer*: Pandro S. Berman.

(TV 1989). *Teleplay*: Gavin Lambert. *Cast*: Elizabeth Taylor (Princess Kosmonopolis), Mark Harmon (Chance Wayne), Rip Torn (Boss Finley), Cheryl Paris (Heavenly Finley), Kevin Geer (Tom Finley), Valerie Perrine, Ronnie Claire Edwards, Ruta Lee. *Director*: Nicolas Roeg. *Producer*: Fred Whitehead.

The aging, drug-addicted movie star Alexandre Del Lago flees Hollywood and shacks up with the young gigolo Chance Wayne in a Gulf Coast hotel. The two boozy lovers profess love insincerely and try to stop the passage of time. Wayne has returned to the town where he once slept with Boss Finely's daughter and gave her a venereal disease so the political kingpin sends his cronies to find him. Alexandre finds out that her last movie is a hit and that her career is not washed up, so she leaves Wayne to be attacked and castrated by Finley's men. While the excessive drama often seemed like a parody of Tennessee Williams's earlier and bet-

ter works, the play still was compelling and with its superb cast and direction managed to run a year. Geraldine Page and Paul Newman reprised their stage performances of Alexandre and Wayne in the 1962 movie and they were matched by Ed Begley's ardent Boss Finley. The film has a garish look to it that emphasizes the squalor of the plot, though the play was cleaned up considerably for the screen. The 1989 television version starred Elizabeth Taylor as Alexandre and she has some notable moments even if the production is rather flat and the rewritten story less than gripping. Rip Torn, who had played Finley's son Tom on stage and in the 1962 film, portrays the Boss himself in this production and he is both gross and magnetic.

Sweet Charity

Palace Theatre, 29 January 1966 (Palace Theatre), a musical comedy by Neil Simon. *Score:* Cy Coleman, Dorothy Fields. *Cast:* Gwen Verdon (Charity Hope Valentine), John McMartin (Oscar Lindquist), Helen Gallagher (Nickie), Thelma Oliver. *Songs:* If They Could See Me Now; I'm a Brass Band; Big Spender; There's Gotta Be Something Better Than This; Where Am I Going?; Baby Dream Your Dream. *Director-choreographer:* Bob Fosse. *Producers*: Robert Fryer, Lawrence Carr, etc. 608 performances.

(Universal 1969). *Screenplay:* Peter Stone. *Score:* Cy Coleman, Dorothy Fields. *Cast:* Shirley MacLaine (Charity Hope Valentine), John McMartin (Oscar Lindquist), Chita Rivera (Nickie), Ricardo Montalban, Sammy Davis, Jr., Paula Kelly, Stubby Kaye. *Songs:* If They Could See Me Now; I'm a Brass Band; Big Spender; There's Gotta Be Something Better Than This; Where Am I Going?; My Personal Property. *Director-choreographer:* Bob Fosse. *Producer:* Robert Arthur.

Loosely based on the Fellini's film *Nights of Cabiria* (1957), this Broadway vehicle for dancing star Gwen Verdon featured a bright, funny script by Neil Simon and a brassy, contemporary score by Cy Coleman and Dorothy Fields but the show was all Verdon's. The episodic plot followed the misadventures of taxi dancer Charity who always loses in love but never loses hope. Bob Fosse directed and choreographed the dance-heavy show but it was the valiant Verdon who tirelessly carried the musical on her shoulders. Considered by Hollywood to be too old to play the young Charity on screen, Verdon was passed over and Shirley MacLaine was cast in the role. Fosse again staged the piece but MacLaine, as capable as she was in her singing, dancing and acting, could not hold the movie together and it is rather disjointed, coming to life at times and falling flat in other spots. The movie does preserve much of Fosse's stage dances and offers some vibrant supporting performances.

Sweet Kitty Bellairs

December 9, 1903 (Belasco Theatre), a play by David Belasco. *Cast*: Henrietta Crosman (Kitty Bellairs), Charles Hammond (Lord Verney), John E. Kellerd (Lord Standish), Katherine Florence (Lady Standish), Edith Crane, Antoinette Walker, Mark Smith, Jr., Jane Cowl. *Director-producer:* David Belasco. 231 performances.

(Lasky 1916). *Screenplay*: James Young. *Cast*: Mae Murray (Kitty Bellairs), Tom Forman (Lord Verney), Belle Bennett, Lucille Young, Joe King. *Director*: James Young. *Producer*: Jesse Lasky.

(Warner 1930). *Screenplay*: J. Grubb Alexander. *Cast*: Claudia Dell (Kitty Bellairs), Walter Pidgeon (Lord Varney), Ernest Torrence, Lionel Belmore, Perry Askam, June Collyer. *Director*: Alfred E. Green.

The Irish lassie Kitty Bellairs hopes to rise in British society but her rival Lady Standish always seems to be in her way. When both Kitty and the Lady find themselves hiding behind the curtains in a soldier's bedroom, it is Kitty who steps forward and saves Lady Standish from scandal. But in the end Kitty gets the man she loves and a place in high society. Playwright-producer David Belasco based his story on a British play and his production captured the 18th-century period beautifully. That and Henrietta Crosman's sparkling performance as Kitty helped the play to run several months. The 1916 silent screen version starred Mae Murray and was popular enough to warrant an early talkie in 1930 with Claudia Dell as the heroine. The movie has impressive production values but the story sinks under the weight of all the sets and costumes and the

film was a box office failure. The original American play was made into the Broadway operetta *Kitty Darlin'* in 1917.

Sweethearts

September 8, 1913 (New Amsterdam Theatre), an operetta by Harry B. Smith, Fred De Gresac. *Score:* Victor Herbert, Robert B. Smith. *Cast:* Christie MacDonald (Princess Sylvia), Thomas Conkey (Prince Franz), Ethel Du Fre Houston (Dame Paula), Tom McNaughton (Mikel Mikeloviz), Edwin Wilson. *Songs:* Pretty as a Picture; Sweethearts; Angelus; Jeanette and Her Little Wooden Shoes; Every Lover Must Meet His Fate. *Director:* Fred Latham. *Choreographer:* Charles Morgan, Jr. *Producers:* Louis Werba, Mark Luescher. 136 performances.

(MGM 1938). *Screenplay:* Dorothy Parker, Alan Campbell, Noel Langley. *Score:* Victor Herbert, Robert B. Smith, Robert Wright, George Forrest. *Cast:* Jeanette MacDonald (Gwen Marlowe), Nelson Eddy (Earnest Lane), Frank Morgan (Felix Lehman), Mischa Auer (Leo Kronk), Ray Bolger (Hans), Terry Kilburn, Reginald Gardiner, Herman Bing, Douglas McPhail, Gene Lockhart. *Songs:* Pretty as a Picture; Sweethearts; Summer Serenade; Wooden Shoes; Every Lover Must Meet His Fate; On Parade. *Director:* W. S. Van Dyke. *Choreographer:* Albertina Rasch. *Producer:* Hunt Stromberg.

This European-style operetta has the kind of plot that gives the genre a bad name. A princess is abducted as a baby and raised by a family who runs a laundry in Belgium. The prince who was betrothed to marry her stumbles on the laundress years later, they fall in love without knowing each other's true identity, and the two end up ruling as king and queen. As with most operettas, it was only the music that counted and the Victor Herbert score did not disappoint. The movie version wisely discarded the stage plot and replaced it with a contemporary tale about a pair of operetta singers, married to each other, who are driven apart by greedy businessmen. Jeanette MacDonald and Nelson Eddy were the stars and they seem to be having more fun on the screen than in any of their other operetta movies. *Sweethearts* does not seem as dated as most of Hollywood's operettas of the 1930s and there is much to enjoy in the musical.

The Sword and the Rose see When Knighthood Was in Flower

A Tailor Made Man

August 27, 1917 (Cohan & Harris Theatre), a comedy by Harry James Smith. *Cast*: Grant Mitchell (John Paul Bart), Helen MacKellar (Tanya Huber), Gus Weinberg (Mr. Huber), Theodore Friebus (Dr. Sonntag), Frank Burbeck (Abraham Nathan), Minna Gayle Haynes, Lotta Linthicum, John A. Boone. *Director*: Sam Forrest. *Producer*: George M. Cohan. 398 performances.

(Ray Productions 1922). *Screenplay*: Albert Ray. *Cast*: Charles Ray (John Paul Bart), Tom Ricketts (Anton Huber), Ethel Grandin (Tanya Huber), Stanton Heck (Abraham Nathan), Victor Potel. *Director*: Joseph De Grasse. *Producer*: Charles Ray.

(MGM 1931). *Screenplay*: Edgar Allan Woolf. *Cast*: William Haines (John Paul Bart), Dorothy Jordan (Tanya), Joseph Cawthorn (Huber), Marjorie Rambeau, William Austin. *Director*: Sam Wood.

Although John Paul Bart is only a drudge in a tailor's shop, he has his heart set on marrying the boss's rich daughter Tanya Huber but she is courted by a well-dressed dandy from high society. So Bart borrows some fancy duds from the shop one night and goes out on the town where he is the toast of society, catching the eye of a classy heiress and offered a Wall Street job. Of course it all falls apart when they find out Bart is a fake but by then he was won the heart of Tanya. The bright comedy was a hit during the war years, even though it was based on a German play, and it afforded character actor Grant Mitchell one of his best roles. A silent film version was made in 1922 and a talkie in 1931, though neither enjoyed the same kind of success that the play had. But the light comic William Haines was quite amusing as the hero in the latter movie.

Take a Chance

November 26, 1932 (Apollo Theatre), a musical comedy by B. G. DeSylva, Laurence Schwab, Sid Silvers, etc. *Score:* Richard A. Whiting, Nacio Herb Brown, Vincent Youmans, B. G. DeSylva , etc. *Cast:* Jack Haley (Duke Stanley), Ethel Merman (Wanda Brill), Jack Whiting (Kenneth Raleigh), Sid Silvers (Louie Webb), June Knight (Toni Ray), Mitzi Mayfair (Consuelo Raleigh), Oscar Ragland. *Songs:* Rise 'n' Shine; Eadie Was a Lady; You're an Old Smoothie; Should I Be Sweet?; Turn Out the Lights. *Director:* Edgar MacGregor. *Choreographer:* Bobby Connolly. *Producers:* Laurence Schwab, B. G. DeSylva. 243 performances.

(Paramount 1933). *Screenplay:* Lawrence Schwab. *Score:* Richard A. Whiting, Nacio Herb Brown, Vincent Youmans, B. G. DeSylva , etc. *Cast:* Lillian Roth (Wanda Hill), James Dunn (Duke Stanley), Cliff Edwards (Louie Webb), June Knight (Toni Ray), Charles "Buddy" Rogers (Kenneth Raleigh), Lilian Bond. *Songs:* Rise 'n' Shine; It's Only a Paper Moon; Should I Be Sweet?; New Deal Rhythm; Come Up and See Me Sometime; Turn Out the Lights. *Directors:* Lawrence Schwab, Monte Brice. *Producer:* Lawrence Schwab.

This show started out as a revue about American history called *Humpty Dumpty* but it was in such trouble on the road that the producers turned it into a book musical about the backstage doings of a revue called *Humpty Dumpty*. The story was routine at best but the performers, particularly Ethel Merman and Jack Haley, were in top form and the songs were memorable. The film version kept the hackneyed plot but dropped Merman and Haley and some of the songs. Like the play, *Take a Chance* only came to life on screen with the production numbers. Of particular interest is Lillian Roth's spirited rendition of "Rise `n' Shine" and the interpolation of the then little-known "It's Only a Paper Moon."

Take Her, She's Mine

December 21, 1961 (Biltmore Theatre), a comedy by Phoebe and Henry Ephron. *Cast*: Art Carney (Frank Michaelson), Phyllis Thaxter (Anne Michaelson), Elizabeth Ashley (Mollie Michaelson), June Harding, Jean McClintock, Heywood Hale Broun, Louise Sorel, Walter Moulder, Paul Geary. *Director*: George Abbott. *Producer:* Harold Prince. 404 performances.

(Fox 1963). *Screenplay*: Nunnally Johnson. *Cast*: James Stewart (Frank Michaelson/Narrator),

Sandra Dee (Mollie Michaelson), Audrey Meadows (Anne Michaelson), Robert Morley, Philippe Forquet, John McGiver, Bob Denver. *Director-producer*: Henry Koster.

When Frank Michaelson's daughter Mollie goes off to college, he is despondent and it takes his loving wife, his sloppy teenage younger daughter, and some rumba lessons to help him get through the separation pains. Critics dismissed the thin comedy but audiences identified with Art Carney's frustrated father role and the play ran over a year. The 1963 film added some complications to the play's non-plot but the predictable generation gap scenes were only padding. As on stage, the father is the source of the humor and James Stewart handles the character's comic miseries with a polish that is far better than his material.

Talk Radio

May 28, 1987 (Public Theatre), a play by Eric Bogosian. *Cast*: Eric Bogosian (Barry Champlain), Zach Grenier (Sid Greenberg), John C. McGinley (Stu Noonan), Peter Onorati (Bernie), Robyn Peterson (Linda), Mark Metcalf, Linda Atkinson. *Director*: Frederick Zollo. *Producer:* New York Shakespeare Festival. 210 performances.

(Cineplex-Odeon 1988). *Screenplay*: Eric Bogosian, Oliver Stone. *Cast*: Eric Bogosian (Barry Champlain), Ellen Greene (Ellen), Alec Baldwin (Dan), John C. McGinley (Stu), Leslie Hope, John Pankow, Michael Wincott. *Director*: Oliver Stone. *Producers*: Edward Pressman, etc.

Cleveland radio DJ Barry Chamberlain's controversial talk show, in which he insults callers and slurs every race and religion, has gotten so popular that a national network is interested in picking up the show. But one night Barry goes berserk, having a nervous breakdown on the air and then is silent for forty seconds of dead air. The brash, intense play was an Off Broadway hit and Eric Bogosian's performance was deemed as shattering as his writing. All the action of the play was in the radio studio but the 1988 movie opened up the story, showed Barry in other situations outside of the studio, and generally helped flesh out the character. The film is well directed and Bogosian's screen Barry rivals his stage performance, but the abrasive piece does tend to wear thin after a while.

Tall Story

January 29, 1959 (Belasco Theatre), a comedy by Howard Lindsay, Russel Crouse. *Cast*: Robert Elston (Ray Blent), Hans Conreid (Leon Solomon), Nina Wilcox (June Ryder), Marc Connelly (Charles Osman), Marian Winters (Myra Solomon), Robert Wright (Harmon Nagel), Jamie Smith, Ray Merritt, Mason Adams, Ralph Stantley, John Astin. *Director*: Herman Shumlin. *Producers:* Emmett Rogers, Robert Weiner. 108 performances.

(Warner 1960). *Screenplay*: Julius J. Epstein. *Cast*: Anthony Perkins (Ray Blent), Jane Fonda (June Ryder), Ray Walston (Prof. Sullivan), Marc Connelly (Charles Osman), Anne Jackson (Myra Sullivan), Murray Hamilton, Elizabeth Patterson, Bob Wright. *Director-producer*: Joshua Logan.

Howard Nemerov's novel *The Homecoming Game* about college life was turned into a satirical comedy that poked fun at both students and faculty. Ray Blent, Custer College's basketball star, needs money so he can marry June Ryder so he accepts plenty of cash to throw an important game. Ray is not dumb but he flunks two exams on purpose so that he will be benched. But the college pressures the two professors who gave the exams to allow Ray to retake them and when he gets high grades it restores his self-esteem. For a play that employed a large cast and many set changes, it was a rather slight comedy but it managed a profitable run all the same. The movie was less successful, though it did afford a noticeable screen debut for Jane Fonda as June and gave Anthony Perkins one of his more wholesome roles. The comedy is uneventful but the cast is mostly amusing and the direction is brisk if not polished.

Tea and Sympathy

September 30, 1953 (Ethel Barrymore Theatre), a play by Robert Anderson. *Cast*: Deborah Kerr (Laura Reynolds), John Kerr (Tom Lee), Leif

Erickson (Bill Reynolds), Florida Friebus, Richard Midgley, John McGovern, Dick York, Alan Sues. *Director*: Elia Kazan. *Producer:* Playwrights' Company. 712 performances.

(MGM 1956). *Screenplay*: Robert Anderson. *Cast*: Deborah Kerr (Laura Reynolds), John Kerr (Tom Lee), Leif Erickson (Bill Reynolds), Edward Andrews, Darryl Hickman, Norma Crane, Dean Jones. *Director*: Vincente Minnelli. *Producer*: Pandro S. Berman.

The first mainstream American play to deal with homophobia, this tender drama is still a thought-provoking piece of writing even though the subject has been handled many times since then. At a New England boarding school, both the teachers and students pick on the shy, delicate Tom Lee and suspect he is a homosexual. Only the housemaster's wife Laura Reynolds understands the boy and offers him tea and sympathy. She knows her own overly-masculine husband is confused about his sexuality but suspects Tom is more sensitive than gay. In the end she discreetly offers herself to the youth, saying "Years from now—when you talk of this—and you will!—be kind." The drama was more disturbing to audiences than shocking and it caused enough interest to run two years. Deborah Kerr and John Kerr (no relation to each other) gave poignant performances as Laura and Tom and got to reprise the roles on screen in 1956 (as did Leif Erickson as Laura's husband) but the movie turns the homosexual issue into some vague problem about being a team player and the story is told in artificial terms. An honest portrayal of homophobia on the screen in 1956 would have been a tall order but the movie didn't have to be this blind.

The Teahouse of the August Moon

October 15, 1953 (Martin Beck Theatre), a comedy by John Patrick. *Cast*: David Wayne (Sakini), John Forsythe (Capt. Fisby), Paul Ford (Col. Wainwright Purdy II), Mariko Nikki (Lotus Blossom), Harry Jackson, Larry Gates, Maoe Kondo. *Director*: Robert Lewis. *Producer:* Maurice Evans. 1,027 performances. Pulitzer Prize, Tony Award.

(MGM 1956). *Screenplay*: John Patrick. *Cast*: Marlon Brando (Sakini), Glenn Ford (Capt. Fisby), Paul Ford (Col. Wainwright Purdy II), Machiko Kyo (Lotus Blossom), June Negami, Eddie Albert, Henry Morgan. *Director*: Daniel Mann. *Producer*: Jack Cummings.

Vern Sneider's comic novel, about the American occupation of Japan after the war, was adapted for the stage and given a big, bright production with colorful characters and a merry cast. In their efforts to "Americanize" the residents of a small Okinawan village, the military officials seem to stumble into one blunder after another, as commented on by the cunning interpreter Sakini who serves as a kind of narrator for the play. David Wayne shone as Sakini and Paul Ford was hilarious as the befuddled Col. Purdy. The play won all the major awards and ran over three years on Broadway, though it is little revived today. Ford reprised his stage performance in the big-budget 1956 film but Marlon Brando replaced Wayne as Sakini and his portrayal of the Japanese character is more interesting than humorous. But the rest of the cast is marvelously funny and the colorful production values make the screen version as much fun as the play. The failed 1970 Broadway musical *Lovely Ladies, Kind Gentlemen* was based on the comedy.

The Tender Trap

October 13, 1954 (Longacre Theatre), a comedy by Max Shulman, Robert Paul Smith. *Cast*: Robert Preston (Joe McCall), Ronny Graham (Charlie Reader), Kim Hunter (Sylvia Crewes), Janey Riley, Julia Meade, Parker McCormick, Joey Faye, Jack Manning. *Director*: Michael Gordon. *Producer:* Clinton Wilder. 102 performances.

(MGM 1955). *Screenplay*: Julius J. Epstein. *Cast*: Frank Sinatra (Charlie Reader), David Wayne (Joe McCall), Debbie Reynolds (Julie Gillis), Celeste Holm (Sylvia Crewes), Lola Albright, Carolyn Jones. *Director*: Charles Walters. *Producer*: Lawrence Weingarten.

Research chemist Joe McCall works for a pharmaceutical company but dreams of being his own boss and making enough money to keep his demanding wife and kids happy. When he thinks he has discovered a new cure for the common cold, he goes to New York to have it tested and stays with his swinging bachelor pal Charlie Reader. Joe envies his friend's wild lifestyle and even toys with having an affair himself, but when the cold cure turns out to be a bust Joe returns home just as Charlie falls into the tender trap and weds a pretty lab assistant. The unpretentious comedy boasted a gifted cast but audiences only kept it on the boards for three months. The play was fashioned into a screen vehicle for Frank Sinatra in 1955 by turning the playboy Charlie into the central character and having Debbie Reynolds as an actress who traps him in love and marriage. Joe was reduced to a supporting character but as David Wayne played him he was a delight. The cast has a breezy, likable tone and the comedy, though more of a time capsule about 1950s gender attitudes than a gripping story, is still entertaining.

That Certain Feeling see *King of Hearts*

That Championship Season

September 14, 1972 (Booth Theatre), a play by Jason Miller. *Cast*: Richard A. Dysart (Coach), Charles Durning (George Sikowski), Paul Sorvino (Phil Romano), Walter McGinn, Michael McGuire. *Director*: A. J. Antoon. *Producer*: New York Shakespeare Festival. 700 performances. Pulitzer Prize, Tony Award.

(Cannon 1982). *Screenplay*: Jason Miller. *Cast*: Robert Mitchum (Coach Delaney), Bruce Dern (George Sikowski), Paul Sorvino (Phil Romano), Stacy Keach, Martin Sheen, Arthur Franz. *Director*: Jason Miller. *Producers*: Yoram Globus, Menahem Golan.

(TV 1999). *Teleplay*: Jason Miller *Cast*: Paul Sorvino (Coach), Tony Shalhoub (George Sikowski), Vincent D'Onofrio (Phil Romano), Terry Kinney, Gary Sinise, Susan M. Carr, Denise Kaye. *Director*: Paul Sorvino. *Producer*: Steve Greener.

Four men living in a small Pennsylvania city have managed to ruin their lives but they can look fondly back to when they were high school basketball players and their team

won the state championship. Each year on the anniversary of the event they have a reunion at the home of the retired-coach who led them to victory. But the gathering turns sour as past regrets and current animosities surface and even the memory of the championship seems hollow. The tightly-knit drama took place in real time and built powerfully as the evening wore on. The cast of unknowns was superior (the play would launch the careers of Paul Sorvino and Charles Durning) and the drama was directed with precision and care. The Off Broadway production won all the major awards, moved to Broadway, and enjoyed a long run followed by many regional theatre mountings. A film version was not immediately forthcoming because the intimate little drama was so stagebound in its structure and theatricality. When a movie was made in 1982, it foolishly tried to open up the action and move the reunion to different locales but it was still a filmed play. The screen cast consisted of talented veterans yet the acting is disappointing. Robert Mitchum's coach lacks energy and the rest seems more tired and depressed than interesting. Even Sorvino, recreating his stage role, is only a shadow of the character he first created. Sorvino was old enough in 1999 to play the coach in a television production and he comes off much better, though the other cast members are uneven. The studio production makes no attempt to expand the play and consequently works better because of it.

These Three see *The Children's Hour*

They Knew What They Wanted

November 24, 1924 (Garrick Theatre), a play by Sidney Howard. *Cast*: Richard Bennett (Tony), Pauline Lord (Amy), Glenn Anders (Joe), Charles Kennedy, Allen Atwell, Robert Cook. *Producer*: Theatre Guild. 192 performances. Pulitzer Prize.

(RKO 1940). *Screenplay*: Robert Ardrey. *Cast*:

Charles Laughton (Tony), Carole Lombard (Amy), William Gargan (Joe), Harry Carey, Frank Fay, Joseph E. Bernard. *Director*: Garson Kanin. *Producer*: Erich Pommer.

The middle-aged Italian immigrant Tony sees the pretty waitress Amy in a San Francisco restaurant and, when he returns to his vineyard in the Napa Valley, he writes a letter proposing marriage, enclosing a photo of his handsome young hired hand Joe as himself. When Amy arrives at the vineyard and learns the truth, her despondency leads her to an affair with Joe and she gets pregnant. Tony wants to marry her all the same and Amy slowly grows to love him. Although it seems to be a very contrived play today with stilted dialogue (including ridiculous broken English for Tony), the comedy-drama was a great success in its day, helped no doubt by the superlative performances by some of Broadway's top stars. A silent movie version, retitled *A Secret Love*, was made in 1928 with Pola Negri as Amy and an early talkie in 1930, called *A Lady to Love*, starred silent screen star Vilma Banky whose speaking voice was disappointing, though Edward G. Robinson was excellent as Tony. The 1940 remake featured Charles Laughton as Tony and Carole Lombard as Amy and both rose above the clumsy dialogue to give touching performances. Laughton's Italian dialect is a bit showy yet he manages to be affecting all the same. The supporting cast is also fine, though the movie seem awkwardly directed at times. While the play is rarely revived, the 1956 musical version called *The Most Happy Fella* is still a stageworthy piece.

Thieves

April 7, 1974 (Broadhurst Theatre), a comedy by Herb Gardner. *Cast*: Marlo Thomas (Sally Cramer), Richard Mulligan (Martin Cramer), Dick Van Patten (Charlie), Ann Wedgeworth (Nancy), Irwin Corey (Joe Kaminsky), David Spielberg, William Hickey, Alice Drummond, Haywood Nelson, Sammy Smith. *Director*: Charles Grodin. *Producers:* Richard Scanga, Charles Grodin. 312 performances.

(Brut 1977). *Screenplay*: Herb Gardner. *Cast*:

Marlo Thomas (Sally Cramer), Charles Grodin (Martin Cramer), Irwin Corey (Joe Kaminsky), Anne Wedgeworth (Nancy), Hector Elizondo, Gary Merrill, Mercedes McCambridge, John McMartin. *Directors*: John Berry, Albert T. Viola. *Producer*: George Barrie.

This slice-of-life comedy about the residents of a Manhattan high-rise apartment building was a series of vignettes (some funny, some wistful) that critics thought forced and hollow but audiences enjoyed, particularly the performances by some familiar television stars. Some of the cast reprised their roles in the 1977 movie and what charm they had on stage was lost in the crude, phony production that never seemed like a film or a play. This time audiences did not find the stereotypes amusing and the picture was a box office bomb.

This Is the Army

July 4, 1942 (Broadway Theatre), a musical revue. *Score:* Irving Berlin. *Cast:* Ezra Stone, Burl Ives, Gary Merrill, Julie Oshins, Robert Sidney, Alan Manson, Earl Oxford. *Songs:* This Is the Army, Mr. Jones; I Left My Heart at the Stage Door Canteen; Mandy; I'm Getting Tired So I Can Sleep; Oh, How I Hate to Get Up in the Morning; The Army's Made a Man of Me. *Directors:* Ezra Stone, Joshua Logan. *Choreographers:* Robert Sidney, Nelson Barclift. *Producer:* "Uncle Sam." 113 performances.

(Warner 1943). *Screenplay:* Casey Robinson, Claude Binyon. *Score:* Irving Berlin. *Cast:* George Murphy (Jerry Jones), Joan Leslie (Eileen Dibble), Ronald Reagan (Johnny Jones), Charles Butterworth (Eddie Dibble), George Tobias (Maxie Stoloff), Rosemary DeCamp (Ethel), Dolores Costello, Una Merkel, Ezra Stone, Earl Oxford, Kate Smith. *Songs:* This Is the Army, Mr. Jones; I Left My Heart at the Stage Door Canteen; We're on Our Way to France; God Bless America; I'm Getting Tired So I Can Sleep; Oh, How I Hate to Get Up in the Morning; The Army's Made a Man of Me; With My Head in the Clouds. *Director:* Michael Curtiz. *Choreographers:* LeRoy Prinz, Robert Sidney. *Producer:* Hal B. Wallis.

While some of this wartime musical revue was a matter of flag waving and lifting morale, much of it was good-humored as it poked fun at military life. Irving Berlin wrote the songs and appeared on stage to sing his World War One favorite "Oh, How I Hate to Get Up in the Morning." The cast was comprised of enlisted men and all the proceeds from the box office went to the Emergency Relief Fund. The film version also donated its profits to the Fund but it was a much more commercial affair with name actors and large production numbers that often resembled military parades. Most of Berlin's songs were kept and a dull backstage plot, about putting on an all-soldier revue for the boys going off to war, was added. The film is a product of its time and, as such, captures the era truthfully.

A Thousand Clowns

April 6, 1962 (Eugene O'Neill Theatre), a comedy by Herb Gardner. *Cast*: Jason Robards, Jr. (Murray Burns), Sandy Dennis (Sandra Markowitz), Barry Gordon (Nick Burns), William Daniels (Albert Amundson), A. Larry Haines (Arnold Burns), Gene Saks (Leo Herman). *Director*: Fred Coe. *Producers*: Fred Coe, Arthur Cantor. 428 performances.

(United Artists 1965). *Screenplay*: Herb Gardner. *Cast*: Jason Robards (Murray Burns), Barbara Harris (Sandra Markowitz), Martin Balsam (Arnold Burns), Barry Gordon (Nick Burns), Gene Saks (Leo Herman), William Daniels (Albert Amundson). *Director-producer*: Fred Coe.

This comedy about nonconformity was refreshingly different in its day, a few years before fighting the system became more common. Unemployed comedy writer Murray Burns has to swallow his pride and try to rejoin the work force in order to keep the city's Social Services Department from putting his abandoned nephew Nick into a foster home. Robards's over-the-top performance, on both stage and screen, proved that one of America's most serious actors was also expert at comedy. Much of the Broadway cast was retained for the film and, under the same producer-director, it became a faithful screen version without looking too stagy. Interesting sidelight: the catchy title song for the movie was written by saxophonist Gerry Mulligan and his wife, Broadway-stage star Judy Holliday who died of cancer before the film was released.

Three Men on a Horse

January 30, 1935 (Playhouse Theatre), a farce by John Cecil Holm, George Abbott. *Cast*: William Lynn (Erwin Trowbridge), Sam Levene (Patsy), Shirley Booth (Mabel), Joyce Atling (Audrey Trowbridge), Fleming Ward (Clarence Dobbins), James Lane, Millard Mitchell, Teddy Hart, Richard Huey, Edith Van Cleve. *Director*: George Abbott. *Producer*: Alex Yokel. 835 performances.

(Warner 1936). *Screenplay*: Laird Doyle. *Cast*: Frank McHugh (Erwin Trowbridge), Sam Levene (Patsy), Joan Blondell (Mabel), Carol Hughes (Audrey Trowbridge), Allen Jenkins, Teddy Hart, Guy Kibbee, Eddie Anderson, Edgar Kennedy. *Director*: Mervyn LeRoy. *Producer*: Samuel Bischoff.

Greeting card poet Erwin Trowbridge has a knack for picking horses in the racing column of the newspaper but never bets himself. When some racketeers find out about his talent they gobble him up and try to make a fortune. But the minute Erwin places his own money on a horse, his talent disappears and he returns to writing syrupy verse. The raucous comedy has remained an audience favorite from the start, though rarely has the original production, directed by George Abbott with a brilliant cast of comic actors, been bested. The 1936 movie retained Sam Levene from the stage and his portrayal of the lovable mobster Patsy is a classic of sorts. The film is well paced and the performances are vigorous but the screen version doesn't glow like the play. A 1959 television production featured Carol Channing and Johnny Carson. Oddly, two Broadway musicals were made from the play but both failed to run: *Banjo Eyes* in 1941 and *Let It Ride!* in 1961.

The Tiger

February 4, 1963 (Orpheum Theatre), a play by Murray Schisgal. *Cast*: Anne Jackson (Gloria), Eli Wallach (Ben). *Director*: Arthur Storch. *Producer*: Claire Nichtern. 200 performances.

The Tiger Makes Out (Columbia 1967). *Screenplay*: Murray Schisgal. *Cast*: Anne Jackson (Gloria), Eli Wallach (Ben), Bob Dishy, Ruth White, John Harkins, Roland Wood, Charles Nelson Reilly. *Director*: Arthur Hiller. *Producer*: George Justin.

Ben abducts the stranger Gloria and brings her to his sloppy apartment not for anything illicit but to vent his philosophical ideas about the world. The unwilling Gloria eventually warms up to the neurotic Ben and the two plan to meet again. This short farce was part of a double bill of one-acts that enjoyed a healthy run Off Broadway and introduced playwright Murray Schisgal to New Yorkers. The playlet was really an extended acting exercise for veteran performers Eli Wallach and Anne Jackson and they were hilarious in it. A screen version of the short play would need quite a bit of opening up and the 1967 movie, retitled *The Tiger Makes Out*, attempted to do so but it still came down to a one-scene, one-joke piece. Wallach and Jackson reprised their stage performances but on the screen they seem loud and obvious even for a surreal farce.

The Tiger Makes Out see *The Tiger*

The Time of the Cuckoo

October 1 5, 1952 (Empire Theatre), a play by Arthur Laurents. *Cast*: Shirley Booth (Leona Samish), Dino Di Luca (Renato de Rossi), Lydia St. Clair (Signora Fioria), Jane Rose (Mrs. McIlhenny), Daniel Reed (Mr. McIlhenny), Donald Murphy, Geraldine Brooks, Ruggero Romor. *Director*: Harold Clurman. *Producers:* Robert Whitehead, Walter Fried. 263 performances.

Summertime (Lopert 1955). *Screenplay*: H. E. Bates, David Lean. *Cast*: Katharine Hepburn (Jane Hudson), Rossano Brazzi (Renato de Rossi), Isa Miranda (Signora Fiorini), Darin McGavin, Mari Aldon, Andre Morell. *Director*: David Lean. *Producer*: Ilya Lopert.

Although the American spinster Leona Samish vacations in Venice to see the sights, she is hoping for a little romance as well. She gets it in the form of a kindly, enchanting Italian merchant Renato de Rossi. Leona is crushed when she learns he is married but departs Venice with no regrets. The charming comedy-drama was well received, especially Shirley Booth's funny, heartbreaking performance as Leona. The play was opened

up to include some stunning Venice locations in the 1955 film version called *Summertime*. Katharine Hepburn's spinster (now called Jane Hudson) was very different from Booth's, yet was engaging in its own unique way and the warm Rossano Brazzi was a splendid foil for Hepburn's chilly persona. The highly romantic film was directed by David Lean who kept the tale from turning too sentimental. The unsuccessful 1965 Broadway musical *Do I Hear a Waltz?* was based on the original play.

The Time of Your Life

October 25, 1939 (Booth Theatre), a play by William Saroyan *Cast*: Eddie Dowling (Joe), Julie Haydon (Kitty Duval), Edward Andrews (Tom), Gene Kelly (Harry), Len Doyle (Kit Carson), Will Lee, Grover Burgess, Curt Conway. *Directors*: Eddie Dowling, William Saroyan. *Producer:* Theatre Guild. 185 performances. Pulitzer Prize.

(United Artists 1948). *Screenplay*: Nathaniel Curtis. *Cast*: James Cagney (Joe), Jeanne Cagney (Kitty Duval), Wayne Morris (Tom), James Barton (Kit Carson), William Bendix, Ward Bond, Broderick Crawford, Gale Page, Paul Draper, James Lydon, Richard Erdman, Pedro de Cordoba, Tom Powers. *Director*: H. C. Potter. *Producer*: William Cagney.

(TV 1976). *Teleplay*: William Saroyan. *Cast*: Nicholas Surovy (Joe), Patti Lupone (Kitty Duval), Norman Snow (Tom), David Schramm (Kit Carson), Kevin Kline, Benjamin Hendrickson, Mary Lou Rosato, Sam Tsoutsouvas, Richard Ooms. *Director*: Kirk Browning. *Producer*: Lindsay Law.

This one-of-a-kind play by William Saroyan mixed comedy with pathos and realism with dreams to present a unique microcosm of the American character. Into a San Francisco waterfront saloon comes a variety of characters with a dream: the streetwalker Kitty looking for a home, the wealthy Joe hoping to bring happiness, a pinball addict trying to make the highest score, a hoofer aching to make the big time, and so on. Some succeed and some don't but each is alive and living the dream. The poetic play was given a beautiful Broadway production that balanced the work's many moods. Audiences were not put off by the strangeness of the piece and it enjoyed a successful run. The 1948 film boasts a quality cast and some have the eccentric essence of the characters but the movie is flatly realistic and seems to take everything that is dreamed of literally. An abridged 1958 television production featured Franchot Tone, Dan Dailey, Susan Strasberg, and Ann Sheridan while a 1976 television broadcast retained most of the script and came closest to the play. Based on a touring production, this version featured a young cast, some of whom would later become famous.

To Gillian on Her 37th Birthday

March 22, 1984 (Circle in the Square Downtown), a play by Michael Brady. *Cast*: David Rasche (David), Frances Conroy (Kevin), Noelle Parker (Cindy), Cheryl McFadden (Gillian), Sarah Jessica Parker (Rachel), Jean DeBaer (Esther), Richmond Hoxie (Paul). *Director*: Pamela Berlin. *Producers*: Ensemble Studio Theatre, etc. 46 performances.

(Rastar 1996). *Screenplay*: David E. Kelley. *Cast*: Peter Gallagher (David), Michelle Pfeiffer (Gillian), Wendy Crewson (Kevin), Claire Danes (Rachel), Kathy Bates (Esther), Bruce Altman (Paul), Laurie Fortier (Cindy), Freddie Prinze, Jr. *Director*: Michael Pressman. *Producers*: David E. Kelley, etc.

Although Gillian died in a boating accident two years earlier, her teacher-husband David quietly talks to his dead wife on the porch of their New England beach house. David's daughter Rachel is worried about her still-grieving father and helps set up a date with him and a former student. David resists until Gillian appeared on what would have been her 37th birthday and tells David "The secret is I'm dead. I am very, very, very dead." While the play was popular enough to move to a larger Off Broadway theatre, the run was not long. But the tender drama received many productions later in schools and community theatres. The faithful 1996 movie avoided blowing the little drama up into something momentous, though film stars Peter Gallagher and Michelle Pfeiffer played David and Gillian. The acting throughout is first-rate and the direction is delicate and unfussy.

Tobacco Road

December 4, 1933 (Masque Theatre), a play by Jack Kirkland. *Cast*: Henry Hull (Jeeter Lester), Margaret Wycherly (Ada Lester), Maud Odell (Sister Bessie Rice), Dean Jagger (Lov Besney), Ruth Hunter (Ellie May), Sam Byrd, Patricia Quinn, Ashley Cooper. *Director-producer*: Anthony Brown. 3,182 performances.

(Fox 1941). *Screenplay*: Nunnally Johnson. *Cast*: Charley Grapewin (Jeeter Lester), Elizabeth Patterson (Ada Lester), Marjorie Rambeau (Sister Bessie Rice), Gene Tierney (Ellie May), William Tracy, Dana Andrews, Slim Summerville, Ward Bond, Grant Mitchell. *Director*: John Ford. *Producer*: Darryl F. Zanuck.

Erskine Caldwell's novel, about a shiftless, worthless Georgia family who have no money and no morals, was turned into a giant stage hit that surprised everyone by running over eight years. Critics vilified it and moral leaders denounced it, but it seems everyone went to see the grimy little play. Sharecropper Lester Jetter has lost the farmland of his ancestors through laziness and stupidity and thinks nothing of selling his daughter to a local farmer for seven dollars. When the farmer complains that she will not consummate the marriage, Lester offers him another daughter. The rest of the family is no better, for the son runs over his own mother and kills her with a truck when they have a disagreement. The play is sometimes produced today as a comedy and it is questionable how seriously playgoers took the piece in the 1930s. By the next decade it seemed pretty ridiculous because the 1941 movie takes a serio-comic tone and plays the characters as lovable idiots. Of course much of the play was sanitized for the screen but the squalor is genuine enough. The cast is delightfully rustic, especially Charley Grapewin as Jeeter, a role he had played on Broadway late in the long run.

Tomorrow and Tomorrow

January 13, 1931 (Henry Miller Theatre), a play by Philip Barry. *Cast*: Zita Johann (Eve Redman), Harvey Stephens (Gail Redman), Herbert Marshall (Nicholas Hay), Osgood Perkins (Samuel Gillespie), Drew Price, Mary Elizabeth

Forbes, John T. Doyle. *Director-producer:* Gilbert Miller. 206 performances.

(Paramount 1932). *Screenplay:* Josephine Lovett. *Cast:* Ruth Chatterton (Eve Redman), Robert Ames (Gail Redman), Paul Lukas (Dr. Nicholas Hay), Harold Minjir (Samuel Gillespie), Tad Alexander, Walter Wallace, Arthur Pierson. *Director:* Richard Wallace.

Gail and Eve Redman, a childless couple who live in a college town, provide housing for a visiting scholar, Dr. Nicholas Hay, and Eve falls into an affair with the dashing foreign physician. She bares Hay's child but Gail thinks the baby boy is his. Years later, the boy grows up to have a traumatic illness and only Dr. Hay manages to cure the youth. Despite Hay's urging her to leave her husband and have mother and son join him, Eve sticks with her uncomprehending husband. The soap operish drama was not typical of the satiric Philip Barry but the writing was intelligent and the production potent enough that it managed a healthy run in the dark days of the Depression. The play was turned into a slick "women's picture" in 1932 and again the fine cast and solid production values made the movie very satisfying. Just as Herbert Marshall made a suave, engaging Hay on stage, Paul Lukas was similarly appealing as the foreign lover on screen and Ruth Chatterton was laudable as Eve.

Tomorrow the World

April 14, 1943 (Ethel Barrymore Theatre), a play by James Gow, Arnaud d'Usseau. *Cast:* Ralph Bellamy (Michael Frame), Skippy Homeier (Emil Bruchner), Shirley Booth (Leona Richards), Dorothy Sands (Jessie), Joyce Van Patten, Edith Angold, Richard Taber. *Director:* Elliott Nugent. *Producer:* Theron Bamberger. 500 performances.

(United Artists 1944). *Screenplay:* Ring Lardner, Jr., Leopold Atlas. *Cast:* Frederic March (Mike Frame), Skippy Homeier (Emil Buckner), Betty Field (Leona Richards), Agnes Moorehead (Jessie), Edith Angold, Joan Carroll. *Director:* Leslie Fenton. *Producers:* Lester Cowan, David Hall.

University professor Michael Frame takes in his orphaned pre-teen nephew Emil from Germany and the boy is so indoctrinated with Nazi teachings that he mouths off Hitler-like slurs all the time and even attempts to spy for the Germans. But Michael and his sister have patience with the youth and, with the help of an understanding school teacher, finally convince Emil to view the world through less prejudiced eyes. The play was an obvious propaganda piece yet it was so well written and the characters were much more complex than simple stereotypes that the drama proved to be very compelling. The acting was skillful, particularly Ralph Bellamy as Michael, Shirley Booth as the teacher, and the young Skippy Homeier as Emil. Homeier reprised the role in the 1944 movie in which Frederic March was Michael and Betty Field played the teacher. Again the whole cast is excellent and the film is intelligently done, avoiding the excess that must have been tempting. Though no longer topical, the movie still is effective.

Too Many Girls

October 18, 1939 (Imperial Theatre), a musical comedy by George Marion, Jr. *Score:* Richard Rodgers, Lorenz Hart. *Cast:* Marcy Westcott (Consuelo Casey), Hal LeRoy (Al Terwilliger), Mary Jane Walsh (Eileen Eilers), Desi Arnaz (Manuelito), Eddie Bracken (Jojo Jordan), Richard Kollmar (Clint Kelley), Van Johnson. *Songs:* I Didn't Know What Time It Was; Give It Back to the Indians; Love Never Went to College; Spic and Spanish; I Like to Recognize the Tune. *Director-producer:* George Abbott. *Choreographer:* Robert Alton. 249 performances.

(RKO 1940). *Screenplay:* John Twist. *Score:* Richard Rodgers, Lorenz Hart. *Cast:* Lucille Ball (Consuelo Casey), Richard Carlson (Clint Kelley), Ann Miller (Pepe), Eddie Bracken (Jojo Jordan), Frances Langford (Eileen Eilers), Hal LeRoy (Al Terwilliger), Desi Arnaz (Manuelito), Van Johnson. *Songs:* I Didn't Know What Time It Was; Love Never Went to College; Spic and Spanish; You're Nearer; Heroes in the Fall. *Director-producer:* George Abbott. *Choreographer:* LeRoy Prinz.

A college musical with romance and the requisite football game, this Rodgers and Hart show contained a vibrant score and introduced such talents as Eddie Bracken, Desi Arnaz, and Van Johnson. Four bodyguards disguised as football players accompany a high-spirited heiress to college in New Mexico to keep an eye on her for her rich daddy. Of course she falls for one of the boys and that causes trouble for the lovers, the team, and the school. Director George Abbott and much of the Broadway cast were reunited for the movie with Lucille Ball, then in the glamour phase of her career, as the heiress. Only a few of the songs were cut so the result is not only entertaining but the most accurate cinema record of a Rodgers and Hart musical.

Top Banana

November 1, 1951 (Winter Garden Theatre), a musical comedy by Hy Kraft. *Score:* Johnny Mercer. *Cast:* Phil Silvers (Jerry Biffle), Judy Lynn (Sally Peters), Eddie Hanley (Danny), Rose Marie (Betty Dillon), Jack Albertson (Vic Davis), Bob Scheerer (Tommy), Lindy Doherty (Cliff Lane), Joey and Herbie Faye. *Songs:* If You Want to Be a Top Banana, Only If You're in Love; I Fought Every Step of the Way; The Man of the Year This Week; A Word a Day; My Home Is in My Shoes; Sans Souci. *Director:* Jack Donohue. *Choreographer:* Ron Fletcher. *Producers:* Paula Stone, Mike Sloan. 350 performances.

(United Artists 1954). *Screenplay:* Hy Kraft. *Score:* Johnny Mercer. *Cast:* Phil Silvers (Jerry Biffle), Judy Lynn (Sally Peters), Danny Scholl (Cliff Lane), Rose Marie (Betty Dillon), Jack Albertson (Vic Davis), Johnny Coy, Joey and Herbie Faye. *Songs:* If You Want to Be a Top Banana, Only If You're in Love; I Fought Every Step of the Way; The Man of the Year This Week; A Word a Day; My Home Is in My Shoes; Sans Souci. *Director:* Alfred E. Green. *Choreographer:* Ron Fletcher. *Producers:* Al Zugsmith, Ben Peskay.

A musical comedy vehicle for Phil Silvers, the plot concerned a vaudeville comic who has a television show and is at odds with the sponsors over introducing a romantic singing duo to the program. It was a thin story but was happily interrupted by the clowning of Silvers and other outstanding comics from variety, including Rose Marie, Jack Albertson, and Herbie and Joey Faye. The show ran a year but has all but disappeared except for a bizarre movie version that simply brought the cameras into the Winter Garden Theatre and filmed the proceedings without an audience present.

Watching these savvy comics go through their routines to absolute silence is truly an odd and disquieting experience. There is even a silent curtain call at the end of the film! It is perhaps the most accurate recreation of a Broadway musical on film, yet it captures none of the fun the audiences must have had in the theatre.

Torch Song Trilogy

June 10, 1982 (Little Theatre), a play by Harvey Fierstein. *Cast:* Harvey Fierstein (Arnold Beckoff), Estelle Getty (Mrs. Beckoff), Court Miller (Ed), Paul Joynt (Alan), Diane Tarleton, Fisher Stevens. *Director:* Peter Pope. *Producers:* Kenneth Waissman, etc. 1,222 performances. Tony Award.

(New Line 1988). *Screenplay:* Harvey Fierstein. *Cast:* Harvey Fierstein (Arnold), Anne Bancroft (Ma), Matthew Broderick (Alan), Brian Kerwin (Ed), Karen Young, Eddie Castrodad, Ken Page, Charles Pierce. *Director:* Paul Bogart. *Producers:* Ronald K. Fierstein, Howard Gottfried.

Drag queen Arnold Beckoff thinks he has found the love of his life in Ed, a man he picks up in a gay bar one night. But Ed is undecided about his sexuality and gives up Arnold to get engaged to Laurel. When Arnold has a new boy friend, Alan, Laurel invites them all to a weekend in the country which turns into a game of musical beds. Years later, Ed's marriage to Laurel is floundering and he returns to Arnold who has adopted the gay teenager David to raise. Arnold's mother mourns her late husband just as Arnold mourns Alan who was killed in a gay-bashing incident. They realize that their sorrow is the same and Arnold takes comfort in his love for Alan, David, Ed, and his mother. Originally three one-act plays previously presented Off Broadway, they were combined into a long but totally engrossing comedy-drama that was as humorous as it was heartbreaking. The trilogy was so successful it transferred to Broadway for a long run and won several awards, the first gay play to do so. Playwright Harvey Fierstein played Arnold on stage and in the 1988 film and it was a uniquely compassionate performance even as it was sometimes hilarious. The three plays were greatly edited to fit into a feature-length movie (the middle play was severely edited) but the screen version was just as uncompromising and direct as the Broadway production. Along with Fierstein, Matthew Broderick as Alan and Anne Bancroft as Ma were the standouts in the expert cast.

A Touch of the Poet

October 2, 1958 (Helen Hayes Theatre), a play by Eugene O'Neill. *Cast:* Eric Portman (Cornelius Melody), Helen Hayes (Nora Melody), Kim Stanley (Sara Melody), Betty Field, Curt Conway, Art Smith, Tom Clancy. *Director*: Harold Clurman. *Producer*: Robert Whitehead. 284 performances.

(TV 1974). Teleplay: Eugene O'Neill. *Cast:* Fritz Weaver (Cornelius Melody), Nancy Marchand (Nora Melody), Roberta Maxwell (Sara Melody), Carrie Nye, Donald Moffat, John Phaelen. *Director*: Kirk Browning. *Producer*: David Griffiths.

The pompous Irish American Cornelius Melody brags about his days as a soldier under General Wellington and drinks away all the profits at the inn he owns outside of Boston. His long-suffering wife Nora and his outspoken daughter Sara put up with his nonsense but when Sara loves an aristocratic youth and his family objects to the low-class Irish family, Melody goes off in a drunken rage to fight a duel. But he returns humiliated and in disgust he shoots his prize mare, his one link to his illustrious past. The drama is the only surviving work from a multi-play series of dramas that Eugene O'Neill was writing at the end of his life. The series was to follow the history of one family over 150 years but this one piece of the whole stands on its own as a complete and fascinating work. Eric Portman was larger than life as Melody while Helen Hayes and Kim Stanley were quietly ardent as his wife and daughter. The drama has been revived on occasion and a television version was made in 1974 with a distinguished cast led by Fritz Weaver as Melody and Nancy Marchand and Roberta Maxwell as wife and daughter. It is obviously a studio production with humble production values but the power of the play is still there.

Tovarich

October 15, 1936 (Plymouth Theatre), a play by Robert Sherwood. *Cast*: John Halliday (Prince Mikail), Marta Abba (Grand Duchess Tatiana), Jay Fassett (Charles Dupont), Frederic Worlock (Count Brekenski), Ernest Lawford (Chauffournier-Dubieff), Margaret Dale (Fernande Dupont), Adora Andrews, Cecil Humphreys. *Director-producer:* Gilbert Miller. 356 performances.

(Warner 1937). *Screenplay*: Casey Robinson. *Cast*: Claudette Colbert (Grand Duchess Tatiana), Charles Boyer (Prince Mikail), Melville Cooper (Charles Dupont), Basil Rathbone, Anita Louise, Isabel Jeans, Morris Carnovsky. *Director-producer*: Anatole Litvak.

Prince Mikail and the Grand Duchess Tatiana flee to Paris when the Romanoffs are overthrown but they put the czar's money that they have been entrusted with into a bank, waiting for the Communists to be ousted and for the royal family to be restored. To earn a living in the meantime, the aristocratic couple takes work as servants in a rich and eccentric Parisian household and keep their identity a secret. But eventually they are found out, Russia demands the money back, and the prince and duchess happily continue on as working folk. Robert Sherwood adapted Jacques Deval's Paris hit for Broadway and, while it retained a European flavor, there was something definitely America about the comedy. The 1937 screen version afforded a charming vehicle for Charles Boyer and Claudette Colbert as the blue-blooded couple and they were surrounded by marvelous character actors who were directed with flair. The joke of seeing aristocracy playing servants may pall today but in its time the film was a refreshing and droll delight. The 1963 Broadway musical version of the story, also called *Tovarich*, starred Jean-Pierre Aumont and Vivien Leigh.

Toys in the Attic

February 25, 1960 (Hudson Theatre), a play by Lillian Hellman. *Cast*: Maureen Stapleton (Carrie Berniers), Anne Revere (Anna Berniers), Jason Robards (Julien Berniers), Irene Worth (Albertine Prine), Rochelle Oliver, Percy Rodriguez, Charles McRae. *Director*: Arthur Penn. *Producer:* Kermit Bloomgarden. 556 performances.

(United Artists 1963). *Screenplay*: James Poe. *Cast*: Dean Martin (Julian Berniers), Geraldine Page (Carrie Berniers), Wendy Hiller (Anna Berniers), Gene Tierney (Albertine Prine), Yvette Mimieux, Larry Gates, Nan Martin. *Director*: George Roy Hill. *Producer*: Walter Mirisch.

Spinster sisters Anna and Carrie Berniers have little in their lives but their gad-about brother Julian so when he marries Lily the friction between the three woman grows until it destroys Julian's career. Lillian Hellman's last play was an intriguing character study filled with unspoken tension and sublimated sensuality. The superior cast gave memorable performances under the watchful direction of Arthur Penn and the Broadway production ran a year and a half. The 1963 film adaptation diluted the script and offered an uneven cast that failed to satisfy. Wendy Hiller and Geraldine Page are transparent but effective as the sisters and Dean Martin seems weightless as Julian, making the character shallow rather than dissolute.

The Traveling Lady

October 27, 1954 (Playhouse Theatre), a play by Horton Foote. *Cast*: Kim Stanley (Georgette Thomas), Jack Lord (Slim Murray), Lonny Chapman (Henry Thomas), Brooke Seawell (Margaret Rose), Calvin Thomas, Mary Perry, Helen Carew, Katherine Squire. *Director*: Vincent J. Donehue. *Producer:* Playwrights' Company. 30 performances.

Baby, the Rain Must Fall (Columbia 1965). *Screenplay*: Horton Foote. *Cast*: Lee Remick (Georgette Thomas), Steve McQueen (Henry Thomas), Don Murray (Slim), Josephine Hutchinson, Ruth White, Paul Fix, Charles Watts. *Director*: Robert Mulligan. *Producer*: Alan J. Pakula.

Georgette Thomas arrives at a small Texas town with her daughter to be reunited with her husband Henry when he gets out of jail. But she soon learns that he has been released and is already in trouble again with the law. Georgette turns to the widower Slim Murray for comfort and eventually love. The rural drama accurately captured the locale and attitude of the residents but

the play lacked excitement and only lasted a month. All the same, Hollywood filmed the story in 1965 as *Baby, the Rain Must Fall* and gave it an impressive cast led by Steve McQueen as Henry, Lee Remick as Georgette, and Don Murray as Slim. The movie is well acted and filmed but only the charisma of the stars are of interest. Although it failed at the box office, over the years the film has gained a reputation as a forgotten gem.

Tribute

June 1, 1978 (Brooks Atkinson Theatre), a play by Bernard Slade. *Cast*: Jack Lemmon (Scottie Templeton), Robert Picardo (Jud), Rosemary Prinz (Maggie Stratton), A. Larry Haines (Lou Daniels), Tresa Hughes, Catherine Hicks, Ann Dodge, Joan Welles. *Director*: Arthur Storch. *Producer:* Morton Gottlieb. 212 performances.

(Tiberius 1980). *Screenplay*: Bernard Slade. *Cast*: Jack Lemmon (Scottie Templeton), Robby Benson (Jud Templeton), Lee Remick (Maggie Stratton), John Marley (Lou Daniels), Kim Cattrall, Colleen Dewhurst, Gale Garnett. *Director*: Bob Clark. *Producers*: Garth H. Drabinsky, etc.

Scottie Templeton is a beloved Hollywood fixture, a cheery press agent always good for a laugh with his many friends. But the one person Scottie has not won over is his grown son Jud. Knowing that he is dying of cancer, Scottie tries to make amends before it's too late and succeeds to a degree. The comedy-drama was framed by a jokey tribute held for Scottie but that couldn't disguise the thin and tired plot and characters. Jack Lemmon played Scottie with electric energy and warmth and his sparkling performance allowed the play to run half a year. Lemmon reprised the role in the clumsy 1980 screen version but, as delightful as he is, he cannot save the melodramatics of the piece. Robby Benson is mawkish as the son and Lee Remick and Colleen Dewhurst are wasted in underdeveloped supporting characters.

The Trip to Bountiful

(TV 1953). *Teleplay*: Horton Foote. *Cast*: *Director*: Lillian Gish (Mrs. Carrie Watts), Eileen Heckart (Jessie Mae Watts), Eva Marie Saint

(Thelma), John Beal (Ludie Watts), Charles Slader, Will Hare, Dennis Cross. *Director:* Vincent J. Donehue. *Producer:* Fred Coe.

November 3, 1953 (Henry Miller Theatre), a play by Horton Foote. *Cast:* Lillian Gish (Mrs. Carrie Watts), Jo Van Fleet (Jessie Mae Watts), Eva Marie Saint (Thelma), Gene Lyons (Ludie Watts), Will Hare, Frank Overton. *Director:* Vincent J. Donehue. *Producers:* Theatre Guild, Fred Coe. 39 performances.

(Bountiful Film Partners 1985). *Screenplay:* Horton Foote. *Cast:* Geraldine Page (Mrs. Watts), Carlin Glynn (Jessie Mae), Rebecca de Mornay (Thelma), John Heard (Ludie Watts), Richard Bradford, Kevin Cooney. *Director:* Peter Masterson. *Producers:* Horton Foote, etc.

The elderly Mrs. Carrie Watts is so unhappy living with her son and his scolding wife that she boards a bus back to her hometown of Bountiful, Texas, where she revisits old haunts and comes to realize the past is dead. Texas playwright Horton Foote wrote this character drama for television in 1953 and that same year it showed up on Broadway with Lillian Gish reprising her poignant performance as Mrs. Watts. While all the acting in the Broadway production was estimable, the play was too uneventful for playgoers and the drama only lasted a month. But interest in the play was kept alive with various regional productions and thirty-three years later it was filmed with Geraldine Page giving a moving performance as Mrs. Watts, winning an Oscar for her efforts. This time the piece was better received by audiences and the quiet little drama was a modest box office hit. The film is slow and atmospheric yet the fine acting throughout makes it interesting enough.

True to the Army see *She Loves Me Not*

True West

December 23, 1980 (Public Theatre), a play by Sam Shepard. *Cast:* Peter Boyle (Lee), Tommy Lee Jones (Austin), Louis Zorich (Saul Kimmer), Georgine Hall (Mom). *Director:* Robert Woodruff. *Producer:* New York Shakespeare Fes-

tival. 24 performances.

(TV 1984). *Teleplay:* Sam Shepard. *Cast:* John Malkovich (Lee), Gary Sinise (Austin), Sam Schacht (Saul Kimmer), Margaret Thompson (Mom). *Director:* Allan A. Goldstein. *Producers:* Howard Grossman, John H. Williams.

(Cheyenne 2000). *Screenplay:* Sam Shepard. *Cast:* Bruce Willis (Lee), Chad Smith (Austin), Andrew Alburger (Saul Kimmer), Danielle Kennedy (Mom). *Director:* Gary Halvorson. *Producers:* Marc Bauman, etc.

Screenwriter Austin is working on a Western and housesitting his mother's California home while she is on vacation when his brother Lee, a slovenly small-time crook and vagrant, moves in and starts to trash the place. The two brothers are opposites yet after a few weeks Austin starts to pick up Lee's derelict manner while Lee cleans up his act and works on the screenplay. The rivalry climaxes in a bloody fight that somewhat purges the animosity between the two brothers. Sam Shepard's most produced play, it was a notorious flop when first presented Off Broadway in a misconceived production that the playwright publicly disavowed. But a brilliant revival from Chicago in 1982 ran in New York for nearly three years and established the tragicomedy's reputation. Some of the Chicago actors remade the play for television in 1984 and, studio-bound as it is, the characters throb with life. Unknowns Gary Sinise and John Malkovich were outstanding as Austin and Lee; the play and television versions helped make them stars. A movie remake in 2002 starred Bruce Willis as Lee with Chad Smith as Austin and despite all the shouting and violence the film rarely captured Shepard's ideas, reducing the play to melodramatics and theatrical posing.

The Tunnel of Love

February 13, 1957 (Royale Theatre), a comedy by Joseph Fields, Peter DeVries. *Cast:* Tom Ewell (Augie Poole), Nancy Olson (Isolde Poole), Sylvia Dansel (Estelle Novick), Darren McGavin (Dick Pepper), Elisabeth Fraser (Alice Pepper), Elizabeth Wilson. *Director:* Joseph Fields. *Producer:* Theatre Guild. 417 performances.

(MGM 1958). *Screenplay*: Joseph Fields, Jerome Chodorov. *Cast*: Doris Day (Isolde Poole), Richard Widmark (Augie Poole), Gia Scala (Estelle Novick), Gig Young (Dick Pepper), Elizabeth Fraser (Alice Pepper), Elizabeth Wilson. *Director*: Gene Kelly. *Producers*: Joseph Fields, Martin Melcher.

Peter DeVries's odd, satirical novel on suburban life was turned into a Broadway comedy that ran a year despite mixed notices and a questionable storyline. Augie and Isolde Poole have been unsuccessful in having a baby so they start proceedings with an adoption agency. But when Estelle Novick from the agency comes to interview the couple, Isolde has walked out after an argument, leaving Augie to begin an affair with Estelle. Soon both Isolde and Estelle are pregnant and accusations fly all over the place until the Pooles get back together and decide to leave the suburbs for the city. The 1958 movie sanitized the plot in places (Augie was drunk and wasn't sure if he seduced Estelle or not) and concentrated on the couple's efforts to overcome red tape and adopt. The acting is uneven and the direction unsteady. The film can be viewed as a bold sex comedy or a tasteless farce, depending on your point of view.

Twentieth Century

December 29, 1932 (Broadhurst Theatre), a comedy by Ben Hecht, Charles MacArthur. *Cast*: Moffatt Johnston (Oscar Jaffe), Eugenia Leontovich (Lily Garland), Etienne Giradot (Matthew Clark), William Frawley, Roy Roberts, Henry Sherwood, James Spottswood, Dennie Moore. *Director*: George Abbott. *Producers*: George Abbott, Philip Dunnung. 152 performances.

(Columbia 1934). *Screenplay*: Ben Hecht, Charles MacArthur, etc. *Cast*: John Barrymore (Oscar Jaffe), Carole Lombard (Lily Garland), Walter Connolly, Roscoe Karnes, Charles Lane, Ralph Forbes, Edgar Kennedy, Etienne Girardot. *Director-producer*: Howard Hawks.

This vivacious American farce lampoons show business (both Broadway and Hollywood) as it gives actors a chance to play wild-eyed, larger than life characters. Destitute theatre producer Oscar Jaffe boards the train Twentieth Century Limited in Chicago with the hopes of convincing his former-flame, the movie star Lily Garland, to give up the movies and come back to work for him on Broadway. The train ride has the couple arguing, accusing, and eventually falling back in love, and a handful of eccentric characters on board keep the atmosphere chaotic. The Broadway production was a modest hit but the comedy did even better in revivals over the years. The 1934 movie gave John Barrymore one of his best farce roles in Oscar and he is matched with a zesty performance by Carole Lombard as Lily. The screenplay opens up the action, the first half of the film about Oscar and Lily's past together and then the second half on board the train. The screwball comedy is directed with razor-sharp timing by Howard Hawks and the supporting cast is filled with delightful character actors. A 1956 television version starred Orson Welles and Betty Grable and the play was the basis for the 1978 Broadway musical *On the Twentieth Century*.

27 Wagons Full of Cotton

April 19, 1955 (Playhouse Theatre), a one-act play by Tennessee Williams. *Cast*: Maureen Stapleton (Flora Meighan), Myron McCormick (Jake Meighan), Felice Orlandt (Silva Vicarro). *Director*: Vincent J. Donehue. *Producers:* Charles Bowden, Richard Barr. 47 performances.

Baby Doll (Warner 1956). *Screenplay*: Tennessee Williams. *Cast*: Carroll Baker (Baby Doll), Eli Wallach (Silva Vacarro), Karl Malden (Archie Lee Meighan), Mildred Dunnock (Aunt Rose), Lonny Chapman, Eades Hogue, Noah Williamson. *Director*: Elia Kazan. *Producers*: Elia Kazan, Tennessee Williams.

27 Wagons Full of Cotton (TV 1990). *Teleplay*: Tennessee Williams. *Cast*: Lesley Ann Warren (Flora), Peter Boyle (Jake), Ray Sharkey (Silva). *Director*: Don Scardino. *Producer*: A& E Television.

Tennessee Williams's "Mississippi Delta comedy" is a three-character one-act play that was first produced as part of a bill with Leonard Bernstein's one-act opera *Trouble in Tahiti* in 1955. The sly, immoral farmer Jake knows he can get a better price for his cotton if his sluttish wife Flora has a sexual liaison with the buyer Silva Vicarro, so he manipulates things to his profit. The odd but intriguing little play was expanded by Williams into the 1956 film *Baby Doll* that upset censors (and the Catholic Legion of Decency who condemned it) with its frank and grotesque portrayal of crude sexuality. In the screenplay, the husband (now called Archie) has been married to his thumb-sucking child-wife Baby Doll for two years but they cannot consummate the marriage until her upcoming twentieth birthday. Silva seduces Baby Doll before Archie gets to as a way of revenge and the eager, oversexed wife has no problem with the arrangement. Although much of the film seems like a nasty joke, it does manage to sizzle with sensuality and the Elia Kazan-directed movie has a stark yet hypnotic look to it. The performances are a bit over the top but enjoyable in a sleazy way that both tantalizes and repulses. The original play was turned into a television production in 1990 and, played more realistically, it has its own fascination. The trio of actors is first rate and the intimate comedy-drama plays well decades after it was considered so provocative.

The Twilight of the Golds

October 21, 1993 (Booth Theatre), a play by Jonathan Tolins. *Cast*: David Groh (Walter), Raphael Sbarge (David), Judith Scarpone (Phyllis), Jennifer Grey (Suzanne), Michael Spound (Rob). *Director*: Arvin Brown. *Producers:* Charles H. Duggan, etc. 29 performances.

(TV 1997). *Teleplay*: Jonathan Tolins, Saul Bass. *Cast*: Garry Marshall (Walter), Brendan Fraser (David), Faye Dunaway (Phyllis), Jennifer Beals (Suzanne), Jon Tenney (Rob), Jill Bernstein, Mark Shunkey, Sean O'Bryan, Rosie O'Donnell, John Schlesinger. *Director*: Ross Kagan Marks. *Producer*: Paul Colichman, etc.

A married couple are expecting a baby but when genetic tests reveal that the child will grow up to be homosexual they decide to abort it, despite the protests from the gay Uncle David. The abortion is botched and the couple will not be able to have any children

in the future. This heavy-handed allegory was generally trounced upon by the critics but some playgoers thought it a thought-provoking drama. It ran less than a month on Broadway but all the same a television version was made in 1997 and it was later given limited release as a feature film. Some of the cast give noteworthy performances, such as Brendan Fraser's acerbic David, while others are histrionic and annoying. If one accepts the fantasy premise then there is something here worth watching.

Two Against the World see Five Star Final

Two for the Seesaw

January 16, 1958 (Booth Theatre), a play by William Gibson. *Cast*: Henry Fonda (Jerry Ryan), Anne Bancroft (Gittel Mosca). *Director*: Arthur Penn. *Producer:* Fred Coe. 750 performances.

(United Artists 1962). *Screenplay*: Isobel Lennart. *Cast*: Shirley MacLaine (Gittel Mosca), Robert Mitchum (Jerry Ryan), Edmond Ryan, Elizabeth Fraser, Eddie Firestone. *Director*: Robert Wise. *Producer*: Walter Mirisch.

Omaha lawyer Jerry Ryan separates from his wife and goes to New York City to lose himself, only to meet the kookie, unconventional Gittel Mosca and fall into an affair with her. But after a while the romance turns to reality and the two part knowing that they are too different to remain together. The slight but affecting two-character play depended on strong performances and it got them on stage with Henry Fonda and, in her Broadway debut, Anne Bancroft. The comedy-drama was opened up somewhat for the 1962 screen version but despite the added characters and many locales it still came down to a two-character piece. Shirley MacLaine is a sprightly Gittel but Robert Mitchum's quiet, low-key Jerry seems to advocate sleep rather than romance. The film is beautifully filmed by Robert Wise but lacks energy. The play was turned into the Broadway musical *Seesaw* in 1973.

The Two Mrs. Carrolls

August 3, 1943 (Booth Theatre), a play by Martin Vale. *Cast*: Victor Jory (Geoffrey Carroll), Elisabeth Bergner (Sally Carroll), Irene Worth (Cecily Harden), Richard Stapley (Guy Pennington), Margery Maude, Philip Tonge, Stiano Braggiotti. *Director*: Reginald Denham. *Producers:* Robert Reud, Paul Czinner. 585 performances.

(Warner 1947). *Screenplay*: Thomas Job. *Cast*: Humphrey Bogart (Geoffrey Carroll), Barbara Stanwyck (Sally Carroll), Alexis Smith (Cecilia Latham), Ann Carter (Beatrice Carroll), Patrick O'Moore (Charles Pennington), Nigel Bruce, Isobel Elsom. *Director*: Peter Godfrey. *Producer*: Mark Hellinger.

Sally Carroll, the second wife of artist Geoffrey, has been weakening of late and cannot understand why. While Geoffrey has an affair with the attractive new neighbor Cecily Harden, his first wife Harriet visits Sally and warns her that Geoffry once tried to kill her with a slow-acting poison. The two Mrs. Carrolls get help from a friend, Guy Pennington, who locks Geoffrey in the house and calls the police. Rather than surrender, Geoffrey takes a lethal dose of poison. The thrilling melodrama boasted a first-rate cast (including Irene Worth as Cecily in her Broadway debut) and ran a year and a half, followed my many community theatre productions. A British television production of the play was made in 1947 and that same year Hollywood released a movie version with Humphrey Bogart as Geoffrey Carroll. The tough Bogart seems miscast as the psychotic artist and Barbara Stanwyck gives one of her more melodramatic performances so the film is a bit much at times. But some of the supporting players are excellent and the climax still has punch.

Uncle Tom's Cabin

July 18, 1853 (Purdy's National Theatre), a melodrama by George L. Aiken. *Cast*: J. Lingard (Uncle Tom), J. J. Prior (George Harris), Mrs. J. J. Prior (Eliza), Cordelia Howard (Eva), Mrs. G. C. Howard (Topsy), N. B. Clare (Simon Legree). *Producer:* 325 performances.

(Peerless 1914). *Screenplay*: Edward McWade. *Cast*: Sam Lucas (Uncle Tom), Teresa Michelena (Eliza), Marlie Eline (Eva), Roy Applegate (Simon Legree), Boots Wall (Topsy), Walter Hitchcock (George Shelby). *Director*: William Robert Daly. *Producer*: J. V. Ritchey.

(Paramount 1918). *Screenplay*: J. Seale Dawley. *Cast*: Marguerite Clark (Eva/Topsy), Sam Hardy (Simon Legree), Frank Losee (Uncle Tom), Florence Carpenter (Eliza). *Director*: J. Searle Dawley. *Producer*: Adolph Zukor.

There were several stage versions of Harriet Beecher Stowe's controversial novel about slavery in the South but this 1853 adaptation was the most successful, breaking records in its out-of-town tryout and on Broadway where it ran a year. The melodrama returned to New York and every other city many times over the next six decades, making it the play seen by more playgoers than any other in the history of the American theatre. Like the novel, the melodrama was instrumental in fanning the fires of the abolitionist movement leading to the Civil War, yet even after the war *Uncle Tom's Cabin* remained a theatre favorite. In 1879 alone there were forty-nine different road companies touring the country. At least eight screen versions were made, starting with a 1903 film with Siegmund Lubin as the villain Simon Legree. Two versions were released in 1910, one with Frank H. Crane and Anna Rosemond as the slaves Uncle Tom and Eliza, and the other featuring Genevieve Tobin as the innocent Eva. The two most popular movies were the 1914 and 1918 versions, the latter starring Marguerite Clark in the very different roles of Eva and Topsy. The 1927 film is a good example of a well-meaning effort to condemn slavery yet the African American characters are played with such exaggerated mannerisms that the movie ends up being very offensive. By 1930 the touring companies of *Uncle Tom's Cabin* had faded away so there was no interest in making talking films of the story. But a 1987 television production re-examined the piece and offered a revised look at the characters as flesh-and-blood creations rather than the stereotypes they had become.

Uncommon Women and Others

November 17, 1977 (Marymount Manhattan Theatre), a play by Wendy Wasserstein. *Cast*: Jill Eikenberry (Kate Quin), Swoozie Kurtz (Rita Altabel), Glenn Close (Leilah), Alma Cuervo (Holly Kaplan), Ann McDonough (Samantha Stewart), Cynthia Herman (Susie Friend), Ellen Parker (Muffet DiNicola), Anna Levine (Carter), Josephine Nichols (Mrs. Plumm). *Director*: Steven Robman. *Producer*: Phoenix Theatre. 22 performances.

(TV 1979). *Teleplay*: Wendy Wasserstein. *Cast*: Jill Eikenberry (Kate Quin), Swoozie Kurtz (Rita Altabel), Meryl Streep (Leilah), Alma Cuervo (Holly Kaplan), Ann McDonough (Samantha Stewart), Cynthia Herman (Susie Friend), Ellen Parker (Muffet DiNicola), Josephine Nichols (Mrs. Plumm), Anna Levine (Carter). *Directors*: Merrily Mossman, Steven Robman. *Producer*: Phyllis Geller.

Five classmates from an exclusive all-women's college gather six years after graduation and look back on their school years through a series of flashbacks. Wendy Wasserstein's first play, the comedy was satirical at times, nostalgic at other times, but always truthful and incisive. Like her later works, the play dealt with women's decisions in life and the paradox of being female while trying to compete in a male-dominated career world. The comedy was praised during its limited Off Broadway run and it was later revived in New York and at venues across the country, particularly colleges. The 1979 television production was also responsible for getting the play known outside of Manhattan. Although it is studio-bound and simply filmed, the remarkable cast and the firm direction make the production a stimulating experience. Future stars Swoozie Kurtz and Meryl Streep are matched by the other young performers who never slip into the stereotypic.

Under Cover

August 26, 1914 (Cort Theatre), a thriller by Roi Cooper Megrue. *Cast*: William Courtenay (Steven Denby), DeWitt C. Jennings (Inspector Taylor), Lily Cahill (Ethel Cartwright), William Draycott (Mr. Harrington), Lucile Watson (Mrs. Harrington), Phoebe Foster, Ralph Morgan. *Director*: Felix Edwards. *Producer*: Selwyn & Co. 349 performances.

(Paramount/Artcraft 1916). *Screenplay*: Doty Hobart. *Cast*: Hazel Dawn (Ethel Cartwright), Owen Moore (Steven Denby), William Courtleigh, Jr. (Monty Vaughn), Ethel Fleming (Amy Cartwright), Frank Losee, Ida Darling. *Director*: Robert G. Vignola.

This suspense melodrama about retrieving some stolen jewels had a tightly-knit plot in which the hero walks into a trap set by a detective. But the story was made more intriguing by having the action of the last act take place while a previous act is occurring in a different room. The gimmick and the solid production allowed the thriller to run for a year on Broadway. The 1916 silent screen version told the story in a convention manner so it was more a routine melodrama rather than the unique stage work.

Under the Red Robe

December 28, 1896 (Empire Theatre), a play by Edward E. Rose. *Cast*: William Faversham (Gil de Berault), Viola Allen (Renée de Cochefort), J. E. Dodson (Cardinal Richelieu), Lewis Baker (Henri de Cocheforet), Robert Edeson, Jane Harwar. *Producer*: Charles Frohman. 216 performances.

(Cosmopolitan 1923). *Screenplay*: Bayard Veiller. *Cast*: Robert B. Mantell (Cardinal Richelieu), Alma Rubens (Renee de Cocheforet), Otto Kruger (Henri de Cocheforet), John Charles Thomas (Gil de Berault), William Powell (Duke of Orleans), Ian Maclaren (King Louis XIII), Genevieve Hamper, Mary MacLaren, George Nash. *Director*: Alan Crosland.

(New World 1937). *Screenplay*: Lajos Biró, etc. *Cast*: Conrad Veidt (Gil de Berault), Annabella (Lady Marguerite), Raymond Massey (Cardinal Richelieu), Romney Brent (Marius), Sophie Stewart, Wyndham Goldie, Lawrence Grant. *Director*: Victor Sjostrom. *Producer*: Robert Kane.

Stanley Weyman's swashbuckling novel, about intrigue and heroism in the time of Cardinal Richelieu, was adapted into a popular melodrama that was a hit on Broadway and in London. Gil de Berault has angered the powerful Cardinal and is told be must betray the brother of his beloved Renée de Cochefort or die. But Berault manages to outwit the Cardinal and his men and get his sweetheart as well. The tale was first filmed as a 1915 silent short but the 1923 version was an opulent, action-packed movie with a fine cast and magnificent decor by the famous designer Joseph Urban. The 1937 British-American remake is less excessive on scenery but even better in its storytelling. Conrad Veidt as Berault, Annabella as Renée, and Raymond Massey as the Cardinal have a slightly mocking tone to their delivery of the purple prose and the action sequences are first-rate.

Under the Yum Yum Tree

November 16, 1960 (Henry Miller Theatre), a comedy by Lawrence Roman. *Cast*: Gig Young (Hogan), Dean Jones (Dave Manning), Sandra Church (Robin Austin), Nan Martin (Irene Wilson). *Director*: Joseph Anthony. *Producers:* Frederick Brisson, Roger L. Stevens. 173 performances.

(Columbia 1963). *Screenplay*: David Swift. *Cast*: Jack Lemmon (Hogan), Dean Jones (Dave Manning), Edie Adams (Irene Wilson), Carol Lynley (Robin Austin), Paul Lynde, Bill Bixby, Phil Arnold, Imogene Coca. *Director*: David Swift. *Producer*: Frederick Brisson.

Free-spirited Robin Austin wants her fiancé Dave Manning to move into the San Francisco apartment left her by her aunt but Dave refuses until he meets the lecherous landlord Hogan and decides he'd better keep his eye on Robin. But Dave will not sleep with Robin until they are married and when he suspects that Hogan has had a fling with Robin in his absence he insists that Robin come with him to Reno for a quick marriage ceremony. The slightly naughty, only slightly funny play managed to override mixed notices and run six months. The 1963 movie turned Hogan into the main character and Jack Lemmon had fun playing the leering landlord. Dean Jones reprised his Dave from the stage and Carol Lynley was Robin, now two college students living together and being distracted by Lemmon and the eccentric neighbors. A sex comedy that quickly dated, it was risque enough in the pre-sexual revolution days to become a box office success.

Under Two Flags

February 5, 1901 (Garden Theatre), a play by Paul M. Potter. *Cast*: Blanche Bates (Cigarette), Francis Carlyle (Bertie Cecil), Campbell Gollan (Marquis of Chateauroy), Maclyn Arbuckle, Francis Carlyle, Rose Snyder, Edward S. Abeles. *Director*: David Belasco. *Producers:* Charles Frohman, David Belasco. 135 performances.

(Fox 1916). *Screenplay*: J. Gordon Edwards. *Cast*: Theda Bara (Cigarette), Herbert Heyes (Bertie Cecil), Stuart Holmes (Chateauroy), Stanhope Wheatcroft (Berkeley Cecil), Joseph Crehan, Charles Craig. *Director-producer*: J. Gordon Edwards.

(Universal 1922). *Screenplay*: Tod Browning, etc. *Cast*: Priscilla Dean (Cigarette), James Kirkwood (Cpl. Victor), John Davidson (Sheik Ben Ali Hammed), Stuart Holmes (Chateauroy), Ethel Grey Terry, Bobby Mack. *Director*: Tod Browning. *Producer*: Carl Laemmle.

(Fox 1936). *Screenplay*: W. P. Lipscomb, Walter Ferris. *Cast*: Ronald Colman (Sgt. Victor), Claudette Colbert (Cigarette), Victor McLaglen (Doyle), Rosalind Russell (Lady Cunningham), Gregory Ratoff (Ivan), Nigel Bruce, C. Henry Gordon, John Carradine. *Director*: Frank Lloyd. *Producer*: Darrel F. Zanuck.

In French North Africa, the bold and wily camp follower Cigarette fights Bedouin tribes and braves desert dust storms to be reunited with her sweetheart. The famous adventure story was first told in a novel by "Ouida" and there were various stage adaptations that toured the country. The popular Blanche Bates played the heroine in this spectacular Broadway production that even included Cigarette's faithful horse Cochise. Four movies were made of the tale, starting with a 1912 silent short. The 1916 film starred the vampy Theda Bara as Cigarette and the 1922 remake featured Priscilla Dean. The 1936 talkie filled out the story somewhat and pitted Ronald Colman, torn between the torrid Cigarette of Claudette Colbert and the aristocratic Rosalind Russell, against the snarling villain Victor McLaglen. It has a far-fetched plot but the performers are first-rate and the location shooting in Arizona recreates the Sahara and the various outposts impressively.

The Unsinkable Molly Brown

November 3, 1960 (Winter Garden Theatre), a musical comedy by Richard Morris. *Score:* Meredith Willson. *Cast:* Tammy Grimes (Molly Tobin), Harve Presnell (Johnny Brown), Cameron Prud'homme (Shamus Tobin), Edith Meiser, Monty Dalmes. *Songs:* I Ain't Down Yet; I'll Never Say No to You; Belly Up to the Bar, Boys; Colorado, My Home; Are You Sure? *Director:* Dore Schary. *Choreographer:* Peter Gennaro. *Producers:* Theatre Guild, Dore Schary. 532 performances.

(MGM 1964). *Screenplay:* Helen Deutsch. *Score:* Meredith Willson. *Cast:* Debbie Reynolds (Molly Tobin), Harve Presnell (Johnny Brown), Ed Begley (Shamus Tobin), Jack Kruschen, Hermione Baddeley. *Songs:* I Ain't Down Yet; I'll Never Say No to You; Belly Up to the Bar, Boys; Colorado, My Home; He's My Friend. *Director:* Charles Walters. *Choreographer:* Peter Gennaro. *Producer:* Lawrence Weingarten.

A robust musical comedy by the creator of *The Music Man*, it was based on an historic character but always left like a brassy Broadway show. The episodic plot followed the uneducated hick Molly as she works her way out of poverty, marries prospector Leadville Johnny Brown, discovers then loses a fortune, enters high society, survives the sinking of the *Titanic*, and becomes a folk hero of sorts. Meredith Willson's score was tuneful, bouncy, and catchy and Tammy Grimes was in top form as Molly. But she was passed over for the screen version and pretty, petite Debbie Reynolds was miscast in the role. Harve Presnell got to reprise his stage Johnny but much of the score was cut and replaced with postcard-like scenery and long dance sequences. The film is mildly enjoyable but far from the raucous good time it was in the theatre.

Up in Central Park

January 27, 1945 (New Century Theatre), a musical comedy by Herbert and Dorothy Fields.

Score: Sigmund Romberg, Dorothy Fields. *Cast:* Wilbur Evans (John Matthews), Maureen Cannon (Rosie Moore), Betty Bruce (Bessie O'Cahane), Noah Berry (William Marcy Tweed), Maurice Burke, Robert Rounseville. *Songs:* Close as Pages in a Book; April Snow; Carousel in the Park; When You Walk in the Room; The Big Back Yard. *Director:* John Kennedy. *Choreographer:* Helen Tamiris. *Producer:* Michael Todd. 504 performances

(Universal 1948). *Screenplay:* Karl Tunberg. *Score:* Sigmund Romberg, Dorothy Fields. *Cast:* Deanna Durbin (Rosie Moore), Dick Haymes (John Matthews), Albert Sharpe (Timothy Moore), Vincent Price (Boss Tweed), Tom Powers (Rogan), Thurston Hall, Hobart Cavanaugh, Howard Freeman. *Songs:* Carousel in the Park; When You Walk in the Room; Oh Say, Do You See What I See? *Director:* William A. Seiter. *Choreographer:* Helen Tamiris. *Producer:* Karl Tunberg.

Although it arrived years after the golden age of operetta on Broadway, there was more than a touch of the old genre in Sigmund Romberg's lovely score. In 1870s New York, a muckraker exposes the graft in the building of Central Park but falls in love with the daughter of a Boss Tweed crony. The story was an atmospheric recreation of the period rather than a hard-hitting look at politics and the songs were filled with a nostalgic warmth. The two hits were "Close As Pages in a Book" and "April Snow," both of which were cut when the musical was filmed as a vehicle for Deanna Durbin. Dick Haymes was her wooden love interest and Vincent Price snarled as Boss Tweed. The result was neither a pleasing musical nor an interesting drama.

Up in Mabel's Room

January 15, 1919 (Eltinge Theatre), a farce by Wilson Collison, Otto Harbach. *Cast:* John Cumberland (Garry Ainsworth), Hazel Dawn (Mabel Essington), Enid Markey (Geraldine), Frederick Sutton, Lucy Cotton, Harry C. Bradley, Evelyn Gosnell. *Director:* Bertram Harris. *Producer:* A. H. Woods. 229 performances.

(PDC 1926). *Screenplay:* Tay Garnett. *Cast:* Marie Prevost (Mabel Ainsworth), Harrison Ford (Garry Ainsworth), Phyllis Haver (Sylvia Wells), Harry Myers (Jimmy Larchmont), Sylvia Breamer

(Alicia), Paul Nicholson, Carl Gerard. *Director:* E. Marsh Hopper. *Producer:* Al Christie.

(United Artists 1944). *Screenplay:* Tom Reed. *Cast:* Marjorie Reynolds (Geraldine Ainsworth), Dennis O'Keefe (Gary Ainsworth), Gail Patrick (Mabel Essington), Mischa Auer (Boris), Charlotte Greenwood (Martha), Lee Bowman, John Hubbard, Binnie Barnes. *Director:* Allan Dwan. *Producer:* Edward Small.

A door-slamming bedroom farce of the classic variety, the plot revolved around the innocent newlywed Garry Ainsworth who once gave his old girl friend Mabel an undergarment as a gift. He goes to her room to retrieve it without his wife finding out but once there everyone he wishes to avoid shows up. Using such a contrived premise, the merry play managed to keep the comic complications flying and it delighted playgoers for over seven months. The bewitching Hazel Dawn starred as Mabel on Broadway and the equally alluring Marie Prevost played her in the 1926 silent screen version. The 1944 talkie tried to update the story somewhat but the silly premise remained the same as Dennis O'Keeke played a professor who must get the evidence out of Gail Patrick's room. As old-fashioned as it was, the movie still entertained and the actors were sportive and endearing .

The Vagabond King

September 21, 1925 (Casino Theatre), an operetta by Brian Hooker, Russell Janney, W. H. Post. *Score:* Rudolf Friml, Brian Hooker. *Cast:* Dennis King (Francois Villon), Carolyn Thomson (Katherine de Vaucelles), Max Figman (Louis XI), Jane Carroll (Huguette du Hamel), Herbert Corthell. *Songs:* Only a Rose; Song of the Vagabonds; Hugette Waltz; Love Me Tonight; Love for Sale; Some Day; Nocture. *Director:* Max Figman. *Choreographer:* Julian Alfred. *Producer:* Russell Janney. 511 performances.

(Paramount 1930). *Screenplay:* Herman J. Mankiewicz. *Score:* Rudolf Friml, Brian Hooker, etc. *Cast:* Dennis King (Francois Villon), Jeanette MacDonald (Katherine deVaucelles), Lillian Roth (Huguette), O.P. Heggie (Louis XI), Warner Oland (Thibault), Lawford Davidson, Arthur Stone, Thomas Ricketts. *Songs:* Song of the Vagabonds; Hugette Waltz; Love Me Tonight;

Love for Sale; Some Day; If I Were King; Mary, Queen of Heaven. *Director:* Ludwig Berger. *Producer:* Adolph Zukor.

(Paramount 1956). *Screenplay:* Ken Englund, Noel Langley. *Score:* Rudolf Friml. Brian Hooker, etc. *Cast:* Oreste Kirkop (Francois Villon), Kathryn Grayson (Katherine du Vaucelles), Rita Moreno (Huguette), Walter Hampden (Louis XI), Cedric Hardwicke (Tristan), William Prince, Leslie Nielsen. *Songs:* Only a Rose; Song of the Vagabonds; Hugette Waltz; Watch Out for the Devil; This Same Heart. *Director:* Michael Curtiz. *Choreographer:* Hanya Holm. *Producer:* Pat Duggan.

The swashbuckling tale of the poet-outlaw Francois Villon, who repels the forces of King Louis XI of France, outwits the gallows, and marries a French aristocrat all in one day, had been previously popular as the play and film *If I Were King* (qv). This operetta version featured a rousing score by Rudolf Friml that produced a handful of song favorites and the show was one of the longest-running of the decade. The first film version in 1930 was a rather primitive affair that boasted two-color Technicolor but was rather heavy handed in its storytelling. Although Dennis King got to reprise his stage Villon and Jeanette MacDonald was in fine voice as the aristocrat Katherine, the best performance was given by Lillian Roth as the peasant martyr Huguette. The remake in 1956 is a stronger production and comes closer to the stage work. The Maltese tenor Oreste may not be everyone's idea of Villon but fine performances were given by Kathryn Grayson as Katherine and Rita Moreno as Huguette.

Very Warm for May

November 17, 1939 (Alvin Theatre), a musical comedy by Oscar Hammerstein. *Score:* Jerome Kern, Oscar Hammerstein. *Cast:* Jack Whiting (Johnny Graham), Grace McDonald (May Graham), Eve Arden (Winnie Spofford), Hiram Sherman (Ogden Quiler), Frances Mercer (Liz Spofford), Donald Brian (William Graham), Richard Quine (Sonny Spofford), Hollace Shaw, Avon Long, Max Showalter. *Songs:* All the Things You Are; Heaven in My Arms; In the Heart of the Dark; In Other Words; That Lucky Fellow; Seventeen. *Directors:* Vincente Minnelli,

Oscar Hammerstein. *Choreographers:* Albertina Rasch, Harry Losee. *Producer:* Max Gordon. 59 performances.

Broadway Rhythm (MGM 1944). *Screenplay:* Dorothy Kingsley, Harry Clork. *Score:* Jerome Kern, Oscar Hammerstein, Gene de Paul, Ron Raye, Ralph Blane, Hugh Martin, etc. *Cast:* George Murphy (Johnny Demming), Ginny Simms (Helen Hoyt), Lena Horne (Fernway de la Fer), Nancy Walker (Trixie Simpson), Charles Winninger (Sam Demming), Gloria DeHaven (Patsy Demming), Ben Blue, Kenny Bowers, Eddie Anderson. *Songs:* All the Things You Are; Milkman, Keep Those Bottles Quiet; Brazilian Boogie, Somebody Loves Me, Irresistible You; Who's Who in Your Love Life?; Pretty Baby; Oh You Beautiful Doll; What Do You Think I Am? *Director:* Roy Del Ruth. *Choreographers:* Robert Alton, Jack Donohue. *Producer:* Jack Cummings.

Jerome Kern's last Broadway musical was not a success but it did leave behind one of his greatest songs: "All the Things You Are." The lackluster libretto was about a romance at a summer stock company and the cast included no stars so its box office appeal was very limited. Yet all the songs were noteworthy, even if they did not become standards like the aforementioned ballad. It was the only thing that Hollywood kept when the show was filmed as *Broadway Rhythm*. The rest of the screen score was by a variety of songsmiths, none by Kern. The plot was changed to a tired backstage tale about a producer trying to mount his new Broadway musical but it afforded room for many production numbers. More impressive is the appearance of such young and exciting talents as Lena Horne, Gloria DeHaven, Ginny Simms, and Nancy Walker. It is a mishmash of a movie musical but is filled with worthwhile moments.

A View from the Bridge

September 29, 1955 (Coronet Theatre), a drama by Arthur Miller. *Cast:* Van Heflin (Eddie Carbone), Eileen Heckart (Beatrice), Jack Warden (Marco), Gloria Marlowe (Catherine), Richard Davalos (Rodolpho), J. Carroll Naish (Alfieri), Tom Pedi, David Clarke, Antony Vorno. *Director:* Martin Ritt. *Producers:* Kermit Bloomgarden, etc. 149 performances.

(Transcontinental 1961). *Screenplay:* Norman Rosten. *Cast:* Raf Vallone (Eddie Carbone), Maureen Stapleton (Beatrice), Raymond Pellegrin (Marco), Carol Lawrence (Catherine), Jean Sorel (Rodolpho), Morris Carnovsky (Alfieri), Harvey Lembeck, Vincent Gardenia, Frank Campanella, Mickey Knox. *Director:* Sidney Lumet. *Producer:* Paul Graetz.

The Brooklyn longshoreman Eddie Carbone takes in two relatives from Italy who have entered the country illegally but when one of them shows an interest in his pretty niece Catherine, Eddie gets furious and turns the immigrants in to the authorities. The guilt is too great so Eddie kills himself. Arthur Miller's play took the form of a classic tragedy with the neighborhood lawyer serving as a one-man Greek chorus. Originally presented as a long one-act with *A Memory of Two Mondays* (qv), the drama was later revised and expanded into a full-length play which has seen many revivals on Broadway and regionally. The 1961 French film version featured an American cast but was shot in several languages. It has a stiff, formal look begetting a tragedy yet the performances are vividly realistic and many of the scenes are quite moving. The tragic ending, on the other hand, is on a grand, almost-operatic scale so it tends to be more impressive than affecting.

Visit to a Small Planet

February 7, 1957 (Booth Theatre), a comedy by Gore Vidal. *Cast:* Cyril Ritchard (Kreton), Philip Coolidge (Roger Spelding), Eddie Mayehoff (Gen. Tom Powers), Sibyl Bowan, Sarah Marshall, Conrad Janis, Grenadier Saadi. *Director:* Cyril Ritchard. *Producers:* George Axelrod, Clinton Wilder. 388 performances.

(Paramount 1960). *Screenplay:* Edmund Beloin, Henry Garson. *Cast:* Jerry Lewis (Kreton), Fred Clark (Maj. Roger Spelding), Joan Blackman, John Williams, Jerome Cowan, Earl Holliman, Gale Gordon, Lee Patrick. *Director:* Norman Taurog. *Producer:* Hal B. Wallis.

The sophisticated, puckish Kreton arrives on earth from his distant planet with the hopes of observing the Civil War that he has read about back home. Instead he lands in the home of the television commentator Roger Spelding in 1957 just as the celebrity is visited by the hawkish General Tom Powers. Kreton is fascinated by all the military talk and hopes to instigate a world war just for his amusement. Fortunately he fails so Kreton merrily departs hoping to return again someday during a time of warfare. Gore Vidal's wry satire used fantasy sparingly and the emphasis was on the witty tossing back and forth of ideas. But the comedy was not so cerebral that it didn't entertain playgoers for a year on Broadway. Some of the success could be attributed to Cyril Ritchard who directed the production and played Kreton with a pixie-like glee that was both eccentric and endearing. The 1960 movie was a travesty of Vidal's play, butchered as it was into a vehicle for Jerry Lewis who played a moronic spaceman who falls for a pretty earthling. Even as a Lewis film it disappoints and what is left of the satire turns into third-rate sit-com nonsense.

The Voice of the Turtle

December 8, 1943 (Morosco Theatre), a play by John Van Druten. *Cast*: Margaret Sullavan (Sally Middleton), Elliott Nugent (Bill Page), Audrey Christie (Olive Lashbrooke). *Director*: John Van Druten. *Producer:* Alfred de Liagre, Jr. 1,557 performances.

(Warner 1947). *Screenplay*: John Van Druten, Charles Hoffman. *Cast*: Eleanor Parker (Sally Middleton), Ronald Reagan (Bill Page), Eve Arden (Olive Lashbrooke), Wayne Morris, Kent Smith, John Emery. *Director*: Irving Rapper. *Producer*: Charles Hoffman.

Stood up by his date, serviceman Bill Page spends his weekend leave in the apartment of the actress Sally Middleton and by the time he must leave the two have fallen in love. The intimate comedy-drama was refreshing in its anti-sentimentality and avoidance of many romantic clichés. Rather, the twosome were very matter-of-fact about the situation and their emotions which made the play more believable. The 1947 screen version opened up the three-character piece by adding locations and other characters but much of the intimacy survived. Ronald Reagan and Eleanor Parker played the lovers and Eve Arden took most of the laughs as

the outspoken friend who unwittingly brings them together.

Wait Until Dark

February 2, 1966 (Ethel Barrymore Theatre), a thriller by Frederick Knott. *Cast*: Lee Remick (Susy Hendrix), Robert Duvall (Harry Roat, Jr.), James Congdon (Sam Hendrix), Mitchell Ryan (Mike Talman), Julie Herrod, Val Bisoglio. *Director*: Arthur Penn. *Producer:* Fred Coe. 373 performances.

(Warner 1967). *Screenplay*: Robert and Jane Howard-Carrington. *Cast*: Audrey Hepburn (Susy Hendrix), Alan Arkin (Harry Roat, Jr.), Efrem Zimbalist, Jr. (Sam Hendrix), Richard Crenna, Jack Weston, Samantha Jones. *Director*: Terence Young. *Producer*: Mel Ferrer.

Three drug traffickers search for a doll stuffed with heroin and find it is in the apartment of the blind Susy Hendrix whose husband is out of town. After much threatening and some double crossing among the men, Susy is left to play a deadly game of cat and mouse in her dark apartment with the one remaining murderer. Much of the melodrama was talky and contrived in order to set up the climatic scene but when it came the payoff was worth it. The frightening thriller ran nearly a year on Broadway and later saw many community theatre productions. The 1967 movie improved upon the plot by making the buildup to the big scene more interesting and opening up the action so that final confrontation in Susy's apartment was the only confined space in the film. Audrey Hepburn was as convincing as she was beautiful as the blind Susy and Alan Arkin, as the deadliest of her three tormentors, was chilling in his unemotional cruelty.

The Wash

November 6, 1990 (City Center Stage II), a play by Philip Kan Gotanda. *Cast*: Sab Shimono (Nobu Matsumoto), Nobu McCarthy (Masi Matsumoto), Diane Takei (Marsha Matsumoto), Jodi Long, George Takei, Shizuko Hoshi, Marshall Factora, Carol A. Honda. *Director*: Sharon Ott. *Producer:* Manhattan Theatre Club. 16 performances.

(American Playhouse 1988). *Screenplay*: Philip Kan Gotanda. *Cast*: Mako (Nobu Matsumoto), Nobu McCarthy (Masi Matusumoto), Patti Yasutake (Marsha), Marion Yue, Peter Fitzsimmons, Ken Narasaki. *Director*: Michael Toshiyuki Uno. *Producer*: Calvin Skaggs.

After many years of marriage, the Japanese American couple Nobu and Masi Matsumoto separate and each makes tentative steps to start a new life. But Masi still returns to her husband each week to collect and drop off his laundry. Encouraged by their grown children, they each seek new relationships and when Masi decides to marry a widower she asks for a divorce and says she will no longer be doing Nobu's wash. The unpretentious, poignant drama was first produced in California before a limited run Off Broadway where it was warmly received. The 1988 movie also was modest in its goals but proved very effective with its straightforward direction and heartfelt acting. Seasoned Asian actor Mako was particularly fine as the confused Nobu who cannot understand the new ways of the world.

Watch on the Rhine

April 1, 1941 (Martin Beck Theatre), a play by Lillian Hellman. *Cast*: Lucile Watson (Fanny Farrelly), Paul Lukas (Kurt Mueller), Mady Christians (Sarah), George Coulouris (Count de Brancovis), Helen Trenholme, Ann Blyth, Eric Roberts, Peter Fernandez. *Director-producer:* Herman Shumlin. 378 performances.

(Warner 1943). *Screenplay*: Lillian Hellman, Dashiell Hammett. *Cast*: Bette Davis (Sara Muller), Paul Lukas (Kurt Muller), Lucile Watson (Fanny Farrelly), George Coulouris (Count de Brancovis), Geraldine Fitzgerald, Beulah Bondi, Donald Woods, Henry Daniell. *Director*: Herman Shumlin. *Producer*: Hal B. Wallis.

Sarah Mueller, her German husband Kurt, and their children flee the Nazis and go to the Washington, DC, home of Sarah's mother Fanny. A German count visiting there recognizes Kurt and attempts to blackmail him. Kurt kills the count and then decides to return to Germany and fight against the Nazis. Although it was another propaganda play during the war years, Lillian

Hellman's characters were many-layered and the ideas expressed were not simple jingoism. The outstanding cast was led by Paul Lukas as Kurt and when he reprised the performance in the 1943 film he won the Oscar. Also from the stage was George Coulouris as the count and Lucile Watson as Fanny, joined by Bette Davis as Sarah. It is a talky film that remains stage-bound on the screen but the dialogue is stimulating and the splendid performances are still fresh.

The Water Engine

December 20, 1977 (Public Theatre), a play by David Mamet. *Cast*: Dwight Schultz (Charles Lang), Patti Lupone (Rita/Lily), David Sabin, Bill Moor, Michael J. Miller, Barbara Tarbuck, Dominic Chianese, Colin Stinton. *Director*: Steven Schachter. *Producer:* New York Shakespeare Festival. 79 performances.

(TV 1992). *Teleplay*: David Mamet *Cast*: William H. Macy (Charles Lang), Patti Lupone (Rita Lang), Joe Mantegna, John Mahoney, Joanna Miles, Mike Nussbaum, Charles Durning, Treat Williams. *Director*: Steven Schacter. *Producer*: Donald P. Borchers.

When amateur inventor Charles Lang creates an engine in 1934 that runs on water for fuel, he hopes to sell the patent and secure the future for himself and his sister Rita. But big business thugs and crooked lawyers try to steal the invention and end up murdering Lang and Rita and destroying the plans in order to maintain the status quo. Yet Lang has left a copy of the blueprints with a young science-minded boy who may someday bring the invention to light. The "American fable" was told in the format of a radio broadcast which allowed the multi-scened story to flow easily. The play was successful enough Off Broadway it was moved to Broadway where it did not last long but was picked up by schools and community theatres. The 1992 television production eschewed the radio format and with its murky direction and rewritten scenes the new version was more confusing than intriguing. The large cast included many top players but the acting was uneven and ranged in style from surrealistic to gritty realistic.

Waterloo Bridge

January 6, 1930 (Fulton Theatre), a drama by Robert E. Sherwood. *Cast*: Glenn Hunter (Roy Cronin), June Walker (Myra), Cora Witherspoon, Eunice Hunt, Florence Edney. *Director*: Winchell Smith. *Producer:* Charles Dillingham. 64 performances.

(Universal 1931). *Screenplay*: Benn Levy, Tom Reed. *Cast*: Douglass Montgomery (Roy Cronin), Mae Clark (Myra), Doris Lloyd, Frederick Kerr, Enid Bennett, Bette Davis. *Director*: James Whale. *Producer*: Carl Laemmle, Jr.

(MGM 1940). *Screenplay*: S. N. Behrman, etc. *Cast*: Robert Taylor (Roy Cronin), Vivien Leigh (Myra), Lucile Watson, Virginia Field, Maria Oupenskaya, C. Aubrey Smith. *Director*: Mervyn LeRoy. *Producers*: Sidney Franklin, Mervyn LeRoy.

Gaby (MGM 1956). *Screenplay*: Albert Hackett, Frances Goodrich, Charles Lederer. *Cast*: Leslie Caron (Gaby), John Kerr (Gregory Wendell), Cedric Hardwicke, Taina Elg, Margalo Gillmore, Scott Marlowe. *Director*: Curtis Bernhardt. *Producer*: Edwin Knopf.

During World War One, the American soldier Roy Cronin gets leave in London where he meets the pretty American Myra on Waterloo Bridge one night. He falls in love with her not knowing she is an unemployed actress who has turned to prostitution. Roy learns the truth just before he returns to the front but gives her money and takes out an insurance policy in her name before he goes. The unsentimental drama was well written and acted with skill but audiences and critics were unenthusiastic so the production only ran two months. Yet three movies were made of the tale, though all made major changes in the script. The 1931 version featured Douglass Montgomery as Roy who married the American ballerina Myra in London; when he is missing in action his family cuts her off without a cent so she turns to prostitution. It was much more romantic than the play yet the look of the film was dark and gritty even and Mae Clarke was outstanding as Myra. The 1940 remake was even more romantic and, with Robert Taylor and Vivien Leigh as the lovers, very popular. The script returned somewhat back to the play but cleaned up the more objectional spots. The entire cast and the direction are lush, bigger than life, yet effective. The story was remade yet again in 1956 as *Gaby* with Leslie Caron as a French ballerina in love with soldier John Kerr. The movie is updated, given a happy ending, and generally flattened out until it seems inconsequential. The performers disappoint and the story fails to convince.

Way Down East

February 7, 1898 (Manhattan Theatre), a play by Lottie Blair Parker, Joseph R. Grismer. *Cast*: Phoebe Davies (Annie Moore), James O. Barrows (Squire Bartlett), Howard Kyle (David Bartlett), Minnie Dupree, George Backus, Homer Granville. *Producers:* William A. Brady, Florenz Ziegfeld. 152 performances.

(Griffith 1920). *Screenplay*: Anthony Paul Kelly. *Cast*: Lillian Gish (Anna Moore), Richard Barthelmess (David Bartlett), Burr McIntosh (Squire Bartlett), Kate Bruce, Mary Hay. *Director-producer*: D. W. Griffith.

(Fox 1935). *Screenplay*: Howard Estabrooke, William Hurlbut. *Cast*: Rochelle Hudson (Anna Moore), Henry Fonda (David Bartlett), Russell Simpson (Squire Bartlett), Slim Summerville, Margaret Hamilton, Edward Trevor, Andy Devine, Spring Byington. *Director*: Henry King. *Producer*: Winfield R. Sheehan.

Annie Moore was seduced and became pregnant but the baby died so she sets off to start life anew where no one knows her. She gets a job as a servant at the Bartlett estate but when Squire Bartlett learns of her past he turns Annie out and she makes her way through a violent snowstorm. The son, David Bartlett, has grown to love Annie so he rides out and rescues her then persuades the family to accept her. This classic melodrama had all the standard stage conventions, from the forlorn heroine to the storm, but there was honesty in the characterization and the emotional tug it created was not as manufactured as most "mellerdramers" of the day. The play was a success in New York and on the road for over twenty years and Phoebe Davies, who originated the role of Annie on Broadway, played it over 4,000 times during her career. Four screen versions were made of the tale, the first in 1908 being only a silent short. A 1914 movie told the story in more detail but it was the 1920 version by D. W. Griffith that became a silent screen classic with its famous scene of Annie, played by Lillian Gish, caught on an ice floe rushing down the river. The melodrama was filmed on a giant scale so that the story seemed almost epic in scope; clichéd or not, it is still impressive. The 1935 remake looked very old-fashioned amidst the smart, sassy movies of the Depression era and the stilted dialogue would have come across better on title cards than from the mouths of Rochelle Hudson and Henry Fonda as the lovers. It is also a disappointing film in its action sequences but there are some expert character actors to be found in the cast.

West Side Story

September 26, 1957 (Winter Garden Theatre), a musical play by Arthur Laurents. *Score:* Leonard Bernstein, Stephen Sondheim. *Cast:* Larry Kert (Tony), Carol Lawrence (Maria), Chita Rivera (Anita), Art Smith (Doc), Mickey Calin (Riff), Ken LeRoy (Bernardo), Lee Becker Theodore, David Winter. *Songs:* Tonight; Maria; Somewhere; Gee, Officer Krupke; America; Cool; I Feel Pretty; A Boy Like That; I Have a Love; Something's Comin'; One Hand, One Heart. *Director:* Jerome Robbins. *Choreographers:* Jerome Robbins, Peter Gennaro. *Producers:* Harold Prince, Robert E. Griffith. 732 performances.

(Mirisch/United Artists (1961). *Screenplay:* Ernest Lehman. *Score:* Leonard Bernstein, Stephen Sondheim. *Cast:* Natalie Wood (Maria), Richard Beymer (Tony), Rita Moreno (Anita), George Chakiris (Bernardo), Russ Tamblyn (Riff), Simon Oakland, John Astin, David Winter, Eliot Feld, Anthony Teague. *Songs:* Tonight; Maria; Somewhere; Gee, Officer Krupke; America; Cool; I Feel Pretty; A Boy Like That; I Have a Love; Something's Comin'; One Hand, One Heart. *Directors:* Robert Wise, Jerome Robbins. *Choreographer:* Jerome Robbins. *Producer:* Robert Wise. Academy Award.

This innovative Broadway musical, an updating of *Romeo and Juliet* set in gang-infiltrated New York, used dance is ways not seen previously in the theatre. Jerome Robbins's choreography was an explosion of restlessness, bitterness, even sexual tension.

Leonard Bernstein's music was often jazzy and contemporary yet he used old opera techniques, such as the exhilarating quintet right before the rumble. Newcomer Stephen Sondheim provided the knowing lyrics and the whole production held together impressively, allowing the audience to even accept ballet on the ghetto sidewalks. While the Broadway show was well received and ran over two years, *West Side Story* became a revival favorite only after the popular film version. Many of the creative talents were retained for the movie and the musical was filmed both on the streets of New York and in a studio. Robbins's ballet-like steps struck some movie audiences as silly in the context of a real setting but many accepted the musical's premise and helped make the movie version very successful. The choreography remains the highlight of the film, almost matched by the beloved score. While there were many vibrant supporting performances, Natalie Wood and Richard Beymer as the modern Juliet and Romeo were lacking and the film seemed to succeed in spite of them. But what is good about *West Side Story* remains very good with repeated viewings.

The West Side Waltz

November 19, 1981 (Ethel Barrymore Theatre), a play by Ernest Thompson. *Cast:* Katharine Hepburn (Margaret Mary Elderdice), Dorothy Loudon (Cara Varnum), David Margulies, Regina Baff, Don Howard. *Director:* Noel Willman. *Producers:* Robert Whitehead, etc. 126 performances.

(TV 1995). *Teleplay:* Ernest Thompson. *Cast:* Shirley MacLaine (Margaret Mary Elderdice), Liza Minnelli (Cara Varnum), Jennifer Gray, August Schellenberg, Richard Gilliland. Hal Williams. *Director:* Ernest Thompson. *Producers:* Mitchell Blumberg, etc.

Retired pianist Mary Margaret Elderdice is getting old and is told by her nosy neighbor Cara Varnum that the two of them should share the same apartment so there will be someone to look after her. Mary Margaret refuses Cara's offer and hires a kookie young actress as a companion instead. But after Mary Margaret matches the girl up with a lawyer, she relents and asks Cara to move in with her. The thin, unconvincing play ran four months only because Katharine Hepburn (in her last stage role) played Mary Margaret and her performance was as spry and zesty as the play was dull. The slight story was opened up in the 1995 television production and it boasted a star cast and added scenes but what it really needed was Hepburn. Most of the performances embarrass (Liza Minnelli even wears a fat suit and gray wig to play Cara) and the direction cannot decide if the piece is a comedy or a drama.

What Price Glory?

September 5, 1924 (Plymouth Theatre), a drama by Maxwell Anderson, Laurence Stallings. Cast: Louis Wolheim (Capt. Flagg), William Boyd (First Sergeant Quirt), Leyla Georgie (Charmaine), Clyde North, Brian Donlevy, George Tobias, Fuller Mellish, Jr. *Director-producer:* Arthur Hopkins. 435 performances.

(Fox 1926). *Screenplay:* Maxwell Anderson, Malcolm Stuart Boyland, James T. O'Donohoe. *Cast:* Victor McLaglen (Capt. Flagg), Edmund Lowe (Quirt), Dolores Del Rio (Charmaine), William V. Mong, Phyllis Haver, Barry Norton, Leslie Fenton, Sammy Cohen, Ted McNamara. *Director:* Raoul Walsh.

(Fox 1952). *Screenplay:* Maxwell Anderson, Henry and Phoebe Ephron. *Cast:* James Cagney (Capt. Flagg), Dan Dailey (Quirt), Corinne Calvet (Charmaine), Robert Wagner, Marisa Pavan, James Gleason, William Demarest. *Director:* John Ford. *Producer:* Sol C. Siegel.

Arguably the best American play written about World War One, the drama was shocking in its time because of its profane and brutally honest dialogue as well as its callous approach to patriotism. Soldiers Flagg and Quirt are friendly enemies whose rivalry keeps them on their toes. But when they both crave the French girl Charmaine, their robust camaraderie is threatened, but only temporarily. The silent film version that came out two years later solved the profanity problem by only hinting at the coarse dialogue in its titles. It remains an enthralling war film with vibrant performances under Raoul Walsh's vigorous direction. Also, a

musical theme written to accompany the film became very popular as the waltz song "Charmaine," probably the first hit song to come from a film. The 1952 remake of *What Price Glory?* was forced to clean up much of the play's dialogue for sound and John Ford's film made for an interesting if unremarkable war movie.

When Knighthood Was in Flower

January 14, 1901 (Criterion Theatre), a play by Paul Kester. *Cast:* Julia Marlowe (Mary Tudor), Bruce McRae (Charles Brandon), Charles Harbury (Henry VIII), Wilfred North, David Torrence, Vernon Clarges. *Producer:* Charles Frohman. 176 performances.

(Cosmopolitan 1922). *Screenplay:* William LeBaron, Luther Reed. *Cast:* Marion Davies (Mary Tudor), Forrest Stanley (Charles Brandon), Lyn Harding (Henry VIII), Theresa Maxwell Conover, Pedro de Cordoba, Ruth Shepley. *Director:* Robert G. Vignola.

The Sword and the Rose (Disney 1953). *Screenplay:* Lawrence Edward Watkins. *Cast:* Glynis Johns (Mary Tudor), Richard Todd (Charles Brandon), James Robertson Justice (Henry VIII), Michael Gough, Jane Barrett, Peter Copley. *Director:* Ken Annakin. *Producer:* Perce Pearce.

Charles Major's popular novel about romance in Tudor England was adapted for the stage with plenty of scenery and big emotions that critics disdained but playgoers enjoyed. Mary Tudor is told by her brother, King Henry VIII of England, that she must forget her love for the lowly Charles Brandon and marry King Louis XII of France. Instead she and Charles elope. But they are caught, Mary weds Louis, and only years later after the death of the French king are the lovers reunited. The renowned Shakespearean actress Julia Marlowe played Mary in New York and on the road for two seasons, earning her enough money to return to Shakespeare again. The story was ideal for the screen and the play was made into two silent films: a 1908 version with Linda Avidson as Mary and a 1922 remake starring Marion Davies. The later is a very elaborate and over-produced spectacle built to show off the pretty Davies but, as was usually the case, the pert actress was never as effective in serious pieces as she was in comedies. In 1953 the story was told again in *The Sword and the Rose*, a colorful and handsome production filmed in England by Disney. Glynis Johns is a sly Mary and Richard Todd is a bland Charles but the movie is enjoyable enough without being anything special.

When Ladies Meet

October 6, 1932 (Royale Theatre), a comedy by Rachel Crothers. *Cast*: Frieda Inescort (Mary Howard), Herbert Rawlinson (Rogers Woodruff), Selena Royale (Claire), Spring Byington (Bridget Drake), Walter Abel (Jimmie Lee), Robert Lowes, Auguste Aramini. *Director*: Rachel Crothers. *Producer:* John Golden. 191 performances.

(Cosmopolitan-MGM 1933). *Screenplay*: Leon Gordon, John Meehan. *Cast*: Myrna Loy (Mary Howard), Frank Morgan (Rogers Woodruff), Ann Harding (Claire), Alice Brady (Bridget), Robert Montgomery (Jimmie Lee), Martin Burton, Luis Alberni. *Director*: Harry Beaumont. *Producer*: Lawrence Weingarten.

(MGM 1941). *Screenplay*: S. K. Lauren, Anita Loos. *Cast*: Joan Crawford (Mary Howard), Herbert Marshall (Rogers Woodruff), Greer Garson (Claire), Robert Taylor (Jimmie Lee), Spring Byington (Bridget), Rafael Storm, Mona Barrie, Max Willenz. *Director*: Robert Z. Leonard. *Producers*: Orville O. Dull, Robert Z. Leonard.

Novelist Mary Howard writes a book about a woman who falls in love with a married man then meets his wife. Life copies art because soon after finishing the book Mary meets Claire Woodruff, the wife of the publisher Rogers whom she loves. But the two rivals for Rogers's affection find that they have more in common with each other than with him so both drop him. The knowing comedy was Rachel Crothers's last play and it was typical of her sly insight into women and their views of men. The sophisticated piece found modest success on Broadway and was turned into a movie in 1933 with Myrna Loy and Ann Harding as the two women who meet. It is a stylish film with much of the sparkling stage dialogue in tact

and the acting on a very breezy but pointed level. Alice Brady and Frank Morgan tend to steal some of the scenes with their comic finesse. The popular 1941 remake was less satisfactory even though it boasted a top-flight cast and expensive production values. Joan Crawford and Greer Garson make valiant efforts to fight over Herbert Marshall but they don't seem to believe it and neither does the camera.

When the Boys Meet the Girls see *Girl Crazy*

When You Comin' Back, Red Ryder?

December 6, 1973 (Eastside Playhouse), a play by Mark Medoff. *Cast*: Kevin Conway (Teddy), Bradford Dourif (Stephen), Elizabeth Sturges (Angel), Addison Powell, Robyn Goodman, Joe Jamrog, James Kiernan, Kristen Van Buren. *Director*: Kenneth Frankel. *Producers:* Elliot Martin, Circle Repertory Theatre. 302 performances.

(Melvin Simon 1979). *Screenplay*: Mark Medoff. *Cast*: Marjoe Gortner (Teddy), Peter Firth (Stephen), Stephanie Faracy (Angel), Candy Clark, Anne Ramsey, Dixie Harris, Lee Grant, Hal Linden, Pat Hingle. *Director*: Milton Katselas. *Producers*: Marjoe Gortner, Paul Maslansky.

The noisy, psychotic drug runner Teddy arrives at a remote New Mexico diner and humorously taunts the customers and the staff, then turns violent and forces them at gunpoint to humiliate themselves by doing whatever he tells them to do. The explosive little drama received mixed reviews and was considered either a potent, revealing play or a cheap rip-off of *The Petrified Forest* (qv). The Off Broadway production had a strong cast and was a surprise hit, followed by productions in regional theatres and colleges. The 1979 movie version also boasted a gifted cast but the story seemed more contrived and drawn out on the screen and the drama grew less interesting with each passing minute.

Where's Charley?

October 11, 1948 (St. James Theatre), a musical comedy by George Abbott. *Score:* Frank Loesser. *Cast:* Ray Bolger (Charley Wykeham), Allyn McLerie (Amy Settigue), Byron Palmer (Jack Chesney), Doretta Morrow (Kitty Verdun), Horace Cooper (Mr. Spettigue), Paul England (Sir Francis Chesney), Jane Lawrence (Lucia D'Alvadorez), Cornell MacNeil. *Songs:* Once in Love With Amy; Make a Miracle; My Darling, My Darling; At the Red Rose Cotillion.; The New Ashmolean Marching Society and Students' Conservatory Band. *Director:* George Abbott. *Choreographer:* George Balanchine. *Producers:* Cy Feuer, Ernest Martin. 792 performances.

(Warner 1952). *Screenplay:* John Monks, Jr. *Score:* Cast: Ray Bolger (Charley Wykeham), Allyn McLerie (Amy Spettigue), Robert Shackleton (Jack Chesney), Mary Germaine (Kitty Verdun), Horace Cooper (Mr. Spettigue), Howard Marion Crawford, Margaretta Scott. *Songs:* Once in Love With Amy; Make a Miracle; My Darling, My Darling; At the Red Rose Cotillion; The New Ashmolean Marching Society and Students' Conservatory Band. *Director:* David Butler. *Choreographer:* Michael Kidd. *Producer:* Gerry Blattner.

This musicalization of the classic British farce *Charley's Aunt* afforded Ray Bolger his best Broadway role and marked Frank Loesser's first Broadway score. Dressed up like his maiden aunt in order to secure a chaperone for some young ladies visiting his Oxford digs, Bolger turned the old drag routine into a fine art. The showstopper of the evening was "Once in Love With Amy" which he delivered in an old-time vaudeville style complete with audience participation. It is fortunate that Bolger got to reprise his Charley on the screen and much of the plot and score also were carried over but it is not a very impressive film. Parts of the movie were shot on Oxford locations but they do not blend comfortably with the studio scenes. The slow pace also hurts one's enjoyment of the musical. But Bolger, even in a paler version of his stage antics, is still worth watching.

White Cargo

November 5, 1923 (Greenwich Village Theatre), a play by Leon Gordon. *Cast:* Richard Stevenson (Langford), Annette Margules (Tondeleyo), A. E. Anson (Witzel), Frederick Roland (Ashley), Conway Wingfield, J. Malcolm Dunn. *Director:* Leon Gordon. *Producer:* Earl Carroll. 702 performances.

(WP Films 1930). *Screenplay:* J. B. Williams. *Cast:* Maurice Evans (Langford), Gypsy Rhouma (Tondeleyo), John F. Hamilton (Ashley), Leslie Farber, Sebastian Smith, Humberston Wright, Tom Helmore. *Director:* J. B. Williams. *Producers:* Arthur Barnes, J. B. Williams.

(MGM 1942). *Screenplay:* Leon Gordon. *Cast:* Richard Carlson (Langford), Hedy Lamarr (Tondeleyo), Bramwell Fletcher (Ashley), Walter Pidgeon (Witzel), Reginald Owen, Frank Morgan, Clyde Cook, Henry O'Neil. *Director:* Richard Thorpe. *Producer:* Victor Saville.

At a remote rubber plantation in the West African jungle, the new white manager Langford arrives and is immediately smitten with the whorish half-caste Tondeleyo. Soon they are living together then Langford gets a missionary to marry them. But the marriage is not a happy one and Langford turns to drink and Tondeleyo tries to poison him. But another white man catches her, forces Tondeleyo to drink the poison, and Langford is sent back to civilization. While some critics called the play tasteless and obscene it became one of the biggest Broadway hits of the 1920s with several road company upsetting censors across the country. In 1929 a British silent film was made of the play but it was delayed and released the next year with sound. Maurice Evans played Langford and Gypsy Rhouma was the alluring Tondeleyo. It is a primitive movie with crude sound mixing but the torrid story still comes across. A more polished screen version came out in 1942 with Hedy Lamarr giving one of her most seductive performances as Tondeleyo. The plot had dated poorly and some of the actors seemed to be playing broad melodrama but the movie was enjoyable in an uninvolving way.

Who Was That Lady? see Who Was That Lady I Saw You With?

Who Was That Lady I Saw You With?

March 3, 1958 (Martin Beck Theatre), a comedy by Norman Krasna. *Cast*: Peter Lind Hayes (David Williams), Ray Walston (Michael Haney), Mary Healy (Ann Williams), William Swetland, Gregory Morton, Larry Storch, Roland Winters. *Director*: Alex Segal. *Producer*: Leland Hayward. 208 performances.

Who Was That Lady? (Columbia 1960). *Screenplay*: Norman Krasna. *Cast*: Tony Curtis (David Wilson), Dean Martin (Michael Haney), Janet Leigh (Ann Wilson), James Whitmore, John McIntyre, Barbara Nichols, Joi Lansing. *Director*: George Sidney. *Producer*: Norman Krasna.

When chemistry professor David Williams is caught kissing an appreciative co-ed by his wife Ann, he appeals to his friend Michael Haney to help him get out of the fix. Haney is a television writer and concocts a story for Ann that he and David are secret agents for the FBI and that the co-ed was a spy. Ann believes them but so do some real spies and soon the two pretenders are caught up in FBI intrigues and foreign agents. The silly comedy was well plotted and plausible in its own silly way and the likable performers helped keep the play on the boards for six months. The comedy had various locations so it was not difficult for playwright Norman Krasna to open up the action in his screenplay for the 1960 movie. Tony Curtis and Janet Leigh are enjoyable as David and Ann, as is Dean Martin in a role that fit his playboy persona. The film also benefits from some fine location shooting and detailed sets including one showing the basement of the Empire State Building which the drugged David mistakes for a Russian submarine.

Whoopee

December 4, 1928 (New Amsterdam Theatre), a musical comedy by William Anthony McGuire. *Score:* Walter Donaldson, Gus Kahn. *Cast:* Eddie Cantor (Henry Williams), Ruth Etting (Leslie Daw), Paul Gregory (Wanenis), Ethel Shutta (Mary Custer), Tamara Geva (Yolandi), Frances Upton. *Songs:* Makin' Whoopee; Love Me or Leave Me; Until You Get Somebody Else; I'm Bringing a Red Red Rose. *Director:* William Anthony McGuire. *Choreographers:* Seymour Felix, Tamara Geva. *Producer:* Florenz Ziegfeld. 379 performances.

(Goldwyn/United Artists 1930). *Screenplay:* William Conselman. *Score:* Walter Donaldson, Gus Kahn. *Cast:* Eddie Cantor (Henry Williams), Eleanor Hunt (Sally Morgan), Paul Gregory (Wanenis), Ethel Shutta (Mary Custer), John Rutherford, Spencer Charters, Chief Caupolican. *Songs:* Makin' Whoopee; My Baby Just Cares for Me; I'll Still Belong to You; Stetson; A Girl Friend of a Boy Friend of Mine. *Director:* Thornton Freeland. *Choreographer:* Busby Berkeley. *Producers:* Samuel Goldwyn, Florenz Ziegfeld.

The diminutive comic Eddie Cantor had one of his greatest Broadway triumphs playing the hypochondriac Henry Williams who goes out West for his health but instead gets mixed up in an elopement, a jealous sheriff, and a tribe of Indians. It was a silly libretto tailored to Cantor's talents and it was further enhanced by some terrific songs, including the torchy "Love Me or Leave Me" sung by Ruth Etting. Cantor made his sound movie debut with the 1930 screen version and it instantly made him a movie star. The haphazard plot is pretty much the same but many of the songs were dropped for new ones, in particular the jaunty standard "My Baby Just Cares for Me." Etting and her torch number were gone as the film concentrated on the farcical aspects of the stage show. Another plus is the film debut of choreographer Busby Berkeley whose eye for the absurd and the geometric can be seen even in this first effort.

Who's Afraid of Virginia Woolf?

October 13, 1962 (Billy Rose Theatre), a play by Edward Albee. *Cast*: Uta Hagen (Martha), Arthur Hill (George), George Grizzard (Nick), Melinda Dillon (Honey). *Director*: Alan Schneider. *Producers*: Richard Barr, etc. 664 performances. Tony Award.

(Warner 1966). *Screenplay*: Ernest Lehman. *Cast*: Richard Burton (George), Elizabeth Taylor (Martha), George Segal (Nick), Sandy Dennis (Honey). *Director*: Mike Nichols. *Producer*: Ernest Lehman.

Tacitern college professor George and his loud-mouthed wife Martha have a stormy marriage but there is an understanding between the two of them that others cannot see. But during one long, drunken night in which they entertain a new faculty member and his wife, George and Martha go too far and it results in the destruction of their illusion that they have a son. One of the most explosive and heartfelt of all American dramas, the play was Edward Albee's first full-length work and probably his best. Uta Hagen and Arthur Hill played Martha and George with relish, finding the humor and savagery in the characters. Although the award-winning play ran two years on Broadway, Hollywood was fearful of the property because of its foul language, lack of action, and adult subject matter. But Ernest Lehman's screenplay softened some of the racier words and opened up the action slightly so that director Mike Nichols (in his first movie job) could film the verbal battles and quiet scenes in various locations. He also used active camera work to create tension in moments that were limited to one space. Richard Burton and Elizabeth Taylor as George and Martha gave what is arguably the best screen performances of their careers and the same might be said for George Segal and Sandy Dennis as the younger couple. Here is a rare case of a great American play becoming a superlative movie.

Will Success Spoil Rock Hunter?

October 13, 1955 (Belasco Theatre), a comedy by George Axelrod. *Cast*: Jayne Mansfield (Rita Marlowe), Orson Bean (George MacCauley), Walter Matthau (Michael Freeman), Martin Gabel (Irving LaSalle), William Thourlby, Harry Clark, Tina Louise. *Director*: George Axelrod. *Producer:* Jule Styne. 444 performances.

(Fox 1957). *Screenplay*: Frank Tashlin. *Cast*: Jayne Mansfield (Rita Marlowe), Tony Randall (Rockwell P. Hunter), John Williams (Irving LaSalle), Betsy Drake (Jenny Wells), Joan Blondell (Violet), Henry Jones, Mickey Hargitay, Lili Gentle. *Director-producer*: Frank Tashlin.

The nerdy journalist George MacCauley makes a deal with the devil, dis-

guised as an agent, that he can get anything he wishes, each wish costing George ten per cent of his soul. First he wishes for the sexy movie star Rita Marlowe, then to be a studio head, then win an Oscar, and so on. But as his wishes start to run out, George panics and makes a new deal with playwright Mike Freeman who is going through a dry spell. The devil will make Mike's script a success and the wishes will transfer from George to Mike. The plotting may have been messy and the dialogue sometimes forced, but the comedy overrode poor notices to run over a year. Of the sprightly cast, most of the applause went to Walter Matthau as the "playwrote" Mike but it was sex symbol Jayne Mansfield as Rita that made the box office hum. She reprised the role in the 1957 movie which made so many changes in the script that Mansfield's character was one of the few things left from the play. Tony Randall played an ad executive who bills himself as a great lover and Mansfield was the spokesperson for a sexy lipstick. The film is mostly a satire on television commercials and the power of celebrity in America and as such it is entertaining. But the screenplay was even more scattered than the play was and many jokes fell flat, coming in rapid succession as uttered by a cast directed to race through the proceedings.

Winged Victory

November 20, 1943 (44th Street Theatre), a play by Moss Hart. *Cast*: Edmund O'Brien (Irving Miller), Mark Daniels (Allan Ross), Don Taylor (Pinky Scariano), Anthony Ross, Gary Merrill, Philip Bourneuf, Ray Middleton, Elisabeth Fraser, Martin Ritt, Peter Lind Hayes, Karl Malden, Lee J. Cobb, Olive Deering, Kevin McCarthy, Red Buttons, Barry Nelson, Phyllis Avery, Grant Richards. *Director*: Moss Hart. *Producer:* U. S. Army Air Forces. 212 performances.

(Fox 1944). *Screenplay*: Moss Hart. *Cast*: Lon McCallister (Frankie Davis), Jeanne Crain (Helen), Edmund O'Brien (Irving Miller), Don Taylor (Danny Scariano), Judy Holliday (Ruth), Lee J. Cobb, Peter Lind Hayes, Red Buttons, Barry Nelson, Karl Malden, Garry Merrill, Martin Ritt. *Director*: George Cukor. *Producer*: Darryl F. Zanuck.

Three Air Force recruits go through basic training then serve on the bomber "Winged Victory" where one of them is injured but the three are undaunted as they continue the war effort. The large-cast propaganda drama was produced too raise money for the Army Emergency Relief Fund, which it did with success. Most of the cast consisted of unknowns but many later went on to become famous. The 1944 film version was also a fundraiser but used stars in featured or cameo roles. All the same, it too boasted some future names. The movie is competently done and manages to inspire without too much blind patriotism.

Wings

January 28, 1979 (Lyceum Theatre), a drama by Arthur Kopit. *Cast*: Constance Cummings (Emily Stilson), Mary-Joan Negro (Amy), James Tolkan (Billy), Carl Don, Betty Pelzer. *Director*: John Madden. *Producers*: Kennedy Center, Yale Repertory Theatre, etc. 113 performances.

(TV 1983). *Teleplay*: Arthur Kopit. *Cast*: Constance Cummings (Emily Stilson), Mary-Joan Negro (Amy), James Tolkan (Billy), Frances Bay, Phil Leeds. *Director*: John Madden. *Producer*: American Playhouse.

Silver-haired Emily Stilson, who was once an aviatrix and aerial stunt performer, suffers a stroke and we experience it from her point of view. Over the next two years she gradually learns to regain some of her powers of speech and movement as visions of her past flying efforts act as commentary on Emily's recovery. This delicate drama, rather atypical of the absurdist playwright Arthur Kopit, was first produced at Yale, then played Off Broadway before transferring to Broadway for a critically-acclaimed run. Constance Cummings's performance as Emily was considered a high-flying feat of its own and she got to reprise the role in the 1983 television production along with most of the cast. While the studio version utilizes some camera and editing tricks to convey the mind of Emily, the theatricality of the play is lost. All the same, for Cummings's performance alone the video is memorable. A musical version of the play, also called *Wings*, was produced Off Broadway in 1993 and was generally applauded.

Winterset

September 25, 1935 (Martin Beck Theatre), a play by Maxwell Anderson. *Cast*: Burgess Meredith (Mio), Richard Bennett (Judge Gaunt), Margo (Miriamne), Eduardo Ciannelli, Harold Johnsrud, Morton L. Stevens, Theodore Hecht. *Director-producer*: Guthrie McClintic. 195 performances.

(RKO 1936). *Screenplay*: Anthony Veiller. *Cast*: Burgess Meredith (Mio), Edward Ellis, (Judge Gaunt), Margo (Miriamne), Eduardo Ciannelli, Maurice Moscovitch, Paul Guilfoyle. *Director*: Alfred Santell. *Producer*: Pandro S. Berman.

In hopes of clearing the name of his father, who was unjustly accused and convicted of murdering a paymaster, Mio goes to the judge who ruled in the case years ago but finds he is mentally incompetent and unable to shed any light on the matter. But Miriamne, the sister of a man who witnessed the crime, is able to help Mio and the two fall in love while searching for the culprits. It leads them to the gangsters who were responsible for the murder. They kill Mio and, when Miriamne threatens to reveal the truth, they kill her as well. The blank-verse drama was based on the famous Sacco and Vanzetti case but playwright Maxwell Anderson turned what might have been a political piece into one of the few American tragedies. Both Burgess Meredith and Margo reprised their Mio and Miriamne in the 1936 screen version (it was his film debut) and both are affecting even if the movie itself seems stiff and talky at times. The stylized stage production (including Jo Meilziner's famous suggestive waterfront setting) allowed the poetic drama to create its own existence; the film is shot in shadows and mist but just seems confusing. Also, Anderson's blank verse is gone and there is a happy ending. Yet the movie is still quite effective and has a hypnotic quality. An early television broadcast of the drama was made in 1945 with John McQuade as Mio and a 1959 television version featured George C. Scott, Piper Laurie, and Martin Balsam.

Wit

October 6, 1998 (MCC Theatre), a play by Margaret Edson. *Cast*: Kathleen Chalfant (Vivian Bearing), Helen Stenborg (E. M. Ashford), Paula Pizzi, Alec Phoenix, Walter Charles. *Director*: Derek Anson Jones. *Producer:* MCC Theatre. 545 performances. Pulitzer Prize.

(TV 2001). *Teleplay*: Emma Thompson, Mike Nichols. *Cast*: Emma Thompson (Vivian Bearing), Eileen Atkins (E. M. Ashford), Christopher Lloyd, Audra McDonald, Harold Pinter, Jonathan M. Woodward. *Director*: Mike Nichols. *Producers*: Simon Bosanquet, etc.

Dr. Vivian Bearing, a noted English literature scholar and expert on John Donne, tells the audience that she is diagnosed with ovarian cancer. In a series of scenes in which she undergoes clinical treatments, Vivian talks about literature to help her maintain her sanity. The play was moving without being very dramatic but both critics and playgoers praised the honest, uncompromising performance of Kathleen Chalfant as Vivien. Emma Thompson played her in the 2001 television production and, with director Mike Nichols, co-wrote the adaptation which opened the story up and showed different characters in Vivian's life. It was intelligently done and beautifully filmed but again it was the central performance that kept the production from turning into another disease-of-the-week television movie.

The Witching Hour

November 18, 1907 (Hackett Theatre), a play by Augustus Thomas. *Cast*: John Mason (Jack Brookfield), Jennie A. Eustace (Helen Whipple), Morgan Conan (Clay), George Nash (Frank Hardmuth), Janet Dunbar (Viola Campbell), William Sampson, Ethel Winthrop, Harry S. Hadfield. *Producer:* Shuberts. 212 performances.

(Frohman 1916). *Screenplay*: Anthony Paul Kelly. *Cast*: C. Aubrey Smith (Jack Brookfield), Marie Shotwell (Helen Whipple), Jack Sherrill (Clay), Robert Conness (Frank Hardmuth), Freeman Barnes. *Director*: George Irving.

(Famous Players 1921). *Screenplay*: Julia Crawford Ives. *Cast*: Elliott Dexter (Jack Brookfield), Mary Alden (Helen Whipple), A. Edward Sutherland (Clay), Robert Cain (Fran Hard-

muth), Winter Hall, Ruth Renick, Charles West, Fred Turner. *Director*: William Desmond Taylor. *Producer*: Jesse L. Lasky.

(Paramount 1934). *Screenplay*: Salisbury Field, Anthony Veiller. *Cast*: John Halliday (Jack Brookfield), Judith Allen (Nancy Brookfield), Tom Brown (Clay), Ralf Harolde (Frank Hardmuth), Guy Standing, William Frawley, Richard Carle. *Director*: Henry Hathaway. *Producer*: Anthony Veiller.

Jack Brookfield has never stopped loving Helen Whipple even though she married another man, so years later, when Helen's son Clay is accused or murder, Jack comes to his defense. He uses telepathy to reach the jury, sending word to them that the D. A. Hardmuth has a murder in his past and is railroading the boy. Clay is acquitted and Hardmuth tries to shoot Jack, but he uses his hypnotic powers to get the D. A. to drop his gun. The play was the talk of the town with its engrossing story and original use of telepathy in a drama. Two silent movies were made of the play, the 1916 film featuring a young C. Aubrey Smith as Jack Brookfield and a 1921 version with Elliott Dexter in the role. Both were successful enough to warrant a talkie in 1934 but the plot had changed so much that Jack was now hypnotizing Clay into taking blame for a murder he didn't commit. John Halliday plays Jack and he is surrounded by a strong cast which makes the melodrama still interesting enough.

Within the Law

September 11, 1912 (Eltinge Theatre), a play by Bayard Veiller. *Cast*: Jane Cowl (Mary Turner), Dodson Mitchell (Edward Gilder), Orme Caldara (Richard), William B. Mack (Joe Garson), Arthur Paulding, John Willard, Florence Nash. *Director*: Holbrook Blinn. *Producer:* American Play Company. 541 performances.

(Vitagraph 1917). *Screenplay*: Eugene Mulin. *Cast*: Alice Joyce (Mary Turner), Walter McGrail (Gilder), Harry T. Morey (Joe Garson), Anders DeGarde, Eugene O'Rourke, Adele DeGarde. *Director*: William P. S. Earle.

(First National 1923). *Screenplay*: Frances Marion. *Cast*: Norma Talmadge (Mary Turner), Lionel

Belmore, Eddie Boland, Lew Cody, Ward Crane, Helen Ferguson. *Director*: Frank Lloyd.

Paid (MGM 1930). *Screenplay:* Charles MacArthur, Lucien Hubbard. *Cast:* Joan Crawford (Mary Turner), Kent Douglass (Bob Gilder), Robert Armstrong (Joe Garson), Purnell Pratt (Edward Gilder), Marie Prévost, John Miljan, Polly Moran. *Director-producer:* Sam Wood.

Within the Law (MGM 1939). *Screenplay*: Edith Fitzgerald, Charles Lederer. *Cast*: Ruth Hussey (Mary Turner), Tom Neal (Gilder), Paul Kelly (Joe Garson), William Gargan, Rita Johnson, Paul Cavanaugh. *Director*: Gustav Machaty. *Producer*: Lou L. Ostrow.

Innocent Mary Turner was accused of theft by her employer, Edward Gilder, and sentenced to prison for three years. When she is released she takes her revenge by organizing a gang of crooks who work just "within the law" and see that Gilder's business falters. She also weds Gilder's son Richard, then reveals to her former boss that she has stolen his wealth and his name. But having avenged herself, Mary realizes that she truly loves Richard and even her hatred of the elder Gilder has waned. The thought-provoking "problem play" was a hit on Broadway and gave Jane Cowl one of her most renowned roles. A 1916 silent film featured Muriel Starr as Mary, Alice Joyce played her in the 1917 remake, and Norma Talmadge essayed the role in the 1923 version. An early talkie in 1930 called *Paid* starred Joan Crawford (her first major talking role and one that made her a star) as Mary while Ruth Hussey played her in the 1939 remake again titled *Within the Law*. While details changed in the five different films, the plots always concentrated on Mary's vengeance and how it softened because of her love for Richard.

Without Love

November 10, 1942 (St. James Theatre), a play by Philip Barry. *Cast*: Katharine Hepburn (Jamie Coe Rowan), Elliott Nugent (Patrick Jamieson), Audrey Christie (Kitty Trimble), Robert Chisholm (Richard Hood), Robert Shayne, Neil Fitzgerald, Ellen Morgan. *Director*: Robert Sinclair. *Producer:* Theatre Guild. 113 performances.

(MGM 1945). *Screenplay*: Donald Ogden Stewart. *Cast*: Spencer Tracy (Pat Jamieson), Katharine Hepburn (Jamie Rowan), Lucille Ball (Kitty Trimble), Keenan Wynn, Carl Esmond, Patricia Morison, Felix Bressart. *Director*: Harold S. Bucquet. *Producer*: Lawrence Weingarten.

The diplomat Patrick Jamieson cannot find housing in wartime Washington so the puritanical spinster Jamie Coe Rowan offers to let him stay with her in her late father's home. In order to avoid scandal the two marry but agree that it will be a marriage without love or sex. Of course the twosome eventually fall into a romance and it ends up being a marriage of both love and sex. Critics were not enthused about the script but with Katharine Hepburn playing Jamie the production ran several months. Elliott Nugent was Hepburn's Patrick on stage but the 1945 movie paired her with her favorite costar Spencer Tracy and the dynamics of the story changed somewhat. Jamie was now a widow and Patrick an inventor but the living arrangements and the predictable results were the same. The Hepburn-Tracy chemistry was there but the story was not as interesting as they were and it was one of the least successful of the team's screen efforts.

The Wiz

January 5, 1975, (Majestic Theatre), a musical fantasy by William F. Brown. *Score:* Charlie Smalls. *Cast:* Stephanie Mills (Dorothy), Tiger Haynes (Tinman), Andre De Shields (Wiz), Ted Ross (Lion), Hinton Battle (Scarecrow), Clarice Taylor, DeeDee Bridgewater, Mabel King. *Songs:* Ease on Down the Road; Be a Lion; Home; If You Believe; Slide Some Oil to Me; He's the Wizard; Don't Nobody Bring Me No Bad News. *Director:* Geoffrey Holder. *Choreographer:* George Faison. *Producer:* Ken Harper. 1,672 performances. Tony Award.

(Universal 1978). *Screenplay:* Joel Schumacher. *Score:* Charlie Smalls, Quincy Jones. *Cast:* Diana Ross (Dorothy), Nipsey Russell (Tinman), Michael Jackson (Scarecrow), Ted Ross (Lion), Richard Pryor (Wiz), Lena Horne, Mabel King, Theresa Merritt. *Songs:* Ease on Down the Road; Be a Lion; Home; If You Believe; Slide Some Oil to Me; He's the Wizard; Don't Nobody Bring Me No Bad News; Is This What Feeling Gets?; End of the Yellow Brick Road. *Director:* Sidney

Lumet. *Choreographer:* Louis Johnson. *Producer:* Rob Cohen.

With unknown actors, untried writers, and a nightmarish tryout tour, this Motown-like retelling of *The Wizard of Oz* opened on Broadway with low expectations (the producers posted the closing notice on opening night) before becoming the sleeper hit of the decade. The show was more a joyous celebration of talent than a cohesive musical play but audiences and critics embraced the vibrant goings-on and it ran for years. The stage work avoided comparisons with the classic 1939 film by using an African American idiom throughout and placing the songs differently than in the screen version. But when *The Wiz* was filmed, the debacle on screen was so bizarrely wrong that it was hard to believe it was based on the same story. Pop singer Diana Ross was considered the only bankable black actress for the part so teenage Dorothy became an adult schoolteacher in Harlem who has such low self-confidence that she spend most of her life hiding in her bedroom. The land of Oz was a glitzy version of various spots in New York City, which made no sense logically or geographically. The expensive production managed to get little bang for its buck and much of the movie is a non-event with a couple of fun performances hiding under all that makeup. The saddest aspect of the film is the effect it had on the stage work; the musical is rarely revived today and many believe it is because of the numbing film version.

The Women

December 26, 1936 (Ethel Barrymore Theatre), a comedy by Clare Boothe. *Cast*: Margalo Gillmore (Mary Haines), Ilka Chase (Sylvia Fowler), Phyllis Povah (Edith Potter), Betty Lawford (Crystal Allen), Margaret Douglas (Countess De Lage), Jane Seymour, Adrienne Marden, Marjorie Main, Jessie Busley, Audrey Christie, Ruth Hammond. *Director*: Robert B. Sinclair. *Producer:* Max Gordon. 657 performances.

(MGM 1939). *Screenplay*: Anita Loos, Jane Murfin. *Cast*: Norma Shearer (Mary Haines), Rosalind Russell (Sylvia) Fowler), Joan Craw-

ford (Crystal Allen), Mary Boland (Countess De Lave), Paulette Goddard, Phyllis Povah, Marjorie Main, Lucile Watson, Ruth Hussey, Virginia Weidler. *Director*: George Cukor. *Producer*: Hunt Stromberg.

The Opposite Sex (MGM 1956). *Screenplay*: Fay Kanin, Michael Kanin. *Score:* Nicholas Brodszky, Ralph Freed, Sammy Cahn, etc. *Cast*: June Allyson (Kay Hilliard), Dolores Gray (Sylvia Fowler), Joan Collins (Crystal Allen), Agnes Moorehead (Countess), Ann Sheridan, Anne Miller, Charlotte Greenwood, Sam Levene, Joan Blondell, Leslie Nielsen, Jeff Richards. *Songs:* Now Baby Now; Young Man With a Horn; A Perfect Love; Rock and Roll Tumbleweed; The Opposite Sex. *Director*: David Miller. *Producer*: Joe Pasternak.

A gaggle of women of the Park Avenue set professes to be friends with each other but are more interested in spreading the dirt about the others. When they learn that the husband of sweet, non-vindictive Mary Haines is keeping another woman, they make sure she finds out about it. But even though Mary goes through with the divorce she never stops loving him and is more than ready to take him back when his remarriage fails. The core of the comedy was a love story but what made the play so entertaining were all of the female characters on the fringe who painted a nasty but fascinating picture of American women. Some of Broadway's favorite actresses were in the cast and the stylish production presented all the characters, costumes, and sets with polish. The 1939 movie featured some of Hollywood's favorite female stars and the acting ranged from the weepy sentiments of Norma Shearer (as Mary) to the vampy sexuality of Joan Crawford to the hilarious bitchiness of Rosalind Russell. The all-woman cast was directed with style by George Cukor and the movie managed to be mean and funny. The 1956 remake, called *The Opposite Sex*, turned the story into a musical and added all the male characters that were only spoken about in the play and earlier film. But adding songs and men did nothing for the story and the flatly directed movie was neither nasty nor funny enough. A few of the performers have some sparkle but the songs do not so even as a musical the remake disappoints.

The Wonder Bar

March 17, 1931 (Nora Bayes Theatre), a musical comedy by Irving Caesar, Aben Kandel. *Score:* Robert Katscher. *Cast:* Al Jolson (Monsieur Al), Patsy Kelly (Electra Pivonka), Arthur Treacher (Lord Cauldwell), Rex O'Malley (Ramon Colmano), Wanda Lyon (Liane Duval), Vernon Steele, Al Segal. *Songs:* Trav'lin' Alone; Good Evening, Friends; The Dance We Do for Al; Something Seems to Tell Me; The Dying Flamingo; Valse Amoureuse. *Director:* William Millison. *Choreographer:* Albertina Rasch. *Producer:* Morris Guest. 76 performances.

Wonder Bar (Warner/First National 1934). *Screenplay:* Earl Baldwin. *Score:* Harry Warren, Al Dubin. *Cast:* Al Jolson (Al Wonder), Dolores Del Rio (Inez), Dick Powell (Tommy), Kay Francis (Liane Renaud), Ricardo Cortez (Harry the Gigolo), Hugh Herbert (Corey Pratt), Guy Kibbee, Henry O'Neill, Hal LeRoy. *Songs:* Wonder Bar; Don't Say Goodnight; Why Do I Dream These Dreams?; Vive La France; Goin' to Heaven on a Mule. *Director:* Lloyd Bacon. *Choreographer:* Busby Berkeley. *Producer:* Robert Lord.

One of Al Jolson's last Broadway shows, this musical set in the swanky Paris cabaret of the title had much to recommend even though its run was cut short when the star left New York to return to Hollywood. Jolson played the owner of the club who has to deal with various low-life types, particularly a dancer who is trying to steal his female attraction, and he proved to be as magnetic on stage even when he did not resort to his blackface, "Mammy"-crooning persona. The film version retained Jolson but added more characters and subplots so the movie does not feel like a Jolson vehicle. Much of it is quite enjoyable and the supporting cast was first rate. But one production number staged by Busby Berkeley stands out as in very bad taste for any era: "Goin' to Heaven on a Mule," in which Jolson donned blackface and was joined by dozens of stereotypic "Negro" angels eating watermelon and pork chops at St. Peter's Gate.

Wonderful Town

February 25, 1953 (Winter Garden Theatre), a musical comedy by Joseph Fields, Jerome Chodorov. *Score:* Leonard Bernstein, Betty Comden, Adolph Green. *Cast:* Rosalind Russell (Ruth Sherwood), Edith Adams (Eileen Sherwood), George Gaynes (Robert Baker), Cris Alexander (Frank Lippencott), Jordan Bentley, Henry Lascoe, Dody Goodman, Dort Clark, Nathanial Frey. *Songs:* Ohio; One Hundred Easy Ways; Conga; A Little Bit in Love; A Quiet Girl; Wrong Note Rag. *Director:* George Abbott. *Choreographer:* Donald Saddler. *Producer:* Robert Fryer. 559 performances.

(TV 1958). *Teleplay:* Joseph Fields, Jerome Chodorov. *Score:* Leonard Bernstein, Betty Comden, Adolph Green. *Cast:* Rosalind Russell (Ruth Sherwood), Jacquelyn McKeever (Eileen Sherwood), Sydney Chaplin (Robert Baker), Cris Alexander (Frank Lippencott), Jordan Bentley, Dort Clark, Joseph Buloff, Jack Fletcher. *Songs:* Ohio; One Hundred Easy Ways; Conga; A Little Bit in Love; A Quiet Girl. *Directors:* Mel Ferber, Herbert Ross. *Choreographer:* Robert Beaumont. *Producer:* Robert Fryer.

Although *My Sister Eileen* (qv) had been a popular play, movie, and musical film, the story was musicalized again for Broadway as a vehicle for Rosalind Russell (who had starred in the non-musical film). She played the Ohio writer Ruth Sherwood who comes to New York City with her pretty sister Eileen to find success and love. Some of their misadventures were dropped to make room for the sensational songs and dances scored by Leonard Bernstein, Betty Comden, and Adolph Green. The show ran nearly two years but, because of the musical *My Sister Eileen* film, it was not put on the screen. Yet a fine television production in 1958 featured Russell and a few other cast members from the stage and it is a lively, highly entertaining record of an outstanding musical performance as well as a delightful piece of entertainment.

The World of Suzie Wong

October 14, 1958 (Broadhurst Theatre), a play by Paul Osborn. *Cast:* William Shatner (Robert Lomax), France Nuyen (Susie Wong), Ron Randall (Ben Jeffcoat), Sarah Marshall (Kay Fletcher), Noel Leslie, Stephen C. Cheng. *Director:* Joshua Logan. *Producers:* David Merrick, etc. 508 performances.

(Worldfilm 1960). *Screenplay:* John Patrick. *Cast:* William Holden (Robert Lomax), Nancy Kwan

(Suzie Wong), Michael Wilding (Ben Marlowe), Sylvia Syms (Kay O'Neill), Jacqui Chan, Laurence Naismith. *Director*: Richard Quine. *Producer*: Ray Stark.

Richard Mason's novel, about the romance between an American artist in Hong Kong and the prostitute he hopes to reform, was adapted for the stage with competency, though most critics found it an old-fashioned tale with a oriental twist. But audiences were moved by the romantic story and the play ran over a year. The 1960 film has gorgeous Hong Kong locations to add to the exotic flavor of the plot but the romance is still more soap opera than drama. Nancy Kwan is alluring as the prostitute Suzi Wong but William Holden is so low-key as the artist that there's more romance in the scenery than in the lovers.

Years Ago

December 3, 1946 (Mansfield Theatre), a comedy by Ruth Gordon. *Cast*: Patricia Kirkland (Ruth Jones), Fredric March (Clinton Jones), Florence Eldridge (Mrs. Jones), Richard Simon (Fred Whitmarsh), Bethel Leslie, Seth Arnold, Jennifer Bunker, Frederic Persson. *Director*: Garson Kanin. *Producer:* Max Gordon. 206 performances.

The Actress (MGM 1953). *Screenplay*: Ruth Gordon. *Cast*: Spencer Tracy (Clinton Jones), Jean Simmons (Ruth Gordon Jones), Teresa Wright (Annie Jones), Anthony Perkins (Fred Whitmarsh), Ian Wolfe, Kay Williams, Maru Wikes, Norma Jean Nilsson. *Director*: George Cukor. *Producer*: Lawrence Weingarten.

Young but ambitious Ruth Jones has decided to become an actress but before she goes to New York she has to convince her curmudgeonly father who wants Ruth to be a physical education teacher, her worried mother, and the Harvard grad who wants to marry her. Ruth Gordon based the autobiographical play on her own youth and filled the tale with humorous and affectionate characters in a small-town setting. Fredric March stole the show as the grumpy father who fights any form of change (for example, he refuses to allow a telephone in his house) but eventually softens up and pawns his prize telescope to pay for Ruth's start in New York. March won the Tony Award (it was the first year it was given) but Spencer Tracy was cast as the father in the 1953 screen version called *The Actress* and it was a delightfully low-key comic performance. Jean Simmons was Ruth, Teresa Wright her mother, and Anthony Perkins (in his film debut) was her suitor. All have a warm, domestic charm and the comedy is quietly amusing rather than a joke-fest. George Cukor directed with restraint and the nostalgic piece still pleases, although it failed at the box office when first released.

Yellow Jack

March 6, 1934 (Martin Beck Theatre), a play by Sidney Howard, Paul de Kruif. *Cast*: John Miltern (Walter Reed), Geoffrey Kerr (Stackpoole), Robert Shayne (Harkness), Robert Keith (Jesse W. Lazear), Barton MacLane (James Carroll), Eduardo Ciannelli (Aristides Agramonte), Katherine Wilson, George Nash, Whitford Kane. *Director-producer:* Guthrie McClintic. 79 performances.

(MGM 1938). *Screenplay*: Edward Chodorov, Sidney Howard, etc. *Cast*: Robert Montgomery (John O'Hara), Virginia Bruce (Frances Blake), Lewis Stone (Major Reed), Andy Devine (Charlie Spill), Henry Hull, Henry O'Neill, Charles Coburn, Buddy Ebsen, Janet Beecher, Sam Levene. *Director*: George B. Seitz. *Producer*: Jack Cummings.

The renowned Dr. Walter Reed struggles to determine the cause of yellow fever as he treats American soldiers infected with the disease in Cuba at the end of the 19th century. Since only humans suffer from it, most doctors believe that yellow fever is contracted by human contact. But the Cuban Dr. Carlos Findlay argues that it is spread by mosquitoes. Four young soldiers are paid to act as guinea pigs and when they are bitten by the mosquitoes they contract the disease, proving Dr. Findlay's theory. The somber subject kept the drama from finding box office success but the production was praised for its intelligent script, fine acting, and stunning mutli-level scenery. Much of the integrity of the drama was lost in the 1938 movie in which a love interest for one of the guinea pigs was added and the scientific aspects of the tale were romanticized. The large, talented cast does its best but too many performances are hindered by the melodramatic dialogue.

Yentl see Yentl, the Yishiva Boy

Yentl, the Yeshiva Boy

December 17, 1974 (Brooklyn Academy of Music), a play by Leah Napolin, Isaac Bashevis Singer. *Cast*: Tovah Feldshuh (Yentl), John V. Shea (Avigdor), Neva Small (Hadass), Hy Anzell, Ron Lagomarsino, Rita Karin. *Director*: Robert Kalfin. *Producer:* Chelsea Theatre Center. 48 performances.

Yentl (MGM/United Artists 1983). *Screenplay*: Jack Rosenthal, Barbra Streisand. *Score:* Michel Legrand, Alan and Marilyn Bergman. *Cast*: Barbra Streisand (Yentl/Anshel), Mandy Patinkin (Avigdor), Amy Irving (Hadass), Nehemiah Persoff (Papa), Steven Hill, Allen Corduner, Ruth Goring. *Songs*: Papa, Can You Hear Me?; The Way He Makes Me Feel; No Wonder; Where Is It Written? *Director*: Barbra Streisand. *Choreographer*: Gillian Lynne. *Producers*: Rusty Lemorande, Barbra Streisand.

The Polish rabbi's daughter Yentl rather study the Torah than get married so when her father dies she disguises herself as a male student and continues her education at a Yeshiva. But Yentl's true identity is discovered when she weds the fiancée of her friend so she sets out for new lands where she believes a woman has a better future. Isaac Bashevis Singer's short story made an enchanting fable on stage and Tovah Feldshuh was deemed exceptional as Yentl. The limited Off Broadway run was very popular so the production transferred to Broadway the next season where it only had a modest run. Barbra Streisand saw the role as an ideal musical vehicle for the screen so she co-wrote, co-produced, and starred in the 1983 movie which was a box office success. The story is romanticized on screen and the fine songs are used to convey Yentl's thoughts rather than as production numbers. It is a beautifully filmed movie with Eastern European locations and artfully staged by first-time director Streisand. Her performance as Yentl met with mixed notices but everyone agreed that Mandy Patinkin and Amy Irving were superb as Yentl's friend and wife. Although it is too long and some sections move too slowly, the movie is often brilliant.

Yes, My Darling Daughter

February 9, 1937 (Playhouse Theatre), a comedy by Mark Reed. *Cast*: Peggy Conklin (Ellen Murray), Boyd Crawford (Douglas Hall), Violet Heming (Constance Nevins), Lucile Watson (Ann Whitman Murray), Nicholas Joy (Titus Jaywood), Margaret Curtis, Charles Bryant. *Director-producer*: Alfred de Liagre, Jr. 405 performances.

(Warner 1939). *Screenplay*: Casey Robinson. *Cast*: Priscilla Lane (Ellen Murray), Jeffrey Lynn (Doug Hall), Roland Young (Titus Jaywood), Fay Bainter (Ann Murray), May Robson (Granny Whitman), Genevieve Tobin (Aunt Connie), Ian Hunter. *Director*: William Keighley. *Producer*: Hal B. Wallis.

Ellen Murray is engaged to Douglas Hall and she decides to spend a weekend with him in his apartment. Ellen's mother is outraged, though she herself was a flapper in earlier days and advocated free love. Ellen and Douglas go through with the illicit tryst but he feels so guilty afterwards that he insists they wed immediately. While this kind of coy sex comedy would be the rage in the late 1950s and early 1960s, this play was a decade ahead of its time and was just shocking enough to draw audiences for over a year. Yet Hollywood frowned on such behavior so in the 1939 film the two lovers elope and get married instead of spending a weekend in sin. As with the play, the mother and other relatives were more fun than the couple itself and the screen cast was expert at this kind of comedy.

Yokel Boy

July 6, 1939 (Majestic Theatre), a musical comedy by Lew Brown. *Score:* Sam Stept, Lew Brown, Charles Tobias. *Cast:* Buddy Ebsen (Elmer Whipple), Judy Canova (Judy), Dixie

Dunbar (Tiny), Phil Silvers (Punko Parks), Lois January (Mary Hawkins), Jackie Heller, Mark Plant, Ralph Riggs, Lew Hearn. *Songs:* Comes Love; It's Me Again; Let's Make Memories Tonight; I Know I'm Nobody; I Can't Afford to Dream; The Ship Has Sailed. *Director-producer:* Lew Brown. *Choreographer:* Gene Snyder. 208 performances.

(Republic 1942). *Screenplay:* Russell Rouse, Isabel Dawn. *Score:* Sam Stept, Lew Brown, Charles Tobias, etc. *Cast:* Eddie Foy, Jr. (Joe Ruddy), Roscoe Karnes (Al Deavers), Albert Dekker (Bessie Malone), Joan Davis (Molly Malone), Alan Mowbray (R. B. Harris), Mikhail Rasumny, Lynne Carver, Marc Lawrence. *Songs:* Comes Love; It's Me Again; Let's Make Memories Tonight; I Can't Afford to Dream; Jim Caesar. *Director:* Joseph Santley.

Pretty much forgotten now, this musical comedy about Hollywood was a hit in its day because of the hilarious performances by newcomers Buddy Ebsen, Phil Silvers, and Judy Canova. The satirical plot concerned country bumpkin Ebsen whose sweetheart goes West to become a movie star so he follows to protect her from the amorous clutches of Tinsel Town. Canova played a hillbilly who belted out three numbers in her broad, clowning style. While the score was not memorable, the farcical piece pleased audiences for six months. The second-class studio Republic Pictures bought the property in order to feature Canova but by the time the movie was made, Canova was out, as was the rest of the cast and most of the plot. The film's yokel is Eddie Foy, Jr., who has watched so many flicks in his local movie house that he can accurately predict audience attendance and satisfaction levels. A corrupt studio assistant tries to use the yokel to save Hollywood millions of dollars but gangsters horn in on the racket and the plot dissolved into a muddle. The film was not a success but Republic later used Canova in a series of cheap musical comedies that kept the studio solvent for years.

You Can't Take It with You

December 14, 1936 (Booth Theatre), a comedy by George S. Kaufman, Moss Hart. *Cast:* Henry Travers (Martin Vanderhof), Josephine Hull (Penny), Frank Wilcox (Paul), Margot Stevenson (Alice), Jess Barker (Tony Kirby), William J. Kelly (Mr. Kirby), Paula Trueman (Essie), George Heller, George Tobias, Ruth Attaway, Mitzi Hajos. *Director:* George S. Kaufman. *Producer:* Sam H. Harris. 837 performances. Pulitzer Prize.

(Columbia 1938). *Screenplay:* Robert Riskin. *Cast:* Jean Arthur (Alice Sycamore), James Stewart (Tony Kirby), Lionel Barrymore (Grandpa Martin Vanderhof), Edward Arnold (Anthony P. Kirby), Mischa Auer (Boris), Spring Byington (Penny Sycamore), Ann Miller (Essie), Samuel Hinds, Donald Meek, H. B. Warner, Dub Taylor, Eddie Anderson. *Director-producer:* Frank Capra. Academy Award.

Members of the Sycamore family are considered lovable eccentrics not because they are all that radical or unconventional but because they enjoy life and avoid the worries and frustrations that plague most people. Grandpa, for example, hasn't paid any taxes for years and treats the federal tax investigator with warmth and charm as he refused to pay. When the pretty Alice Sycamore falls for the son of a strait-laced businessman, she invites the family to the Sycamore home but they arrive a day early and see the kookie household at its worst. Alice wins her beau all the same and life continues merrily at the Sycamores. One of the most beloved (and produced) of all American comedies, the George S. Kaufman and Moss Hart play creates its own kind of cockeyed reality and never seems to date. The Broadway production featured a dream cast of character actor favorites but the farce also found favor on the road, in revival, and in every kind of theatre venue. As surefire as the script was, Hollywood didn't trust it and in the 1938 screen version made many changes, few of them improvements on the original. The focus moved from Grandpa to the wealthy Mr. Kirby, the father of Alice's beau Tony. Director Frank Capra chose to contrast the free-spirited life at the Sycamores with the cold, aggressive world of big business. This proves interesting for a while but weighs the movie down and the last reels are no longer comic but preachy about the integrity of the common man. Despite this, the film has outstanding performances (James Stewart is particularly nimble in the expanded role of Tony) and was very popular at the box office. Television versions of the play were made in 1945 with Robert Ober as Grandpa, 1947 with Findlay Currie, and 1979 with Art Carney. A wonderful Broadway revival with Jason Robards as the family patriarch was broadcast in 1984 and a television series based on the comedy was run in 1987-1988 with Harry Morgan as Grandpa.

Zooman see *Zooman and the Sign*

Zooman and the Sign

December 7, 1980 (Theatre Four), a play by Charles Fuller. *Cast*: Giancarlo Esposito (Zooman), Ray Aranha (Reuben Tate), Mary Alice (Rachel Tate), Carl Gordon, Frances Foster, Alvin Alexis, Terrance Terry Ellis, Steven A. Jones, Carol Lynn Maillard. *Director*: Douglas Turner Ward. *Producer:* Negro Ensemble Company. 33 performances.

Zooman (TV 1995). *Teleplay*: Charles Fuller. *Cast*: Louis Gossett, Jr. (Rueben Tate), Charles Dutton (Emmett), Cynthia Martells (Rachel), Khalik Kain (Zooman), Hill Harper, Tommy Hollis, Julio Oscar Mechoso. *Director*: Leon Ichaso. *Producers*: James B. Freydberg, Michael Manheim.

The hyperactive street punk Zooman accidentally kills a little girl while shooting at a rival gang then flees. When none of the neighbors will come forward to give information to the police, the parents of the dead girl hang a sign on their door condemning their fellow citizens. Members of the neighborhood harass the family but the father perseveres. Zooman is also upset about the sign and when he returns late one night to take it down he is mistaken for an intruder and shot down. The father then puts up a new sign expressing his sadness over the way events turned out. One of the best African American plays of the decade, the limited run Off Broadway was so popular the drama was brought back the next season. The faithful television production in 1995 was titled simply *Zooman* but little of the plot, characters, or power of the play were cut. The stage production featured some of the finest African American actors in New York and the television version boasted a masterful cast of stage, film, and television actors as well. Louis Gossett, Jr., as the little girl's father, is outstanding.

Zoot Suit

March 25, 1979 (Winter Garden Theatre), a play by Luis Valdez. *Cast*: Edward James Olmos (El Pachuco), Daniel Valdez (Henry Reyna), Mike Gomez (Joey Castro), Lupe Ontiveros (Dolores Reyna), Tony Plana (Rudy Reyna), Rose Portillo (Della Barrios), Angela Moya, Abel Franco, Roberta Delgado Esparza, Miguel Delgado. *Director*: Luis Valdez. *Producers:* Shuberts, etc. 41 performances.

(Universal 1982). *Screenplay*: Luis Valdez. *Cast*: Daniel Valdez (Henry Reyna), Edward James Olmos (El Pachuco), Charles Aidman (George Shearer), Tyne Daly (Alice Bloomfield), John Anderson, Abel Franco, Mike Gomez, Alma Martinez, Lupe Ontiveros. *Director*: Luis Valdez. *Producer*: Peter Burrell.

In the 1940s, a gang of Chicano youths who sport zoot suits are accused of a murder at the Sleepy Lagoon reservoir in Los Angeles. When they are tried and sentenced and their appeal fails, there is rioting in the streets. Based on a true incident, the play took an unrealistic approach to telling he story, using songs at times and having the episodic scenes tied together by a zoot-suited narrator called El Pachuco. The drama was a huge success in California but only managed a brief run in New York were it was the first Hispanic play produced on Broadway. The 1982 movie is more satisfying than the stage work as it uses flashy camera techniques to tell the story and capture the fervor of the times, even though it is filmed in a theatre with distracting cutting away to the audience. Edward James Olmos reprised his stage performance as El Pachuco and he is indeed riveting to watch.

Bibliography

Allvine, Glendon. *The Greatest Fox of Them All.* New York: Lyle Stuart, 1969.

Aylesworth, Thomas G. *Broadway to Holly-wood.* New York: W. H. Smith, 1985.

Balio, Tino. *United Artists.* Madison: University of Wisconsin Press, 1976.

Banham, Martin (ed.). *The Cambridge Guide to Theatre.* New York: Cambridge University Press, 1992.

Bawden, Liz-Anne. *The Oxford Companion to Film.* New York: Oxford University Press, 1985.

The Best Plays. 82 Editions. Editors: Garrison Sherwood and John Chapman (1894–1919); Burns Mantle (1919–1947); John Chapman (1947–1952); Louis Kronenberger (1952–1961); Henry Hewes (1961–1964); Otis Guernsey, Jr. (1964–2000); Jeffrey Eric Jenkins (2000–2001). New York: Dodd, Mead, 1894–1988; New York: Applause, 1988–1993; New York: Limelight, 1994–2001.

Blum, Daniel. *A Pictorial History of the Silent Screen.* New York: Putnam, 1953.

_____, and John Willis. *A Pictorial History of the American Theatre, 1860–1980.* (5th Ed.) New York: Crown, 1981.

Bordman, Gerald. *American Musical Theatre: A Chronicle.* (3rd Ed.) New York: Oxford University Press, 2001.

_____. *American Theatre: A Chronicle of Comedy and Drama, 1869–1914.* New York: Oxford University Press, 1994.

_____. *American Theatre: A Chronicle of Comedy and Drama, 1914–1930.* New York: Oxford University Press, 1995.

_____. *American Theatre: A Chronicle of Comedy and Drama, 1930–1969.* New York: Oxford University Press, 1996.

_____, and Thomas S. Hischak. *The Oxford Companion to American Theatre.* (3rd Ed.) New York: Oxford University Press, 2004.

Cohen, Paul Marantz. *Silent Film and the Triumph of American Myth.* New York: Oxford University Press, 2001.

Crowther, Bosley. *The Lion's Share: The Story of an Entertainment Empire.* New York: E. P. Dutton, 1957.

Drew, William S. *Speaking of Silents.* Vestal, N.Y.: Vestal, 1989.

Druxman, Michael B. *The Musical from Broadway to Hollywood.* New York: Barnes, 1980.

Eames, John Douglas. *The MGM Story.* New York: Crown, 1975.

_____. *The Paramount Story.* New York: Crown, 1985.

Everson, William K. *American Silent Film.* New York: Oxford University Press, 2000.

Eyman, Scott. *The Speed of Sound.* New York: Simon & Schuster, 1997.

Feuer, Jane. *The Hollywood Musical.* Bloomington: Indiana University Press, 1982.

Fitzgerald, Michael G. *Universal Pictures: A Panoramic History.* Westport, Conn.: Arlington House, 1977.

Ganzl, Kurt. *Ganzl's Encyclopedia of the Musical Theatre.* New York: Schirmer, 1993.

Geduld, Harry M. *The Birth of the Talkies.* Bloomington: Indiana University Press, 1975.

Green, Stanley. *Broadway Musicals Show by Show.* (5th Ed.) Milwaukee: Hal Leonard, 1999.

_____. *Encyclopedia of Musical Film.* New York: Oxford University Press, 1981.

_____. *Encyclopedia of the Musical Theatre.* New York: Dodd, Mead, 1976.

Halliwell, Leslie. *Halliwell's Film Guide*. (7th Ed.) New York: Harper & Row, 1989.

Hawes, William. *Filmed Television Drama, 1952–1958*. Jefferson, N.C.: McFarland, 2002.

_____. *Live Television Drama, 1946–1951*. Jefferson, N.C.: McFarland, 2001.

Henderson, Mary C. *Theater in America*. New York: Harry N. Abrams, 1986.

Hirschhorn, Clive. *The Hollywood Musical*. (Revised 2nd Ed.) New York: Crown, 1983.

_____. *The Universal Story*. New York: Crown, 1981.

_____. *The Warner Bros. Story*. New York: Crown, 1979.

Hischak, Thomas S. *American Theatre: A Chronicle of Comedy and Drama, 1969–2000*. New York: Oxford University Press, 2001.

_____. *Film It with Music: An Encyclopedic Guide to the American Movie Musical*. Westport, Conn.: Greenwood, 2001.

_____. *Stage It with Music: An Encyclopedic Guide to the American Musical Theatre*. Westport, Conn.: Greenwood, 1993.

_____. *The Theatregoer's Almanac*. Westport, Conn.: Greenwood, 1997.

Jacobs, Lewis. *The Rise of the American Film*. New York: Harcourt, Brace, 1939.

Jewell, Richard B., and Vernon Harbin. *The RKO Story*. New York: Arlington House, 1982.

Katz, Ephraim. *The Film Encyclopedia*. (3rd Ed.) New York: HarperPerennial, 1998.

Klepper, Robert K. *Silent Films, 1877–1996*. Jefferson, NC: McFarland, 1999.

Konigsberg, Ira. *The Complete Film Dictionary*. (2nd Ed.) New York: Penguin, 1997.

Lasky, Betty. *RKO: The Biggest Little Major of Them All*. Englewood Cliffs, N.J.: Prentice Hall, 1984.

Lewis, David H. *Broadway Musicals*. Jefferson, N.C.: McFarland, 2002.

Maltin, Leonard. *Movie and Video Guide*. (2003 Ed.) New York: Penguin Putnam, 2002.

Mast, Gerald. *A Short History of the Movies*. Indianapolis: Pegasus, 1971.

Matthew-Walker, Robert. *Broadway to Hollywood: The Musical and the Cinema*. London: Sanctuary, 1996.

McCann, Richard Dyer. *The Silent Film*. Lanham, Md.: Rowman & Littlefield, 1997.

McNeil, Alex. *Total Television*. (4th Ed.) New York: Penguin, 1996.

Norton, Richard C. *A Chronology of American Musical Theatre*. New York: Oxford University Press, 2002.

Sennett, Ted. *Warner Brothers Presents*. Secaucus, N.J.: Castle, 1971.

Shipman, David. *The Story of Cinema*. New York: St. Martin's, 1982.

Theatre World. 56 editions. Editors: Daniel C. Blum (1946–1964), John Willis (1964–2000); New York: Norman McDonald, 1946–1949; New York: Greenberg, 1949–1957; Philadelphia: Chilton, 1957–1964; New York: Crown, 1964–1991; New York: Applause, 1991–2000.

Thomas, Lawrence B. *The MGM Years*. New York: Arlington House, 1971.

Thomas, Tony, and Aubrey Solomon. *The Films of 20th Century–Fox*. Secaucus, N.J.: Citadel, 1979.

Walker, Alexander. *The Shattered Silents*. New York: William Morrow, 1979.

Wilmeth, Don B., and Tice Miller (eds.). *Cambridge Guide to American Theatre*. New York: Cambridge University Press, 1993.

Name Index

Title Index